GUINNESS WORLD RECORDS 2005

Dedicated to Norris McWhirter MBE
1925–2004

MANAGING EDITOR
Claire Folkard

SENIOR EDITOR
Jackie Freshfield

EDITORS
Carla Masson
Rob Dimery

DESIGN CONCEPT & CREATION
55 DESIGN
Matt Purkiss-Webb
Paul Deacon
Mel Fisher

COVER DESIGN
Ron Callow at Design 23

HEAD OF PICTURE/MEDIA DESK
Betty Halvagi

PICTURE RESEARCH
Maureen Kane
Caroline Thomas
Louise Thomas

PRODUCTION DIRECTOR
Patricia Langton

PRODUCTION CO-ORDINATOR
Colette Concannon

PRINTING AND BINDING
MOHN Media Mohndruck GmbH
Gütersloh,
Germany

TECHNICAL CONSULTANT (COVER)
Esteve Font Canadell

COLOUR ORIGINATION
Resmiye Kahraman
Colour Systems,
London, UK

KEEPER OF THE RECORDS
Stewart Newport

RESEARCH TEAM
Stuart Claxton
Jerramy Fine
David Hawksett
Keely Hopkins
Kim Lacey
Hein Le Roux
Chris Marais
Susan Morrison
Della Torra Howes

PROOFREADING
Craig Glenday
Ben Way

INDEX
Susan Bosanko

ACCREDITATION   Guinness World Records Limited has a very thorough accreditation system for records verification. However, whilst every effort is made to ensure accuracy, Guinness World Records Limited cannot be held responsible for any errors contained in this work. Feedback from our readers on any point of accuracy is always welcomed.

ABBREVIATIONS AND MEASUREMENTS   Guinness World Records Limited uses both metric and imperial measurements (US imperial in brackets). The only exception is for some scientific data, where metric measurements only are universally accepted, and for some sports data. Where a specific date is given the exchange rate is calculated according to the currency values that were in operation at the time. Where only a year date is given the exchange rate is calculated from December of that year. 'One billion' is taken to mean one thousand million. 'GDR' (the German Democratic Republic) refers to the East German state which unified with West Germany in 1990. The abbreviation is used for sports records broken before 1990. The Union of Soviet Socialist Republics split into a number of parts in 1991, the largest of these being Russia. The Commonwealth of Independent States replaced it and the abbreviation 'CIS' is used mainly for sporting records broken at the 1992 Olympic Games.

Guinness World Records Limited does not claim to own any right, title or interest in the trademarks of others reproduced in this book.

GENERAL WARNING   Attempting to break records or set new records can be dangerous. Appropriate advice should be taken first and all record attempts are undertaken entirely at the participant's risk. In no circumstances will Guinness World Records Limited have any liability for death or injury suffered in any record attempts. Guinness World Records Limited has complete discretion over whether or not to include any particular records in the book.

©2004 Guinness World Records Ltd
A HIT Entertainment plc Company

GUINNESS WORLD RECORDS 2005

Contents

Feats of engineering

Science & technology

Art & media

Music & entertainment

Sport

Introduction

This year marks the 50th anniversary of the first edition of what is now known as *Guinness World Records.*

In 2003, the 100-millionth copy of the book was published – a staggering achievement in publishing history, making *Guinness World Records* the biggest selling copyright book ever. From its relatively humble beginnings, today the book is sold in 100 countries around the world and translated into 23 languages.

The origins of the book date back to a shooting party in County Wexford,

Ireland, in 1951, when Sir Hugh Beaver (above), Managing Director of Guinness Brewery, was involved in a dispute as to whether or not the golden plover was Europe's fastest game bird. To his frustration, he was unable find a book that could give him an accurate answer.

It occurred to Sir Hugh that disputes such as this must happen often, especially in social gatherings, and so a book that could provide all the answers would be in great demand. At the time, the record-breaking athlete Chris Chataway was working as an underbrewer at Guinness's Park Royal Brewery in London and he recommended Norris and Ross McWhirter (both left), whom he had met at athletic events, to Sir Hugh as the ideal people to compile such a book. At the time, the McWhirters were running a fact-finding agency and publishing company in London, specializing in athletics records. Indeed, when Roger Bannister (above right) broke the four-minute-mile barrier on 6 May 1954, with a time of 3 min 59.4 sec, it was Norris McWhirter who announced the record-breaking time at that historic event. This was one of the 'new' athletics records to make it into the first edition. Sir Hugh liked the idea of a book of superlatives and commissioned the twins to create what was to become the first edition of *The Guinness Book of Records*.

After a busy year of research into the fastest and the slowest, the biggest and the smallest, the heaviest and the lightest, and the longest and the shortest of everything, the first copy was printed and bound on 27 August 1955. An instant success, the book was quickly recognized as the authoritative source of records in Britain and around the world.

Although the death of Norris McWhirter (pictured below right with the first edition of *The Guinness Book of Records*) in April 2004 in some ways marked the end of an era, the legacy of the iconic book he and his brother Ross created all those years ago lives on. Over the years, Norris inspired generations of children, delighting them with his encyclopedic knowledge and remarkable ability to recall records in a moment – as regularly demonstrated on the long-running BBC TV children's programme, *Record Breakers*.

As well as his famous television partnership with the late Roy Castle, he also worked with Sir David Frost (above right) on Sir David's American Guinness Specials from 1973 to 1988. Sir David remembers Norris as 'a man with a passion for facts and the accuracy of them, but also a man who had a heart-warming appreciation of man's ingenuity and determination to succeed. He loved to recount anecdotes about the remarkable individuals he had met over the years, whether they were Olympic record holders or people who had established records in fields that nobody else might have ever wished to attempt – like Mark Gottlieb, the underwater violinist, or Frank Freer, the man who peeled the world's longest unbroken apple peel. In their different ways, in Norris's eyes they were all superlatives.'

Today around 3.5 million copies of *Guinness World Records* are sold annually, demonstrating that humankind's desire for knowledge combined with a passion to be a Guinness World Record holder is undiminished. Now a household name around the world, no other enterprise collects, confirms, accredits and presents world record data with the same investment in comprehensiveness and authenticity.

Although no longer part of or associated with the Guinness Brewery, *Guinness World Records* remains the global authority on world records. This year's edition offers some unique features: we tell the story behind some of the most famous world records, and also hear from a selection of record breakers themselves in a number of fascinating and exclusive interviews.

As ever, remember that you don't have to be a movie star or world-class athlete to have a Guinness World Record. You just need to have the determination and dedication to succeed!

If you want to approach us with an idea for a record, turn to the back page to find out how.

Fifty years of change

1955–2005

The world's population has more than doubled since the first edition of *Guinness World Records* (formerly *The Guinness Book of Records*) went on sale in 1955. Here we chart some other key changes that have taken place over the past 50 years.

1955: the first edition

The Guinness Book of Records was launched in the same year that a truck driver from Mississippi named Elvis Presley (USA) signed for RCA Victor. Fast-food entrepreneur Ray Kroc (USA, left) opened his first McDonald's restaurant in April of that year, and Walt Disney (USA) opened a theme park in Anaheim, California, USA.

Other firsts

Competing with Guinness for bookshelf space in 1955 were JRR Tolkien's (UK) *The Lord of the Rings: The Return of the King* and Ian Fleming's (UK) third James Bond novel *Moonraker*.

Playing on the jukebox was Bill Haley and His Comets' (USA, below right) 'Rock Around the Clock' (which is still the biggest selling single by a band) and the rights to the design of the 'Pluto Platter' – the toy that would be better known as the 'Frisbee' – were sold by the inventor Walter Morrison (USA) to the Wham-O toy company.

Births and deaths

In 1955 three giants of modern communications were born: Bill Gates (USA), Tim Berners-Lee (UK) – the inventor of the World Wide Web – and Apple Macintosh co-founder Stephen Jobs (USA). The year also saw the deaths of Sir Alexander Fleming (UK) – the bacteriologist who discovered the effects of penicillin – and the physicist Albert Einstein (USA, b. Germany, below left).

The world today is a very different place, of course. Over the past five decades we've seen the advent of space travel and satellite communication, the creation of a global marketplace, the seemingly limitless expansion of the Internet coupled with an equally astonishing miniaturization of technology, and a worldwide population explosion (about 1,000 more people will be born in the time it takes you to read this page).

Charting the change

Here's a selection of Guinness World Records – past and present – that illustrate some important changes that have taken place over the last 50 years. Figures from 1955 are taken from the first edition of *The Guinness Book of Records* and are quoted verbatim.

2005

★ **World population (2005): 6.31 billion**

★ **Remotest known body**
Using the Hubble Space Telescope and the Keck Observatory, astronomers from the California Institute of Technology (USA) have discovered a small and compact system of stars around 2,000 light years across, with a redshift of 7.0. This corresponds to a distance of around 13 billion light years away.

★ **Highest football transfer fee**
The highest transfer fee quoted for a player is a reported 13 billion Spanish pesetas (£47 million or £66 million) for Zinedine Zidane (France) from Juventus to Real Madrid on 9 July 2001.

1955

★ **World population (1955): 2.56 billion**

★ **Remotest known body**
The first record published in the first edition of GWR!
The universe is the entirety of space and matter. The remotest known heavenly bodies are extra-galactic nebulae at a distance of some 1,000 million light years or 6,000,000,000,000,000,000,000 miles. There is reason to believe that even remoter nebulae exist but, since it is possible that they are receding faster than the speed of light (670,455,000 mph) [1,078,992,732 km/h], they would be beyond man's 'observable horizon'.

★ **Highest football transfer fee**
The world record transfer fee is the 105,000,000 lire (£60,375 or $167,000) paid in May 1952 by Napol to Genoese Atlanta for the former Swedish International Hans Jeppson, 27.

Did you know... not all the records have been broken?

Here are some records that haven't been broken in 50 years!

Tallest man
The tallest man in medical history for whom there is irrefutable evidence is Robert Pershing Wadlow (USA), who when last measured on 27 June 1940 was 2.72 m (8 ft 11.1 in) tall.

Longest solar eclipse
A total eclipse of the Sun that took place on 20 June 1955 west of the Philippines lasted for 7 min 8 sec. The maximum possible duration of an eclipse of the Sun is 7 min 31 sec.

Longest reign as world heavyweight boxing champion
Joe Louis (USA) was champion for 11 years 252 days, from 22 June 1937 – when he knocked out James Joseph Braddock (USA) in the eighth round in Chicago, Illinois, USA – until announcing his retirement on 1 March 1949. During his reign, Louis made a record 25 defences of his title.

Largest concrete dam
The Grand Coulee dam on the Columbia River, Washington, USA, has a concrete volume of 8,092,000 m³ (285,766,282 ft³) to a weight of 19,595,000 tonnes (43,199,528,900 lb). It was completed in 1942 at a cost of $56 million (£14 million), has a crest length of 1,272 m (4,173 ft) and is 168 m (550 ft) high.

Best selling record
In 1955, Irving Berlin's (USA) 'White Christmas' had sold 18 million copies. By 2005, sales exceeded 100 million copies. Bing Crosby's (USA) recording of this song accounts for more than 50 million copies.

Largest office building
The Pentagon, in Arlington, Virginia, USA, built to house the US Defense Department's offices and completed in January 1943, is the world's largest office building. Each of the outermost sides is 281 m (921 ft) long and the perimeter of the building measures about 1,405 m (4,610 ft). Its five storeys enclose a floor area of 604,000 m² (149.2 acres), the corridors total 28 km (17.5 miles) in length, and there are 7,754 windows to be cleaned. There are over 26,000 military and civilian employees working in the building.

Largest stadium
The Maracanã Municipal Stadium (below) in Rio de Janeiro, Brazil, has a standard capacity of 205,000 spectators, 155,000 of whom can be seated. It was built for the 1950 football World Cup and housed a crowd of 199,854 for the final match of the tournament, Brazil v. Uruguay, on 16 July 1950 – the greatest ever attendance for a sporting event.

Most expensive bottle of wine
The most expensive commercially available bottle of wine is the Chateau d'Yquem Sauternes (1787), priced between £16,843 and £40,282 ($56,000 and $64,000) depending on the retailer.

Highest paid TV performer
The world's highest paid TV actor per episode is Ray Romano (USA), who earned $1.8 million (£1.2 million) per episode of *Everybody Loves Raymond* (CBS, USA) for the eighth series in 2004/05.

Largest passenger liner
The Cunard Line's *Queen Mary 2*, which made its maiden voyage in January 2004, is 345 m (1,132 ft) long and has a beam (width) of 41 m (135 ft). At approximately 150,000 gross registered tonnes (grt), *Queen Mary 2* is nearly three times larger than *Titanic* (46,000 grt), and has space for 2,620 passengers and 1,253 crew.

Most expensive bottle of wine
The most expensive bottle of wine obtainable would be a bottle of Feinste Trockenbeeran Auslese of 1949 or any other good vintage. This is a white wine made in the Rhine Valley in very small quantities from specially selected grapes and retails at £8 ($22) or more.

Highest paid TV performer
The biggest contract ever signed for television appearances was between Jackie Gleason, the American comedian, and the Columbia Broadcasting System on behalf of the Buick Division of General Motors, in December 1954. Under this contract, Jackie Gleason will receive £2.5 million ($7 million) over the next two years for a once-weekly half-hour programme.

Largest passenger liner
The *Queen Elizabeth*, of the Cunard fleet, is the largest passenger vessel in the world and also has the largest displacement of any ship in the world, with a gross tonnage of 83,673. She has an overall length of 1,031 feet (314.2 m), and is 118 feet 7 inches (387.17 m) in breadth. She is powered by steam turbines which develop about 200,000 hp (149,140 kw).

GWR on TV

From BBC TV's *Record Breakers* to FOX's *Guinness World Records: Primetime*, Guinness World Records on television has always been loved for the programmes' celebration of amazing achievements. Today Guinness World Records appears on TV in around 85 countries!

GWR comes to TV

Guinness World Records' most famous television past is, of course, BBC TV's *Record Breakers*, which appeared on UK TV screens for over 30 years. Fronted by the energetic and enthusiastic Roy Castle (below, right, with Norris McWhirter and a model of Robert Wadlow), the show featured a weekly array of record attempts, along with the chance to put Norris McWhirter 'on the spot' and test his encyclopedic record knowledge – a test that he famously only failed once!

In the 1980s, Sir David Frost fronted *The Spectacular World of Guinness Records* – a show featuring many more weird and wonderful human achievements – which ran successfully for six years.

Guinness World Records: Primetime

The end of the 1990s saw the arrival of a spectacular new show launched in the USA on the FOX network. *Guinness World Records: Primetime* was a dramatic, exciting show that has since gone on to be shown around the world in over 75 countries, including Canada, Brazil, the Seychelles, the Philippines and the Czech Republic.

L'Été de Tous les Records

After a hugely successful initial run in 2003, 2004 saw the return of *L'Été de Tous les Records* – a fun summertime roadshow that travelled each week to a different location in France. An entertaining mixture of record attempts by local people combined with some impressive feats by established record holders, the show was a huge hit. Fronted by well-known TV sports presenter Pierre Sled, the show also featured Barry White as the Guinness World Records official judge, who, with his catchphrase 'Are you ready?', proved immensely popular.

Guinness World Records: Die Grössten Weltrekorde

An exciting new show launched in Germany in 2004 – a two-hour special presented by Oliver Welke, with celebrated professional boxer Henry Maske as the Guinness World Records judge. Four new records were set on the show, including Wim Hof's famous ice endurance record (opposite, bottom right) – he managed to stay in the ice box for an incredible 1 hr 7 min. Broadcast live from the studio, the show was a huge success, and is to be followed by a second one in autumn 2004.

Guinness World Records: Fifty Years, Fifty Records

In celebration of the 50th anniversary, this year sees the long-awaited return of Guinness World Records to the UK TV screens in the form of a two-hour live extravaganza broadcast from a massive sound stage in London on 11 September – almost 50 years to the day since the historic first meeting between Sir Hugh Beaver and the McWhirter twins. Over the duration of the show an attempt will be made to break 50 records – an impressive record in itself!

Opposite, clockwise from top: Oliver Welke, host of *Guinness World Records: Die Grössten Weltrekorde*; the 2003 *L'Été de Tous les Records* team; Wim Hof (Netherlands) on *Guinness World Records: Die Grössten Weltrekorde*; Georges Christen (Luxembourg), holder of the record for most telephone directories torn in two minutes, on *L'Été de Tous les Records*; Shridhar Chillal (India), owner of the world's longest nails on a single hand, on *Guinness World Records: Primetime*.

★ GWR TV

★ GWR TV

★ GWR TV

★ GWR TV

★ GWR TV

Human beings

Contents

Extreme bodies
Human beings

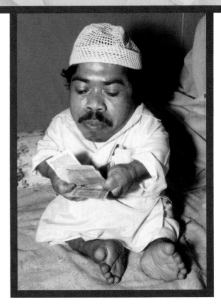

« Longest tongue

Stephen Taylor's (UK, left) tongue measures 9.4 cm (3.7 in) from the tip to the centre of his closed top lip. It was measured at Westwood Medical Centre, Coventry, Warwickshire, UK, on 29 May 2002.

Shortest man ⩘

The shortest mature human of whom there is independent evidence was Gul Mohammed (India, above).

On 19 July 1990, he was examined at Ram Manohar Hospital, New Delhi, India, and found to measure a height of 57 cm (22.5 in).

★ **Tallest living man**
After seven measurements taken over the course of 22–23 April 1999 in Tunis, Tunisia, Radhouane Charbib's (Tunisia) height was confirmed as 2.35 m (7 ft 8.9 in).

★ **Tallest woman**
Zeng Jinlian (China) measured 2.48 m (8 ft 1.75 in) when she died on 13 February 1982.

★ **Tallest living woman**
When last measured, Sandy Allen (USA) was 2.31 m (7 ft 7.25 in) tall. Her birth weight was a normal 2.95 kg (6 lb 7 oz) but her abnormal growth began almost immediately. She stood 1.9 m (6 ft 3 in) by the age of 10 and was 2.16 m (7 ft 1 in) at the age of 16.

★ **Shortest woman**
Pauline Musters (Netherlands, b. 26 February 1876) measured 30 cm (12 in) at birth, and at nine years of age was 55 cm (21.5 in) tall and weighed only 1.5 kg (3 lb 5 oz). When she died of pneumonia with meningitis on 1 March 1895 in New York City, USA, aged 19, a post-mortem examination showed her to be 61 cm (24 in) tall. Her 'vital statistics' were 47-48-43 cm (18.5-19-17 in).

★ **Shortest living woman**
Madge Bester (South Africa) is only 65 cm (25.5 in) tall. She suffers from *Osteogenesis imperfecta* (characterized by brittle bones and other deformities of the skeleton) and is confined to a wheelchair.

★ **Heaviest man**
The heaviest person in medical history was Jon Brower Minnoch (USA), who had suffered from obesity since childhood. He was 1.85 m (6 ft 1 in) tall and weighed 178 kg (28 st) in 1963, 317 kg (50 st) in 1966 and 442 kg (69 st 9 lb) in September 1976. In March 1978, Minnoch was admitted to University Hospital, Seattle, USA, where consultant endocrinologist Dr Robert Schwartz calculated that Minnoch must have weighed more than 635 kg (100 st), much of which was water accumulation due to his congestive heart failure.

★ **Heaviest woman**
Rosalie Bradford (USA) is claimed to have registered a peak weight of 544 kg (85 st) in January 1987.

★ **Living person with the largest hands**
Hussain Bisad (Somalia), who resides in the UK, has hands measuring 26.9 cm (10.59 in) from the wrist to the tip of his middle finger.

★ **Longest ear hair**
Radhakant Bajpai (India) has hair sprouting from the centre of his outer ears (middle of the pinna) that measures 13.2 cm (5.19 in) at its longest point.

★ **Longest hair**
The longest documented hair belonged to Hoo Sateow (Thailand), a tribal medicine man from Muang Nga, Chang Mai, Thailand. On 21 November 1997, his hair was unravelled and officially measured at 5.15 m (16 ft 11 in) long. He stopped cutting his hair in 1929 at the age of 18.

★ **Longest fingernails on a single hand**
The aggregate measurement of the five nails on the left hand of Shridhar Chillal (India) was 7.05 m (23 ft 1.5 in) on 4 February 2004. His thumbnail measured 158 cm (62.2 in), his index fingernail 131 cm (51.5 in), his middle fingernail 138 cm (54.3 in), his ring fingernail 140 cm (55.1 in) and his little fingernail 138 cm (54.3 in). Chillal last cut his nails in 1952.

★ **Largest chest measurement**
Robert Earl Hughes (USA) had a chest measurement of 315 cm (124 in).

Heaviest twins »

Twins Billy Leon (1946–79) and Benny Lloyd (1946–2001) McCrary, alias McGuire (both USA, right), were normal in size until the age of six. By November 1978, Billy and Benny weighed 337 kg (53 st 1 lb) and 328 kg (51 st 9 lb) respectively, and each had a waist measuring 2.13 m (84 in). Both died from heart failure.

★ GWR TALKS TO
Lee Redmond

Lee Redmond (USA, right) holds the record for the longest fingernails. She hasn't cut her nails since 1979, and has grown and manicured them to a total length of 7.51 m (24 ft 7.8 in).

Why did you grow your nails?
I didn't want to – they were really healthy and I decided to grow them to see how long they'd get before they twisted out of shape. But they never did twist so I just grew them!

Would you ever cut them?
I trim them back once in a while, but cut them clear off? No way! Psychologists have said my nails were a shield I'd put up to stop men getting near me. And you know what? All my fans are male!

Have you ever bitten your nails?
Oh, I just couldn't imagine it! People chew their nails because they're lacking a certain mineral in their body. They tell me that

if a bomb was to go off, I could go into a shelter and live off my fingernails!

Is it true that some people want to buy your nails?
Yeah – I turned down $10,000 when they were just nine inches (22.8 cm)! It was for a TV show – I was asked along with the lady with the longest hair. I didn't accept, but she had over 7 ft (2.13 m) of hair cut off! My nails are priceless!

What kind of reaction do your nails usually get?
It used to be negative. Now, so many people have seen me in the Guinness World Records books and on TV shows, they're more amazed by them. People see the difference between my nails and those on the man from India [Shridhar Chillal, see page 14]: they want to know how I keep my nails looking so much better than he does.

So, what's your secret?
You are what you eat, for one thing – the nail is nothing but protein – so I eat high protein. But they get dry and brittle so I soak them in warm olive oil.

Do you worry about damaging them in your sleep?
No – they just hang off the side of the bed! I don't even think about it.

How do you get dressed?
My nails are like an extension of my fingers, so I just slide them down the sleeves as usual. Now that gravity has pulled my nails straighter they're much easier to slip through. I just can't put on anything that goes over my head because I can't co-ordinate putting my hands up and feeding the nails through, so everything has to come up over my bottom!

How does it feel to be in the book?
It's an honour. I get asked to sign a lot of books! I use them to teach self-esteem classes. I really think it helps kids:

meeting me and seeing me in the books gets their minds going, knowing they can do anything.

One more question! How do you go to the bathroom?
That's usually the first question people ask! I usually say 'Very carefully... and I don't have haemorrhoids!'

Tallest man
Human beings

The record for the tallest man ever was held by Robert Pershing Wadlow (USA, below), who stood at 2.72 m (8 ft 11.1 in). His record is one of the most popular Guinness World Records and is recognized as a true classic.

Early days
Robert Pershing Wadlow (USA) was born at 6:30 am in Alton, Illinois, USA, on 22 February 1918 to Addie and Harold Wadlow (both USA). Robert was the eldest of five children. He had two sisters and two brothers, all of whom were of normal height and weight. His birth weight of 3.85 kg (8 lb 8 oz) gave no indication of the amazing growth that was to come. In fact, Robert grew at a normal rate until the age of two, when he underwent a double hernia operation. From then on, he grew at an astonishing speed so that by the age of five he stood 1.63 m (5 ft 4 in) tall and weighed 48 kg (7 st 7 lb). By the age of nine he was able to carry his 1.8-m (5-ft 11-in), 77-kg (12-st) father up the stairs of the family home. With a peak daily food consumption of 8,000 calories, his greatest recorded weight was 223 kg (35 st) on his 21st birthday.

Robert's Guinness World Records
As well as being the tallest man in medical history for whom there is irrefutable evidence, he also holds Guinness World Records for the largest hands and feet. His hands measured 32.3 cm (12.75 in) from the wrist to the tip of his middle finger, and his feet were 47 cm (18.5 in) long – his shoes were size 36 (UK) or 37AA (USA). When he was 12 years old doctors found that he had an over-active pituitary gland, the source of the human growth hormone somatotropin. Corrective surgery was dangerous and not guaranteed to work, so his parents let nature take its course.

Robert's everyday life
Robert tried to lead as normal a life as possible. He enjoyed photography and collecting stamps, and at 13 years old he became the world's tallest boy scout when he measured 2.23 m (7 ft 4 in). By the time he reached 18 he was 2.53 m (8 ft 3.5 in) tall – his clothing required three times as much cloth as normal sized clothes and his massive size 36 shoes cost $100 a pair. Robert's younger brother Harold once recalled on *Guinness World Records: Primetime* how his brother went about his day-to-day living: 'He had to duck to go through all doorways. No room on a bus, no room on a train, no seats, no airplane, everything was made for a person six feet tall or under. He probably wished that he wasn't as tall as he was and wanted a normal life, which he couldn't possibly live.'

Incredible feet!

Robert had his shoes custom-made by the International Shoe Company, and when he was aged 20 he was invited to become a goodwill ambassador for the firm. Robert and his father made an extensive tour around the western USA, promoting the company who made his shoes free of charge. His brother Harold commented:

'He couldn't go anywhere without being stared at and drawing a crowd. Some people would bother him, you know, because of his height. They might come up behind him and pinch his leg or something else, you know, or even maybe try to kick him in the shins, make sure he wasn't on stilts.'

Robert Wadlow pictured above with his family (from left to right): brother Eugene, mother Addie with brother Harold Jr, sister Betty, father Harold and sister Helen.

When did he break the record?

Robert gained a place in the history books when he exceeded 2.53 m (8 ft 3.5 in) in 1936, beating the record held by Irishman Patrick Cotter O'Brien who measured 2.46 m (8 ft 1 in) before he died in 1806.

Why did he die so young?

Apart from the difficulties associated with his abnormal height, Robert was very healthy, but for many years he was troubled by medical problems with his huge feet. He had poor circulation in his long legs as well as limited sensation in his feet and did not feel any rubbing or chafing until blisters had formed.

In July 1940, when aged 22, Robert was provided with a brace designed to strengthen his ankles. However, the brace was poorly fitted and a septic blister formed on his right ankle. His poor circulation and lack of sensation meant that the blister went unnoticed for some days and by the time he arrived in Manistee, Michigan, a week later to make a guest appearance, a fatal infection had set in.

Robert passed away in his sleep at 1:30 am on 15 July 1940. He was buried in Oakwood Cemetery in his hometown of Alton, Illinois. The 3.28-m-long (10-ft 9-in) coffin was carried by 12 men. Out of respect, the town of Alton closed for the day and over 40,000 people signed the register at his funeral. After Robert's death, his family destroyed most of his belongings as they did not want collectors to put his personal items on display.

Robert Wadlow height chart

Age	Height	Weight
5	1.63 m (5 ft 4 in)	48 kg (7 st 7 lb)
8	1.83 m (6 ft)	77 kg (12 st)
9	1.89 m (6 ft 2.25 in)	82 kg (12 st 12 lb)
10	1.99 m (6 ft 5 in)	95.6 kg (15 st)
11	2.00 m (6 ft 7 in)	-
12	2.10 m (6 ft 10.5 in)	-
14	2.26 m (7 ft 5 in)	137 kg (21 st 7 lb)
15	2.34 m (7 ft 8 in)	161 kg (25 st 5 lb)
16	2.40 m (7 ft 10.24 in)	170 kg (26 st 10 lb)
17	2.45 m (8 ft 0.38 in)	143 kg (22 st 7 lb)
18	2.53 m (8 ft 3.5 in)	-
19	2.58 m (8 ft 5.5 in)	218 kg (34 st 4 lb)
20	2.61 m (8 ft 6.75 in)	-
21	2.65 m (8 ft 8.25 in)	223 kg (35 st)
22.4	2.72 m (8 ft 11.1 in)	199 kg (31 st 5 lb)

Robert Wadlow is remembered by his family as a 'quiet young man who overcame a unique handicap, and who was an inspiration to all of those that knew him'. His record remains one of the most popular and memorable in the 50-year history of *Guinness World Records*.

How big is your hand compared with Robert's?

« Largest sesamoid bone

The patella or knee cap (left) is the largest sesamoid bone in the human body. Sesamoids are ovoid like the seeds of the sesame plant and most are only a few millimetres in diameter. They are usually embedded tendons close to joints or where the tendons angle sharply round bone. Their function is to take compression when a tendon is going around a joint, as when kneeling.

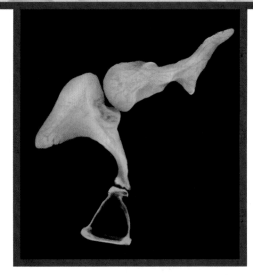

Smallest joint ⌃

The smallest joint is in the ear, between the smallest bone, the stapes or stirrup bone (above, bottom), and the incus bone (above, middle). The stapes measures a mere 2.6–3.4 mm (0.1–0.13 in) in length and weighs 2–4.3 mg (0.03–0.066 grains).

★ Largest muscle
Muscles normally account for 40% of human body weight in men and 35% in women. The bulkiest of the 639 named muscles in the human body is usually the *gluteus maximus* or buttock muscle, which extends the thigh. However, in pregnancy the uterus or womb can increase from about 30 g (1 oz) to over 1 kg (2 lb 3 oz) in weight.

★ Smallest muscle
The smallest muscle in the human body is the *stapedius*, which controls the stapes in the ear. The muscle is less than 0.127 cm (0.05 in) long.

★ Most active muscle
It has been estimated that the eye muscles move more than 100,000 times a day. Many of these rapid eye movements take place during the dreaming phase of sleep.

★ Longest muscle
The longest muscle in the human body is the *sartorius*, which is a narrow ribbon-like muscle running from the pelvis and across the front of the thigh to the top of the tibia below the knee. Its action is to draw the lower limb into the cross-legged position.

★ Longest bone
Excluding a variable number of sesamoids (small rounded bones), there are 206 bones in the adult human body, compared with about 300 for children (as they grow, some bones fuse together). The thigh bone, or femur, is the longest. It constitutes 27.5% of a person's stature normally, and may be expected to be 50 cm (19.75 in) long in a man measuring 1.8 m (6 ft) tall. The longest recorded bone was a femur measuring 76 cm (29.9 in), which belonged to Constantine, a German giant.

★ Largest internal organ
The largest organ in the human body, the adult liver can weigh between 1.2 and 1.5 kg (2 lb 10 oz and 3 lb 4 oz) – about one thirty-sixth of the total body weight. Located behind the lower ribs and below the diaphragm, it performs over 100 separate bodily functions and can measure up to 22 cm (8.6 in) long and 10 cm (3.9 in) wide.

★ Largest gall bladder
On 15 March 1989, at the National Naval Medical Center in Bethesda, Maryland, USA, Prof Bimal C Ghosh (USA) removed a gall bladder weighing 10.4 kg (23 lb) from a 69-year-old woman.

★ Largest gallstone
The largest gallstone reported in medical literature was one of 6.29 kg (13 lb 14 oz) removed from an 80-year-old woman by Dr Humphrey Arthure (UK) at Charing Cross Hospital, London, UK, on 29 December 1952.

★ Largest bladder stone
Dr Kadri Al-Ban removed from one of his patients, Mohammed Ali A Al-Muleiki (both Yemen), a vesical (bladder) stone weighing 260 g (9.17 oz) and with a diameter of about 7 cm (2.75 in) at the Al-Kadri Clinic, Ibb, Yemen, on 25 October 1998.

★ Rarest blood group
A type of Bombay blood (sub-type h-h) has so far been found only in a Czechoslovak nurse in 1961 and in a brother (Rhesus positive) and sister (Rhesus negative) named Jalbert in Massachusetts, USA, reported in February 1968. Using the ABO system, one of 14 systems, group AB occurs in less than 3% of persons in the UK and 1% in the USA.

★ Most common blood group
On a world basis, Group O is the most common blood group (46%), but in some countries, for example Norway, Group A predominates.

★ Largest artery
The aorta is 3 cm (1.18 in) in diameter where it leaves the heart and by the time it ends at the level of the fourth lumbar vertebra, it is about 1.75 cm (0.68 in) in diameter.

Longest life of a cell ⌃
Brain cells (above) last for life. By way of comparison, bone cells may live for only 10–30 years.

★ Largest vein
The inferior vena cava, which returns the blood from the lower half of the body to the heart and is slightly larger than the aorta, is the largest vein in the body.

★ Largest cell
The megakaryocyte, a blood cell, measures 0.2 mm (0.007 in). It is found in the bone marrow and produces the 'stickiest' particles in the body – the platelets – which play an important role in blood clotting.

★ Smallest cell
The brain cells in the cerebellum measure about 0.005 mm (0.0001968 in) or 5 microns.

★ Longest cell
Motor neurons are some 1.3 m (4 ft 3.12 in) long; they have cell bodies (grey matter) in the lower spinal cord with axons (white matter) that carry nerve impulses from the spinal cord down to the big toe. The cell systems that carry certain sensations (vibration and positional sense) back from the big toe to the brain are even longer. Their uninterrupted length, from the toe and up the posterior part of the spinal cord to the medulla of the brain, is about equal to the height of the body.

★ Most abundant cell
The body contains in the region of 30 billion red blood cells (erythrocytes), approximately 5×10^{12} in every litre of blood (8.75×10^{12} in every pint). The function of these cells is to carry oxygen around the body.

★ Longest-lived human cells
The cells of Henrietta Lacks (USA) are still alive and being grown in laboratories worldwide decades after her death from cancer on 4 October 1951 when she was 31. A single cell was removed and was subsequently found to lack chromosome 11, which is now known as the 'tumour suppressor'. As a result of this biological error, the cell is immortal and is one of the most helpful tools in biomedical research.

★ Fastest turnover of body cells
The body cells with the shortest life are in the lining of the alimentary tract, where the cells are shed every three to four days.

★ Longest memory of a cell
A lymphocyte is a type of white blood cell that is part of the body's immune defence system. As successive generations of lymphocytes are produced during one's life, they never forget an enemy.

★ Heaviest brain
In December 1992, Dr George T Mandybur (USA), at the University of Cincinnati, Ohio, USA, reported the weight of a 30-year-old male's brain as being 2.3 kg (5 lb 1.1 oz).

★ Lightest brain
The lightest 'normal' or non-atrophied brain on record was one weighing 680 g (1 lb 8 oz). It belonged to Daniel Lyon (Ireland), who died aged 46 in New York, USA, in 1907. He was just over 1.5 m (5 ft) in height and weighed 66 kg (145 lb). A normal adult brain weighs in the region of 1.4 kg (3 lb).

★ Highest hyperacuity
The human eye is capable of judging relative position with remarkable accuracy, reaching limits of between 3 and 5 seconds of arc. In April 1984, Dr Dennis M Levi (USA) of the College of Optometry, University of Houston, Texas, USA, repeatedly identified the relative position of a thin bright green line within 0.85 seconds of arc. This is equivalent to a displacement of some 6 mm (0.25 in) at a distance of 1.6 km (1 mile).

★ Strongest joint
The hip joint is the strongest and one of the most stable joints as the head of the femur fits almost perfectly into the socket of the pelvis.

★ Most mobile joint
The shoulder joint is the most mobile and as a result is the joint that is easiest to dislocate.

« Farthest eyeball popper

Kim Goodman (USA, left) can pop her eyeballs to a distance of 11 mm (0.43 in) beyond her eye sockets. Her eyes were measured on the set of the television show *Guinness World Records: Primetime* in Los Angeles, California, USA, on 13 June 1998. Kim first discovered her unique and somewhat startling talent when she was accidentally hit on the head with a hockey mask and one of her eyeballs popped out much further than normal. Ever since that day, Kim's eyes would protrude out of her head every time she yawned, and she has now taught herself to pop her eyes out on cue.

★ Earliest successful artificial eye
On 17 January 2000, it was announced that Jeremiah Teehan (USA), who lost his sight after a blow to his head 36 years before, could see again thanks to an artificial eye developed by William Dobelle (USA). Jeremiah became the second person to receive surgery of this kind, and the first to have had successful results.

★ Largest plate inserted in human skull
Tom Thompson (USA) had a titanium plate measuring 15 x 11 cm (5.9 x 4.33 in) inserted into the left side of his head by neurosurgeons at DeKalb General Hospital, Decatur, Georgia, USA, on 30 April 1971. The surgery took place after he had been struck by a car and was pronounced dead on arrival at the local hospital.

★ Strangest diet
Michel Lotito (France), known as Monsieur Henri Mangetout, has been eating metal and glass since 1959. Gastroenterologists have X-rayed his stomach and have described his ability to consume 900 g (2 lb) of metal per day as unique.

★ Heaviest object removed from stomach
The heaviest object extracted from a human stomach was a ball of hair weighing 2.53 kg (5 lb 3 oz) from a 20-year-old female compulsive swallower in the South Devon and East Cornwall Hospital, UK, on 30 March 1895.

★ Oldest patient to undergo surgery
The greatest recorded age at which anyone has undergone an operation is 111 years 105 days for a hip operation on James Henry Brett Jr (USA) on 7 November 1960.

★ Farthest distance travelled by a human voice
The normal intelligible outdoor range of the male human voice in still air is 180 m (590 ft). Silbo, the whistled language of the Spanish-speaking inhabitants of the Canary Island of La Gomera, is intelligible under ideal conditions at 8 km (5 miles).

There is a recorded case, under optimal acoustic conditions, of a Silbo speaker being heard at a distance of 17 km (10.5 miles) across still water at night.

★ Highest G force endured non-voluntarily
Racing driver David Purley (UK) survived a deceleration from 173 km/h (108 mph) to zero in 66 cm (26 in) in a crash at Silverstone, Northamptonshire, UK, on 13 July 1977. He endured 179.8 G and suffered 29 fractures, three dislocations and six heart stoppages.

★ Highest blood sugar level
Alexa Painter (USA) survived a blood sugar level 20.7 times above average at 139 mmol/litre (2,495 mg/decalitre) when she was admitted to the Community Hospital of Roanoke, Virginia, USA, to be treated for severe diabetic ketoacidosis on 30 December 1991 at the age of two. The normal blood sugar range is between 4.4 and 6.6 mmol/litre (80–120 mg/dl).

★ Longest medical operation
The most protracted operation reported lasted for 96 hours and was performed in Chicago, Illinois, USA, on 4–8 February 1951 when an ovarian cyst was removed from Gertrude Levandowski (USA). During the operation her weight fell 280 kg (44 stone or 616 lb) to 140 kg (22 stone or 308 lb).

★ Earliest heart transplant patient
The first heart transplant was performed on Louis Washkansky (South Africa), aged 55, at the Groote Schuur Hospital, Cape Town, South Africa, between 1 am and 6 am on 3 December 1967, by a team of 30 headed by Prof Christiaan Barnard (South Africa). The donor was Denise Ann Darvall (South Africa), aged 25. Washkansky lived for 18 days.

First hand ⌃
transplant

During a 14-hour operation in Lyon, France, in 1998, an international team of eight surgeons attached the hand of a dead man to the wrist of 48-year-old Clint Hallam (Australia, above).

Furthest traced descendant by DNA »

Adrian Targett (UK) has been linked through some 300 generations and shown to be a direct descendant, on his mother's side, of Cheddar Man, a 9,000-year-old skeleton (right), one of the oldest complete skeletons found in Great Britain in 1903.

★ **Longest heart transplant survival**
Sammy Katy King (USA) survived 24 years 142 days after having received a 24-year-old male's heart at Stanford University, Palo Alto, California, USA, on 4 April 1975.

★ **Earliest recipient of an artificial heart**
On 1–2 December 1982, at the Utah Medical Center, Salt Lake City, Utah, USA, 61-year-old Barney Clark (USA) became the first recipient of an artificial heart, a Jarvik 7. The patient died on 23 March 1983, 112 days later.

★ **Longest artificial heart transplant survival**
After his heart transplant on 25 November 1984, William J Schroeder (USA) survived 620 days.

★ **Longest cardiac arrest**
The longest cardiac arrest is four hours in the case of fisherman Jan Egil Refsdahl (Norway), who fell overboard into the icy waters off Bergen,

Norway, on 7 December 1987. He was rushed to nearby Haukeland Hospital after his body temperature fell to 24°C (75°F) and his heart stopped beating. He made a full recovery once he was connected to a heart-lung machine.

★ **Earliest successful kidney transplant**
The first successful kidney transplant in a human was performed by RH Lawler (USA) at Little Company of Mary Hospital, Chicago, Illinois, USA, on 17 June 1950.

★ **Most fluid removed after hydronephrosis**
A 35-year-old Egyptian patient suffering from hydronephrosis – an enlargement of the kidney caused by a blockage of normal urine flow – had 22 litres (38.7 pints) of urine removed from his kidney on 16 June 1999, at the Bugshan Hospital, Jeddah, Saudi Arabia. (The kidney's normal urine capacity is 3–5 ml or 0.105–0.175 fl oz.) The kidney was eventually removed on

6 July 1999, measuring 50 x 40 x 25 cm (19.6 x 15.7 x 9.8 in) and weighing 700 g (24.6 oz).

★ **Most sets of teeth**
Cases of the growth of a third set of teeth in late life have been recorded several times. A reference to a case in France of a fourth dentition, known as Lison's case, was published in 1896.

★ **Most lightning strikes survived**
The only man in the world to be struck by lightning seven times was ex-park ranger Roy C Sullivan (USA), the 'human lightning conductor' of Virginia, USA. A single lightning strike is

made up of several 100 million volts (with peak current in the order of 20,000 amps).

★ **Longest survivor of a porcine aortic valve replacement**
Harry Driver (UK) received a porcine (pig's) aortic valve replacement on 12 April 1978 under surgeon Dr John Keats (UK). It functioned for 25 years 238 days until it was replaced by another on 16 March 2004 by Dr Philip Kay (UK).

★ **Fastest sneeze**
The highest speed at which expelled particles from a sneeze have been measured to travel is 167 km/h (103.6 mph).

Rarest « form of conjoined twins

The most extreme form of conjoined twins is known as *dicephales tetrabrachius dipus* (two heads, four arms and two legs). The only fully reported example of this is Masha and Dasha Krivoshlyapovy (USSR, left), who were born on 3 January 1950 and died within 17 hours of each other on 17 April 2003, aged 53 years 104 days.

Most children delivered ⌃ at a single birth to survive

Bobbie McCaughey (USA) gave birth to a set of septuplets (above) on 19 November 1997 at the University Hospital, Iowa, USA. Conceived by in-vitro fertilization, the four boys and three girls were delivered after 31 weeks by Caesarean section, and weighed between 1,048 g and 1,474.3 g (2 lb 5 oz and 3 lb 4 oz). Another set of surviving septuplets were born eight weeks prematurely on 14 January 1998 to Hasna Mohammed Humair (Saudi Arabia). The four boys and three girls were born at the Abha Obstetric Hospital, Aseer, Saudi Arabia.

★ Lightest birth
A premature baby girl weighing 280 g (9.87 oz) was reported to have been born on 27 June 1989 at the Loyola University Medical Center, Illinois, USA. The lowest birthweight recorded for a surviving infant, of which there is definite evidence, is 283 g (10 oz) in the case of Marian Taggart (UK), who was born six weeks premature in 1938 in South Shields, Tyne & Wear, UK.

★ Heaviest birth
Anna Bates (Canada), who measured 2.27 m (7 ft 5.5 in), gave birth to a boy weighing 10.8 kg (23 lb 12.8 oz) and 76 cm (30 in) in length at her home in Seville, Ohio, USA, on 19 January 1879, but the baby died 11 hours later.

★ Most premature baby
James Elgin Gill was born to Brenda Gill (Canada) on 20 May 1987 in Ottawa, Ontario, Canada, 128 days (18 weeks) premature and weighing 624 g (1 lb 6 oz). The normal human gestation period is 280 days (40 weeks).

★ First 'Siamese' twins
The term 'Siamese' was first applied to conjoined twins in connection with the celebrated Chang and Eng Bunker, born at Meklong, Siam (now Thailand), on 11 May 1811. They were joined by a cartilaginous band at the chest. In April 1843 the twins married sisters Sarah and Adelaide Yates (USA) and fathered 10 and 12 children respectively. The twins died within three hours of each other on 17 January 1874, aged 62 years 251 days.

★ Oldest mother
It was reported that Rosanna dalla Corte (Italy, b. February 1931) gave birth to a baby boy on 18 July 1994 when she was 63 years old.

★ Most albino siblings
Of the eight children born to George and Minnie Sesler (both USA), four of their five sons were born with the rare genetic condition albinism. John, George, Kermit and Kenneth were all born with translucent skin, pinkish-blue eyes and white hair.

★ Most generations born on leap day
The only verified example of a family producing three consecutive generations born on 29 February is that of the Keoghs. Peter Anthony (Ireland, b. 1940), his son Peter Eric (UK, b. 1964) and his granddaughter Bethany Wealth (UK, b. 1996) all celebrate their birthdays every four years.

★ Most generations born on the same day
Four families hold this record. Ralph Betram Williams (USA) was born on 4 July 1982 in Wilmington, North Carolina, USA. His father, grandfather and, in 1876, his great-grandfather were also born on 4 July.
Veera Tuulia Tuijantyär Kivistö (Finland), born in 1997, shares her birthday of 21 March with her mother (b. 1967), her grandfather (b. 1940) and great-grandfather (b. 1903).
Maureen Werner (USA) was born on 13 October 1998 and shares her birthday with her mother (b. 1970), her grandfather (b. 1938) and great-grandmother (b. 1912).
Jacob Camren Hildebrandt (USA) was born in 2001 and shares his birthday of 23 August with his father (b. 1966), his grandmother (b. 1944) and great-grandmother (b. 1919).

★ Most children delivered at a single birth
The highest recorded number of children born at a single birth is nine to Geraldine Brodrick (Australia) at the Royal Hospital for Women, Sydney, Australia, on 13 June 1971. None of the children (five boys and four girls) lived for more than six days.

★ Most consecutive generations of twins
Three consecutive generations of the Roy family (Canada) have given birth to twins: Joyce Roy, a twin born 22 May 1951, gave birth to Diane and Carole on 17 January 1973. Diane gave birth to twin boys Derek and Ricky (b. 16 December 1999) and Carole had twin girls Kelly and Ashley (b. 12 May 2001).

Oldest »
woman ever

The greatest fully authenticated age to which any human has ever lived is 122 years 164 days by Jeanne Louise Calment (France, right). Born on 21 February 1875, she died at a nursing home in Arles, southern France, on 4 August 1997.

Centenarians surviving beyond their 113th year are extremely rare: the present absolute proven limit of human longevity is just over 122 years. Data on centenarians has shown that only one 115-year life can be expected in 2.1 billion lives.

★ **Oldest living woman**
Hendrikje Van Andel-Schipper (Netherlands, b. 29 June 1890) took the title of the world's oldest living woman at the age of 113 years 335 days on 29 May 2004.

★ **Oldest living man**
American Fred Hale (b. 1 December 1890) became the world's oldest living man on 5 March 2004 at the age of 113 years 95 days.

★ **Oldest man ever**
Born on 29 June 1865, the oldest man ever recorded was Shigechiyo Izumi (Japan), who was listed as a six-year-old in Japan's first census of 1871. He died on 21 February 1986 aged 120 years 237 days.

Oldest living people since 1955

Name	Country born	Born	Died	Country died	Age
1. Betsy Baker	UK	20 August 1842	24 October 1955	USA	113 years 65 days
2. Martha Graham	USA	December 1844	25 June 1959	USA	114 years c.180 days
3. James Henry Brett Jr	USA	25 July 1849	10 February 1961	USA	111 years 200 days
4. James Hull	UK	23 April 1852	9 September 1961	Australia	109 years 139 days
5. Lovisa Svensson	Sweden	20 November 1853	17 February 1963	Sweden	109 years 89 days
6. Kiet Portier-Tan	Netherlands	13 May 1855	21 April 1963	Netherlands	107 years 343 days
7. John Mosely Turner	UK	15 June 1856	21 March 1968	UK	111 years 280 days
8. Johanna Booyston	South Africa	17 January 1857	16 June 1968	South Africa	111 years 151 days
9. Marie Bernatkova	Czech Republic	22 October 1857	alive October 1968		111 years +days
10. Ada Roe	UK	6 February 1858	11 January 1970	UK	111 years 339 days
11. Josefa Salas Mateo	Spain	14 July 1860	27 February 1973	Spain	112 years 228 days
12. Alice Stevenson	UK	10 July 1861	18 August 1973	UK	112 years 39 days
13. Elizabeth Watkins	UK	10 March 1863	31 October 1973	UK	110 years 235 days
14. Mito Umeta	Japan	27 March 1863	31 May 1975	Japan	112 years 65 days
15. Niwa Kawamoto	Japan	5 August 1863	16 November 1976	Japan	113 years 103 days
16. Shigechiyo Izumi	Japan	29 June 1865	21 February 1986	Japan	120 years 237 days
17. Mamie Eva Keith	USA	22 March 1873	20 September 1986	USA	113 years 182 days
18. Mary McKinney	USA	30 May 1873	2 February 1987	USA	113 years 248 days
19. Anna Williams	UK	2 June 1873	27 December 1987	UK	114 years 208 days
20. Florence Knapp	USA	10 October 1873	11 January 1988	USA	114 years 93 days
21. Carrie White [1]	USA	18 November 1874	14 February 1991	USA	116 years 88 days
22. Jeanne Calment	France	21 February 1875	4 August 1997	France	122 years 164 days
23. Marie-Louise Meilleur	Canada	29 August 1880	16 April 1998	Canada	117 years 230 days
24. Sarah Knauss	USA	24 September 1880	30 December 1999	USA	119 years 97 days
25. Eva Morris	UK	8 November 1885	2 November 2000	UK	114 years 360 days
26. Marie Bremont	France	25 April 1886	6 June 2001	France	115 years 42 days
27. Maud Farris Luse	USA	21 January 1887	18 March 2002	USA	115 years 56 days
28. Kamato Hongo	Japan	16 September 1887	31 October 2003	Japan	116 years 45 days
29. Mitoyo Kawate	Japan	15 May 1889	13 November 2003	Japan	114 years 182 days
30. Ramona Trinidad Iglesias-Jordan [2]	Puerto Rico	31 August 1889	29 May 2004	Puerto Rico	114 years 272 days
31. Hendrikje Van Andel-Schipper	The Netherlands	29 June 1890			113 years 335 days*

[1] Authentication called into question by census data   *still living as of 29 May 2004

[2] Title given to Charlotte Benkner (USA, b. 16 November 1889, d. 14 May 2004 aged 114 years 181 days) on 13 November 2003 aged 113 years 362 days and withdrawn on 29 March 2004 following receipt of documentation supporting Ramona Trinidad Iglesias-Jordan's claim.

Most ≪ spoons balanced on the face

Jonathan Friedman (USA) was able to balance 13 stainless-steel spoons on his face (one on each ear, two on each cheek, two on his chin, one on his lips, one on his nose and three on his forehead). He balanced them for 2 minutes at Lake Oswego, Oregon, USA, on 30 March 2004, aged 12.

Guinness World Records photographed Jonathan in November 2003 balancing nine spoons (left).

Youngest solo ⌃ circumnavigation

The youngest person to sail solo around the world is David Griffiths Dicks (Australia, above) who was 18 years 41 days old when he completed his circumnavigation back to Freemantle, Western Australia, in a time of 264 days 16 hr 49 min on 16 November 1996.

★ **Youngest physician**
Balamurali Ambati (USA, b. 29 July 1977) became the world's youngest doctor when he graduated from the Mount Sinai School of Medicine in New York City, USA, on 19 May 1995 at the age of 17.

★ **Youngest actor to receive star billing**
Leroy Overacker (USA, b. 12 May 1932), known on screen as 'Baby Leroy', was chosen at the age of six months to play opposite Maurice Chevalier in *A Bedtime Story* (USA, 1933).

★ **Youngest consultant**
On 15 April 2000, supermarket chain Tesco announced that it had procured the services of seven-year-old Laurie Sleator (UK) to advise senior executives on the Pokémon craze that was sweeping the globe. His advice contributed to Tesco selling over £1 million ($1.55 million) worth of Pokémon goods over the Easter weekend. Laurie was remunerated in the form of Pokémon products.

★ **Youngest billionaire**
The world's youngest billionaire is His Serene Highness 12th Prince Albert von Thurn und Taxis (Germany, b. 24 June 1983) with an estimated net worth of $2.1 billion (£1.14 billion) according to the *Forbes* Rich List 2004. On his 18th birthday he became the sole heir of a royal family fortune that includes extensive landholdings, real estate, castles, works of art and businesses.

★ **Youngest person to visit both poles**
The youngest person to have visited both geographical poles is Jonathan Silverman (USA, b. 13 June 1990), who reached the North Pole on 25 July 1999 and the South Pole on 10 January 2002, aged 11 years 211 days.

★ **Youngest person to visit the North Pole**
Alicia Hempleman-Adams (UK, b. 8 November 1989) stood at the geographic North Pole at the age of 8 years 173 days on 1 May 1998, the youngest person ever to have done so.

She flew to the pole to meet her father, the well-known adventurer David Hempleman-Adams (UK), at the end of his successful trek to the pole.

★ **Youngest person to walk to the South Pole**
Andrew Cooney (UK, b. 9 April 1979) became the youngest person to walk from the edge of the Antarctic continent to the South Pole, when he arrived there at the age of 23 years 268 days on 2 January 2003, 54 days after setting out.

★ **Youngest person to travel to all seven continents**
The youngest person to have travelled to all seven continents is Tanya Daniella Donkin (South Africa) who visited her seventh continent on 16 November 2000 at the age of 3 years 319 days. All her travels were with her parents, Dave and Irene Donkin (both South Africa). Tanya was born in South Africa (Africa) on 2 January 1997; landed in Zurich, Switzerland (Europe) on 20 February 1997; in Buenos

Aires, Argentina (South America) on 14 December 1997; on Deception Island (Antarctica) on 28 December 1997; in Miami, USA (North America) on 17 December 1998; in Sydney, Australia (Australasia) on 17 December 1999; and in Dubai, United Arab Emirates (Asia) on 16 November 2000.

★ **Youngest published male author**
At the age of six, Dennis Vollmer (USA, b. 21 July 1980) wrote and illustrated *Joshua Disobeys* and had it commercially published by Landmark Editions, Inc., of Kansas City, Missouri, USA, after his story won a national student writing contest in 1987.

★ **Youngest published female author**
The youngest commercially published female author is Dorothy Straight (USA, b. 25 May 1958), who wrote *How the World Began* in 1962, aged only four. It was published by Pantheon Books in August 1964.

Youngest ⌃ published cook

Justin Miller (USA, b. 10 January 1990; above) was seven years old when *Cooking with Justin: Recipes for Kids (And Parents)* was published in 1997. Apart from writing, he also advises the Marriott Hotel chain on its children's menus.

Youngest ⌄ radio presenter

On 16 January 1999, Cody Morton (Canada, b. 12 June 1988; below) hosted a show on CHOO FM in Tofino, British Columbia, Canada, aged 10 years 218 days.

★ **Youngest figure skating world champion**
The youngest female winner of a world title is Tara Lipinski (USA, b. 10 June 1982), who won the individual title on 22 March 1997 aged just 14 years 286 days.

★ **Youngest Wimbledon competitor**
The youngest Wimbledon competitor was Mita Klima (Austria) who was just 13 years old in the 1907 singles competition.

★ **Youngest person to win a match at Wimbledon**
The youngest person to win a match at Wimbledon is Jennifer Capriati (USA, b. 29 March 1976), who was aged 14 years 89 days when she competed in her first Wimbledon tennis match on 26 June 1990.

★ **Youngest football World Cup player**
The youngest player to play in football's premier tournament is Souleymane Mamam (Togo) who played for Togo against Zambia aged 13 years 310 days in a preliminary qualifying game on 6 May 2001.

★ **Youngest professional artist**
Dante Lamb (USA, b. 16 November 1999) is the youngest artist to have his work purchased and displayed. Dante's abstract paintings hang in the Monkey Love Dessert Bar & Gallery, St Simons Island, Georgia, USA, and his first piece sold on 6 October 2003 for $85 (£50) when he was only three years old.

★ **Most consecutive pea shooting World Championships**
The most consecutive pea shooting World Championships won is three by Mike Fordham (UK) in 1983–85 and David Hollis (UK) in 1999–2001. Hollis was also the youngest World Champion, aged just 13 when he scooped the title in 1999. The Championships are held every year in Witcham, Cambridgeshire, UK.

★ **Youngest international gymnast**
Pasakevi Voula Kouna (Greece, b. 6 December 1971) was aged 9 years 299 days at the start of the Balkan Games at Serres, Greece, on 1 October 1981, when she represented Greece.

★ **Youngest world line dance champion**
Siobhan Dunn (UK, b. 30 June 1991) won the Junior World Line Dance Championship in Nashville, Tennessee, USA, on 10 January 1998 aged just 6 years 194 days.

★ **Youngest TV presenter**
The world's youngest presenter of a regular television programme is Sheridan Jobbins (Australia) who, at the age of nine, began hosting *Cooking With Sheri* (Channel 7, Australia) in April 1969. The five-minute weekly (and then daily) show continued to air nationally for three consecutive years, ending when she was 11 years old. In total, 26 episodes were filmed.

★ **Youngest solo rap artist**
Jordy Lemoine (France, b. 14 January 1988) was at No.1 in the French charts with techno/house rap 'Dur dur d'être Bébé' ('It's Hard to Be a Baby') at the age of four and a half in September 1993. The song later entered the US *Billboard* chart.

★ **Youngest DJ**
Llewellyn Owen aka 'DJ Welly' (UK, b. 21 February 1992) headlined at London's Warp Club on 1 May 2000 aged 8 years 70 days. Welly was paid the standard rate for headlining DJs, £125 ($190) an hour. Since his professional debut, he has headlined at famous clubs such as Ministry of Sound (UK).

★ **Youngest film director-writer-producer**
Lex the Wonderdog (Netherlands, 1973), a thriller of canine detection, was written, produced and directed by Sydney Ling (Netherlands, b. 20 November 1959) when he was 13 years old. He was the youngest ever director of a professionally made feature-length film.

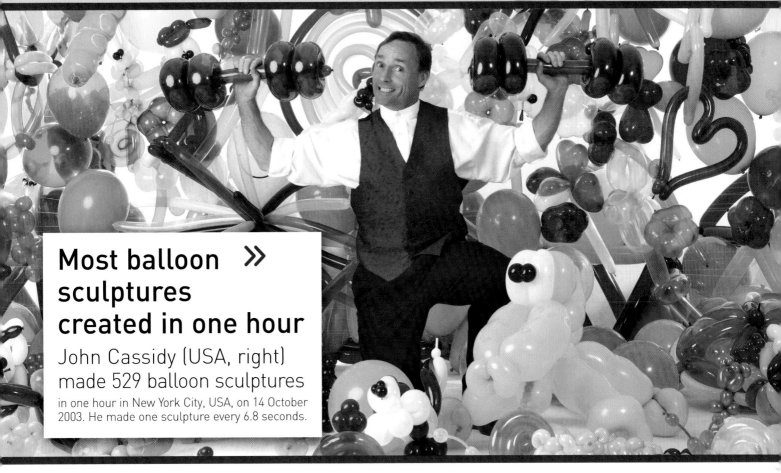

Most balloon » sculptures created in one hour

John Cassidy (USA, right) made 529 balloon sculptures in one hour in New York City, USA, on 14 October 2003. He made one sculpture every 6.8 seconds.

★ **Most body skips in a minute**
Ved Prakash Sharma (India) was able to 'skip' with his arms while handcuffed, by stepping through his arms and bringing them up and over his head, a total of 27 times in a minute at Bhim Stadium, Bhiwani, India, on 15 August 2003.

★ **Furthest basketball slam dunk from a trampoline**
Jonathon Thibout (France) managed to slam dunk a basketball from a trampoline placed 5.8 m (19 ft) from the back board of the net on the set of L'Eté de tous les Records, Port Leucate, France, on 29 August 2003.

★ **Greatest distance zorbing**
The greatest distance travelled by a zorb ball in a single roll is 323 m (1,059 ft 8.5 in) by Rich Eley (UK) near Glynde, East Sussex, UK, on 10 May 1999. During the attempt, the zorb reached a record speed of 49.8 km/h (31 mph). The zorb originated in New Zealand and is a large, round, bouncy ball that can accommodate one person. As it rolls, the person strapped inside rolls too. A zorb ball weighs approximately 89 kg (198 lb), and keeps the 'zorbonaut' in an air cushion about 60 cm (2 ft) off the ground.

★ **Most divisions of a human hair**
Alfred West (UK) succeeded in splitting a human hair 17 times into 18 parts on eight occasions. All the divisions were made from the same point.

★ **Tallest coin column**
The tallest single column of coins ever stacked on the edge of a coin was built by Dipak Syal (India) on 3 May 1991 and comprised 253 Indian one-rupee pieces on top of a vertical five-rupee coin.

★ **Greatest number of skips on a tightrope**
Walfer Guerrero (Colombia) achieved 1,250 consecutive turns skipping with a rope on a high wire at the Wereldcircus Carré, Haarlem, The Netherlands, on 1 June 1995. The tightrope was 9.6 m (31 ft 5 in) high.

★ **Most 'ducks and drakes'**
The record for the most consecutive skips of a stone on water is 40, held by Kurt Steiner (USA). The cast was achieved at the Pennsylvania Qualifying Stone Skipping Tournament held at Riverfront Park, Franklin, Pennsylvania, USA, on 14 September 2002.

★ **Most tennis balls held in the hand**
Francisco Peinado Toledo (Spain) placed 18 tennis balls in his left hand and held them for 10 seconds at Valencia, Spain, on 18 September 2003.

★ **Furthest toss of a cow pat**
The record distances in the country sport of throwing dried cow pats, or 'chips', depend on whether or not the projectile may be 'moulded into a spherical shape'. The greatest distance achieved under the 'non-sphericalization and 100 per cent organic' rule (established in 1970) is 81.1 m (266 ft), by Steve Urner (USA) at the Mountain Festival, Tehachapi, California, USA, on 14 August 1981.

★ **Most tea cups caught on the head while unicycling**
In 1952, unicyclist Rudy Horn (Germany) became the first person to throw six cups and saucers with his feet and balance them on his head, while mounted on a unicycle. He rounded off this feat by adding a teaspoon and a lump of sugar. At the time he was performing with the Bertram Mills Circus at Olympia, London, UK.

★ **Most powerful lungs**
The inflation of a standard 1,000-g (35-oz) meteorological balloon to a diameter of 2.44 m (8 ft) against set times was achieved by Manjit Singh (UK) in 42 minutes at Rushley Pavilion Centre, Leicester, UK, on 16 September 1998.

Most basketballs ⌃ spun simultaneously

Michael Kettman (USA) spun 28 basketballs simultaneously on 25 May 1999 at Guinness World Records, London, UK. He is pictured above, setting his previous record of 25 in 1998.

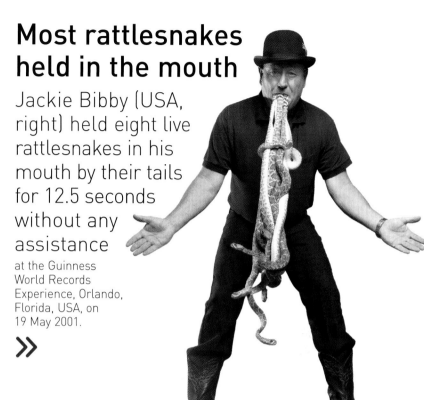

Most rattlesnakes held in the mouth

Jackie Bibby (USA, right) held eight live rattlesnakes in his mouth by their tails for 12.5 seconds without any assistance at the Guinness World Records Experience, Orlando, Florida, USA, on 19 May 2001.

»

★ GWR TALKS TO
Ashrita Furman

Ashrita Furman (USA, below) holds an amazing total of 19 Guinness World Records, including the fastest mile travelled on a pogo-stick – 12 min 16 sec set at Iffley Field, Oxford, UK, on 24 July 2001. His latest record successes include balancing 23 milk crates with a total weight of 39.92 kg (88.01 lb) on his chin for 11.23 seconds on 17 June 2002 at Jamaica, New York, USA, and the record for the running a mile while balancing a full milk bottle on his head, which he achieved in a record time of 8 min 27 sec at the TSV 1880 Sports Association Track, Starnberg, Germany, on 9 November 2003.

You set your first record in 1979. Why did you choose the jumping jacks (star jumps) record?
Well, I knew how to do it! At first I tried juggling – 100,000 throws and it took all night – but there was no category! So I trained for the jumping jacks record.

How do you get the inspiration for your records?
I take inspiration from all sorts of different places. Most records are already in the book, but I'm more open minded now; anything is possible. I like the idea of people competing for the same record. It just comes down to 'Can I do better?' It's fun to create your own category but it's also a challenge to break an existing record – you have a certain standard to reach.

What do you think about your versatility record?
I'm really chuffed. A lot of it is just down to having an active imagination. The fastest milk bottle mile, the hula-hooping record – they were just off the top of my head.

What's the attraction of breaking records all over the world?
I travel a lot anyway, so while I'm away I try to break records. I really wanted to go to Antarctica because I wanted to have set records on all seven continents. Someone I know in the Argentinian Navy got me a flight over to the Antarctic where I was able to set my 'fastest mile on a pogo-stick' record.

How do you train for pogo-sticking in Antarctica?
It's difficult! It was certainly not the best place to set a pogo-stick record but it was a fantastic adventure! I almost got blown off the pogo by a helicopter leaving the base and at about the 0.75-mile point the spring of the pogo-stick got more and more sluggish until it froze and I fell off! Fortunately we had a spare.

What's your next record attempt going to be?
I'll try skipping again, then glass balancing, then something in China. Maybe a somersault record. My current record is 8,341 forward rolls in 10 hr 30 min over 19.67 km (12 miles). I set it in 1986, but now I think I'm fitter.

What do you do to keep fit?
I go to the gym and I run a couple of times a week. Skipping keeps you in great shape. And I juggle shot-puts!

What would you say to young people wanting to break records?
I became interested in breaking records as a kid and I still feel like a big kid! My dream was to get in the book and I didn't think I could and now I have 19 records. Everyone has a special talent. I really believe there is something that everyone can do that will get you into Guinness World Records.

Lifelong achievements
Human beings

Oldest barefoot ⌃ waterskier

George Blair, aka Banana George, (USA, above, b. 22 January 1915)

successfully waterskied barefoot on Lake Florence, Winter Haven, Florida, USA, at the age of 87 years 18 days on 10 February 2002.

★ Longest working career as a barber

Peter J Vita (USA, b. 30 April 1910) has been cutting hair professionally since 1922. Mr Vita started his career in his father's barbershop when he was 12 years old. He opened his own barbershop in 1930 where he worked until 1988, before moving his business to Port Chester, New York, USA, where he continues today.

★ Longest working career in the merchant navy

From 2 May 1953 until 23 June 1969, Robert Morris (UK, b. 16 September 1928) served as cook on a total of 50 ships.

★ Longest working career as a bartender

Angelo Cammarata (USA) started his career as a bartender on 7 April 1933 when Prohibition was repealed. He served beer at his family's grocery store on the stroke of midnight and was still working in his own bar *Cammarata Days* in July 1998 – 69 years later.

★ Longest working career as a radio DJ

Ray Cordeiro, aka 'Uncle Ray', (UK, b. 12 December 1924) has been a regular disc jockey since 1949, first working for the station Rediffusion Ltd (Hong Kong) and then moving to (the now) Radio Television Hong Kong on 15 September 1960. He still hosts a regular four-hour nightly show called *All the Way with Ray* transmitted 10 pm until 2 am Monday to Friday.

★ Oldest working mime artist

American mime artist Arnold Jones (USA, b. 13 January 1914) is still working six hours a day, five days a week entertaining crowds in Hollywood, California, USA. He has been a professional mime artist for over 70 years, starting at the age of 14 as 'The Mechanical Man' at fairs across America's Midwest.

★ Longest working career as a circus bandmaster

Merle Evans (USA) was bandmaster with Ringling Brothers–Barnum & Bailey Circus for 50 years. Between 1919 and 1969 he led the band for about 30,000 performances, never missing a show.

★ Longest career as a radio actor in the same role

Norman Painting (UK) took part in the first broadcast of BBC Radio 4's *The Archers* on 1 January 1951 and is still in the series as Philip Archer.

★ Oldest chorus line member

The oldest 'showgirl' who is still regularly performing in a chorus line is Beverly Allen (USA, b. 4 November 1917). A member of The Fabulous Palm Springs Follies, her jitterbug routine – in which her partner lifts her over his head to spin her 'head-over-heels' – has become an audience favourite.

★ Longest working career as a stadium announcer

Walter Miceli (Brazil) has been the stadium announcer at the Estádio de São Januário, Rio de Janeiro, Brazil, home of Club de Regatas Vasco da Gama, since 12 February 1947.

★ Oldest BASE jumper

James Talbot Guyer (USA, b. 16 June 1928) parachuted off the 148-m-high (486-ft) Perrine Bridge, Idaho, USA, on 2 August 2002 aged 74 years 47 days.

★ Longest distance covered over a working career

Stanley E Rychlicki (USA) walked for 37 years of his 40-year career as a 'pipeline inspector' and covered a distance of 220,288 km (136,880 miles), sometimes walking in excess of 32 km (20 miles) daily in Pennsylvania and New York, USA.

Fastest time to ︽ type one to one million

Les Stewart (Australia, above) has typed the numbers one to one million manually in words on 19,990 quarto sheets. Starting in 1982, his target to become a 'millionaire' became a reality on 7 December 1998.

Longest ≫ working career as a salsa artist

Celia Cruz (Cuba, right) was a leading salsa artist for 50 years and recorded over 50 albums. She began her career singing with Cuba's then-leading band Sonora Matancera in 1950, before leaving Cuba permanently to pursue a career in the USA in 1960. She recorded some 20 gold LPs and received more than 100 awards.

★ **Oldest dance instructor**
Gisel Weser (Germany, b. 1 February 1921) is the oldest dancing teacher, having worked at Triebel-Hölzer (founded 1883) in Lutherstadt Eisleben, Saxony-Anhalt, Germany, since 1949. She became head of the school in 1968 and continues to teach.

★ **Oldest bell ringer**
Reginald Bray (UK, b. 28 October 1902) is an active member of the bell-ringing team of St Cyr and St Julitta, Newton St Cyres, Devon, UK. He rang bells on 30 October 2003, two days after his 101st birthday, and continues bell-ringing today.

★ **Oldest authors**
The oldest male author is Constantine Kallias (Greece, b. 26 June 1901), who published a 169-page paperback entitled *A Glance of My Life* in February 2003 at the age of 101.
Sisters and co-authors A Elizabeth Delany and Sarah Louise Delany published *The Delany Sisters' Book of*

Everyday Wisdom in October 1994, when Sarah Louise was 105 years old and Elizabeth was 103.

★ **Oldest competitive billiards player**
Jim Turton (UK, b. 2 January 1909) has been playing competitive billiards since 1924.

★ **Oldest competitive pool player**
Wesley Walker (USA, b. 24 April 1916) plays for Southern Vending in the Valley National 8-Ball Association league in Oklahoma, USA.

★ **Longest working career as a builder**
Edward William Beard (UK, 1878–1982) retired in October 1981 after 85 years with the firm he founded in 1896.

★ **Oldest drivers**
Two male drivers were issued with new driving licenses at the advanced age of 104: Fred Hale Sr (USA, b. 1 December 1890 – currently the oldest living man) was issued with his license in

February 1995, and drove until it expired on his 108th birthday in 1998. Layne Hall (USA), whose date of birth is uncertain (b. 24/25 December 1884 or 15 March 1880), was issued with a license on 15 June 1989 when he was either 104 (according to his death certificate) or 109 (according to his driving license). It was valid until his birthday in 1993, but he died on 20 November 1990.
The oldest female driver was Maude Tull (USA), who took to driving aged 91 after her husband died'. She was issued a renewal on 5 February 1976 when aged 104.

★ **Oldest competing aerobatic pilot**
Ian Metcher (Australia) was 85 years old when he won the basic aerobatics section of the Western Australia Light Aircraft Championships at Jandakot Airport near Fremantle, Australia, on 24 February 2001.

★ **Oldest person to abseil**
Mary Maughan (UK, b. 3 October 1908) abseiled

down a 38-m (124-ft) cliff in Parrock Quarry, Ambleside, Cumbria, UK, on 30 June 2000 when aged 91 years 8 months and 27 days.

★ **Oldest person to 'loop the loop'**
On 21 May 1998, 95-year-old Adeline Ablitt (UK, b. 1903) flew in a glider as it performed a loop over the Soaring Centre, Leicestershire, UK.

★ **Most blood donated**
Maurice Creswick (South Africa) has donated blood for a record 59 consecutive years since 1944, giving his record 336th unit of blood on 9 July 2003. Having given blood since turning 18, he has donated a total of 188.9 litres (41.5 gal).

★ **Oldest working general practitioner**
Dr Kauromal M Chandiramani (India, b. 9 May 1899) practised as a general practitioner in Mumbai (Bombay), India, for 75 years 198 days from 22 September 1923 to 9 May 1999 – his 100th birthday.

Mass participation
Human beings

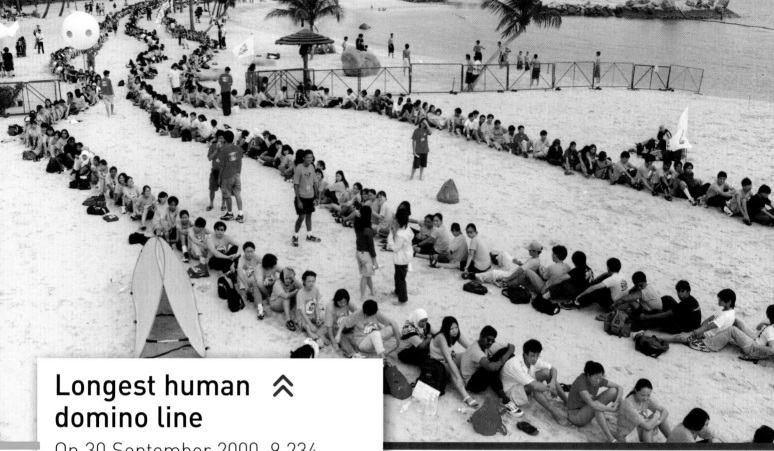

Longest human ⌃⌃ domino line

On 30 September 2000, 9,234 students aged 18-21 from NYAA Poly Connects formed
a human domino chain (above) stretching 4.2 km (2.6 miles) across Siloso Beach, Sentosa Island, Singapore.

★ Largest human chain
On 23 August 1989 up to 2 million people joined hands to form a human chain 595 km (370 miles) long across Estonia, Latvia and Lithuania, commemorating the 50th anniversary of the non-aggression treaty between the USSR and Nazi Germany.

★ Largest human rainbow
The world's largest human rainbow comprised 11,273 staff, students, alumni and families from Hong Kong Polytechnic University, and was formed at the Hong Kong Stadium, Hong Kong, China, on 6 October 2002.

★ Largest human national flag
A total of 10,371 spectators at the Scotland against Germany football game on 10 September 2003 in Westfalenstadion, Dortmund, Germany, formed the shape and colours of the German flag in the south grandstand. Participants wore coloured T-shirts and caps to form the black, red and gold flag.

★ Largest walking bus
On 8 October 2003 the Royal Borough of Kingston-upon-Thames and Transport for London (both UK) organized a 'walking bus' of 1,109 people to the schools of Fern Hill Primary, St Agatha's Catholic Primary and Latchmere Infants and Junior Schools (all UK).

★ Largest human logo
On 24 July 1999, 34,309 people organized by Realizar Eventos Especias gathered at the National Stadium of Jamor, Lisbon, Portugal, to create the Portuguese logo for Euro2004, as part of the successful Portuguese bid to UEFA to hold the European Football Championships in 2004.

★ Longest human conveyor belt
A conveyor belt consisting of 1,000 students from the University of Guelph, Canada, was formed on 7 September 1998. A surfboard was transported along its length.

★ Largest group hug
A total of 5,117 students, staff and friends from St Matthew's Secondary School in Orleans, Ontario, Canada hugged each other for 10 seconds on 23 April 2004 in support of The Force, a local cancer charity.

★ Largest circle dance
The greatest number of participants in a circle formation dance were the 6,748 people who performed the hokey cokey at Bangor, Co. Down, UK, as part of the VE Day anniversary celebrations on 6 May 1995.

★ Largest locomotion dance
A total of 669 people danced the Locomotion for seven minutes in the grounds of Haydon Bridge High School, Hexham, Northumberland, UK, on 19 October 2001.

★ Largest game of musical chairs
On 5 August 1989, the largest game of musical chairs began with 8,238 participants at the Anglo-Chinese School in Singapore. Three and a half hours later, the game ended with the lucky 15-year-old winner Xu Chong Wei on the last chair.

★ Largest simultaneous yodel
The world's largest simultaneous yodel involved 937 people all yodelling the popular Swiss song 'Von Luzern uf Wäggis zue' for more than one minute. The event was staged at the Ravensburger Spieleland, Meckenbeuren, Germany, on 5 October 2002.

≪ Largest yoga class

Manoj Gupota (India) led a yoga class of 6,315 people (left) at

Pandit Ravishankar Shukla (Wright Town) Stadium, Jabalpur, India, on 13 February 2003.

Most people brushing their ≫ teeth in the same venue

A total of 10,240 students brushed their teeth simultaneously for at least 60 seconds at Ai Guo Road, Luohu District, Shenshen City, China, on 20 September 2003. The event was organized by Health Bureau of Luohu District, Education Bureau of Luohu District and the Chamber of Commerce of Luohu District and sponsored by Colgate-Palmolive (Guangzhou) Co. Ltd.

★ Most people on unicycles

On 18 May 2003, 100 students from the circus school Circus Jopie travelled on unicycles for a distance of 350 m (1,150 ft) at Utrecht, The Netherlands. Their first attempt was in a single line wearing a 450-m-long (1,475-ft) dragon costume. Unfortunately, the costume separated in two halves during the journey.

★ Most people sitting on one chair

On 20 September 2002, 407 pupils from Otto-Hahn-Gymnasium (high school) in Springe, Germany, sat on one chair at the same time. The unbroken line of pupils, each seated on the knees of the person behind, measured 60.7 m (199 ft 1.2 in) long.

★ Largest unsupported circle

The largest number of people in an unsupported circle (where you sit on the lap of the person behind you) is 10,323, achieved by employees of the Nissan Motor Company at Komazawa Stadium, Tokyo, Japan, on 23 October 1982.

★ Most people skipping rope simultaneously

On 2 April 2003, a total of 1,356 schoolchildren skipped ropes simultaneously at Bishopston School, Swansea, UK.

★ Largest snowball fight

The world's largest snowball fight involved 2,473 participants (1,162 against 1,311) and took place at Triel in the ski resort of Obersaxen-Mundaun at Graubunden, Switzerland, on 18 January 2003.

★ Largest dog walk

A total of 4,372 dogs took part in the Catherine Cookson Great North Dog Walk, organized by Anthony Carlisle (UK). The walk was held on 22 June 2003 and started from Gypsies Green Stadium, South Shields, UK.

★ Largest simultaneous 'dog stay'

Dogs for the Disabled and Pets at Home organized a 'dog stay' involving a record 514 dogs on 16 August 2003 at The Wag and Bone Show, Ascot, Berkshire, UK.

★ Largest cookery lesson

Princess Household Appliances BV (Netherlands) organized a cookery lesson involving 357 students who were taught how to make paella by Cas Spijkers (Netherlands) on 15 June 2003 at Estepona, Marbella, Spain.

★ Largest water balloon fight

On 13 September 2003 the University at Buffalo, New York, USA, played host to a water balloon fight involving 422 students throwing 5,214 water balloons.

★ Largest simultaneous whoopee cushion sit

The UK's CBBC Xchange TV show organized a simultaneous whoopee cushion sit involving 1,504 participants at Tottenham Hotspur Football Club's ground, White Hart Lane, London, UK, on 13 January 2004.

★ Most people simultaneously slimed

On 27 October 2003, during Nickelodeon's Slimetime Live show at Universal Studios in Orlando, Florida, USA,

762 people were simultaneously slimed by around 568 litres (125 gal) of green slime.

★ Most people to pop balloons simultaneously

On 22 January 2004, 1,603 basketball fans popped balloons simultaneously during halftime of the Metro State against Fort Hays State University men's basketball game at Gross Memorial Coliseum at Hays, Kansas, USA.

★ Most couples kissing simultaneously

A total of 5,327 couples kissed simultaneously for 10 seconds on 14 February 2004 as part of the Close-up Lovapalooza festival in Manila, Philippines.

★ Largest sleepover/ pyjama party

On 1 February 2003, McLean Bible Church and Dulles Town Center, Virginia, USA, hosted a sleepover party for 1,045 students. All participants wore pyjamas and slept on the floor in sleeping bags.

Team efforts
Human beings

Fastest 4-x-100-m ⌃⌃ sack relay race

The 4-x-100-m sack relay race, held on 17 June 2003 at Ivanhoe Grammar School, Mernda, Victoria, Australia, was won in 2 min 29.09 sec. The members of the winning team were Patrick Holcolmbe (above, second from left), James Osbourne (fifth from left), Luke MacFarlane (sixth from left) and Andrew Rodaughan (second from right, all Australia).

★ Fastest men's wheelie-bin race

On 21 February 1999, at Westfield Devils Junior Soccer Club, Launceston, Tasmania, Australia, Shaun Viney and Aaron Viney (both Australia) completed a 110-m (360-ft 9.6-in) wheelie-bin race in 31.1 seconds.

★ Fastest women's woolsack race

The 'Mega Movers' team of four ladies completed the woolsack World Championships in Tetbury, Gloucestershire, UK, in 3 min 52.01 sec on 25 May 1989. The event involves competitors racing up and down a steep hill while carrying a 27.21-kg (60-lb) bag of wool on their shoulders.

★ Fastest 31-legged race over 50 m

Students from the Sugikami Elementary school in the Kumamoto Prefecture, Japan, ran a 31-legged race covering a total of 50 m (164 ft) in 8.94 seconds at Yokohama Arena, Japan, on 23 November 2002.

★ Farthest distance covered in a lawn mower race

Ian Dobson, Robert Jones and Steve Williams (all UK) of the team 'Extreme Headless Chickens' covered 504.7 km (313.6 miles) in the annual 12-hour lawn mower race at Wisborough Green, UK, on 29–30 August 1998, organized by the British Lawn Mower Racing Association.

★ Longest supermarket trolley push

A team of 801 staff from Woolworths, BCC and Jack-the-Slasher supermarkets took turns to push a supermarket shopping trolley from Cairns to Brisbane, Queensland, Australia, covering 1,767 km (1,098 miles) in 36 days, from 20 June to 26 July 1987.

★ Farthest distance to push a bed

A team of nine employees from Bruntsfield Bedding Centre, Edinburgh, UK, pushed a wheeled hospital bed 5,204 km (3,233.65 miles) between 21 June and 26 July 1979.

★ Fastest time to dismantle a car

A team from Espoon Ammattioppilaitos technical school (Finland) consisting of Tapio Heino, Panu Natunen, Aaro-Pekka Nousiainen, Sami Rissanen, Sampo Vuolteenaho, Ahmed Abdirizag, Mikael Gorski, Janne Spanow and Juha Määttä (all Finland) dismantled a five-door saloon car in 35 minutes on 28 November 2001. All parts were removed except for the bodywork, chassis and axles.

★ Fastest time to swap an engine

A team of four mechanics – Stefan Klotz, Ralf Kaelche, Markus Jung and Stefan Worner (all Germany) – took the engine from one Volkswagen Beetle and installed it into another, then drove the car 5 m (16 ft 5 in) in a time of 1 min 37 sec on the set of *Guinness – Die Show der Rekorde*, Munich, Germany, on 17 January 1999.

★ Most people on a motorcycle wheelie

On 12 June 1998, a total of nine people, led by Todd Colbert (USA), did a motorcycle wheelie in Lake Whales, Florida, USA.

★ Most people crammed into a Smart car

A total of 13 girls from Team IGA-Optic (Germany) crammed into a Smart car on the set of *Guinness – Die Show der Rekorde*, Munich, Germany, on 2 April 1999.

Farthest wheelchair ⋀ push over 24 hours

A team of 75 volunteers pushed a wheelchair a distance of 386.2 km (240 miles) in 24 hours at Copeland Stadium, Whitehaven, Cumbria, UK, on 8–9 September 2000 (above). The event was organized by the Maryport branch of the Cumbria Cerebral Palsy Society.

Fastest Boeing 737 ⋀ 100-m pull by a team

On 27 January 2001, a team of 10 Royal Marine reserves (UK, above) pulled a Boeing 737-300, weighing 37 tonnes (81,500 lb), over a distance of 100 m (328 ft) in 43.2 seconds at Manchester Airport, UK.

★ **Most plaster casts applied in an hour by a team**
A team of 10 people applied forearm plaster casts (one per person) to 825 volunteers in an hour at the main square of Herentals, Belgium, on 5 July 2003. The event was organized to celebrate the 750th year of Herentals Hospital.

★ **Most faces painted in an hour by a team**
At an attempt organized by Face2Face International (UK), a team of five people consisting of Susan Howard, Rosemary Jones, Emma Edworthy, Ann Ardern and Andrew Griffiths (all UK) painted a total of 239 faces in an hour, using a minimum of three colours per face at Crealy Park, Exeter, Devon, UK, on 1 August 2003.

★ **Longest daisy chain**
The longest daisy chain measured 2.12 km (1.31 miles) and was made in seven hours by a team of 16 villagers from Good Easter, Chelmsford, Essex, UK, on 27 May 1985.

★ **Fastest loaf from field to oven**
On 21 August 1999, a team led by baker John Haynes and farmer Peter Rix (both UK) at Alpheton, Suffolk, UK, took 18 min 11.4 sec to produce 13 loaves from growing wheat.

★ **Most trees planted in an hour**
A team of 96 people, including schoolchildren from St Therese's School and other volunteers (all UK) from Neath Port Talbot, planted 4,100 trees in one hour on 8 April 2003. The event was organized by Neath Port Talbot County Borough Council (UK) and held at Margam Country Park, West Glamorgan, UK.

★ **Largest human mobile**
The largest human mobile was made up of 24 people from the Height Rescue Fire Department Team, at Fire station 33, Veddel, Hamburg, Germany, on 14 June 2003. Suspended from a crane, the lowest point of the mobile was 50 m (164 ft) off the ground.

★ **Most heads shaved in an hour by a team**
A team of 10 hairdressers shaved a total of 56 heads in one hour at the Victoria Oval, Dubbo, New South Wales, Australia, in aid of the Cancer Council's Relay for Life on 28 September 2002.

★ **Fastest time to pop 1,000 balloons**
A team of 37 participants (all UK) popped 1,000 balloons in 1 min 44 sec on the set of *Blue Peter* at the BBC Television Centre, London, UK, on 7 November 2003.

★ **Largest can pyramid built in 30 minutes**
On 23 September 2000, the Malaysia can team, consisting of students from the INTI College Subang Jaya, built a pyramid created from 9,455 empty aluminium drinks cans in 24 minutes at the Midvalley Mega Mall in Kuala Lumpur,

Malaysia. It had a square base of 30 x 30 cans, measuring 1.98 x 1.98 m (6 ft 6 in x 6 ft 6 in).

★ **Farthest distance travelled by a team on a water slide in 24 hours**
Harald Bachmann, Markus Ullmann, Jörg Hofmann, Robert Bachmann, Franz Walter, Werner Müller, Aaron Pfeffer, Dominik Radler and Stefan Wolf (all Germany) slid a total distance of 676.974 km (420.652 miles) together on a 102-m (334-ft) waterslide in 24 hours at Kempten, Germany, on 12 and 13 July 2002.

★ **Longest reading-aloud marathon by a team**
Phillipp Haag, Eduard Maier, Martina Holdermann, Sabrina Holzäpfel, Simone Jordan and Franziska Sobe (all Germany) from Calmbach Secondary School, Bad Wildbad, Germany, read aloud for a record 75 hours between 16 and 19 July 2003.

« Heaviest aircraft pulled by an individual

David Huxley (Australia, left) pulled a Boeing 747-400 weighing 187 tonnes (412,264 lb) a distance of 91 m (298 ft 6 in) in 1 min 27.7 sec on 15 October 1997 in Sydney, Australia.

Bed of nails concrete block break ⌃

Chad Netherland (USA, above) had 21 concrete blocks weighing a total of 314.21 kg (692 lb 10.8 oz) placed on his chest and then broken with a 7.25-kg (16-lb) sledgehammer while he lay on a bed of nails at The Great Lakes Aquarium, Duluth, Minnesota, USA, on 9 November 2003.

★ **Heaviest aircraft pull by wheelchairs**
A team of eight members of the Suffolk Braves Wheelchair Basketball Club (UK) pulled a Cessna 421 Eagle executive aircraft weighing 4 tonnes (8,818 lb) a distance of 500 m (1,640 ft) in 16 min 20 sec on 9 December 1998 at Marshall Airport, Cambridge, England.

★ **Longest duration aircraft restraint**
Using ropes looped around his arms, Ilkka Nummisto (Finland) prevented the take-off of two Cessna aeroplanes pulling in opposite directions for 54 seconds at Räyskälä Airport, Finland, on 1 August 2001.

★ **Fastest 50-m caravan pull**
Juan Antonio Valdecantos Mayor (Spain) pulled a caravan weighing 705 kg (1,554 lb) a distance of 50 m (164 ft) in a time of 17.95 seconds at the studios of *El Show de los Récords*, Madrid, Spain, on 22 November 2001.

★ **Heaviest vehicle pulled by hair**
The heaviest vehicle to have been pulled by the hair alone over a distance of 30 m (98 ft) is a double-decker bus weighing 7,874 kg (17,359 lb), by Letchemanah Ramasamy (Malaysia) at Bruntingthorpe Proving Ground, Leicestershire, UK, on 1 May 1999.

★ **Heaviest vehicle pulled by teeth**
Walter Arfeuille (Belgium) used his teeth to pull eight railway carriages with a total weight of 223.8 tonnes (493,570 lb) over a distance of 3.2 m (10 ft 5 in) along rails at Diksmuide, Belgium, on 9 June 1996.

★ **Heaviest train pulled by beard**
Ismael Rivas Falcon (Spain) pulled a train weighing 2,753.1 kg (6,069 lb) over a distance of 10 m (32 ft 9.6 in) using only his beard at the studios of *El Show de los Récords*, Madrid, Spain, on 15 November 2001.

★ **Heaviest vehicle pulled over 100 ft**
Kevin Fast (Canada) pulled a truck weighing 25,180 kg (55,512 lb) over a distance of 30.48 m (100 ft) along Queen Street, Cobourg, Ontario, Canada, on 7 June 2003.

★ **Heaviest ship pulled by teeth**
Omar Hanapiev (Russia) pulled the 576-tonne (1,269,861-lb) tanker *Gunib* a distance of 15 m (49 ft 2.4 in) using a rope connected only to his teeth, on 9 November 2001 at Makhachkala, Russia.

★ **Heaviest boat pulled**
David Huxley (Australia) pulled the *Delphin*, weighing in at 1,006 tonnes (2,217,847 lb), with a cargo of 175 cars plus passengers over a distance of 7 m (23 ft) on 19 November 1998 in Rostock, Germany.

★ **Heaviest truck pulled by arm**
The heaviest truck pulled with an arm-wrestling move weighed 3,259.3 kg (7,185 lb 7 oz). Oscar Olaria Paris and Mariano Macor Stopello (both Spain) set the record on *El Show de los Récords* in Madrid, Spain, on 4 October 2001.

★ **Heaviest human pyramid**
Tahar Douis (Morocco) supported 12 members of the Hassani Troupe (three levels in height) with a total weight of 771 kg (1,700 lb) at the BBC television studios, Birmingham, UK, on 7 December 1979.

★ **Heaviest deadlift with the little finger**
The heaviest deadlift with the little finger is 89.6 kg (197 lb 8 oz) by Barry Anderson (UK) on 14 October 2000 at the Bass Museum, Burton-upon-Trent, Staffordshire, UK.

Greatest weight ≪ balanced on teeth

Frank Simon (Hungary, left) lifted a 61.8-kg (136-lb) motorcycle above his head and balanced it on his teeth for 10 seconds on the set of *El Show de los Récords* in Madrid, Spain, on 4 October 2001. He is pictured here demonstrating his skills with another bike at Red Rock Canyon, Nevada, USA.

★ **Greatest weight lifted by nipples**
Sage Werbock (USA) lifted a total weight of 21.9 kg (48 lb 4.2 oz) suspended from his pierced nipples for five seconds at the Tritone Bar in Philadelphia, Pennsylvania, USA, on 20 May 2003.

★ **Greatest weight lifted by teeth**
Walter Arfeuille (Belgium) lifted weights totalling 281.5 kg (620 lb 10 oz) a distance of 17 cm (6.75 in) off the ground using only his teeth in Paris, France, on 31 March 1990.

★ **Greatest weight balanced on the head**
The greatest weight ever balanced on the head and held for 10 seconds is 188.7 kg (416 lb), by John Evans (UK) who lifted 101 bricks at BBC Television Centre, London, UK, on 24 December 1997.

★ **Most boat lifts**
Sami Heinonen and Juha Räsänen (both Sweden) continuously lifted a boat and 10 crew with a combined weight of 653.2 kg (1,440 lb) 10 cm (4 in) off the ground a total of 24 times on 9 October 2000 on the set of *Guinness World Records*, at Studio Werne, Helsinki, Finland.

★ **Greatest weight of bricks lifted**
Fred Burton (UK) lifted a horizontal row of 20 bricks, weighing a total of 102.73 kg (226 lb 7 oz), and held them at chest height for two seconds on 5 June 1998 at Cheadle, Staffordshire, UK.

★ **Most weight sustained on the body**
Eduardo Armallo Lasaga (Spain) lay beneath 1,399.8 kg (3,086 lb) of concrete blocks on the set of *El Show de los Récords*, Madrid, Spain, on 18 October 2001.

★ **Greatest weight lifted by beard**
The heaviest weight lifted with a human beard is 61.3 kg (135 lb) when Antanas Kontrimas lifted Ruta Cekyte (both Lithuania) off the ground for 15 seconds on 18 August 2001 at the VIII International Country Festival 2001, Visaginas, Lithuania.

★ **Longest four-finger hang**
Daniel Dulac (France) was hoisted up to a bar housing two finger holds (as used in artificial climbing walls). Using just two fingers of each hand, he was suspended for 2 min 18.1 sec on the set of *L'Émission des Records*, Paris, France, on 14 May 2002.

★ **Fastest time to bend an iron bar and fit it into a suitcase**
Firas Kichi (Spain) bent an iron bar 6 m (19 ft 7.2 in) long and with a diameter of 12 mm (0.47 in) a total of 16 times to fit it into a suitcase measuring 50 x 70 x 20 cm (19.6 x 27.5 x 7.87 in), all within 38.61 seconds on the set of *El Show de los Récords*, Madrid, Spain, on 14 December 2001.

★ **Most telephone directories torn in three minutes**
Mike West (USA) ripped 30 telephone books, each containing 1,052 pages, from top to bottom, at Eclectics Training Center, New Albany, Indiana, USA, on 14 December 2002.

★ **Longest duration joust lifting**
Raymond Janin (France) held a joust measuring 2.8 m (9 ft 2.16 in) long and weighing 3 kg (6 lb 8.53 oz) horizontally at shoulder height for 26 seconds on the set of *L'Été de Tous les Records*, Sete, France, on 21 August 2003.

★ **Most flips of a 25-kg weight in a minute**
Johnny Lindström (Sweden) flipped over a 25-kg (55-lb 1.54-oz) weight with one hand a total of 24 times in a minute on the set of *Guinness World Rekords*, Stockholm, Sweden, on 24 November 2001.

Staying power
Human beings

Longest guitar marathon by ⌄ an individual

Sanjeev Babu (India, below centre) played a guitar for 24 hr 30 min from 14 to 15 August 2003 at the YMCA Ground, Trivandrum, Kerala, India.

★ **Longest banjo marathon**
Doug Young (USA) played a banjo for 24 hr 57 sec at the Good/Bad Art Collective, Brooklyn, New York City, USA, on 12–13 May 2001.

★ **Longest church organ marathon**
On 20–21 June 2003, Roelof Hamberg (Netherlands) played a church organ for 32 hours at the Joris Church, St Jorissant, Venlo, The Netherlands.

★ **Longest drumming marathon**
Allister Brown (UK) played the drums for 58 hr 17 min on 8–10 September 2003 at the Lisburn School of Music, Lisburn, County Antrim, Northern Ireland.

★ **Longest percussion marathon**
Hermes Arango Saenz (Colombia) played nine different percussion instruments for 40 hours in Medellín, Colombia. The instruments played were: drum kit, kettledrums, congas,

bongos, guiro, dominican guiro, cumbiemberan maracas, salsa maracas and bell. The marathon started at 6 am on 2 August 2001 and finished at 10 pm on 3 August 2001.

★ **Longest tuba marathon**
The longest tuba marathon by an individual lasted for 24 hr 8 min and was achieved by Rodney Kenny (UK), on 16–17 August 2002 at The Salvation Army, Gosport, Hampshire, UK.

★ **Longest karaoke marathon featuring multiple participants**
Organized by Mark Pearson (UK), the karaoke marathon at the Keighley Festival, Keighley, West Yorkshire, UK, featured 85 different acts and continued for 80 hours from 14 to 18 June 2003.

★ **Longest singing marathon by an individual**
ACE Anderson (USA) sang continuously for 49 hr 30 min at Washington County Regional Park, Hurricane, Utah, USA, on 27–29 June 2003.

★ **Longest club DJ marathon**
Club DJ Martin Boss (USA) performed a mixing session that lasted 74 hours at Vinyl Frontier in Orlando, Florida, USA, from 1 to 4 February 2002.

★ **Longest radio DJ marathon**
DJ Christoph Stöckli's (Switzerland) broadcast on Radio Extra Bern, Bern, Switzerland, lasted for 105 hours. He began his marathon attempt at 6 am on 24 July and finally closed his programme at 3 pm on 28 July 2002.

★ **Longest joke-telling marathon**
Working on the basis that a joke must have a beginning, a middle and an end, Mike Hessman (USA) told 12,682 jokes in 24 hours on 16–17 November 1992.

★ **Longest dance party**
The 'Heart Health Hop', a dance party marathon organized by St Joseph® Aspirin, held at the Rock and Roll Hall of Fame

and Museum, Cleveland, Ohio, USA, began on 29 July 2003 with 42 dancers, 41 of whom completed the marathon after 52 hr 3 min on 31 July 2003.

★ **Longest ironing marathon**
Eufemia Stadler (Switzerland) ironed continuously for 40 hours while standing at an ironing board on 16–18 September 1999. She ironed a total of 228 shirts.

★ **Longest rocking chair marathon**
Garry Hamilton (UK) rocked on a rocking chair continuously from 24 to 26 August 1999 for 21 hours at the Hilton Hotel, Glasgow, UK.

★ **Longest card-playing marathon**
Gareth Birdsall, Simon MacBeth, Finn Clark, Gad Chadha, Sonia Zakrezewski, Tim West-Meads, Sebastian Kristensen and David Gold played bridge for 72 hr 9 min at St John's Wood Bridge Club, London, UK, from 31 October to 3 November 2003.

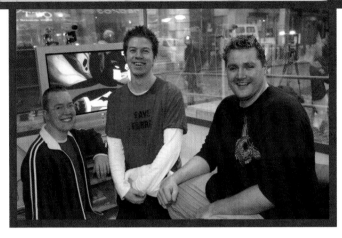

Longest TV-watching ⌃ marathon

Nick Tungatt, Adam King, Steven Hayes (all UK, above from left to right) and Sam Beatson (UK)
continually watched television screens for 47 hr 16 sec from 4 to 6 December 2002, in an event sponsored by CNX at Covent Garden, London, and at The Printworks, Manchester, UK.

Most consecutive ⌃ Texas skips

Andrew Rotz (USA, above) achieved 11,123 consecutive Texas skips at the National Convention of the Wild West Arts Club in Las Vegas, Nevada, USA, on 11 March 2003, smashing the previous record set at 4,011. The attempt took 3 hr 10 min to complete. A Texas skip is a vertical loop that is repeatedly pulled from one side of the body to the other. With each pass, the roper jumps through the centre of the loop.

★ **Longest time spent on a bed of nails by a woman**
Geraldine Williams (UK, aka Miranda, Queen of the Fakirs) lay on a bed of sharp nails 15.2 cm (6 in) tall and 5 cm (2 in) apart for 30 hours on 18–19 May 1977.

★ **Longest lecture marathon**
Errol ET Muzawazi (Zimbabwe) talked on the subject of democracy for 62 hr 30 min from 12 to 15 December 2003 at a student residence at Politechnika Wroclawska, Wroclaw, Poland.

★ **Longest quiz master marathon**
Quiz master Gavin Dare (UK) asked a total of 3,668 questions continuously in 32 hr 15 min at The Goff's Oak Public House, Hertfordshire, UK, from 25 to 26 October 2003.

★ **Farthest pool-rescue marathon**
The farthest pool-rescue distance is 19,300 m (63,320 ft) and was completed by the Wong Tai Sin District Life Saving Society at Morse Park Swimming Pool, Kowloon, Hong Kong, China, on 31 August 2002. A total of 386 trained lifesavers towed a mannequin for a distance of 50 m (164 ft) each for 8 hr 27 min.

★ **Fastest backwards-run marathon**
Timothy Bud Badyna (USA) ran a marathon backwards in 3 hr 53 min 17 sec in Toledo, Ohio, USA, on 24 April 1994.

★ **Longest parasailing marathon**
Berne Persoon (Sweden) parasailed for 24 hr 10 min on Lake Graningesjön, Sweden, on 19–20 July 2002.

★ **Longest sustained ball control by a female**
Cláudia Martini (Brazil) juggled a regulation soccer ball for 7 hr 5 min 25 sec non-stop using her feet, legs and head without the ball ever touching the ground at Caxias do Sul, Brazil, on 12 July 1996.

★ **Longest skiing marathon**
Christian Flühr (Germany) skied non-stop for 168 hours at Tyrol, Westendorf, Austria, on 8–15 March 2003. During that time he skied a combined distance of 6,600.03 km (4,101.06 miles) and a combined altitude of 906,036 m (2,972,559 ft).

★ **Longest duration for underwater kissing**
Antonio de la Rosa Suarez (Spain) was able to stay underwater at the bottom of a water-filled tank for 6 min 13.49 sec by being given air through kisses from Nerea Martinez Urruzola and Vanesa de la Rosa Suarez (both Spain), who took it in turns to swim down to him. The attempt was made at the studios of El Show de los Récords, Madrid, Spain, on 22 November 2001.

★ **Longest spinning marathon**
The record for the longest spinning (static cycling) marathon belongs to Jennifer Johnston (USA) who cycled for 73 hr 13 min continuously at the National Fitness and Racquet Club, Klamath Falls, Oregon, USA, from 8 to 11 November 2003.

Pushing the limits
Human beings

Greatest altitude ⌃ reached by helium-filled toy balloons

Ian Ashpole (UK, above) achieved the highest flight powered by toy helium balloons, reaching 3,350 m (11,000 ft) on 28 October 2001 over Chatteris, Cambridgeshire, UK. Owing to the low air pressure at this altitude, some of the 600 balloons (each with a diameter of 90 cm, or 3 ft) burst, forcing him to parachute to safety. Ian is shown here during a non-record-related stunt: he lies in a hammock suspended between hot-air balloons, then free-falls out of the hammock and parachutes to the ground.

★ Highest dry-air temperature endured
During US Air Force experiments held in 1960, the highest dry-air temperature endured by heavily clothed volunteers was measured at 260°C (500°F).

During the same tests, the highest dry-air temperature endured by naked volunteers was measured at 205°C (400°F). Temperatures of 140°C (284°F) in saunas have been found quite bearable.

★ Longest time to remain standing motionless
Om Prakash Singh (India) stood motionless, except for involuntary blinking, for 20 hr 10 min 6 sec on 13–14 August 1997. Om Prakash Singh started his attempt on the eve of the golden jubilee of India's independence as an homage to unknown martyrs.

★ Longest time spent balancing on one foot
Arulanantham Suresh Joachim (Sri Lanka) balanced on one foot for 76 hr 40 min at Uihara Maha Devi Park Open Air Stadium, Sri Lanka, from 22 to 25 May 1997.

★ Longest time spent balancing on a tightrope
Jorge Ojeda-Guzman (USA) spent 205 days, from 1 January to 25 July 1993, on a wire 11 m (36 ft) long and 10.7 m (35 ft) above ground.

During his time on the tightrope, he entertained crowds by walking, dancing and balancing on a chair.

★ Farthest distance walked backwards
The greatest exponent of reverse pedestrianism was Plennie L Wingo (USA), who completed his 12,875-km (8,000-mile) transcontinental walk from Santa Monica, California, USA, to Istanbul, Turkey, from 15 April 1931 to 24 October 1932.

★ Longest firewalk
Gérard Moccetti (Switzerland) walked 50.5 m (165 ft 8 in) over embers with an average temperature of 665°C (1,230°F) at Scairedo, Barbengo, Ticino, Switzerland, on 19 January 2003.

★ Longest time to endure full-body ice contact
Wearing only swimming trunks, Wim Hof (Netherlands) was able to stand in a tube filled with ice cubes for 1 hr 7 min, beating his previous record by 56 seconds at the studios of Guinness World Records: Die Grössten Weltrekorde on 23 January 2004.

★ Longest time spent in a balloon
The Fédération Aéronautique Internationale (FAI) endurance record for a gas and hot-air balloon is 19 days 21 hr 47 min. It was set by Brian Jones (UK) and Bertrand Piccard (Switzerland) between 1 and 21 March 1999, when they flew from Chateau d'Oex, Switzerland, and landed 500 km (300 miles) from Cairo, Egypt.

★ Greatest height to jump on to an airbag
On 7 August 1997, Stig Günther (Denmark) jumped from a height of 104.5 m (342 ft) off a crane on to an air bag measuring 12 x 15 x 4.5 m (39 x 49 x 15 ft). His impact speed was about 145 km/h (90 mph).

★ Longest full-body burn (without oxygen)
Stig Günther (Denmark) endured a full-body burn without oxygen supplies for 2 min 6 sec in Copenhagen, Denmark, on 13 March 1999.

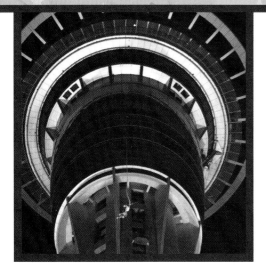

Highest bungee ⌃ jump from a building

AJ Hackett (New Zealand, above) leaped off the Sky Tower

Casino, the highest building in Auckland, New Zealand, plunging 180.1 m (590 ft 10 in) on 5 October 1998. His fall ended just 12 m (40 ft) above the concrete pavement before he rebounded.

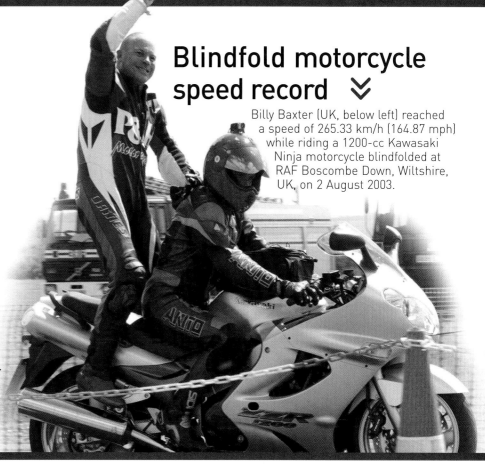

Blindfold motorcycle speed record ⌄

Billy Baxter (UK, below left) reached a speed of 265.33 km/h (164.87 mph) while riding a 1200-cc Kawasaki Ninja motorcycle blindfolded at RAF Boscombe Down, Wiltshire, UK, on 2 August 2003.

★ **Highest bungee jump by altitude**
Curtis Rivers (UK) performed a bungee jump from a hot-air balloon at 4,632 m (15,200 ft) over Puertollano, Spain, on 5 May 2002.

★ **Highest bungee jump from a structure**
Chris Allum (New Zealand) jumped 251 m (823 ft 6 in) from the New River Gorge Bridge, West Virginia, USA, in 1992.

★ **Deepest freshwater cave scuba dive**
On 23 August 1996, Nuno Gomes (South Africa) scuba-dived to a depth of 282.6 m (927 ft 2 in) at the Boesmansgat Cave in the Northern Cape province of South Africa. Essentially a very deep sinkhole, the cave at the surface resembles a small lake with vertical sides.

★ **Deepest seawater scuba dive**
The deepest scuba dive was one of 307.8 m (1,010 ft) made by John Bennett (UK)

on 6 November 2001 off Escarcia Point, Puerto Galera, The Philippines. The descent, aided by a weighted sled, took just over 12 minutes, while the ascent took 9 hr 36 min to allow for decompression.

★ **Highest shallow dive**
Danny Higginbottom (USA) dived from 8.9 m (29 ft 2 in) into 30 cm (12 in) of water at the studios of *Guinness World Records: Die Grössten Weltrekorde* on 23 January 2004.

★ **Longest scuba dive in open freshwater**
Jerry Hall (USA) spent 71 hr 39 min 40 sec underwater in South Holston Lake, Bristol, Tennessee, USA, using scuba gear between 6 and 9 August 2002.

★ **Longest scuba submergence using one air tank**
Mick Brown (UK) remained underwater for 7 hr 15 min 44 sec, breathing off a single standard 12-litre scuba tank,

in a swimming pool at Walton-on-the-Naze, Essex, UK, on 1 February 2003.

★ **Blindfold car speed record**
Mike Newman (UK) reached 232.960 km/h (144.755 mph) in a Jaguar XJR at Elvington Airfield, North Yorkshire, UK, on 13 August 2003.

★ **Highest speed on a quad bike (ATV)**
Graham 'G-Force' Hicks, a deaf-blind daredevil from Peterborough, Cambridgeshire, UK, reached 167.4 km/h (104.02 mph) on a quad bike, or ATV (all-terrain vehicle), at Bruntingthorpe Proving Ground, Leicestershire, UK, on 22 June 2002. He received instructions from his pillion rider Rob Hall, who told him where to steer via a system of touch-based commands.

★ **Longest time spent on 'Wall of Death'**
Martin Blume (Germany) spent 7 hr 13 sec on a 'Wall of Death' in Berlin, Germany, on 16 April 1983. He rode a Yamaha XS 400

over 12,000 laps on a wall with a diameter of 10 m (33 ft), averaging 48 km/h (30 mph) over 292 km (181.5 miles).

★ **Longest time to keep an aircraft airborne**
Robert Timm and John Cooke (both USA) kept their Cessna 172 Hacienda aloft for 64 days 22 hr 19 min 5 sec, from 4 December 1958 to 7 February 1959. They took off from McCarran Airfield, Las Vegas, Nevada, USA, and landed at the same place after covering a distance equivalent to six times round the world, with refuelling taking place in the air.

★ **Greatest distance flown in a wing suit**
Skydiver Adrian Nicholas (UK) flew 16 km (10 miles) in a wing suit over Yolo County, California, USA, on 12 March 1999. He exited the plane at 10,317 m (33,850 ft) and reached speeds of approximately 241 km/h (150 mph). He 'flew' for 4 min 55 sec and only opened his parachute 152 m (500 ft) from the ground.

Against the odds
Human beings

Highest fall survived ⌃ without a parachute

Vesna Vulovic (Yugoslavia, above) was 23 and working as a Jugoslavenski Aerotransport hostess when the DC-9 she was working aboard blew up on 26 January 1972. Vulovic survived a fall inside a section of tail unit from 10,160 m (33,333 ft) over Srbsk, Kamenice, Czechoslovakia (now Czech Republic), despite breaking many bones. She was in a coma for 27 days and remained in hospital for 16 months. On the left is one of her rescuers, Zdenko Kubik.

Most deaths on ⌃ Mount Everest in one day

On 10 May 1996, a blizzard with winds of up to 145 km/h (90 mph) and temperatures of -40°C (-40°F) claimed the lives of eight climbers on Mount Everest – the most in one day. Dr Seaborn 'Beck' Weathers (USA, above) was trapped on the South Col of Mount Everest for 16 hours. He lost his right hand, part of his left hand and his nose owing to frostbite.

★ Lowest body temperature survived
The lowest authenticated body temperature is 14.2°C (57.5°F), the rectal temperature for Karlee Kosolofski (Canada), then aged two, on 23 February 1994. She had accidentally been locked outside her home for six hours in a temperature of -22°C (-8°F). Despite severe frostbite, which meant the amputation of her left leg above the knee, she made a full recovery.

★ Most operations endured
From 22 July 1954 to the end of 1994, Charles Jensen (USA) had 970 operations to remove tumours associated with basal cell naevus syndrome.

★ Longest underwater submergence survival
In 1986, two-year-old Michelle Funk (USA) made a full recovery after spending 66 minutes underwater in a swollen creek.

★ Deepest underwater escape with no equipment
The greatest depth from which an underwater escape has been made without any equipment is 68.6 m (225 ft) by Richard A Slater from the rammed submersible Nekton Beta off Catalina Island, California, USA, on 28 September 1970.

★ Longest time trapped in a lift
At the age of 76, Kively Papajohn (Cyprus) was trapped in her apartment block lift for six days from 28 December 1987 to 2 January 1988. She survived the cold and beat dehydration by rationing out some fruit, vegetables and bread that she had in her shopping bag.

★ Longest fall survived in a lift
Betty Lou Oliver (USA) survived a plunge of 75 storeys (over 300 m or 1,000 ft) in a lift in the Empire State Building in New York City, USA, on 28 July 1945, after an American B-25 bomber crashed into the building in thick fog, severing all the lift's cables.

★ Highest fall survived down a lift shaft
Stuart Jones (New Zealand) fell 23 storeys (70 m or 229 ft 7 in) down a lift shaft while carrying out structural work on the roof of a temporary lift car at the Midland Park Building, Wellington, New Zealand, in May 1998. He suffered multiple injuries, including a broken hip, an open fracture in his left lower leg, a broken left knee cap and a broken rib.

★ Longest time adrift at sea
The longest known time that anyone has survived adrift at sea is approximately 484 days, by the Japanese Captain Oguri Jukichi and one of his sailors, Otokichi. Their ship was damaged in a storm off the Japanese coast in October 1813 and they drifted in the Pacific before being rescued by an American ship off California, USA, on 24 March 1815.

★ Longest time adrift at sea alone
The longest recorded survival alone on a raft is 133 days by Second Steward Poon Lim (Hong Kong) of the UK Merchant Navy, whose ship, the SS Ben Lomond, was torpedoed in the Atlantic 910 km (565 miles) west of St Paul's Rocks at 11:45 am on 23 November 1942.

He was finally picked up by a Brazilian fishing boat off Salinópolis, Brazil, on 5 April 1943 and was able to walk ashore.

Longest post-earthquake survival by a cat »

On 21 September 1999, an earthquake struck Taiwan, killing an estimated 2,400 people. Eighty days later in December 1999, a cat (right) was discovered alive in Taichung after being trapped by a message board that had fallen during the quake, pinning it to the ground in the rubble of a collapsed building. The cat, dehydrated and barely breathing, weighed less than half the weight of a healthy cat of its size. It was rushed to a veterinary hospital where it made a full recovery.

★ **Longest survival without food and water**

The longest recorded case of survival without food and water is 18 days by Andreas Mihavecz (Austria), then aged 18. He was put into a holding cell on 1 April 1979 in a local government building in Höchst, Austria, but totally forgotten by the police. On 18 April 1979, he was discovered close to death.

★ **Longest survival with heart outside body**

Christopher Wall (USA, b. 19 August 1975) is the longest known survivor of the condition ectopia cordis, in which the heart lies outside the body at birth. The mortality rate is high, with most patients not living beyond 48 hours, but Wall still lives with the condition.

★ **Longest time survived without a pulse**

The longest time a human has survived without a pulse in their vascular system is three days. Julie Mills (UK) was at the point of death from severe heart failure and viral myocarditis when, on 14 August 1998, cardiac surgeons at The John Radcliffe Hospital, Oxford, UK, used a non pulsatile blood pump (AB180) to support her for one week. Her heart recovered in this time and the pump was removed.

★ **Greatest ever life-saving operation at sea**

The greatest ever rescue at sea was that of 2,735 people from the American aircraft carrier *CV-2* USS *Lexington* on 8 May 1942 after it had been sunk between Australia and New Caledonia in the Battle of the Coral Sea.

★ **Greatest rescue at sea without loss of life**

All 2,689 people on board the American vessel *Susan B Anthony* survived when it was sunk off Normandy, France, on 7 June 1944.

★ **Largest object removed from human skull**

The largest object removed from a human skull is a 20-cm (8-in) survival knife with a serrated blade, which was plunged into the head of 41-year-old Michael Hill (USA) on 25 April 1998. Michael survived the operation and the next day astonished doctors by being able to speak and function normally, although the years to come proved that the knife had permanently damaged his memory and paralysed his left hand.

★ **Most hangings survived**

There is a tie for this record. The survivor of the most legal hanging attempts is Joseph Samuel (Australia), a 22-year-old who was sentenced to death for murder in Sydney, Australia. On 26 September 1803, the first attempt at execution failed when the rope broke. The second attempt failed when the rope stretched so much that the victim's feet touched the ground. At the third attempt, the second replacement rope broke, after which Samuel was reprieved.

In Exeter, Devon, UK, in 1885, John Lee (UK) also survived three attempted hangings. On each occasion that his hanging was due to take place, the trap door failed to open.

★ **Longest surviving headless chicken**

On 10 September 1945, a Wyandotte chicken called Mike had its head chopped off but went on to survive for 18 months. Mike's owner, Lloyd Olsen (USA), fed and watered the headless chicken directly into his gullet with an eyedropper. Mike eventually choked to death on a corn kernel in an Arizona motel.

★ **Longest survival of a sheep in a snowdrift**

On 24 March 1978, Alex Maclennan (UK) found one ewe still alive after he had dug out 16 dead sheep buried in a snowdrift for 50 days near the River Skinsdale on Mrs Tyser's Gordonbush Estate in Sutherland, Highland, UK, after the great January blizzard in that year. The sheep's hot breath had created air-holes in the snow, and the animal had gnawed its own wool for protein.

Longest motorcycle ⋁ ride by a team

Chris and Erin Ratay (both USA, below) covered 163,061 km (101,322 miles) on separate

motorcycles on a journey that covered 50 countries on six continents. They departed from Morocco on 21 May 1999 and returned home to New York City, USA, on 6 August 2003.

Fastest circumnavigation by male sailing solo ⋀

Francis Joyon (France, above) carried out a solo non-stop circumnavigation in the 27-m

(88-ft 6-in) trimaran *IDEC* in a time of 72 days 22 hr 54 min 22 sec, from 22 November 2003 to 3 February 2004.

★ GWR TALKS TO
Sir Ranulph Fiennes

Explorer Sir Ranulph Fiennes (UK, above) currently holds four Guinness World Records: the first pole-to-pole circumnavigation, the longest self-supporting trek (2,170 km or 1,350 miles during a 94-day trek with fellow Briton Michael Stroud), which was also the longest unsupported Antarctic trek and the fastest Antarctic crossing. The last record comprised the 4,185-km (2,600-mile) transantarctic leg of the 1980–82 Trans-Globe Expedition from Sanae to Scott Base, and was achieved in 55 days, from

28 October 1980 to 11 January 1981. The expedition reached the South Pole on 15 December 1980. For this record-breaking attempt, Sir Ranulph was accompanied by Oliver Shepard and Charles Burton (both UK).

How did you come to be an explorer?
I spent eight years in the Army and led a number of adventure training journeys. When I left the Army in 1970 I extended these activities to make a career out of expedition organizing and leading: the expeditions became a way of life.

What drives you to take on these great challenges?
To keep at 'the top of the tree' internationally in expedition work it was, through the 70s, 80s and 90s, necessary to attempt the biggest available geographical challenges and succeed, where possible, before my rivals.

What do you consider to be your greatest achievement to date?
If pressed to name which of the expeditions over a 32-year period I am most proud of I would find it very difficult to be specific. I'd say it was the discovery of the lost city of Ubar. It took me a period of 26 years on and off, and some seven separate expeditions between 1968 and 1991, before I finally discovered the site in the oasis of Shis'r in Dhofar, Oman.

What other challenges do you wish to take on in the future?
There are various challenges in the pipeline but the rule of our expedition group is to discuss them as little as possible to avoid others getting there first.

How do you prepare for some of these expeditions/challenges?
Our group has usually prepared for expeditions with meticulous care and by choosing the best available team, equipment and advisors. This includes physical fitness and nutrition experts. Fitness regimes and special diets alter according to the nature of each challenge.

What does it mean to you to have a Guinness World Record?
Many sponsors, without whom our projects would be impossible, respect the internationally accepted judgment of Guinness World Records as to what does or does not constitute a world record. Also the ability to cite Guinness World Records we've previously achieved always helps when requesting sponsorship.

What advice would you offer anyone seeking a similar career?
I usually recommend joining the Royal Geographical Society and taking advantage of its unique Expedition Advisory Centre, the nerve centre of 90% of all ongoing UK expedition work.

Who inspired you as a child?
As a child in South Africa I was inspired by stories about my father (killed in World War II, four months before I was born) and about his father, both of whom led adventurous lives in often remote regions. Later on I was inspired by the desert travels of Wilfred Thesiger and the polar travels of Wally Herbert.

Fastest time to visit ⌃ all NFL stadiums

Peter Baroody (USA, above) watched a complete National Football League (NFL) match at all 31 NFL stadiums in the USA in just 107 days, from 5 September to 22 December 2002. He began in New York City and finished in Kansas City.

32 Games
31 Stadiums
17 Weeks
30,000 Miles

★ **Longest lifeboat journey**
When his ship, the *Endurance*, became trapped in Antarctic sea-ice, Sir Ernest Shackleton (UK) and his 28-strong crew had to abandon her. Their three lifeboats set course for Elephant Island, 161 km (100 miles) to the north. Once there, and knowing that rescue was unlikely, Shackleton selected five of his best men to sail the largest lifeboat, the 6.85-m-long (22-ft 6-in) *James Caird*, towards a whaling station in South Georgia, 1,287 km (800 miles) away. In a journey that is still regarded as one of the greatest rescue journeys of all time, Sir Ernest and his men reached the island after 17 days, on 19 May 1916.

★ **Longest non-stop ocean voyage by raft**
During the Raft Transpacific Expedition, the raft *Nord*, captained by Andrew Urbanczyk (USA), sailed from Half Moon Bay, California, USA, to the US-owned Pacific island of Guam, a straight-line distance of 5,110 nautical miles (9,463 km or 5,880 miles), in 136 days from 26 August 2002 to 28 January 2003.

★ **Fastest circumnavigation by a crewed sailing vessel**
Millionaire adventurer Steve Fossett (USA) and a crew of 13 sailed around the world non-stop in 58 days 9 hr 32 min aboard the 38-m (125-ft) catamaran *Cheyenne*, from 7 February to 5 April 2004. The voyage started and finished at Le Stiff Lighthouse, Ushant, France.

★ **Longest motorcycle ride**
Emilio Scotto (Argentina) covered more than 735,000 km (457,000 miles) through 214 countries and territories on a motorcycle from 17 January 1985 to 2 April 1995.

★ **Fastest solo unsupported trek to the South Pole**
Fiona Thornewill (UK) walked and skied her way to the South Pole from Hercules Inlet at the edge of the Antarctic continent in 42 days from 30 November 2003 to 10 January 2004. She was pulling a 130-kg (285-lb) sled containing all her supplies and equipment, yet still managed to cover up to 35 km (22 miles) per day.

★ **Most sovereign countries visited in six months**
John Bougen and James Irving (both New Zealand) visited 191 of the world's 193 sovereign countries in 167 days 15 hr 39 min from 28 August 2002 to 12 February 2003. Their journey, called the All Nations Quest, was in support of the Save the Children charity.

★ **Fastest time to travel the Pan-American Highway by bicycle**
Giampietro Marion (Italy) cycled the Pan-American Highway, from Prudhoe Bay, Alaska, to Ushuaia, Argentina, in 140 days 6 hr, from 28 June 2000 to 15 November 2000.

★ **Fastest circumnavigation by car**
The record for the fastest circumnavigation by car (under the rules applicable in 1989 and 1991) embracing more than an equator's length of driving (40,750 km or 24,901 road miles) was by Mohammed and Neena Choudhury (India). The journey took 69 days 19 hr 5 min from 9 September to 17 November 1989.

★ **Greatest distance covered in 24 hours by wheelchair**
Rafael Emilio de León Lebrón (Dominican Republic) wheeled himself over 181.147 km (112.5 miles) in 24 hours on 13–14 December 2001 at the Juan Pablo Duarte Centro Olímpico, Santo Domingo de Guzmán, Dominican Republic.

★ **Longest journey by wheelchair**
Rick Hansen, paralysed from the waist down in 1973 as a result of a motor accident, wheeled his wheelchair 40,075.16 km (24,901.55 miles) through four continents and 34 countries. He started his journey from Vancouver, British Columbia, Canada, on 21 March 1985 and arrived back there on 22 May 1987.

Natural world

Contents

Nearest «
extrasolar planet

On 7 August 2000, a team led by Dr William Cochran (USA) of the University of Texas McDonald Observatory announced their discovery of the nearest planet outside the Solar System. The planet, which is probably slightly larger than Jupiter, orbits the star Epsilon Eridani (an artist's impression of the planet is shown left). This star, only 10.5 light years away, is one of the closest stars to the Sun.

★ **Brightest nebula**

The Orion Nebula (M42 or Messier 42 – ie number 42 in Charles Messier's 1781 catalogue of nebulous objects) is the brightest nebula in the sky with an apparent magnitude of 4. Located in the 'sword' of the constellation Orion, only the brightest central part of this vast diffuse cloud of gas and dust is easily visible to the naked eye.

★ **Brightest supernova remnant**

The Crab Nebula (M1) in the constellation of Taurus is the brightest supernova remnant in the sky, with a magnitude of 8.4. It is around 6,300 light years distant. One light year is the distance light travels in a year, about 9.5 trillion km (6 trillion miles).

★ **Deepest note in the universe**

The deepest note in the universe is caused by acoustic waves generated by a super-massive black hole in the centre of the Perseus cluster of galaxies, 250 million light years away. The sound, which propagates through the extremely thin gas surrounding the black hole, is a B flat, 57 octaves below middle C. This is more than a million billion times lower than a human ear can detect. The sound waves are estimated to have been consistently produced by the black hole for around 2.5 billion years. They were discovered using observations by the Chandra X-Ray Observatory, by astronomers led by Professor Andrew Fabian, Cambridge University, Cambridge, UK.

★ **Biggest globular cluster in the Milky Way**

Omega Centauri, in the constellation of Centaurus, is the most massive of the roughly 140 globular clusters surrounding our galaxy. Consisting of several million stars whose combined mass equates to five million Suns, it is just visible to the naked eye. It is around 10 times more massive than the other large globular clusters and some astronomers have suggested that it is the remnants of the nucleus of another galaxy which merged with ours billions of years ago.

★ **Coldest place in the Milky Way**

The Boomerang Nebula, a cloud of dust and gases 5,000 light years from Earth, has a temperature of -272°C (-457.6°F). It is formed by the rapid expansion of gas and dust flowing from its central star.

★ **Nearest globular cluster**

The nearest globular cluster to the Earth is M4. It is located in the constellation of Scorpius at a distance of around 5,600 light years and is visible through binoculars and small telescopes as a fuzzy smudge.

★ **Most distant object in the universe**

Astronomers from Caltech (USA), using the Hubble Space Telescope and the Keck Observatory, have discovered a small and compact system of stars around 2,000 light years across, with a redshift of 7. This corresponds to a distance of around 13 billion light years away. These results were announced in February 2004.

★ **Most distant planet with an atmosphere**

On 27 November 2001 astronomers using the Hubble Space Telescope announced the discovery of an atmosphere on a planet orbiting another star. This unnamed planet orbits the star HD209458, 150 light years away. It was discovered in 1999 thanks to the wobble its gravity inflicts upon HD209458 as it orbits it.

★ **Most massive extrasolar planet**

Announced in January 2001, the discovery of the planet HD168443 orbiting a star 123 light years away challenges conventional definitions of planets. Jupiter, the largest planet in our Solar System, weighs more than all the other planets and moons combined. But HD168443 is 17 times more massive even than Jupiter.

Flattest star »

The least spherical star in our galaxy studied to date is the southern star Achenar (Alpha Eridani, right).

Observations made between 11 September and 12 November 2002 using the Very Large Telescope (VLT) Interferometer at the European Southern Observatory's Paranal Observatory, in Atacama, Chile, have revealed that Achenar is spinning so rapidly that its equatorial diameter is more than 50% greater than its polar diameter. The results were released on 11 June 2003.

« Greatest explosion ever

Most astronomers now believe that the universe began around 13.7 billion years ago in a cataclysmic explosion called the Big Bang (shown left in an artist's impression). All the matter and energy in the universe had its origins in this event, along with time itself. One second after the Big Bang, the temperature was around ten thousand million degrees, or around six hundred times hotter than the interior of the Sun.

★ Most massive star visible to the naked eye
Eta Carinae is a rare supergiant some 9,000 light years from Earth. With a mass estimated at between 100 and 200 times that of the Sun, it is one of the most massive stars in the galaxy. It is just visible to the naked eye with a magnitude of 6.21.

★ Oldest planet in the Milky Way
The oldest planet discovered so far in our galaxy is an extrasolar planet in the globular cluster M4, some 5,600 light years from Earth.

With an estimated age of at least 10 billion years, this distant planet is more than twice as old as our Solar System. Its discovery was announced in July 2003.

★ Oldest star in the Milky Way
The oldest star identified to date in the Milky Way galaxy is HE0107-5240, a giant star around 36,000 light years from Earth. Its age is measured by its composition: when the universe formed, it consisted of hydrogen with some helium. As it evolved, the rest of the chemical elements appeared, formed by nuclear synthesis in stars. HE0107-5240 has almost no metal content in it, meaning it must have formed from clouds of gas consisting of almost pure hydrogen and helium when the universe was young. It could date back to the very beginning of the universe, around 13.7 billion years ago.

★ Most luminous star in the galaxy
The latest observations of LBV1806-20, a star 45,000 light years from Earth, indicate it is between five and 40 million times more luminous than the Sun. It has a mass of at least 150 times that of the Sun and has a diameter at least 200 times greater.

★ Farthest object visible by the naked eye
The most remote heavenly body visible to the naked eye is the Andromeda Galaxy in the constellation of Andromeda (M31, magnitude 3.47), a spiral galaxy 2.2 million light years away. Under good observation conditions the spiral galaxy in Triangulum (M33, magnitude 5.79), can be seen by the naked eye at a distance of 2.53 million light years.

★ Largest galaxy
The central galaxy of the Abell 2029 galaxy cluster, 1,070 million light years distant in Virgo, has a major diameter of 5.6 million light years – 80 times the diameter of our own Milky Way galaxy – and a light output equivalent to two trillion (2×10^{12}) Suns.

★ Closest planet to a star
A Jupiter-sized gas giant orbits the star OGLE-TR-3. This 'hot Jupiter' orbits just 3.5 million km (2.1 million miles) from its parent star and has an orbital period of just 28 hr 33 min. OGLE-TR-3 is a G-type star (similar to the Sun) some 4,900 light years away. The planet was discovered using the Optical Gravitational Lensing Experiment, and announced in April 2003.

Largest recorded ⌄ solar flare

On 4 November 2003, the Sun unleashed a solar flare rated as an X28 event by the Space Environment Center of the National Oceanic and Atmospheric Administration (NOAA) in Boulder, Colorado, USA. Considered a major event, X-class flares are the most powerful and can cause planet-wide radio disruption. Images of solar flares (left) and other phenomena are captured daily by the Extreme ultraviolet Imaging Telescope (EIT) on board the SOHO spacecraft.

Largest cyclone ⌃ in the Solar System

The Great Red Spot (above) on the planet Jupiter is the largest cyclone in the Solar System. It varies in size but can be up to 40,000 km (24,800 miles) long and 14,000 km (8,700 miles) wide.

★ Fastest winds in the Solar System
The planet Neptune has the fastest winds anywhere in the Solar System. Measured by NASA's *Voyager 2* probe in 1989, they blow at around 2,400 km/h (1,500 mph).

★ Most distant object in the Solar System
The minor planet 1999DG8 was discovered by a team of astronomers led by Brett Gladman (Canada) from the Canadian Institute of Theoretical Physics, using the 3.6-m (11.81-ft) Canada-France-Hawaii Telescope (USA) in February 1999. With a diameter of around 100 km (62 miles), this icy body was around 9 billion km (5.6 billion miles) from the Sun when it was observed on two different nights. Because its orbit has yet to be properly calculated, 1999DG8 could follow a path which takes it closer to or further from the Sun.

★ Hottest place in the Solar System
Although no one has ever visited there, the very centre of the Sun is the hottest place in the Solar System. The latest estimates of the temperature are 15.6 billion°C. The pressure in the core is also immense, around 250 billion times the pressure at sea level on Earth. It is here that around 600 million tonnes of hydrogen are fused into helium every second. This ongoing nuclear reaction is what makes the Sun shine.

★ Closest moon to a planet
Of all the moons in the Solar System, the one that orbits closest to its planet is the tiny Martian satellite Phobos. Phobos is 9,378 km (5,827 miles) from the centre of Mars – which corresponds to 5,981 km (3,716 miles) above the Martian surface. Using the surface-to-surface measurement, Phobos is roughly 60 times closer to Mars than the Moon is to Earth.

★ Largest corona
Coronae (roughly circular features surrounded by multiple cocentric ridges) are so far unique to the planet Venus. They were discovered by the US *Magellan* spacecraft, which orbited the planet from 10 August 1990 to 11 October 1994. The largest is Artemis Corona, which has a diameter of 2,100 km (1,300 miles). Planetary scientists are in disagreement on the origin of coronae, but it seems likely that they are the result of hot magma welling up from the Venusian mantle.

★ Largest canyon in the Solar System
The Valles Marineris canyon on the planet Mars has an overall length of around 4,500 km (2,800 miles). At its widest it is 600 km (370 miles) across and is also up to 7 km (4.3 miles) deep. It is named after the *Mariner 9* spacecraft which discovered it in 1971.

★ Satellite with the thickest atmosphere
Saturn's large moon Titan has the thickest atmosphere of any moon in the Solar System, and exerts a surface pressure of 1.44 bar. Consisting mainly of nitrogen gas, Titan's atmosphere is the most similar to our own in the Solar System.

Most volcanically »
active body

Photographs of Jupiter's moon Io (right), taken from the *Galileo* spacecraft, revealed enormous volcanic eruption plumes reaching hundreds of kilometres into space. Io's activity is driven by tidal energy – the result of gravitational interactions between Jupiter, Io and one of the other moons, Europa. Io is so active that it has turned itself inside out during its lifetime.

⌃ Highest mountain in the Solar System

The peak of Olympus Mons (above) on Mars rises 25 km (15 miles) above

its base – nearly three times the height of Mt Everest. Despite its great height, Olympus Mons has a very gentle slope and is therefore designated a shield volcano: it is over 20 times wider than it is high.

★ **Largest observed coma**
The coma (the cloud around the nucleus in the head of a comet) on a comet seen in 1811 was thought to be around 2 million km (1.2 million miles) in diameter.

★ **Highest volcanic eruption**
On 6 August 2001 NASA's *Galileo* spacecraft performed a close flyby of Jupiter's volcanically active satellite, Io. Over the following months, as the data was transmitted back to Earth, scientists realised that the spacecraft had passed through the top of a 500-km (310-mile) high volcanic plume. This is the highest volcanic eruption plume ever witnessed in the Solar System.

★ **Most distant moon from a planet**
Announced by the International Astronomical Union on 3 September 2003, S/2003 N1 orbits Neptune at an average distance of approximately 49.5 million km (31 million miles). It has an orbital period of approximately 26 years and measures around 38 km (24 miles) across.

★ **Fastest planet**
Mercury, which orbits the Sun at an average distance of 57.9 million km (35.9 million miles), has an orbital period of 87.9686 days, thus giving the highest average speed in orbit of 172,248 km/h (107,030 mph). This is almost twice as fast as the Earth.

★ **Largest planet**
Jupiter has an equatorial diameter of 143,884 km (89,405 miles) and a polar diameter of 133,708 km (83,082 miles). It has a mass 317.828 times – and a volume 1,323.3 times – that of the Earth.

★ **Smallest planet**
The discovery of Pluto by Clyde William Tombaugh (USA) of the Lowell Observatory, Flagstaff, Arizona, USA, was announced on 13 March 1930. The planet has a diameter of 2,324 km (1,444 miles) and a mass 0.0022 that of the Earth.

★ **Largest moon compared to its planet**
Charon, the only known satellite of Pluto, has a diameter of 1,270 km (790 miles). Pluto itself is only 2,324 km (1,444 miles) across. The Pluto-Charon System is regarded by some as a 'double planet'.

★ **Hottest planet**
Venus has an average temperature of around 480°C (896°F). This scorching heat is hot enough to melt lead and, coupled with the atrocious atmosphere, makes exploration of the surface by probes very difficult. If you were to step on to the surface of Venus you would be simultaneously crushed by the pressure, incinerated by the heat, dissolved by the sulphuric acid and suffocated by the carbon dioxide.

★ **Planet with the longest day**
While the Earth takes 23 hr 56 min 4 sec to complete one rotation, Venus takes 243.16 'Earth days' to spin once through 360°. As Venus is closer to the Sun, its year is shorter than Earth's, lasting only 224.7 days, so a day on Venus is actually longer than its year. Another Venusian curiosity is that it rotates backwards compared with all of the other major planets (apart from Uranus, which spins on its side).

★ **Planet with the shortest day**
Jupiter spins around on its axis once every 9 hr 55 min 29.69 sec.

★ **Most powerful aurorae in the Solar System**
The aurorae on Jupiter are around 1,000 times more powerful than the aurorae seen on Earth. Jupiter's aurorae are caused by energetic particles from the Sun being channelled on to the planet's poles by Jupiter's magnetic field and causing atoms in its upper atmosphere to glow like the gas in a neon tube. This process produces around a million megawatts of energy, enough to power 100 major cities on Earth.

Greatest snowfall in 12 months

Over a 12-month period from 19 February 1971 to 18 February 1972, 31,102 mm (102 ft 0.5 in) of snow fell at Paradise, Mt Rainier, Washington, USA. ⌄

⌃ Most powerful short-term natural climate change

The El-Niño Southern Oscillation occurs as a result of cyclic warming of the eastern and central Pacific Ocean. Apart from the seasonal effects of the Earth moving around the Sun, it is the most powerful short-term natural climate change on Earth. The entire cycle of El Niño and La Niña (its cooler counterpart and opposite) lasts between three and seven years. It causes unusual weather conditions all around the world, particularly notable in the 1982/83 and 1997/98 events.

★ GWR TALKS TO
Professor Joshua Wurman

Professor Joshua Wurman (USA, above), a professional 'storm chaser', runs the Center for Severe Weather Research in Boulder, Colorado, USA. He operated the University of Oklahoma's 'Doppler on Wheels' mobile weather observatory when they measured the highest winds ever, during the Bridgecreek/Moore/Oklahoma City tornado that caused F5 damage and nearly 40 deaths. The wind speed on this occasion was between 452 and 516 km/h (281-321 mph).

How long have you been a storm chaser?
Professionally, since 1995; for recreation, since 1992.

What was it that inspired you to do this as a career?
Interest in nature combined with the excitement of a young science that had big questions to be answered.

How close do you get to tornadoes?
We have been hit by weak tornadoes, but we usually stay 1.6-4.4 km (1-3 miles) away from the centres.

What is your favourite part of the job?
Discovering new things. Observational scientists like myself are the inheritors of the tradition of exploration. In past centuries, explorers got on boats and charted new places, in the future they may get on spaceships. Now, the reachable unknowns are inside tornadoes and hurricanes, in deep sea trenches, etc, and present day explorers are to be found there.

What has been the scariest moment in your career?
I don't have a particularly scary moment that I can recall. It sounds boring, but we actually are very, very safe. We are constantly tracking the course of the tornado – its strength and size – and plotting escape routes if necessary.

What does it mean to you to have a Guinness World Record?
Since I was a very small child, I read the Guinness book every year and memorized a lot of it. As an adult, to finally, have a record in the book is great.

★ Greatest depth of snow
The greatest depth of snow on the ground was 11.46 m (37 ft 7 in) measured at Tamarac, California, USA, in March 1911.

★ Most destructive geomagnetic storm
The most destructive geomagnetic storm ever recorded was the 'Great Geomagnetic Storm' of 13 March 1989, which was classified G5 (the most severe) on the space weather scale. The result of an abnormally strong solar wind, it caused major disruption to the power grid all over North America and changed the orbit of a satellite. The solar wind is a stream of particles radiating from the Sun into the Solar System, and it is this phenomenon that is responsible for the northern and southern lights (aurora borealis, aurora australis).

Most tornadoes in 24 hours ⌃

The record number of tornadoes in a 24-hour period is 148. They swept through the southern and mid-western states of the USA on 3–4 April 1974. This region of America is often referred to as 'Tornado Alley'.

★ **Lowest temperature in an inhabited area**
The coldest permanently inhabited place is the Siberian village of Oymyakon (pop. 4,000), 63°16'N, 143°15'E (700 m or 2,300 ft), in Russia, where the temperature reached -68°C (-90°F) in 1933. An unofficial -72°C (-98°F) has been published more recently.

★ **Lowest temperature on Earth**
A low of -89.2°C (-128.6°F) was registered at Vostok, Antarctica (altitude 3,420 m or 11,220 ft), on 21 July 1983.

★ **Clouds with the greatest vertical range**
The cloud form with the greatest vertical range is cumulonimbus, which has been observed to reach a height of nearly 20,000 m (65,600 ft) in the tropics – that's nearly three times the height of Mt Everest.

★ **Longest lightning flash**
At any time, around 100 lightning bolts per second hit the Earth. Typically, the actual length of these bolts can be around 9 km (5.5 miles). In 1956 meteorologist Myron Ligda (USA) observed and recorded a lightning flash, using radar that covered a horizontal distance of 149 km (93 miles) inside clouds.

★ **Greatest pressure drop measured in a tornado**
The greatest pressure drop ever measured inside a tornado was 100 millibars. It was recorded by severe storms researcher Tim Samaras (USA), who successfully placed an instrument probe in the path of an F4 tornado, near Manchester, South Dakota, USA, on 24 June 2003.

★ **Driest place**
For the period between 1964 and 2001, the average annual rainfall for the meteorological station in Quillagua, in the Atacama Desert, Chile, was just 0.5 mm (0.02 in). This discovery was made during the making of the documentary series *Going to Extremes*, by Keo Films in 2001.

★ **Largest hole in the ozone layer**
Scientists at NASA's Goddard Space Flight Center, Maryland, USA, detected the largest hole so far seen in the ozone layer in September 2000. With an area of around 28.3 million km² (11 million miles²), this hole above Antarctica is roughly three times the area of the USA. The ozone layer in the stratosphere (about 12–45 km or 7–28 miles above the ground) shields the Earth's surface from the Sun's damaging ultraviolet (UV-B) rays.

★ **Greatest display of solar halos**
On 11 January 1999, at least 24 types of solar halo were witnessed by scientists at the geographic South Pole. Solar halos are formed by sunlight being reflected and refracted by ice crystals in the atmosphere, causing rings around the Sun. Atmospheric conditions at the South Pole are conducive to this type of phenomenon.

★ **Oldest fossilized raindrops**
On 15 December 2001, Indian geologist Chirananda De announced his discovery of the fossilized imprints of raindrops in ancient rocks in the lower Vindhya Range, Madhya Pradesh, India. These fossils prove that rain fell on Earth at least 1.6 billion years ago.

★ **Greatest annual rainfall**
By average annual rainfall, the world's wettest place is Mawsynram, Meghalaya, India, with 11,873 mm (4,678 in) of rain per annum.

Largest land gorge ⌃

The largest land gorge in the world is the Grand Canyon (above) on the Colorado River in north-central Arizona, USA. It extends from Marble Gorge to the Grand Wash Cliffs, over a distance of 446 km (277 miles). It averages 16 km (10 miles) in width and 1.6 km (1 mile) in depth.

Highest natural arch ⌃

The red sandstone Rainbow Bridge (above) on Lake Powell National Monument, Utah, USA, is the highest natural arch in the world. It is only 82.3 m (270 ft) long, but is a massive feature rising to a height of 88.4 m (290 ft). The Rainbow Bridge was formed when an ancient stream eroded away some of the weaker sedimentary rock in the area, leaving the natural bridge behind.

★ Coolest erupting lava
The natrocarbonatite lava of the volcano Oldoinyo Lengai, Tanzania, erupts at temperatures of 500–600°C (930–1,110°F). Common basaltic lavas erupt at temperatures between 1,100 and 1,200°C (2,010 and 2,190°F).

★ Tallest sea stack
Ball's Pyramid near Lord Howe Island (Australia) in the Pacific Ocean is 561 m (1,843 ft) high but has a base axis of only 200 m (660 ft).

★ Largest active volcano
Mauna Loa, Hawaii, USA, is the largest active volcano. It has the shape of a broad gentle dome 120 km (75 miles) long and 50 km (31 miles) wide (above sea level), with lava flows that occupy more than 5,125 km^2 (1,980 miles^2) of the

island. It has a total volume of 42,500 km^3 (10,200 miles^3), of which 84.2% is below sea level.

★ Largest geode
A geode is a rock cavity filled with minerals – most are small enough to fit in the palm of a human hand. The largest geode discovered to date is near Almería, Spain. It forms a mineral-lined cave 8 m (26 ft) long, 2 m (6 ft) wide and 2 m (6 ft) high, and is around six million years old.

★ Deepest valley
The Yarlung Zangbo valley, in Tibet, has an average depth of 5,000 m (16,400 ft). In 1994 explorers discovered that its deepest point was 5,382 m (17,657 ft). The peaks either side of the valley – Namche Barwa (7,753 m or 25,436 ft) and Jala Peri (7,282 m or 23,891 ft) – are

just 21 km (13 miles) apart with the Yarlung Zangbo river flowing between them at an elevation of 2,440 m (8,000 ft).

★ Deepest canyon
The Vikos Gorge in the Pindus mountains of northwest Greece is 900 m (2,950 ft) deep with only 1,100 m (3,600 ft) between its rims. Gorges in many countries have a higher depth/width ratio, but none are as deep.

★ Oldest confirmed impact on Earth
On 23 August 2002, a team of US scientists led by Gary Byerly and Donald Lowe (both USA) announced their discovery of a 3.47-billion-year-old asteroid impact on Earth. They had studied ancient rock samples from Australia and South Africa and analysed the spherules contained within. These tiny particles are a common by-product of meteoritic strikes and, along with local zircon crystals, were used to date the impact. The spherule beds in the rock indicate that the impacting

body had a rough diameter of around 20 km (12 miles). No crater has been found, as the Earth's geological processes have erased it.

★ Highest continent
Excluding its ice shelves, Antarctica has an average elevation of 2,194 m (7,198 ft) above the OSU91A Geoid (similar to, but more accurate than, sea level).

★ Largest geological feature discovered from space
The Richat Structure in the Sahara Desert of Mauritania is an almost circular, multi-ringed sedimentary basin with a diameter of around 50 km (30 miles). Originally thought to be an impact crater, it is now believed to be the eroded remains of an uplifted sedimentary dome. The distinctive 'bull's-eye' shape was discovered from orbit by US astronauts Jim McDivitt and Ed White during the *Gemini IV* mission in June 1965.

Largest modern-day landslide ⌃

The landslide on Mt St Helens, Washington, USA (above), was the largest ever observed by a survivor. On 18 May 1980, about 2,800 million m³ (96,000 million ft³) of rock slipped off the mountain immediately prior to the volcanic eruption. This is equivalent to a block of earth nearly 1.2 km (0.8 miles) high, wide and long.

★ Largest liquid body on Earth

The largest liquid body on Earth is its outer core. The inner core is solid iron/nickel and measures around 1,221 km (758 miles) across. This is surrounded by the liquid outer core, with a thickness of 2,259 km (1,403 miles). The outer core has a total volume of around 1.719×10^{20} m³. It represents around 29.3% of Earth's mass and 16% of Earth's volume, or 100 times the volume of water in Earth's oceans.

★ Largest doline

Xio Zhai Tien ('The Great Doline'), situated in the Sichuan region of central southern China, measures 500 m (1,600 ft) across and 660 m (2,100 ft) deep. Dolines are basins formed when limestone caves subside.

★ Largest sandstone monolith

Uluru, also known as Ayers Rock, is a huge exposed sandstone monolith that rises 348 m (1,143 ft) above the surrounding desert plain in Northern Territory, Australia. It is 2.5 km (1.5 miles) long and 1.6 km (1 mile) wide.

★ Fastest land mass on Earth

Owing to convection currents in the Earth's mantle, all the continental plates slowly move relative to each other. The greatest movement occurs at the Tonga microplate, near Samoa, which is moving further into the Pacific at a rate of 24 cm (9.4 in) per year.

★ Deepest permafrost

Permafrost more than 1,370 m (4,500 ft) deep was reported from the upper reaches of the Viluy River, Siberia, Russia, in February 1982.

★ Largest steam rings

The active volcano Mount Etna in Sicily, Italy, is the tallest and most active volcano in Europe. A complex physical process is causing it to emit huge steam rings, similar to more familiar smoke rings. Etna's steam rings are around 200 m (650 ft) across and can last for around 10 minutes, as they slowly drift upwards to a height of about 1,000 m (3,300 ft) above the volcanic vent.

★ Weakest region in the Earth's magnetic field

The Southern Magnetic Anomaly, found off the coast of Brazil, is a region in the Earth's magnetic field that is some 30% weaker than the average for the whole planet. This 'dip' is due to eccentricities in the Earth's core, and causes increased doses of radiation in satellites passing over this region.

★ Longest day on Earth

The tidal bulges in the Earth's oceans caused by the gravitational effect of the Moon are gradually transferring momentum from the Earth's rotation to the Moon's orbit. As a result, the Earth's rotation is slowing at a rate of around 0.02 seconds per century, and each day is a little longer than the day before. Therefore, the longest day is always today.

★ Oldest volcanic rocks on Earth

Volcanic rocks dated at 3.825 billion years have been discovered in the Inukjuak area in the northern reaches of the province of Québec, Canada. The precise dating of the rocks was performed by the University of Québec, Montréal, and the Simon Fraser University in British Columbia (both Canada).

Highest mountain
Natural world

The highest mountain in the world is Mount Everest. Its peak rises to 8,848 m (29,028 ft 9 in) – the highest point in the world.

Mount Everest is situated in the eastern Himalayas – its summit ridge separates Nepal and Tibet. It was discovered to be the world's highest mountain in 1856 by the Survey Department of the Government of India. Measurements from theodolite readings taken in 1849 and 1850 gave the first accurate measurement and revealed the peak to be the world's highest.

Naming Everest
The mountain was named after Col. Sir George Everest (UK), who was Surveyor-General of India from 1830 to 1843, and who, in fact, pronounced his name 'Eve-rest' as opposed to 'Ever-est'. Mount Everest is also known by the Tibetan name Chomolungma (Goddess Mother of the World) and by the Nepali name Sagarmatha (Forehead in the Sky).

Climbing Everest
Many human triumphs and tragedies have been played out on Everest's slopes. George Mallory (UK) was one of the first to lead an expedition to climb the peak, in 1921. He perished not far from the summit on his 1924 expedition and his body was discovered in 1999. The challenge to climb the highest mountain has not waned since the peak was first conquered in 1953 by Sherpa Tenzing Norgay (Nepal) and Sir Edmund Hillary (New Zealand).

A record-breaking mountain
Mount Everest has been the inspiration for many Guinness World Records: from the simple fact of being the world's highest peak, to being the venue for the world's highest-altitude concert. Many of the records achieved on Everest are broken regularly – and some of the current record holders are featured on these pages. As the world's highest peak, Everest will always attract adventurous climbers and records will continue to be broken on its slopes.

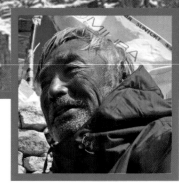

★ Fastest ascent of Everest
Lakpa Gelu Sherpa (Nepal) made a successful ascent of Mount Everest in 10 hr 56 min 46 sec on 26 May 2003, the fastest ever climb from Base Camp to the summit.

★ Longest stay on the summit
Babu Chhiri Sherpa (Nepal) stayed at the summit of Mount Everest for 21 hours without using bottled oxygen in May 1999. Most climbers stay less than an hour. He climbed Mount Everest again just weeks later, becoming the first person to climb the mountain twice in the same season.

★ Most conquests
Apa Sherpa (Nepal) completed his 13th successful climb of Mount Everest when he reached the summit on 26 May 2003. Dates of his climbs are: 1990, 1991, 1992 (spring and autumn), 1993, 1994, 1995, 1997, 1998, 1999, 2000, 2002 and 2003.

★ Oldest man to reach the summit
Yuichiro Miura (Japan) reached Mount Everest's summit aged 70 years 222 days on 22 May 2003, becoming the oldest person ever to have done so. Miura, a professional skier, formerly achieved fame by skiing down Everest from 8,000 m (26,246 ft) in 1970.

Mount Everest was first conquered at 11:30 am on 29 May 1953, when the summit was reached by Edmund Percival Hillary (New Zealand) and Sherpa Tenzing Norgay (Nepal, both left). The successful expedition was led by Col. (later Hon. Brigadier) Henry Cecil John Hunt (UK).

How did you become involved in mountaineering?

When I was 16 years old I travelled with a school party 200 miles (320 km) south to the Tongariro National Park, and that was the first time I saw snow, really heavy winter snow, and for ten days I skied and scrambled around the snowy mountainside. I was by now pretty big and strong, and I revelled in this new experience. There was no doubt that it changed my life. I'd found something that I could enjoy and do well and it became an important part of my existence.

How did you come to be involved in the 1953 Everest Expedition?

I did a great deal of mountaineering in New Zealand and Europe, so I'd become a pretty competent climber. Then four of us decided to go to the Himalayas and we climbed a number of peaks well over 20,000 ft (6,090 m). Eric Shipton – the famous explorer/ mountaineer – invited two of us to join him. He'd just got permission to approach Everest from the south side, which nobody had done before. So I sort of got swept in.

During the ascent did you experience doubts that you'd reach the summit?

I was never completely confident at any stage that I was going to get to the top. My whole attitude was that I would tackle any problems that I happened to meet, hopefully overcome them, and then if all went well I'd get up to the south summit and finally to the top. And that's the way it worked out. I've always felt that if there's a big challenge ahead of you, and you're absolutely confident that you can do it, why bother starting – it's not worth the effort to give it a crack. But that wasn't the case with Everest – I didn't really know whether or not I would be successful, so I was determined to give it everything I had.

What was for you the single biggest challenge?

Probably the most demanding bit was on the summit ridge, this rock step around 40 ft (12 m) high, which nowadays they call the Hillary Step. I had to find a way up this so I wiggled and jammed between the rock and the ice cornice, never knowing if the ice would break off, but I did it. That was the first time I was confident that I was going to be successful.

What are your thoughts on how Everest is tackled today?

I don't like the increasing commercialization of Himalayan mountaineering. If you have $60,000 you can more or less buy your way into an expedition and be conducted up the mountain. We were in Kathmandu recently and there were 15 expeditions located at Base Camp on the south side of Everest, and another 15 on the north side – literally hundreds of people trying to climb the mountain, many with little or no experience, being conducted by more experienced leaders. I strongly believe that the number of expeditions on the mountain at any one time should be reasonably limited. To have 30 expeditions on the mountain at any one time is absolutely ridiculous. There's no challenge to it, and that's the whole point.

Why was climbing Everest an important thing to have done?

It was the biggest and the best, so it was the major challenge. And of course I'd read so much about George Mallory and Andrew Irvine and the enthusiastic climbers in the 1920s and 1930s, which had built up a feeling that it would be great to have a chance to have a crack at the mountain, to see if we could get up it too.

Could you tell us a bit about your work with the Sherpas?

As I got older I became more interested in the welfare of the Sherpa people and have worked with charitable institutions for 40 years building schools, hospitals, and many other projects for the Sherpas. We've also helped train their teachers. We love doing it – it's no sacrifice as far as we're concerned. We're very fond of our Sherpa friends and they work hard on these projects too, so it's been a very satisfying experience.

Is there somebody that you particularly admire?

To me Ernest Shackleton epitomized the great explorer, the man who could deal with great problems when they arose, the man who kept his team alive, kept their spirit up.

Do you have any unfulfilled ambitions?

Well I'm pretty ancient, you know, I'm fast approaching 85, but I'm still very energetic about raising funds for Sherpa projects and I'm still very enthusiastic on environmental matters as well, and with the re-establishing of the forests in the Mount Everest area. So, the environment and the welfare of the mountain people, I would say, are now my main motivations in life.

★ **Oldest woman to reach the summit**
Tamae Watanabe (Japan) reached the summit of Mount Everest at the age of 63 years 177 days at 9:55 am on 16 May 2002, becoming the oldest woman ever to do so. More than 50 people reached the summit on the same day.

★ **Earliest solo summit**
Reinhold Messner (Italy) was the first to successfully climb Mount Everest solo, reaching the summit on 20 August 1980. It took him three days to make the ascent from his base camp at 6,500 m (21,325 ft), and the climb was made all the more difficult by the fact that he did not use bottled oxygen.

The largest tabular iceberg measured over 31,000 km² (12,000 miles²).

The flat-topped, blocky iceberg was 335 km (208 miles) long and 97 km (60 miles) wide – that's larger than Belgium – and was sighted 240 km (150 miles) west of Scott Island in the Southern Ocean, Antarctica, by the USS *Glacier* on 12 November 1956.

★ **Deepest point in the ocean**
The deepest part of the ocean is 'Challenger Deep', which lies at a depth of 10,911 m (35,797 ft) in the Marianas Trench in the Pacific Ocean. It is named after HM Survey Ship *Challenger II*, which discovered it in 1951, although it was first reached in 1960 by the manned US Navy bathyscaphe *Trieste*. The record depth – almost 11 km (7 miles) – was confirmed in March 1995 by the unmanned Japanese probe *Kaiko*.

★ **Largest continuous ocean current system**
The Thermohaline Conveyor is a vast global system of ocean circulation driven by differences in sea water density and salinity. It transports cold and salty deep water from the North Atlantic down to the Southern Ocean where it then travels east and north to the Indian and Pacific Oceans. Here it rises and becomes warm, travelling back westwards where it sinks again in the North Atlantic. The entire cycle can last for a thousand years.

★ **Greatest submarine mountain range**
The submarine Mid-Ocean Ridge extends 65,000 km (40,000 miles) from the Arctic Ocean to the Atlantic Ocean, around Africa, Asia and Australia, and under the Pacific Ocean to the west coast of North America. Its greatest height is 4,200 m (13,800 ft) above the base ocean depth.

★ **Fastest ocean current**
During the monsoon, the Somali current in the northern Indian Ocean flows at 12.8 km/h (9 mph).

★ **Highest ocean temperature**
The highest temperature recorded in the ocean is 404°C (759°F) for a hydrothermal vent measured by an American research submarine some 480 km (300 miles) off the American west coast in 1985.

★ **Largest ocean**
Excluding adjacent seas, the Pacific Ocean represents 45.9% of the world's oceans and covers 166,241,700 km² (64,186,000 miles²) in area. The average depth is 3,940 m (12,925 ft).

★ **Largest area of calm water**
An area known as the Sargasso Sea in the north Atlantic Ocean covers about 6.2 million km² (2.4 million miles²) of relatively still water. Its surface is largely covered by sargassum seaweed.

★ **Longest river**
From its farthest stream in Burundi, the Nile extends 6,695 km (4,160 miles) in length. Credited as the longest river, the Nile's main source is Lake Victoria in East Africa.

★ **Greatest river flow**
The Amazon discharges an average of 200,000 m³/sec (7.1 million ft³/sec) into the Atlantic Ocean, increasing to more than 340,000 m³/sec (12 million ft³/sec) in full flood. The lower 1,450 km (900 miles) average 17 m (55 ft) in depth, but the river has a maximum depth of 124 m (407 ft). The flow of the Amazon is 60 times greater than that of the Nile.

★ **Largest basin**
The vast Amazon river basin covers around 7,045,000 km² (2,720,000 miles²). It has countless tributaries, including the Madeira, which at 3,380 km (2,100 miles) is the longest tributary in the world, being surpassed in length by only 17 rivers.

★ **Deepest brine pool**
The Orca Basin in the Gulf of Mexico lies 2,200 m (7,200 ft) below sea level. This 7 x 21-km (4 x 13-mile) depression is filled with water that has a salt content of around 300 g/litre (48 oz/gal) – around eight times saltier than the Gulf itself. Effectively a hypersaline lake at the bottom of the sea, the salinity is caused by salt leaching out of the salt deposits under the sediment on the sea floor.

★ **Largest inland island**
The largest inland island (ie land surrounded by rivers) is Ilha do Bananal, Brazil, at 20,000 km² (7,700 miles²).

Highest waterfall

The Salto Angel (below) on a branch of the Carrao River, Venezuela, is the highest waterfall (as opposed to vaporized 'Bridal Veil') in the world.

It has a total drop of 979 m (3,212 ft) – the longest single drop being 807 m (2,648 ft). The Angel Falls were named after the American pilot Jimmie Angel, who recorded them in his log book on 16 November 1933. The falls, known by the native Venezuelans as Churun-Meru, had been reported by the Spanish explorer Ernesto Sánchez la Cruz in 1910.

Largest lagoon

Lagoa dos Patos ('Lagoon of Ducks', above), located near the seashore in Rio Grande do Sul, southernmost Brazil, is 280 km (174 miles) long and extends over 9,850 km² (3,803 miles²). It has a maximum width of 70 km (44 miles), and is separated from the Atlantic Ocean by long sand strips.

★ **Largest freshwater island**
The largest island surrounded mostly by freshwater is the Ilha de Maraj in the mouth of the Amazon River, Brazil, which measures 48,000 km² (18,500 miles²).

★ **Largest lake island**
The largest island in a lake is Manitoulin Island, which covers an area of 2,766 km² (1,068 miles²) in the Canadian section of Lake Huron.

★ **Saltiest lake**
Don Juan Pond in Wright Valley, Antarctica, is so salty that it remains liquid even at temperatures as low as -53°C (-63.4°F). The percentage of salt by weight is 40.2%, compared with 23.1% and 3.38% for the Dead Sea and the world's oceans respectively.

★ **Greatest waterfall annual flow**
On the basis of the average annual flow, the greatest waterfall in the world is the Boyoma Falls in the Congo (former Zaïre), with a flow of 17,000 m³/sec (600,000 ft³/sec). The flow of the Guaíra (Cascade of the Seven Waterfalls) on the Paraná River between Brazil and Paraguay attained a rate of 50,000 m³/sec (1,750,000 ft³/sec), although the closing of the Itaipú Dam gates in 1982 ended this claim to fame. However, it now holds the record for the greatest waterfall submerged by a reservoir.

★ **Highest tides**
The greatest tides occur in the Bay of Fundy, which divides the peninsula of Nova Scotia, Canada, from the USA's north-easternmost state of Maine and the Canadian province of New Brunswick. Burncoat Head in the Minas Basin, Nova Scotia, Canada, has the greatest mean spring range, with 14.5 m (47 ft 6 in). A tide range of 16.6 m (54 ft 6 in) was recorded at springs in Leaf Basin in Ungava Bay, Québec, Canada, in 1953.

★ **Largest polynya**
The largest area of open sea surrounded by sea ice ever recorded measured around 275,000 km² (106,000 miles²). It occurred in the Weddell Sea, off Antarctica, during the winter months of 1974, 1975 and 1976. This spectacularly large polynya was discovered using satellite imagery.

★ **Largest atoll**
The slender 283-km (176-mile) coral reef of Kwajalein, in the Marshall Islands in the central Pacific Ocean, encloses a lagoon of 2,850 km² (1,100 miles²).

★ **Largest atoll land area**
Christmas Atoll in the Line Islands in the central Pacific Ocean has an area of 649 km² (251 miles²), of which 321 km² (124 miles²) is land.

★ **Most southerly ocean**
The most southerly part of any ocean is located at 87°S, 151°W, at the snout of the Scott Glacier, 320 km (200 miles) from the South Pole.

Prehistoric life
Natural world

Largest « crocodile ever

Sarchosuchus imperator (left) was a prehistoric crocodile species that lived around 110 million years ago. Fossilized remains found in the Sahara Desert suggest that this creature took around 50–60 years to grow to its full length of 11–12 m (37–40 ft).

★ **Largest dinosaur skull**
Torosaurus ('piercing lizard'), a ceratopsid, had the largest skull of all known land animals. A herbivore, *Torosaurus* measured around 7.6 m (25 ft) in length and weighed up to 8 tonnes (17,600 lb). Its skull measured up to 3 m (9 ft 10 in) in length and weighed up to 2 tonnes (4,400 lb).

The largest single dinosaur skull ever found measures 3.2 m (10 ft 6 in) in height and belonged to a *Pentaceratops* ('five horn lizard') skeleton.

★ **Dinosaur with the longest tail**
The diplodocid *Diplodocus* ('double beamed') was a long-necked sauropod dinosaur from the late Jurassic period (155 to 145 million years ago). It had a tail length of up to 13–14 m (43–45 ft).

★ **Oldest fossilized animal food store**
In November 2003 a team of scientists from the University of Bonn (Germany) announced their discovery of a 17 million-year-old fossilized rodent burrow – probably for a hamster or a squirrel – containing more than 1,200 fossilized nuts.

★ **Oldest known marsupial**
The *Deltatheridium* ('little delta (tooth) beast') found in Mongolia's Gobi Desert in November 1988 has been estimated by scientists to be 80 million years old. This means it lived among dinosaurs and that marsupials possibly originated here.

★ **Oldest fossilized embryos**
Around 100 embryos of *Markuelia hunanensis* – an extinct species of worm – were discovered in Hunan, southern China, by a team from Bristol University (UK) and Beijing University (China). They date back around 500 million years. The discovery was announced in January 2004.

★ **Largest carnivore ever**
A skeleton of *Giganotosaurus carolinii*, the largest predatory dinosaur, was discovered in Neuquen, Patagonia, Argentina,

in 1995. It was 12.5 m (41 ft) long, and weighed 8 tonnes (17,600 lb). The bones suggest that it is taller than *Tyrannosaurus rex*. It lived about 110 million years ago – 30 million years before *T. rex.*

★ **Longest prehistoric tusks**
The average length for the tusks of the straight-tusked elephant *Hesperoloxodon antiques germanicus*, which lived about two million years ago in what is now Germany, was 5 m (16 ft 4.75 in).

★ **Largest duck-billed dinosaur**
The duck-billed *Lambeosaurus* ('Lambes lizard') grew to 9–15 m (30–50 ft) long and weighed roughly 5.6 tonnes (12,000 lb). A herbivore that lived during the Cretaceous period, it roamed the Earth in herds 65–83 million years ago.

★ **Longest dinosaur**
The longest vertebrate on record was a diplodocid excavated in 1980 from New Mexico, USA. It was named

Seismosaurus halli, ('earth-shaking lizard') and estimated to be 39–52 m (128–170 ft) long based on comparisons of individual bones. In 1999, the bones were reconstructed at the Wyoming Dinosaur Center and measured 41 m (134 ft).

★ **Largest herbivorous dinosaur**
Sauropod dinosaurs, a group of long-necked, long-tailed, four-legged plant-eaters, lumbered around most of the world during the Jurassic and Cretaceous periods 65–208 million years ago. The largest measured 40 m (131 ft) and weighed up to 100 tonnes (220,000 lb).

★ **Oldest spider in amber**
A spider trapped in amber has been dated at 125–135 million years old. From the family Linyphiidae, it was found in Lebanon and analysed by David Penney and Paul Selden (both UK) and announced on 26 December 2002.

Largest and most complete
Tyrannosaurus rex skeleton »

The largest, most complete and best preserved *Tyrannosaurus rex* skeleton ever found is 'Sue' (right). It measures 4 m (13 ft) tall and 12.5 m (41 ft) long and is approximately 90% complete.

It was found in South Dakota, USA, on 12 August 1990 by explorer Sue Hendrickson (USA), after whom the dinosaur has been named. The skeleton is currently displayed at The Field Museum, Chicago, Illinois, USA.

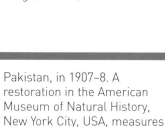

★ Oldest spider silk

The oldest spider silk in the world dates from the Early Cretaceous Period, more than 120 million years ago, and was described in the journal *Nature* by Swiss researcher Dr Samuel Zschokke from the University of Basel. The strand is 4 mm (0.1 in) long and has tiny glue droplets which, in modern-day spiders, are used to catch insects. The specimen was recovered in 1969 from amber beds located near Jezzine, Lebanon, but it was only in 2003 that its importance was recognized.

★ Largest prehistoric mammal

The largest prehistoric mammal was *Indricotherium* (also *Baluchitherium* or *Paraceratherium*) of the family Hyrachyidae, a long-necked, hornless rhinocerotid that roamed across western Asia and Europe roughly 35 million years ago. It was first known from bones discovered in the Bugti Hills of Baluchistan, Pakistan, in 1907–8. A restoration in the American Museum of Natural History, New York City, USA, measures 5.4 m (17 ft 9 in) to the top of the shoulder hump and 11.2 m (37 ft) in total length.

★ Earliest prehistoric salamanders

The earliest salamanders date back 165 million years and thousands of fossilized remains have been discovered in volcanic ash beds in China and Mongolia. These animals are related to the salamanders that now inhabit North America and Asia.

★ Longest prehistoric snake

The longest prehistoric snake was the python-like *Gigantophis garstini*, which inhabited what is now Egypt around 38 million years ago. Parts of a spinal column and a small piece of jaw discovered at Fayum in the Western Desert indicate a length of roughly 11 m (36 ft). This is 1 m (3 ft 3 in) longer than the present-day longest snake.

★ Most dinosaur footprints discovered in one place

About ten different dinosaurs are thought to have made the 100 or more impressions in China's north-west Gansu Province. The prints date from around the junction of the late Jurassic and early Cretaceous periods, 140 million years ago. One of the footprints was approximately 1.5 m (5 ft) long and 1.2 m (4 ft) wide.

★ Largest prehistoric insect

The dragonfly *Meganeura monyi* lived around 280 million years ago. Fossil remains (ie impressions of wings) discovered at Commentry, France, indicate a wing expanse of up to 70 cm (27.5 in). This compares with the largest dragonfly living today (*Megaloprepus caeruleata*) from Central and South America which has been measured up to 120 mm (4.72 in) in length with a wingspan of up to 191 mm (7.52 in).

★ Largest prehistoric bird

The largest prehistoric bird was the flightless *Dromornis stirtoni*, a huge emu-like creature that lived in central Australia between 25,000 and 15 million years ago. Fossil leg bones found near Alice Springs, Northern Territory, Australia, in 1974 indicate that the bird must have stood around 3 m (10 ft) tall and weighed about 500 kg (1,100 lb).

★ Largest armoured dinosaur

Ankylosaurus ('armoured lizard'), a herbivore protected with thick plates covering the skin, also had a double row of spikes running down from the back of its head to its club tail. Measuring 7.5–10.7 m (24 ft 7 in–35 ft) long, 1.8 m (6 ft) wide and 1.2 m (4 ft) tall, it had plates to protect its eyes and only its belly was left unplated. The last, and at 4 tonnes (8,800 lb), the largest of the ankylosaurids, it lived in the late Cretaceous period, about 65–70 million years ago.

« Largest eyes on a mammal

The Philippine tarsier (*Tarsius syrichta*, left) is one of the world's smallest primates. They have a tail measuring 135–275 mm (5.3–10.8 in), a head and body length of 85–160 mm (3.3–6.3 in) and their large forward-pointing eyes have a diameter of 16 mm (0.6 in). Their eyes are so enormous that they would be equivalent to grapefruit-sized eyes in a human being. They are the only primates, along with animals from the Galago genus, able to turn their heads through 180° in each direction. Tarsiers live in the forests of Borneo, Sumatra and the Philippines.

★ Largest land mammal

The adult male African elephant (*Loxodonta africana*) typically stands 3–3.7 m (9 ft 10 in–12 ft 1 in) at the shoulder and weighs 4–7 tonnes (8,800 lb–15,400 lb). The largest specimen ever recorded measured 4.16 m (13 ft 7 in) in a projected line from the highest point of the shoulder to the base of the forefoot, indicating a standing height of about 3.96 m (12 ft 11 in).

★ Smallest elephant species

The world's smallest elephant is the Borneo pygmy, which is 30% smaller than the Asian elephant (*Elephas maximus*). An adult male measures 1.7–2.6 m (5 ft 6 in–8 ft 6 in) tall, whereas the female is 1.5–2.2 m (4 ft 11 in–7 ft 2 in). The average estimated weight is 2,500 kg (5,500 lb). The current population is under 2,000, all living in Borneo, Malaysia, where they were confirmed as being a separate sub-species in September 2003, following DNA research funded by the World Wildlife Fund.

★ Longest gestation period for a mammal

The Asian elephant (*Elephas maximus*) has an average gestation period of 650 days (over 21 months) and a maximum of 760 days (over two years) – more than two and a half times that of humans.

The shortest mammalian gestation period is 12–13 days and is common in a number of species, including the Virginia opossum (*Didelphis virginiana*) of North America, and the rare water opossum or yapok (*Chironectes minimus*) of central and northern South America.

★ Fastest mammal on land over short distances

When measured on level ground over a short distance, the cheetah (*Acinonyx jubatus*) can maintain a steady maximum speed of approximately 100 km/h (62 mph). However, research completed by Prof Craig Sharp (UK) of Brunel University, London, UK, in 1965 recorded accurate speeds of 104.4 km/h (64.3 mph) for a 35-kg (77-lb) adult female over a distance of 201.2 m (660 ft).

★ Fastest mammal on land over long distances

The pronghorn (*Antilocapra americana*) is the fastest land animal when measured steadily over a long distance. These antelope have been observed to travel continuously at 56 km/h (35 mph) for as far as 6 km (4 miles). The pronghorn is found in western USA, south-western Canada and parts of northern Mexico.

★ Largest litter for a wild mammal

The greatest number of young born to a wild mammal at a single birth is 31 (30 of which survived) in the case of a tail-less tenrec (*Tenrec ecaudatus*), a hedgehog-like insectivore found in Madagascar.

★ Largest mouth for a land animal

The hippopotamus (*Hippopotamus amphibious*) of Africa can open its jaws to almost 180°. In a fully grown male hippo, this equates to an average gape of 1.2 m (4 ft). Although they are herbivores, hippos have canine teeth that typically measure 71 cm (28 in) and which continually grow. The largest canine recorded for a hippo is 122 cm (48 in).

★ Fastest heartbeat in a mammal

The shrew (family Soricidae) has the fastest heartbeat of any mammal, with a rate of 1,200 beats per minute, which is similar to that of a hummingbird when hovering. Shrews are roughly the size of a thumb and weigh a tiny 4.5 g (0.15 oz).

★ Largest structure built by a land animal

Beavers (*Candor canadensis*) of North America use mud, wood, vegetation and stones to dam up water and form a pond, then build a lodge for winter refuge. The largest lodge ever recorded was 12.1 m (40 ft) across and 4.8 m (16 ft) high, and the longest beaver dam measured 1.5 km (0.9 miles) long.

Largest mammal to build a nest

⋙ The largest mammal to construct a nest is the gorilla (*Gorilla gorilla*, left) of Africa, where adult males measure 1.7–1.8 m (5 ft 6 in–5 ft 9 in) tall and weigh 136–227 kg (300–500 lb). Everyday, the gorillas each create a new ground nest from the surrounding vegetation. The nests are circular and typically measure 1 m (3 ft 3 in) in diameter.

Tallest ⋙ mammal

The giraffe (*Giraffa camelopardalis*, below), found in the dry savannah and open woodland areas of sub-Saharan Africa, is the tallest mammal. An adult male giraffe typically measures 4.6–5.5 m (15–18 ft) tall.

★ **Mammal with the most names**
In the English language alone, the puma (*Puma concolor*) has over 40 names, including cougar, mountain lion, red tiger and Florida panther.

★ **Highest living mammal**
The large-eared pika (*Ochotona macrotis*) has been recorded at a height of 6,130 m (20,100 ft) in Asian mountain ranges.
The yak (*Bos mutus*) found in Tibet and China climbs to an altitude of 6,100 m (20,000 ft) when foraging.

★ **Largest colony of mammals**
The black-tailed prairie dog (*Cynomys ludovicianus*), a rodent of the family Sciuridae found in the western USA and in northern Mexico, builds large colonies. One single 'town' discovered in 1901 contained about 400 million individuals and was estimated to cover 61,400 km² (23,706 miles²) – the size of the Republic of Ireland.

★ GWR TALKS TO
Sir David Attenborough

Sir David Attenborough (UK, above) has had the longest working career as a writer and presenter of TV nature programmes. His first series, *Zoo Quest* (BBC, UK), was broadcast in 1954 and his most recent, the BBC's *Life of Mammals*, was broadcast in the UK in 2002.

What has been the most enjoyable TV series to put together?
Life on Earth. At the time it was the most ambitious series ever produced by the BBC Natural History Unit. It was seen by an estimated 500 million viewers and people still comment on the impact that the series had.

Have you ever been attacked by any animals?
No, never. Usually the only scary moments are when human beings are involved. But having said that, I was once filming in Kenya with Iain Douglas Hamilton, the elephant expert, and we were on the receiving end of a nasty rhino charge which wrecked our Land Rover.

Is there any particular creature that fascinates you over and above all others?
I have a private passion about birds of paradise which are found only in New Guinea and its offshore islands. Their courtship displays are simply ravishing and many have never been filmed. Once when we were trying to film Wilson's Bird of Paradise, we'd been waiting in the bird hide since before dawn and the sound recordist waiting some distance away told me that he knew when the bird arrived as he heard my heartbeat double!

If you could bring back any extinct species of plant or animal what would it be?
A giant plant-eating dinosaur.

Do you intend to keep on making television wildlife programmes?
I'm doing what I want to do and as long as people want me to go on doing it, I'll continue. I don't know what I'd do otherwise!

What advice would you give any budding naturalist?
Learn all you can about animals.

What does it mean to you to have a Guinness World Record?
It's something with which to surprise my friends!

« Longest bills

The longest bill belongs to the Australian pelican (*Pelecanus conspicillatus*, left). On average, it is 34–47 cm (13–18.5 in) long.

The longest beak in relation to overall body length is that of the sword-billed hummingbird (*Ensifera ensifera*) found in the Andes from Venezuela to Bolivia. The beak measures 10.2 cm (4 in) making it longer than the bird's actual body (excluding the tail).

Highest density ⌄ of feathers

The penguin (below) has the highest density of feathers. In his book, *The General Biology and Thermal Balance of Penguins* (1967), Dr Bernard Stonehouse (UK) counted 11–12 feathers per cm^2 (70 per in^2) in emperor, Adélie, yellow-eyed and little (blue) penguins. Each feather has its own small muscles associated with it to allow control. On land the feathers stay erect to trap air, insulating them; in the water they flatten to form a watertight barrier.

★ Largest bird
The largest living bird is the North African ostrich (*Struthio camelus camelus*). Male examples of this ratite (flightless) sub-species have been recorded up to 2.75 m (9 ft) tall and weighing 156.5 kg (345 lb).

★ Smallest bird
The smallest bird is the bee hummingbird (*Mellisuga helenae*) of Cuba and the Isle of Youth. Males measure 57 mm (2.25 in) in total length, half of which is taken up by the bill and tail, and weigh only 1.6 g (0.05 oz). Females are slightly larger. This is believed to be the lowest weight limit for any warm-blooded animal.

★ Most abundant bird
The red-billed quelea (*Quelea quelea*), a seed-eating weaver of the drier parts of sub-Saharan Africa, has an estimated adult breeding population of 1.5 billion. At least 200 million of these 'feathered locusts' are slaughtered annually without reducing this overall number.

★ Highest G force experienced by a bird
American experiments have shown that the beak of the red-headed woodpecker (*Melanerpes erythrocephalus*) hits the bark of a tree with an impact velocity of 20.9 km/h (13 mph), subjecting the brain to a deceleration of about 10 G when the head snaps back.

★ Longest feathers
The longest feathers grown by any bird were recorded in 1972 on a phoenix fowl or Yokohama chicken (a strain of red junglefowl, *Gallus gallus*) whose tail covert measured 10.6 m (34 ft 9.5 in). It was owned by Masasha Kubota (Japan). The longest feathers on a bird found in the wild (ie not bred for ornamental purposes) are those of the male crested Argus pheasant (*Rheinhartia ocellata*), whose feathers reach 1.73 m (5 ft 8 in).

★ Fastest bird swimmer
The gentoo penguin (*Pygoscelis papua*) has a maximum speed of about 27 km/h (17 mph).

★ Shortest bills
The shortest bills in relation to body length belong to the smaller swifts (the Apodidae family), and in particular to the glossy swiftlet (*Collocalia esculenta*), whose bill is almost non-existent.

★ Fastest wingbeat of a bird
During courtship, the ruby-throated hummingbird (*Archilochus colubris*) can produce a wingbeat rate of 200 beats/sec as opposed to the normal 90 beats/sec of all other hummingbirds.

★ Highest flying birds
The highest altitude recorded for a bird is 11,300 m (37,000 ft) for a Ruppell's vulture (*Gyps rueppellii*) that collided with an aeroplane over Abidjan, Ivory Coast, on 29 November 1973. The impact damaged one of the aircraft's engines, but the plane landed safely.

★ Largest bird's nest
A pair of bald eagles (*Haliaeetus leucocephalus*), and possibly their successors, built a nest near St Petersburg, Florida, USA, that measured 2.9 m (9 ft 6 in) wide and 6 m (20 ft) deep. When it was examined in 1963 it was estimated to weigh more than 2 tonnes (4,400 lb).

★ Smallest bird's nest
Hummingbirds build the smallest nests. That of the vervain hummingbird (*Mellisuga minima*) is about half the size of a walnut shell, while the deeper but narrower nest of the bee hummingbird (*M. helenae*) is thimble-sized.

★ Smallest bird egg
The smallest egg laid by any bird is that of the vervain hummingbird (*Mellisuga minima*) of Jamaica and two nearby islets. Two specimens measuring less than 10 mm (0.39 in) in length weighed a minute 0.365 g (0.0128 oz) and 0.375 g (0.0132 oz).

Keenest »
vision of
all birds

Large birds of
prey have the
keenest vision
as they can
detect a target
object at a distance three
or more times greater
than that achieved by
humans. A peregrine
falcon (*Falco peregrinus*,
right) can spot a pigeon
at a range of over 8 km
(5 miles) under ideal
conditions.

★ **Most airborne land bird**
The common swift (*Apus apus*)
remains airborne for two to
four years, during which time
it sleeps, drinks, eats and even
mates on the wing. It has been
calculated that a young swift
completes a non-stop flight of
500,000 km (310,000 miles)
between fledging and its first
landing at a potential nesting
site some two years later.

★ **Most airborne bird**
The most airborne of all birds
is the sooty tern (*Sterna
fuscata*) which, after leaving
the nesting grounds as a
youngster, remains aloft for
three to 10 years while
maturing, settling on water
occasionally, before returning
to land to breed as an adult.

★ **Fastest land bird**
The world's fastest bird on land
is the ostrich (*Struthio camelus*),
which can reach speeds of
up to 50 km/h (30 mph) when
running. Unlike most birds,
the ostrich cannot fly, and
therefore uses its powerful legs
to sprint at such speeds. The

ostrich has one of the largest
strides of any animal – it can
exceed 7 m (23 ft) at full pace.

★ **Fastest bird
in level flight**
The fastest fliers in level flight
are found among the ducks
and geese (Anatidae). Some
powerful species such as the
red-breasted merganser
(*Mergus serrator*), the eider
(*Somateria mollissima*), the
canvasback (*Aythya valisineria*)
and the spur-winged goose
(*Plectropterus gambensis*) can
probably reach 90–100 km/h
(56–62 mph) on rare occasions.

★ **Slowest-flying bird**
The slowest-flying birds are the
American woodcock (*Scolopax
minor*) and the Eurasian
woodcock (*S. rusticola*), which
have been timed during
courtship displays at only
8 km/h (5 mph) without stalling.

★ **Largest penguin colony**
The largest penguin colony is on
Zavodovski Island in the South
Sandwich Islands. Approximately
two million chinstrap penguins

(*Pygoscelis antarctica*) breed on
the slopes of the island, which
is an active volcano. Chinstraps
get their name from a thin line
of black feathers that runs
under their chin. They are also
considered the most common
penguins in the world with a
population of around 12 million,
mainly found in the Antarctic.

★ **Smallest bird of prey**
The smallest bird of prey in the
world is a title held jointly by
the black-legged falconet
(*Microhierax fringillarius*) of
southeast Asia and the white-
fronted or Bornean falconet
(*Microhierax latifrons*) of northwestern Borneo. Both species
have an average length of
14–15 cm (5.5–6 in), including
a 5-cm (2-in) tail, and a weight
of about 35 g (1.25 oz).

★ **Longest migration
by a bird**
The Arctic tern (*Sterna
parasidaea*) migrates the
greatest distance of any bird
species. It breeds north of the
Arctic Circle and then flies
south to the Antarctic for the

northern winter and then back
again, a round trip of about
35,000 km (21,750 miles).

★ **Longest incubation**
An egg of the mallee fowl
(*Leipoa ocellata*) of Australia,
took 90 days to hatch,
compared with its normal
62 days.

★ **Lowest temperature
endured by a bird**
The lowest temperature
endured by any bird is an
average of -20°C (-4°F) by the
breeding emperor penguin
(*Aptenodytes forsteri*) on the
Antarctic sea ice where
windspeeds can vary between
25 and 75 km/h (16 and 47 mph).

★ **Largest wingspan of any
living species of bird**
A male wandering albatross
(*Diomedea exulans*) of the
southern oceans holds the
record with a wingspan of
3.63 m (11 ft 11 in). The bird
was caught by members of the
Antarctic research ship USNS
Eltanin in the Tasman Sea on
18 September 1965

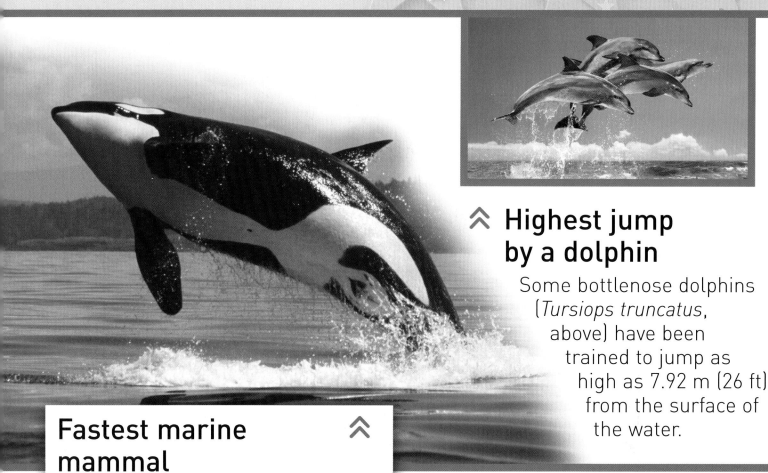

⯆ Highest jump by a dolphin

Some bottlenose dolphins (*Tursiops truncatus*, above) have been trained to jump as high as 7.92 m (26 ft) from the surface of the water.

Fastest marine mammal ⯆

On 12 October 1958, a bull killer whale (*Orcinus orca*, above) an estimated 6.1–7.6 m (20–25 ft) long was timed at 55.5 km/h (34.5 mph) in the northeastern Pacific.

Similar speeds have also been reported for Dall's porpoise (*Phocoenoides dalli*) in short bursts.

★ Smallest whale
There are two contenders for the smallest cetacean: Hector's dolphin (*Cephalorhynchus hectori*) and vaquita (*Phocoena sinus*), which grow to only 1.2 m (3 ft 11 in) long.

★ Largest animal brain
The brain of the sperm whale or cachalot (*Physeter macrocephalus*) weighs approximately 9 kg (19 lb 13 oz). In comparison the weight of a bull African elephant's brain reaches 5.4 kg (11 lb 14 oz) and a human brain is, on average, 1.4 kg (3 lb). Sperm whales are found in all waters except the polar regions. They get their name from the waxy spermaceti oil produced by the spermaceti organ on their heads.

★ Largest offspring
In the two months before it is born, a blue whale (*Balaenoptera musculus*) increases in weight by as much as 2 tonnes (4,400 lb) – it grows about 1,000 times faster than a human baby in the womb. The newborn calf is 6–8 m (19–26 ft) long and weighs 2–3 tonnes (4,400–6,600 lb). Everyday, the baby drinks about 200 litres (350 pints) of its mother's milk and gains as much as 90 kg (198 lb) in weight – the same as the weight of an adult human being. By the time it is weaned at seven months old it has roughly doubled in length and weighs an amazing 20 tonnes (44,000 lb). The blue whale is the world's largest mammal.

★ Greatest weight loss
During her seven-month lactation period, a 120-tonne (264,000 lb) female blue whale (*Balaenoptera musculus*) can lose up to 25% of her bodyweight nursing her calf.

★ Slowest heartbeat in a mammal
The mammal that is presumed to have the slowest heartbeat of any warm-blooded animal is the blue whale (*Balaenoptera musculus*), with between four and eight beats per minute – dependent upon whether or not the whale is diving. By comparison the average adult human heart beats at 70 beats per minute. Blue whales also have the largest heart of any animal and their heartbeat can be heard up to 32 km (20 miles) away underwater.

★ Largest jaw for a mammal
The largest jaw ever recorded on a mammal measured 5 m (16 ft 5 in) and belonged to a male sperm whale (*Physeter macrocephalus*) nearly 25.6 m (84 ft) in length. The massive lower jaw is now exhibited in the Museum of Natural History, London, UK. Sperm whales are also the largest-toothed whales.

★ Densest fur
The sea otter (*Enhydra lutris*) has over 100,000 hairs per cm^2 (650,000 per in^2). Most of the world's sea otters are found off the coast of Alaska, USA.

★ Oldest pinniped
A pinniped is a carnivorous aquatic mammal with flipper-like limbs. The greatest proven age for a pinniped was estimated by scientists at the Limnological Institute in Irkutsk, former USSR, to be 56 years for the female Baikal seal (*Phoca sibirica*) and 52 years for the male.

Largest pinniped ⌄

The largest of the 34 known species of pinniped is the southern elephant seal (*Mirounga leonina*, below) of the sub-Antarctic islands. Bulls average 5 m (16 ft 6 in) in length from the tip of the inflated snout to the tips of the outstretched tail flippers, have a maximum girth of 3.7 m (12 ft) and weigh about 2,000–3,500 kg (4,400–7,720 lb).

The largest accurately measured specimen of the elephant seal was a bull, killed at Possession Bay, South Georgia, on 28 February 1913, that weighed at least 4 tonnes (8,800 lb) and measured 6.5 m (21 ft 4 in) after flensing (stripping of the blubber or skin).

★ **Smallest pinniped**
The smallest pinniped, by a small margin, is the Galapagos fur seal (*Arctocephalus galapagoensis*). Adult females average 1.2 m (3 ft 11 in) in length and weigh about 27 kg (60 lb). Males are usually considerably larger, averaging 1.5 m (4 ft 11 in) in length and weighing around 64 kg (141 lb).

★ **Rarest seal**
With less than 400 remaining, the rarest seal species is the Mediterranean monk seal (*Monachus monachus*), found in remote and undisturbed areas of the Mediterranean Sea and northwest African coast. Its closest relative, the Caribbean monk seal (*M. tropicalis*), is already extinct.

★ **Largest grey seal colony**
Over 100,000 grey seals (*Halichoerus grypus*) arrive at Sable Island off Nova Scotia, Canada, every winter to breed. After 18 days the resulting pups are then left to fend for themselves. The grey seal's name *Halichoerus grypus* comes from the Greek meaning 'hook-nosed sea pig'.

★ **Largest amphibian**
The largest of the amphibians are the giant salamanders (family Cryptobranchidae) of which there are three species. The record holder is the Chinese giant salamander (*Andrias davidianus*), which lives in mountain streams in north-eastern, central and southern China. One record-breaking specimen collected in Hunan Province measured 1.8 m (5 ft 11 in) in length and weighed a massive 65 kg (143 lb).

★ **Smallest newt**
The smallest newt or salamander is the Mexican lungless salamander (*Bolitoglossa mexicana*), which only grows to about 2.54 cm (1 in), including the tail.

★ **Largest frog**
A specimen of the African goliath frog (*Conraua goliath*) captured in April 1889 on the Sanaga River, Cameroon, by Andy Koffman (USA) had a snout-to-vent length of 36.8 cm (14.5 in) and an overall length of 87.6 cm (34.5 in) with its legs extended.

★ **Smallest toad**
The smallest toad is the sub-species *Bufo taitanus beiranus* of Africa, the largest specimen of which measured only 24 mm (0.94 in) long.

★ **Most paternal amphibian**
The West European midwife toad (*Alytes obstetricans*) takes its name from the behaviour of the male. When the female lays its eggs, the male fertilizes them and then winds the string of eggs (which can be 0.9–1.2 m or 3–4 ft long) around his thighs. The male, who is only 7.6 cm (3 in) long, carries the eggs in this manner for up to four weeks. When the eggs are ready to hatch, the toad swims into suitable water for the tadpoles to be released.

« Most ferocious freshwater fish

Attracted to blood and frantic splashing, a school of piranhas (left) can completely strip an animal as large as a horse of its flesh within minutes, leaving only its skeleton.

The most ferocious piranhas are those of the genera *Serrasalmus* and *Pygocentrus*, found in the large rivers of South America.

⌃ Slowest fish

The swimming ability of sea horses (family Syngnathidae, above) is severely limited by a rigid body structure – only their pectoral and dorsal fins can move rapidly. Sea horses propel themselves along in an erect posture, never attaining speeds of more than 0.016 km/h (0.001 mph). Incapable of swimming against the current, they hang on to coral and marine plants with their prehensile tails to avoid being swept away.

★ Largest fish
The largest fish is the rare plankton-feeding whale shark (*Rhincodon typus*), which is found in the warmer areas of the Atlantic, Pacific and Indian Oceans. The largest scientifically recorded example was 12.65 m (41 ft 6 in) long, 7 m (23 ft) round the thickest part of the body and weighed an estimated 15–21 tonnes (33,000–46,200 lb). It was captured off Baba Island, near Karachi, Pakistan, on 11 November 1949.

★ Largest predatory fish
The largest predatory fish is the rare great white shark (*Carcharodon carcharias*). Adult specimens average 4.3–4.6 m (14–15 ft) in length, and generally weigh 520–770 kg (1,150–1,700 lb). There are many claims of huge specimens up to 10 m (33 ft) in length and, although few have been properly authenticated, there is plenty of circumstantial evidence to suggest that some great whites grow to more than 6 m (20 ft) in length.

★ Largest freshwater fish
The largest fish to spend their whole life in fresh or brackish water are the rare Mekong giant catfish (*Pangasius gigas*), principally of the Mekong River basin in southeast Asia, and *Pangasius sanitwongsei*, principally of the Chao Phraya River basin, Thailand, both of which are reputed to attain a length of 3 m (10 ft) and weigh 300 kg (660 lb). However, *Arapaima giga* of South America is reported to attain a length of 4.5 m (14 ft 9 in), but weighs only 200 kg (440 lb).

★ Heaviest bony fish
The heaviest bony fish in the ocean is the sunfish (*Mola mola*), which has been recorded weighing 2 tonnes (4,400 lb) and measuring 3 m (10 ft) from fin tip to fin tip.

★ Deepest fish
The fish that lives at the greatest recorded depth is a species of cusk-eel (family Ophidiidae) called *Abyssobrotula galatheae*. The 20-cm-long (8-in) fish has been collected from the Puerto Rico Trench in the Atlantic Ocean at a depth of 8,370 m (27,460 ft).

★ Longest fish migration
Many fish species undertake long annual migrations between their feeding grounds. The longest straight line distance known to have been covered by a marine fish is 9,335 km (5,800 miles) for a bluefin tuna (*Thunnus thynnus*) that was dart tagged off Baja, California, Mexico, in 1958 and caught 483 km (300 miles) south of Tokyo, Japan, in April 1963. During its journey, its weight increased from 16 kg (35 lb) to 121 kg (267 lb).

For freshwater fish, the European eel (*Anguilla anguilla*) holds the record. It spends between seven and 15 years in fresh water in Europe then suddenly changes into breeding condition and begins a marathon journey that may take it from land-locked waters to the Atlantic, where it heads for the species' spawning grounds in the Sargasso Sea. The entire journey – between 4,800 and 6,400 km (3,000 and 4,000 miles) – takes about six months.

★ Highest living fish
The highest living fish is the Tibetan loach (Cobitidae), found at an altitude of 5,200 m (17,000 ft) in the Himalayas.

★ Fastest fish
The cosmopolitan sailfish (*Istiophorus platypterus*) is considered to be the fastest species of fish over short distances, although practical problems make it difficult to establish precise measurements of its speed. In a series of trials carried out at the Long Key Fishing Camp, Florida, USA, one sailfish took out 91 m (300 ft) of line in three seconds, which is equivalent to a velocity of 109 km/h (68 mph), compared with 96 km/h (60 mph) for the cheetah at high speed.

Most poisonous edible fish ⌃

The most poisonous fish are the pufferfish (*Tetraodon*, above) of the Red Sea and Indo-Pacific region that deliver a fatal toxin called tetrodotoxin, one of the most powerful non-proteinous poisons. Less than 0.1 g (0.004 oz) is enough to kill an adult person in as little as 20 minutes. In Japan, the pufferfish is served as a delicacy known as fugu-sashi. Improper preparation of this dish can cause fatal poisoning so only specially licensed cooks are allowed to prepare it.

Most venomous mollusc «

The two closely related species of blue-ringed octopus *Hapalochlaena maculosa* and *H. lunulata* (left) – found around the coasts of Australia and parts of southeast Asia – carry a neurotoxic venom so potent that their relatively painless bite can kill a human in a matter of minutes. It has been estimated that each individual, which measures just 10 cm (4 in) in length, carries sufficient venom to cause the paralysis (or even death) of 10 adult people.

★ Lightest fish
The lightest of all vertebrates is the dwarf goby (*Schindleria praematurus*), which weighs only 2 mg (equivalent to 14,184 to the ounce) and is 12–19 mm (0.47–0.74 in) long. It is found throughout the Indo-Pacific.

★ Largest eye
The Atlantic giant squid (*Architeuthis dux*) has the largest eye of any animal – living or extinct. It has been estimated that the record example from Thimble Tickle Bay, Newfoundland, Canada, found in 1878 had eyes measuring 40 cm (15.75 in) in diameter – almost the width of an open *Guinness World Records* book.

★ Largest squid
The largest intact specimen of a squid ever found was an immature female of the species *Mesonychoteuthis hamiltoni* that was caught in March 2003 in the Ross Sea, Antarctica. It had a total length of 5 m (16 ft), a mantle length of 2.5 m (8 ft) and weighed

150 kg (330 lb). This species swims to a depth of 2,000 m (6,500 ft) and is an aggressive killer, eating large prey like Patagonian toothfish, *Dissostichus eleginoides*, which can grow to more than 1.8 m (6 ft) long. Mantle length (not total length) is the standard measure in cephalopods.

★ Animal with the most chromosomes
The king crab has 208 pairs of chromosomes per cell. By comparison, humans have 23 pairs of chromosomes in each cell.

★ Most heat-tolerant water-based organism
The most heat-resistant organism discovered to date is strain 121, a microbe belonging to the ancient group of bacteria-like organisms called archae. Strain 121 was discovered in superheated water from hydrothermal vents at the bottom of the Pacific Ocean. This organism can survive temperatures of 121°C (249.8°F).

★ Most dangerous sea urchin
The most dangerous sea urchin is the flower sea urchin (*Toxopneustes pileolus*). Toxin from the spines and pedicellaria (small pincer-like organs) causes severe pain, respiratory problems and paralysis in humans.

★ Deepest starfish
The greatest depth from which a starfish has been recovered is 7,584 m (24,881 ft) for a specimen of *Porcellanaster ivanovi* collected by the Soviet research ship *Vityaz* in the Marianas Trench in the Pacific Ocean c. 1962.

★ Smallest starfish
The asterinid sea star (*Patiriella parvivipara*) discovered on the west coast of Eyre Peninsula, South Australia in 1975 has a maximum radius of only 4.7 mm (0.18 in) and a diameter of less than 9 mm (0.35 in).

★ Largest concentration of crustaceans
The largest single concentration of crustaceans ever recorded was a swarm of krill (*Euphausia superba*), estimated to weigh 10 million tonnes, tracked by US scientists off Antarctica in March 1981.

★ Largest crustacean
The largest of all marine crustaceans is the giant spider crab (*Macrocheira kaempferi*). A specimen with a claw-span of 3.7 m (12 ft 1.5 in) weighed 18.6 kg (41 lb).
The largest freshwater crustacean is the crayfish or crawfish (*Astacopsis gouldi*), found in the streams of Tasmania, Australia. It has been measured up to 61 cm (2 ft) in length and may weigh as much as 4.1 kg (9 lb).

★ Largest oyster
In 1999 a common oyster (*Ostrea edulis*) taken from Chesapeake Bay, Virginia, USA, weighed in at 3.7 kg (8 lb) and measured 30.5 cm (12 in) long and 14 cm (5 in) wide.

Fastest flying « insect

Acceptable modern experiments have established that the highest maintainable airspeed of any insect, including the deer bot fly (*Cephenemyia pratti*), hawk moths (Sphingidae, left), horseflies (*Tabanus bovinus*) and some tropical butterflies (Hesperiidae), is 39 km/h (24 mph), rising to a maximum of 58 km/h (36 mph) for the Australian dragonfly (*Austrophlebia costalis*) for short bursts.

★ **Fastest wingbeat of an insect**
The fastest wingbeat of any insect under natural conditions is 62,760 per minute by a tiny midge of the genus *Forcipomyia*. The muscular contraction-expansion cycle of 0.00045 seconds, necessary for such rapid wing beats, further represents the fastest muscle movement ever measured.

★ **Heaviest insect**
The heaviest insects are the goliath beetles (family Scarabaeidae) of equatorial Africa. *Goliathus regius*, *G. meleagris*, *G. goliathus* (=*G. giganteus*) and *G. druryi* are the largest. In measurements of one series of males (females are smaller), the lengths from the tips of the small frontal horns to the end of the abdomen were up to 11 cm (4.3 in), with weights of 70–100 g (2.5–3.5 oz).

★ **Largest colony of ants**
The largest recorded colony of ants stretches 6,000 km (3,700 miles) from northern Italy, through France to the Atlantic coast of Spain, and is made up of a species of Argentine ant (*Linepithema humile*) introduced into Europe around 80 years ago. The ants have shown the ability to recognize each other even though they may come from opposite ends of the colony.

★ **Largest dragonfly**
Megaloprepus caeruleata of Central and South America has been measured up to 120 mm (4.7 in) in length with a wing-span up to 190 mm (7.5 in).

★ **Largest butterfly**
The huge and poisonous Queen Alexandra's birdwing (*Ornithoptera alexandrae*) of Papua New Guinea may have a wingspan that exceeds 280 mm (11 in) and weigh over 25 g (0.9 oz).

★ **Largest millipede**
The largest millipede is a full-grown African giant black millipede (*Archispirostreptus gigas*) owned by Jim Klinger (USA). It measures 38.7 cm (15.2 in) in length, 6.7 cm (2.6 in) in circumference and has 256 legs. The average length for this type of millipede is between 16 and 28 cm (6.5 and 11 in).

★ **Largest grasshopper**
An unidentified species of grasshopper from the border of Malaysia and Thailand measures 25.4 cm (10 in) in length and is capable of leaping 4.6 m (15 ft).

★ **Highest jump by an insect**
The best jumping performance by an insect is the froghopper (spittle bug, *Philaenus spumarius*) which can reach heights of 70 cm (28 in) or more than 115 times its body length.

★ **Longest insect**
The longest-known specimen of *Pharnacia kirbyi*, a stick insect from the rainforests of Borneo, is in the Natural History Museum in London, UK. It has a body length of 328 mm (12.9 in) and a total length, including the legs, of 546 mm (21.5 in). In the wild this species is often found with some legs missing because they are so long and easily trapped when the insect sheds its skin.

★ **Largest scorpion**
One of the *Heterometrus swannerdami* species, found during World War II in the village of Krishnarajapuram, India, measured 29.2 cm (11.5 in) in overall length from the tips of the pedipalps or 'pincers' to the end of the sting.

★ **Most venomous scorpion**
The Tunisian fat-tailed scorpion (*Androctonus australis*) is responsible for 80% of stings and 90% of deaths from scorpion stings in North Africa.

★ **Heaviest scorpion**
The large black West African species *Pandinus imperator* can weigh up to 60 g (2 oz). It can also measure between 13 and 18 cm (5 and 7 in) in length, the same average length as the hand of an adult human being.

Largest ≪ wasp nest

A wasp nest found by Yoichiro Kawamura (Japan, left) on 18 May 1999 at Yonegaoka, Japan, had a circumference of 2.45 m (8 ft) and weighed 8 kg (17 lb 8 oz).

Oldest insect ⩓

The longest-lived insects are the splendour beetles (Buprestidae, above). On 27 May 1983 a specimen of *Buprestis aurulenta* appeared from the timber staircase in a house in Essex, UK, after at least 47 years as a larva.

Fastest moving insect ≫

Periplaneta americana, a large tropical cockroach of the family Dictyoptera (right), clocked a record speed of 5.4 km/h (3.36 mph),

or 50 body lengths per second, at the University of California at Berkeley, USA, in 1991. There are about 4,000 species of cockroaches, known mainly from the tropics, as they prefer warm, humid climates.

★ **Smallest spider**
The smallest known spider is *Patu marplesi* (family Symphytognathidae) of Western Samoa. A specimen (male) found in moss at an altitude of 600 m (2,000 ft) in Madolelei, Upolu, in January 1965 measured 0.43 mm (0.017 in) overall – about the size of a full stop on this page.

★ **Largest spider**
The largest known spider is a male goliath bird-eating spider (*Theraphosa blondi*) collected by members of the Pablo San Martin Expedition at Rio Cavro, Venezuela, in April 1965. It had a record leg-span of 28 cm (11 in) – sufficient to cover a dinner plate. This species is found in the coastal rainforests of Surinam, Guyana and French Guiana, but isolated specimens have also been reported from Venezuela and Brazil.

★ **Heaviest spider**
Female bird-eating spiders (family Theraphosidae) are more heavily built than males,

and in February 1985 Charles J Seiderman (USA) captured a female example near Paramaribo, Surinam, that weighed a record 122.2 g (4.3 oz) before its death from moulting problems in January 1986. Other measurements included a maximum leg-span of 267 mm (10.5 in), a total body length of 102 mm (4 in) and 25-mm-long (1-in) fangs.

★ **Most venomous spider**
The Brazilian wandering spiders of the genus *Phoneutria*, and particularly the Brazilian huntsman (*P. fera*), has the most active neurotoxic venom of any living spider. Its venom is so potent that only 0.006 mg (0.00000021 oz) is sufficient to kill a mouse. *Phoneutria* are usually dark in colour and have a body-and-leg spread of approximately 17 cm (6.75 in). These large and highly aggressive creatures often enter human dwellings and hide in clothing or shoes. When disturbed, they bite

furiously several times, and hundreds of accidents involving these species are reported annually.

★ **Strongest spider**
The strongest spider is the Californian trapdoor spider (*Bothriocyrtum californicum*), which is able to resist a force 38 times its own weight attempting to open its trapdoor: a silken structure covering the entrance to its underground burrow. If the average adult male human being weighs 82 kg (180 lb) it would be similar to a man trying to hold a door closed while it was being pulled on the other side by the weight of a small jet.

★ **Largest continuous area of spider webs**
The largest continuous areas of spider webs are created by members of the Indian genus *Stegodyphus*. They build huge three-dimensional

interwoven and overlapping webs that have been known to cover vegetation in a continuous silken mass for several kilometres.

★ **Simplest spider web**
The simplest web is that of the species of the genus *Miagrammopes*, found in Africa, Australia and North America. They have reduced their web to a single strand averaging 1 m (3 ft) long. This is woven between two small branches.

★ **Strongest spider's web**
The American house spider (*Achaearenea tepidariorum*) spins an irregular cobweb strong enough to ensnare and hold small mice.

★ **Oldest spider**
The oldest spider recorded lived for an estimated 26–28 years. It was a female of the tropical bird-eaters (family Theraphosidae) that was collected in Mexico in 1935.

Oldest chelonian ⌄

The greatest authenticated age recorded for a chelonian is at least 188 years, achieved by a Madagascar radiated tortoise (*Astrochelys radiata*, below) that was presented to the Tonga royal family by Captain Cook (UK) in either 1773 or 1777. The animal was called Tui Malila and remained in their care until its death in 1965.

Largest ≫ crocodilian

The largest reptile in the world is the estuarine or saltwater crocodile (*Crocodylus porosus*, above), which ranges throughout the tropical regions of Asia and the Pacific. The Bhitarkanika Wildlife Sanctuary in Orissa State, India, houses four protected estuarine crocodiles measuring more than 6 m (20 ft) in length, the largest being over 7 m (23 ft) long. There are several unauthenticated reports of specimens up to 10 m (33 ft) in length.

★ Oldest living chelonian
Harriet, one of three giant tortoises (*Geochelone nigra porteri*) collected by Charles Darwin (UK) from the Galapagos Islands in 1835, is thought to be the world's oldest resident at 173 years old. Born in November 1830, she currently resides at the Australia Zoo, near Brisbane, Queensland, Australia.

★ Deepest dive by a chelonian
In May 1987 Dr Scott Eckert (USA) reported that a leatherback turtle (*Dermochelys coriacea*) fitted with a pressure-sensitive recording device had reached a depth of 1,200 m (3,937 ft) off the Virgin Islands in the West Indies.

★ Largest chelonian
The leatherback turtle (*Dermochelys coriacea*) averages 1.8–2.1 m (6–7 ft) from the tip of the beak to the end of the tail (with a carapace of 1.52–1.67 m or 5–5 ft 6 in). They measure about 2.1 m (7 ft) across the front flippers and can weigh up to 450 kg (1,000 lb).

★ Fastest chelonian
The highest speed claimed for any reptile in water is 35 km/h (22 mph) by a frightened Pacific leatherback turtle (*Dermochelys coriacea*).

★ Largest tortoise
The largest specimen was a Galapagos tortoise (*Chelonoidis nigra*) named Goliath, who resided at the Life Fellowship Bird Sanctuary in Seffner, Florida, USA, from 1960 to 2002. He was 135.8 cm (4 ft 5 in) long, 102 cm (3 ft 4 in) wide and 68.5 cm (2 ft 3 in) high, and weighed 417 kg (920 lb).

★ Oldest crocodilian
The greatest authenticated age for a crocodilian is 66 years – achieved by a female American alligator (*Alligator mississippiensis*) that arrived at Adelaide Zoo, South Australia, on 5 June 1914 when she was two years old. She died on 26 September 1978.

★ Most dangerous lizard
With a length of up to 60 cm (24 in), the Gila monster (*Heloderma suspectum*) is a large, heavily built, brightly coloured lizard that lives in the arid parts of Mexico and southwestern USA. They have eight well-developed venom glands in their lower jaws and carry enough venom to kill two adult humans. The venom is not injected but seeps into the wound inflicted when the Gila monster bites its victim with its sharp, fragile teeth. Because of this, a lizard may continue to hang on after it has bitten and actively chew for several minutes. In one study of 34 people bitten by these animals, there were eight fatalities. The lizard only attacks when provoked.

★ Largest lizard
The largest lizard is the Komodo dragon (*Varanus komodoensis*), otherwise known as the Komodo monitor or ora, found on the Indonesian islands of Komodo, Rintja, Padar and Flores. Males average 2.25 m (7 ft 5 in) in length and weigh about 59 kg (130 lb). The largest accurately measured specimen was a male presented to an American zoologist in 1928 by the Sultan of Bima. For a short period in 1937 it was put on display in St Louis Zoological Gardens, Missouri, USA, by which time it was 3.10 m (10 ft 2 in) long and weighed 166 kg (365 lb).

Oldest snake ≪

The greatest reliable age recorded for a snake is 40 years 3 months and 14 days for a male common boa (*Boa constrictor*, above) named Popeye, who died at Philadelphia Zoo, Pennsylvania, USA, on 15 April 1977.

★ Longest lizard
The slender Salvadori or Papuan monitor (*Varanus salvadorii*) of Papua New Guinea has been reliably measured at up to 4.75 m (15 ft 7 in) in length. Nearly 70% of its total length is taken up by the tail.

★ Fastest lizard
The highest burst of speed recorded for any reptile on land is 34.9 km/h (21.7 mph), is achieved by *Ctenosaura*, a spiny-tailed iguana from Central America.

★ Fastest land snake
The fastest land snake is the aggressive black mamba (*Dendroaspis polylepis*) of southeastern, tropical Africa. The snake can reach speeds of 16–19 km/h (10–12 mph) in short bursts over level ground.

★ Heaviest living snake
The heaviest living snake is a Burmese python (*Python molurus bivittatus*) that weighed 182.5 kg (403 lb) on 20 November 1998. She is 25 years old, 8.22 m (27 ft) long and has a girth of 71.1 cm (28 in). Known as 'Baby', she lives at the Serpent Safari Park in Gurnee, Illinois, USA, and is owned by Lou Daddano (USA). Snakes continue to grow throughout their lives, so Baby is still growing.

★ Longest snake
The reticulated python (*Python reticulatus*) of southeast Asia, Indonesia and the Philippines regularly exceeds 6.25 m (20 ft 6 in), and the record length is 10 m (32 ft 9.5 in) for a specimen shot in Celebes, Indonesia, in 1912.

★ Longest venomous snake
The longest venomous snake is the king cobra (*Ophiophagus hannah*), also called the hamadryad, which measures 3.65–4.5 m (12–15 ft) in length and is found in southeast Asia and India. The king cobra can stand tall enough to look an adult human in the eye and its head is as big as a man's hand. Its venom can stun the nervous system and cause asphyxiation while other toxins start digesting the paralysed victim. The venom in a single bite from a king cobra is enough to kill an elephant or 20 people.

★ Most venomous land snake
The small-scaled fierce snake or taipan (*Oxyuranus microlepidotus*) measures up to 1.7 m (5 ft 7 in) and is found mainly in the Diamantina River and Cooper Creek drainage basins in Queensland and western New South Wales, Australia. In a single strike, a taipan can inject 60 mg (0.002 oz) of venom, sufficient to quickly paralyse a small marsupial, but also more than enough to kill several human adults. The average venom yield after milking is 44 mg (0.00155 oz) but one male specimen yielded 110 mg (0.00385 oz) – enough to kill 250,000 mice. Fortunately this species only lives in the arid deserts of central eastern Australia and no human death has been reported from its bite.

★ Heaviest venomous snake
The heaviest venomous snake is probably the eastern diamondback rattlesnake (*Crotalus adamanteus*) of the southeastern USA, which weighs 5.5–6.8 kg (12–15 lb) and is 1.52–1.83 m (5–6 ft) in length. The heaviest on record weighed 15 kg (33 lb) and was 2.36 m (7 ft 9 in) long.

Smallest living dog ⌃

The smallest living dog in terms of length is Tiny Pinocchio (above),

who measured 20.3 cm (8 in) long on 23 May 2003. Tiny Pinocchio is owned by Linda Skeels-Hopson (USA). The smallest dog in terms of height is Whitney, a Yorkshire terrier who measured 7.6 cm (3 in) to the shoulder on 26 November 2002. Whitney is owned by Christopher and Patricia Sheridan (both UK).

Tallest and longest dog ⌃

Harvey, a Great Dane owned by Charles Dodman (UK, both above), stands at 105.41 cm (41.5 in) tall

and measures 231.14 cm (91 in) from nose to tip. Great Danes are one of the tallest dog breeds, with an average height from the ground to the top of the shoulder of around 75 cm (29.5 in).

★ Fastest car window opening by a dog

The world record for the fastest time a dog has unwound a non-electric car window is 13 seconds and belongs to Striker, a border collie owned and trained by Francis Gadassi (Hungary). The record was set on 14 August 2003 in Québec City, Canada. Striker used his paw and nose to perform the record attempt.

★ Longest dog tongue

Brandy, a boxer owned by John Scheid (USA), had a tongue that measured 43 cm (17 in).

★ Smallest dog ever

The smallest dog was a fist-sized dwarf Yorkshire terrier owned by Arthur Marples (UK). Fully grown, this tiny dog stood 7.11 cm (2.8 in) at the shoulder and measured 9.5 cm (3.75 in) from its nose to the tip of its tail.

★ Highest jump by a dog

The world record for the highest jump cleared by a dog is 167.6 cm (66 in), achieved by Cinderella May A Holly Grey, a greyhound owned by Kathleen Conroy and Kate Long (both USA), at the Purina Dog Chow Incredible Dog Challenge show, Gray Summit, Missouri, USA, on 3 October 2003.

★ Largest dog litter

Three dogs are on record as having given birth to 23 puppies. An American foxhound belonging to W Ely (USA) is the first dog to have recorded this feat on 19 June 1944. Between 6 and 7 February 1975 a St Bernard belonging to R and A Rodden (USA) had 14 of its puppies survive. A Great Dane belonging to M Harris (UK) had 16 of its litter survive in June 1987.

★ Longest ears on a dog

The longest ears on a dog each measured 33.2 cm (13 in) in length when they were measured on 11 December 2003. They belong to a basset hound called Jack vom Forster Wald, who lives with his owners, Claudia and Carsten Baus, in Fulda, Germany.

★ Most tennis balls held in the mouth by a dog

Augie, a golden retriever owned by the Miller family (USA), successfully gathered and held five regulation-sized tennis balls in his mouth on 6 July 2003.

★ Oldest horse ever

The greatest age reliably recorded for a horse is 62 years for Old Billy (foaled 1760), bred by Edward Robinson, Woolston, Lancashire, UK. Old Billy died on 27 November 1822.

★ Oldest donkey ever

The donkey with the oldest documented age is Suzy, who reached the age of 54 in 2002. Suzy was owned by Beth Augusta Menczer (USA). The average lifespan of a donkey is 25–30 years.

« Tallest living horse

Goliath (left) measured 19 hands 1 in (195.58 cm or 77 in) on 24 July 2003.

Goliath is owned by Priefert Manufacturing, Inc., (USA) and is a male black Percheron draft horse, whose pedigree name is Prince Jordan of Lakeview. On average, he eats 22.6 kg (50 lb) of hay and drinks 113.5 litres (30 gallons) of water per day.

Largest horn circumference

Lurch (below), an African watusi steer owned by Janice Wolf (USA), had a horn circumference of 95.25 cm (37.5 in) when measured on 6 May 2003. Although they are not the longest horns on record, Lurch's horns are each approximately 2.1 m (7 ft).

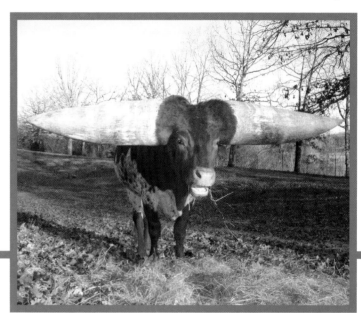

★ Oldest pony ever

The world's oldest pony was Sancho, a Welsh/Arab cross who reached the age of 54 years in 2003. Sancho was owned by Elizabeth Saunders (UK) and was discovered by the Veteran Horse Society, North Pembrokeshire, UK. The pony died in August 2003.

★ Oldest living rabbit

The world's oldest living rabbit is Baby, a Holland Lop born in August 1990 and owned by Kayla and Sue Bulos (both USA). House rabbits usually live for around 7–10 years.

★ Oldest rabbit ever

A wild rabbit named Flopsy was caught on 6 August 1964 and died 18 years and 10 months later at the home of LB Walker (Australia).

★ Longest rabbit ears

The longest rabbit ears measured 79 cm (31.1 in) in a complete span on 1 November 2003 at the American Rabbit Breeders Association National Show in Wichita, Kansas, USA. The ears belong to an English Lop called Nipper's Geronimo, who is owned by Waymon and Margaret Nipper (USA).

★ Highest rabbit high jump

The highest rabbit high jump is 46 cm (18 in), achieved by Golden Flame, a castor satin rabbit belonging to Sam Lawrie (UK), on 29 August 2002.

★ Largest mouse litter

A mouse belonging to M Ogilvie (UK) gave birth to a litter of 34 on 12 February 1982, 33 of which survived.

★ Smallest breed of domestic hamster

The Roborovski hamster (Phodopus roborovskii) typically grows to a length of 4–5 cm (1.5–2 in). These hamsters originate from Mongolia and northern China.

★ Largest hamster litter

On 28 February 1974 a hamster belonging to the Miller family (USA) gave birth to a litter of 26. The average amount is eight babies per litter.

★ Largest cat litter

On 7 August 1970 a Burmese/Siamese cross cat owned by V Gane (UK) gave birth to 19 kittens, four of which were stillborn.

★ Oldest kinkajou in captivity

The oldest living kinkajou (Potos flavus) in captivity is Huggy Bear, who turned 27 years 6 months old in January 2004 and belongs to Sonja Pedersen (USA). A kinkajou is a member of the raccoon family.

★ Oldest goat ever

The world's oldest goat was McGinty, who lived to the age of 22 years 5 months. Until her death in November 2003, she was owned by Doris C Long (UK).

★ Oldest caged parrot

The longest lived caged parrot was Prudle, owned by Iris Frost (UK). Prudle was captured in 1958 and lived to the age of 35. Before dying in 1994, Prudle had learned over 800 words and could even conduct polite conversation.

★ Cat with the most toes

Jake, a male ginger tabby cat, has 28 toes, with seven on each paw, as counted by a veterinarian on 24 September 2002. Jake lives in Bonfield, Ontario, Canada, with his owners Michelle and Paul Contant (Canada).

Unusual plants
Natural world

Largest flower

The mottled orange-brown and white parasite *Rafflesia arnoldii* (right) has the largest of all blooms. These attach themselves to the cissus vines in the jungles of southeast Asia. They measure up to 91 cm (3 ft) across, weigh up to 11 kg (24 lb) and their petals are 1.9 cm (0.75 in) thick.

»

Smallest ⯬ seed

Epiphytic orchids (orange epiphytic orchid, below) produce 992.25 million seeds per gram (28,130 million per oz). The largest seed is that of the giant fan palm or double coconut (*Lodoicea maldivica*). The single-seeded fruit weighs up to 20 kg (44 lb) and can take 10 years to develop.

★ GWR TALKS TO
Ron Hildebrant

Ron Hildebrant (USA) has spent much of his life tracking down the record-breakers of the tree world. He helped to measure the tallest living tree, the 112.6-m (396-ft 4.8-in) Stratosphere Giant (see right) in August 2000, and he's more than happy to share his enthusiasm for trees with *Guinness World Records* readers!

What exactly is a tree hunter?
A tree hunter is someone who looks for the biggest, tallest and oldest trees. Sometimes unusual ones are sought, such as rare specimens or those with unusually shaped trunks or strange branching, but most of the time tree hunters are searching for trees with measurable parameters – such as height, diameter or age.

Redwoods are the tallest trees in the world. What is the most amazing one you have seen?
I'd say the late great Dyerville Giant, which fell after a storm in March 1991. It was, until then, the world's tallest tree, being 113.4 m (372 ft) high, and indeed the tallest tree of modern times. It was 5.06 m (16.6 ft) in diameter and perhaps up to 2,500 years old – I haven't yet determined its exact age – and had a trunk volume of 807 m³ (28,500 ft³), making it one of the largest redwoods of modern times. After its fall I discovered it had at one time been even taller – 119 to 122 m (390 to 400 ft) high a couple of centuries ago.

You've seen the world's tallest tree. How old is it?
Yes, I have; this is the well-named Stratosphere Giant, which towers very, very high, at 112.6 m (369 ft 4.8 in) as of 2002 – and is still growing. I recently did an accurate age estimate of the tree after having greatly improved my methods for coast redwoods, and it's about 1,600 years old, plus or minus about a 100 years or so.

How do you measure a tree?
In the pre-laser days it was a lot of grunt work – we'd lay out tapelines, plumbing tree tops from three places and using a good surveyor's transit. It required taking slope angles into account, but the hardest part was adjusting for leaning or off-centred tree tops. In the mid-1990s, the laser came out. These revolutionary devices have greatly reduced the time, labour and effort involved, and are extremely accurate. With the laser, leaning tops are no longer an issue, for a direct measurement is determined by the laser itself. We can point and shoot at a tree and get a reading accurate to within a few feet in just seconds.

How do you become a tree hunter?
If you're willing to invest in some good tools and you have some good maths skills in algebra and trigonometry and keep yourself in good physical shape, that's a good start. It's helpful to know how a particular tree species behaves in certain environments, making it easier to find particular types of trees. A background in botany, geology, meteorology, soils and ecology are all a big plus. Expect to do plenty of hiking: in some of my hikes I do 16 km (10 miles) or more in a day, or hike up to 3,350 m (11,000 ft) or more in elevation. Finally, expect to fail in your quests now and then, but never give up!

Oldest living individual tree ⌃

The oldest living individual tree is the ancient bristlecone pine (*Pinus longaeva*) called Methuselah (above), which is 4,733 years old. It was found by Dr Edmund Schulman (USA) in the White Mountains, California, USA, and dated in 1957.

★ Tallest living tree
The world's tallest living tree is the Stratosphere Giant which measured 112.6 m (369 ft 4.8 in) as of 2002. This coast redwood (*Sequoia sempervirens*) was discovered by Chris Atkins (USA) in August 2000 in the Rockefeller Forest of the Humboldt Redwoods State Park, California, USA.

★ Fastest growing tree
The fastest recorded rate of growth for any tree (discounting bamboo, which is classified as a woody grass) is 10.74 m (35 ft 2.8 in) in 13 months, or approximately 2.8 cm (1.1 in) per day by an *Albizzia falcata* planted on 17 June 1974 in Sabah, Malaysia.

★ Earliest tree
The earliest surviving species of tree is the maidenhair (*Ginkgo biloba*) of Zhejiang, China, which first appeared about 160 million years ago during the Jurassic era. It was rediscovered by Engelbert Kaempfer (Germany) in 1690. It has been grown in Japan since c. 1100, where it was known as ginkyou (silver apricot) and is now known as ichou.

★ Oldest tree ever documented
The oldest age for a tree ever recorded is for a bristlecone pine (*Pinus longaeva*) known as Prometheus, which was cut down from Mt Wheeler in Nevada, USA, in 1963 and dated at approximately 5,200 years old. Although 4,867 rings were counted – the most ever – the tree was growing in a harsh environment which slowed its development, and so its actual age has been adjusted to approximately 5,200 years old.

★ Largest prey for carnivorous plants
Of all the carnivorous plants or pitcher plants, the ones that digest the largest prey belong to the Nepenthaceae family (genus *Nepenthes*). Both the *Nepenthes rajah* and *N. rafflesiana* have been known to consume frogs, birds and even rats, digesting their prey using enzymes. These species are commonly found in the rainforests of Asia, notably Borneo and Indonesia.

★ Most dangerous stinger
New Zealand's tree nettle (*Urtica ferox*) has been known to kill dogs and horses. Its stinging hairs inject potent toxins into the skin. The tree nettle can grow up to 3 m (10 ft) in height. Fine white stinging hairs line its green leaves and contain many toxins, the main ones being histamine, 5-hydroxytryptamine, acetylcholine and formic acid.

★ Smelliest flower
Also known as the corpse flower, the *Amorphophallus titanum* is the smelliest flower on Earth. When it blooms, it releases an extremely foul odour – comparable to that of rotten flesh – that can be smelled half a mile away. This plant is native to the Sumatran rainforests and very few have flowered in Europe or the USA since first discovered in 1878.

★ Tallest wild cactus
The tallest cacti ever recorded is a cardon (*Pachycereus pringlei*) found in the Sonoran Desert, Baja California, Mexico. It measures 19.2 m (63 ft) and was discovered by Marc Salak and Jeff Brown (both USA) in April 1995. Its incredible height is about the same as the combined height of four giraffes.

Horticultural giants
Natural world

Heaviest lemon

The heaviest lemon (below) weighed 5.26 kg (11 lb 9.7 oz) on 8 January 2003 and was grown by Aharon Shemoel (Israel) on his farm in Kefar Zeitim, Israel. The lemon's circumference was 74 cm (29 in) and 35 cm (13.7 in) high and it grew with another large lemon.

★ **Longest courgette**
A courgette measuring 1.93 m (76 in) on 22 September 2003 was grown by Sher Singh Kanwal (USA) in his garden in Niagara Falls, New York, USA.

★ **Longest beetroot**
A beetroot grown by Richard Hope (UK) measured 6.146 m (20 ft 2 in) on 27 September 2003 at the Llanharry Giant Vegetable Championships, Rhondda Cynon Taff, UK.

★ **Most heads on one sunflower**
A sunflower plant with 837 heads was grown by Melvin Hemker (USA). The heads were counted on 18 September 2001.

★ **Largest rose bush**
A specimen of the rose bush Lady Banks (*Rosa banksiae*), known as Banks at Tombstone, Arizona, USA, has a trunk circumference of 4.09 m (13 ft 5 in), stands roughly 2.75 m (9 ft) high and covers an area of 743 m² (8,000 ft²). The bush is supported by 77 posts, and 250 people can sit under the arbour.

★ **Largest home-grown lily bloom**
A lily bloom measuring 59 cm (23.2 in) long on 21 March 2002 was grown by Natividad Rico Pérez (Spain) at her home in Monóvar, Alicante, Spain.

★ **Largest gourd circumference**
Robert Weber (Australia) grew a gourd with a circumference of 1.77 m (69.6 in) and presented it at the Australasian Giant Pumpkin and Vegetable Competition in Victoria, Australia, on 7 April 2001.

★ **Largest tomato truss**
A record 185 tomatoes were counted on a tomato plant grown by Joe Hallam (UK) on 19 August 2003.

★ **Tree with most different fruit**
The record for the most fruits produced from the same tree is five: apricot, cherry, nectarine, plum and peach. The fruit species were grafted on to a prune tree in 2000 by Luis H Carrasco E (Chile).

Heaviest Fruit and Vegetables

Fruit/Vegetable	Weight	Name & Venue	Date
Apple	1.67 kg (3 lb 11 oz)	Alan Smith (UK), Linton, Kent, UK	1997
Beetroot	23.4 kg (51 lb 9 oz)	Ian Neale (UK), Shepton Mallet, Somerset, UK	2001
Brussels sprout	8.3 kg (18 lb 3 oz)	Bernard Lavery (UK), Llanharry, Rhondda Cynon Taff, UK	1992
Cabbage	56.24 kg (124 lb)	Bernard Lavery (UK), Llanharry, Rhondda Cynon Taff, UK	1989
Cantaloupe melon	28.8 kg (63 lb 8 oz)	Bill Rogerson (USA), Robersonville, North Carolina, USA	1997
Carrot	8.61 kg (18 lb 13 oz)	John Evans (USA), Palmer, Alaska, USA,	1998
Cauliflower	24.6 kg (54 lb 3 oz)	Alan Hattersley (UK), Sheffield, UK	1999
Celery	28.7 kg (63 lb 4.8 oz)	Scott and Mardie Robb (both USA), Palmer, USA	2003
Cherry	21.69 g (0.76 oz)	Gerado Maggipinto (Italy), Sammichele di Bari, Italy	2003
Courgette	29.25 kg (64 lb 8 oz)	Bernard Lavery (UK), Llanharry, Rhondda Cynon Taff, UK	1990
Cucumber	12.4 kg (27 lb 3 oz)	Alfred J Cobb (UK), Shepton Mallet, Somerset, UK	2003
Garlic head	1.19 kg (2 lb 10 oz)	Robert Kirkpatrick (USA), Eureka, California, USA	1985
Gooseberry	61.04 g (2.15 oz)	K Archer (UK), Scholar Green, Cheshire, UK	1993
Gourd	42.8 kg (94 lb 5 oz)	Robert Weber (Australia), Victoria, Australia	2001
Grapefruit	3.065 kg (6 lb 12 oz)	Debbie Hazelton (Australia), Queensland, Australia	1995
Leek	8.1 kg (17 lb 13 oz)	Fred Charlton (UK), Somerset, UK	2002
Lemon	5.26 kg (11 lb 9.7 oz)	Aharon Shemoel (Israel) Kefar Zeitin, Israel	2003
Mango	1.94 kg (4 lb 4 oz)	John Painter (USA), Bokeelia, Florida, USA,	1999
Marrow	61.23 kg (135 lb)	John Handbury (UK), Temple Normanton, Chesterfield, UK	1998
Onion	7.24 kg (15 lb 15.5 oz)	Mel Ednie (UK), Anstruther, Fife, UK	1994
Parsnip	3.8 kg (8 lb 6 oz)	Norman Lee Craven (Canada), Toronto, Ontario, Canada.	2003
Peach	725 g (25.6 oz)	Paul Friday (USA), Coloma, Michigan, USA	2002
Pear	2.1 kg (4 lb 8 oz)	Warren Yeoman (Australia), Arding, New South Wales, Australia	1999
Pineapple	8.06 kg (17 lb 12 oz)	E Kamuk (Papua New Guinea), Ais Village, West New Britain Province, Papau New Guinea	1994
Potato	3.5 kg (7 lb 11 oz)	K Sloane (UK), Patrick, Isle of Man, UK	1994
Pumpkin	606.7 kg (1,337 lb 9 oz)	Charles Houghton (USA), Massachusetts, USA	2002
Quince	2.34 kg (5 lb 2 oz)	Edward Harold McKinney (USA), Citronelle, Alabama, USA	2002
Radish	31.1 kg (68 lb 9 oz)	Manubu Oono (Japan), Kagoshima, Japan	2003
Squash	436 kg (962 lb)	Steve Hoult (Canada), Toronto, Ontario, Canada	1997
Strawberry	231 g (8.14 oz)	G Andersen (UK), Folkstone, Kent, UK	1983
Swede	34.35 kg (75 lb 12 oz)	Scott Robb (USA), Palmer, Alaska, USA	1999
Sweet potato	22.5 kg (49 lb 9oz)	Belinda Love (Australia), Gingin, Western Australia	1998
Tomato	3.51 kg (7 lb 12 oz)	G Graham (USA), Edmond, Oklahoma, USA	1986

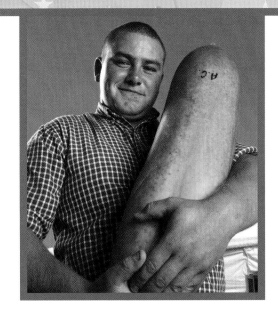

Tallest Plants

Plant	Height	Name & Venue	Date
Bean	14.1 m (46 ft 3 in)	Staton Rorie (USA), Rienzi, Mississippi, USA	2003
Celery	2.74 m (9 ft)	Joan Priednieks (UK), Westonzoyland, Somerset, UK	1998
Cactus (homegrown)	21.3 m (70 ft)	Pandit S. Munji (India), Dharwad, Karnataka, India	2004
Chrysanthemum	4.34 m (14 ft 3 in)	Bernard Lavery (UK) Spalding, Lincolnshire, UK	1995
Dandelion	100 cm (39.3 in)	Ragnar Gille and Marcus Hamring (both Sweden) Uppsala, Sweden	2003
Fuchsia	6.58 m (21 ft 7 in)	The Growing Place (UK), Spalding, Lincolnshire, UK,	2003
Papaya tree	13.4 m (44 ft)	Prasanta Mal (India), Arambagh, Hooghly, India	2003
Parsley	1.39 m (55 in)	Danielle, Gabrielle and Michelle Kassatly, (all USA), San Jose, California, USA.	2003
Pepper	4.87 m (16 ft)	Laura Liang (USA), Irvine, California	1999
Periwinkle	2.19 m (7 ft 2 in)	Arvind, Rekha, Ashish and Rashmi Nema (all India), Indrapuri, Bhopal, India	2003
Petunia	5.8 m (19 ft 1 in)	Bernard Lavery (UK), Llanharry, Rhondda Cynon Taff, UK	1994
Potato or brinjal	5.5 m (18 ft 0.5 in)	Abdul Masfoor (India), Karnataka State, India.	1998
Rose bush	3.38 m (11 ft 1 in)	Kathleen Mielke-Villalobos (USA), San Diego, California, USA	2003
Sunflower	7.76 m (25 ft 5.5 in)	M Heijms (Netherlands), Oirschot, Netherlands	1986
Tomato	19.8 m (65 ft)	Nutriculture Ltd (UK), Mawdesley, Lancashire, UK	2000

Heaviest cucumber

Alfred J Cobb (UK) grew a cucumber (held above by Mr Atherton) weighing 12.4 kg (27 lb 5.3 oz). It was presented at the National Amateur Gardening Show's UK National Giant Vegetables Championship at Shepton Mallet, Somerset, UK, on 5 September 2003.

★ GWR TALKS TO
Bernard Lavery

From monster corn cobs to fantastic fuchsias, Bernard Lavery's (UK, below right) records for giant fruit, vegetables and plants are some of the best loved Guinness World Records. He currently holds 12 records, including the longest gourd, which grew to 12.6 m (41 ft 4 in) in 1992, and the longest corn cob, which grew to a length of 92 cm (36.25 in) in 1994.

How did you get involved in growing giants?
I first caught the 'growing' bug over 20 years ago while growing my first pumpkin (right). Although this didn't break any records, the pleasures I got from the experience were immense and soon multiplied when I directed my efforts to a whole range of different vegetable subjects. In 1985 I organized the first UK Giant Vegetable Championships in Cardiff.

How do you grow giant vegetables?
The most important factor is to use the varieties of seeds that have the genetic capabilities to produce larger than average specimens. It's then adviseable to obtain some advice from books or other giant growers. If these options are unavailable then you must just have a go yourself. You must remember that when you make a mistake another year will have to pass before you can try again. The second most important thing you must have is the presence of 'Lady Luck'. If she's sitting on your shoulder then you're half way there.

What would you like to grow that you haven't tried?
The aubergine would be my choice for a new challenge. I've grown some large ones already, but nowhere near a world weight.

Can you eat these giants after they have been shown?
Giant vegetables are much the same as ordinary sized ones. When they're young and freshly harvested they are superb, but when they're grown on to well past their best, then like ordinary ones, they become tough and tasteless.

What is the record you are most proud of?
I am most proud of the record I set in 1991 for the longest carrot that measured 5.14 m (16 ft 10.5 in).

What's your best advice for growing giant plants?
Just try to enjoy it. It's a real challenge to stretch Mother Nature to her limits and beyond, but if at first you don't succeed then try, try again. It's magical when you succeed.

Modern world

Contents

« Highest life expectancy

Japan had the highest life expectancy at birth in 2002 with a total population average of 81.1 years (77.5 years for men and 84.7 years for women).

⌄ Lowest life expectancy

According to 2001 data, life expectancy at birth in the Republic of Botswana in Africa is only 37.1 years (36.8 years for men and 37.5 years for women).

★ Largest country
Russia's total area covers 11.5% of the world's total land area – 17,075,400 km² (6,592,848 miles²). It is 70 times larger than the UK, with a population of 144,417,000 in 2001.

★ Most maritime boundaries
The country with the largest number of maritime boundaries is Indonesia, with 19 (including boundaries with disputed territorial claims).

★ Most land boundaries
The countries with the most land boundaries are China and Russia, both with 14. China's are: Mongolia, Russia, North Korea, Vietnam, Laos, Burma (Myanmar), India, Bhutan, Nepal, Pakistan, Afghanistan, Tajikistan, Kyrgyzstan and Kazakhstan. These extend for 24,000 km (14,900 miles). Russia has boundaries with Norway, Finland, Estonia, Latvia, Lithuania, Poland, Belarus, Ukraine, Georgia, Azerbaijan, Kazakhstan, China, Mongolia and North Korea. These boundaries extend for 19,900 km (12,365 miles).

★ Country of origin for most refugees
The country from which most people seek asylum is Iraq. According to the 2002 figures from the United Nations High Commission for Refugees (UNHCR), 51,000 Iraqis applied for political asylum to one of 37 industrialized nations. The total number of applications made in 2002 was 587,400.

★ Country receiving most applications for political asylum
According to figures from UNHCR, of the 587,400 applications for political asylum that were submitted in 2002, the country that received the highest number was the UK with 111,606 (19%).

★ Country with most administrative divisions
The UK has a record 235 administrative divisions.

★ Country from which the most countries have gained independence
A total of 62 countries have gained independence from the UK.

★ Country with the most official languages
The Republic of South Africa has 11 official languages: English, Afrikaans, isiZulu, isiXhosa, Sesotho, Setswana, Sepedi, Xitsonga, siSwati, isiNdebele and Tshivenda.

★ Highest and lowest inflation
Zimbabwe has the highest inflation according to the Economist Intelligence Unit 2003 forecast, with consumer prices rising at over 300%. Hong Kong currently has the lowest inflation at -2.5 %.

★ Highest and lowest cost of living
According to the Economist Intelligence Unit's Worldwide Cost of Living Survey of January 2003 (for December 2002 results), Japan's capital city, Tokyo, is the most expensive city in the world. Harare, the capital of Zimbabwe, is the world's cheapest.

★ Most and least taxed country
In Denmark the highest rate of personal income tax is 62.9%, with the basic rate of income tax starting at 43.7% (June 2003). The lowest taxed countries are Bahrain and Qatar, where the rate, regardless of income, is nil. For both nations, oil provides over half of government revenues.

Highest and lowest ⌃⌃ government revenues

The country that produced the highest government revenues

from taxation per km² of physical land is the Vatican City (above) with $476,363,636 (£302,031,217) as of 2001. The lowest is the Democratic Republic of the Congo with only $115 (£72) per km² of land.

★ **Highest and lowest GNI per capita**

According to the World Bank Atlas, the country with the highest Gross National Income (GNI) for 2002 was Bermuda, which overtook Luxembourg with $38,830 (£25,627). The Democratic Republic of Congo had the lowest GNI per capita with $90 (£59). GNI is the total value of goods and services produced by a country in one year, divided by its population. GNI per capita shows what part of a country's GNI each person would have if it was divided equally.

★ **Country with the largest energy consumption**

The USA is the world's largest consumer of both fossil fuels (coal, oil and natural gas) and commercial energy (fossil fuels plus nuclear and hydro power). In 1998 it consumed a total of 1,937 million tonnes of oil equivalent (Mtoe) of fossil fuels and 2,147 Mtoe of commercial energy. The total world energy consumption of fossil fuels was 7,624 Mtoe

and the world total energy consumption of commercial fuel was 8,477 Mtoe.

★ **Most densely populated country**

Monaco has a population density of 16,476 per km² (42,840 per mile²) in 2003. Its population that year was 32,130 with a total area of 1.95 km² (0.75 miles²). This equates to each person having 60.6 m² (652 ft²) of land.

★ **Most sparsely populated country**

In 2001, Mongolia had a population of 2,435,000 in an area of 1,564,160 km² (603,930 miles²), giving a density of 1.6 people to every 1 km² (4 people to every 1 mile²).

★ **Most populous country**

In 2003, China had an estimated population of 1,286,975,468 – higher than that for the whole world 150 years ago, when the world population stood at 1,260,000,000. The UN's predicted population for China in 2025 is 1.48 billion.

★ **Least populous country**

The Vatican City, or Holy See, had approximately 911 inhabitants in 2003. The Vatican is the world's smallest country.

★ **Largest population of children**

In the Marshall Islands, in the north of the Pacific Ocean, 39.1% of the population were under the age of 15 in 2003. Out of an estimated total population of 56,429, approximately 22,063 individuals were aged between 0 and 14 years.

★ **Most bombed country**

The most heavily bombed country has been Laos. It has been estimated that between May 1964 and 26 February 1973 some 2.26 million tonnes

(5 billion lb) of bombs were dropped along the North to South Ho Chi Minh Trail supply route to South Vietnam.

★ **Country with highest military expenditure per capita**

Israel has the highest military expenditure per capita, with $1,487.68 (£819.07) spent per person as of 2003. Israel had a population of 6,258,000 in 2001.

★ **Country with lowest military expenditure per capita**

From available figures, the country that spends the least money on military expenditure is Swaziland, with $17.80 (£9.80) per person as of 2003. Swaziland had a population of 1,104,000 in 2001.

Longest reigning queen ⟱

The longest reigning queen is Victoria (below), Queen of Great Britain and, from 1876, Empress of India. She ruled for 63 years 216 days, from 1837 to 1901.

⟪ Youngest reigning monarch

Swaziland's King Mswati III (left) was crowned on 25 April 1986 when aged 18 years 6 days. He was born Makhosetive, the 67th son of King Sobhuza II.

★ Longest lived prime minister
The longest lived prime minister of any country was Antoine Pinay (France) who was born on 30 December 1891 and died on 13 December 1994 aged 102 years 348 days. He was his country's prime minister from March to December 1952.

★ Most re-elected prime minister
Lebanese prime minister Rashid Karami was first elected in 1955 and then officially re-elected seven additional times between 1958 and 1976. His final term of office was in 1984, when most people hoped he would end the country's civil war, but he was assassinated

in 1987 by a bomb thrown at his helicopter. Karami served in 1955–56; 1958–60; 1961–64; 1965–66; 1966–68; 1969–70; 1975–76 and 1984–87.

★ Longest ruling party
The party with the longest uninterrupted spell in government is the PRI (Partido Revolucionario Institucional) of Mexico, which won every Mexican presidential election from 1929 to 2000 when it lost to the PAN (Partido de Accion Nacional).

★ Youngest president
Jean-Claude Duvalier (Haiti, b. 3 July 1951) succeeded his father, François Duvalier, as Haitian president for life on 22 April 1971, becoming the

world's youngest president at the age of 19 years 293 days. He served as President of Haiti until 1986.

★ Longest serving living president
General Gnassingbe Eyadema (Togo) became President of the Togolese Republic on 14 April 1967 after leading a coup to oust President Nicolas Grunitzky.

★ Oldest president
Joaquin Balaguer was president of the Dominican Republic in 1960–62, 1966–78 and 1986–96. He ultimately left office at the age of 89, having held the presidency for no fewer than 22 years.

★ Youngest UN ambassador
Laura Sweeting (UK, b. 1 June 1984) became the United Nations' youngest Goodwill Ambassador on 9 June 2000. The 16-year-old schoolgirl's role in the Water4Life Appeal/ Children Helping Children

campaign raised awareness of the fact that over 5,000 people die each day because of the lack of clean water.

★ Youngest current head of state
Yahya Jammeh (b. 25 May 1965) became President of the Provisional Council and Gambian head of state following a military coup on 26 July 1994. On 27 September 1996, he was elected president following a return to civilian government.

★ Longest serving mayor
The longest recorded mayoralty was that of Edmond Mathis (France), who served as Mayor of Ehuns, Haute-Sàne, France, for 75 years (1878–1953).

★ Youngest mayor
The youngest mayor on record is Shane Mack (USA), born on 15 November 1969. Shane was elected Mayor of Castlewood, South Dakota, USA, at the age of 18 years 169 days on 3 May 1988 and held office for eight years.

Largest parliament ⌃

The largest legislative assembly in the world is the National People's Congress (NPC, above) of the People's Republic of China.

The 10th National People's Congress, elected at the beginning of 2003, is composed of 2,985 deputies legally elected by 35 electoral units nationwide. It is comprised of 31 provinces, autonomous regions and municipalities, Hong Kong and Macao special administrative regions, and the Chinese People's Liberation Army. Every minority ethnic group has an appropriate number of representatives in the NPC.

★ **Wealthiest queen**
Owing to rising UK property values, the net worth of Queen Elizabeth II (UK) has increased nearly 60% in the last year. *Forbes World's Richest People 2004* estimates her wealth at £358.8 million ($660 million).

★ **Largest political constituency**
The Kalgoorlie Australian federal parliamentary constituency in Western Australia covers more than 2,600,000 km² (1,000,000 miles²), an area greater than the whole of Western Europe. The constituency measures 2,250 km (1,400 miles) from north to south and 1,600 km (1,000 miles) from east to west, and covers the whole state of Western Australia except for Perth in the southwest.

★ **Most votes for a chimp in a political campaign**
In the 1988 mayoral elections campaign in Rio de Janeiro, Brazil, the anti-establishment 'Brazilian Banana Party' presented a chimpanzee called Tião as their candidate. The chimp came third out of 12 candidates, taking just over 400,000 votes. Known for his moody temper, the chimp's campaign slogan was 'Vote monkey – get monkey'. Tião died in 1996 aged 33. Tião means 'Big Uncle' in Portuguese.

★ **Heaviest monarch**
In September 1976, King Taufa'ahau Tupou IV of Tonga recorded a weight of 209.5 kg (462 lb). He is 1.9 m (6 ft 3 in) tall. By 1985 he was reported to have slimmed down to 139.7 kg (307 lb); in early 1993 he was 127.0 kg (279 lb); and by 1998 he had lost further weight as a result of a fitness programme.

★ **Oldest ruling house**
The Emperor of Japan, Akihito (b. 23 December 1933), is the 125th in line from the first Emperor, Jimmu Tenno, whose reign was traditionally from 660 BC to 581 BC but more probably dates from c. 40 BC to c.10 BC.

★ **Largest royal family**
There are more than 4,200 royal princes and more than 40,000 other relatives in the Saudi royal family.

★ **Longest reigning living queen**
Born on 21 April 1926, Queen Elizabeth II (UK) is currently the longest reigning living queen.

She succeeded to the throne on 6 February 1952 on the death of her father, King George VI. She is Queen of the United Kingdom and Head of the Commonwealth. The year 2002 saw the Queen's Golden Jubilee, marking 50 years since her accession.

★ **Longest reigns ever**
Minhti, King of Arakan (now part of Burma [Myanmar]), is reputed to have reigned for 95 years between 1279 and 1374, but the longest well-documented reign of any monarch was that of Phiops II (also known as Pepi II), or Neferkare, a Sixth-Dynasty pharaoh of ancient Egypt. His reign began c. 2281 BC, when he was six years old, and is believed to have lasted around 94 years.

Musoma Kanijo, although not a monarch, was chief of the Nzega district of Tanganyika (now part of Tanzania) and reputedly reigned for more than 98 years from 1864, when he was eight years old, until his death on 2 February 1963.

Largest olive cultivator ⌃

Spain is the world's leading cultivator of olives, producing 970,000 tonnes (2.1 billion lb) of olives annually.

The principal olive-producing regions are Catalonia and Andalusia. Spain and Italy together account for 54% of the total amount of olive oil produced worldwide.

Highest solar energy ⌃ use per capita

At 1.82 W per capita, Switzerland has the highest solar energy usage in the world.

The picture above shows a photovoltaic generating plant installed at a government office building in Berne, Switzerland.

★ Largest solar power facility

In terms of nominal capacity, the largest solar electric power facility in the world is the Harper Lake Site (LSP VIII & IX) in the Mojave Desert, California, USA, operated by UC Operating Services (USA). The two solar electric generating stations (SEGS) at Harper Lake have a nominal capacity of 160 MW (80 MW each). The station site covers 518 ha (1,280 acres) and houses 400,000 solar collectors – mirrors that concentrate solar energy – over a 400-ha (1,000-acre) area.

★ Largest solar-slate roof

In 1999, a former grain storage facility in Berne, Switzerland, was fitted with a 2,050-m^2 (22,000-ft^2) solar-slate roof comprising 16,650 photovoltaic cell-embedded slates known as Sunslates. The project was planned and engineered by Atlantis Energy Ltd, and generates 167,000 kWh (kilowatt-hours) of electrical energy, which is fed into the city's electricity grid. The total investment in the project was 2.6 million Swiss francs (£1.1 million or $1.7 million).

★ Most environmentally friendly country

The country regarded as the most environmentally sustainable is Finland, which heads the Environmental Sustainability Index (ESI) compiled in 2002 by the World Economic Forum.

Based on 20 core indicators covering five broad areas – environmental systems (eg air and water quality), reducing environmental stress (eg pollution levels), reducing human vulnerability to environmental degradation, social and institutional capacity to respond to environmental threats, and contribution to global stewardship – Finland scored 73.9 out of 100. The lowest was Kuwait with 23.9.

★ Largest producer of energy

In 2001 the USA produced 75,295 petajoules of commercial energy, including solid, liquid and gaseous fuels as well as primary electricity. A petajoule is 1,000,000,000,000,000 joules.

★ Fastest forest depletion

Burundi, Central Africa, suffers the fastest decrease in forested area with an average loss of 9% every year between 1990 and 2000. If this rate was permanently sustained, Burundi's forested areas would be completely cleared in just over 11 years.

★ Largest deforestation

The greatest deforestation rate is in Brazil where, between 1990 and 2000, an average of 22,264 km^2 (8,596 miles^2) of forest was cleared every year. This is equivalent to a country the size of Wales.

★ Largest reforestation

The greatest reforestation rate is in China where between 1990 and 2000 enough trees were replanted every year to cover an average area of 18,063 km^2 (6,974 miles^2). This is equivalent to a country the size of Kuwait.

★ Highest carbon dioxide emissions

The USA has the highest emissions of CO_2, one of the key gases responsible for the 'greenhouse effect'. The USA emitted 5,789 million tonnes (11,578 billion lb) of CO_2 in 2001, a 1.1% decrease on the previous year. The decrease in CO_2 emissions in 2001 was reportedly due to a reduction in US economic growth from 3.8% in 2000 to 0.3% in 2001.

Largest ≫ turkey farm

The world's largest turkey farm belongs to Bernard Matthews plc (UK). The farm is situated in North Pickenham, Norfolk, UK, and processes 1 million turkeys per year.

★ **Highest carbon dioxide emissions per capita**
The United Arab Emirates (UAE) has the highest carbon dioxide (CO_2) emissions per capita. In 1999 the emissions level reached 31.25 tonnes (68,750 lb) of CO_2 per capita. The total amount of CO_2 emissions for the UAE in 1999 was 88 million tonnes (190 billion lb).

★ **Greatest shrinkage of a lake**
The Aral Sea, on the border between Uzbekistan and Kazakhstan, has lost more than 60% of its area and approximately 80% of its volume since 1960. From 1960 to 1998, the lake decreased in area from 68,000 km^2 (26,300 miles^2) to 28,700 km^2 (11,000 miles^2) and in volume from approximately 1,040 km^3 (250 miles^3) to 180 km^3 (43 miles^3). The water level has dropped about 18 m (60 ft) in the same time period. This dramatic shrinkage is almost entirely due to the large amounts of water being extracted from the major rivers that feed it. This water is diverted for irrigation purposes.

★ **Greatest modern loss of agricultural land to aridity**
The greatest rate at which land has become arid in modern times has been experienced in Portugal where, since 1970, over 51% of agricultural land can no longer support agriculture at former levels.

★ **Highest glass recycling rate**
Switzerland leads the world in recycling glass. An estimated 91% of glass products sold in Switzerland are recycled.

★ **Highest paper recycling rate**
Germany recycles between 70% and 80% of its consumption of paper and cardboard per year.

★ **Waste generation**
The USA produces the most municipal waste per capita according to figures issued by the Organization for Economic Cooperation and Development in 2001. The estimated figure stands at 760 kg (1,675 lb) per capita.

★ **Highest proportion of organic farming**
In Austria an estimated 10% of agricultural land is farmed organically. Austria has more than 20,000 organic farms. Although Italy is believed to have around 40,000 organic farms, they represent a lower proportion of the total land organically farmed.

★ **Most polluted major city**
Mexico City is the world's most polluted major city and the most polluted capital city. The city is classified as having serious problems associated with sulphur dioxide, suspended particulate matter, carbon monoxide and ozone (in all of which World Health Organization guidelines are exceeded by more than a factor of two), plus moderate to heavy pollution for lead and nitrogen dioxide. Factors contributing to the high pollution levels include the high altitude and geographical location, as high emissions from industry and vehicles are trapped by surrounding mountains.

★ **Most acidic acid rain**
A pH reading of 1.87 was recorded at Inverpolly Forest in the Scottish Highlands, UK, in 1983, and a reading of 2.83 was recorded over the Great Lakes, USA/Canada, in 1982. These are the lowest pH levels ever recorded in acid precipitation, making it the most acidic acid rain; pH values range from 0 to 14, with 7 being neutral.

★ **Worst oil spill disaster**
The worst oil spill occurred as a result of a marine blow-out beneath the drilling rig *Ixtoc I* in the Gulf of Campeche, Gulf of Mexico, on 3 June 1979. The oil slick had reached 640 km (400 miles) by 5 August 1979. The spill was capped on 24 March 1980, following a loss of up to 500,000 tonnes (140 million gal or 636 million litres) of oil.

War & peace
Modern world

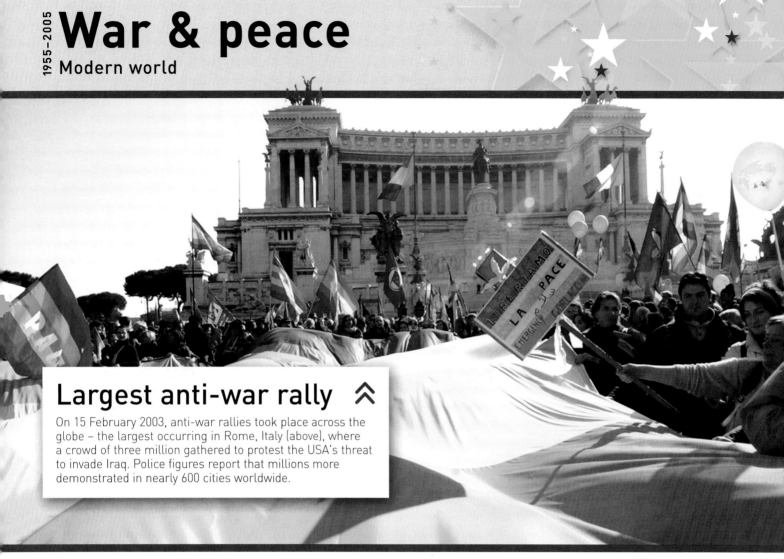

Largest anti-war rally ⌃

On 15 February 2003, anti-war rallies took place across the globe – the largest occurring in Rome, Italy (above), where a crowd of three million gathered to protest the USA's threat to invade Iraq. Police figures report that millions more demonstrated in nearly 600 cities worldwide.

★ Largest tank battle

The largest tank battle ever is generally acknowledged to be the Battle of Kursk during World War II. On 12 July 1943, in the Prokhorovka region near the Russian town of Kursk, a total of 1,500 German and Russian tanks amassed for close-range fighting. By the end of the day both sides had lost over 300 tanks.

★ Costliest civil war

The costliest civil war, in terms of the number of lives lost during combat and in events directly relating to the war, is the Russian Civil War of 1917–22. It is estimated that the former Soviet Union lost 939,755 soldiers, and over eight million civilians died following armed attacks, famine and disease.

★ Longest continuous period of civil war

The longest period of continuous civil warfare lasted for 254 years from 475 to 221 BC in China, and is known as the Warring States Period. Feudal lords in seven major state kingdoms sought dominance over each other in numerous intensive battles. King Ying Zheng of the Qin state was eventually victorious, becoming the first emperor (Qin Shihuang) of a unified China.

★ Most nationalities in one military force

As of January 2004 the French Foreign Legion had 7,622 men serving in its ranks, with a diverse range of nationalities from 136 countries. Legionnaires serve in France and around the world.

★ Youngest modern conscripts

In March 1976 President Francisco Macías Nguema of Equatorial Guinea (deposed in August 1979) decreed compulsory military service for all boys aged between seven and 14 years old. The edict stated that any parent that refused to hand over his or her son 'will be imprisoned or shot'.

★ Longest-serving military mule

The unit mascot for the 853 AT Coy ASC (MA Mules) was a Spanish mule called Pedongi, who was on active service with the Indian Army from 4 May 1965 until her death on 25 March 1998 aged 37. Her name was derived from the first battle area she was sent to at Pedong, northeast India.

★ Largest contributors to peacekeeping

Canada and Fiji have been part of almost all 55 United Nations (UN) peacekeeping operations.

★ Longest-running peacekeeping operation

The UN Truce Supervision Organization (UNTSO) has been in place since June 1948. UNTSO is based in Jerusalem but maintains military posts throughout the Middle East.

★ Largest current peacekeeping force

The largest current peacekeeping force is the UN Mission in Liberia (UNMIL).

On 19 September 2003 the UN Security Council agreed to the deployment of a 15,000-strong force on 1 October 2003 for a 12-month stay. Following the civil war, a cease-fire was signed in June 2003, but the UNMIL mandate is there to ensure that peace is maintained and that humanitarian relief is supplied, as well as to support the establishment of democratic elections.

★ Largest peacekeeping deployment ever

The United Nations Protection Force (UNPROFOR), which was deployed in the former Yugoslavia from February 1992 to March 1995, reached a maximum strength of 39,922 military personnel in September 1994. Serious fighting in Croatia began in June 1991 when that Republic and its northern neighbour, Slovenia, declared themselves independent from Yugoslavia, and Serbs living in Croatia, supported by the Yugoslav People's Army, opposed this move.

Earliest use of marine mammals in defence

In 1970–1971 during the Vietnam War, five US Navy bottlenose dolphins (*Tursiops truncatus*, left) were sent to Cam Ranh Bay, Vietnam, to defend US military boats from enemy swimmers. The most recent deployment of dolphins in active duty was during the Umm Qasr mission in the waters off Iraq in March 2003. Dolphins were trained by the US to detect underwater mines in the Gulf, so that military boats and ships loaded with humanitarian aid could pass safely. The dolphins did not touch the mines, but released a balloon showing their location.

Highest percentage of military personnel

In North Korea (above) in 1999, 5.05% of the total population of 21,386,000 (or one for every 19 people) was a member of the armed forces.

★ Most expensive peacekeeping operation
UNPROFOR cost $4.6 billion (£2.96 billion) from February 1992 to March 1995. This cost covers all missions deployed during this period, and equates to just under $3 million (£1.93 million) per day.

★ Bloodiest UN peacekeeping operation
The conflict in the Balkans led to more fatalities than any other UN peacekeeping mission. The total number of fatalities for all missions in the region is 268, including 210 fatalities in UNPROFOR alone.

★ Peacekeeping mission with most contributing nations
The United Nations Mission in Bosnia and Herzegovina (UNMIBH) drew troops from 44 different nations until the end of its mandate on 31 December 2002. UNMIBH was an umbrella organization over-seeing the activities of the International Police Task Force (IPTF) that was set up in Bosnia and Herzegovina after the United Nations Protection Force (UNPROFOR) mission came to an end in 1995.

★ Largest humanitarian agency
The UN World Food Programme (WFP) is the largest humanitarian agency in the world. The organization was established in 1963 and to date has delivered 68.7 million tonnes (151 billion lb) of food to over 1.2 billion people in 100 countries, with a total cost of $32 billion (£19.1 billion).

★ Largest single humanitarian operation
The largest and most expensive humanitarian operation ever undertaken was feeding the 27.1 million people of Iraq following the 2003 war. The food-aid operation, organized by the WFP, began on 1 April 2003 and finished in October 2003 with 2.2 million tonnes (4.8 billion lb) of food commodities being delivered under a budget of $1.5 billion (£927 million).

★ Largest and longest running humanitarian airdrop
The WFP has been in southern Sudan since 1992. Drought, civil war, flooding and remote locations mean that an average of 2.5 million people suffer from food shortages annually. At its peak, the WFP operated 14 aircraft per day, each making three trips and delivering an average of 16 tonnes (352,000 lb) of food per drop.

★ Most Nobel Peace Prizes
The International Committee of the Red Cross, founded in Geneva, Switzerland, in 1893, has received three awards for Peace: 1917, 1944 and 1963. The latter award was shared with the League of the Red Cross Societies.

★ Largest demonstration
A figure of 2.7 million demonstrators was reported from China for a demonstration against the USSR in Shanghai on 3–4 March 1969 following border clashes.

★ Largest landlocked navy
Paraguay, a totally landlocked South American state, has a navy with 3,595 personnel (in 2000). The navy operates on the nation's major rivers, the Paraguay and Paraná. Military service in Paraguay is compulsory; for those opting for naval service the period in uniform is two years.

★ Oldest air force
The earliest autonomous air force is the Royal Air Force (UK), the origins of which can be traced back to 1878 when the War Office commissioned the building of a military balloon. The Royal Air Force itself came into existence on 1 April 1918. The British were not the first to utilize balloons, however. The French used them for military observations at the Battle of Fleurus in June 1794 during the French Revolutionary Wars.

Crime & punishment
Modern world

« Largest heroin seizure

According to the Drug Enforcement Administration (DEA) the largest heroin seizure (left) took place in Bangkok, Thailand, on 11 February 1988 when 1,277 kg (2,816 lb) was seized. It had an estimated street value of £45.5 million ($75 million).

Highest-ranking camel «

The world's highest-ranking law-enforcement camel is BERT (USA, left), who was accepted as Reserve Deputy Sheriff for the Los Angeles County Sheriff's Department in San Dimas, California, USA, on 5 April 2003 and who regularly goes on patrol with his handler Nance Fite (USA). Born on 3 March 1997, BERT, which stands for 'Be Enthusiastic Responsible and True', is a dromedary (one hump). He weighed 802 kg (1,770 lb) on 27 May 2003 and stands at a height of 208 cm (82 in) to the top of his hump, although he will not be considered fully grown until he is eight years old.

★ Highest murder rate per capita

According to the seventh UN Survey of Crime Trends and Operations of Criminal Justice Systems, covering the period 1998–2000, Colombia has the most recorded intentional homicides per capita, with 65 murders per 100,000 people.

★ Most murders by a doctor

Family doctor Harold Shipman (UK) murdered 215 of his patients between 1975 and 1998. Shipman killed his elderly victims, most of whom were women, with high doses of diamorphine injections. In January 2000, he was sentenced to a life term in prison for the 15 murders of which he was found guilty. Shipman hanged himself in his prison cell on 13 January 2004.

★ Greatest mass arrest

The greatest mass arrest reported in a democratic country was that of 15,617 demonstrators rounded up on 11 July 1988 by South Korean police to ensure security in advance of the 1988 Olympic Games in Seoul.

★ Largest white-collar crime

In February 1997, copper trader Yasuo Hamanaka (Japan) pleaded guilty to fraud and forgery in connection with illicit trading that cost the Japanese company Sumitomo an estimated $2.6 billion (£1.37 billion) accumulated over a 10-year period of unauthorized transactions.

★ Highest rate of gun ownership

Among countries not at war or suffering civil unrest, the USA has the highest rate of civilian gun ownership. Surveys in 1999 found that around 40% of US households have at least one firearm. The USA has over 200 million guns – more than the number of adults in the country.

★ Largest reward for counter-terrorism

In July 2003, the US government approved the payment of a $30-million (£16.4-million) reward to the informant who led US forces to Saddam Hussein's (Iraq) two eldest sons, Uday and Qusay (both Iraq), in Mosul, Iraq. The $15 million (£8.2 million) for each is the largest ever paid by the USA under its Rewards for Justice programme.

★ Fastest recorded speed on public roads

Andrew Osborne (UK) was sentenced to 28 days in prison at Aylesbury Magistrates Court on 16 July 2003 after being clocked in March 2003 travelling at 252 km/h (158 mph) on his 1200-cc Kawasaki motorcycle at Tingewick bypass, Bucks, UK.

★ Longest serving judge

The oldest recorded active judge was Judge Albert R Alexander (USA). He was enrolled as a member of the Clinton County Bar, Missouri, USA, in 1926 and was later the magistrate and probate judge of Clinton County until his retirement aged 105 years 8 months on 9 July 1965.

★ Most viewed trial

A daily average of 5.5 million Americans watched live coverage of the OJ Simpson (USA) trial on three major cable television networks between 24 January and 3 October 1995. Simpson, an American football player and actor, was on trial for the 12 June 1994 murder of his ex-wife, Nicole, and a waiter, Ronald Goldman (both USA). He was acquitted of the charges when the jury reached a verdict of not guilty on 3 October 1995.

Earliest system of fingerprinting ⌃

The first effective system of identification by fingerprints –

the science of dactylography – was instituted in 1896 by Edward Henry (UK), an Inspector General of police in British India, who eventually became Commissioner of Metropolitan Police in London.

★ GWR TALKS TO
Lois Gibson

Since 1982, over 150 criminals have been identified and brought to justice in Texas, USA, thanks to the detailed composites drawn by forensic artist Lois Gibson (USA, above). This figure represents the record for most criminals positively identified from one artist's composites.

How did you become a forensic artist?
I became a forensic artist because someone tried to kill me for fun when I was 21. My attacker got into my apartment and choked me for about half an hour straight. I couldn't bring myself to tell the authorities, but about six weeks later I got lost in Los Angeles and was driving by a house just as my attacker was being arrested. This changed my life. I want my witnesses to have that wonderful feeling when they know their attacker is caught.

What did you do next?
After the attack, I got a Bachelor of Fine Arts With Honors from the University of Texas in Austin and went on to produce about 3,000 fine-art portraits for tourists. Then I moved to Houston, and was amazed to discover that they had had over 700 murders there that year. One day it just hit me: I could draw attackers' faces from witnesses' descriptions. I approached the Houston Police Department, who had no one doing that at the time. Every third sketch I did helped solve a crime, but it took them seven years to give me that job!

Four years later I went to the FBI Academy in Quantico, Virginia, and completed the Forensic Art Course there. Now I teach this profession at Northwestern University in Evanston, Illinois.

Do you work for different police forces across the USA or is it always the same one?
I work at the Houston Police Department, but cities and counties near and far bring witnesses to me.

How long have you been doing it? Do you get better with practice?
I've been a forensic artist for 21 years. One definitely gets better with practice, way better.

How long does it take to do each drawing?
Now my drawings take one hour. In the beginning it took almost three hours. If I have a reclusive witness who definitely doesn't want to talk, I can do the sketch in 25 minutes. If the witness needs to talk a lot, it can take two hours.

Talk us through your procedure.
I start at the top and go down. So, hair, forehead, eyebrows, eyes, nose, lips, chin, throw on the ears if they are seen, neck, shoulders in that order.

Do you do drawings digitally?
No, I draw everything by hand. It is much faster to draw by hand than with a computer... and way more accurate.

What does it mean to you to have a Guinness World Record?
It makes all that brutal, heart-wrenching work seem worthwhile. Since I deal with armed officers, I never say my sketch actually solved a case – indeed, the sketch can only help the officers make an arrest. But my fellow and future forensic artists need to know that forensic art can help solve cases.

Guinness World Records has given me a forum to spread compositry to other countries in the world besides the USA and Canada. All those countries need forensic artists too!

Largest global brand ⌄

According to a study released by AC Nielsen, the largest global brand in the world based on sales is Coca-Cola, which in 2002 had sales of $19 billion (£13 billion). The brand is present in over 200 countries.

Largest ⌃ company merger

America Online (AOL), the largest Internet company, announced a $350,000 million (£213,000 million) merger with media corporate Time Warner on 10 January 2000. The completed merger created AOL Time Warner, the world's largest media company. The brands owned by the new company include AOL, Time, CNN, Warner Bros, Netscape, Sports Illustrated, TNT and Cartoon Network.

in net income in 12 months. Exxon's refineries can handle over 6 million barrels daily.

revenues of $48,005 million (£30,333 million) in the fiscal year ending March 2003. The company reported more than 119.7 million subscribers worldwide as of March 2003. It operates in 28 countries on five continents.

★ Largest corporate bankruptcy
In terms of assets, the largest corporate bankruptcy amounted to $103.9 billion (£65.8 billion) filed by the telecommunications company WorldCom, Inc. on 21 July 2002.

★ Largest corporation
Based on revenues, the largest corporation as of 2003 was integrated oil company ExxonMobil (USA), which had revenues of $246,738 million (£138,781 million).

★ Highest share value
On 27 March 2000 the share price of Yahoo! Japan stood at JPY120.4 million ($1.12 million). Yahoo! Japan is the nation's dominant information portal, and the scarcity of the stock contributed to the dramatic

rise in price. Japanese company Softbank owns 41.93% of the company, with US-based Yahoo! owning 33.49%. Yahoo! Japan's share price has increased 4,700% since December 1998.

★ Largest publishing company
With 80,632 employees, the world's largest printing and publishing company is Bertelsmann AG (Germany). In 2002 the company had revenues of $19,192 million (£11,965 million) with profits of $972 million (£606 million).

★ Greatest annual profit
In 2001, integrated oil company ExxonMobil (USA) announced profits of $15,320 million (£10,932 million), which represented a 13.5% growth

★ Largest music company
Universal Music Group (USA) is the largest music company with revenues of $6,276 million (£3,455 million) as of December 2002. Based in New York, USA, the Universal Music Group has more than 12,000 employees, operates in 71 countries and had an estimated worldwide market share in 2002 of 24.4%.

★ Largest retail company by number of outlets
By the end of January 2003, Wal-Mart (USA) operated 4,688 retail stores worldwide.

★ Largest mobile telecommunications company
Vodafone Group Plc (UK) is the world's largest mobile telecommunications group, with

★ Oldest stock exchange
The Stock Exchange in Amsterdam, The Netherlands, was founded in 1602. It dealt in printed shares of the United East India Company of The Netherlands in the Oude Zijds Kapel.

★ Largest lottery
By the end of January 2004, ticket sales for the UK's National Lottery (launched in November 1994) had reached £45 billion ($81 billion).

★ Richest woman
Alice Walton (USA), daughter of Sam Walton, founder of the world's largest retailer Wal-Mart, and Helen, his widow, each have an estimated net worth of $20 billion (£11 billion) according to the Forbes 2004 Rich List.

Largest company by assets

American multi-national motor manufacturer Ford Motor Company (USA, left) is the largest company in the world in terms of assets (excluding banks and financial institutions). At June 2003, its assets were worth a total of $311,791 million (£189,113 million).

«

★ GWR TALKS TO
Bill Gates

Bill Gates (USA, above) is Chairman and Chief Software Architect of Microsoft Corporation. As well as being the world's richest living person, worth $46.6 billion (£25.4 billion) in March 2004 according to *Forbes* magazine, Bill and his wife Melinda hold the record for the largest single private charitable donation ($6 billion or £4.2 billion), which they made to their own Bill & Melinda Gates Foundation. The foundation itself holds the record for the largest single

donation to AIDS research ($25 million or £15.08 million) and is also the world's largest charitable foundation. Its largest donation was $1 billion (£700 million) over 20 years for minority student scholarships, via the Gates Millennium Scholars Program.

How and when did you first become interested in technology and computers?
When I was 13, my school installed a teletype machine that connected to a mainframe computer in downtown Seattle. From that point on, my friends and I spent most of our free time writing programs and figuring out how to make the computer do interesting things.

What are you working on for Microsoft now?
My job is to figure out new ways to make computers more useful, and work with our software developers

and product groups to set the technical direction for the company. Right now I'm working on a number of projects, including the next major release of our Windows operating system.

What do you think will be the interesting developments in technology in the near future?
Everything from the TV to the refrigerator is taking on the intelligence and connectivity of the PC, and this opens up some amazing new possibilities. I think computers will change our lives more in the next ten years than they have in the past 20.

What personal achievement are you most proud of?
Although it's great that I get to do the work I love and have been very successful at it, I'm proudest of my three children.

What does your charity do and what is the most satisfying part of running it?
The Bill & Melinda Gates Foundation focuses most of its efforts on long-term global

health issues. We have a tremendous opportunity to improve the quality of life for billions of people by treating and preventing disease, improving child and reproductive health, and slowing the spread of HIV and other global health threats. My wife and I are privileged to work with some of the world's smartest people to develop sustainable solutions to problems that affect a large percentage of the world's population.

What does it mean to have a Guinness World Record?
It's a great honour, but I'm just happy that I've been able to use what I have to help improve people's lives.

What advice would you give to any young people who would like to follow in your footsteps?
Most important of all is to choose work that you are truly passionate about. If you really love what you do, you'll barely notice how hard you work at it.

≪ Highest and lowest health budget

The USA has the largest health expenditure at $3,724 (£2,359) per capita according to the World Health Organization's World Health Report 2000. Somalia has a health budget of only $11 (£6.80) per capita.

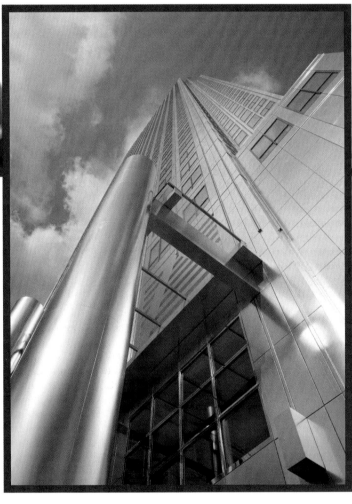

★ Most and least hospital beds

According to 2002 data, Switzerland has one bed per 155 people. Niger has only one hospital bed per 2,000 people.

★ Most and least physicians

In Monaco there is one physician for every 170 people. The country with the highest number of people per physician is Malawi with 49,118 people for every one doctor.

★ Most prevalent allergic disease

Bronchial asthma affects up to 150 million people worldwide, with deaths from the condition reaching 180,000 each year. Globally, it is estimated that the economic costs associated with this disease exceed those of tuberculosis and HIV/AIDS combined.

★ Most common infectious disease

The common cold is almost universal, afflicting everyone but those living in isolated communities or in Antarctica (no virus will survive the extreme cold). There are at least 40 cold viruses that are airborne or transmitted by direct contact.

★ Highest number of people with HIV/AIDS

In the Republic of South Africa one in nine people are affected by HIV/AIDS. In 2001, out of a total population of 43.5 million, 4.7 million people carried the virus.

★ Highest death rate from infectious disease

The west African island-republic of São Tomé and Princípe has 241 deaths from infectious diseases per 100,000 annually.

★ Leading cause of death

In industrialized countries, diseases of the heart and of blood vessels (cardiovascular disease) account for more than 50% of deaths. The most common are heart attacks and strokes, generally due to atheroma (degeneration of the arterial walls) obstructing the flow of blood.

Most and least expensive office location ⋀

Based on March 2003 prices, London (UK, above) has the most expensive office space in the world. Cost per m² including rent, taxes and service charges is £1,014 ($1,596). Where country-comparable data is available, Sandton in Johannesburg, South Africa, is the least expensive location for office space. Cost per m², allowing for similar expenses, is £79 ($125).

Lowest and highest ≫ spending on education

Somalia allocates just 0.4% of its Gross National Income (GNI) to primary, secondary and tertiary education. The USA spent 5.4% of its GNI on education in 1997.

★ **Largest school by pupils**
The largest school in terms of pupils is the City Montessori School in Lucknow, India, which had a record enrolment for the 2003/04 academic year of 27,911 pupils on 24 September 2003.

★ **Oldest university**
The oldest existing and continually operating educational institution is the University of Karueein, founded in AD 859 in Fez, Morocco.

★ **Longest lesson**
Murry Burrows (Australia) taught biology to his class of 26 students at Laidley State High School, Queensland, Australia, for 54 hours on 15–17 April 2003.

★ **Most expensive course**
The Ivor Spencer International Finishing School for Young Ladies and Gentlemen, London, UK, began a one-month £77,500 ($126,000) 'finishing' course in 1998. Students stayed at a top London hotel, went to the ballet and opera, and took lessons in protocol, etiquette, food, wine, cooking and style.

★ **Oldest doctorate**
On 12 May 2000, Elizabeth Eichelbaum (USA) received her doctorate in Education from the University of Tennessee, USA, at the age of 90 years 58 days.

★ **Longest time to complete a degree**
Robert FP Cronin (UK) began his biology degree on 9 February 1948 at Princeton University, New Jersey, USA, and graduated on 30 May 2000, 52 years 111 days later at the age of 73 years 272 days. He is the world's oldest graduate.

★ **Longest elapsed time before a class reunion**
The 1929 class of Miss Blanche Miller's Kindergarten and Continuation School, Bluefield, West Virginia, USA, had their first reunion after 70 years. Ten members of the class had died but of the remaining group, 55% were in attendance.

★ **Largest school reunion**
A total of 2,521 former pupils of Pestalozzi School, Guben, Germany, attended the school's 100th anniversary celebrations on 29 June 2002.

★ **Longest annual class reunion**
The Cherokee County Community High School's class of 1929 held its 74th class reunion in Columbus, Kansas, USA, on 7 June 2003. Of the original class of 110, 30 graduates remain, but only nine could make the reunion.

★ **Largest employer**
Indian Railways had 1,583,614 regular employees when it was last assessed in March 1997. The Indian Railways' wage bill for the period 1996–97 worked out at a massive 105,145,000,000 rupees ($2.1 billion or £1.5 billion).

★ **Longest working career**
The longest working life has been the 98 years worked by Shigechiyo Izumi (Japan), who began work goading draught animals at a sugar mill at Isen, Tokunoshima, Japan, in 1872. He retired as a sugar-cane farmer in 1970 aged 105. He attributed his long life to 'God, Buddha and the Sun'.

★ **Highest and lowest rates of unemployment**
According to information available in 2002, the country with the highest rate of unemployment is Liberia with 70% of its labour force not in paid employment. Andorra and the South Pacific island of Nauru had the lowest rate of unemployment for any country with 0%.

★ **Longest working career in a single company**
Thomas Stoddard (USA) started working at Speakman Company, Delaware, USA, on 16 February 1928 as a 16-year-old mailboy. He remained an employee of the plumbing and pipe-fitting company until his retirement (as a member of the board of directors) 75 years later on 16 February 2003, when he was 91 years old.

« Highest apple consumption

In 1998, China consumed the greatest amount of apples in the world overall with a total of 14.694 million tonnes (32.3 billion lb) or 11.6 kg (25 lb 9 oz) per capita. Assuming an apple weighs 150 g (5.2 oz), this is equivalent to 77 apples per person. Moldova consumes the most apples per person, with 70.9 kg (156 lb 4.9 oz) consumed per person in 1998. The country got through 310,000 tonnes (682 million lb) of apples in that year – equivalent to 472 per person.

Highest vodka consumption ⩘

Russia is the leading vodka consumer with 14.5 litres (25.5 pints) per capita consumed in 1999. Considering that there are a proportion of Russians who do not drink, it is estimated that 80% of adult men consume, on average, 220 half-litre (0.87 pints) bottles of vodka per year.

★ **Highest bread consumption**
As of 2000 the country with the largest per capita consumption of bread was Turkey with 199.6 kg (440 lb) per person. Turkish people eat more than three times their own body weight in bread annually.

★ **Highest baked bean consumption**
The country with the largest annual consumption of baked beans per capita is the UK with 5.3 kg (11 lb 10 oz) per person according to surveys in 1999.

★ **Highest chocolate consumption**
In Switzerland, the average person consumed 11.5 kg of chocolate (25 lb 6 oz) during 2000. This is equivalent to 230 50-g (1.76-oz) bars a year.

★ **Largest consumption of cigarettes**
The world's largest consumer of cigarettes, in terms of volume purchased, is China with 1.69 trillion sold in 2002. With a global consumption in 2000 of 5.5 trillion this means that approximately one in every three cigarettes smoked today is smoked in China.

★ **Highest wine consumption**
Luxembourg consumes an average of 63.3 litres (111.3 pints) of wine annually per person. The smallest measurable wine consumer is Egypt, where the average yearly wine consumption is about two tablespoons.

★ **Highest alcohol consumption**
The alcohol consumption rate is highest in Ireland where 12.3 litres (21.6 pints) of pure alcohol per person is consumed annually according to surveys done in 2000. This intake is based on the amount of pure alcohol consumed within wine, beer and spirits.

★ **Highest beer consumption**
The Czech Republic consumes 160 litres (281 pints) of beer annually per person as of 2000. The country that consumed the greatest volume of beer in the same year was the USA with 24,376 million litres (42,895 million pints). This is equivalent to a per capita consumption of 89 litres (156 pints).

★ **Highest tea consumption**
In Ireland, the average annual consumption of tea is 2.69 kg (5 lb 14 oz) per capita, the equivalent of 1,184 cups per person each year.

★ **Highest organic produce sales**
Denmark has annual organic retail sales of £220 million ($349.2 million) in a population of 5.3 million, averaging sales of £41.51 ($65.88) per capita.

★ **Greatest fast food expenditure**
In 2000, Americans spent over $110 billion (£166 billion) on fast food – more than on higher education, personal computers or new cars. On any one day approximately 25% of adults in the USA visit a fast food outlet. The typical American eats roughly three hamburgers and four orders of french fries a week. The USA has more than 300,000 fast food restaurants.

★ **Most meat waste**
The country that wastes the most bovine meat (beef and veal) per year is Argentina, where 332,000 tonnes (730 million lb) was thrown away in 1998.

★ **Most and least telephones**
Monaco has the most telephones per 1,000 people with 1,000 receivers as of 1998. Nauru in the South Pacific has the least with 0.2 per 1,000 people in 1998.

★ **Country with most mobile phones**
There were 69,209,000 mobile phones in the USA in 1998. By contrast only 35 million people in the USA were mobile phone subscribers in 1996.

★ **Most Internet users**
As of the end of 2001, Sweden had 554.18 Internet users per 1,000 people.

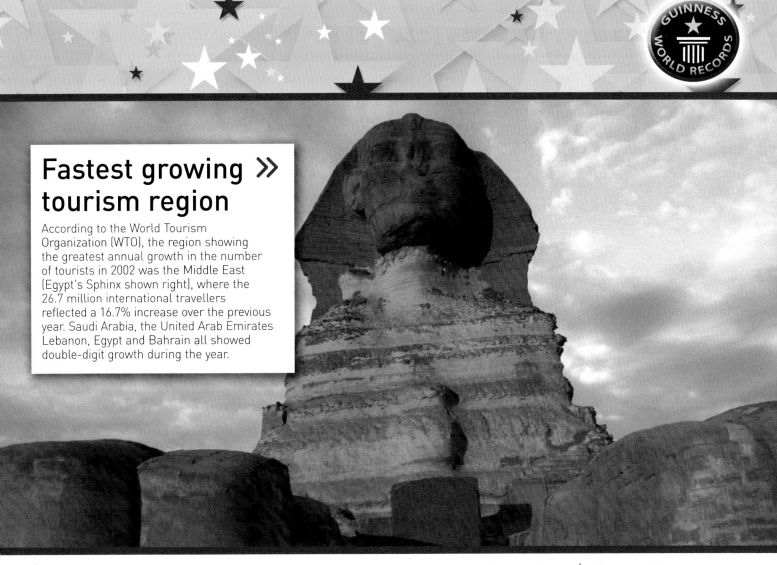

Fastest growing »
tourism region

According to the World Tourism Organization (WTO), the region showing the greatest annual growth in the number of tourists in 2002 was the Middle East (Egypt's Sphinx shown right), where the 26.7 million international travellers reflected a 16.7% increase over the previous year. Saudi Arabia, the United Arab Emirates Lebanon, Egypt and Bahrain all showed double-digit growth during the year.

★ **Most TV sets**
The country with the most televisions is China, which had 400 million TV sets in 1997.

★ **City to hold the most wedding ceremonies**
Las Vegas, Nevada, USA, has over 100 chapels performing approximately 8,400 marriage ceremonies per month – that's about 280 per day or one wedding every 5 mins 17 sec.

★ **Highest divorce rate**
As of September 2002, the country with the highest divorce rate was the Maldives, with 10.97 divorces per 1,000 inhabitants each year.

★ **Longest marriage**
Wesley and Stella McGowen (both USA) have been married since 6 February 1920 – over 84 years.

★ **Biggest tourist spenders**
The biggest overseas travel spenders are US citizens, who in 2002 spent $58 billion (£36.8 billion) while on holiday in foreign countries (excluding airfares) according to the World Tourism Organization.

★ **Highest earnings from tourism**
Despite a fall of 7.4% in 2002, the USA remains the world leader in terms of earnings from international tourism, taking $66.5 billion (£44.3 billion) in that year. This is equivalent to a world market share of 14%.

★ **Most popular tourist destination**
According to the WTO, in 2002 France attracted 77 million international visitors, singlehandedly accounting for 11% of all international travellers in that year.

★ **Most visited theme park**
An estimated 16.5 million people passed through the gates of Tokyo Disneyland in 2000. During the 1990s, the park had an estimated 179,112,000 visitors, making it the most visited park of the decade. This is well above the total population of the country (about 126 million).

★ **Most popular form of international travel**
According to the WTO, 43.7% of tourists visiting foreign countries in 1998 arrived by air, compared with 41.4% who travelled by road.

★ **Busiest airport for international passengers**
According to the Airports Council International, London's Heathrow Airport handled 53.79 million passengers arriving from, or departing to, destinations outside the UK during 2001.

★ **Busiest airport by number of aircraft**
A total of 909,535 aircraft take-offs and landings were made during 2001 at O'Hare International Airport, Chicago, Illinois, USA. In terms of the number of passengers served, O'Hare is in second place behind Atlanta's Hartsfield International.

★ **Highest and lowest rate of car ownership**
The wealthy European state of Luxembourg has 576 cars per 1,000, or one for every 1.7 people. By contrast Somalia and the former Soviet republic of Tajikistan jointly have the world's lowest rate of car ownership, with 0.1 cars per 1,000 people, or one car per 10,000 people.

★ **Longest traffic jam**
The longest traffic jam ever stretched 176 km (109 miles) northwards from Lyon towards Paris, France, on 16 February 1980. The biggest jam in terms of the number of cars was estimated to involve 18 million cars crawling bumper-to-bumper on the East-West German border on 12 April 1990.

★ **Best-selling car**
The Ford Focus was the world's best-selling car in 2000 (the latest year for which statistics are available), with global sales of 941,938. This means that one in every 40 cars sold worldwide was a Focus.

Highest pilgrimage ≫

A route (below) on Mount Kailash
(or Khang Rimpoche) in western Tibet,
which measures 53 km (33 miles), reaches an altitude of 6,714 m
(22,028 ft). The mountain is sacred to followers of Buddhism,
Jainism, Hinduism and Bonpo, a pre-Buddhist religion.

Largest church ⩘

The largest church in the world is
the Basilica of Our Lady of Peace
(Notre Dame de la Paix, above) at Yamoussoukro, the legal
and administrative capital of Ivory Coast/Côte d'Ivoire. It was
completed in 1989 at a cost of $164 million (£100 million) and
has a total area of 30,000 m² (322,917 ft²) with seating for 7,000
people. Including its golden cross, it is 158 m (518 ft) high.

★ **Largest religious structure**
The largest religious structure
ever built is Angkor Wat (City
Temple), enclosing 162.6 ha
(401 acres) in Cambodia. It was
built to honour the Hindu god
Vishnu by the Khmer King
Suryavarman II in the period
1113–50. Its curtain wall
measures 1,280 m (4,200 ft),
and its population, before it
was abandoned in 1432, was
80,000. The whole complex of
72 major monuments, begun
c. AD 900, extends over 24.8 km
(15.4 miles).

★ **Largest Buddhist temple**
The largest Buddhist temple
in the world is Borobudur,
near Yogyakarta, central Java,
Indonesia, built between
AD 750 and 842. The 60,000-m³
(2,118,880-ft³) stone structure
is 34.5 m (113 ft) tall and its
base measures 123 x 123 m
(403 x 403 ft).

★ **Largest cathedral**
The world's largest cathedral is
the Gothic church of the Diocese
of New York, USA, St John the
Divine, which has a floor area

of 11,240 m² (120,986 ft²),
equivalent to 43 tennis courts.
The nave is the longest in the
world at 183.2 m (601 ft). (In
comparison, Notre Dame de
Paris is 130 m (427 ft) long.)
The vaulted roof reaches a
height of 37.8 m (124 ft),
around 10 storeys above floor
level. The cornerstone was laid
on 27 December 1892 but,
incredibly, the building is only
two-thirds complete.

★ **Largest Hindu
    temple in use**
Srirangam Temple, at
Tiruchirappalli, Tamil Nadu,
India, is the world's largest
Hindu temple. Dedicated to the
Hindu god Vishnu, the temple
complex covers an area of
63.1 ha (156 acres) with a
perimeter of 9,934 m (32,592 ft).

★ **Largest
    monolithic church**
The largest monolithic (or rock-
hewn) church is Bet Medhane
Alem in Lalibela, Ethiopia. The
structure measures 33.5 m
(110 ft) long, 23.5 m (78 ft) wide
and 11 m (36 ft) high. It was

carved from volcanic rock in
the 12th or 13th century AD by
King Lalibela.

★ **Largest mosque**
The largest mosque is
Shah Faisal Mosque, near
Islamabad, Pakistan. The total
area of the complex is 18.97 ha
(46.87 acres), with the covered
area of the prayer hall being
4,800 m² (51,666 ft²). The
mosque can accommodate
100,000 worshippers in the
prayer hall and the courtyard
plus a further 200,000 people
in the adjacent grounds.

★ **Largest synagogue**
The largest synagogue in the
world is Temple Emanu-El on
Fifth Avenue at 65th Street,
New York City, USA, which
has a total area of 3,523 m²
(37,922 ft²). The synagogue's
main sanctuary is able to
accommodate 2,500 people,
while the adjoining Beth-El
Chapel seats 350. When these
and the Temple's other three
sanctuaries are in use, a
combined total of 5,500 people
can be accommodated.

★ **Temple at highest altitude**
The Rongbuk temple, between
Tingri and Shigatse in Tibet,
China, is situated at an altitude
of approximately 5,100 m
(16,700 ft). It is just 40 km
(25 miles) from Mount Everest.

★ **Most valuable
    sacred object**
The 15th-century gold Buddha
in Wat Trimitr Temple in
Bangkok, Thailand, has the
highest intrinsic value of any
sacred object. It is 3 m (10 ft)
tall and weighs an estimated
5.5 tonnes (12,125 lb). As of
January 2004's price of gold
($415 or £226 per fine ounce),
it is now worth $78 million
(£39.8 million). The gold under
the plaster exterior was found
only in 1954.

★ **Largest statue of
    the Virgin Mary**
The largest statue of the Virgin
Mary with Jesus measures
14 m (46 ft) high and stands on
a 17-m-tall (55-ft 9-in) base. It
was unveiled on 8 September
2003 and stands overlooking
the city of Haskovo, Bulgaria.

Most Muslim pilgrims ⌃

The annual pilgrimage (Hajj) to Mecca, Saudi Arabia (above), attracts greater numbers than any other Islamic mission – an average of two million people a year from 140 countries.

★ Largest single tomb
The Mount Li tomb – the burial place of Qin Shihuang, the first emperor of a unified China – was constructed during his reign, from 221 to 210 BC, and is situated 40 km (25 miles) east of Xian, China. The two walls around the grave measure 2,173 x 974 m (7,129 x 3,195 ft) and 685 x 578 m (2,247 x 1,896 ft).

★ Most Christian pilgrims
The House of the Virgin Mary at Loretto, Italy, receives a total of 3.5 million pilgrims (as opposed to tourists) a year, over three times the number visiting the more famous shrine at Lourdes, France. The basilica of St Antony at Padua, Italy, receives a similar number of pilgrims a year.

★ Largest religious crowd
The greatest recorded number of people assembled with a common purpose was an estimated 20 million who gathered at the Hindu festival of Kumbh Mela, held at the confluence of the Jumna, the Ganges and the mythical 'Saraswati' rivers at Allahabad (Prayag), Uttar Pradesh, India, on 30 January 2001.

★ Tallest cemetery
The permanently illuminated Memorial Necrópole Ecumônica, in Santos, near São Paulo, Brazil, is 10 storeys high and occupies an area of 1.8 ha (4.4 acres). Construction on the cemetery began in March 1983 and the first burial was on 28 July 1984.

★ Longest papal reign
The longest papal reign was that of Pius IX (Giovanni Maria Mastai-Ferretti, Italy), who was pope for 31 years 236 days between 1846 and 1878. St Peter (c. AD 33-67), the first pope, is said to have been head of the Church for 34 years, although his papacy cannot be dated accurately.

★ Fastest growing religion
Islam is the fastest growing religion in the world. In 1990, 935 million of the world's population were Muslims; however, the estimate for January 2004 is 1.4 billion, or 23% of the world's population. Although the religion originated in Arabia, in 2002 around 80% of all believers lived outside the Arab world.

★ Longest pole-sitting by an individual
The monk St Simeon the Stylite (c. AD 386-459) spent about 39 years on a stone pillar on the Hill of Wonders, near Aleppo, Syria – the longest time someone has remained on top of a pole. He did so as an act of self-persecution for people's sins, and in order to be nearer to God. The Church of St Simeon or Qalaat Samaan was built in honour of the monk and houses the ruins of the column. St Simeon's pole-sitting feat is the longest standing record to be chronicled in the book of Guinness World Records.

★ Oldest Koran
The Holy Koran Mushaf of Othman, owned by the Muslim Board of Uzbekistan, once belonged to Caliph Othman (c. AD 588-656), third successor to the Prophet Mohammed. Only about half of the original 706 pages survive. The parchment-made Mushaf Koran was compiled between AD 646 and 656.

Most pumpkins carved in one hour ⌃

School teacher and sports coach Steven Clarke (USA, above) set a new world record when he carved 42 pumpkins in one hour for the Halloween celebrations of CBS TV's *The Early Show* on 31 October 2002 in New York, USA. He also holds the record for fastest pumpkin carver, having sculpted a single jack o'lantern in just 54.72 seconds.

★ Most participants in a ribbon-cutting ceremony
There were 3,238 participants in the ribbon-cutting ceremony at the official launch of Raffles The Plaza and Swissotel The Stamford hotels in Singapore on 6 January 2002. The ribbon was 4,203 m (13,789 ft) long.

★ Fastest youth team in a woolsack race
In May 1997, The Raggy Dolls team from Sir William Romney School (UK) completed the World Woolsack Championship race in a record time of 3 min 20.01 sec. The Annual Woolsack Champion Races, held in Tetbury, Glos, UK, involve relay teams of four runners that run up and down a steep hill while carrying a huge 27.2-kg (60-lb) bag of wool on their shoulders.

★ Tallest erected maypole
A maypole 38.89 m (127 ft 7 in) tall was erected in New Westminster, British Columbia, Canada, on 20 May 1995. A maypole dance was performed around it on 27 May 1995.

★ Most participants in a ground-breaking ceremony
On 27 September 2003, 2,453 people dug with shovels simultaneously to break the ground for the new Providence Newberg Medical Center in Newberg, Oregon, USA.

★ Largest bonfire
The largest bonfire measured 37.5 m (123 ft) high, and had a base of 8 m² (86 ft²) and an overall volume of 800 m³ (28,251 ft³). The event was organized by Kure Commemorative Centennial Events Committee and lit on 9 February 2003 at Gohara-cho, Hiroshima, Japan, as part of a traditional ceremony to encourage good health and a generous harvest.

★ Thickest make-up
The thickest three-dimensional make-up is Chutti, unique to the southwest Indian Kathakali dance-theatre tradition. The villainous Redbeard characters have mask-like attachments that are built up using rice paste and paper and which extend 15 cm (6 in) from the face. The make-up takes hours to apply and the colours used, together with the styles of the costumes, denote the different nature of each of the characters.

★ Largest annual gathering of women
In February or March each year, over 1 million women gather at the Attukal Bhagavathy Temple, Thiruvananthapuram, Kerala, India, for the 'Pongala' offering. The women, who come from all religions and communities in Kerala, gather with their cooking pots to perform a ritual for the health and prosperity of their families. The highest ever attendance was 1.5 million women at the festival on 23 February 1997. The ceremony, which involves cooking rice as an offering to the deity, lasts six hours.

★ Largest gathering of giant papier-mâché models
A total of 215 papier-mâché giants, made by 88 organizations, were gathered at Solsona, Catalonia, Spain, on 6 July 2003 to celebrate the third annual Colla Gegantera del Carnaval de Solsona. The origins of this tradition are unknown, although many European countries have adopted the practice of having these giants dance down the streets as part of their festival celebrations. In Catalonia, the earliest known records are from the 14th century when models of the biblical characters David and Goliath were created for the procession of the feast of Corpus Christi in Barcelona, Spain.

Fastest snail ⌄

The annual World Snail Racing Championships held every July at Congham, Norfolk, UK,

is conducted on a 33-cm (13-in) circular course outside St Andrews Church. The 'runners' (below) race from the centre to the perimeter. Some race several times as they are divided into heats to cater for the 150 snail competitors who enter every year. The all-time record holder is a snail named Archie, trained by Carl Bramham (UK), who sprinted to the winning post in 2 min 20 sec in 1995.

Largest ⌃ annual food fight

On the last Wednesday in August the town of Buñol near Valencia, Spain, holds its annual tomato festival, the Tomatina (above).

In 1999, 25,000 people spent one hour at this giant food fight throwing about 125 tonnes (275,500 lb) of tomatoes at each other. From the backs of lorries, attendants dump the red fruit on to the streets for people to scoop up and throw. By the time the food fight is over, the streets and everyone on them is saturated with sloppy tomato paste. Rivers of tomato juice, as much as 30 cm (12 in) deep, run through the town until area fire engines come in to hose down the streets and the people on them. The Tomatina was first held in 1944.

★ **Longest firework waterfall**
The 'Niagara Falls' measured 3,125.79 m (10,255 ft 2.5 in) when ignited on 24 August 2003 at the Ariake Seas Fireworks Festival, Fukuoka, Japan.

★ **Largest jazz festival**
The Festival International de Jazz de Montreal in Québec, Canada, lasts 11 days over June and July each year and attracts more than 1.5 million people who watch around 400 concerts.

★ **Largest beer festival**
Oktoberfest '99 (Munich, Germany), held 18 September–5 October, was visited by

7 million people who consumed a record 5.8 million litres (1.27 million gal) of beer in 11 beer tents covering an area as large as 50 soccer pitches.

★ **Largest maple syrup festival**
The 36th annual Elmira Maple Syrup Festival held in Elmira, Ontario, Canada, attracted 66,529 people on 1 April 2000.

★ **Largest frogs' leg festival**
The Fellsmere Frogs' Leg Festival held in Fellsmere, Florida, USA, annually attracts 75,000 visitors. Between 18 and 21 January 2001, more than

3,000 kg (6,600 lb) of battered fried frogs' legs were served during the free four-day festival to a total of 13,200 diners.

★ **Largest garlic festival**
The three-day Gilroy Garlic Festival, held each summer in Gilroy, California, USA, attracts 130,000 people, who can sample garlic-flavoured food ranging from meat to ice cream. The event begins with the lighting of a 7.6-m-high (25-ft) garlic bulb effigy.

★ **Longest festival snake**
On 27 August 2000, 500 people were required to carry a monstrous 82.8-m-long (271-ft 7-in), 2-tonne (4,400-lb) serpent made of bamboo and rice straw through the village of Sekikawa, Japan, in honour of the 12th annual Taishita Monja Festival.

★ **Largest audience at a camel wrestling festival**
At the 1994 Camel Wrestling Festival in Selçuk, Turkey, 20,000 people gathered to watch 120 dromedaries wrestle in a

2,000-year-old stadium in Ephesus. There are around 1,200 specially bred wrestling camels in Turkey – known as tulu camels – and the sport extends over the Marmara, Aegean and Mediterranean coasts of western Turkey.

★ **Largest monkey buffet**
The Kala Temple (also known as Monkey Temple) in Lopburi province, north of Bangkok, Thailand, provides an annual spread of tropical fruit and vegetables weighing 3,000 kg (6,600 lb) for the local population of about 2,000 monkeys to enjoy.

★ **Largest origami paper crane**
On 20–21 January 2001, an origami paper crane with a wingspan of 78.19 m (256 ft 6 in) was folded by 1,000 people at the Odate Jukai Dome in Odate City, Japan. The participants, mostly residents of Odate, spent eight hours on the first day sticking 80 pieces of paper together, creating a sheet of 80 m² (861 ft²). It took another 8 hr 40 min to fold the crane.

Material world

Contents

Most expensive mass-produced yo-yo

Cold Fusion and Cold Fusion GT yo-yos, manufactured by Playmaxx Inc., (USA) retail between $150 and $250 (£90 and £150). There is also a special version called Gold Fusion (below), which is plated with 24 carat gold and sells for between $200 and $300 (£120 and £180). In 1998 Playmaxx, Inc., generated approximately $96 million (£57.9 million) in retail sales and was given the Craze of the Year Award by the British Toy Association.

Most valuable grass

On 17 May 2000, Ken Bates (UK), then Chairman of Chelsea Football Club, paid £20,000 ($29,884) for a piece of turf from London's Wembley Stadium. The area of grass is fondly remembered by English football fans as the spot on the goal line where, during the 1966 World Cup final against Germany, the ball landed for the controversial goal scored by Geoff Hurst (above right, with German goalkeeper Hans Tilkowski). At this rate, the entire pitch would have cost around £800 million ($1.2 billion).

The cage-cup is so called because the body and base of the vessel are completely surrounded by a delicate network or 'cage' of glass. Cage-cups were owned by the very wealthiest of Roman society, and this is the only remaining example known to be in private hands.

★ Most valuable bicycle
An 1891 diamond-frame safety bicycle was sold at Phillips, London, UK, in August 1999 for £105,000 ($170,310), breaking the previous record for a bicycle sold at auction by over 200%.

★ Most valuable glass
A record £520,000 ($1,078,480) was paid at auction for a Roman glass cage-cup of c. AD 300 known as the 'Constable-Maxwell cage-cup'. It measures 17 cm (7 in) in diameter and 10 cm (4 in) in height, and sold at Sotheby's, London, UK, on 4 June 1979 to Robin Symes (UK) on behalf of the British Rail Pension Fund.

★ Most valuable single music manuscript
The greatest amount a single-page music manuscript has raised at auction is £1,326,650 ($1,932,398), paid for the earliest draft of Ludwig van Beethoven's (Germany) Ninth Symphony at Sotheby's, London, UK, on 17 May 2002. The buyer was an anonymous telephone bidder.

★ Most valuable music manuscripts
The auction record for a musical manuscript is £2,585,000 ($4,340,215), paid by UK dealer James Kirkman at Sotheby's, London, UK, on 22 May 1987 for a 508-page, 21.6 x 16.5-cm (8.5 x 6.5-in) bound volume of nine complete symphonies written in Wolfgang Amadeus Mozart's (Austria) hand.

★ Most valuable coin collection
The highest price ever paid for a coin collection is $44.9 million (£31.8 million) for the Eliasberg Collection, which was sold over three auctions in 1982, 1996 and 1997 at Bowers and Merena Galleries, New Hampshire, USA. From the 1930s until 1950, Louis E Eliasberg Snr (USA), a leading Baltimore financier, attempted and accomplished what had never been tried before – to collect an example of every major US coin variety from the 1793 half cent to the 1933 double eagle.

★ Most valuable clock
The world record for a clock sold at auction is £1,926,500 ($3,001,294), paid for a Louis XVI ormulu-mounted ebony grande sonnerie astronomical perpetual calendar regulateur de parquet at Christie's, London, UK, on 8 July 1999.

★ Most valuable carpet
A Louis XV Savonnerie carpet measuring 5.4 x 5.8 m (18 x 19 ft), which was probably made for Louis XV's Château de la Mouette c. 1740–50, fetched $4,406,000 (£2,993,512) at Christie's, New York, USA, in November 2000.

★ Most valuable philatelic item
A letter to wine merchants in Bordeaux, France, dated 1847 and franked with 1d (one penny) and 2d (two penny) first-issue stamps from Mauritius was bought anonymously in under a minute for CHF6,123,750 ($4,075,165 or £2,811,639) in a sale conducted by David Feldman (Ireland) at the Hotel International in Zürich, Switzerland, on 3 November 1993.

Most valuable edible fungus

A white truffle (*tuber magnatum pico*) ⌄
weighing 1 kg (2 lb 3 oz) was sold

in November 2002 for a record $35,000 (£22,011) at the annual charity truffle auction held simultaneously in Los Angeles, New York, USA, and Alba in northern Italy, where the giant fungus was unearthed. It was bought by Joe Pytka (USA), owner of the Bastide restaurant in Los Angeles, California, USA, and prepared by head chef Alain Giraud (France, right, with the truffle).

★ **Most valuable kaleidoscope**
A fine English kaleidoscope in a mahogany case (c.1830) sold at Christie's, London, UK, in November 1999 for £45,500 ($74,934).

★ **Most valuable comic**
The world's most valuable comic is the 1939 'Pay Copy' of *Marvel Comics* No. 1, which was sold to Jay Parrino's The Mint (USA) for $350,000 (£240,533) in November 2001. It is called the 'Pay Copy' because some of its pages have notations relating to the payments to the creators of each piece.

★ **Most valuable horse**
Cash Run, a six-year-old broodmare, was purchased on behalf of the Coolmore Stud for $7,100,000 (£4,186,814) by John Magnier (Ireland) in Lexington, Kentucky, USA, on 3 November 2003.

★ **Most valuable letter**
The highest price ever paid on the open market for a single signed letter was $748,000 (£418,228). This was paid on

5 December 1991 at Christie's, New York, USA, for a letter written by Abraham Lincoln (USA) on 8 January 1863 defending the Emancipation Proclamation. It was sold to Profiles in History of Beverly Hills, California, USA.

★ **Most valuable jewel**
A 'D' colour internally flawless pear-shaped diamond weighing 100.1 carats was sold for CHF19,858,500 (£10,548,444 or $16,561,171) at Sotheby's, Geneva, Switzerland, on 17 May 1995. 'D' is the highest grade given to diamonds and indicates that the diamond is the finest white.

★ **Most valuable jewellery collection**
The world's largest jewellery collection, which included a Van Cleef and Arpels 1939 ruby and diamond necklace, belonged to Wallis Simpson, the Duchess of Windsor (USA). It realized £31,380,197 ($50,427,977) when sold at Sotheby's, Geneva, Switzerland, on 3 April 1987.

★ **Most valuable telephone number**
The most valuable telephone number is 8888-8888. It was bought by a bidder representing Sichuan Airlines Co. Ltd (China) on 19 August 2003 for 2.33 million yuan ($280,723 or £177,209) during an auction in Chengdu, China, of more than 100 telephone numbers. Eight is considered lucky in China as it is similar to the Cantonese word for 'getting rich'.

★ **Most valuable Old Master painting**
The Massacre of the Innocents by Peter Paul Rubens (Netherlands) was sold at Sotheby's, London, UK, for a record £49.5 million ($76.7 million) on 10 July 2002 to David Thomson (Canada), chairman of the Thomson Newspapers empire.

★ **Most valuable Old Master drawing**
The record for most valuable Old Master drawing is held jointly between *The Risen Christ* by Michelangelo Buonarroti

(Italy) sold in July 2000 and *Horse and Rider* by Leonardo da Vinci (Italy) sold in July 2001. Both raised £8,143,750 ($12,212,449 [2000] and $11,440,340 [2001]) at Christie's, London, UK.

★ **Most valuable photograph**
Athènes, 1842, a photograph taken of the Athenian Temple of Olympian Zeus on the Acropolis in Athens, Greece, sold at Christie's, London, UK, for £565,250 ($922,488) on 20 May 2003. It was taken in 1842 by the 19th-century French artist and historian Joseph Philibert Girault de Prangey.

★ **Most valuable illuminated manuscript**
The Rothschild Prayerbook (c.1505), an illuminated manuscript, sold for £8,580,000 ($13,400,000) at Christie's, London, UK, on 8 July 1999. For the four-hour-long sale, 380 seats had been pre-booked and 70 phones were in use. The entire sale made nearly three times its high pre-sale estimate.

Largest « bobblehead

Standing 3.35 m (11 ft) tall and in the likeness of game show host Chuck Woolery (left), the world's largest bobblehead weighs 408 kg (900 lb).

It was created by the Game Show Network (USA) and displayed at McCormick Place, Chicago, Illinois, USA, on 8 June 2003. The head on this oversized novelty item really bobbles.

Largest rubber ⩓ band ball

John J Bain (USA, above) constructed a rubber band ball with a circumference of 4.59 m (15 ft 1 in) that weighed 1,415.2 kg (3,120 lb) when measured on 22 October 2003 at the Port Contractors in Wilmington, Delaware, USA.

★ **Largest condom**
A 21.94-m-tall (72-ft) condom was fitted over the obelisk in the Place de la Concorde, Paris, France, on 1 December 1993 to mark World AIDS Day. The condom was funded by Italian clothes firm Benetton.

★ **Largest beer bottle**
A beer bottle measuring 2.54 m (8 ft 4 in) tall and 2.17 m (7 ft 1.5 in) in circumference was unveiled at the Shepherd Neame Brewery in Faversham, Kent, UK, on 27 January 1993. It took 13 minutes to fill the bottle with 625.5 litres (137.5 gal) of Kingfisher beer.

★ **Largest beach towel**
A beach towel depicting the Walt Disney character Mickey Mouse measures 9.4 x 14.46 m (30 ft 10 in x 47 ft 5 in). It was manufactured by Maiden Sunshine (Spain) and displayed at the textile fair 'Textile Hogar' held in Valencia, Spain, on 25 January 2000.

★ **Largest continental broom**
On 3 January 2002 a continental (witch's) broom constructed by Comitato Festeggiamenti Campagnari (Italy) measured 22.19 m (72 ft 9.5 in). The handle alone measured 12.11 m (39 ft 8.75 in).

★ **Largest boomerang**
A boomerang made from wood, plywood and steel and measuring 1.81 m (5 ft 11.25 in) from tip to tip was successfully thrown by Heikki Niskanen (Finland) at Kuopio, Finland, on 5 June 2000. The boomerang travelled past the qualifying 20-m (65-ft) mark and returned into the accuracy circle from where it was thrown.

★ **Largest ceramic plate**
A plate created by the Inatsu Town Planning Association (Japan) on 14 August 1996 measured 2.8 m (9 ft 2 in) in diameter. Made from 1,220 kg (2,690 lb) of clay, it was left to dry out for five months before being painted and finally baked in a kiln for seven days.

★ **Largest flag draped**
The American 'Superflag' owned by 'Ski' Demski (USA) measures 154 x 78 m (505 x 255 ft) and weighs 1.36 tonnes (3,000 lb). It was made by Humphrey's Flag Co. (USA), delivered to Demski on 14 June 1992 and unfurled in 1996 at the Hoover Dam on the

Colorado River, Arizona/Nevada, USA, to mark the passing of the Olympic Torch.

★ **Largest disco ball**
Derek Dyer (USA) has built a disco ball 10 ft (3 m) in diameter that weighs 453.5 kg (1,000 lb). It was unveiled at the Salt Palace in Salt Lake City, Utah, USA, on 31 December 2002.

★ **Largest drum**
A drum made from Japanese cedar and cowhide measuring 4.80 m (15 ft 9 in) in diameter, 4.95 m (16 ft 3 in) deep and weighing 2,000 kg (4,400 lb) was built by the Asano Taiko Company Ltd (Japan). The final section of the drum was completed just a few hours before its first performance on 1 January 2001.

★ **Largest kettle**
A copper kettle that stood 0.9 m (3 ft) high, with a 1.8-m (6-ft) girth and a 90-litre (20-gal) capacity, was built in Taunton, Somerset, UK, c. 1800, for the hardware merchants Fisher and Son.

Largest dental caps

Dental caps approximately 50 cm (19 in) long, 13 cm (5 in) in diameter and weighing 13 kg (28 lb) each were fixed on to a pair of cracked tusks belonging to Spike (below), a resident Asian elephant at the Calgary Zoo, Alberta, Canada, during a 3 hr 30 min operation on 4 July 2002. The stainless steel caps were designed and manufactured by the Southern Alberta Institute of Technology with metal donated by Corus Steel and adhesive by 3M (all Canada).

Largest accordion ⌃

The largest playable accordion in the world (above) is 2.53 m (8 ft 3.5 in) tall, 1.9 m (6 ft 2.75 in) wide, 85 cm (2 ft 9.5 in) deep, and weighs approximately 200 kg (440 lb). The instrument, built by Giancarlo Francenella (Italy), was begun in 2000 and finished in 2001. The giant accordion took over 1,000 hours to create and features 45 treble piano keys, 120 bass buttons and 240 reeds. Built on a 5:1 ratio from the original, the instrument is made of wood (fir, cedar, mahogany and walnut), metals (aluminium and steel), cardboard, cloth and special varnishes.

★ **Largest flute**
The largest playable flute is 1.52 m (5 ft) long and 8.89 cm (3.5 in) in diameter and was made out of PVC by Dinesh Shandilya (India) in 1996.

★ **Largest fountain pen**
A pen made by Zbigniew Rozanek (Poland) in 1991 measured 2.22 m (7 ft) long and 11 cm (4 in) in diameter and had a 48-cm (18-in) nib. The weight of the pen, including ink, was 9.5 kg (20 lb). Without ink it weighed 3.3 kg (7 lb).

★ **Largest jukebox**
A jukebox named 'The Wall', which stood 12.6 m (41 ft 4 in) high and 19.2 m (63 ft) wide, was built by Namco Ltd (Japan) and unveiled in Sunshine Namjatown, Tokyo, Japan, in July 1996. Various features on the jukebox come to life when the music begins.

★ **Largest hourglass**
The largest hourglass stands 1.06 m (42 in) tall with a diameter of 38 cm (15 in). Built by Bob Ciscell (USA), the hourglass contains 29.4 kg (65 lb) of sand, which takes eight hours to run through.

★ **Largest carpet of flowers**
A carpet of flowers measuring 2,040 m² (21,958 ft²) was created by the Dubai Municipality at the Dubai Shopping Festival, Dubai, UAE, on 12 February 2003.

★ **Largest set of windchimes**
A 5.1-m-tall (16-ft 8-in) set of windchimes built by Steve Kubler (USA) in May 2002 stands in front of the West Point Town Hall, Alabama, USA.

★ **Largest piggy bank**
A piggy bank called Pink Pig measured 3.28 m tall, 5 m long and 7.9 m in circumference (10 ft 9 in x 16 ft 8 in x 26 ft 2 in) on 8 November 2002. Pink Pig is owned by C Michael Davenport (USA).

★ **Largest wreath**
An advent wreath measuring 50 m (164 ft) in diameter was made from fir by Otter-Zentrum Hankensbüttel and Landfrauen Isenhagener (both Germany) on 25 November 2002.

★ **Longest paperclip chain made by an individual**
Between 13 and 14 February 2004, Dan Meyer (USA) created a paperclip chain 1,627.6 m (5,340 ft) long, consisting of 54,030 3-cm-long (1.2-in) clips. The chain is nearly three times longer than the height of the CN Tower in Toronto, Canada.

★ **Largest garland**
A 4,434-m (14,550-ft) paper flower garland (or lei) was made by local citizens at the Hyatt Regency Waikiki, Honolulu, Hawaii, USA, on 19 December 1992.

★ **Largest ball of string**
From 1989 to 1992, JC Payne (USA) amassed enough string to create a ball 4.03 m (13 ft 2.5 in) in diameter and 12.65 m (41 ft 6 in) in circumference.

Largest autographed ⌄ drumstick collection

Since 1980, Peter Lavinger (USA, below) has accumulated over 1,300 drumsticks, all of which have been played and handed to him by drummers from various popular bands, including Ringo Starr of The Beatles. He caught his first drumstick from the front row of a Good Rats concert in 1980.

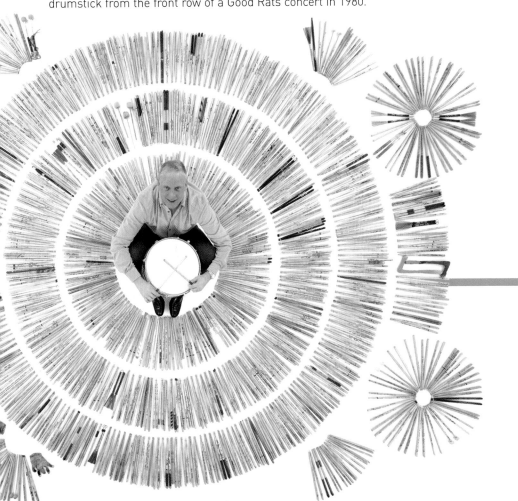

Largest ⌃ collection of yo-yos

John 'Lucky' Meisenheimer (USA, above) has a collection of 4,251 yo-yos, which he has amassed since 1971. His current collection is housed in 23 custom-made cases and is estimated to be worth around $100,000 (£63,167).

He also has a photo of himself with his all-time football hero Paul Merson.

★ **Largest collection of uncut bank notes**
Leigh Follestad (Canada) has 123 sheets of uncut bank notes from 33 countries, representing 73 denominations, which he has been collecting since 1982.

★ **Largest jet-fighter collection**
The world's biggest private collection of jet fighters numbers 110 and belongs to French winemaker Michel Pont. His collection started in 1985 and includes Russian MiGs, British Jaguars and French Mirages. Michel buys the jets from governments, but is not permitted to fly the aircraft over French airspace. He also has a collection of 500 motorbikes, and 24 Fiat Abarth racing cars.

★ **Largest beer bottle collection**
The largest collection of beer bottles in the world is owned by Peter Broeker (Germany), who has amassed 12,548 bottles since 1980. The collection derives from 2,440 different breweries within 153 countries. Peter estimates that if all of his beer bottles were piled one on top of each other they would reach to a height of 3,043 m (9,983 ft), which is almost eight times the height of the Empire State building in New York, USA.

★ **Largest passport collection**
Guy Van Keer (Belgium) owns 7,637 passports and documents used in lieu of passports. They represent 130 countries and passport-issuing authorities, including many countries that no longer exist. The passports date from 1615 to the present day. The collection's most expensive item is a rare Chinese passport from 1898 valued at £28,032 ($52,830).

★ **Largest collection of coloured vinyl records**
Alessandro Benedetti (Italy) has collected 1,180 music records made of coloured vinyl. His collection comprises 866 LPs (792 coloured, 74 with pictures), 291 singles (277 coloured, 14 with pictures) and 23 in unusual shapes.

★ **Largest collection of photographs of professional sporting personalities**
Since 2000, Thomas Gill (UK) has built up a collection of 510 photographs taken of himself with professional footballers. Thomas has photographs of himself with well-known British footballers such as David Beckham, Sir Geoff Hurst and Ryan Giggs.

Largest ›› banana collection

Ken Bannister (USA, right), owner of the International Banana Club Museum in Altadena, California, USA, has 17,000 different banana-related objects that he has amassed since 1972. All are on display in the museum.

★ **Largest collection of royal memorabilia**
Ronny Bragança (Portugal) has a collection of 2,950 pieces of memorabilia relating to Diana, Princess of Wales, which he has accumulated since 1991. He has items from many countries, including Japan, Mexico and Australia. In 1999, he was fortunate enough to purchase a Christmas card signed by Charles and Diana in 1989.

★ **Largest chamber pot collection**
Manfred Klauda (Germany) has amassed 9,400 chamber pots, the earliest dating from the 16th century. Currently his collection can be seen at the Zentrum für Aussergewöhnliche Museen, Munich, Germany.

★ **Largest valid credit card collection**
Walter Cavanagh (USA) has accumulated 1,397 individual valid credit cards. The cost of acquisition to 'Mr Plastic Fantastic' was nil, but they are worth more than $1.65 million (£875,500) in credit. They are kept in a 76.2-m-long (250-ft) wallet – the world's longest.

★ **Largest collection of soft drink cans from the same brand**
Christian Cavaletti (Italy) has a collection of 3,284 different Pepsi cans from 71 different countries. Christian, who has been collecting since 1989, belongs to the two largest soft drink can collectors' clubs: the National Pop Can Collectors (NPCC) and the Pepsi-Cola Collectors Club (PCCC).

★ **Largest ice-lolly stick collection**
Since 1988, Poul Lykke Jepsen (Denmark) has collected 449 different ice-lolly sticks. Poul started collecting lolly sticks after he had eaten two ice creams and noticed that they had different sticks. His collection grew after he got a job as a storage worker in 2001 – his new employers manufactured ice-lolly sticks.

Collections

Collection	Quantity	Holder
airline sickbags	3,307 from 755 airlines	Niek Vermeulen (Netherlands)
airline tags	469 from 115 airlines	Raghav Somani (India)
badges	13,516	Daniel Hedges (UK)
ball-point pens	285,150 from 148 countries	Angelika Unverhau (Germany)
Barbie dolls	1,125	Tony Mattia (UK)
beer cans	75,000 from 125 countries	William B. Christensen (USA)
bottle openers	20,884 from 136 countries	Dale Deckert (USA)
bottled water labels	5,115	Lorenzo Pescini (Italy)
bus tickets (used)	14,000	Yacov Yosipov (Israel)
car bumper stickers	3,230	Bill Heermann (USA)
clothing tags	2,180	Angela Bettelli (Italy)
condoms	1,947	Amatore Bolzoni (Italy)
decorative pins	1,457	Gerhard Kühler (Germany)
five-leaf clovers	31,336	George Kaminski (USA)
fruit stickers	34,500	Antoine Secco (France)
hats	25,777	Tustumena Lodge (USA)
hotel baggage labels	2,016	Robert Henin (USA)
keychains	24,810	Kurt Meadows (USA)
mouse mats	1,947	Daniel Evans (UK)
mugs	4,567	Harold Swauger (USA)
pencils	6,885	Emilio Arenas (Uruguay)
pencil sharpeners	8,514	Demetra Koutsouridou (Greece)
phonecards	4,531 from 239 countries and territories	Harvinder Chohan (Canada)
piggy banks	5,750	Ove Nordström (Sweden)
plasters (unused)	4,500	Brian Viner (UK)
rubber ducks	1,439	Charlotte Lee (USA)
rubber stamps	1,251	James Burton (UK)
shoe horns	1,594	Martien Tuithof (Netherlands)
shot glasses	8,411	Brad Rodgers (USA)
teabag labels	8,661 from 88 countries	Felix Rotler (Germany)
thermometers	4,580	Richard T Porter (USA)
traffic cones	137	David Morgan (UK)

Most valuable model car ⌃

A very rare Dinky green 28 series 2nd Type Bentalls Department Store Promotional Delivery Van with yellow upper side panels and a white roof (above) was sold for £12,650 ($20,147) at Christie's, London, UK, on 14 October 1994. This example is believed to be one of only three known by Christie's experts to have survived.

Most valuable teddy bear ⌃

A Steiff bear named Teddy Girl (above) was sold for £110,000 ($171,600), more than 18 times the estimate and twice the previous world record, by Christie's, London, UK, on 5 December 1994. The buyer was Japanese businessman Yoshihiro Sekiguchi.

★ Largest stitched teddy bear
The bear measuring 11.79 m (38 ft 8.2 in) in length was designed and made by Dana Warren (USA) over a period of six months.

★ Largest model railway engine
A model of *Thomas the Tank Engine* character James, measuring 264 cm high, 150 cm wide, 652 cm long (104 x 59 x 256 in) and weighing nearly 1.52 tonnes (3,351 lb) was built by BBC Visual Effects (UK) for a Thomas the Tank Engine tour in 2003. Models of Thomas, Percy and Gordon were also part of the tour.

★ Largest kite flown
The largest kite ever flown has a total lifting area of 680 m² (7,319.4 ft²). When laid flat, it has a total area of 933 m² (10,042.7 ft²). The 'Megabite', designed by Peter Lynn (New Zealand), measured 64 m (210 ft) long and 22 m (72 ft) wide. The kite was officially measured on 7 September 1997.

★ Longest kite flown
'The Cracken', created by Michel Trouillet (France), measures 1,034.45 m (3,394 ft) in length, with a total mass of 106 kg (233 lb). It was flown by Trouillet and his team on 18 November 1990 in Nîmes, France.

★ Largest spinning top
A team of 25 workers from the Mizushima Plant of Kawasaki Steel Works in Okayama, Japan, created a spinning top measuring 2 m (6 ft 6.75 in) tall and 2.6 m (8 ft 6.25 in) in diameter and weighing 360 kg (793 lb). They spun it for 1 hr 21 min 35 sec on 3 November 1986.

★ Tallest LEGO structure
A LEGO tower built in Tallinn, Estonia, on 18–21 August 1998 reached a height of 24.91 m (81 ft 8.7 in). It consisted of 391,478 plastic, eight-stud toy bricks. Over 6,000 children helped in the construction, which was organized by AS Rekato Ltd (Estonia), to beat the previous record set in Moscow, Russia, in July 1998 by 25 cm (9 in).

★ Longest LEGO structure
A LEGO structure in the shape of a millipede measuring 1,052 m (3,451 ft) and consisting of 2,477,140 bricks, was built by 20,000 children in Bangkok, Thailand, on 27 April 2003.

★ Largest hula hoop spun
The largest hula hoop successfully rotated at least three times around a person's waist had a diameter of 4.08 m (13 ft 4 in). Nozomi Tsuju and Ai Kago (both Japan) rotated the hoop for 30 seconds each at the studios of Nippon Television Network, Tokyo, Japan, on 1 January 2004.

★ Longest Hot Wheels track
The longest Hot Wheels track measured 502.92 m (1,650 ft) and consisted of 2,100 pieces of track, held together by 2,150 connectors. The attempt was organized by Mattel Canada, Inc., for Big Brothers Big Sisters of Canada and was completed on 7 July 2002 at Thunder Alley, Toronto, Ontario, Canada.

★ Largest chess piece
Mats Allanson (Sweden) has made a scaled-up king measuring 4 m (13 ft) high and 1.4 m (4 ft 6 in) in diameter at the base.

Most valuable >> Mickey Mouse toy

A rare clockwork Mickey Mouse motorcycle (c. 1939, right) in its original box sold at Christie's, London, UK, on 16 June 1997 for £51,000 ($83,466).

★ **Earliest chess pieces**
Chessmen found at Nashipur, modern-day Bangladesh, have been dated to c. AD 900 and are the oldest known in existence.

★ **Largest commercially available board game**
Galaxion, manufactured by Cerebe Design International (Hong Kong), is played on a board measuring 83.8 x 83.8 cm (33 x 33 in).

★ **Largest commercially available jigsaw puzzle**
The largest commercially available jigsaw puzzle is made by Ravensburger of Ravensburg, Germany, and measures 2.76 x 1.92 m (9 ft 0.5 in x 6 ft 3.5 in). It has 18,000 pieces – another record for a commercially available jigsaw.

★ **Smallest commercially available jigsaw puzzle**
A 1,000-piece jigsaw puzzle manufactured by Educa Sallent (Spain) measures 46 x 30 cm (18 x 12 in). The miniature puzzles made by Educa Sallent are all made from recycled materials and depict a variety of images, ranging from European landmarks to Disney and Sesame Street characters.

★ **Largest jigsaw puzzle**
A puzzle devised by Great East Asia Surveyors & Consultants Co. Ltd measured 5,428.8 m² (58,435.1 ft²) and consisted of 21,600 pieces in total. It was assembled by 777 people at the former Kai Tak Airport, Hong Kong, China, on 3 November 2002.

★ **Largest set of Russian nesting dolls (matrioshka)**
A 51-piece set of nesting dolls was hand-painted by Youlia Bereznitskaia (Russia). The largest doll is 54 cm (1 ft 9.25 in) in height, while the smallest measures 0.31 cm (0.125 in) in height. The set was completed on 25 April 2003.

★ **Largest ball bath**
The bath had a surface area of 252.9 m² (2,722.2 ft²) with an average depth of 0.4 m (1 ft 4 in) and contained about 130,000 balls. It was made on 30 December 1999 in Plantagebaan, Wouwse Plantage, The Netherlands, by the Stichting Carnaval Wouwse Plantage as part of the festivities for a millennium carnival.

★ **Largest yo-yo**
A yo-yo measuring 3.17 m (10 ft 4 in) in diameter and weighing 407 kg (897 lb) was devised by JN Nichols (Vimto) Ltd (UK) and constructed by engineering students at Stockport College. It was launched by crane from a height of 57.5 m (188 ft 6 in) at Wythenshawe, Greater Manchester, UK, on 1 August 1993 and subsequently yo-yoed about four times.

★ **Largest permanent Monopoly board**
A Monopoly board made of granite and located in San Jose, California, USA, measures 9.44 x 9.44 m (31 x 31 ft). All the playing pieces are proportionally scaled up. The board was opened to the public on 26 July 2002.

Most storeys in a house of cards ≪

The tallest freestanding house of cards was 131 storeys high.

The 7.71-m-tall (25-ft 3.48-in) structure was built by Bryan Berg (USA, left) on 6 November 1999. The house was created using 91,800 cards in the lobby of the casino at Potsdamer Platz, Berlin, Germany, and recorded for the *Guinness die Show der Rekord*. The total weight of the 1,765 packs of cards used was 110 kg (242 lb 8 oz).

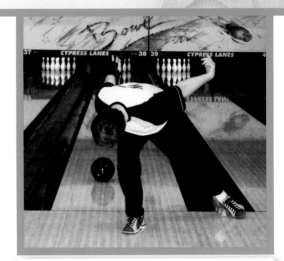

Highest single ⌃ game score when bowling backwards

Del Lawson (USA, above) registered a score of 139 in a single game of backwards bowling at Cypress Lanes, Winter Haven, Florida, USA, on 21 April 2002. He bowled a series of three games with a total score of 376.

★ Most darts bull's-eyes in 10 hours
Perry Prine (USA) hit 1,432 bull's-eyes in 10 hours at the Lake Erie Classic Dart Tournament in Mentor, Ohio, USA, on 27 March 1998.

★ Largest game of Poohsticks
On 22 July 2000 the largest ever game of Poohsticks was played on the River Tweed from the Chain Bridge, Horncliffe, in the Scottish Borders, UK. A total of 2,313 Poohsticks were launched from the bridge to sail downriver to the finishing line at Paxton House Boathouse. A stick stamped 8702 won. Poohsticks is a game invented by AA Milne (UK) of *Winnie the Pooh* fame – Christopher Robin and Pooh threw sticks in the water from one side of a bridge, then ran over to see which stick floated out first on the other side.

★ Farthest wink shot in tiddlywinks
At the Queen's College Tournament, Cambridge, UK, Ben Soares (UK) of the St Andrews Tiddlywinks Society made a wink shot measuring 9.52 m (31 ft 3 in), on 14 January 1995.

★ Most opponents in consecutive chess games
Between 27 and 28 February 2001, Anna-Maria Botsari (Greece) played 1,102 consecutive games of chess against different opponents, with just seven draws and the rest wins, at Kalavryta, Greece.

★ Most simultaneous draughts opponents
Ronald Suki King (Barbados) played 385 games of draughts simultaneously at the Houston International Festival, Texas, USA, on 26 April 1998. King donned rollerskates to move between the 385 games.

★ Largest game of pass the parcel
On 28 February 1998, 3,918 students removed 2,200 wrappers from a parcel measuring 1.5 x 1.5 x 0.5 m (4 ft 11 in x 4 ft 11 in x 1 ft 7 in) in two and a half hours at Nanyang Technological University, Singapore. Owing to the numbers involved, the parcel went round on a trolley and took an hour to complete one circuit.

★ Fastest Jenga tower built to 30 levels
The fastest time to build a stable Jenga tower 30 levels high, within the rules of the game, is 11 min 55 sec by Sabrina Ibrahim, John Chua and Alex Agboola (all UK) on the BBC's *Big Toe Radio Show*, London, UK, on 28 January 2003.

★ Most dominoes set up and toppled single-handedly
Ma Li Hua (China) single-handedly set up and toppled 303,621 dominoes out of a total of 303,628 at Singapore Expo Hall, Singapore, on 18 August 2003. The event was organized by LG Electronics Inc.

★ Most dominoes set up and toppled by a group
The record for most dominoes toppled is 3,847,295 (from a possible 4 million). The attempt was organized by Endemol Netherlands and took place at FEC EXPO, Leeuwarden, The Netherlands, on 15 November 2002. The 4 million dominoes were divided into 51 interconnected projects, all of which related to one central theme.

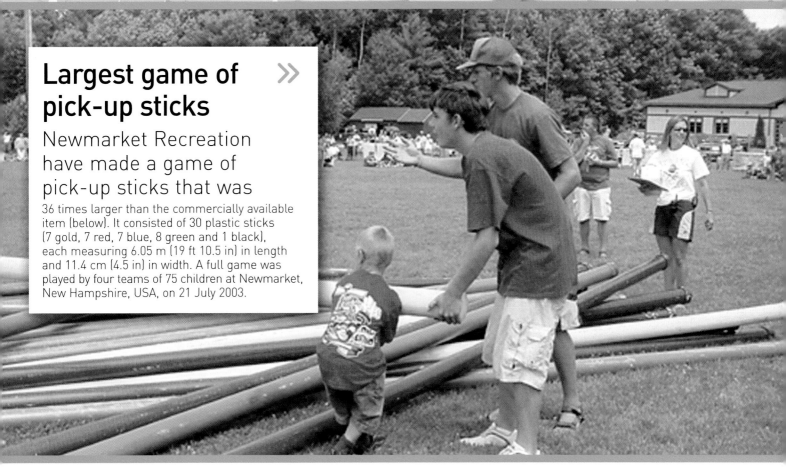

Largest game of pick-up sticks »

Newmarket Recreation have made a game of pick-up sticks that was

36 times larger than the commercially available item (below). It consisted of 30 plastic sticks (7 gold, 7 red, 7 blue, 8 green and 1 black), each measuring 6.05 m (19 ft 10.5 in) in length and 11.4 cm (4.5 in) in width. A full game was played by four teams of 75 children at Newmarket, New Hampshire, USA, on 21 July 2003.

★ **Most dominoes stacked on a single domino**
Matthias Aisch (Germany) stacked 726 dominoes on a single vertically standing supporting domino on 28 December 2003 in Radeburg, Germany. The stack remained standing for an hour.

★ **Largest quiz**
A record 888 participants took part in a quiz at the Radisson SAS Hotel, Galway, Ireland, on 14 October 2003. Teams of four answered 10 rounds of 12 questions.

★ **Fastest time to solve a Rubik's cube**
The fastest time to solve a Rubik's cube in an official championship was 16.53 sec by Jess Bonde (Denmark) at the 2003 World Championships in Toronto, Ontario, Canada.

★ **Fastest time to solve a Rubik's cube blindfolded**
The fastest time to solve a Rubik's cube in an official championship while blindfolded is 3 min 56 sec by Dror Vomberg (Israel) at the 2003 World Championships in Toronto, Ontario, Canada.

★ **Highest overall Scrabble score**
Phil Appleby (UK) achieved a Scrabble score of 1,049 on 25 June 1989 at Wormley, Herts, UK. His opponent scored 253 and the margin of victory, 796 points, is also a record.

★ **Largest sack race competition**
A total of 2,095 Dutch students – from Agnieton College and primary schools in Zwolle, Wezep and Hattem, The Netherlands, took part in a sack race on 11 October 2002 in Zwolle, The Netherlands.

★ **Most participants in a wheelbarrow race**
The largest wheelbarrow race involved 318 people (159 pairs) and took place at Alexandra Park, London, UK, on 31 August 2002 in an attempt organized by Starwood Hotels & Resorts, London, UK.

★ **Largest game of leapfrog**
A total of 849 people took part in a game of leapfrog at Brookfield Community School, Chesterfield, Derbyshire, UK, on 26 September 2003.

★ **Highest altitude by a single kite**
Richard P Synergy (Canada) flew a kite to an altitude of approximately 4,422 m (14,509 ft) above the point of take-off on 12 August 2000 near Kincardine, Ontario, Canada. The kite, a high-tech delta, had an area of 25 m² (270 ft²) and was designed and built by Synergy himself. At its maximum altitude the kite had 7.31 km (4.5 miles) of woven kevlar line connecting it to a winch on the ground. The record-breaking flight lasted 8 hr 35 min.

★ **Most powerful games console**
Microsoft's Xbox is powered by a 733-MHz Intel CPU, the fastest of any current games console. Its graphics processor, a custom-designed chip that runs at 250 MHz, is also the field leader. The Xbox's main rivals, the Sony Playstation 2 and Nintendo GameCube, have CPU clock speeds of 300 and 405 MHz respectively, and graphics chips running at 150 and 202.5 MHz respectively.

★ **Best selling Xbox game**
According to *Screen Digest*, the best selling Xbox game is 'Halo', which had sold 4 million units as of December 2003.

★ **Best selling Playstation 2 game**
According to *Screen Digest*, the best selling Playstation 2 game is 'Grand Theft Auto Vice City', which had sold 9 million units as of December 2003.

★ **Best selling GameCube game**
The best selling GameCube game is 'Mario Sunshine', which had sold 3.5 million units as of December 2003 according to *Screen Digest*.

Food & drink 1

« Largest popcorn sculpture

The world's largest popcorn sculpture (left) is 4 m (13 ft) tall and 2.67 m (8 ft 9 in) wide and is made in the likeness of King Kong. The giant popcorn ape was displayed in front of Leicester Square's Odeon cinema, London, UK, on 24 July 2003 to celebrate the 70th anniversary of the original *King Kong* film (USA, 1933).

Largest gingerbread man «

Chefs at the Hyatt Regency Hotel, Vancouver, Canada, made a gingerbread man (above) that measured 4.23 m (13 ft 11 in) high, 1.72 m (5 ft 8 in) wide and 5.08 cm (2 in) deep, on 19 November 2003. The gingerbread figure weighed 168.8 kg (372 lb 1.82 oz).

★ Curly Wurly stretching

Craig Glenday (UK) stretched a Curly Wurly chocolate bar a total distance of 0.91 m (3 ft) in three minutes at the offices of Guinness World Records, London, UK, on 27 June 2003.

★ Fastest sandwich made using only feet

Using just his feet, Rob Williams (USA) made a Bologna cheese and lettuce sandwich, complete with sliced tomatoes, mustard, mayonnaise, sliced pickles and olives on cocktail sticks, in 1 min 57 sec on the set of *Guinness World Records: Primetime*, Los Angeles, California, USA, on 10 November 2000.

★ Fastest time to husk a coconut using only teeth

In 28.06 seconds, Sidaraju S Raju (India) husked a coconut measuring 78 cm (30.7 in) in circumference and weighing 4.74 kg (10 lb 6.4 oz) using only his teeth at the Ravindra Kalashetra, Bangalore, India, on 30 March 2003.

★ Fastest time to drink two pints of stout

Scott Williams (Canada) drank two pints of Guinness in 6.3 seconds on 23 May 2003.

★ Most Brussels sprouts eaten in one minute

Dave Mynard (UK) consumed 43 cooked Brussels sprouts in 1 minute on 10 December 2003.

★ Most ice cream eaten in 30 seconds

Diego Siu (USA) ate 264 g (9.3 oz) of ice cream in 30 seconds at the Central Florida Fair, Orlando, USA, on 2 March 2003.

★ Fastest time to eat raw onion

In only 2 min 40 sec Danny Healy (UK) ate a raw onion weighing 212 g (7.47 oz) at the BBC Television Centre, London, UK, on 15 November 2003.

★ Greatest egg-dropping height

The greatest height from which fresh eggs have been dropped to the ground and remained intact is 213 m (700 ft) by David Donoghue (UK), who dropped a number of eggs from a helicopter on to a golf course in Blackpool, Lancs, UK, on 22 August 1994.

★ Most eggs crushed with wrist

KS Raghavendra (India) crushed 13 eggs with the back of his wrist in 30 seconds at the Sree Rama Vidyalaya School, Bangalore, India, on 9 September 2003.

★ Farthest marshmallow nose-blow

Scott Jeckel (USA) blew a marshmallow out of one nostril a distance of 4.96 m (16 ft 3.5 in), caught in the mouth of Ray Perisin (USA), on the set of *Guinness World Records: Primetime*, Los Angeles, California, USA, on 13 August 1999.

★ Most baked beans eaten in five minutes

Andy Szerbini (UK) ate a total of 226 baked beans in 5 minutes using a cocktail stick at London Zoo, UK, on 18 November 1996.

Most Smarties eaten in three minutes

The record for the most Smarties eaten in three minutes using chopsticks is held by Kathryn Ratcliffe (UK, below), who ate 138 Smarties at the Metro Centre, Gateshead, Tyne and Wear, UK, on 25 October 2003, breaking her own record of 112.

Most expensive burger ⌃

The DB Burger Royale (above), created by chef Daniel Boulud (France), is available on the menu of DB Bistro Moderne, New York, USA, for $59 (£32.47). The original DB burger was created to mark DB Bistro Moderne's opening in 2001, and the restaurant added the DB Royale burger to the menu in January 2003. It is served exclusively in the black truffle season.

★ **Most baked beans flicked**
The largest quantity of baked beans flicked from a bathtub into a bucket is 982 g (34.63 oz) by Jamie Rickers (UK) on GMTV's programme *Up On The Roof*, London, UK, on 30 October 2002.

★ **Most expensive cocktail commercially available**
The Ritz Side Car, costing €400 (£277.25), features on the cocktail menu at Bar Hemingway, in the Hotel Ritz, Paris, France. The cocktail was invented by head barman Frank Meier in 1923 and contains Ritz Fine Champagne 1865 (pre-phylloxéra) Cognac, Cointreau and lemon juice. The cocktail could be bought for just $5 in 1923. (In terms of purchase power, the current-day equivalent of this figure is £37.24.)

★ **Longest champagne cork flight**
Heinrich Medicus (USA) ejected a cork from an untreated and unheated champagne bottle standing 1.22 m (4 ft) from level ground to a distance of 54.18 m (177 ft 9 in) at the Woodbury Vineyards Winery, New York, USA, on 5 June 1988.

★ **Most grapes stuffed in the mouth**
Michael Levinson (Canada) stuffed 54 seedless grapes, weighing 113 g (4 oz), into his mouth on the set of *Guinness World Records: Primetime* in Los Angeles, California, USA, on 27 September 1999.

★ **Most candles on a cake**
The St Ignatius Cub Scouts (USA) lit 12,432 candles on an iced cake measuring 190.5 x 63.5 cm (75 x 25 in) as part of Ohio's bicentennial celebrations on 9 May 2003.

★ **Most champagne bottles sabred in one minute**
Using a sabre, Dean Opsal (USA) cut off the upper portion of the neck from each of 20 champagne bottles at the Coeur d'Alene Resort Hotel, Coeur d'Alene, Idaho, USA, on 31 October 2001. He achieved this in one minute and without shattering the glass, leaving the contents safe to drink.

★ **Most cherry stems knotted in three minutes**
Al Gliniecki (USA) tied 39 cherry stems into knots with his tongue in three minutes at the Guinness World of Records Experience, Orlando, Florida, USA, on 26 January 1999.

★ **Oldest restaurant**
Restaurante Botín in Calle de Cuchilleros, Madrid, Spain, was opened in 1725 by a French cook called Jean Botín and his Asturian wife. Today the restaurant is run by the third generation of the Gonzalez family, Antonio and Jose Gonzalez (all Spain). Located in the heart of Madrid near the Plaza Mayor it now has four floors which retain the original 18th-century interiors as well as the original firewood oven.

Food & drink 2
Material world

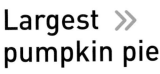

Largest >> pumpkin pie

The largest pumpkin pie (below) weighed 189.6 kg (418 lb).

It was made by the Windsor Certified Farmers Market and the Windsor High School Culinary Arts Program (both USA) and served at the Farmers Market, Windsor, California, USA, on 26 October 2003. The pie was 1.936 m (6 ft 4 in) in diameter and 7.62 cm (3 in) deep.

★ Longest sesame twist
The longest sesame twist measured 1.5 m (4 ft 10.8 in) and was made by chefs at Guifa Xiang, Tianjin, China, on 1 December 1999. A sesame twist is a traditional Chinese delicacy made from fried dough with a crispy stuffing.

★ Largest bag of cookies
The largest bag of cookies was made by Loblaws Supermarkets Ltd and was 3.29 m (10 ft 8 in) high, 2.13 m (7 ft) deep and 1.14 m (45 in) wide. It contained 3,852 trays, each with 26 cookies, making a total of 100,152. It went on display at Loblaws Wonderland Market, London, Ontario, Canada, between 6 and 7 September 2001.

★ Largest lollipop
The largest lollipop weighed 2,158.7 kg (4,759 lb 1.6 oz) and was made by Franssons (Sweden) for a festival in Gränna, Sweden, on 27 July 2003. The lollipop was 1.98 m (6 ft 6 in) wide, 3 m (9 ft 10 in) long and 24 cm (9.5 in) thick and was peppermint-striped like traditional Gränna rock.

★ Largest marzipan sweet
The world's largest pistachio marzipan sweet weighed 4.2 tonnes (9,255 lb) and was made by 225 chefs in an event organized by Spacetel Syria at Hamadanya Stadium, Aleppo, Syria, on 1 July 2003.

★ Largest bowl of pasta
The largest ever bowl of pasta weighed 1,480 kg (3,265 lb), excluding the weight of the bowl. It was created by Nintendo of America, Inc., in conjunction with Buca Di Beppo restaurants (USA) on 22 August 2002 in Washington Square, San Francisco, USA. The fibreglass bowl measured 0.91 m (3 ft) high and 3.048 m (10 ft) wide.

★ Longest salami
A salami measuring 151.89 m (498 ft 3.6 in) was made by the Association of Friulian Butchers and the Udine Chamber of Commerce (both Italy) and was displayed at the Piazza San Giacomo, Udine, Italy, on 13 October 2002. The average circumference of the salami was 14 cm (5.5 in) and the entire salami weighed 269 kg (590.8 lb).

★ Largest serving of fish and chips
The largest serving of fish and chips had a combined weight of 32.66 kg (72 lb) and was made by Fedics Food Services, Port Elizabeth, Eastern Cape, South Africa, on 22 November 2003. Individually, the fish weighed 14.30 kg (31 lb 8 oz) and the chips weighed 18.36 kg (40 lb 8 oz).

★ Largest cup of coffee
On 29 January 2002, Ettore Diana and Luca Braguti (both Italy) made a 1,500-litre (329.95-gal) cappuccino at the Hotel Leon d'Oro, Verona, Italy.

★ Largest tea bag
The world's largest tea bag was made by Lipton Yellow Label of Lever Brothers Pakistan Ltd on 22 June 2002. The tea bag weighed 8.9 kg (19 lb 10 oz) and was displayed at the Avari Towers Hotel, Karachi, Pakistan. The giant tea bag measured 3.18 m (10 ft) long and 2.21 m (7 ft 3 in) wide, and attached to the tea bag was a string measuring 4.26 m (14 ft) long. The bag was made from original filter paper and contained 7 kg (15 lb 7 oz) of black tea. It is estimated that 3,500 cups of tea could be made from the tea bag.

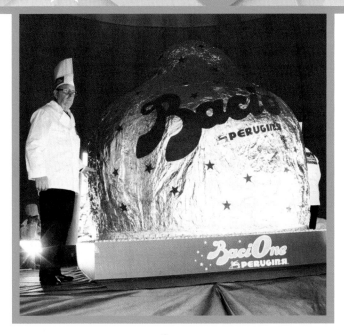

Largest ⋀ individual chocolate

The largest single chocolate is a 5,980-kg (13,183-lb) BaciOne (above). Made by Nestlé (Italy), it was displayed at the Perugina factory, San Sisto, Italy, on 26 October 2003.

Largest wedding cake ⋁

The largest wedding cake ever (below) weighed 15,032 lb (6,818.40 kg) and was made by chefs at the Mohegan Sun Hotel and Casino, Uncasville, Connecticut, USA, and displayed at their New England bridal showcase on 8 February 2004.

★ Largest box of popcorn

On 11 September 2003, BR Turbo (Brazil) filled a huge box with popcorn, 24.92 m³ (880 ft³) in volume, at the Mercado Público, Porto Alegre, Rio Grande do Sul, Brazil. It took them 5 hr 59 min to fill the box.

★ Largest cocktail

The world's largest cocktail was a 26,645-litre (5,861-gal) margarita made on 17 May 2001 by staff at Jimmy Buffett's Margaritaville and Mott's, Inc., Universal City Walk, Orlando, Florida, USA.

★ Largest pizza

On 8 December 1990, the largest pizza ever was baked at the Norwood Hypermarket, Johannesburg, South Africa. It was 37.4 m (122 ft 8 in) in diameter and took about 39 hours to prepare and cook.

★ Largest pizza commercially available

Paul Revere's Pizza (USA) will bake and deliver a pizza with a 1.21-m (4-ft) diameter and an area of 1.17 m² (12.59 ft²). The pizza, named the 'Ultimate Party Pizza', is sold at $99.99 (£54.63). It comprises 4.81 kg (170 oz) of dough, 1.36 litres (48 fl oz) of sauce, various meats and vegetables, and about 2.25 kg (5 lb) of cheese.

★ Largest milkshake

The Comfort Diners, Parmalat USA, and the American Dairy Association (all USA) made the world's largest milkshake, with a volume of 22,712.47 litres (4,996 gal) in New York, USA, on 1 August 2000.

★ Largest box of chocolates

Marshall Field's, Chicago, Illinois, USA, created a box of Frango mint chocolates weighing 1,463 kg (3,226 lb) on 14 November 2002.

★ Longest hot dog

The world's longest hot dog measured 10.5 m (34 ft 5.25 in). It was made by students from the University of Pretoria and displayed at the Sonop Hostel, Pretoria, South Africa, on 18 October 2003.

★ Largest candy cane

Employees of Fabiano's Chocolates and Ice Cream (USA) made a candy cane measuring 11.14 m (36 ft 7 in) long and 10.1 cm (4 in) in diameter at Lansing City Market, Michigan, USA, on 5 December 1998.

★ Largest bubblegum bubble blown from the mouth

The greatest reported diameter for a bubblegum bubble blown from the mouth under the strict rules of this highly competitive activity is 58.4 cm (23 in), and was achieved by Susan Montgomery Williams (USA) at the ABC-TV studios in New York City, USA, on 19 July 1994.

★ Largest bubblegum bubble blown through the nose

After pre-chewing for at least an hour, Joyce Samuels (USA) blew, from her nose, a bubblegum bubble with a diameter of 28 cm (11 in) on the set of Guinness World Records: Primetime, Los Angeles, California, USA, on 10 November 2000.

★ Fastest jellybean sorting using a straw

The fastest time in which 30 Jelly Belly jellybeans have been sorted into five flavours using a drinking straw is 1 min 3.58 sec by Euan Hamilton (UK) in a competition organized by the Beano comic (UK) in May 2004.

Feats of engineering

Contents

« Tallest monumental column

The tapering column (left) on the bank

of the San Jacinto River near Houston, Texas, USA, is 173.7 m (570 ft) tall, 14 m (47 ft) square at the base and 9 m (30 ft) square at the observation tower. Built between 1936 and 1939 to commemorate the Battle of San Jacinto (21 April 1836), it is surmounted by a star weighing 200 tonnes (440,000 lb).

Largest stadium roof ⌃

The transparent acrylic glass 'tent' roof over the Munich Olympic Stadium, Germany (above) measures 85,000 m² (915,000 ft²) in area. It rests on a steel net supported by masts.

★ Largest ice village
A village of 140 'igloos' – huts constructed solely of ice – was built near the famous Icehotel at Jukkasjärvi, Sweden, to accommodate 700 employees of Tetra Pak International during a conference at the hotel in December 2002. Each hut had a diameter of 4.3 m (14 ft) and was 2.1 m (7 ft) tall. The igloos slept up to five people each and were constructed of around 50 m³ (1,765 ft³) of ice.

★ Largest wooden building
Built in 1912, the Woolloomooloo Bay Wharf, Sydney, Australia, is 400 m (1,312 ft) long, 63 m (206 ft) wide and stands on 3,600 piles. The building on the wharf is five storeys high, 350.5 m (1,150 ft) long and 43 m (141 ft) wide with a floor area of 64,000 m² (688,890 ft²), and has been converted into a marina complex and hotel apartments.

★ Tallest residential-only building
The tallest purely residential building in the world is the 21st Century Tower in Dubai,

UAE, which has 54 floors and tops out at 269 m (882 ft). Its main roof is at 189.7 m (622 ft). However, the roof of the 264-m (866-ft) Tower Palace 3 Tower G, in Seoul, South Korea, is also its highest point, meaning that it can accommodate 69 floors of living space. Both towers were completed in 2003.

★ Tallest obelisk
The world's tallest obelisk is the Washington Monument in Washington DC, USA. It stands 169 m (555 ft) tall and was completed in 1884 to honour George Washington, the first president of the United States. An obelisk is a tapered four-sided column, usually with a pointed top.

★ Tallest free-standing structure
The tallest free-standing structure on Earth is the Petronius oil and gas drilling platform, which stands 570 m (1,870 ft) above the ocean floor in the Gulf of Mexico. Operated by Texaco, the platform began commercial production on

21 July 2000. The highest point on the platform, the vent boom, stands in excess of 610 m (2,000 ft) above the ocean floor. The tallest free-standing structure on land is the 553.34-m (1,815-ft 5-in) CN Tower in Toronto, Canada.

★ Largest airport roof
The Hajj Terminal at the £2.8-billion ($5.3-billion) King Abdul-Aziz Airport near Jeddah, Saudi Arabia, which was designed to cater for the annual influx of pilgrims, is the world's largest roofed structure, covering a total area of 150 ha (370 acres).

★ Largest airport terminal
The Hong Kong International Airport passenger terminal building is 1.3 km (0.8 miles) long and covers 550,000 m² (5.92 million ft²). The baggage hall of this gargantuan structure is as big as the Yankee Stadium in New York, USA, and could hold five Boeing 747s parked wingtip to wingtip. The terminal is designed to accommodate

45 million passengers a year and handles 460 flights a day. It contains 3 km (1.8 miles) of moving walkways, 55,000 m² (592,000 ft²) of glass cladding and around 117,000 m² (1.25 million ft²) of carpeting.

★ Largest soccer stadium
The Maracanã Municipal Stadium in Rio de Janeiro, Brazil, has a standard capacity of 205,000 spectators, 155,000 of whom can be seated. It was built for the 1950 Football World Cup and housed a crowd of 199,854 for the final match of the tournament, Brazil v. Uruguay, on 16 July 1950 – the greatest ever attendance for a sporting event. The oval stadium is 32 m (105 ft) high and the distance between the middle of the field and the furthest spectator is 126 m (413 ft).

★ Longest stadium roof span
The longest roof span is 240 m (787 ft 4 in) for the major axis of the elliptical Texas Stadium, completed in 1971 at Irving, Texas, USA.

Largest palace »

The Imperial Palace in the centre of Beijing, China (above), covers a rectangle measuring 960 x 750 m (3,150 x 2,460 ft) over an area of 72 ha (178 acres). The outline survives from the construction of the third Ming emperor, Yongle (1402–24), but owing to constant reconstruction work, most of the intra-mural buildings (five halls and 17 palaces) are from the 18th century.

★ Largest retractable roof

The world's largest retractable roof covers the SkyDome, home of the Toronto Blue Jays baseball team, near the CN Tower in Toronto, Canada. Completed in June 1989, the roof covers 3.2 ha (8 acres), spans 209 m (685 ft) at its widest and rises to 86 m (282 ft). It weighs 11,000 tonnes (24.6 million lb) and takes 20 minutes to open fully. When retracted, the entire field and 91% of the seats are uncovered. The stadium has a capacity of 67,000 for concerts, 55,000 for Canadian football and 50,600 for baseball.

★ Largest stadium with air-supported roof

The Pontiac Silverdome Stadium in Detroit, Michigan, USA, has a capacity of 80,311. The 4-ha (10-acre) translucent roof covering the 235 x 183-m (770 x 600-ft) octagonal stadium is held up by pressurized air provided by 25 large fans. Made from flexible Teflon-coated fibreglass, the roof is 62 m (202 ft) high. The air pressure in the stadium causes no discomfort and is within the limits of natural atmospheric pressure variations. The building is equipped with revolving doors to ensure that the air doesn't leak out as people enter.

★ Largest residential palace

The Istana Nurul Iman – the palace of the Sultan of Brunei in the capital Bandar Seri Begawan – was completed in January 1984 at a reported cost of £300 million ($422 million). It is the largest residence in the world, with a floor space of 200,000 m² (2,152,780 ft²), 1,788 rooms and 257 lavatories.

★ Largest pyramid

The largest pyramid, and the largest monument ever built, is the Quetzalcóatl Pyramid at Cholula de Rivadavia, 101 km (63 miles) southeast of Mexico City. It is 54 m (177 ft) tall, and its base covers nearly 18.2 ha (45 acres). Its volume has been estimated at 3.3 million m³ (116.5 million ft³), compared with a volume of 2.4 million m³ (84.8 million ft³) for the Pyramid of Khufu, or Cheops, at Giza.

★ Largest hotel

The MGM Grand Hotel and Casino, Las Vegas, Nevada, USA, consists of four 30-storey towers on a 45.3-ha (112-acre) site. The hotel has 5,005 rooms, with suites of up to 560 m² (6,000 ft²) a 15,200-seat arena, and a 13.3-ha (33-acre) theme park.

★ Tallest door

Each of the four doors in the NASA Vehicle Assembly Building near Cape Canaveral, Florida, USA, is 140 m (460 ft) high, as tall as a 35-storey building. They were originally designed to allow fully assembled Saturn and Apollo rockets to pass through them.

★ Highest clock

The world's highest two-sided clock is 177 m (580 ft) above street level on top of the Morton International building, Chicago, Illinois, USA.

★ Largest shopping centre

West Edmonton Mall in Edmonton, Alberta, Canada, covers an area of 492,386 m² (5.3 million ft²). The mall cost CAN$1.2 billion (£700 million or $927 million) to build and features over 800 stores and services, as well as 11 major department stores.

★ Tallest air-traffic control tower

The 130-m (425-ft) tower at Kuala Lumpur International Airport, Malaysia, is the world's tallest air-traffic control tower. Its design imitates an Olympic torch.

Tallest structures
Feats of engineering

From earliest times man has aimed for the sky, originally to glorify a secular ruler or religious deity, but now to gain international prestige.

Foundations

Built as a tomb for a god-king, Egypt's Great Pyramid at Giza was probably the world's tallest building for 3,500 years, from 2,500 BC until the construction of the great European cathedrals in the Middle Ages. The modern era of tall buildings was heralded by the completion in 1889 of the 312-m-high (1,023-ft) Eiffel Tower in Paris, France. And from La Tour Eiffel onwards, it has been big business, rather than religion, that has driven the construction of ever taller buildings. There is enormous prestige attached to being the home of the world's tallest structure – and some recent record holders are featured here (to scale).

The advent of skyscrapers

During the early 20th century, the USA dominated the race to be the home of the world's tallest building. New York is still the most famous home of the 'skyscraper', as these giants became known. New York's tallest ever buildings were the Twin Towers of the World Trade Center, dedicated in 1973 but destroyed in the terrorist atrocity of 11 September 2001. The north tower was the taller of the two and stood an amazing 417 m (1,368 ft) high. The World Trade Center was the tallest building for a relatively short time, as in 1974 Chicago's Sears Tower was completed and took the title. Sears held on to that record for over 20 years.

Competition from Asia

From the 1990s, the USA has had some stiff competition from Asia, and in 1996 the title of world's tallest building passed to the 88-storey, 452-m (1,483-ft) Petronas Twin Towers in Kuala Lumpur, Malaysia. The completion of the 508-m (1,667-ft) Taipei 101 in Taipei, Taiwan, in 2004 means that the title remains in Asia for now, but several new proposed buildings, including the new Freedom Tower on the site of the World Trade Center in New York City, USA, and the Burj Dubai in the United Arab Emirates – whose final height will not be made public until it is completed – means that the crown is likely to change hands several times in the near future.

1931 Empire State Building
New York City, New York, USA
Height to tip of antenna: **449 m (1,472 ft)**
Height to roof: **381 m (1,250 ft)**

1974 Sears Tower
Chicago, Illinois, USA
Height to tip of antenna: **527 m (1,728 ft)**
Height to roof: **442 m (1,450 ft)**

1996 Petronas Twin Towers
Kuala Lumpur, Malaysia
Height to tip of spire: **452 m (1,483 ft)**
Height to roof: **378.6 m (1,242 ft)**

Tallest freestanding structure

But no building standing today is as tall as the world's tallest structure on land – the CN Tower in Toronto, Ontario, Canada. This communications tower is entirely freestanding and has no residential or office space. 'Topped out' in April 1975, it measures a staggering 553.33 m (1,815 ft 5 in).

The future...

Skyscraper buffs will continue to argue as to which of the world's architectural gems constitute the world's tallest building. There are plans being drawn up all over the world for new high rise buildings so perhaps when *Guinness World Records* celebrates its centenary in 2055, there will be a building in existence that's twice the height of the current record holder!

2004 Taipei 101
Taipei, Taiwan
Height to tip of spire:
508 m (1,666 ft)
Height to roof: **448 m (1,470 ft)**

1975 CN Tower
Toronto, Ontario, Canada
Height to tip of spire/
antenna: **553.33 m
(1,815 ft 5 in)**

★ GWR TALKS TO
Ron Klemenic

Chairman, Council on Tall Buildings & Urban Habitat (CTBUH), the body that decides which building is the world's tallest.

Who makes the decision on the tallest building for the CTBUH?
There's a committee of about a dozen people, and it's made up of architects and engineers from around the world.

How does the CTBUH define the height of a building?
Our definition was put together by Fazlur Khan, the structural engineer on the Sears Tower in Chicago, who said that the height of the building should be measured from the elevation of the main entrance of the building to the top of the architecture. So you then have to interpret what the 'top of the architecture' is. For the Sears Tower it's pretty clear – it's to the elevation of the main flat roof. Here, for instance, the antennae don't count, because if you remove them the fundamental appearance of the building doesn't change, it's still the same from an architectural point of view. Whereas if you removed the spire from the Chrysler Building in New York it doesn't look like the Chrysler building any longer. That's really how the Petronas Towers captured the title, because if you were to remove the the architectural spires, somehow the buildings wouldn't look the same.

Why is the CN Tower not considered to be the tallest building in the world?
The CN Tower is the tallest free-standing structure in the world, but we don't consider it to be a building; it's a tower. The reason we look at it that way is because the lions' share of the tower is not occupiable space, it's simply a tower or a shaft.

Would you agree that since 9/11 the days of the skyscraper are numbered?
It certainly doesn't appear to be the case. In North America there aren't really any proposals for anything that would surpass the Sears Tower, aside from the proposed Freedom Tower in New York. It's mostly driven by economics – once buildings get above 80 storeys or so, they start to lose their economic viability.

However, when we look at Asia and the Middle East, there's still great interest in designing the tallest building in the world, and in Dubai there's a building being planned right now [the Burj Dubai] that would surpass everything that I'm aware of in terms of height.

So having the tallest building is all about prestige?
For sure. For instance, the Petronas Towers remain only partially occupied, because the economy of Malaysia really can't support those buildings as economic entities. But they were symbolic for the Malaysian economy and people.

Is there a theoretical upper limit to tall buildings?
From a structural point of view, there really is not; the limitations are primarily economic. I doubt that the new building in Dubai makes any sound financial sense. However, there's an individual behind that project who has the financial fortitude to fund it, despite the fact that it might never make him any money from leasing space. However, it may pay for itself in other ways, such as notoriety.

What are the biggest challenges facing anyone planning to build the tallest building in the world?
Certainly if you want it to be a revenue-producing, profitable enterprise, one of the greatest challenges is moving people around. In other words, the amount of space the lifts consume as a ratio of the floor that's remaining to be leased. As you go taller and taller, you need more and more lifts to get the people up and down, and at some point – roughly around 80 storeys – the floor area consumed by the lifts is so great that the area remaining to lease is too small to make the building economically viable. So one of the technical challenges is advances in lift technology.

[At the time of going to press, the CTBUH had not yet officially confirmed Taipei 101 as the tallest building, because it had not yet been opened for business.]

Constructions
Feats of engineering

Longest wall ⌃

The Great Wall of China (above) has a main-line length of 3,460 km (2,150 miles) – nearly three times the length of the UK – plus 3,530 km (2,195 miles) of branches and spurs. Construction of the wall began during the reign of Qin Shi Huangdi (221–210 BC). The height of the Great Wall varies from 4.5 to 12 m (15 to 39 ft) and it is up to 9.8 m (32 ft) thick. It stretches from Shanhaiguan, on the Gulf of Bohai, to Yumenguan and Yangguan.

★ Largest solar energy roof

A huge solar energy roof was installed to cover the exposition hall at the Floriade 2002 flower festival, Haarlemmermeer, The Netherlands. The area of the roof is 26,110 m² (281,045 ft²) and it has a generating capacity of 2.3 MW. It was created by Nuon Renewables. The festival opened on 6 April 2002 and ran until 20 October 2002.

★ Furthest distance to move a bridge

London Bridge proved unable to handle increasing volumes of traffic in the 20th century. It was auctioned in 1962 to Robert McCulloch (USA) for $2,460,000 (then £876,068). The bridge was dismantled and moved brick by brick to Lake Havasu City, Arizona, USA, where it was reassembled and opened in 1971. It had been moved a total of 8,530 km (5,300 miles). Legend has it that McCulloch had bought the wrong bridge – he had presumed he was buying the more decorative Tower Bridge.

★ Highest causeway

In the mid-1990s, a causeway was constructed to replace a Bailey bridge that spanned Khardungla Pass, Ladakh, India. (A Bailey bridge is made out of prefabricated sections and is named after its inventor, Sir Donald Bailey.) At one time, this Bailey bridge had the highest altitude of any road bridge in the world: 5,602 m (18,380 ft). However, because of constant damage from avalanches it was replaced by the causeway.

★ Longest cable suspension bridge

The main span of the Akashi-Kaikyo road bridge, which links the Japanese islands of Honshu and Shikoku, is 1,990.8 m (1.24 miles) long. The overall suspended length, with side spans, is 3,911.1 m (2.43 miles). Two towers rise 297 m (974 ft 5 in) above water level and the two main supporting cables are 1.12 m (44 in) in diameter, making both the tower height and the cable diameter world

records. Work on the bridge began in 1988 and it was opened to traffic on 5 April 1998.

★ Longest bridge-tunnel

The Chesapeake Bay bridge-tunnel, which opened to traffic on 15 April 1964, extends 28.4 km (17.65 miles) from the Eastern Shore region of the Virginia Peninsula to Virginia Beach, USA. The longest bridged section is Trestle C, at 7.34 km (4.56 miles), and the longest tunnel is the Thimble Shoal Channel Tunnel, at 1.75 km (1.09 miles).

★ Longest cantilever bridge

The Québec Bridge (Pont de Québec) over the St Lawrence River, Canada, has the longest cantilever truss span of any bridge in the world, measuring 549 m (1,800 ft) between the piers and 987 m (3,239 ft) overall. It carries a railway track and two carriageways.

Work started in 1899, and the bridge was finally opened to traffic on 3 December 1917, having cost CAN$22.5 million (£4.7 million or $22.5 million) and 87 lives.

★ Longest Tibetan bridge

The longest Tibetan bridge (a bridge made entirely from rope) has a span of 362 m (1,187 ft). It connects the islands of Procida and Vivara, Italy, and was constructed by the Sportchallengers (Italy) organization. The bridge was completed on 15 July 2001.

★ Highest bridge

The world's highest bridge spans the Royal Gorge of the Arkansas River in Colorado, USA, at 321 m (1,053 ft) above the water. It is a suspension bridge with a main span of 268 m (880 ft). The bridge took six months to construct and was completed on 6 December 1929.

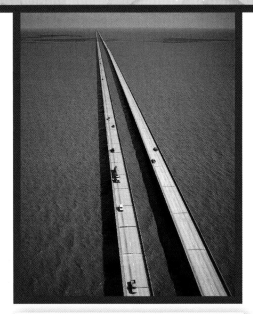

Longest steel arch bridge ⌄

The Lupu Bridge (below), Shanghai, China, which stretches across the Huangpu River, has a span of 550 m (1,804 ft). The bridge took three years to construct and opened on 28 June 2003. It is 32 m (104.9 ft) longer than the previous record holder, the New River Gorge Bridge, near Fayetteville, West Virginia, USA.

Longest bridge ⌃

In 1969, the Second Lake Pontchartrain Causeway, which joins Mandeville and Metairie, Louisiana, USA, and is 38.42 km (23.87 miles) long, was completed. It is shown above with the First Causeway, built in 1956.

★ **Deepest road tunnel**
The Hitra Tunnel in Norway, linking the mainland to the island of Hitra, reaches a depth of 264 m (866 ft) below sea level. It is 5.6 km (3.47 miles) long, with three lanes, and was opened in December 1994. The tunnel was built to provide an all-weather link to Hitra island across the turbulent waters of the Norwegian Sea.

★ **Longest big-ship canal**
The Suez Canal links the Red Sea and the Mediterranean Sea. It took 10 years to build, employing a workforce of 1.5 million people – 120,000 of whom perished during the construction – and finally opened on 17 November 1869. The canal runs from Port Said lighthouse to Suez Roads. It is 162.2 km (100.8 miles) long, with a minimum width of 300 m (984 ft) and a maximum width of 365 m (1,198 ft).

★ **Longest cycleway bridge**
A cycleway bridge 237.6 m (779 ft 6 in) in length spans the 17 tracks at Cambridge Railway Station, UK.

★ **Longest floating bridge**
The Second Lake Washington Bridge, Seattle, Washington State, USA, has a total length of 3.839 km (2.39 miles), with a floating section measuring 2.291 km (1.42 miles). The bridge was built at a total cost of $15 million (£5.35 million) and was finally completed in August 1963.

★ **Longest wooden bridge**
The Lake Pontchartrain Railroad Trestle, Louisiana, USA, which connects the cities of New Orleans and Kenner, is 9.369 km (5.82 miles) long. Construction began on the bridge in February 1882 and was completed in September

of that year. When it opened in 1883, the bridge originally stretched for 34.6 km (21.49 miles). It is made from reinforced creosoted yellow pine timber.

★ **Longest plastic bridge**
The longest reinforced-plastic span bridge is at the Aberfeldy Golf Club at Aberfeldy, Perth and Kinross, UK. The main span is 63 m (206 ft 8 in) and the overall bridge is 113 m (370 ft 9 in) long.

★ **Longest sewage tunnel**
When it is complete, the Chicago TARP (Tunnels and Reservoir Plan) in Illinois, USA, will involve 211 km (131 miles) of machine-bored sewer tunnels 2.7 to 10 m (9 to 33 ft) in diameter. The system helps to control pollution and flooding and will service 3.9 million people in 52 communities over an area of 971 km^2 (375 miles^2).

★ **Longest road and rail bridge system**
Japan's Seto Ohashi Bridge consists of six bridge sections stretching a distance of 9.4 km (5.8 miles). The bridge, which opened on 10 April 1988 (100 years after it was first proposed by the Japanese authorities), joins the city of Kurashiki on the island of Honshu with Sakaide City on the island of Shikoku.

★ **Tallest structure**
The KVLY-TV tower, a stayed television transmitting mast between Fargo and Blanchard, North Dakota, USA, is 629 m (2,063 ft) tall. The tower and its anchors cover 64 ha (160 acres), an area equivalent to 130 American football fields. The total weight of steel in the tower is 392 tonnes (864,500 lb), and the total length of the guy wires is 12.2 km (7.6 miles).

Most visited garden ⌄
with paying visitors

The most visited garden for which an admission charge applies is the Royal Botanic Gardens, Kew, Surrey, UK (below), which has an average of one million paying visitors per year. The 132-ha (326-acre) site has 40 historically important buildings and collections of more than 40,000 species of plants. Kew Gardens became a United Nations World Heritage site on 3 July 2003.

Largest temporary ⌃
corn maze and pathway

Stewarts GardenLands Maize Maze (above) covered an area of 68,271 m² (16.9 acres) when it opened on 10 July 2003 in Christchurch, Dorset, UK. The maze, which has a central lobster shape, was designed by Adrian Fisher (UK) and created by Martin and Susie Stewart (both UK). A 14.22-km-long (8.83-mile) pathway in the maze holds the record for the longest path in a temporary maze.

★ Largest garden
In the late 17th century, André Le Nôtre (France) created a magnificent garden for King Louis XIV at Versailles, France. The gardens and parkland were created out of what had once been marshland. They cover more than 6,070 ha (15,000 acres), of which the famous formal garden covers 100 ha (247 acres).

★ Oldest botanical gardens
The Orto Botanico in Padua, Italy, was created in 1545. The original design of a circular central plot (which symbolizes the world) surrounded by a ring of water remains, as does the gardens' original purpose – to serve as a place for scientific research.

★ Largest rose garden
The Roseto di Cavriglia in Cavriglia, Italy, has more than 7,500 varieties of rose.

★ Largest scented garden
The largest scented garden is at the Kirstenbosch National Botanical Gardens on the slopes of Table Mountain, Cape Town, South Africa. The Fragrance Garden includes a Braille Trail and many aromatic plants offering the opportunity for blind and visually impaired visitors to enjoy the plants.

★ Smallest park
Circular in shape, Mill Ends Park, located on a safety island on SW Front Avenue, Portland, Oregon, USA, measures a tiny 60.96 cm (24 in) diameter and 2,917.15 cm² (452.16 in²) in area. On 17 March 1948 it was designated as a city park, for snail races and as a colony for leprechauns, at the behest of the city journalist Dick Fagan (USA).

★ Largest saltwater garden park
The largest gardens irrigated by salt water are those that form the Zayed Project for Seawater Irrigation, on the coast of the Arabian Gulf in Abu Dhabi, United Arab Emirates. The gardens measure 20,000 m² (215,278 ft²) and contain 22,000 specimens from 40 types of plants, all of which tolerate pure salt water or a saltwater/freshwater mixture, either naturally or by genetic modification.

★ Largest permanent hedge maze and pathway
The largest permanent hedge maze is the Peace Maze at Castlewellan Forest Park, Co Down, Northern Ireland, UK, which has a total area of 11,215 m² (2.77 acres) and a total path length of 3.51 km (2.18 miles). The maze opened on 12 September 2001 and was designed by Beverley Lear (UK) and created by the Forest Service, Northern Ireland, UK, assisted by members of the public. The 3.51-km-long (2.18-mile) pathway holds the record for the longest pathway in a permanent hedge maze.

Oldest topiary garden ≪

Topiary (left) is the art of clipping bushes and shrubs into ornamental shapes. The topiary garden at Levens Hall, Cumbria, UK, features designs that are more than 300 years old and were initially planted and trained during the 1690s. The topiary shapes in the garden include a judge's wig and umbrellas.

★ Oldest cultivated decorative plant

The oldest species of plant cultivated and used for decoration is the rose (Rosa). Documents dating back to AD 50 suggest that ancient Romans grew the flowers in plantations and local hothouses to ensure a year-round supply of medicinal extracts, cooking ingredients and ornamentation.

★ Largest plant conservatory

The Eden Project, near St Austell, Cornwall, UK, consists of two giant transparent domes, or 'biomes'. The largest of these, the humid tropics biome, stands 55 m (180 ft) tall, covers 25,390 m² (273,295 ft²) and has a total volume of 415,730 m³ (14.681 million ft³). The smaller warm temperate biome has 6,540 m² (70,395 ft²) of floor space and a volume of 85,620 m³ (3.02 million ft³).

★ Largest seed collection

The Millennium Seed Bank Project at Wakehurst Place Garden, West Sussex, UK, had 6,655 identified species preserved in its cold store as of 4 July 2003. In total there are three million individual seeds preserved in the underground frozen vault. This amounts to 15,613 collections and represents approximately 2.8% of the world's flora.

★ Largest herbarium

The largest herbarium contains 8,880,000 species of preserved plants and is in the Muséum National d'Histoire Naturelle, Paris, France.

★ Oldest vine

Scientific measurement of the 'Old Vine' in Maribor, Slovenia, carried out in 1972 established that it was then at least 350 years old and may have been up to 400 years old.

★ Largest vineyard

A vineyard in the Languedoc region of France extends over the Mediterranean slopes between the Pyrénées and the Rhône in the départements Gard, Hérault, Aude and Pyrénées-Orientales. It covers an area of 840,000 ha (2,075,685 acres), 52.3% of which is 'monoculture viticole', ie consisting only of wine crops.

★ Tallest and longest hedge

The Meikleour beech hedge in Perthshire, UK, was planted in 1746 by Jean Mercer and Robert Murray Nairne (both UK) to define the eastern border of their land. The hedge is 540 m (1,771 ft) long and averages 30 m (98 ft) in height.

★ Largest permanent tree maze

Designed by Erik and Karen Poulsen (both Denmark), the Samso Labyrinten on the Island of Samso in Denmark has an area of 60,000 m² (645,835 ft²) and its path measures 5,130 m (16,830 ft). It was created in September 1999 and opened to the public on 6 May 2000.

★ Oldest hedge maze

The maze in the gardens of Hampton Court Palace, Surrey, UK, was built for King William III of England. Designed by royal gardeners George London and Henry Wise (both UK), it was planted between 1689 and 1695 using hornbeam Carpinus. The maze covers an area of 0.2 ha (0.5 acres), with a total path length of 800 m (0.5 miles).

★ Longest running horticultural show

The Shropshire Horticultural Society's 'Shrewsbury Flower Show' celebrated its 116th event on 15–16 August 2003. The annual show has been held since 1875 at the Quarry Showground, Shrewsbury, UK, but stopped during the war years 1914–18 and 1940–46.

The earliest documented horticultural show, a 'carnation and gooseberry' display held in July 1836, was organized by the Salop Horticultural Society in Shropshire, UK.

★ Largest horticultural library

The Royal Horticultural Society's Lindley Library in London, UK, has more than 50,000 books. The library was established in 1861, and is named after the botanist John Lindley (UK).

Theme parks & rides
Feats of engineering

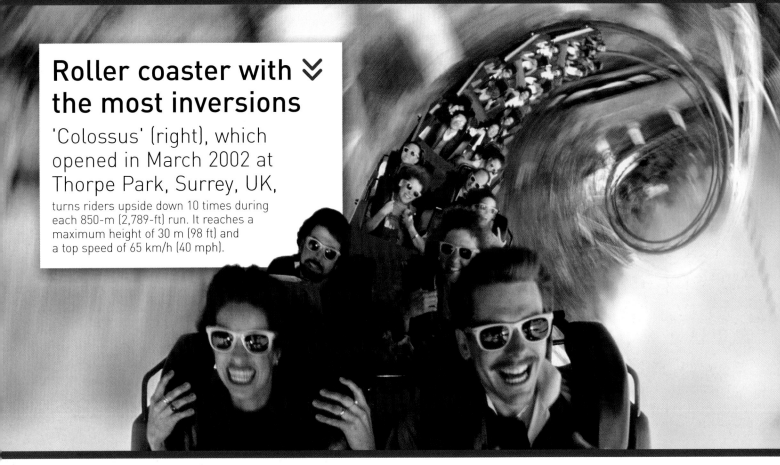

Roller coaster with ⬇ the most inversions

'Colossus' (right), which opened in March 2002 at Thorpe Park, Surrey, UK, turns riders upside down 10 times during each 850-m (2,789-ft) run. It reaches a maximum height of 30 m (98 ft) and a top speed of 65 km/h (40 mph).

★ **Oldest operating amusement park**
Bakken, located in Klampenborg, Denmark, opened in 1583. It features over 150 attractions, including a wooden roller coaster dating from 1932.

★ **Greatest number of roller coasters in an amusement park**
In 2003, both Six Flags Magic Mountain in Valencia, California, USA, and Cedar Point near Sandusky, Ohio, USA, opened their 16th roller coaster to the public.

★ **Largest amusement resort**
Walt Disney World in Orlando, Florida, USA, is set in 12,140 ha (30,000 acres) – twice the size of Manhattan. It opened on 1 October 1971 and cost $400 million (£164 million).

★ **Amusement park with the most rides**
Six Flags Great Adventure in Jackson, New Jersey, USA, has a total of 71 different mechanical rides. The park, which now boasts 12 roller coasters, opened its doors on 4 July 1974 and covers a total area of 56.6 ha (140 acres).

★ **Largest indoor amusement park**
The world's largest shopping mall, West Edmonton Mall, Alberta, Canada, is home to Galaxyland, which covers 37,160 m² (400,000 ft²). It holds 30 skill games and 27 rides and attractions, including 'Mindbender' – a 14-storey, triple-loop roller coaster – and 'Drop of Doom', a 13-storey free-fall ride.

★ **Largest wave pool**
According to the World Waterpark Association, the largest wave pool covers around 1.6 ha (4 acres) and can be found at Siam Park City, Bangkok, Thailand.

★ **Longest full-circuit roller coaster**
'Steel Dragon', which opened on 1 August 2000 at Nagashima Spaland, Mie, Japan, is the longest full-circuit roller coaster at 2,479 m (8,133 ft), and the tallest full-circuit roller coaster, rising to 95 m (311 ft 8 in) above ground level. It has the longest drop of any full-circuit roller coaster – 93.5 m (306 ft 9 in).

★ **Tallest amusement park big wheel**
The 'Dai-Kanransha' big wheel, at Pallet Town grounds, Tokyo, Japan, stands 115 m (377 ft) from the base of its pedestal to the top of the wheel. It has a revolution velocity of 0.06 rpm, a wheel diameter of 100 m (328 ft) and can can carry up to 384 passengers.

★ **Largest observation wheel**
The 'British Airways London Eye', designed by London architects David Marks and Julia Barfield (both UK) has a diameter and height of 135 m (443 ft). Constructed on London's South Bank, it made its first 'flight' on 1 February 2000, with regular service commencing the following month. The wheel continuously turns during normal operation. Each of the 32 fully enclosed capsules, carrying up to 25 passengers, completes a full 360° rotation every 30 minutes.

★ **Greatest capacity observation wheel**
Walter Bassett (UK) constructed his first and largest observation wheel for the Oriental Exhibition, at Earl's Court, London, UK, in 1895. It had 10 first-class and 30 second-class cars, each carrying 30 people. The wheel could carry a maximum of 1,200 passengers to a height of 84 m (276 ft). The wheel was scrapped in 1906.

★ **Longest walk-through horror house**
'Labyrinth of Terror' at Fujikyu Highland Amusement Park, Yamanashi Prefecture, Japan, is a hospital-themed house of horrors that opened on 19 July 2003. It has a 616-m (2,021-ft) walk-though course, which takes visitors between 30 and 40 minutes to complete.

Largest indoor ⌃ water park

The Ocean Dome (above) at Sheraton Resort Phoenix Sengaia near Miyazaki, Japan, is 300 m (984 ft) long, 100 m (328 ft) wide and 38 m (125 ft) high and contains a beach 140 m (459 ft) long.

Fastest full-circuit roller coaster ≫

The world's fastest and tallest roller coaster is 'Top Thrill Dragster' (right), a hydraulically launched 'strata-coaster' at Cedar Point, near Sandusky, Ohio, USA, which reaches its maximum speed of 193 km/h (120 mph) just four seconds after launch. The ride, which opened in May 2003, is 128 m (420 ft) tall, 853 m (2,800 ft) long and cost $25 million (£16.6 million) to build.

★ Tallest and fastest wooden roller coaster

The first hill of 'Son of Beast' at Paramount King's Island in Kings Mills, Ohio, USA, is 66.4 m (218 ft) high, making it the tallest wooden roller coaster in the world. The ride, which is roughly as high as a 16-storey building, opened in April 2000. It was built by Roller Coaster Corporation of America, and is also the world's fastest wooden coaster at 126 km/h (78.3 mph).

★ Steepest wooden roller coaster

'Colossos' at Heide-Park near Soltau, Germany, has the steepest drop of any wooden roller coaster, with an angle of 61°. The 1,500-m (4,921-ft) ride lasts for 2 min 25 sec, during which it can reach speeds of up to 120 km/h (74.6 mph).

★ Oldest continually operating roller coaster

'The Scenic Railway' at Luna Park, St Kilda, Victoria, Australia, opened to the public on 13 December 1912 and has remained in operation ever since. This traditional wooden coaster was designed by La Marcus Adna Thompson (USA), who is regarded as the father of the modern roller coaster.

★ Highest average age for a roller-coaster ride

The highest average age of roller coaster passengers is 75.25 years, set by a group of 32 riders on the 'Big Dipper' at Blackpool Pleasure Beach, Lancashire, UK, on 24 September 2003.

★ Longest roller-coaster marathon

Richard Rodriguez (USA) rode the Expedition GeForce and Superwirbel roller coasters at Holiday Park, Hassloch, Germany, for 192 hours (8 days) non-stop, from 20 to 28 August 2003.

★ Most roller coasters ridden in 24 hours

The greatest number of different roller coasters ridden in a 24-hour period is 74, a feat achieved by Philip A Guarno, Adam Spivak, John R Kirkwood and Aaron Monroe Rye (all USA) on 9 August 2001. The four rode coasters in 10 parks in four US states, using helicopters to travel between each park.

★ Longest inner-tube water slide

The 266.5-m-long (874-ft 4-in) 'Triple Saurus' slide at Shibamasa World Water Amusement Park in Fukui, Japan, opened on 7 July 2001. The longest of three similar slides attached to the same tower, it stands 26.5 m (86 ft 11 in) high.

★ Tallest vertical-drop amusement ride

'The Giant Drop' at Dreamworld, near Coomera, Queensland, Australia, drops from a height of 119 m (390 ft), giving riders a terrifying five seconds of free-fall time before being brought to a halt by electromagnetic brakes.

★ Oldest operating carousel

The Vermolen Boden-Karussel at Efteling Theme Park in Kaatsheuvel, The Netherlands, was built in 1865. It was originally powered by horses, but was later restored and is now electrically driven.

Longest small-scale ⌃⌃ model railway track

The Great American Railway (above) has a total track length of more than 15,250 m (50,000 ft) of H0 scale (1:87.1) track and is the star exhibit at the Northlandz attraction

in Flemington, New Jersey, USA. The model railway and its miniature world covers an area of 4,645 m² (50,000 ft²), including 4,000 buildings and over half a million lichen trees, and is the culmination of 25 years of single-handed work for Bruce Williams Zaccagnino (USA, pictured above).

★ **Earliest railway**
As early as 1550, wagons running on wooden rails were used for mining at Leberthal, Alsace, France.

★ **Earliest public electric railway**
On 12 May 1881, a public electric railway opened at Lichtervelde near Berlin, Germany. It was 2.5 km (1.5 miles) long, ran on 100 V current and carried 26 passengers at up to 48 km/h (30 mph).

★ **Longest train**
The longest freight train was 7.35 km (4.57 miles) long, and consisted of 682 ore cars pushed by eight powerful diesel-electric locomotives. Assembled by BHP Iron Ore (Australia), it travelled 275 km (171 miles) from the company's Newman and Yandi mines to Port Hedland, Western Australia, on 21 June 2001.

★ **Longest model train**
The longest model train was 70.2 m (230 ft 3 in) in length and consisted of 650 wagons hauled by four locomotives. It was run by the Arid Australia model railway group in Perth, Western Australia, on 3 June 1996. The train was built in the H0 scale of 1:87.1, meaning it was the equivalent length of a full-scale train measuring 6.11 km (3.8 miles).

★ **Heaviest train pulled by single locomotive**
The heaviest train ever hauled by a single engine is believed to be one of 15,545 tonnes (34.2 million lb) made up of 250 freight cars stretching 2.5 km (1.6 miles) and pulled by the *Matt H Shay* (No. 5014), a steam engine that ran on the Erie Railroad in the USA from 1914 until 1929.

★ **Largest steam locomotive**
The largest steam locomotives are generally considered to be the 4-8-8-4 'Big Boys', which were built by the American Locomotive Company between 1941 and 1944. They are 39.85 m (130 ft 9 in) long and weigh 508.02 tonnes (1.12 million lb), including their tenders.

★ **Largest railway station by number of platforms**
In terms of the number of platforms, the world's largest railway station is Grand Central Terminal, Park Avenue and 42nd Street, New York City, USA. It was built from 1903 to 1913 and has 44 platforms situated on two underground levels, with 41 tracks on the upper level and 26 on the lower. The station covers 19 ha (47 acres), and around 550 trains and 200,000 commuters use it daily.

★ **Fastest speed on a national rail system**
Atlantique, a French SNCF high-speed TGV train, achieved a speed of 515.3 km/h (320.2 mph) between Courtalain and Tours, France, on 18 May 1990.

★ **Highest sustained average train speed**
The highest average speed by a train over a distance in excess of 1,000 km (621 miles) is 306.37 km/h (190.37 mph) by a French Societé Nationale des Chemins de fer Français (SNCF) Train à Grande Vitesse (TGV) travelling between Calais and Marseille on 26 May 2001. The unmodified train covered the 1,067 km (663 miles) between the cities in 3 hr 29 min, reaching a top speed of 366 km/h (227 mph).

Fastest steam locomotive

The London North Eastern Railway 'Class A4' (4-6-2) No. 4468 *Mallard* (below, later numbered 60022) recorded a speed of 201 km/h (125 mph) over a distance of 402 m (1,319 ft) while hauling seven coaches weighing 243 tonnes (535,722 lb) gross down Stoke Bank, near Essendine, (now) Rutland, UK, on 3 July 1938.

Fastest average speed for a scheduled train journey ⌃

The West Japan Railway Company operates its 500-Series Nozomi bullet trains (above), or 'shinkansen', at an average speed of 261.8 km/h (162.7 mph) on the 192-km (119-mile) line between Hiroshima and Kokura on the island of Honshu, Japan.

★ **Fastest railed vehicle**
A four-stage rocket-sled system accelerated an 87-kg (192-lb) payload to a speed of 2,886 m/s (9,468 ft/s) in 6.031 seconds at Holloman High Speed Test Track, Holloman Air Force Base, New Mexico, USA, on 30 April 2003. This is equivalent to a speed of 10,385 km/h (6,453 mph).

★ **Fastest diesel train**
The former British Rail (UK) inaugurated its HST (High Speed Train) daily service between London, Bristol and South Wales on 4 October 1976 using InterCity 125 trains. One of these holds the world speed record for diesel trains, at 238 km/h (148 mph), set on a test run between Darlington, Durham, and York, North Yorkshire, UK, on 1 November 1987.

★ **Fastest train in regular public service**
The magnetically levitated (maglev) train linking China's Shanghai International Airport to the city's financial district reaches a top speed of 431 km/h

(267.8 mph) on each 30-km (18-mile) run. The train, which was built by Transrapid International (Germany), had its maiden run on 31 December 2002.

★ **Fastest maglev train**
The MLX01, a manned superconducting magnetically levitated (maglev) train operated by the Central Japan Railway Company and Railway Technical Research Institute, reached a speed of 581 km/h (361 mph) on the Yamanashi Maglev Test Line, Yamanashi Prefecture, Japan, on 2 December 2003.

★ **Highest railway line**
At La Cima, Peru, the standard-gauge (1,435-mm or 56.5-in) track on the main line between

Lima and La Oroya reaches 4,818 m (15,806 ft) above sea level as it crosses the Andes. There are 67 tunnels and 59 bridges on the line. However, in 2001, China began building the Qinghai–Tibet railway, which is planned to reach a height of 5,072 m (16,640 ft).

★ **Highest railway station**
Cóndor Station on the metre-gauge (39-in) Río Mulatos–Potosí line in Bolivia lies at an altitude of 4,786 m (15,702 ft).

★ **Longest railway platform**
The platform at Kharagpur Station, West Bengal, India, is 833 m (2,733 ft) in length.

★ **Least extensive metro**
The Carmelit underground system in Haifa, Israel, is just 1,800 m (5,905 ft) long. The Carmelit, which opened in 1959, is a funicular railway running at a gradient of 12 degrees and is the only metro in Israel. The line, which starts at Paris Square and finishes at Carmel Central, has six stations.

★ **Longest monorail**
The Osaka Monorail in Osaka, Japan, has a total length of 22.2 km (13.8 miles). Fully operational since August 1997, the monorail runs between Osaka International Airport and Hankyu Railway Minami Ibaraki Station, with a second stage running between Hankyu and Keihan Railway Kadomashi Station.

Fastest electric car ⌃

On 22 October 1999, the *White Lightning* electric streamliner (above), driven by Patrick Rummerfield (USA), achieved a speed of 395.821 km/h (245.951 mph) at the Bonneville Salt Flats, Utah, USA. With its slender, aerodynamic carbon-fibre body, the 7.62-m (25-ft) *White Lightning* looks more like a rocket than a car and can reach a speed of 161 km/h (100 mph) in eight seconds.

Earliest internal-combustion car ⌄

The first successful petrol-driven car, the Motorwagen (below), built by Karl Friedrich Benz (Germany), ran at Mannheim in late 1885. The three-wheeler weighed 254 kg (560 lb) and could reach 13–16 km/h (8–10 mph). Its single-cylinder engine delivered 0.63 kW (0.85 hp) at 400 rpm. It was patented on 29 January 1886.

★ **Earliest full-scale automobile**
Nicolas-Joseph Cugnot (France) made a military steam tractor for the Paris Arsenal in October 1769 with a top speed of 4 km/h (2.5 mph). Cugnot's second, larger tractor, completed in May 1771, survives in the Conservatoire Nationale des Arts et Métiers in Paris, France.

★ **Fastest production car**
On 31 March 1998, Andy Wallace (UK) drove a standard McLaren F1 production car at 386.46 km/h (240.14 mph) at the Volkswagen Proving Ground, Wolfsburg, Germany. Various de-tuned track cars have been licensed for road use but are not normal production models.

★ **Fastest steam car**
On 19 August 1985, Robert E Barber (USA) broke the 79-year-old speed record for a steam car when *Steamin' Demon*, built by Barber-Nichols Engineering Co. (USA), reached 234.331 km/h (145.607 mph) at Bonneville Salt Flats, Utah, USA.

★ **Fastest wheel-driven vehicle**
The highest speed achieved by a wheel-driven car is 659.808 km/h (409.986 mph), with a peak speed of 696.331 km/h (432.692 mph), by Al Teague (USA) in *Spirit of '76* at Bonneville Salt Flats, Utah, USA, on 21 August 1991.

★ **Fastest diesel-engined car**
Virgil W Snyder (USA) drove a diesel-powered streamliner called *Thermo King-Wynns* at 379.413 km/h (235.756 mph) at Bonneville Salt Flats, Utah, USA, on 25 August 1973.

★ **Fastest open-road race**
The fastest road race in the world is the Silver State Classic on Route 318, Nevada, USA, in which drivers maintain average speeds in excess of 305 km/h (190 mph) over the 145-km (90-mile) course. The highest ever average speed attained was 334.38 km/h (207.78 mph), set by Chuck Shafer and Gary Brockman (both USA) in May 2000.

★ **Most valuable car**
The greatest confirmed price paid for a car is $15 million (£8.45 million) for the 1931 Bugatti Type 41 'Royale' Sports Coupé by Kellner. It was sold by Nicholas Harley (UK) to the Meitec Corporation of Japan on 12 April 1990.

★ **Most expensive production car**
The Mercedes-Benz CLK/LM cost $1,547,620 (£957,100) when launched in 1997. It can travel from 0 to 100 km/h (62 mph) in 3.8 seconds and has a top speed of 320 km/h (200 mph).

★ **Most valuable pop memorabilia**
John Lennon's 1965 Phantom V Rolls Royce was bought for $2,229,000 (£1,703,000) by Jim Pattison, Chairman of the Expo 86 World Fair in Vancouver, Canada, at Sotheby's, New York, USA, on 29 June 1985.

★ **Longest car**
Jay Ohrberg (USA) created a 30.5-m-long (100-ft) 26-wheeled limousine. Its many features include a king-sized water bed and a swimming pool with diving board. It can be driven as a rigid vehicle or adapted to bend in the middle, and was designed for use in films and displays.

★ **Largest production car**
The largest car produced for private use was the Bugatti Type 41 'Royale', known in the UK as the 'Golden Bugatti', which was assembled at Molsheim, France, by the Italian Ettore Bugatti. First built in 1927, it measures over 6.7 m (22 ft) in length with a bonnet of more than 2.13 m (7 ft) long.

★ **Most powerful production car**
The 5,998-cc V12 engine of the Ferrari Enzo is claimed by its makers to generate 492 kW (660 hp) of power, making it the most powerful car ever to enter series production. Ferrari claims that the Enzo reaches 100 km/h (62 mph) in 3.65 seconds and has a top speed of 349 km/h (217 mph).

Fastest production pick-up truck »

A standard 2004 Dodge Ram SRT-10 pick-up truck (right),

driven by National Association for Stock Car Auto Racing (NASCAR) driver Brendan Gaughan (USA), reached a speed of 248.783 km/h (154.587 mph) at the DaimlerChrysler Proving Grounds, Chelsea, Michigan, USA, on 2 February 2004.

★ **Best selling two-seater sports car**
Mazda (Japan) has sold in excess of 677,000 units of its MX-5 Miata sports car. Production began in April 1989.

★ **Highest car mileage**
A 1966 Volvo P-1800S owned by Irvin Gordon (USA) had covered in excess of 3,572,342 km (2,219,751 miles) by March 2004. The car is still driven on a daily basis and covers more than 160,000 km (100,000 miles) per year, thanks in part to being driven to numerous events in Europe and the USA.

★ **Longest journey by solar electric vehicle**
The *Radiance*, a sleek solar car built by the Queen's University Solar Vehicle Team (Canada), travelled 7,043 km (4,376 miles) across Canada from Halifax, Nova Scotia, to Vancouver, British Columbia, from 1 to 29 July 2000. *Radiance* was built for the annual World Solar Challenge between Darwin and Adelaide in Australia, and achieved second place in 1999.

★ **Longest lawnmower ride**
Gary Hatter (USA) travelled 23,487 km (14,594 miles) in 260 consecutive days between 31 May 2000 and 14 February 2001 on his Kubota BX2200-60 mower. Starting in Portland, Maine, he passed through all contiguous US states, as well as Canada and Mexico, ending his trip in Daytona Beach, Florida.

★ **Longest-manufactured production car**
The Morgan 4/4 has been in production since December 1935. Produced by the Morgan Motor Car Company (UK), all Morgans are hand-built and take an average of 23 days to make. The company's total production for all four of its models is around 540 per year.

★ **Longest single-model vehicle parade**
A total of 2,728 VW Beetles took part in a parade organized by the Volkswagen Aficionado Club of Brazil on a race track near Sao Paulo, Brazil, on 1 May 1995.

★ **Most 360-degree spins ('doughnuts') in a production car in one minute**
Alistair Weaver (UK) performed 22 doughnuts in one minute in a 1.8-litre Caterham Superlight at Elvington Airfield, North Yorkshire, UK, on 8 April 2002.

★ **Longest ramp jump by car**
The longest ramp jump, with the vehicle landing on its wheels and driving on, is 72.23 m (237 ft) by Ray Baumann (Australia) in a Chrysler VH Valiant at Ravenswood International Raceway, Perth, Western Australia, on 23 August 1998.

★ **Longest ramp jump in a limousine**
Michael Hughes (USA) jumped a distance of 31.4 m (103 ft) in a 3-tonne (6,600-lb) Lincoln Town Car stretched limousine at Perris Auto Speedway, Perris, California, USA, on 28 September 2002.

★ **Largest car park**
West Edmonton Mall in Edmonton, Alberta, Canada, is the world's largest shopping and entertainment centre and also houses the largest car park. The parking area can hold 20,000 vehicles, with overflow facilities on an adjoining lot for an additional 10,000 cars.

★ **Largest automobile producer by country**
In 2002, the USA manufactured around 12.27 million vehicles, according to the Organization Internationale des Constructeurs d'Automobiles (OICA).

★ **Largest car engine**
The production cars with the largest engines were the US Pierce-Arrow 6-66 Raceabout of 1912–18, the US Peerless 6-60 of 1912–14 and the Fageol of 1918. Each had an engine of 13.5 litres (823.8 in³).

Land speed record
Feats of engineering

Man has always been obsessed with speed. But it was the invention and refinement of the automobile that heralded a new century of land speed record breaking. Here are some highlights.

How it all began
In the first edition of *Guinness World Records* (formerly *The Guinness Book of Records*) back in 1955, the land speed record was held by John Cobb (UK) and stood at 634.39 km/h (394.19 mph). But this was by no means the first record set. Land speed record attempts as we know them date back to **1898** when Count Gaston de Chasseloup-Laubat (France) did a single run through a measured kilometre, and registered an average speed of 63.13 km/h (39.24 mph). In **1904**, Henry Ford sought to prove the speed of his new automobiles and duly set a new record in the Ford *Arrow* on the frozen Lake St Clair in Michigan, USA. He reached an average speed of 147.04 km/h (91.37 mph), but said that it scared him so much he never wanted to race again.

Breaking the 100-mph barrier
The 100-mph barrier was broken later in **1904** when Louis Emile Rigolly drove through the kilometre at 166.64 km/h (103.55 mph) and the land speed record went back to France. **1904** also marks the birth of the Fédération Internationale de l'Automobile (FIA), the governing body of motor sport worldwide, who officiate at every attempt on the land speed record. The rules have changed little over the years: the challenging car has to make two timed runs in opposite directions over a measured mile (or kilometre) within one hour.

Early triumphs
Perhaps the most famous attempts on the record were by Malcolm Campbell and later his son Donald (both UK). On 4 February **1927** Campbell Snr drove the Napier-Campbell *Bluebird* to 281.45 km/h (174.88 mph) on the beach at Pendine, Carmarthenshire, UK. Rivalry between Campbell Snr and Major Henry Seagrave (UK) drove the record through the 300-mph barrier on 3 September **1935** when Campbell achieved an average speed of 484.62 km/h (301.13 mph) on the Bonneville Salt Flats, Utah, USA.

UK/US rivalry
John Cobb's (UK) record speed of 634.39 km/h (394.19 mph), set in his *Railton Mobil Special* in **1947**, stood for nearly 16 years. The 400-mph barrier was eventually breached by Craig Breedlove (USA) in **1963**, driving the *Spirit of America*. Breedlove reached an average speed of 655.72 km/h (407.45 mph), although the record was disallowed at the time as the FIA did not recognize the use of jet power for land speed attempts.

Donald Campbell claimed the land speed record for Britain again on 17 July **1964** at Lake Eyre, Australia, in *Bluebird*, powered by a gas turbine engine. His 648.73-km/h (403.10-mph) record was the only one not set in the USA during that period of record attempts.

The second half of the **1960s** saw a battle for the record between two Americans: Art Arfons and Craig Breedlove. Arfons triumphed, achieving a speed of 927.87 km/h (576.55 mph) in *Green Monster* on the Bonneville Salt Flats on 7 November **1965**.

Through the sound barrier
Advances in technology meant that breaking the sound barrier was becoming an increasingly real prospect. In **1970** Gary Gabelich (USA) drove through the 1,000-km/h barrier in *Blue Flame*, reaching a speed of 1,001.66 km/h (622.40 mph), and on 4 October **1983**, Richard Noble (UK) set a new record of 1,019.46 km/h (633.47 mph) in *Thrust 2* in the Black Rock Desert, Nevada, USA.

The next challenge was to build and drive a land speed vehicle that would break the sound barrier. This was achieved in October **1997**, when RAF fighter pilot Andy Green (UK), driving in the 10-tonne, twin-jet-engine *Thrust SSC* (below), did the unimaginable by achieving a speed of 1,227.98 km/h (763.03 mph), or Mach 1.02. Green made the two runs through the measured mile, each time generating a shockwave in front of the car and a massive sonic boom. This record, which still stands, came almost 100 years after the first record was set in 1898.

1904
Henry Ford: Ford *Arrow*
147.04 km/h (91.37 mph)

1935
Malcolm Campbell: *Bluebird*
484.62 km/h (301.13 mph)

1947
John Cobb: *Railton Mobil Special*
634.39 km/h (394.19 mph)

1963
Craig Breedlove: *Spirit of America*
655.72 km/h (407.45 mph)

★ GWR TALKS TO
Richard Noble OBE

Richard Noble (UK, right) set a land speed record of 1,019.46 km/h (633.47 mph) in *Thrust 2* in 1983 and was Project Director for the successful *Thrust SSC* (supersonic car) land speed record attempt in 1997.

Did you have any high-speed experience before *Thrust 2*?
From the driving point of view, no, I had no experience when I started off. As the *Thrust 2* project developed I learnt to fly, and the discipline of flying is much more akin to record breaking than driving a race car.

Why didn't you drive *Thrust SSC* yourself?
I wanted to, but I realized that combining the jobs of driving the car and raising the money was absolutely hopeless. I decided that because I already held the land speed record I would raise the money and run the project.

Why go after the record again?
We actually saw *Thrust SSC* as the third car in a range of three. *Thrust 1* was a very simple, elementary jet-powered vehicle to introduce the project. *Thrust 2* was the record breaker, and *Thrust 3* we saw as being the supersonic car.

What was the biggest challenge?
One was the culture challenge, because we were up against a mass of companies that said it couldn't be done. The second was that the funding was so difficult.

Are you planning to break the record again?
We're very proud of what we've actually achieved, but nobody wants to go back again! The reality was that when we started going supersonic, I think it frightened a lot of us. I was watching this car coming up at supersonic speeds, and I realized what an enormous risk was being run by Andy [Green, the driver]. Andy's comment was that he'd driven the car twice too often, so that was it really.

Is there a limit to this record?
Yes, although it's a long way off. It's all about the human body's ability to withstand acceleration. If you think that 9 G is the upper limit of acceleration that a human can usefully work at, with acceleration of 9 G, speeds of twice or three times the speed of sound are possible. In terms of the car, the forces it experiences are absolutely enormous, so you need something that's as tough as a locomotive or a submarine. To give you an idea, the wheels on *SSC* were turning at 8,000 RPM, which means that you're running 35,000 radial G at the edge of the wheels. You're right at the limits of what materials will do.

Why is this record important?
I think it's very, very important because it's a measure of a man's or a nation's ability to take on a challenge. It's very important because it inspires the next generation to do something similar.

1997
Andy Green: *Thrust SSC*
1,227.98 km/h (763.03 mph) or Mach 1.02

1970
Gary Gabelich: *Blue Flame*
1,001.66 km/h (622.40 mph)

1983
Richard Noble: *Thrust 2*
1,019.46 km/h (633.47 mph)

Land speed records since 1947

Year	Date	Car and driver	km/h	mph
1947	16 Sept	*Railton Mobil Special*: John Cobb	634.39	394.19
1963*	5 Aug	*Spirit of America*: Craig Breedlove	655.72	407.45
1964	17 July	*Bluebird*: Donald Campbell	648.73	403.10
1964	2 Oct	*Wingfoot Express*: Tom Green	664.98	413.20
1964	5 Oct	*Green Monster*: Art Arfons	698.49	434.02
1964	13 Oct	*Spirit of America*: Craig Breedlove	754.33	468.72
1964	15 Oct	*Spirit of America*: Craig Breedlove	846.97	526.28
1964	27 Oct	*Green Monster*: Art Arfons	863.75	536.71
1965	2 Nov	Spirit of America: Craig Breedlove – Sonic I	893.96	555.48
1965	7 Nov	*Green Monster*: Art Arfons	927.87	576.55
1965	15 Nov	*Spirit of America*: Craig Breedlove – Sonic I	966.57	600.60
1970	23 Oct	*Blue Flame*: Gary Gabelich	1,001.66	622.40
1983	4 Oct	*Thrust 2*: Richard Noble	1,019.46	633.47
1997	25 Sept	*Thrust SSC*: Andy Green	1,149.29	714.10
1997	15 Oct	*Thrust SSC*: Andy Green	1,227.98	763.03

* not recognized by FIA

Bikes & motorbikes
Feats of engineering

Highest speed on a human powered vehicle (HPV)

⌄

Sam Whittingham (Canada, below) reached a speed of 130.36 km/h (81 mph) on a flat road surface in his streamlined recumbent bicycle *Varna Diablo* (left) at the World Human Powered Speed Challenge near Battle Mountain, Nevada, USA, on 5 October 2002.

Tallest rideable bicycle ⌃

Brad Graham (Canada, above) successfully rode his SkyCycle, which measures 4.34 m (14 ft 3 in) to the handlebars, on 1 July 2003 at Thunder Bay, Ontario, Canada. The bicycle has only two wheels and no stabilizers of any kind.

★ Most stairs climbed on a bicycle

On 16 October 2003 Javier Zapata (Colombia) climbed 1,318 steps on a bicycle in the Torre Major skyscraper, Mexico City, Mexico, without his feet touching the ground. The building is approximately 225 m (738 ft) high and has 55 storeys. The climb lasted 1 hr 38 min.

★ Longest signposted cycle route

The North Sea Cycle Route is a signposted route that follows the coastline of the North Sea through The Netherlands, Germany, Denmark, Sweden and Norway. It continues through Scotland and England, covering a distance of around 6,000 km (3,700 miles).

★ Furthest distance cycled backwards in one hour

Markus Riese (Germany) cycled 29.1 km (18 miles) backwards in one hour at the Velocipedclubs Darmstadt 1899 eV cycling club, Darmstadt, Germany, on 24 May 2003.

★ Longest snowmobile ramp jump on water

Vance Irwin (Canada) performed a 14.6-m (48-ft) ramp jump on water riding his unmodified Polaris 600 snowmobile at Fox Lake Municipal Park, Hanna, Alberta, Canada, on 1 July 2002.

★ Earliest motorcycle

Gottlieb Daimler built the *Einspur*, a motorized bicycle with internal combustion engine, between October and November 1885 at Bad Cannstatt, Germany. The wooden-framed machine was first ridden by Wilhelm Maybach. It had a top speed of 19 km/h (12 mph) and developed 0.37 kW (0.5 hp) from its single-cylinder 264-cc four-stroke engine at 700 rpm. It was lost in a fire in 1903.

★ Earliest mass-production motorcycle

In 1894 Heinrich and Wilhelm Hildebrand and Alois Wolfmüller (all Germany) opened a motorcycle factory at Munich, Germany. In its first two years, this factory produced over 1,000 machines, each having a water-cooled 1,488-cc twin-cylinder four-stroke engine developing about 1.9 kW (2.5 hp) at 600 rpm.

★ Longest motorcycle ramp jump with passenger

Jason Rennie (UK) jumped his Yamaha YZ250 motorcycle a distance of 29.2 m (96 ft) with his girlfriend Sian Phillips on the back on 12 November 2000, at the Rednall airfield near Oswestry, Shropshire, UK.

★ Longest distance jumped on a trial motorbike

Joachim Hindren (Finland) jumped a distance of 4 m (13 ft) on a trial motorcycle without the use of a ramp at Sipoo, Finland, on 13 October 2001.

★ Tallest rideable motorcycle

Bigtoe, built by Tom Wiberg (Sweden), is 2.3 m (7 ft 6 in) tall at its highest point. The motorcycle has a top speed of 100 km/h (62 mph) and is powered by a Jaguar V12 engine.

★ Longest motorcycle

Rick Dozer, Bill Decker, Rob Moore and William Longest (all USA) built a rideable motorcycle measuring 8.9 m (29 ft 3 in) wheel to wheel. The chopper-style Harley-Davidson monster has forks 4.6 m (15 ft) long and is 1.72 m (6 ft) tall at its highest point. William Longest rode it on a public road near Georgetown, Kentucky, USA, on 15 June 2003.

★ Fastest motorcycle speed

Riding a 7-m-long (23-ft) streamliner named *Easyriders*, powered by two 1,500-cc Ruxton Harley-Davidson engines, Dave Campos (USA) set AMA and FIM absolute speed records with an average of 518.522 km/h (322.101 mph) over two 1-km runs in opposite directions at Bonneville Salt Flats, Utah, USA, on 14 July 1990.

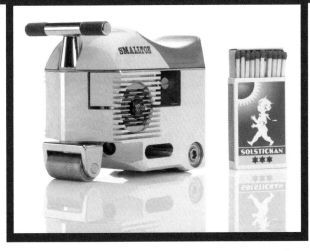

Largest engine capacity for a production model motorcycle

The Triumph Rocket III (below) is powered by a three-cylinder 2,294-cc engine, the largest ever fitted to a production motorcycle. The 320-kg (705-lb) machine produces 104 kW (140 hp) of power and 200 Nm (147 lbf/ft) of torque, making it more powerful than most saloon cars.

Smallest motorcycle ⌃

Tom Wiberg (Sweden) built a motorcycle (above) with a front wheel diameter of 16 mm (0.62 in) and a rear wheel diameter of 22 mm (0.86 in), and rode it for over 10 m (33 ft) in Hökerum, Sweden, in 2003. The micro machine, called *Smalltoe*, has a seat height of 65 mm (2.55 in), weighs 1.1 kg (2.4 lb) and is powered to a top speed of 2 km/h (1.24 mph) by its 0.22-kW (0.3-hp) engine.

★ Fastest motorcycle and trailer
On 28 February 2002 Kevin Smith (UK) reached 224.5 km/h (139.5 mph) on a Kawasaki ZZR1100 while towing a standard Squire D21 trailer at Millbrook Proving Ground, Bedfordshire, UK.

★ Fastest production motorcycle
The Suzuki GSX-1300R Hayabusa is reported to reach speeds of 312 km/h (194 mph), making it the fastest production bike in the world.

★ Highest speed travelled seated backwards on a motorcycle
Szabolcs Borsay (Hungary) reached a speed of 200.726 km/h (124.725 mph) sitting backwards on his Suzuki GSX-R1000 at Balaton Airport, Sármellék, Hungary, on 2 July 2002.

★ Longest solo motorcycle ride by a woman
Benka Pulko (Slovenia) travelled 180,016 km (111,856 miles) on a solo motorcycle journey that took her through 69 countries and seven continents. Her journey started in Ptuj, Slovenia, on 19 June 1997 and ended at the same location precisely 2,000 days later on 10 December 2002.

★ Longest continuous ride while standing on a motorcycle
On 13 December 2002 in Beijing, China, Liu Jichun (China) rode 5.32 km (3.30 miles) while standing on the seat of a motorcycle and without touching the handlebars.

★ Longest motorcycle wheelie
Yasuyuki Kudo (Japan) covered 331 km (205.7 miles) non-stop on the rear wheel of his Honda TLM220R motorcycle at the Japan Automobile Research Institute Proving Ground, at Tsukuba, near Tsuchiura, Japan, on 5 May 1991.

★ Fastest motorcycle wheelie over one kilometre
Christopher McInnes (UK) reached a speed of 203.4 km/h (126.4 mph) while performing a motorcycle wheelie over a kilometre at Elvington airfield, North Yorkshire, UK, on 18 November 2001. He was riding a Suzuki GSX-R750.

★ Longest stoppie (front-wheel wheelie) on motorcycle
Craig Jones (UK) covered 266 m (873 ft) on the front wheel of his Buell XB12R motorcycle at the Florida Evaluation Center, Naples, USA, on 15 August 2003.

★ Largest scooter by engine capacity
The Suzuki Burgman 650 scooter has a 638-cc four-stroke, two-cylinder engine, the largest available on any standard production model today. The 238-kg (524-lb) Burgman went on sale in 2003, with a manufacturer's suggested retail price of $7,699 (£4,750).

★ Largest motorcycle manufacturer
The Honda Motor Company of Japan is the world's largest manufacturer of motorcycles, having sold 8.08 million vehicles globally during the 2002/03 financial year. This figure includes quad motorcycles, or all-terrain vehicles (ATVs), and aquabikes, or personal watercraft (PWCs).

Largest propeller ⌄

A six-bladed propeller (below) weighing 93.5 tonnes (206,100 lb) and measuring 9 m (29 ft 6 in) in diameter was designed and manufactured by Stone Manganese Marine Ltd (UK) for a PO NedLloyd container ship. The six-bladed propeller was cast on 30 January 1997 with 129 tonnes (284,400 lb) of liquid metal.

Earliest hovercraft flight

The first public flight by a full-sized hovercraft was made by the 4-tonne (8,800-lb) Saunders-Roe Nautical One (SR.N1, above) at Cowes, Isle of Wight, UK, on 11 June 1959. With a 680-kg-thrust (1,500-lb) Viper turbojet engine, this craft reached 68 knots (126 km/h or 78 mph) in June 1961. The hovercraft was the brainchild of Sir Christopher Cockerell (UK). ⌃⌃

★ Oldest active sailing ship
The oldest square-rigged sailing vessel that is still sea-going is thought to be the 1,200-tonne (2.64 million-lb) iron barque *Star of India*, built at Ramsey, Isle of Man, UK, in 1863 as the full-rigged ship *Euterpe*. She has been restored and is now preserved as a museum ship in San Diego, California, USA. The *Star of India* still makes occasional day trips under sail.

★ Highest speed on water
Ken Warby (Australia) recorded a speed of 275.97 knots (511.11km/h, or 317.58 mph) in the unlimited-class jet-powered hydroplane *Spirit of Australia* on Blowering Dam Lake, New South Wales, Australia, on 8 October 1978. A hydroplane is a lightweight flat-bottomed boat designed to 'plane' (or skim) just above the surface with only its propellers and rudders in the water.

★ Fastest human powered speed on water
Mark Drela (USA) pedalled the hydrofoil *Decavitator* at a speed of 18.5 knots (34.26 km/h or 21.28 mph) over a 100-m (328-ft) course on the Charles River, Boston, Massachusetts, USA, on 27 October 1991. Hydrofoils are light vessels, the hulls of which are lifted out of the water when in motion by wing-like 'foils' under them.

★ Fastest sailing vessel
On 26 October 1993, the trifoiler *Yellow Pages Endeavour* reached a speed of 46.52 knots (86.15 km/h or 53.53 mph) while on a timed run of 500 m (1,640 ft) at Sandy Point near Melbourne, Victoria, Australia.

★ Fastest propeller-driven boat
Russ Wicks (USA) achieved a speed of 178.61 knots (330.79 km/h or 205.54 mph) in his hydroplane *Miss Freei* on 15 June 2000 at Lake Washington, Seattle, USA. *Miss Freei* was powered by a Lycoming L-7C turbine engine from a Chinook helicopter that generates 2,237 kW (3,000 hp) at 10,000 rpm. In contrast, most cars produce around 90 kW (120 hp) at no higher than 6,000 rpm.

★ Largest passenger liner
The Cunard Line's *Queen Mary 2*, which made its maiden voyage in January 2004, is 345 m (1,132 ft) long, has a beam (width) of 41 m (135 ft) and space for 2,620 passengers and 1,253 crew. At approximately 150,000 gross registered tons (grt), the *Queen Mary 2* is nearly three times larger than *Titanic*, which had a tonnage of 46,000 grt.

★ Largest container ship
The 322.97-m-long (1,059.61-ft) Orient Overseas Container Line (OOCL) SX-class vessels have a registered capacity of 8,063 Twenty-foot Equivalent Units (TEU) of standard containers. The first, OOCL *Shenzhen*, was launched on 30 April 2003. It was built by Samsung Heavy Industries Co., Ltd (South Korea), and is owned and operated by OOCL (China). Capable of carrying 115,000 tonnes (253.5 million lb) of cargo, ships of this size will coast for 8 km (5 miles) when the engine is cut.

★ Largest sailing ship by weight
The *France 2* was a steel-hulled, five-masted barque launched at Bordeaux, France, in 1911. Her hull measured 127.4 m (418 ft) overall and she had a deadweight tonnage (cargo-carrying capacity) of 8,000 tonnes (17.6 million lb). She was wrecked off New Caledonia on 12 July 1922.

Largest steamboat �

The *American Queen* (below), a luxurious traditional steamboat (paddle-wheeled riverboat) launched in 1995, is 127.4 m (418 ft) long and has a displacement of 4,891 tonnes (10.78 million lb). Built at a cost of $65 million (£41 million) by the Delta Queen Steamboat Company (USA), it has six passenger decks and can accommodate around 450 people.

★ **Largest ship**
The world's largest ship of any kind is the oil tanker *Jahre Viking* (formerly the *Happy Giant* and *Seawise Giant*), which has a deadweight tonnage of 564,763 tonnes (1.24 billion lb). The tanker is 458.45 m (1,504 ft) long, has a beam of 68.8 m (226 ft) and a draught of 24.6 m (80 ft 9 in).

★ **Longest sailing ship**
The French-owned sister ships *Club Med I* and *Club Med II* are each 187 m (613 ft) long. They have five aluminium masts and 2,800 m² (30,100 ft²) of computer-controlled polyester sails. Each ship caters for around 400 passengers, with roughly half as many crew members. With their relatively small sail area and powerful engines, they are strictly motor-sailors.

★ **Tallest sailing-ship mast**
The 75.2-m-long (246.7-ft) luxury yacht *Mirabella V*, launched in November 2003, has a single carbon-fibre mast 90 m (295 ft) tall. The largest ever single-masted yacht,

Mirabella V was built by Vosper Thornycroft in Southampton, UK, and is available for hire at a rate of £200,000 ($250,000) per week.

★ **Largest ship ever scrapped**
The 555,051-deadweight-tonne (dwt) ultra-large crude carrier (ULCC) *Sea Giant* was bought by Wirana Shipping Corp. of Singapore in August 2003 for $17.6 million (£10.8 million) to be broken up for scrap metal. The second largest ship ever constructed, the giant tanker was 424 m (1,391 ft) long and 63 m (206 ft) wide.

★ **Fastest hovercraft**
At the 1995 World Hovercraft Championships, Bob Windt (USA) recorded a speed of 137.4 km/h (85.38 mph) on the Rio Douro River, Peso de Regua, Portugal. Windt was driving a streamlined 5.8-m (19-ft) Universal UH19P hovercraft called *Jenny 2* that had an 82-kW (110-hp) V6 car engine driving its two

fans (one at the rear to provide propulsion, and one underneath to provide lift). The speed of the craft was measured over a flying kilometre.

★ **Largest car ferry**
Irish Ferries' *Ulysses*, launched on 1 September 2000, can carry 1,342 cars. The ship is 209 m (685 ft) long and 31 m (104 ft 6 in) wide and has a capacity of 50,938 grt.

★ **Deepest-diving submersible currently in service**
The Japanese research submarine *Shinkai 6500* is a three-person submersible 9.5 m (31 ft) long, 2.7 m (8 ft 10 in) wide and 3.2 m (10 ft 6 in) high. It reached a depth of 6,526 m (21,414 ft) in the Japan Trench off Sanriku, Japan, on 11 August 1989.

★ **Largest shipwreck**
On 12 December 1979, the 321,186-deadweight-tonne (dwt) (708 million-lb) Very Large Crude Carrier (VLCC) *Energy*

Determination blew up and broke in two in the Strait of Hormuz, in the Persian Gulf. Although the ship was not actually carrying any cargo at the time, the value of the hull alone was $58 million (£27 million).

★ **Greatest distance sailed in 24 hours**
On 12 and 13 June 2002 the 33.5-m (110-ft) maxi catamaran *Maiden 2* covered 694.78 nautical miles (1,287.55 km or 800.04 miles) under sail in the North Atlantic. The average speed was 28.95 knots (53.61 km/h or 33.31 mph).

★ **Fastest Atlantic crossing in a monohull yacht**
The monohull yacht *Mari-Cha IV*, captained by Robert Miller (UK), took 6 days 17 hr 52 min 39 sec to cross the Atlantic. It set off from Ambrose Light Tower, New York, USA, on 2 October 2003 and arrived at Lizard Point, Cornwall, UK, on 9 October 2003. A crew of 24 sailed the yacht.

Aircraft 1
Feats of engineering

First power-driven flight ⌃

At 10:35 am on 17 December 1903 near Kitty Hawk, North Carolina, USA, Orville Wright (USA) flew the 9-kW (12-hp) chain-driven *Flyer I* (above) for 36.5 m (120 ft). He travelled for 12 seconds at a speed of 10.9 km/h (6.8 mph) and an altitude of 2.5–3.5 m (8–12 ft).

★ Earliest manned flight
Frenchman François Pilâtre de Rozier is widely regarded as the first person to have flown. On 15 October 1783 he rose 26 m (84 ft) into the air in a tethered hot-air balloon built by the inventors Joseph and Jacques-Etienne Montgolfier (France).

★ Earliest balloon flight
A model hot-air balloon invented by Father Bartolomeu de Gusmão (*né* Lourenço) was flown indoors at the Casa da India, Terreiro do Paço, Portugal, on 8 August 1709.

★ Fastest circumnavigation by balloon
Steve Fossett (USA) flew around the world alone in 13 days 8 hr 33 min in *Bud Light Spirit of Freedom* from 19 June to 2 July 2002. He took off from Northam, Western Australia, and landed at Eromanga, Queensland, Australia.

★ Highest altitude attained by a hot-air balloon
Per Lindstrand (UK) achieved an altitude of 19,811 m (64,997 ft) in a Colt 600 hot-air balloon over Laredo, Texas, USA, on 6 June 1988.

★ Largest working airship
The largest working airship is the WDL 1B, three of which have been built at Mulheim, Germany. Each WDL 1B is 60 m (197 ft) in length and has a volume of 7,200 m³ (254,300 ft³).

★ First jet-engined flight
Flugkapitän Erich Warsitz (Germany) flew a Heinkel He 178 at Marienehe, Germany, on 27 August 1939. It was powered by a Heinkel He S3b turbojet engine weighing 378 kg (834 lb) designed by Dr Hans Pabst von Ohain (Germany).

★ Fastest biplane
The Italian Fiat CR42B, which had a 753-kW (1,010-hp) Daimler-Benz DB601A engine, attained a speed of 520 km/h (323 mph) in 1941.

★ Fastest ever transatlantic flight
Flying a Lockheed SR-71A 'Blackbird' eastwards, Majors James V Sullivan and Noel F Widdifield (both USA) crossed the Atlantic in a time of 1 hr 54 min 56.4 sec on 1 September 1974. The average speed for the New York–London stage of 5,570.8 km (3,461.53 miles) was 2,908.02 km/h (1,806.96 mph). This figure was reduced because of a period spent refuelling from a Boeing KC-135 tanker aircraft.

★ First circumnavigation by an aircraft without refuelling
Richard 'Dick' Rutan and Jeana Yeager (both USA) circumnavigated the world in a westward direction from Edwards Air Force Base, California, USA, from 14 to 23 December 1986. Their aircraft *Voyager* was specially designed by Dick's brother Burt.

★ Fastest air speed
The fastest recorded speed in an aircraft capable of taking off and landing under its own power is 3,529.56 km/h (2,193.17 mph), by Captain Eldon W Joersz and Major George T Morgan Jr (both USA) in a Lockheed SR-71A 'Blackbird' near Beale Air Force Base, California, USA, on a 25-km (15.5-mile) course on 28 July 1976.

★ Fastest air-launched aircraft
The experimental X-15A-2 aircraft flown by USAF test pilot Pete Knight (USA) reached a speed of 7,274 km/h (4,520 mph) over California, USA, on 3 October 1967.

Largest airship »

The world's largest airships were the 213.9-tonne (471,568-lb) German *Hindenburg* (LZ 129, right) and *Graf Zeppelin II* (LZ 130), each of which had a length of 245 m (804 ft) and a hydrogen gas capacity of 200,000 m³ (7,062,000 ft³). The *Hindenburg* first flew in 1936, exploding and crashing on 6 May 1937; the *Graf Zeppelin II* first flew in 1938, although it was decommissioned within a year, broken up for scrap and melted down to build fighter planes.

Largest flying boats
« in passenger service

The Boeing Model 314 'Clipper' aircraft (left) had a wingspan of 46.3 m (152 ft), a length of 32.3 m (106 ft) and a maximum take-off weight of 38.1 tonnes (84,000 lb). Clippers were operated by Pan American Airlines during the 'golden age' of flying boats in the late 1930s.

★ Fastest piston-engined aircraft
On 21 August 1989, in Las Vegas, Nevada, USA, the *Rare Bear*, a modified Grumman F8F 'Bearcat' piloted by Lyle Shelton (USA), set the world record of 850.24 km/h (528.31 mph) for a 3-km (1.8-mile) course, as officially approved by the Fédération Aéronautique Internationale (FAI).

★ Fastest propeller-driven aircraft
The Russian Tupolev Tu-95/142 (NATO code-name 'Bear') long-range bomber is the fastest propeller-driven aircraft in standard production form, with a maximum level speed of 925 km/h (575 mph). First produced in the 1950s, it is still in service with several air forces.

★ Fastest airliner
The Tupolev Tu-144, first flown on 31 December 1968 in the former USSR, was reported to have reached approximately 2,500 km/h (1,600 mph). The aircraft was taken out of service in 1978. The BAC/Aerospatiale Concorde, first flown on 2 March 1969, cruised at up to 2,330 km/h (1,450 mph) and on 21 January 1976 became the first supersonic airliner to be used on passenger services. The Concorde was finally taken out of service by British Airways on 24 October 2003 because it was no longer profitable to run.

★ Largest amphibious aircraft currently in operation
The Russian Beriev A-40 'Albatross' aircraft, which is capable of taking off and landing on both land and water, has a maximum take-off weight of 86 tonnes (189,600 lb), a wingspan of 42.5 m (139 ft) and is 45.7 m (150 ft) long. The 'Albatross' is powered by two turbojet engines with 15,000 kg (33,000 lb) of thrust each. The multi-purpose aircraft can be used for search and rescue, cargo and passenger transport, maritime patrol and military applications.

★ Largest wingspan
The Hughes H4 Hercules flying boat, commonly known as the *Spruce Goose*, has a wingspan of 97.51 m (319 ft 11 in) and a length of 66.65 m (218 ft 8 in). The eight-engined 193-tonne (425,500-lb) aircraft was raised 21 m (70 ft) into the air in a test run of 914 m (3,000 ft), piloted by Howard Hughes (USA) off Long Beach Harbor, California, USA, on 2 November 1947, but never flew again.

★ Largest wingspan of an aircraft currently flying
A modified six-engine version of the Antonov An-124 'Ruslan', known as An-225 'Mriya' ('Dream'), which was built to carry the former Soviet Union space shuttle *Buran*, has a wingspan of 88.4 m (290 ft).

★ Longest flight by an unmanned aircraft
A USAF Northrop Grumman Global Hawk *Southern Cross II* completed a flight of 13,840 km (8,600 miles) on 22 April 2001. The *Southern Cross II*, a full-scale unmanned conventional aircraft, took off from Edwards Air Force Base, California, USA, and landed at RAAF Base Edinburgh, South Australia, 23 hr 23 min later. Global Hawks can stay aloft for over 30 hours at altitudes of 20,000 m (65,000 ft).

★ Highest altitude attained by a propeller-driven aircraft
The unmanned, solar-powered *Helios* prototype flying wing achieved a height of 29,524 m (96,863 ft) over the Hawaiian island of Kauai on 13 August 2001. Commissioned by NASA and developed by AeroVironment, Inc., of Monrovia, California, USA, *Helios* is one of a new breed of slow-flying, high-altitude aircraft that its makers believe will present a viable alternative to communications satellites.

★ Greatest passenger load
On 24 May 1991 an El Al Boeing 747 commercial airliner transported 1,088 passengers as part of Operation Solomon, which involved the evacuation of Ethiopian Jews from Addis Ababa, Ethiopia.

Largest objects transported by air ⯆

Though not the heaviest, the largest single objects to be transported by air are the 37.23-m-long (122.17-ft) reusable NASA space shuttles, which are 'piggy-backed' on top of modified Boeing 747 jets from various landing strips back to Florida's Cape Canaveral. The shuttles – *Discovery*, *Atlantis* and *Endeavour* (right) – weigh around 100 tonnes (220,500 lb) each when being transported.

★ GWR TALKS TO
Mike Bannister

For many people, a flight on Concorde was a once-in-a-lifetime taste of real luxury. The aircraft held several Guinness World Records, including those for the fastest transatlantic flight by a commercial aircraft and the fastest aerial circumnavigation. Mike Bannister (UK, above right) piloted Concorde for 22 years altogether, and though the aircraft was taken out of service last year, he cherishes very fond memories of it.

When did you first decide to become a pilot?
When I was a little boy my family used to take holidays on the English south coast and the journey would take us five and a half hours by coach. One day I saw an aeroplane fly overhead while we were on the beach. I worked out the same journey would only take 20 minutes by air and immediately decided I wanted to learn to fly!

How long have you been flying?
I went to pilot training school in 1967, and in 1969 I saw the first flight of Concorde and decided that was what I wanted to fly. I first flew Concorde on 18 August 1977 and worked as a co-pilot and instructor until 1989. I flew other aircraft for a few years and then, in 1995, I was offered the chance to go back to Concorde as Chief Pilot. I flew her 'til her retirement on 25 November 2003.

Is flying Concorde different to flying other aircraft?
Yes, it's a completely different experience. Concorde flew at both supersonic and subsonic speeds, and cruised at twice the altitude of normal aircraft. She was a delight to fly – you could control her using only your fingertips! Because she had a very tough fuselage, the cabin only needed to be pressurized at 5,000 feet; most aircraft are pressurized at 8,000 feet. Also, the aircraft travelled faster than the Earth rotates, so the sun was in effect going backwards and your bodyclock would reset.

This is why you'd feel less jetlagged flying by Concorde. Flying at the edge of space, you could see the Earth's curvature!

Did you have many memorable passengers?
There was a subdued elegance about Concorde, and there were always a lot of business passengers on board. There were also always people taking the trip of a lifetime, and we had a number of celebrities too. After its retirement was announced, the atmosphere on board became more like a party!

What other aircraft have you flown?
I've flown over 100 different types of aircraft over the years but most recently flew a Tiger Moth for the first time.

Finally, what tips would you give to any aspiring pilots?
Whatever you dream of, live your dream – chase it! If you find something you want to do as a child and you do it in your adult life it's very satisfying and leads to a very happy life!

Heaviest production aircraft ⌄

The Ukrainian Antonov An-124 'Ruslan' cargo aircraft (below) has a maximum take-off weight of 405 tonnes (892,000 lb). It has a cargo hold with a usable volume of 1,014 m³ (35,800 ft³).

Largest helicopter ⌃ currently in production

The five-person Russian Mil Mi-26 (above) has a maximum take-off weight of 56,000 kg (123,500 lb). Unladen it weighs 28,200 kg (62,200 lb) and its overall length is 40 m (131 ft). The eight-bladed main rotor has a diameter of 32 m (105 ft) and it is powered by two 8,500-kW (11,400-hp) turbine engines.

★ Fastest aerial circumnavigation

The fastest flight under the Fédération Aéronautique Internationale (FAI) rules, which permit flights that exceed the length of the Tropic of Cancer or Capricorn (36,787.6 km or 22,858.8 miles), was one of 31 hr 27 min 49 sec by an Air France Concorde (Capts Michel Dupont and Claude Hetru, both France) from JFK airport in New York, USA, eastbound via Toulouse, Dubai, Bangkok, Guam, Honolulu and Acapulco on 15 and 16 August 1995. There were 80 passengers and 18 crew on board flight AF1995.

★ Fastest transatlantic flight by a commercial aircraft

A British Airways Concorde took 2 hr 52 min 59 sec to travel the 6,035 km (8,750 miles) between New York (JFK airport) and London (Luton) on 7 February 1996, breaking its own record set in April 1990 by one and a half minutes. The plane, piloted by Captain Leslie Scott (UK), averaged more than 2,011 km/h (1,250 mph).

★ Largest helicopter ever

The Russian Mil Mi-12 was powered by four 4,850-kw (6,500-hp) turboshaft engines and had a rotor diameter of 67 m (219 ft 10 in). It was 37 m (121 ft 5 in) long and had a maximum take-off weight of 103 tonnes (227,000 lb). Only one was ever produced.

★ Longest helicopter flight

Robert Ferry (USA) piloted his Hughes YOH-6A helicopter 3,561.6 km (2,213.1 miles) from Culver City, California, USA, to Ormond Beach, Florida, USA, without landing. He completed his FAI-approved flight on 6 April 1966.

★ Fastest circumnavigation by helicopter

John Williams and Ron Bower (both USA) flew around the world in a Bell 430 helicopter in 17 days 6 hr 14 min 25 sec (average speed of 91.76 km/h or 57.02 mph). They left Fair Oaks, London, UK, on 17 August 1996 and flew west, against prevailing winds, arriving back at Fair Oaks on 3 September 1996.

★ Greatest altitude reached in an autogyro

On 17 April 1998 William B Clem III (USA) flew his home-built Dominator autogyro 7,456 m (24,462 ft) above Wauchula, Florida, USA. It was powered by an 85-kW (115-hp) Rotax 914 engine.

★ Fastest speed in an autogyro

On 18 September 1986, Wing Cdr Kenneth H Wallis (UK) flew his WA-116/F/S autogyro, with a 45-kW (60-hp) Franklin aero-engine, at 193.6 km/h (120.3 mph) over a 3-km (1.8-mile) straight course at Marham, Norfolk, UK.

★ Most powerful jet engine

A General Electric GE90-115B turbofan engine achieved steady state thrust of 568,927 N (127,900 lb) during final certification testing at Peebles, Ohio, USA, in December 2002.

★ Largest ever airline

In the last complete year of the former USSR's existence (1990), the official state airline Aeroflot employed 600,000 people – more than the top 18 US airlines put together at that time. Aeroflot flew 139 million passengers annually with 20,000 pilots along 1,000,000 km (620,000 miles) of domestic routes across 11 time zones.

★ Longest duration flight in a human-powered vehicle

Kanellos Kanellopoulos (Greece) kept his *Daedalus 88* aircraft aloft for 3 hr 54 min 59 sec on 23 April 1988 while pedalling the 115.11 km (71.53 miles) between Heraklion, Crete, and the Greek island of Santorini. His flight ended prematurely when an offshore gust of wind broke off the plane's tail and it crashed into the sea a few metres from shore.

★ Largest parafoil

The largest parafoil parachute has a span of 43.6 m (143 ft) and a surface area of 700 m² (7,500 ft²), nearly one and a half times the size of the wings of a Boeing 747. It was developed by NASA to bring its X-38 craft back to the Earth's surface after re-entering the atmosphere.

Large vehicles
Feats of engineering

Largest land << transport vehicle

The two 2,721-tonne (6 million-lb) crawler-transporters (left) that carry space shuttles to their launch pad at Kennedy Space Center, Florida, USA, are the largest vehicles used for moving objects between two points (though they are not the largest mobile machines). Each one is 40 m (131 ft) wide, 35 m (114 ft) long and runs on eight giant tank-style tracks.

★ Largest land vehicle
The largest machine capable of moving under its own power is the 14,196-tonne (31.3 million-lb) RB293 bucket wheel excavator, an earth-moving machine manufactured by MAN TAKRAF of Leipzig, Germany. Employed in an open-cast coal mine in the German state of North Rhine-Westphalia, it is 220 m (722 ft) long, 94.5 m (310 ft) tall at its highest point and is capable of shifting 240,000 m³ (8.475 million ft³) of earth daily.

★ Longest vehicle
The longest land vehicles ever made were the overland supply trains built by RG Le Tourneau, Inc., of Longview, Texas, USA, for the US Army. One example: the Arctic Snow Train, owned by the famous wire-walker Steve McPeak (USA), had 54 wheels, was 174.3 m (572 ft) long and had a gross weight of around 400 tonnes (880,000 lb). The Snow Train had a top speed of 32 km/h (20 mph), and it was driven by a crew of six when used as an overland train for the military.

★ Longest road train
A road train 1,235 m (4,052 ft) long and comprising 87 trailers and a single prime mover was assembled near Mungindi, New South Wales, Australia, on 29 March 2003 at the Mighty Mungindi Truck and Trailer Pull.

★ Largest fork-lift truck
In 1991 Kalmar LMV of Lidhult, Sweden, manufactured three counterbalanced fork-lift trucks capable of lifting loads up to 90 tonnes (198,500 lb) at a load centre of 2.4 m (7.87 ft). They were built for a great man-made river project in Libya comprising two separate pipelines, one 998 km (620 miles) long, running from Sarir to the Gulf of Sirte, and the other 897 km (557 miles) long, running from Tazirbu to Benghazi.

★ Largest bulldozer
The Komatsu D575A Super Dozer is the world's largest bulldozer, weighing in at 152.6 tonnes (336,425 lb). Its 7.4 x 3.2-m (24.27 x 10.66-ft) blade has a capacity of 69 m³ (2,437 ft³). The 11.72-m-long (38-ft 5-in) pusher moves on tank-style tracks and is powered by an 858-kW (1,150-hp) turbocharged diesel engine.

★ Largest two-axle dumper truck
The T-282, manufactured by the Liebherr Mining Equipment Co. (USA), is the world's largest two-axle dump truck, with a payload capacity of around 327 tonnes (720,900 lb). The diesel-electric-powered vehicle is 14.47 m (47 ft 6 in) long, 8.7 m (28 ft 7 in) wide, 7.3 m (24 ft) high, and weighs around 201 tonnes (443,100 lb).

★ Largest front-end loader
The largest wheel-driven front-end loader is the LeTourneau L-2350, which weighs 262 tonnes (578,000 lb) and can lift up to 72.5 tonnes (160,000 lb) in its 40.5-m³-capacity (1,430-ft³) bucket. This massive earth-mover is powered by a giant diesel engine that develops 1,715 kW (2,300 hp).

★ Largest dragline excavator
Big Muskie, a walking earth-moving machine weighing 13,200 tonnes (29.1 million lb), was the largest ever dragline excavator, weighing as much as nearly 10,000 saloon cars. It stood at the Central Ohio Coal Co.'s Muskingham open-cast coal mine in Ohio, USA, but was dismantled in 1999.

Tallest limousine

The world's tallest limousine (below) measures 3.33 m (10 ft 11 in) from the ground to the roof.

Built by Gary and Shirley Duval (both Australia), it has an eight-wheel independent suspension system and sits on eight monster truck tyres. It has two separate engines and took a little over 4,000 hours to build.

Largest ⋀ monster truck

Bigfoot 5 (above) is 4.7 m (15 ft 4 in) tall with 3-m-tall (10-ft) tyres and weighs 17,200 kg (38,000 lb). It was built in the summer of 1986 and is one of a fleet of 17 *Bigfoot* trucks created by Bob Chandler (USA). Now permanently parked in St Louis, Missouri, USA, it makes occasional exhibition appearances at local shows.

★ **Largest operating dragline excavator**
The largest operating dragline excavator is the Bucyrus 2570WS, which is based at Peak Downs mine in Queensland, Australia, and weighs 7,271 tonnes (16 million lb). It has a boom length of 109.7 m (360 ft) to carry its giant 120-m³ (4,238-ft³) bucket, which is in turn suspended from 14.3-cm-thick (5.62-in) cables.

★ **Largest shovel**
The largest mechanical shovel ever built was the Marion 6360 stripping shovel, which had an operating weight of around 13,000 tonnes (28.6 million lb) and a bucket capacity of 137 m³ (4,860 ft³). It had a reach of 72 m (236 ft), a dumping height of 46.6 m (153 ft), and was in service at an open-cast coal mine near Percy, Illinois, USA, until 1991, when it was taken out of service after a fire.

★ **Largest operating shovel**
The largest mechanical shovel currently in use is the Bucyrus 1950B stripping shovel – known

as 'The Silver Spade' – which weighs in at approximately 6,350 tonnes (14 million lb). It operates at an open-cast coal mine near New Athens, Ohio, USA.

★ **Largest hydraulic shovel excavator**
The RH 400-2000 hydraulic shovel excavator manufactured by O&K Mining (Germany) is the largest of its kind in the world. The giant crawler, which is capable of filling the world's largest dumper truck in just six passes, weighs 900 tonnes (1,985,000 lb) and has a shovel capacity of 51.7 m³ (1,825.7 ft³). The top of the driver's cab is 10.2 m (33 ft 6 in), or around three storeys, above the ground, and the machine is powered by a 3,280-kW (4,400-hp) Cummins diesel engine, which is fed by a 16,000-litre (3,519-gal) fuel tank.

★ **Tallest mobile crane**
The Demag CC 12600, made by Mannesmann Dematic, is 198 m (650 ft) high in

its tallest configuration, which comprises a 120-m (394-ft) 'fixed jib' attached to a 114-m (374-ft) near-vertical boom. It has a maximum lifting capacity of 1,600 tonnes (3.5 million lb) at a 22-m (72-ft) radius and is so large that it requires 100 trucks to transport all of its different parts to a site.

★ **Largest tyre**
Standing 4 m (13 ft 1 in) tall and weighing more than 4 tonnes (8,800 lb), the world's largest tyres are built by Michelin to fit on to the world's biggest dump trucks.

★ **Longest ramp jump in a monster truck**
Bigfoot 14, driven by Dan Runte (USA), jumped 61.5 m (202 ft) over a Boeing 727 passenger jet on 11 September 1999 at Smyrna Airport, Tennessee, USA. He was the first person ever to achieve this feat.

★ **Fastest speed in a monster truck**
Dan Runte (USA) reached a speed of 111.5 km/h (69.3 mph) in *Bigfoot 14* on 11 September 1999 at Symrna Airport, Nashville, Tennessee, USA, the highest speed ever recorded in a monster truck. The speed was recorded during the run-up to the longest ever monster truck jump of 61.5 m (202 ft).

★ **Longest bus**
The articulated DAF Super CityTrain buses of the Democratic Republic of Congo are 32.2 m (105 ft) long and can carry 350 passengers comfortably. Each bus weighs 28 tonnes (61,700 lb) unladen.

★ **Largest bus fleet**
The Andhra Pradesh State Road Transport Corporation (India) operates around 18,900 buses on 8,678 routes, carrying an estimated 13 million passengers every day.

Science & technology

Contents

Least ≪ dense solid

Lawrence Livermore National Laboratory (USA) has produced an aerogel (left) with a density of just 1.9 mg/cm^3 (0.47 grains/in^3).

Aerogels are nanoporous, lightweight solids that physically resemble 'solid smoke'. Aerogels also have the lowest refractive index and the highest thermal insulation of any solid material.

★ **Most accurate kilogramme**
The kilogramme is the only Système International (SI) base unit of measurement whose definition is still based on a physical prototype. The world's most accurate kilogramme is a cylinder of platinum and iridium that was made in 1889. It is maintained at the Bureau International des Poids et Mesures (BIPM) at Sèvres near Paris, France.

★ **Smallest microchain drive**
The links on a microchain drive created by Sandia National Laboratories in Albuquerque, New Mexico, USA, and announced in January 2002, are only 50 micrometres apart. The microchain is constructed of silicon and is designed to transmit power in micro-electromechanical devices.

★ **Darkest man-made substance**
A black coating composed of a nickel-phosphorus alloy, first developed by researchers in the USA and India in 1980, reflects just 0.16% of visible light,

making it around 25 times less reflective than conventional black paint. In 1990, the Anritsu Corporation (Japan) refined this coating to produce the darkest version so far. In 2002, the National Physical Laboratory, UK, developed a new method for the commercial manufacturing of this coating.

★ **Lowest man-made temperature**
Scientists at the Massachusetts Institute of Technology, Cambridge, USA, led by Aaron Leanhardt (USA), announced in September 2003 that they had achieved a temperature of 450 picokelvin above absolute zero (0.00000000045° above absolute zero).

★ **Most powerful pulsed neutron spallation source**
ISIS, at the Rutherford Appleton Laboratory, Chilton, Oxfordshire, UK, is the world's most powerful pulsed neutron source. Covering the size of a soccer field, it produces 4×10^{16} fast neutrons per second. These are focused into beams in a neutron

microscope, which allows scientists to study, at a microscopic scale, the atomic and molecular arrangements that give materials their unique properties.

★ **Longest continuous observational science data**
Astronomers have access to a continuous set of observational data of the sunspot number (number of sunspots on the Sun) dating back to 1750.

★ **Quietest place on Earth**
Ultra-sensitive tests carried out on 21 January 2004 at the Anechoic Test Chamber, Orfield Laboratories, Minneapolis, Minnesota, USA, gave a background noise reading of -9.4 decibels A-weighted (dBA).

★ **Longest-running laboratory experiment**
The Pitch Drop Experiment has been running since 1930 at the University of Queensland, Australia. It consists of black pitch contained in a glass funnel, with the entire apparatus

enclosed in a container. It demonstrates that pitch is actually an extremely viscous liquid. Once the stem of the funnel was cut, the pitch slowly began to drip. In late 2000, the eighth drop fell. From this experiment it has been possible to show that the viscosity of pitch is about 100 billion times that of water. There is enough pitch left for this experiment to run for another hundred years.

★ **Smallest abacus**
In November 1996, scientists at the IBM Research Division's Zurich laboratory built an abacus with individual molecules as beads, each with a diameter of less than one nanometre (one millionth of a millimetre). The IBM scientists succeeded in forming stable rows of 10 molecules along steps just one atom high on a copper surface. The steps acted as rails, similar to the earliest form of the abacus, which had grooves instead of rods to keep the beads in line.

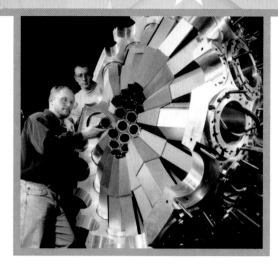

Most sensitive ⌃ gamma ray detector

Gammasphere (above) at the

Argonne National Laboratory, Illinois, USA, is a gamma ray 'microscope' used in nuclear physics research. It is a cylinder measuring 3 m (10 ft) high, pierced with 110 gamma ray detectors. These focus inwards to a central target area that is bombarded with ions from a particle accelerator.

Highest-intensity ⌄ focused laser

The Vulcan laser (right) at the Rutherford Appleton Laboratory, Chilton, Oxfordshire, UK, is the highest-intensity focused laser in the world. Following its upgrade, which was completed in 2002, it is now capable of producing a laser beam with an irradiance (focused intensity) of 10^{21} W/cm^2.

★ **Discoverer of greatest number of elements**
Albert Ghiorso (USA) has discovered or co-discovered 12 chemical elements since he began his scientific career in 1942. The first was element 95, americum, in 1944. Albert is still at the Lawrence Berkeley Laboratory, California, USA, where he has worked since 1946.

★ **Shortest flash of light**
In February 2004 a team of physicists led by Dr Ferenc Krausz (Austria) of Vienna University of Technology, Vienna, Austria, announced that they had created pulses of ultraviolet laser light lasting just 250 attoseconds (250 x 10^{-16} seconds). Using these attosecond light pulses, they were able to observe electrons in neon atoms and distinguish between events just 100 attoseconds apart.

★ **Largest telescope**
The twin Keck telescopes, on the summit of Hawaii's dormant Mauna Kea volcano, are the largest optical and infrared telescopes. Each of them is eight storeys tall and weighs 300 tonnes (661,000 lb). Both Kecks have a 10-m (32-ft 9.6-in) mirror comprising 36 hexagonal segments that act together to create a single reflective surface. Keck I began scientific observations in May 1993 and Keck II began in October 1996.

★ **Largest robotic telescope**
The Liverpool Telescope, owned by the Astrophysics Research Institute (ARI) of Liverpool John Moores University, UK, has a main mirror with a diameter of 2 m (6 ft 6.72 in). Located on La Palma, Canary Islands, Spain, it was designed for observing invisible and near-infrared wavelengths and achieved first light on 27 July 2003.

★ **Highest-resolution optical image**
The highest-resolution image ever taken shows details smaller than 20 billionths of a metre across. Using a technique called 'near-field Raman scattering', a team at the University of Rochester, New York, USA, led by Professor Lukas Novotny (USA), was able to image individual carbon nanotubes with visible light. The research was announced in March 2003.

★ **Most powerful X-ray generator**
The Z Machine at the Sandia National Laboratories in Albuquerque, New Mexico, USA, can, very briefly, generate X-rays with a power output roughly the equivalent to 80 times that of all the world's electrical generators.

★ **Largest Van de Graaff generator**
In 1931 Dr Robert J Van de Graaff built the largest Van de Graaff generator at the Massachusetts Institute of Technology, USA. It was originally used to help with research into high-energy X-rays and atom smashing, and is now on permanent display at the Thomson Theater of Electricity at the Boston Museum of Science, USA. It consists of two columns each with a 4.57-m-wide (15-ft) hollow aluminium sphere at the top. Originally the two spheres were oppositely charged, which resulted in lightning-like discharges of 5 million volts. Today, both spheres are joined together and discharge to props and grounded probes, rather than discharging to each other.

★ **Greatest altitude achieved by a laser-powered craft**
On 2 October 2000, Lightcraft Technologies (USA) successfully flew a 12.2-cm-diameter (4.8-in) craft to a height of 71 m (233 ft), powered only by light. They used a US Army 10-kW (13.4-hp) pulsed carbon dioxide laser on the ground, fired upwards at the 51-g (1.8-oz) craft, which reflects the light backwards to a point just beneath it. The resulting expansion of the superheated air provides the craft with thrust. These test flights took place at the White Sands Missile Range, New Mexico, USA.

Hardest element ≫

Carbon (C) has three different allotropes (different configurations of atoms),

but the diamond allotrope, which has an extremely strong lattice structure, has the maximum value of 10 on Moh's relative scale of hardness. Diamonds (below) are formed at least 150 km (93 miles) beneath the Earth's surface, where the pressures and temperatures are great enough to force the carbon atoms to adopt this structure.

Weakest force ≪

Four fundamental forces in the universe account for all interactions

between matter and energy. They are the strong nuclear, weak nuclear, electromagnetic and gravitational forces. The weakest of these is gravity. A good example of how much weaker gravity is compared to, say, electromagnetism, is that it is easy for a toy magnet to pick up a handful of nails while the whole of Earth's gravity is trying to pull them back down. The strongest force is the strong nuclear.

★ Heaviest and lightest quarks
Of the six 'flavours' of quarks (sub-atomic particles) – known as 'up', 'down', 'top', 'bottom', 'strange' and 'charmed' – the heaviest is the top quark, which has a mass of 170 giga-electron-volts (GeV). It was discovered in February 1995 at Fermilab, Batavia, Illinois, USA. The lightest are the 'up' and 'down' quarks, both at 0.15 GeV.

★ Fastest speed possible
The speed of light is achieved only by light and other forms of electromagnetic radiation, eg radio waves, infrared radiation and X-rays. The speed of light varies depending on what it is travelling through. Light travels fastest through a vacuum, where its velocity is 299,792,458 m/s (around 300,000 km/s or 186,000 miles per second). This means that when you look at the Moon, you see it as it was about 1.3 seconds ago, and the Sun as it was around 8.3 minutes ago.

★ Most common element
Hydrogen (H) represents over 90% of all matter in the universe and 70.68% of all matter in the Solar System. Iron (Fe) is the most common element on Earth, making up 36% of its mass, and molecular nitrogen (N_2) is the most common element in the atmosphere at 75.52% by mass or 78.08% by volume.

★ Rarest element on Earth
Only around 25 g (0.9 oz) of the element astatine (At) occurs naturally in the Earth's crust. Astatine was discovered in 1931 by Fred Allison and EJ Murphy (both USA).

★ Element with the highest melting and boiling point
Of all the metals, tungsten (W) has the highest melting point at 3,414°C (6,177°F) and the highest boiling point at 5,847°C (10,557°F). The graphite form of carbon (C) sublimes directly to vapour at 3,704°C (6,699°F) and can be obtained as a liquid only from above a temperature of 4,730°C (8,546°F) and a pressure of 10 megapascals (100 atmospheres).

★ Most ductile element
One gram of gold (Au) can be drawn to 2.4 km (1.5 miles), or 1 oz to 69 km (43 miles).

★ Oldest biological molecules
Biological molecules extracted from the rib of an iguanodon – a huge herbivorous dinosaur – found in a quarry in Surrey, UK, have been dated at around 125 million years old. The research was carried out by Liverpool University, the University of Wales and the Natural History Museum (all UK), and the results were announced in September 2003.

★ Oldest living bacteria
Bacteria trapped in suspended animation inside salt crystals for 250 million years have been revived and cultured by US scientists. Designated *Bacillus 2-9-3*, this species is 10 times older than the previous oldest revived bacteria.

Element with the ⌄ lowest melting and boiling point

For metallic elements, mercury (Hg, below) has the lowest melting and

boiling points at -38.829°C (-37.892°F) and 356.62°C (673.92°F) respectively. Helium (He) cannot be obtained as a solid at atmospheric pressure, the minimum pressure required being 2.532 megapascals (24.985 atmospheres) at a temperature of -272.375°C (-458.275°F). Helium also has the lowest boiling point, at -268.928°C (-452.070°F).

★ Most radiation-resistant microbe

The bacterium *Deinococcus radiodurans* (formerly *Micrococcus radiodurans*) can withstand atomic radiation of 6.5 million röntgens, or 10,000 times the level that would be fatal to the average human.

★ Highest microbe

In April 1967 NASA reported that bacteria had been discovered at an altitude of 41.13 km (25.56 miles).

★ Smelliest molecules

Ethyl mercaptan (C_2H_5SH) and butyl seleno-mercaptan (C_4H_9SeH) have an odour reminiscent of a combination of rotting cabbage, garlic, onions, burnt toast and sewer gas. Ethyl mercaptan is added to odourless gas to act as a warning agent.

★ Smelliest substances

The smelliest substances are the man-made 'Who-Me?' and 'US Government Standard Bathroom Malodor', which have five and eight chemical ingredients respectively. 'Who-Me?' was developed by the US military during World War II and was intended to be sprayed on German troops, then occupying France, to humiliate them. Bathroom Malodor smells primarily of human faeces and becomes incredibly repellent to people at just two parts per million. The substance was originally created to test the power of deodorizing products.

★ Lightest known particle

Neutrinos are the lightest known particles in the universe, with a maximum mass of 0.000000000000000 000000000000000000018 kg. Neutrinos come in three varieties – electron, muon and tau neutrinos. The mass is an average of the three types.

★ Oldest irrational number

An irrational number is a number that cannot be expressed as a fraction or an integer. The first irrational number discovered was the square root of 2, by Hippasus of Metapontum (then part of Magna Graecia, southern Italy) in around 500 BC.

★ Lowest temperature possible

Temperature is a direct result of the vibrations of the atoms or molecules that make up matter. The coldest that any substance can be is when there is no vibration in its atoms or molecules. This is referred to as absolute zero, and is at 0 K (zero Kelvin) or -273.15°C (-459.67°F). Absolute zero has never been achieved in an Earth laboratory, and even in the coldest parts of deep space, the temperature is slightly above absolute zero. There is no upper limit to how hot something can be.

★ Largest known prime number

A prime number is a number that is only divisible by 1 and itself. The largest known prime number is $2^{20,996,011}-1$, which contains 6,320,430 digits. It was discovered by Michael Shafer (USA), a chemical engineering student, on 17 November 2003. Shafer was running software on his computer as part of the Great Internet Mersenne Prime Search, or GIMPS.

★ Greatest time dilation

The most time dilation experienced by an individual is around 1/50th of a second, for Russian cosmonaut Sergei Avdeyev. This is a consequence of the 747 days 14 hr 22 min he has spent in low Earth orbit, travelling at around 27,000 km/h (17,000 mph). Relative to people on Earth, Avdeyev has 'time travelled' 1/50th of a second into the future, a phenomenon consistent with Albert Einstein's Theory of Relativity.

★ Longest time survived in space by bacteria

From 7 April 1984 to 11 January 1990, *E. Coli* bacteria cells survived unshielded onboard NASA's Long Duration Exposure Facility satellite in low Earth orbit. The satellite and its 57 experiments were retrieved by the space shuttle *Challenger*.

Largest ancient stone circle ⌃⌃

The 11.5-ha (28.4-acre) earthworks and stone circles of Avebury, Wiltshire, UK (above), which were 'rediscovered' in 1646, represent the UK's largest prehistoric monument and largest henge (a circular area, often containing a circle of stones or wooden posts). The earliest calibrated date in the area of this Neolithic site is c. 4200 BC. The work is 365 m (1,200 ft) in diameter with a ditch 12 m (40 ft) wide around the perimeter.

★ **Largest prehistoric building**
Archaeological tests reveal that a 5,000-year-old structure, probably a temple, discovered at a sacred Stone Age site at Stanton Drew, Somerset, UK, had a diameter of 90 m (295 ft) and was at least six times the size of Stonehenge. The building is estimated to have been 10 m (33 ft) high, possibly with a thatched roof supported by more than 400 wooden columns, each approximately a metre in diameter, forming nine rings.

★ **Earliest places of worship**
Many archaeologists are of the opinion that the decorated Upper Palaeolithic caves of Europe (c. 30,000–10,000 BC) were used as places of worship or religious ritual.

★ **Earliest alphabet**
The earliest known example of alphabetic writing is that found on clay tablets showing the 32 cuneiform (wedge-shaped) letters of the Ugaritic alphabet, a now-extinct Semitic language of Syria. The tablets were found in 1929 at Ugarit (now Ras Shamra), Syria and were dated to around 1450 BC.

★ **Earliest castle**
The 20-storey Gomdan or Gumdan Castle, in the old city of Sana'a, Yemen, dates from before AD 200 and is now a UNESCO World Heritage site.

★ **Earliest parliament**
The earliest known legislative assembly, or *ukkim*, was a bicameral (two-chamber) gathering in Erech, Iraq, in c. 2800 BC.

The oldest recorded legislative body is the Icelandic *Althing* founded in AD 930.

The earliest known use of the term 'parliament' came in an official royal document dating from 19 December 1241, in which the term referred to a summons to King Henry III's Council in England.

★ **Oldest stained glass**
Pieces of stained glass dating back to before AD 850 (some possibly even back to the 7th century) were excavated by Rosemary Cramp (UK) at Monkwearmouth and Jarrow (both UK), set into a window of that date in St Paul's Church, Jarrow, Co. Durham, UK.

★ **Earliest canal**
Early in 1968 archaeologists found relics of canals dating back to c. 4000 BC near Mandali, Iraq.

★ **Earliest zoo**
The earliest known collection of animals was established at modern-day Puzurish, Iraq, by Shulgi, a 3rd-dynasty ruler of Ur from 2097–2094 BC.

★ **Earliest domestication of dogs**
Archaeologists believe that the Palaeolithic humans in East Asia domesticated dogs (*Canis familiaris*) approximately 15,000 years ago by successfully breeding aggression out of wolves (*C. lupus*).

★ **Earliest domestication of horses**
Evidence from Ukraine indicates that the domestication of horses so that they could be ridden may have happened some time before 4000 BC.

★ **Oldest remains of modern humans**
The oldest remains of modern humans discovered so far date back 160,000 years. They consist of two complete crania, belonging to one adult and one child, and fragments from another adult skull. The remains were discovered in Ethiopia by a team of scientists led by Tim White of Berkeley University of California, USA.

Largest geoglyphs ⋀

The so-called 'Nazca lines' are a group of gigantic figures (geoglyphs) engraved on the desert ground of Nazca, Peru, representing plants, animals (monkey, above), insects and a variety of geometric shapes. Most can only be appreciated from the air. The designs occupy a 500-km² (190-mile²) area of land and they average 180 m (600 ft) in length, although one perfectly formed arrow exceeds 490 m (1,600 ft).

Oldest ice body ⋁

In September 1991, the preserved remains of a Neolithic man were discovered, 5,300 years after he had died, by two hikers on a melting glacier in the Tyrolean Alps on the Italian-Austrian border. Analysis of 'Ötzi' (below), as the mummy was named, and his belongings have given a new insight into the technology and culture of central Europe some 5,000 years ago.

★ Oldest hominid footprints
A hominid is any primate of the family Hominidae, which includes modern man (*Homo sapiens*) and his ancestors. The oldest known human-like footprints were discovered in Laetoli, northern Tanzania, in 1978. They belong to two or three hominids striding upright on the ashy plains of the area some 3.6 million years ago. The trackway consists of some 70 footprints in two parallel trails about 30 m (100 ft) long.

★ Oldest mummy
Mummification dates from 2600 BC, or the 4th dynasty of the Egyptian pharaohs. The oldest complete mummy is of Wati, a court musician of c. 2400 BC from the tomb of Nefer in Saqqâra, Egypt, found in 1944.

★ Oldest coin
The earliest coins recorded were made during the reign of King Gyges of Lydia, Turkey, in c. 630 BC, and consisted of electrum, a naturally occurring amalgam of gold and silver.

★ Earliest measures
The *beqa* of the Amratian period of Egyptian civilization, c. 3800 BC, found at Naqada, Egypt, are cylindrical weights with rounded ends. They weigh from 188.7 to 211.2 g (6.66 to 7.45 oz).

★ Oldest industry
Flint knapping, which involves the production of chopping tools and hand axes, dates back 2.5 million years in Ethiopia. The earliest evidence of trading in exotic stone and amber dates from c. 28,000 BC in Europe.

★ Oldest batteries
Around a dozen clay jars, measuring around 13 cm (5 in) long and dating back around 2,000 years, are believed to be the world's oldest electrical cells, or batteries. Some reports claim that they were discovered in the basement of the Baghdad Museum, Iraq, by German archaeologist Wilhelm König in 1938. The jars contain a copper cylinder and an iron rod, along with signs of acidic corrosion. Modern replicas of these objects have been shown to function as rudimentary electrical cells, and it is possible that they were used for electroplating.

★ Oldest Greek vessel excavated
The 'Kyrenia Ship' was built in the early 4th century BC and sank some 80 years later less than a mile off Kyrenia (northern Cyprus), carrying 400 amphorae (clay vessels) of Rhodian wine and volcanic grain from the island of Kos. The vessel, a 15-m-long (49-ft) open boat, was found in 1967 by a Cypriot diver. It is considered to be the finest preserved ship of the late classical period of Greek civilization, the time of Alexander the Great.

★ Earliest use of the wheel
The earliest documented use of the wheel for transport dates back 5,500 years to Mesopotamia (modern Iraq). Previous to this time, humans had moved heavy objects from one place to another by rolling them over logs.

★ Largest Bronze Age copper mine
The Great Orme Mines, Llandudno, UK, contain at least 8 km (5 miles) of accessible tunnels. They were mined for copper from around 1800 BC until the end of the Bronze Age (c. 750 BC). Mining occurred again from 1692 until 1881. The first chambers of the original mines were discovered in 1976.

Fastest-growing Internet service provider ≫

Since its launch by NTT DoCoMo in February 1999, i-Mode has gained more than 40 million subscribers. i-Mode is a Japanese service specifically aimed at mobile phone users.

≪ Earliest e-mail

In 1971, Ray Tomlinson (USA, above) sent the first e-mail as an experiment to see if he could get two computers to exchange a message. It was Ray who decided to use the @ symbol to separate the recipient's name from their location. The first e-mail message was: 'QWERTYUIOP', the letters on the top line of a keyboard.

★ First hypertext browser

In October 1990, Tim Berners-Lee (UK) started work on a global hypertext browser. The result – the World Wide Web – was made available on the Internet in the summer of 1991. Berners-Lee had originally proposed a global hypertext project to let people combine their knowledge in a web of hypertext documents in 1989.

★ Largest Internet search engine

Google, with around 4.28 billion pages, has the largest continually refreshed index of webpages out of all the world's search engines. The company was founded by Larry Page and Sergey Brin (both USA). Google handles 200 million search queries every day – 2,000 a second during peak hours – and has an index of 3 trillion words.

★ Highest-capacity intercontinental Internet route

In 2003, the Internet routes between Europe and the USA/Canada had a bandwidth capacity of 386,221 megabits per second (Mbps). (This is the equivalent of between five and ten full-length DVD movies per second.) The lowest capacity was between Africa and USA/Canada, with a bandwidth capacity of 1,351.5 Mbps.

★ Largest Internet joke vote

Laughlab, an Internet experiment into humour, was conducted by psychologist Richard Wiseman, University of Hertfordshire, Hatfield, UK, and the British Association for the Advancement of Science. The experiment ran from September 2001 to October 2002, during which more than 40,000 jokes were submitted from the worldwide public, and around 2 million votes were cast on which one was the funniest.

If you'd like to find out what the winning joke was, and also see some of the runners-up, then visit our website: www.guinnessworldrecords.com/joke.

★ Most expensive Internet domain name

The Internet domain name business.com was sold by entrepreneur Marc Ostrofsky (USA) on 1 December 1999 for £4.6 million ($7.5 million).

★ Most searched-for plant and animal on the Internet

According to Google, the most searched-for plant on the Internet is the rose.

The most searched-for animal is the domestic cat, according to the same search engine.

★ Largest single e-commerce transaction

American Internet tycoon Mark Cuban (USA) bought a Gulfstream V business jet over the Internet in October 1999. The jet changed hands for $40 million (£25 million).

★ Longest live event streamed over the Internet

Beginning on 21 October 2001, the Canadian Musicians for Liberty Organization held the longest live event ever streamed over the Internet. Around 1,000 musicians, comprising various bands and solo artists, took turns playing live music to a small local audience as well as directly to the Internet (in both video and sound). The concert continued for 181 hours, with breaks of only a few minutes while the acts swapped over. The event was held to raise money for the Canadian Red Cross USA Relief Fund and took place at Touchdowns Bar and Grill, Mississauga, Ontario, Canada.

Most globally connected ⌃ city on the Internet

According to TeleGeography, London, UK, had an international Internet bandwidth of 550 gigabytes per second (Gbps) of Internet traffic in 2003. By contrast, New York City, USA, had an internet bandwidth of 339 Gbps in 2003.

★ **Largest exclusive concert on the Internet**

A record 9,804 people logged on to a concert by Queen drummer Roger Taylor (UK) and five band members for 45 minutes, at the Cyberbarn, Thursley, Surrey, UK, on 24 September 1998. The concert was exclusive because it was held in Taylor's barn and the only audience was via the Internet.

★ **Internet2 land speed record**

Internet2 is a consortium of 206 universities working to develop the next generation of the Internet. On 14 April 2004 an international team of scientists achieved a result of 69,073 terabit-meters per second, by transferring 838.86 gigabytes of data across 16,343 kilometers (10,155 miles) of network in 1588 seconds. This data rate was reached using Internet protocol version 4 (IPv4) and is roughly equivalent to 10,000 typical home broadband internet connections. The start and end points were Luleå, Sweden, and San Jose, California, USA.

★ **Largest Internet café**

The cybercafé easyEverything in Times Square, New York, USA, opened on 28 November 2000 with 760 computer terminals. It now has 648 terminals.

★ **Country with the most Internet users**

According to the International Telecommunication Union, in 2002 the USA had over 159 million Internet users out of a world total of 623.48 million online users.

★ **Most Internet users by continent**

According to the International Telecommunication Union, of the 623.48 million people online worldwide in 2002, 211.36 million were located in Asia.

★ **Largest networked chess computer**

On 30 January 2004, Grand Master Peter Heine Nielsen (Denmark) played a game of chess against ChessBrain, the world's largest networked chess computer. ChessBrain consisted of 2,070 computers located in 56 countries, which simultaneously combined their processing power.

The match, which took place in Copenhagen, Denmark, ended in a draw after 34 moves.

★ **Oldest electronic spam**

The oldest unsolicited mass e-mail was sent at 12:33 pm EDT on 3 May 1978 by Gary Thuerk (USA), who was working for Digital Equipment Corp. (USA). It was sent to 397 e-mail accounts on the Advanced Research Projects Agency Network (ARPAnet) of the US Defense Dept, inviting account holders to a demonstration of the DECSYSTEM-2020, 2020T, 2060 and 2060T computers. ARPAnet is regarded as the predecessor to the Internet.

★ **Oldest Internet bench**

On 6 August 2001, the world's first park bench with free access to the Internet was opened in Bury St Edmunds, Suffolk, UK. The standard park bench was converted by msn.co.uk to allow four people to connect their laptops simultaneously, in an attempt to change the way people use the Internet.

★ **Largest free web-based e-mail provider**

Microsoft's Hotmail had over 170 million active accounts as of February 2004. Every day Hotmail adds 100,000 new users. It is available in 230 countries and has 12 million unique log-ins per month.

Hotmail was launched in 1996 and its name is derived from the html programming language.

Communications

Science & technology

Largest television ⌃ telephone vote

The record for the largest TV phone vote belongs to *American Idol 2* (FOX, USA) on 21 May 2003, when 24 million viewers called in to the final of the show to vote for the winner of the pop contest (10 finalists, above) in Los Angeles, California, USA.

★ Earliest telephone call

The telephone was invented by Alexander Graham Bell (UK), who devised a way of converting human voices into electrical impulses, then back to voices. He filed his patent for the telephone on 14 February 1876 at the New York Patent office, New York, USA. The first intelligible call occurred in March 1876 in Boston, Massachusetts, USA, when Bell phoned his assistant in a nearby room and said 'Mr Watson – come here – I want to see you'.

★ First pole-to-pole telephone call

On 28 April 1999, at 10:30 am (GMT), the first phone call took place between people at the North and South Poles. It was carried out by NASA employees Mike Comberiate and Andre Fortin (both USA). It became a conference call coordinated from NASA's Marshall Space Flight Center, and lasted 45 minutes. Taking part in the call were George Morrow, Tom Carlson, Joel Michalski, Mike Comberiate, Claire Parkinson, Vince Hurley and Ron Ruhlman (all USA).

★ Most international telephone calls by country

According to TeleGeography, of the 155 billion minutes of international phone calls made in 2002, 40.3 billion minutes were made from the USA.

★ Busiest international telephone route

According to TeleGeography, the busiest international telephone route is between the USA and Canada. In 2002, there were some 10.9 billion minutes of two-way traffic between the two countries.

★ Largest fleet of ocean sensors

ARGO is a global network of free-floating ocean sensors designed to monitor global ocean-current patterns. The sensors drift at depths of up to 2,000 m (6,560 ft) then rise in order to transmit data via satellites. By 8 January 2004, there were 996 active floats, with a total of 3,000 planned by 2006.

★ Largest carrier of international phone calls

According to TeleGeography, in 2002 the largest carrier of international telephone calls, in terms of outgoing traffic, was AT&T Corp. (USA), with 12,796.5 million minutes of communications.

★ Longest telephone cable

The world's longest submarine telephone cable is FLAG (Fibre-optic Link Around the Globe), which runs for 27,000 km (16,800 miles) from Japan to the United Kingdom. It links three continents (Europe, Africa and Asia) and 11 countries, and can support 600,000 simultaneous telephone calls.

★ Largest working telephone

The world's largest operational telephone was exhibited on 16 September 1988 at a festival to celebrate the 80th birthday of Centraal Beheer, an insurance company based in Apeldoorn, The Netherlands. It was 2.47 m (8 ft 1 in) high and 6.06 m (19 ft 11 in) long, and weighed 3.5 tonnes (7,700 lb). The handset, which was 7.14 m (23 ft 5 in) long, had to be lifted by crane for a call to be made.

★ Largest telephone conference call

On 29 September 2003, US Presidential Democrat candidate Howard Dean (USA) conducted a telephone conference call from Los Angeles, California, USA, with his supporters. The greatest number of people simultaneously connected for at least 10 seconds was 3,466.

Largest switchboard ⩘

The switchboard at the Pentagon, Arlington, Virginia, USA, has 34,500 lines handling nearly 1 million calls a day through 161,000 km (100,000 miles) of telephone cable (Pentagon switchboard of 1950, above). Its busiest ever day was 6 June 1994 – the 50th anniversary of D-Day – when there were 1,502,415 calls.

Earliest mobile telephone ⩘

The idea for a portable phone was conceived at Lucent Technologies' Bell Labs, New Jersey, USA, in 1947. The first actual portable phone handset was invented by Martin Cooper (USA, above) of Motorola, who made the first call on 3 April 1973 to his rival, Joel Engel, research head at Bell Labs. The first commercial mobile phone network was launched in Japan in 1979.

★ Most mobile phones per capita
According to statisticians NationMaster.com, Taiwan had 106.45 mobile phones per 100 people in 2002.

★ Fastest text message sent around the world
On 20 February 2002, at the 3GSM World Congress in Cannes, France, Logica sent a text message around the world by forwarding it to mobile phones in six countries in six continents, and finally back to the original phone in Cannes. The message was received back in France only 3 min 17.53 sec after the original sender began typing in the message.

★ Largest animal sound archive
The world's largest animal sound archive, the British Library Sound Archive, London, UK, was established in 1969 and currently holds more than 130,000 wildlife recordings of sound-producing animals from all geographical areas. The sounds are used in numerous industries such as zoology, conservation and television production – and some have even been sold as mobile phone ringtones!

★ Fastest time to type a mobile text message
James Trusler (UK) typed a set text of 160 characters on his mobile phone in a time of 1 min 7 sec on the live TV show The Panel, Ten Network, Sydney, NSW, Australia, on 24 September 2003.

★ Earliest instant telecommunication
The telegraph system, invented by Samuel Morse (USA), was the first form of instant communication that was applied commercially. The first link, from Washington DC to Baltimore, Maryland, USA, was completed by May 1844. Morse sent the first message and soon the arrangements of dots and dashes was called Morse Code.

★ Loudest signalling device
The Chrysler air raid sirens are the loudest sirens ever, capable of producing 138 decibels at a distance of 30 m (100 ft) – so loud that a normal person would be deafened within 60 m (200 ft) of one during operation.

★ Largest live satellite radio broadcast
On 13 February 2002, Ana Ann's (UK) debut single 'Ride' was uplinked from the offices of Worldspace, London, UK, to Worldspace's AfriStar satellite and then beamed down to western Europe, the whole of Africa and the Middle East.

★ Oldest commercial satellite station
Goonhilly Satellite Earth Station on the Lizard Peninsula, Cornwall, UK, has 59 antennae of various sizes in operation. 'Arthur' (Goonhilly One) began operation on 11 July 1962 and continues to carry telephony and data traffic around the world. It received the first live transatlantic television signals from the Telstar satellite.

★ Earliest communications satellite
Echo 1 (sometimes called Echo 1A) was launched on 10 July 1962 from Cape Canaveral, Florida, USA. It was a 30-m-diameter (98-ft) balloon with a reflective aluminium coating, allowing radio and television signals to be passively reflected back to Earth. It ceased operations on 24 May 1968.

★ Largest civil communications satellite
The Astra 1-K was built by Alcatel Space (France). It had a mass of 5,250 kg (11,570 lb) and, fully deployed, would have been 37 m (121 ft) in length and 6.6 m (21 ft 7 in) in height. Upon its launch on 26 November 2002 its Russian Proton booster failed, leaving the satellite stranded in low Earth orbit. It was safely de-orbited on 10 December 2002 over the Pacific Ocean.

Space exploration
Science & technology

'There are things that are known and things that are unknown; in between is exploration' **– Anonymous**

The 'space race'

The first edition of *Guinness World Records* (formerly *The Guinness Book of Records*) was published six years before the first manned spaceflight by Yuri Gagarin (USSR) in 1961. In a special address to the US Congress in the same year, President John F Kennedy (USA) announced the ambitious goal of landing an American on the Moon and returning him safely to Earth before the end of the 1960s. This sparked the 'space race' between the USA and the USSR that dominated the latter half of the 20th century, such that by the end of 2004 – a mere 101 years since the first flight by Orville Wright (USA) – man has stood on the surface of the Moon and sent probes to other planets and there is now a permanent space station orbiting Earth.

Early landmarks

The first man-made object to orbit the Earth was *Sputnik 1*, launched by the USSR on 4 October 1957. It remained in orbit until 4 January 1958. This was followed by *Sputnik 2* on 3 November 1957, which remained in orbit until 13 April 1958.

Sputnik 2 had a passenger – a dog named Laika. America's first foray into space was on 31 January 1958, when *Explorer 1*, the first US satellite, lifted off from Cape Canaveral, Florida, USA. The year 1958 was also the year of the foundation of the National Aeronautics and Space Administration (NASA), who have controlled the American space programme ever since.

Lunar success

Since the 1950s, advances in science and technology have enabled man to continue to push back the boundaries of space exploration. Some eight years after Yuri Gagarin's (USSR) first space flight, Neil Armstrong (USA) took that 'giant leap for mankind' in 1969 when he stepped on to the Moon.

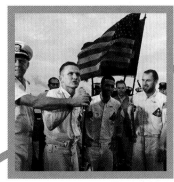

1961
First manned spaceflight

The earliest manned spaceflight was by Cosmonaut Yuri Alekseyevich Gagarin (USSR) in *Vostok 1* on 12 April 1961. *Vostok 1* was launched from the Baikonur Cosmodrome, Kazakhstan, USSR, at 9:07 am and landed near Smelovka, USSR, 115 minutes later. Gagarin ejected from *Vostok 1* 108 minutes into the flight as planned, and landed three minutes after his spacecraft by parachute. The maximum altitude during *Vostok 1*'s 40,868-km (25,394-mile) flight was listed at 327 km (203 miles), with a maximum speed of 28,260 km/h (17,560 mph).

1963
First woman in space

Valentina Tereshkova (USSR) was launched into space on *Vostok 6* on 19 June 1963. At 26, she is the youngest woman ever to undertake such a mission.

1965
First spacewalk

Alexei Arkhipovich Leonov (USSR) was the first person to engage in EVA, or extra-vehicular activity, commonly known as a 'spacewalk', which he accomplished from *Voskhod 2* on 18 March 1965.

1968
First manned lunar mission

On 21 December 1968, *Apollo 8* was launched into space. The crew – Frank Borman, Jim Lovell and Bill Anders (all USA) – were the first men to orbit the Moon. They achieved 10 orbits during their six-day mission.

Did you know...?

- 12 men in total have walked on the Moon.
- 16 nations are participating in the construction of the International Space Station.
- The greatest distance from Earth achieved by humans was when the crew of *Apollo 13* (Jim Lovell, Fred Haise and John Swigert, all USA) were 254 km (158 miles) from the lunar surface, on the far side of the Moon, and 400,171 km (248,655 miles) above the Earth's surface, at 12:21 GMT on 15 April 1970.

More recently, the development of the reusable space shuttle has made possible the construction and development of the International Space Station (ISS) that is now orbiting Earth – a project that has brought together many spacefaring nations. This has allowed scientists to carry out important onboard scientific experiments that benefit mankind. The picture bottom right shows John Herrington (USA) installing new equipment to ISS's Canadarm2 on a scheduled spacewalk. China's first spaceflight in October 2003 was another important landmark in the history of space exploration: China is only the third nation to send a human into orbit.

Next stop Mars?
The exploration of our solar system is an ongoing project: in January 2004, following NASA's successful Mars Exploration Rover mission – which has brought the possibility of landing a human mission on Mars one step closer – President Bush (USA) called on NASA to 'prepare for new journeys to the worlds beyond our own'.

2002
Most space flights by an individual
To date, two astronauts have travelled into space a total of seven times: Jerry Ross (USA, below) flew his seventh mission (STS 110) on board the space shuttle *Atlantis* between 8 and 19 April 2002. Franklin Chang-Dìaz (USA) flew his seventh mission on board the space shuttle *Endeavour* between 5 and 19 June 2002.

2003
Longest maiden flight
Of the three nations to launch humans into space to date, the longest maiden flight is by the Chinese. On 15 October 2003, Chinese 'taikonaut' Yang Liwei was sent into orbit on board the *Shenzou 5* spacecraft on a mission that lasted 21 hr 23 min from launch to touchdown.

1969
First men on the moon
Neil Armstrong (USA), commander of the *Apollo 11* mission, became the first man to set foot on the Moon, on the Sea of Tranquility, at 02:56.15 GMT on 21 July 1969 (22:56.15 EDT on 20 July 1969). He was followed out of the lunar module *Eagle* by Edwin 'Buzz' Aldrin Jr (USA, above) while the command module *Columbia,* piloted by Michael Collins (USA), orbited above.

1972
Longest manned Moon mission
Between 7 and 19 December 1972, the crew of *Apollo 17* stayed on the lunar surface for a record 74 hr 59 min 40 sec. During their stay Eugene Cernan and Harrison 'Jack' Schmitt (who became the twelfth man on the Moon) collected a record 110.4 kg (243 lb 6 oz) of rock and soil during their three EVAs of 22 hr 5 mins.

Innovations from space technology

- Weather prediction
- Satellite navigation & communication
- TV satellite dishes
- Bar coding
- Medical imaging
- CAT scans
- High density batteries
- Flat screen TVs
- Joysticks
- Water purification systems
- Cordless tools
- Pacemakers
- Heart monitors
- Ultrasound scanners
- Digital imaging
- Virtual reality programmes
- Thermal clothing
- Radiation-blocking sunglasses
- Fire-fighting equipment
- Smoke detectors
- Shock-absorbing trainers
- Invisible braces for teeth

Most re-used spacecraft ⌄

NASA's space shuttle *Discovery* (below) was last launched on 10 August 2001

at 4:10 pm CDT. Its mission (STS-105) was to deliver the *Leonardo* cargo module to the International Space Station and to deliver a new crew to the station. This was the 30th mission for *Discovery*, which has been in operation since 30 August 1984.

★ Most accurate measure of the age of the universe

The Wilkinson Microwave Anisotropy Probe (WMAP) was designed to measure the cosmic microwave background of the universe – the heat echo of the Big Bang. The first results from WMAP, released on 11 February 2003, reveal minute temperature differences in the early universe. This has allowed scientists to estimate the age of the universe at 13.7 billion years old, with an error of just 1%.

★ Most people in space at the same time

The greatest number of people in space at any one time is 13. Seven Americans were aboard the space shuttle STS 67 *Endeavour*, three CIS cosmonauts aboard the *Mir* space station, and two cosmonauts and a US astronaut aboard *Soyuz TM21* on 14 March 1995.

★ Most time spent in space

Russian cosmonaut Sergei Avdeyev logged a total of 747 days 14 hr 22 min on three spaceflights to the *Mir* space station between July 1992 and July 1999.

★ Longest manned spaceflight

Russian doctor Valeriy Poliyakov was launched to the *Mir* Space Station aboard *Soyuz TM18* on 8 January 1994 and landed back on Earth in *Soyuz TM20* on 22 March 1995, after a spaceflight lasting 437 days 17 hr 58 min 16 sec.

★ Longest spaceflight by a woman

Shannon Lucid (USA) was launched to the *Mir* space station aboard the US space shuttle STS 76 *Atlantis* on 22 March 1996, and landed aboard STS 79 *Atlantis* on 26 September that year. Her spaceflight, which lasted 188 days 4 hr 14 sec, is the longest spaceflight by a woman. Her stay onboard the space station is also the longest by any US astronaut. Upon returning to Earth, she was awarded the Congressional Space Medal of Honor by President Clinton (USA).

★ Furthest distance travelled on another world

Between 16 January and 23 June 1973, the unmanned Soviet *Lunokhod 2* rover travelled a distance of 37 km (23 miles) on the surface of the Moon, further than any other manned or unmanned lunar or planetary rover.

★ Furthest distance travelled on Mars in one day

On sol 70 (corresponding to 5 April 2004) of NASA's Mars Exploration rover mission, the robotic rover *Opportunity* travelled a total distance of 100 m (328 ft) across Meridiani Planum on Mars. As a comparison, Mars Pathfinder's *Sojourner* rover travelled 102 m (334 ft) during its entire mission in 1997.

★ Greatest spacecraft collision

On 25 June 1997, an unmanned Russian *Progress* supply vehicle weighing 7 tonnes (15,000 lb) collided with the Russian *Mir* space station. Cosmonauts Vasily Tsibliev and Alexander Lazutkin (both Russia) onboard *Mir* had to work quickly to seal a breach in the hull of *Mir*'s *Spektr* module, while US astronaut Michael Foale prepared *Mir*'s *Soyuz* capsule for a possible evacuation. Although the loss of life was avoided, the station was left dangerously low on power and oxygen and temporarily tumbling out of control.

Heaviest manmade object to re-enter Earth's atmosphere

The Russian space station *Mir* (right) was de-orbited during a successful controlled re-entry of Earth's atmosphere on 23 March 2001. After 15 years in space, the 130-tonne (286,500-lb) outpost broke into incandescent pieces and splashed down in the ocean east of New Zealand. »

Oldest astronaut

John Glenn Jr (USA, above) was 77 years 103 days old

when he was launched into space as part of the crew of STS-95 *Discovery* on 29 October 1998. The mission lasted 11 days, landing on 7 November 1998.

Longest spacewalk

Astronauts Jim Voss and Susan Helms (both USA) spent 8 hr 56 min outside in space on 11 March 2001. Their job was to make room on the International Space Station for the Italian cargo module *Leonardo*, which was carried into space by the space shuttle *Discovery*. *Leonardo*'s payload included around 5 tonnes (11,000 lb) of supplies and equipment for the station.

Most durable space station

Mir, the central core module of the *Mir* Space Station (USSR/Russia), was launched into orbit on 20 February 1986. Over the following 10 years, five modules and a docking port for US space shuttles were added to the complex. On 23 March 2001, the space station was de-orbited and destroyed in a controlled re-entry over the Pacific Ocean. More than a hundred people visited the *Mir* Space Station in its 15-year operational history.

Longest orbital survey of an outer planet

NASA's *Galileo* spacecraft was launched on 18 October 1989. It reached the planet Jupiter on 7 December 1995, where it slowed down and entered the orbit of the largest planet in the Solar System. *Galileo*'s survey of Jupiter and its moons represents the first time a manmade probe has orbited a world in the outer Solar System. With its onboard power and communications beginning to fail, *Galileo* burned up in the atmosphere of Jupiter on 21 September 2003. This was a deliberate destruction of the spacecraft, which ensured there was no chance of it inadvertently colliding with Europa (one of Jupiter's 'moons') and contaminating it in the future.

Fastest atmospheric entry

On 7 December 1995, a small probe released by the *Galileo* spacecraft began a fiery descent into the atmosphere of the giant planet Jupiter.

During this, the most difficult atmospheric entry ever, the *Galileo* probe reached a speed of 170,000 km/h (106,000 mph).

Largest planetary rover

Of the three robotic rovers sent to other planets, NASA's twin Mars Exploration rovers *Spirit* and *Opportunity* are the largest. Each has a mass of almost 180 kg (396 lb) and stands 1.44 m (4 ft 9 in) high.

Clearest image of a comet

On 2 January 2004, NASA's *Stardust* spacecraft encountered comet *Wild 2* in order to collect samples of cometary dust for return to Earth. From the closest approach distance of around 236 km (146 miles), the spacecraft was able to obtain images of the icy nucleus at a resolution of just 15 m (50 ft) per pixel.

Most powerful gamma-ray telescope

Launched in 1991, the Compton Gamma-Ray Observatory is the most powerful gamma-ray

telescope to date. After nine years of observations, it re-entered the Earth's atmosphere and burned up on 4 June 2000.

Most distant image of Earth

On 4 February 1990, NASA's *Voyager 1* spacecraft turned its camera back towards the Sun and the planets. After 12.5 years in space, travelling away from Earth, *Voyager 1*'s camera took a picture of our home planet from a distance of almost 6.5 billion km (4 billion miles).

Longest extraterrestrial balloon flight

The twin Soviet spacecraft *Vega 1* and *Vega 2* were launched on 15 December and 20 December 1984 respectively. Both probes encountered Venus in June 1985, and dropped packages into the Venusian atmosphere. Each package split into a lander and a balloon. The *Vega 2* balloon sent data about the Venusian atmosphere for 46.5 hours, before contact was lost.

Highest resolution ≪ digital camera

The world's highest resolution digital camera is MegaCam, with a resolution of 320 million pixels. It is an astronomical camera used on the 3.6-m (11-ft 9.6-in) Canada–France–Hawaii telescope in the summit of Mauna Kea, Hawaii, USA (left). The camera was integrated with the telescope on 28 June 2002.

★ Most detailed human dissection

The Visible Human Project is led by Dr Victor Spitzer (USA) of the University of Colorado. The aim of the project is to create a virtual anatomy 'text book'. Ultimately this digitized virtual body will be part of a medical simulator on which doctors and medical students will learn surgical techniques, in the manner of a pilot learning to fly by using an aeroplane simulator. To create these virtual humans, Dr Spitzer and his team had to perform the most detailed human dissection.

The 'Visible Man' is a real cadaver that was sliced into 1,878 sections. The thickness of each cut was 1 mm (1,000 microns). The 'Visible Woman' cadaver was sliced into 5,189 slices, 0.33 mm (330 microns) thick. Each layer of the sliced cadaver was photographed with a digital camera and stored in a computer. Eventually the recreation of the sliced images will form a minutely detailed 3-D virtual human body.

★ Furthest distance between patient and surgeon

On 7 September 2001, Madeleine Schaal (France) had her gall bladder removed by a robot in an operating room at Strasbourg, France. Her surgeons, Jacques Marescaux and Michel Gagner (both France), remotely operated the ZEUS robotic surgical arms on a secure fibre-optic line from New York, USA, a total distance of 6,222 km (3,866 miles) away.

★ Highest capacity multimedia jukebox

The highest capacity multimedia jukebox available to date is the AV380, with 80 gigabytes of storage space on its internal hard drive. Created by Archos (France), the AV380 can store and play MP3 music tracks as well as MPEG4 video files. It was launched in August 2003.

★ Longest television display

A screen measuring 70.4 m (230 ft 10.8 in) long by 8 m (26 ft 2.4 in) high was built by Mitsubishi Electric (HK) and Mitsubishi Corporation (Japan).

Its installation at the Hong Kong Jockey Club, Shatin Horse Race Course, Hong Kong, China, was completed on 25 May 2003.

★ Smallest colour television screen

MicroEmissive Displays Ltd, Edinburgh, UK, have developed a tiny colour television/video screen that measures just 3.84 x 2.88 mm (0.15 x 0.11 in). The ME1602, which can be linked to video cameras, DVD players and videos, has a resolution of 160 x 120 pixels. It works using organic light-emitting diode technology.

★ Largest computer touchscreen

Mega-mate, the largest computer touchscreen in the world, was developed and built by Displaymate Touchscreens Ltd (UK). Measuring 1 x 3 m (3.28 x 9.84 ft), with an area of 3 m² (32.29 ft²), it was specially commissioned by BRC Imagination Arts for Volkswagen's corporate identity centre in Dresden, Germany, and delivered in November 2001.

★ Lightest document scanner

The Docupen is the lightest A4 document scanner, weighing a mere 49.6 g (1.75 oz). It was released by Planon System Solutions, Inc., Mississauga, Canada, in 2003.

★ Oldest computer mouse

The computer mouse was invented in 1964 by Douglas Engelbart (USA), who was awarded a US patent for it in 1970. It was described in the patent as an 'X-Y position indicator for a display system' and was nicknamed a mouse because of the resemblance of the wire to a tail.

★ Highest-jumping robot

Sandia National Laboratories (USA) have developed experimental 'hopper' robots that use combustion-driven pistons to jump to heights of 9 m (30 ft). The small robots have potential applications in planetary exploration, where several hoppers could be released by a lander to survey the surrounding landscape.

Smallest hard drive

The disk of the smallest hard drive measures

just 2.16 cm (0.85 in) across (below). It was created by Toshiba (Japan) and announced at the international Consumer Electronics Show in Las Vegas, Nevada, USA, in January 2004.

The smallest commercially available hard drives contain a disc just 2.5 cm (1 in) across. Of the models available in February 2004, the highest capacity is 2.2 gigabytes and is manufactured by GS Magicstor, Inc. (China).

Fastest running humanoid robot

QRIO, which stands for 'Quest for Curiosity', is Sony Corporation's latest advanced humanoid autonomous robot (above). It is the world's first bipedal robot capable of running (ie, capable of moving while both legs are off the ground at the same time). QRIO is capable of running at 23 cm/sec (9 in/sec). The robot measures 58 cm (23 in) high and was revealed in September 2003.

vehicles, aircraft, soldiers and commanders. Simulated combat arenas of more than 10,000 km² (3,800 miles²) are used. It was constructed for the UK's Ministry of Defence by Lockheed Martin (USA), and became operational on 1 September 2002.

★ First business computer
LEO I (Lyons Electronic Office) was the first ever business computer. It began operations in November 1951 at the Lyons headquarters, London, UK. The first of its many business applications was the valuation of the weekly output of bread and cakes from Lyons' bakeries. LEO I was supplemented by the more advanced LEO II in May 1957, but continued operations into the 1960s.

★ First stored-program computer
The world's first stored-program computer was the Manchester University Mark I, which incorporated the Williams storage cathode ray tube (patented 11 December 1946). It ran its first program, written by Tom Kilburn (UK), for 52 minutes on 21 June 1948.

★ Earliest microprocessor
The first microprocessor was the 4004 chip, designed and built by Intel (USA). The first one was completed in January 1971. The size of a thumbnail, this first single-processor CPU had the same power as ENIAC (electronic numerical integrator and computer), the room-sized first electronic computer. The 4004 chip had 2,300 transistors and could perform around 100,000 instructions per second.

★ Most sophisticated battlefield simulator
The most sophisticated battlefield computer simulator is the Combined Arms Tactical Trainer. Situated at Warminster, UK, and Sennelager, Germany, it is capable of training more than 850 military personnel at once in an integrated, realistic combat scenario involving

★ Fastest computer
The NEC Earth Simulator at the Yokohama Institute for Earth Sciences, Japan, is capable of 35.6 trillion calculations per second – roughly five times the speed of the previous record holder. Built by HNSX Supercomputers, a division of NEC, the computer is designed to simulate Earth's complex climate in order to predict climate change and global warming, which have severe consequences for Japan.

★ First computer virus
The first computer program to replicate itself surreptitiously (ie a virus) was demonstrated by Fred Cohen, a student at the Massachusetts Institute of Technology, USA, on 11 November 1983.

★ Most powerful quantum computer
Whereas normal computers use a string of zeroes and ones (bits) to represent data, experimental quantum computers use qubits, which can be a zero, one, or simultaneously both. On 20 December 2001, IBM's Almaden Research Center, San Jose, California, USA, announced that they had used a seven-qubit quantum computer to calculate the factors of the number 15.

The computer used a billion billion molecules that have seven nuclear spins for the calculation. Consisting of the nucleii of five atoms of fluorine and two of carbon, these molecules are able to interact with each other as qubits.

⌄ Oldest dated cannon

The Dardanelles Gun (below), cast in Turkey in 1464 for

Sultan Mehmet II, is made from bronze, weighs 16.8 tonnes (37,000 lb) and measures 5.2 m (17 ft) long. It had a range of 1,600 m (5,250 ft) when firing a 600-mm-diameter (23.5-in), 304-kg (670-lb) projectile. The date is engraved on the cannon, which is displayed at the Royal Armouries, Fort Nelson, Hampshire, UK.

Largest suit of ⌄ animal armour

A suit of armour designed for an adult Asian elephant (right) was made in the late 16th or early 17th century in northern India during the Mughul Empire. It weighs 118 kg (260 lb) and, although part of the suit is missing, it is estimated that when complete with its original 8,439 individual metal plates, it would have weighed 159 kg (350 lb). The suit is currently on display at the Royal Armouries Museum in Leeds, UK. It is thought to be the only one of its kind in existence.

★ Largest gun

In the siege of Sevastopol, USSR (now Ukraine), in July 1942 the Germans used a gun with an 80-cm (31.4-in) calibre and a 28.87-m-long (94-ft 5-in) barrel. Built by Krupp (Germany), its remains were discovered near Metzenhof, Germany, in August 1945. When fully assembled, the gun measured 42.9 m (141 ft) in length and weighed 1,344 tonnes (2,963,000 lb).

★ Largest cannon ball

The largest cannon ball has a diameter of 91 cm (36 in) and weighs over 1 tonne (2,204 lb) when filled with its charge of 180 kg (400 lb) of gunpowder. It belongs to the Mallet mortar gun, which was designed by Robert Mallet (Ireland) and completed in March 1857. It is currently on display at the Royal Armouries, Fort Nelson, Hampshire, UK. Mallet's mortar required 35 kg (77 lb) of powder to fire such a projectile to reach its range of 2.4 km (1.5 miles) and to bury the charge to a depth of 9.1 m (30 ft) in soft earth, something that would cause the effect of a small earthquake and ultimately lead to the collapse of structures.

★ Tallest suit of armour

The tallest suit of armour currently on display measures 2.06 m (6 ft 8 in) high. It was traditionally said to have been worn by England's John of Gaunt, Duke of Lancaster in the 14th century, but is actually German in origin and dated to around 1535. It is on display in The White Tower at HM Tower of London, London, UK.

★ Earliest tank

The No.1 Lincoln built by William Foster & Co. Ltd (UK), and modified to become Little Willie, first ran on 6 September 1915. Tanks first saw action with the Heavy Section, Machine Gun Corps (later the Tank Corps) at the Battle of Flers-Courcelette, France, on 15 September 1916. The Mark I 'Male' tank, armed with a pair of 6-pounder guns and four machine guns, weighed 28.4 tonnes (62,610 lb) and was powered by a 78-kW (105-hp) motor, giving a top road speed of 4.8–6.4 km/h (3–4 mph).

★ Fastest tank

A production standard S 2000 Scorpion Peacekeeper tank (complete with appliqué hull armour, ballistic skirts, K10000 replaceable rubber pad track and powered by an RS 2133 high-speed diesel engine) developed by Repaircraft PLC (UK) achieved a speed of 82.23 km/h (51.10 mph) at the QinetiQ vehicle test track, Chertsey, UK, on 26 March 2002. The speed is an average of two consecutive runs in opposite directions.

★ Heaviest tank

The heaviest tank ever was the German Panzerkampfwagen Maus II, which, at 192 tonnes (423,280 lb), weighed as much as 130 modern saloon cars. By 1945 it had only reached the experimental stage and was abandoned. The heaviest operational tank used by any army was the 75.2-tonne (165,780-lb) 13-man French Char de Rupture 2C bis of 1922. It carried a 15.5-cm (6.1-in) howitzer and was powered by two 186-kW (250-hp) engines giving a maximum speed of 12 km/h (7.5 mph).

★ Most heavily armed tank

The Russian T-64, T-72, T-80 and T-90 tanks are all equipped with a 12.5-cm (4.9-in) gun-missile system. The American Sheridan light tank mounts a 15.2-cm (6-in) weapon that is a gun and a missile launcher combined, but this is not a long-barrelled, high-velocity gun of the conventional type. The British Armoured Vehicle Royal Engineers (AVRE) Centurion had a 16.5-cm (6.5-in) low-velocity demolition gun.

Most accurate bomb ⌄

The US-built Joint Direct Attack Munition (JDAM, below), in
operation since 1997, is accurate to +/- 2 m (6 ft 6 in). JDAM is a steerable tailkit attached to existing 'dumb bombs'. After release, the JDAM's location is continually checked by fixes from satellites.

★ Most intelligent handgun
The O'Dwyer Variable Lethality Law Enforcement (VLe) prototype pistol, made by Metal Storm Limited (Australia), has no moving parts: instead, projectiles are fired electronically by a built-in computer processor. The gun can only be fired by someone wearing an authorized transponder ring. The VLe has no magazine – the bullets are stacked behind one another in the barrel, and the handgrip – where the magazine would be on a conventional pistol – contains the electronic control systems. Capable of firing up to three shots in quick succession (within 1/500th of a second), the computer-controlled firing also allows the pistol to fire at a rate equivalent to 60,000 rounds per minute.

★ Earliest use of infrared equipment in battle
Infrared technology was first used in battle during World War II. Electric sniperscopes mounted on top of rifles converted the infrared light from enemy soldiers into visible light, enabling the shooter to fire accurately in darkness.

★ Earliest successful test of a high-powered microwave weapon
A successful test for a high-powered microwave (HPM) weapon on electronic equipment occurred in April 1999 under the observation of the Joint Command and Control Warfare Center of San Antonio, Texas, USA. HPMs are designed to bring maximum disruption to any military or civilian power system by discharging a powerful energy pulse that destroys any electronics within its 300-m (980-ft) range.

★ Country with the most landmines or unexploded ordnance deployed
The Egyptian Government has estimated that 19.7 million mines or unexploded ordnance (UXO) exist in Egypt as of November 2002. Most of the mines in Egypt were planted during World War II. According to the International Campaign to Ban Landmines there are between 85 and 125 million mines buried in countries around the world. In addition, over 200 million are stockpiled.

★ Most widely used firearm
The most widely used firearm is the Automatic Kalashnikov 1947 (AK-47). During the Cold War, the former USSR supplied AK-47s to anti-Western insurgents, and the rifle therefore became a symbol of left-wing revolution. Between 50 and 80 million copies and variations of the AK-47 have been produced globally.

★ Earliest use of smallpox as a biological weapon
During the French and Indian Wars of 1754–1767, British soldiers fighting in North America at that time distributed blankets contaminated with smallpox among the native American Indians. Epidemics followed, killing more than 50% of the affected tribes.

★ Largest radar installation
The largest of the three radar installations in the US Ballistic Missile Early Warning System (BMEWS) is near Thule, Kalaallit Nunaat, Greenland, 1,498 km (931 miles) from the North Pole. Completed in 1960, it cost $500 million (£178.5 million).

★ Earliest use of a graphite bomb
A graphite bomb (G-bomb) was first used in 1991 when Allied forces used it to disable 85% of Iraq's power supplies during the Gulf War. G-bombs work by exploding a cloud of thousands of ultra-fine carbon-fibre wires over electrical installations, short-circuiting electrical systems.

★ Largest non-nuclear conventional weapon in existence
The Massive Ordnance Air Blast (MOAB), a precision-guided weapon, weighs 9,752 kg (21,500 lb). It was first tested by the US Air Force at the Eglin Air Force Armament Center, Florida, USA, on 11 March 2003.

CELEBRATING **50 YEARS** OF RECORDS | 163

Largest battleships in active service since the end of World War II

The battleships USS *Iowa* (above), *New Jersey*, *Missouri* and *Wisconsin* are each 270 m (887 ft) long and have full-load displacements in excess of 41,000 tonnes (90 million lb). All were commissioned during World War II and were in active service at various times until the early 1990s. Each ship is armed with nine 40.64-cm (16-in) guns capable of firing 1,225-kg (2,700-lb) projectiles a distance of 39 km (23 miles), and when operational had a crew complement of around 1,900.

★ Fastest warship
The 23.7-m-long (78-ft), 100-tonne (220,000-lb) US Navy test surface-effect ship *SES-100B* attained a world record 91.9 knots (170 km/h or 105 mph) on 25 January 1980 at the Chesapeake Bay Test Range, Maryland, USA. Similar to hovercraft, surface-effect ships travel on a cushion of air, but also have two sharp rigid hulls that remain in the water. Large fans under the ship create air pressure that is then trapped between the hulls, raising the ship.

★ Largest modern naval battle
The largest purely naval battle of modern times was the World War I Battle of Jutland on 31 May 1916, in which 151 British Royal Navy warships faced 101 German warships. The Royal Navy lost 14 ships and 6,097 men, and the German fleet 11 ships and 2,545 men.

★ Largest amphibious ship
The US Navy's Wasp-class vessels have a full-load displacement of 36,500 tonnes (80.5 million lb) and a length of 257 m (844 ft). Capable of carrying aircraft, large numbers of troops and various landing vessels, their primary role is to land troops on enemy shores. The ships also have 600-bed hospitals (the largest on any ship except for dedicated hospital ships). There are seven Wasp-class ships currently in service.

★ Largest warships
The warships with the largest full-load displacement are the Nimitz-class US Navy aircraft carriers USS *Nimitz, Dwight D. Eisenhower, Carl Vinson, Theodore Roosevelt, Abraham Lincoln, George Washington, John C. Stennis, Harry S. Truman* and *Ronald Reagan*, the last five of which displace approximately 98,550 tonnes (217 million lb). They are 333 m (1,092 ft) long, have an 1.82-ha (4.49-acre) flight deck and are driven by four nuclear-powered 194,000-kW (260,000-shp) geared steam turbines. They can reach speeds in excess of 30 knots (56 km/h or 34.5 mph).

★ Largest stealth ship
The largest ship incorporating stealth technology is the Swedish Visby-class corvette, which is approximately 72 m (236 ft) long and has a displacement of 600 tonnes (1.32 million lb). Developed by the Kockums shipyard (Sweden), the carbon-fibre vessel is lighter than a conventional ship of its size, and features the large flat surfaces used in aircraft to provide low radar visibility. The Visby prototype made its maiden voyage in December 2001.

★ Longest military runway
The runway at Edwards Air Force Base on the west side of Rogers dry lakebed at Muroc, California, USA, is 11.92 km (7.41 miles) in length.

★ Largest air force ever
United States Army Air Corps (now the US Air Force) had 79,908 aircraft in July 1944 and 2,411,294 personnel in March 1944.

★ Fastest combat jet
The fastest combat jet is the Russian Mikoyan MiG-25 fighter (NATO codename 'Foxbat'). The 'Foxbat-B' has been tracked by radar at about Mach 3.2 (3.2 times the speed of sound – 3,395 km/h, or 2,110 mph). The MiG-25 was designed as a high-altitude interceptor and it can take off and climb to an altitude of 35,000 m (114,000 ft) in a little over four minutes.

Earliest ⌄ stealth ship

The US Navy *Sea Shadow* (below) was completed in the mid-1980s but only revealed to the public in 1993.

The bizarre looking twin-hulled ship is 49.98 m (164 ft) long, 20.7 m (68 ft) across and has a full-load displacement of 569 tonnes (1.25 million lb). Built by Lockheed Martin, it has a crew of 10 and a top speed of 18.5 km/h (11.5 mph).

Navy with the ⌃ most aircraft

The US Navy has over 4,000 aircraft in service. It operates around

20 different types of fixed-wing aircraft, including carrier-based F-14 Tomcat, and F/A-18 Hornet (above) fighters, and various reconnaissance, transport, anti-submarine and airborne command-post aircraft. It also operates six different types of helicopters and the unique new V-22 'Osprey' tilt rotor aircraft.

★ Most widely deployed military unmanned aircraft
By early 2004, the 'Predator' unmanned aerial vehicle (UAV) manufactured by General Atomics Aeronautical Systems (USA) had logged more than 65,000 flight hours, of which more than half were in combat areas such as Kosovo, Iraq and Afghanistan. The 100th example of the aircraft, which has a wingspan of 14.84 m (48.7 ft) and a flight endurance time of over 40 hours, was delivered to the US military in February 2004.

★ Longest range air attacks
Seven B-52G 'Stratofortress' bombers left Barksdale Air Force Base, Louisiana, USA, on 16 January 1991 to deliver air-launched cruise missiles against targets in Iraq after the start of the first Gulf War. Each flew 22,500 km (14,000 miles), refuelling four times in flight, with the round-trip mission lasting some 35 hours.

★ Heaviest bomber in service
The Russian Tupolev Tu-160 'Blackjack' bomber has a maximum take-off weight of 275 tonnes (606,270 lb) and a maximum speed of around Mach 2.05 (roughly 2,200 km/h or 1,350 mph). Although a Boeing 747 has a higher maximum take-off weight of 397 tonnes (877,200 lb), the 'Blackjack' is considerably smaller and, crucially, flies more than 2.5 times as fast.

★ Fastest operational bomber
The US variable-geometry or 'swing-wing' General Dynamics FB-111A has a maximum speed of Mach 2.5. The Russian swing-wing Tupolev Tu-22M, which is known to NATO as 'Backfire', has an estimated over-target speed of Mach 2 but could be as fast as Mach 2.5. Mach 2.5 is roughly equivalent to 2,655 km/h (1,650 mph).

★ Largest ever bomber wingspan
The American 10-engined Convair B 36J 'Peacemaker' had a 70.1-m (230-ft) wingspan. The aircraft, which had a maximum take-off weight of 185 tonnes (410,000 lb), was replaced in the 1950s by the Boeing B-52. The 'Peacemaker' had a top speed of 700 km/h (435 mph).

★ Most produced fighter of World War II
Over 36,000 Ilyushin Il-2 'Sturmovik' ground-attack aircraft are said to have been produced in Russia before, during and immediately after World War II, making it the most produced aircraft of that conflict and one of the most numerous combat aircraft ever.

★ Fastest World War II propeller fighter
The German Dornier DO-335 was unique in having a tractive (pulling) propeller in its nose

and a propulsive (pushing) motor behind its cockpit. It had a maximum sustained speed of 665 km/h (413 mph), increasing to 765 km/h (477 mph) with emergency boost. Two models existed – A-1 and A-6 – the latter a two-seater nightfighter. Only 28 were completed before the end of World War II.

★ Top scoring air ace in World War II
The highest officially attributed figure of aircraft shot down by any airman was 352 by Major Erich Hartmann (Germany). In one sortie on the Russian front on 6 November 1943 he shot down a record 13 planes in 17 minutes. His last mission was on 8 May 1945, when he shot down a YAK-7 fighter and later landed his plane to surrender to the British forces. He was handed over to the Russians who tried him for war crimes. He was sent to a work camp for 10 years.

Art & media

Contents

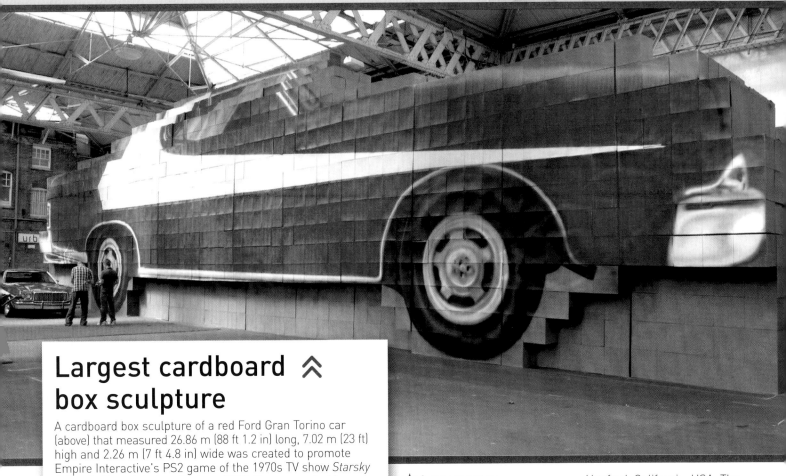

Largest cardboard ⌃ box sculpture

A cardboard box sculpture of a red Ford Gran Torino car (above) that measured 26.86 m (88 ft 1.2 in) long, 7.02 m (23 ft) high and 2.26 m (7 ft 4.8 in) wide was created to promote Empire Interactive's PS2 game of the 1970s TV show *Starsky & Hutch*. Completed on 20 June 2003, it was unveiled in Spitalfields Market, London, UK, by designers from Wreck Age Productions (UK). The sculpture was made by 34 people in just over four days using 4,855 boxes and 286 rolls of tape.

★ Largest apple mosaic
An apple mosaic unveiled on 29 September 2001 at Kivik, Österleden, Sweden, consisted of 25,000 apples. Entitled *Applecheek*, it measured 104 m² (1,119 ft²) and was designed by Emma Karp Laggar and Jan Laggar (both Sweden). Each apple was nailed to a board by a team of eight people to form an abstract image of Earth. Approximately 2.26 tonnes (5,000 lb) of 12 different apple varieties were used.

★ Largest photograph mosaic
Unveiled in Novena Square, Singapore, on 12 July 2003, the world's largest photo mosaic, entitled *Smile Singapore!*, measured 6.24 x 15.24 m (20 ft 6 in x 50 ft) and contained 16,800 individual photographs to create a giant map of Singapore. The mosaic was organized by the Heartware

Network, and each photo represented a minimum $10 donation to charity.

★ Largest ball mosaic
A mosaic containing 11,430 toy balls forming the image of a boy measured 11.2 x 4.5 m (37 x 15 ft) and had a 30.48-m (100-ft) circumference. It was created by Danny O'Connor (USA) and was installed from June 2001 to April 2002 in the Massachusetts Museum of Contemporary Art in North Adams, Massachusetts, USA.

★ Largest balloon mosaic
A mosaic depicting the Chicago skyline was made from 70,884 balloons and measured 17.6 x 26.21 m (58 x 86 ft). It was created by delegates of the International Balloon Arts Convention on 8 March 1999 in the lobby of the Hyatt Regency O'Hare, Rosemont, Illinois, USA.

★ Largest paper flower mosaic
The largest mosaic made of paper flowers measured 231.8 m² (2,496 ft²) and was assembled at East Point City, Tseung Kwan O, Hong Kong, China, on 28 October 2001.

★ Largest flower mural
A flower mural that incorporated 770,000 fresh dahlias measured 1,868.94 m² (20,117 ft²) when it was created on 7 August 2001. It was made by 1,250 people who represented 16 neighbourhoods from the Dahlia Record Committee in Lemelerveld, The Netherlands. The flowers were glued on 900 individual panels, which were then all placed next to each other in a large square to make one continuous image.

★ Largest model made from canned food
On 24 December 1998, a 2.58-m-tall (8-ft 6-in) Christmas tree made from 9,773 cans of food was displayed at the Hanford Mall,

Hanford, California, USA. The tree had an overall volume of 5.07 m³ (179.3 ft³).

★ Oldest paintings
The world's oldest reliably dated paintings were found on the walls of the Chauvet cave in southern France in 1994. The paintings range from 23,000 to 32,000 years old.

★ Largest painting
A painting of the sea that measured 8,586 m² (92,419 ft²) was completed by ID Culture at The Arena, Amsterdam, The Netherlands, to mark the venue's opening on 14 August 1996. The size of the painting is equivalent to nearly four American football fields.

★ Largest finger painting
A finger painting measuring 473.8 m² (5,100 ft²) was completed on 22 July 2003. Its creation was led by artists Jignesh Patel and Munir Rehman (both India) on behalf of the people of Surrey Central, British Columbia, Canada.

Largest nude ⌃⌃ photo shoot

On 8 June 2003, 7,000 volunteers (above) collectively posed in the nude on a street in Barcelona (Spain) for photographer Spencer Tunick (USA).

Largest inflatable sculpture

An inflatable sculpture entitled *Blockhead* (right) is 35 m (114 ft 9.6 in) tall and was created by artist Paul McCarthy (USA) for display in front of the Tate Modern gallery, London, UK, from 19 May until October 2003. *Blockhead* is loosely based on the character Pinocchio.

★ **Largest handprint painting**
A 209.2-m² (2,251.8-ft²) handprint painting was created on 15 November 2002 by 2,541 students organized by the Star Givers of Jeddah, Saudi Arabia. The image, created in honour of Queen Elizabeth II's Golden Jubilee, depicted the monarch's state coach pulled by horses and accompanied by yeoman warders.

★ **Longest painting**
The longest acrylic painting on one continuous canvas measured 2,011.68 m (6,600 ft) on 14 January 2002 at Celestial Court, Toronto, Ontario, Canada, and was created by artist Danny Fong (Canada). The painting, entitled *Thousand Horses*, depicts more than 1,500 horses in different seasons, weather and backgrounds.

★ **Largest outdoor mural**
The Pueblo Levee Project in Pueblo, Colorado, USA, has produced the largest mural in the world at 16,554.8 m² (178,200 ft²). The connected murals are almost 3.21 km (2 miles) long and 17.67 m (58 ft) tall.

★ **Longest drawing**
A drawing that measured 2,820 m (9,251 ft) was created by approximately 2,000 children in Batenburg Square, Sofia, Bulgaria, on 1 June 2003 as part of Children's Day. The theme of the artwork was 'My World'.

★ **Largest painting by numbers**
The largest painting by numbers measures 378 m² (4,068 ft²) and was created at the Island Festival, Dockyard Island, Budapest, Hungary, on 28 July 2003.

★ **Artwork with the most artists**
The 14.63-m-long (48-ft), 2.43-m-high (8-ft) painting *A Little Dab of Texas*, designed by Jim Campbell (USA), was painted by 25,297 people. It was completed on 14 June 1998 after 3 years 7 months. The finished painting was unveiled on 5 September 1998 and exhibited in Washington DC, USA, later that year.

★ **Largest pencil drawing by one artist**
The largest pencil drawing by one artist, entitled *One World, One Song*, has an overall surface area of 185.99 m² (2,002 ft²) and was completed by art teacher TJ Johnson (USA) on 2 August 2002.

★ **Largest photographic exhibition**
A total of 16,609 photographs were displayed by Kodak Greece in the grounds of their head office in Athens on 17 June 2003. The photos had been sent in by Greeks around the world, who had been asked to submit a smiling photo to welcome the return of the Olympic Games in 2004.

★ **Largest matchstick model**
Joseph Sciberras (Malta) constructed an exact scaled-down replica of St Publius Parish Church, Floriana, Malta. It consisted of over three million matchsticks and measured 2 x 2 x 1.5 m (6 ft 7 in x 6 ft 7 in x 4 ft 11 in).

★ **Largest single gallery space**
The Guggenheim Museum in Bilbao, Spain, which opened on 18 October 1997, has 137.16 m (450 ft) of gallery space.

★ **Most valuable piece of Art Nouveau**
A standard lamp in the form of three lotus blossoms by the Daum Brothers and Louis Majorelle (all France) sold for $1.78 million (£1.13 million) at Sotheby's, New York, USA, on 2 December 1989.

Fashion & beauty ★
Art & media

« Most pierced man

Luis Antonio Agüero (Cuba, left) sports 230 piercings on his body and head. His face alone carries more than 175 rings.

The most pierced woman is Elaine Davidson (UK). Between January 1997 and May 2003 she had 1,500 piercings made over her body. Of these, 192 are on her ears, forehead, eye brows, chin, nose and tongue.

Most legs waxed ★ in an hour

Beautician Laura Mitchell (UK, above) hot-waxed 22 pairs of legs (16 men, 6 women) in one hour at the Globe Inn pub, Aberdeen, UK, on 2 May 2002. The legs were fully stripped from the knee to the ankle, on the front, back and sides.

★ Largest Hawaiian shirt
In March 1999, Hilo Hattie (USA), a retailer of Hawaiian fashions from Honolulu, Hawaii, USA, created an aloha shirt with a chest measurement of 4.26 m (14 ft), a waist measurement of 3.5 m (11 ft 6 in) and a neck measurement of 1.53 m (5 ft 0.5 in).

★ Largest jumper
An ecru-coloured cable-stitch jumper made by the company Malhas Carjor of Palmeira, Portugal, on 15 December 1998 had a chest measurement of 2.2 m (7 ft 2 in), a body length of 2.43 m (7 ft 11 in) and a sleeve length of 1.85 m (6 ft). Made from 70% acrylic and 30% wool, it was a scaled-up version of their Trintona design.

★ Largest pair of socks
A pair of nylon socks measuring 1.14 m (45 in) from top to toe and 25 cm (10 in) wide was constructed by Michael Roy Layne (USA) in October 1986 and hung outside City Hall, Boston, USA, to celebrate the Red Sox baseball team winning the American League Championship and entering the World Series.

★ Longest scarf knitted by an individual
Ray Ettinger (USA) knitted a continuous scarf that measured 1,073.8 m (3,523 ft) long and 17.7 cm (7 in) wide on 8 May 2001.

★ Longest zip
The world's longest zip-fastener was laid around the centre of Sneek, The Netherlands, on 5 September 1989. The brass zipper, made by Yoshida Ltd (Netherlands), is 2,851 m (9,353 ft 8 in) long and consists of 2,565,900 metal teeth.

★ Largest underpants
The world's largest pair of cotton underwear (or knickers) measured 9.54 m (31 ft 4 in) wide and 4.9 m (16 ft) tall. It was created by the Exeter Council for Voluntary Service and unveiled on 7 June 2003 at the Exeter County Rugby Ground, Devon, UK.

★ Most scissors used for cutting hair
Bruce Choy (USA) successfully styled a head of hair using eight pairs of scissors in one hand, controlling each pair independently. The record was set at his salon, Flyingshears, in San Francisco, California, USA, on 11 March 2002.

★ Largest sandal
The largest sandal in the world measures 3.93 m (12 ft 10.8 in) long, 1.46 m (4 ft 9.6 in) wide and 1.9 m (6 ft 3 in) high, and was constructed by Pearl Shoes in front of the Milli Shoes showroom, Lahore, Pakistan, in April 2002.

★ Most valuable piece of jewellery
The most valuable piece of jewellery is a pair of 58.6-carat and 61-carat diamond drop earrings bought and sold anonymously for $7.2 million (£2.9 million) at Sotheby's, Geneva, Switzerland, on 14 November 1980 as part of the Magnificent Jewels auction.

★ Most valuable jacket
A jacket that once belonged to rock legend Jimi Hendrix (USA) sold to the Hard Rock Cafe chain for £35,000 ($49,185) at a sale organized by Sotheby's in the London branch of the Hard Rock Cafe (UK) on 19 September 2000.

★ Most body piercings by surgical needles
Brent Moffat (Canada) inserted 700 18-gauge (1.2-cm-long or 0.47-in) surgical needles into his body in 7 hr 19 min at Metamorphosis Custom Piercing and Tattoo, Winnipeg, Manitoba, Canada, on 15 January 2003.

★ Most body piercings in one session
Kam Ma (UK) received a total of 600 new piercings to his body without the aid of an anaesthetic. All piercings were executed by Charlie Wilson (UK) in one continuous session that lasted from 9:15 am to 5:47 pm at Sunderland Body Art, Sunderland, Tyne and Wear, UK, on 26 May 2002.

Largest handbag ⌃

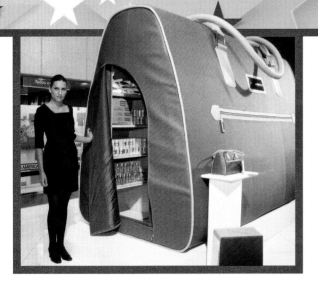

In April 2003, a handbag measuring 3.7 m tall, 3.54 m wide and 1.6 m deep (12 ft 1 in x 11 ft 7 in x 5 ft 3 in) made by the leather accessories company Santa Marinella (Brazil) was unveiled in the Shopping Center, Iquatemi, Brazil. It is an exact replica of the original and made from synthetic leather (stamped lined PVC) with natural cow leather trim. The giant handbag (above) was used to store canned goods for charity.

Smallest waist on a living person ⌃

Cathie Jung (USA, above), who stands 1.72 m (5 ft 8 in) tall, has a tiny 38.1-cm (15-in) waist. Cathie and husband Bob, an orthopaedic surgeon, worked together to develop her tiny waist as part of their enthusiasm for Victorian dress. The 38-year-old mother of three started wearing a six-inch-wide training belt to gradually reduce her waist. Cathie does not eat a special diet or exercise to maintain her waist.

★ Most rhinestones on body
Body artist Maria Rosa Pons Abad (Spain) adorned a model's body with 30,361 rhinestones on the set of *El Show de los Récords*, Madrid, Spain, on 22 November 2001.

★ Most tattooed man
Both Tom Leppard (UK) and Lucky Rich (UK) have approximately 99.9% of their bodies covered in tattoos. Tom, who resides on the Isle of Skye, Scotland, UK, has opted for a leopard print design, with all the skin between the dark spots tattooed saffron yellow. Lucky Rich has had his existing tattoos blacked over, with a white design tattooed on top.

★ Most tattooed woman
The world's most decorated woman is strip artiste Krystyne Kolorful (Canada). Tattoos cover 95% of her body and took 10 years to complete.

★ Fastest 'sheep to suit'
The fastest time to manufacture a three-piece woollen suit, from shearing the sheep to sewing the finished article, is 1 hr 2 min 36 sec, achieved by members of FH Monchengladbach, Germany, on 28 January 1999. The record was broadcast on *Guinness – Die Show Der Rekorde* on 30 January 1999.

★ Largest travelling wardrobe
For her 14-month debut on London's West End stage in *Mame*, Ginger Rogers (USA) arrived in England in 1969 with 118 pieces of luggage. Wisely, she came by ship.

★ Highest annual earnings by a supermodel
According to *Forbes* magazine, Gisele Bundchen (Brazil) took in $12.8 million (£6.95 million) from June 2002 to June 2003, thanks to deals with Victoria's Secret, Christian Dior and Dolce & Gabbana.

★ Longest distance covered on a catwalk by a male model
Between 19 and 21 September 1983, Eddie Warke walked a total distance of 133.7 km (83.1 miles) on a catwalk at Parkes Hotel, Dublin, Republic of Ireland.

★ Most designers represented at one fashion show
A total of 89 different fashion designers from around the world were represented at Paris Fashion Week, France, in 1999. The event as a whole, which averaged 11 catwalk shows per day, outstrips all other international fashion showings and attracts the biggest following.

★ Highest hairstyle
Ladies' hairstyles literally reached their high point in the 1770s. Queen Marie Antoinette's (France) hair was the tallest documented hairstyle. It stood at 91.44 cm (36 in) high in 1775, and was decorated with a mass of ribbons and feathers that made it even higher.

★ Fastest haircut
Trevor Mitchell (UK) cut a full head of hair in 1 min 13 sec on 26 November 1999 at the Southampton City Guildhall, UK, as part of BBC TV South's 'Children in Need' appeal. The event was seen live on BBC TV.

★ Most valuable item of headwear
The Alaskan State Museum bought a native North American Tlingit Kiksadi ceremonial frog helmet dating from c. 1600 for $66,000 (£34,667) at an auction in New York City, USA, in November 1981.

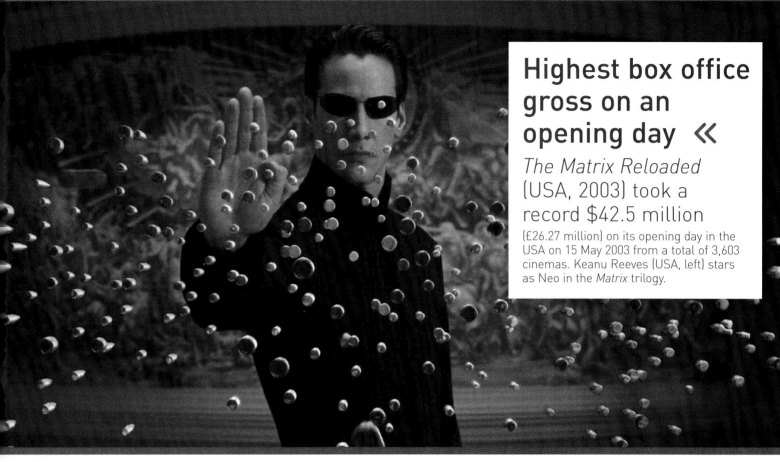

Highest box office gross on an opening day ≪

The Matrix Reloaded (USA, 2003) took a record $42.5 million (£26.27 million) on its opening day in the USA on 15 May 2003 from a total of 3,603 cinemas. Keanu Reeves (USA, left) stars as Neo in the *Matrix* trilogy.

★ **Fastest $100 million box office gross**
Two films have surpassed the $100-million mark in three days. The first was *Spider-Man* (USA, 2002), which opened on 3 May 2002 at 3,615 cinemas, followed by *The Matrix Reloaded* (USA, 2003), which opened on 5 May 2003 at 3,603 cinemas.

★ **Fastest $200 million box office gross**
From its 3 May 2002 opening, *Spider-Man* (USA, 2002) passed the $200-million mark in ten days, taking $223.04 million (£152.412 million) by 12 May and beating the previous record of 13 days set by *Star Wars: Episode 1 – The Phantom Menace* (USA, 1999).

★ **Largest box office loss**
MGM's *Cutthroat Island* (USA, 1995), starring Geena Davis and directed by her then-husband Renny Harlin (both USA), cost over $100 million (£63 million) to produce, promote and distribute, and reportedly earned back just $11 million (£7 million) – 11% of the cost.

★ **Highest box office gross**
James Cameron's (USA) *Titanic* (USA, 1997) was the first film to take $1 billion at the international box office, and had a total box office gross of $1.835 billion (£1.297 billion).

★ **Highest box office gross (inflation adjusted)**
Rising cinema ticket prices mean the all-time top-grossing movies are nearly all recent releases. Although *Gone With The Wind* (USA, 1939) took $393.4 million (then £88 million) at the international box office, in an inflation-adjusted list it comes top with a total gross of $3,785 billion (£2,365.7 billion). In the USA alone, *Gone With The Wind* had 283.1 million admissions compared with 130.9 million for *Titanic*.

★ **Most expensive film made**
Paramount's *Titanic* (USA, 1997), which overran its budget during production, cost just over $200 million (£118.9 million) to make. Originally given a $125-million (£74.3-million) budget, it was

due to have been released in July 1997, but post-production problems set the date back to December 1997, a delay that added to the cost.

★ **Largest pre-production budget for a film**
The war epic *Pearl Harbor* (USA, 2001), which began shooting on 3 April 2000, had a pre-production budget of $145 million (£93.428 million). The eventual total cost was $152.75 million (£107.7 million).

★ **Least expensive feature film made**
The total cost of production for the film *Die Alive* (Canada, 2000), produced and directed by Jean-François Leduc (Canada), was CAN$563.62 ($378.82 or £259.91). It premiered on 26 July 2001 at the Fantasi Film Festival, Montrèal, Canada.

★ **Most prolific film producer**
Since 1963, D Rama Naidu (India) has produced a total of 110 films during his career in Indian cinema.

★ **Living actor with most screen credits**
Actor Christopher Lee (UK) has the most screen credits of any actor alive today, with 211. He has performed in English, French, Canadian, German, Russian, Norwegian, Swedish, Italian, Pakistani, Spanish, Japanese, American, Australian and New Zealand productions, from *Corridor of Mirrors* (UK, 1947) to *Graduation Day* (USA, 2003).

★ **Actress with most leading film roles in a career**
Kinuyo Tanaka (Japan) made her debut role in *Genroku Onna* (Japan, 1924) and performed in a total of 241 films including her final role in *Daichi no Komoriuta* (Japan, 1974).

★ **Actor with most leading film roles in a career**
John Wayne (USA, born Marion Michael Morrison) appeared in 153 movies from *The Drop Kick* (USA, 1927) to *The Shootist* (USA, 1976). In all but 11 of these he played the lead.

Fastest $1 billion box office gross

The Lord of the Rings: The Return of the King (NZ/USA 2003), the final instalment of the trilogy, took $1 billion (£536.7 million) at the international box office in just nine weeks four days from its release on 17 December 2003. It marks only the second film in history to break the billion-dollar barrier, the first being *Titanic* (USA, 1997), which took the same amount in 11 weeks. The film, starring Orlando Bloom (UK, right) as Legolas, had accumulated a worldwide total of $1,005,380,412 (£539,598,761) in ticket sales by 23 February 2004.

Family with most stars on the Hollywood Walk of Fame ⌃

When Drew Barrymore (USA, above) received her star on the Hollywood Walk of Fame on 4 February 2004, she became the seventh member of her family to be so honoured. Stars had previously been awarded to her father John D. Barrymore, her great-uncle Lionel Barrymore, her great-aunt Ethel Barrymore, her grandparents John Barrymore and Dolores Costello and her great-grandfather Maurice Costello.

 Most film roles in a career
Tom London (USA) made the first of his 2,000-plus screen performances in *The Great Train Robbery* (USA, 1903) as the locomotive driver (his job in real life). By 1919 he had starring roles at Universal. His last role was in *The Lone Texan* (USA, 1959).

★ **Most Hollywood film performances in the same role**
William Boyd (USA) played the cowboy Hopalong Cassidy in Paramount's 66 *Hopalong* full-length features beginning with *Hopalong Cassidy* (USA, 1935) and ending with *Strange Gamble* (USA, 1948).

★ **Most stars on the Hollywood Walk of Fame**
Gene Autry (USA), the actor, composer and song writer, has five stars on the Hollywood Walk of Fame strip – numbers 6,384, 6,520, 6,644, 6,667 and 7,000 Hollywood Boulevard – awarded for Recording, Motion Pictures, Television, Radio and Theatre.

★ **Youngest No.1 box office star**
Shirley Temple (USA, b. 23 April 1928) was seven years old when she became No.1 at the box office in 1935, holding the title until 1938.

★ **Oldest No.1 box office star**
Marie Dressler (Canada, 1868–1934) was 64 when she became the No.1 box office star in 1933. Born Leila von Koerber in 1869, she began her film career in 1914 and won the Best Actress Oscar for Min Divot in *Min and Bill* (USA, 1930).

★ **Highest annual earnings by an actor**
The world's top-earning actor is currently Will Smith (USA), who earned an estimated $60 million (£35.7 million) in 2002, according to the 2003 *Forbes* Celebrity 100 list.

★ **Highest annual earnings by an actress**
The world's top-earning actress is currently Jennifer Aniston (USA), who earned an estimated $35 million (£20.8 million) in 2002, according to the 2003 *Forbes* Celebrity 100 list.

★ **Actor in most films grossing over $100 million at the box office**
Harrison Ford (USA) has starred in a total of 15 movies that have grossed over $100 million at the international box office. The highest grossing was *Star Wars* (1997) with $798 million (£564.3 million). Ford also holds the record for highest box office gross for an actor: his 27 films to date have grossed $3,369,662,963 (£1,781,664,973).

★ **Actress in most films grossing over $100 million at the box office**
By February 2004, Julia Roberts (USA) had starred in 11 movies that have grossed at least $100 million (£53.5 million) at the international box office. Her top-grossing film was *Pretty Woman* (USA, 1990), which took $463.4 million (£331 million). Roberts' movies have grossed a record $2,516,318,527 (£1,379,863,198).

★ **Highest-paid actor per film**
Bruce Willis (USA) received $100 million (£61.83 million) for playing Dr Malcolm Crowe in the $55-million (£34-million) film *The Sixth Sense* (USA, 1999) through his salary and a percentage of the film's receipts.

★ **Highest annual earnings by a film producer**
Producer-director Steven Spielberg (USA) topped the 2003 *Forbes* Celebrity 100 list, having earned an estimated $200 million (£119 million) during 2002.

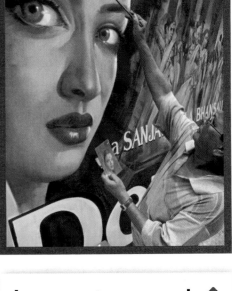

ⅴ Earliest feature-length 'talkie'

Alan Crossland's (USA) *The Jazz Singer* (USA, 1927) premiered on Broadway on

6 October 1927. Warner Bros intended the sound to be confined to music and songs, but Al Jolson (near left with May McAvoy, both USA) ad-libbed some speech, which led to 354 words being spoken in all: 340 by Jolson; 13 by Eugenie Besserer (USA), who played his mother; and one ('Stop!') by Warner Oland (Sweden), who played his father.

Largest annual ⌃ film output

India produces more feature-length films than any other country. A record 948 films were produced in 1990, and in 1994, 754 films were produced in a record 16 languages at India's three major centres of production – Mumbai (Bombay), Calcutta and Madras.

★ **Earliest public screening of a 'talkie'**
The earliest public presentation of sound on film was *The Arsonist* (Germany/USA, 1922), a short drama made using the Tri-Ergon process and shown at the Alhambra cinema, Berlin, Germany, on 17 September 1922. It starred Erwin Baron (USA), who played seven of the nine parts.

★ **Oldest cinema chain**
The Wehrenberg Theatres chain first set up in 1906 with the opening of the Cherokee Theatre in St Louis, Missouri, USA, by former blacksmith Fred Wehrenberg (USA). Still run by the Wehrenberg family today, it currently operates 15 cinemas in the states of Missouri and Illinois.

★ **Largest cinema chain**
Regal Entertainment Group, comprising Regal Cinemas, United Artists Theaters and Edwards Theaters, operates 562 cinemas with 6,119 screens (including two Imax screens) in 39 states of the USA.

★ **First circular cinema**
The world's first circular cinema is located in the European Park of the Moving Image at Futuroscope near Poitiers, France. It consists of nine projectors and nine screens covering a total surface area of 272 m² (2,928 ft²). The process enables the projection of nine electronically synchronized films offering a 360° field of vision.

★ **Largest drive-in cinema by screens**
The Thunderbird Drive-in (also known as the Swap Shop Drive-in), Fort Lauderdale, Florida, USA, which opened with a single screen on 22 November 1963, now has 13 screens of varying sizes, the largest (screen 9) being the original.

★ **Largest drive-in cinema screen ever**
The Algiers Drive-in, Detroit, Michigan, USA, had a screen that measured 65.8 m (216 ft) wide and covered 445.9 m² (4,800 ft²). It first opened on 15 August 1956 to show the western *The Searchers* (USA, 1956). The drive-in originally had a capacity of 1,200, which increased to 1,500 in 1977, but in 1985 the site was sold and is now a shopping centre.

★ **Smallest drive-in cinema**
Both the Harmony Drive-in of Harmony, Pennsylvania, USA, and the Highway 78 Drive-in of Bamberg, South Carolina, USA, could hold no more than 50 cars.

★ **Largest permanent cinema screen**
The Panasonic IMAX Theatre at Darling Harbour, Sydney, Australia, holds the largest fixed projection screen in the world, measuring 35.72 x 29.57 m (117 x 97 ft). It opened in September 1996 and can seat 540 people.

★ **Smallest purpose-built cinema in operation**
Cinema dei Piccoli was built by Alfredo Annibali (Italy) in 1934 in the park of Villa Borghese, Rome, Italy. It now covers an area of 71.52 m² (769.83 ft²). Originally called the Topolino Cinema (after the Italian name for Mickey Mouse), the cinema used a Pathé-Baby 9.5-mm projector and bed sheets for the screen, and played 78 rpm records for background music. Restored in 1991, the cinema has 63 seats, a 5 x 2.5-m (16-ft 4.8-in x 8-ft 2.4-in) screen, stereo sound and air conditioning.

★ **Smallest cinema by seat capacity**
Converted from an old workshop, the smallest cinema to operate as a regular commercial venture is The Screen Room on Broad Street, Nottingham, UK, which has 21 seats. The cinema, owned by Steven Metcalf (UK), opened on 27 September 2002 with the film *Lost in La Mancha* (USA/UK, 2002).

Widest film release ⌃ in a single country

X2 (USA, 2003) was given the widest film release of any film in history

when it opened in the USA at 3,741 cinemas on 2 May 2003. Showing on 7,316 screens, it took $85.6 million (£53.1 million) during the opening weekend, an average of $22,871 (£14,194) per cinema. Famke Jannsen (Netherlands) and Halle Berry (USA, both above) were two of the movie's stars.

★ **Largest audience to attend a film premiere**
A total of 23,930 people attended the premiere of *Brewster McCloud* (USA, 1970) at the Houston Astrodome, Texas, USA, on 5 December 1970. Paying between $2.50 and $50 (then £1.04 and £20.86) per seat, the audience watched the film from a special 70-mm print made for the premiere at a cost of $12,000 (then £5,008), which was projected on to a 47.54 x 18.28-m (156 x 60-ft) screen.

★ **Longest red carpet at a film premiere**
For the premiere of *Pirates of the Caribbean: Curse of the Black Pearl* (USA, 2003), held at Disneyland, Anaheim, California, USA, on 28 June 2003, a red carpet stretched 274 m (900 ft) from Disneyland's entrance along Main Street USA to the Rivers of America in Frontierland.

★ **Longest non-stop cinema show**
A total of 136 feature films were shown consecutively during a 250-hour marathon at the 100 Years of Cinema Festival, Montreal, Canada, from 11 to 22 June 1992.

★ **Movie watching marathon**
An audience of 11 people – Erik Acosta, Dina Agrapides, Eric Bailey, Kim Binal, Wayne Diana, Mark Huang, Cheryl Jones, Daniel Koenig, Ron Mathewson, Allan Press and Nathan Snook – watched 34 films for 66 hr 30 min at an event organized by online DVD rental company Netflix.com at the Times Square Studios, New York City, USA, from 5 to 8 December 2003.

★ **Longest film documentary**
Grandmother Martha (1996), a documentary about the life of ex-actress and entertainer Martha Stelloo (Netherlands), runs for 24 hr 12 min. The film was written, produced and directed by Sydney Ling (Netherlands).

★ **Widest cinema screen**
A temporary screen was used at the 1937 Paris Exposition to show Henri Chrétien's (France) hypergonar films, which were

the precursor of cinerama. The concave screen had a width of 90.5 m (297 ft) and was 9.9 m (33 ft) high.

★ **Country with the most cinemas per capita**
Belarus has more cinemas per capita than any other country in the world, with one cinema for every 2,734 inhabitants. In all, the country has 3,780 cinemas for its population of 10,335,382.

★ **Highest annual cinema attendance**
The largest cinema audience ever in one year was 4.49 billion admissions, achieved in the USA in 1929.

★ **Highest annual cinema attendance per capita**
With a population of 279,384 and a total of 1,531,000 admissions at 46 cinemas

in 2003, Iceland has a greater cinema attendance per capita than any other country. This figure translates as 5,480 visits per 1,000 people per year.

★ **Lowest annual cinema attendance per capita**
Malaysia has a population of 22,662,365 and had a total of 336,000 cinema admissions in 2003. This figure translates as 14.83 visits per 1,000 people per year.

★ **Longest first run of a film in one cinema**
Romance in Lushan (China, 1980) first opened at the Jiangxi Movie Circulation and Screening Company, Lushan, China, on 12 July 1980 and has been shown four times a day since then. As of 8 December 2001 the film had been seen by 1,336,638 patrons.

» Most Oscars won by a film

At the 2004 American Academy Awards ceremony held on

29 February 2004, the third instalment of the *The Lord of the Rings* trilogy, *The Return of the King* (NZ/USA, 2003), won all 11 of its nominations. The film, directed by Peter Jackson, walked away with Best Picture, Best Director, Art Direction, Costume Design, Visual Effects, Sound, Editing, Makeup, Screenplay Based on Material Previously Produced or Published, Original Score and Original Song. Pictured from left to right are Frances Walsh, Peter Jackson and Philippa Boyens (all New Zealand) picking up their Oscars for Best Screenplay.

The Return of the King shares this record of 11 Oscar wins with two other films. The first to achieve the record was *Ben-Hur* (USA, 1959), which won 11 Oscars from 12 nominations on 4 April 1960, followed by *Titanic* (USA, 1997) from 14 nominations on 23 March 1998.

★ **Longest Oscar-winning career**

Katharine Hepburn (USA) had the distinction of having the longest Oscar award-winning career, spanning 48 years 13 days from her first Oscar for *Morning Glory* (USA, 1932) on 16 March 1934 to her last for *On Golden Pond* (USA, 1981) on 29 March 1982.

★ **Most Oscars for acting won by a film**

Both *A Streetcar Named Desire* (USA, 1951) and *Network* (USA, 1976) won three acting Oscars, in 1952 and 1977 respectively. No film has yet won all four acting Oscars.

★ **Most Best Actor wins**

Seven actors have won Best Actor awards twice: Spencer Tracy (USA) for *Captains Courageous* (USA, 1937) and *Boys Town* (USA 1938); Fredric March (USA) for *Dr Jekyll and Mr Hyde* (USA, 1932) and *The Best Years of Our Lives* (USA, 1946); Gary Cooper (USA) for *Sergeant York* (USA, 1941) and *High Noon* (USA, 1952); Marlon Brando (USA) for *On the Waterfront* (USA, 1954) and *The Godfather* (USA, 1972); Jack Nicholson (USA) for *One Flew Over the Cuckoo's Nest* (USA, 1975) and *As Good As It Gets* (USA, 1997); Dustin Hoffman (USA) for *Kramer vs. Kramer* (USA, 1979) and *Rain Man* (USA, 1988); and Tom Hanks (USA) for *Philadelphia* (USA, 1993) and *Forrest Gump* (USA, 1994).

★ **Most Best Actor nominations for the same film**

On 5 March 1936, Clark Gable (USA), Charles Laughton (UK) and Franchot Tone (USA) were all nominated for Best Actor for their performances in *Mutiny on the Bounty* (USA, 1935). The winner was the fourth nominee, Victor McLaglen (UK), for *The Informer* (USA, 1935).

★ **Most Best Actress nominations in the same year**

At the 1929/30 Academy Awards held on 5 November 1930, of the five actresses nominated for Best Actress in a Leading Role, two were nominated twice: Greta Garbo (Sweden) for *Anna Christie* (USA, 1930) and *Romance* (USA, 1930) and Norma Shearer (Canada) for *Their Own Desire* (USA, 1929) and *The Divorcee* (USA, 1930).

★ **Oldest Best Actor winner**

Henry Fonda (USA, 1905–82) won the Best Actor Oscar on 29 March 1982 for his performance as Norman Thayer Jr in *On Golden Pond* (USA, 1981) aged 75 years 317 days.

★ **Oldest Best Actress winner**

Jessica Tandy (UK, 1909–94) won the Best Actress Oscar for *Driving Miss Daisy* (USA, 1989) on 29 March 1990 at the age of 80 years 295 days.

★ **Oldest Best Supporting Actor winner**

The oldest recipient of the Best Supporting Actor award is George Burns (USA, 1896–1996) for his role as Al Lewis in *The Sunshine Boys* (USA, 1975) on 29 March 1976, when he was aged 80 years 68 days.

★ **Most Best Director wins**

John Ford (USA) won an Oscar for Best Director on four occasions: for *The Informer* (USA, 1936), *The Grapes of Wrath* (USA, 1940), *How Green Was My Valley* (USA, 1941) and *The Quiet Man* (USA, 1952).

★ **Oldest actress nominated for an Oscar**

Eva LeGallienne (UK, 1899–1991) was aged 82 years 80 days when she was nominated for the Best Supporting Actress Oscar for her role as Grandma Pearl in *Resurrection* (USA, 1980) for the ceremony held on 31 March 1981.

★ **Oldest actor nominated for an Oscar**

Richard Farnsworth (USA, 1920–2000) was aged 79 years 207 days when the Academy nominated him Best Actor for his role as Alvin Straight in *The Straight Story* (USA, 1999) at the ceremony held on 26 March 2000.

GWR TALKS TO
Keisha Castle-Hughes

Keisha Castle-Hughes (New Zealand) was 13 years 309 days old when she was nominated for Best Actress on 27 January 2004 for her role of Paikea 'Pai' Apirana in *Whale Rider* (NZ/Germany, 2002). She is the youngest person to receive a Best Actress nomination.

How did you get into acting – was it something you always wanted to do?
Yes. However, I didn't think it would happen quite so soon! I hadn't done anything prior to this, not even a school play! A casting director, Diana Rowan, came to my school and asked me to come to a series of workshops and auditions. It went from there.

What aspects of your acting experience have you enjoyed?
We were about halfway through shooting when it suddenly dawned on me that I was really going to be in a film – that I was actually living my dream! The director, Niki Caro, was great to work with. She helped me so much, especially to understand Pai.
I've also travelled extensively for publicity and promotion – to Canada, the USA, Australia, the UK and Japan, and I'll also visit Greece, Spain and China.

What's your favourite movie to watch?
Typically teen – I love *Bring it On*.

Who are your favourite film stars?
Julia Roberts and Johnny Depp.

What's it like being famous suddenly?
I haven't let this experience change my life too much. I just like to do normal kid stuff. I hang out with my friends. We talk about fashion, boys, music, clothes, and just general 'girl stuff'. School is also very important to me. It's always good to get back into it, but I find I really need to be focussed.

Do you get recognised when you are out?
I do. I remember thinking about that before the film came out, wondering what it would be like with people staring at you. It's like I thought it would be – weird!

How does it feel to have a Guinness World Record?
Incredible! Especially since this was my first acting job!

What advice would you give to anyone who wants to go into acting?
If it's what you want to do, go for it! Be sure you have a clear goal in mind and be prepared to work hard. There's a lot of work involved right thoughout the whole acting experience.

★ **Oldest recipient of an Oscar by a performer**
Groucho Marx (USA, 1890–1977) received an Honorary Award in recognition of his brilliant creativity and for the unequalled achievements of the Marx Brothers in the art of motion picture comedy, on 2 April 1974 aged 83 years 182 days.

★ **Youngest Oscar winner**
The youngest Oscar winner is Tatum O'Neal (USA, b. 5 November 1963), who was aged 10 years 148 days when she received the Best Supporting Actress award for *Paper Moon* (USA, 1973) on 2 April 1974.
Shirley Temple was awarded an Honorary Oscar at the age of 6 years 310 days for her achievements in 1934.

★ **Most wins for acting and writing**
Emma Thompson (UK) won Best Actress in 1993 for her role in *Howards End* (UK/Japan, 1992) and was awarded Best Screenplay Based on Material from Another Medium for *Sense and Sensibility* (USA/UK, 1995) in 1996, making her the first person ever to win Oscars for both acting and writing.

★ **Most Oscar-winning generations**
The only family to contain three generations of Oscar winners are the Hustons (all USA). Walter Huston (1884–1950) won Best Supporting Actor for *The Treasure of the Sierra Madre* (USA, 1948). His son John (1906–87) won Best Director for the same film and John's daughter Angelica (b. 8 July 1951) won Best Supporting Actress for *Prizzi's Honor* (USA, 1985).

★ **Most ceremonies presented**
Bob Hope (USA) served as master of ceremony on Oscar night a total of 16 times (alone and in conjunction with others), participating in a record 27 Academy Awards presentations.

★ **Longest speech**
After receiving the Best Actress award for her title role in *Mrs Miniver* (USA, 1942) at the 1942 Academy Awards held on 4 March 1943, Greer Garson (UK) made a speech that lasted 5 min 30 sec.

★ **Most people thanked by an Oscar winner**
On 13 March 1947, Olivia de Havilland (UK/USA; b. Japan) won Best Actress as Josephine Norris in *To Each His Own* (USA, 1946). In her speech she thanked 27 people by their name.

★ **Longest ceremony**
The 71st Academy Awards ceremony, hosted by Whoopi Goldberg (USA) and broadcast by the ABC network, lasted 4 hr 2 min on 21 March 1999.

Most Oscar nominations

Title	Name	Nominated	Won
Actor	Jack Nicholson (USA)	12	2
Actress	Meryl Streep (USA)	13	2
Director	William Wyler (USA)	12	3
Consecutively	Walt Disney (USA)	9	1
Ever	Walt Disney (USA)	64	26
Best Foreign Language Film	France	34	12
Foreign Language Film	*Crouching Tiger, Hidden Dragon* (Taipei, 2000)	10	4
Living person	John Williams (USA)	40	5
Before winning	Randy Newman (USA)	16	1
Without winning	Roland Anderson (USA)	15	0
Without winning (actor)	Richard Burton (UK)	7	0
	*Peter O'Toole (UK)	7	0
Without winning (film)	*The Turning Point* (USA, 1977)	11	0
	The Color Purple (USA, 1986)	11	0
One role	Barry Fitzgerald (Ireland)	2	1

* In 2003 he was finally acknowledged with an Honorary Award.

★ GWR TALKS TO
Vic Armstrong

In a career spanning five decades, Vic Armstrong (UK) has been a stuntman and stunt co-ordinator in more than 250 films, including the Indiana Jones trilogy. He has also doubled for every actor to have played the title role in the James Bond series. He currently holds the record for the most prolific movie stuntman.

Have you ever been badly injured?
I've had my share of injuries – it goes with the territory, as they say. I've broken a leg, shoulder, ribs, nose, arm, collarbone, etc, but even Michael Schumacher crashes his Formula One car occasionally and he is the best in the world at what he does.

Most edited single ⌃ sequence in a movie

For the chariot race scene in *Ben Hur* (USA, 1925, above), editor

Lloyd Nosler (USA) had to compress 60,960 m (200,000 ft) of film into a sparse 228.6 m (750 ft). With a ratio of 267:1, it is the most edited scene in cinema history.

How old were you when you started your career?
I got into stunt work when I was 17 years old by lending a stuntman a horse for the movie *Arabesque* (USA, 1966) with Gregory Peck (USA) and Sophia Loren (Italy). I was then asked to go and ride the horse as there was a big sequence involving lots of big jumps and from that day on all I did was stunt work.

Which film did you enjoy working on the most?
My favourite would have to be *Raiders of the Lost Ark* (USA,1980) – I'm second from left, above – but I also have a soft spot for all the James Bond films I've worked on.

What's the scariest stunt you've been involved with?
All stunts are scary, but one of the scariest was a 30-m (100-ft) fall I did on *The Final Conflict* (UK/USA, 1981).

What advice would you give?
You need to achieve a skill that will make you better than the average person. Mine was riding horses, which came from my days as an amateur steeplechase rider. Then you have to stay cool, calm and collected and analyse each situation to make sure it's safe and within your capabilities.

How do you feel about your Guinness World Record?
I'm very proud: it's a great accolade for me and rates right alongside my Oscar and my BAFTA. I used to read the book when I was a lad: I *never* thought I'd get into it.

What's your favourite Guinness World Record?
I'd go for Tony McCoy (UK), who rode the most steeplechase winners ever. As I started off in life dreaming of doing this, I can really relate to his amazing achievement.

★ Largest film studio
The largest film studio complex in the world is at Universal City, Los Angeles, California, USA. The site, called the Back Lot, opened in 1915 and comprises 561 buildings and 34 sound stages totalling 170 ha (420 acres). Recent films made there by Universal Pictures include *Hulk* (USA, 2003) and *Thunderbirds* (USA, 2004).

★ Largest indoor film set
The UFO landing site built for the climax of Steven Spielberg's *Close Encounters of the Third Kind* (USA, 1977) measured 27 x 137 x 76 m (90 x 450 x 250 ft). Constructed inside a 283,000-m³ (10 million-ft³) dirigible hangar at Mobile, Alabama, USA, the building had six times the capacity of the largest sound stage in Hollywood.

★ Largest production crew for a feature film
The largest number of craftsmen and technicians employed on a dramatic feature was 532 for the World War I flying story *Gunbus* (USA

title *Sky Bandits*; UK, 1986), directed by Zoran Perisic (Yugoslavia) with a cast that included Nicholas Lyndhurst and Adrian Dunbar (both UK).

★ Largest annual film output by a Hollywood studio
The highest output of any Hollywood studio was 101 features made by Paramount in 1921. The highest of the sound era was 68, jointly held by Paramount in 1936 and Warner Bros in 1937.

★ Largest land-based prop
The 18-m-long (60-ft), 12-m-high (40-ft) wooden horse of Troy used in Robert Wise's *Helen of Troy* (USA/Italy, 1954) weighed 81,280 kg (179,191 lb). It took 30 trees and over 453 kg (1,000 lb) of nails to build it.

★ Most retakes for one scene with dialogue
It was claimed that Stanley Kubrick (USA) demanded 127 retakes for a scene with Shelley Duval (USA) in *The Shining* (USA, 1980).

Largest frame format used in film »

Imax (right) uses 70-mm film, three times larger than the standard 35-mm film usually used.

With a dimension of 5 x 7 cm (1.96 x 2.74 in), the film has 15 perforations per frame as opposed to the standard five.

★ **Longest take in a commercially made film**
In *A Free Soul* (USA, 1931), there is a 14-minute uninterrupted monologue by Lionel Barrymore (USA). Since a reel of camera film only lasts ten minutes, the take was achieved by using more than one camera.
Alfred Hitchcock's (UK) *Rope* (USA, 1948) was shot in eight ten-minute takes (apart from one cut to the housekeeper in the first reel). The effect was of one continuous shot, since the action of the story occupied the same time period – 80 minutes – as the length of film.

★ **Longest film shot on a single camera**
Russkij Kovcheg (*Russian Ark;* Russia, 2002), directed by Aleksandr Sokurov (Russia), was the first uncompressed high-definition film. It was shot on a single camera for 90 minutes on 23 December 2001. The final film was shown without any cuts or edits on 22 May 2002 at the Cannes Film Festival,

France, with a running time of 96 minutes (including title sequence and credits).

★ **Longest monologue in a dramatic film**
In *L'Aigle à Deux Têtes* (*The Eagle has Two Heads*, France, 1948) written and directed by Jean Cocteau (France), a 20-minute speech was made by the character Natasha, played by Edwige Feuillère (France).

★ **Most extensive screen test**
To find the actress to play Scarlett O'Hara in *Gone with the Wind* (USA, 1939), MGM shot 45,415 m (149,000 ft) of black-and-white test film and another 3,962 m (13,000 ft) of colour with 60 actresses, none of whom got the part.

★ **Most extensive digital character on film**
Created by WETA Digital, the computer-generated character Gollum in *The Lord of the Rings: The Two Towers* (NZ/USA, 2002) had 250 facial expressions and 300 moving muscles. Gollum's body

movements were based on those of actor Andy Serkis (UK), who filmed every scene in which Gollum appears wearing a unitard body stocking to facilitate the later addition of computer-generated images (CGI).

★ **Longest video documentary about an individual**
A documentary on Elvis Presley (USA) called *The Definitive Elvis Collection* produced by Passport International Productions (USA) is 13 hr 52 min long (including titles). It features over 200 interviews with Elvis's friends, family, fans and co-stars. Production began in January 2000 and it was released on DVD/VHS on 16 July 2002.

★ **Longest running film series**
Over 46 years, 103 features were made about the 19th-century martial arts hero Huang Fei-Hong, starting with *The True Story of Huang Fei-Hong* (Hong Kong, 1949)

and continuing to the latest production, *Once Upon a Time in China 5* (Hong Kong, 1995).

★ **Longest film ever made**
The Cure for Insomnia (USA, 1987), directed by John Henry Timmis IV, is 85 hours long. It premiered in its entirety at the School of the Art Institute of Chicago, Illinois, USA, from 31 January to 3 February 1987.

★ **Most valuable film costume**
A blue and white gingham dress worn by Judy Garland (USA) as Dorothy in the MGM film *The Wizard of Oz* (USA, 1939) was sold at Christie's, London, UK, on 9 December 1999 for £199,500 (then $324,068).

★ **Shortest stuntman**
Measured on 20 October 2003, stuntman Kiran Shah (UK) stands 1.263 m (4 ft 1.7 in) tall. He has performed stunts in 31 movies including being perspective stunt-double for Elijah Wood (USA) in *The Lord of the Rings* trilogy (NZ/USA, 2001–2003).

Longest stop-motion »
feature film

Chicken Run (UK, 2000), directed by Peter Lord and Nick Park (both UK), was released with a running time of 82 minutes and has 118,080 shots filmed using the 'stop-motion' special-effects technique. (A normal live-action feature has between 500 and 1,000 shots.)

Chicken Run also holds the record for the most plasticine used in a feature film. Animators used 2,380 kg (5,247 lb) of plasticine during filming.

★ Largest budget for an animation
Walt Disney's *Tarzan* (USA, 1999), first released on 17 June 1999, was made with a budget of $150 million (then £94 million). It was the first film to use the 'deep canvas' technique, which allows 2-D hand-drawn characters to exist in a 3-D environment.

★ Most successful virtual band
The most successful virtual band is the Gorillaz (UK), with global album sales of 3 million for their eponymous debut, including 1.3 million in the USA and certified sales of 600,000 in the UK. The release peaked at No. 3 on the UK album chart, went top 20 in the USA, and was No.1 on the Eurochart. The animated fourpiece were nominated for six BRIT awards and one Grammy in 2001.

★ Highest box office gross for an animation
Walt Disney's *The Lion King* (USA, 1994) took $777.9 million (then £486.1 million) at the box office. The film starred the voices of Rowan Atkinson (UK) as Zazu the hornbill, Jeremy Irons (UK) as Simba's uncle Scar and Whoopi Goldberg (USA) as Shenzi the hyena.

★ Highest box office gross for an animation (inflation adjusted)
Walt Disney's first full-length feature film, *Snow White and the Seven Dwarfs* (USA, 1937), took $184.9 million (then £37,378,867) at the box office worldwide – equivalent to $1,633,582,523 (£1,020,989,077) today.

★ Fastest $100 million box office gross for an animation
Finding Nemo (USA, 2003), the computer-animated film from Walt Disney and Pixar Animation Studios, cost $94 million (then £78.9 million) to make and reached the $100 million mark at the US box office in eight days from its release on 30 May 2003 at 3,374 cinemas.

★ Most expensive computer-animated film
Monsters, Inc. (USA, 2001), from Walt Disney and Pixar Animation Studios, had a budget of $115 million (£78.6 million).

★ Earliest animal cartoon
Old Doc Yak, a tailcoated billy goat in striped pants, was brought to the screen by *Chicago Tribune* cartoonist Sidney Smith (USA) in a Selig Polyscope series started in July 1913. It was Smith's much-loved animal cartoon characters who gave animated films a distinct appeal of their own as suitable entertainment for children.

★ First feature colour cartoon
The earliest full-length colour cartoon talkie was Argentina's *Peludópolis*, made in 1931 by Quirino Cristiani (Argentina).

★ Earliest colour cartoon series
The Red Head Comedies (USA, 1923), each a satire of an historical event by the Lee-Bradford Corporation, was the very first cartoon series.

★ First full-length cartoon
The earliest full-length feature cartoon was *El Apóstol* (Argentina, 1917), written and directed by Federico Valle (Argentina), with a running time of 70 minutes. Compiled from 58,000 drawings, it took 12 months to finish.

★ Earliest cartoon talkie release
Dave and Max Fleischer's (both Austria) *Come Take a Trip in my Airship* (USA, 1924) opened with the animated figure of a woman in a white dress chattering as the lead-in to the song.

★ First all-talking cartoon
On 1 September 1928, Paul Terry's (USA) *Dinner Time* (USA, 1928) was premiered at the Mark Strand Theatre, New York, USA.

Longest » cartoon series 'talkie'

Between 1933 and 1957, Max Fleischer's (Austria) *Popeye the Sailor Man* (right) had 233 one-reelers and a single two-reeler (*Popeye the Sailor Meets Sinbad the Sailor*; USA, 1936) in the cinema. The series was first aired on television in September 1956, making it the longest running syndicated cartoon series.

Highest box office ⌃ gross for an animation on an opening weekend

Finding Nemo (USA, 2003, above) directed by Andrew Stanton and Lee Unkrich (both USA) opened in the USA on 30 May 2003 to take $70,251,710 (£42,954,271) at the box office from 3,374 cinemas. The tale of a father fish trying to find his son features the voices of Albert Brooks, Ellen DeGeneres and Willem Dafoe (all USA).

★ **Cartoon character most often portrayed on screen**
Zorro, created by Johnston McCulley (USA), has been portrayed in a record 69 films. He was also the first comic-strip character to be the subject of a major feature film, *The Mark of Zorro* (USA, 1920).

★ **Most valuable cartoon poster**
A film poster for a Walt Disney film short, *Alice's Day At Sea* (USA, 1924), depicting Alice astride a fish above the waves, was sold at Christie's, London, UK, in April 1994 for £23,100 (then $34,072).

★ **Earliest cartoon merchandise**
Pat Sullivan's (USA) Felix the Cat, who appeared in 1919 as the animal that 'kept on walking', was not only the first cartoon character to attain the celebrity of a human star, but was, in 1924, also the first to be an image on packaging. Felix was then merchandized as a phenomenally successful cuddly toy two years later.

★ **Most characters voiced by one artist in a TV cartoon series**
Kara Tritton (UK) voiced 198 cartoon characters for 75 episodes over six series of *Blues Clues* (Nick Jr, UK). Kara gave voices to furniture (Postbox, Paper Recycling Bin), food (Mr Salt and Mrs Pepper), animals (Owl, Hippo), ghosts, planets and people.

★ **Longest working career for a cartoon voice-over**
For the first few weeks, the original cinema series *Popeye* was voiced by William Costello (USA). Then in 1934, for the film *Let You and Him Fight*, Jack Mercer (USA) took over the role and voiced

the character for the next 45 years and 294 productions, including the TV cartoons.

★ **Most valuable colour animation cell**
One of the 150,000 colour cells (a clear plastic sheet to which animation drawings are traced and then hand painted) from Walt Disney's *Snow White and the Seven Dwarfs* (USA, 1937) was sold by art dealer Guthrie Courvoisier (USA) in 1991 for $222,525 (then £115,000).

★ **Most valuable black-and-white animation cell**
On 16 May 1989, a black-and-white drawing from Walt Disney's *The Orphan's Benefit* (USA, 1934), depicting Donald Duck being punched by an orphan, raised $286,000 (£174,390) at Christie's, New York, USA.

★ **Fastest script-to-screen animation production**
KliK Animation in Montreal, Canada, produced and aired a topical one-minute animation,

entitled *Le JourNul de François Pérusse*, on the same day. It premiered on 8 February 1999 after the 6 pm news on the Canadian TVA network.

★ **Longest full-length film made without a camera**
Frame by frame, artist José Antonio Sistiaga (Spain) painted his 75-minute animated one-man production, *Scope, Colour, Muda* (Spain, 1970) directly on to the film stock. It took him 17 months between 1968 and 1970 to complete.

★ **Most Emmy awards won for an animated TV series**
By September 2003, *The Simpsons* (FOX, USA) had won a total of 20 Emmy awards: eight for Outstanding Animated Program (one hour or less) in 1990, 1991, 1995, 1997, 1998, 2000, 2001 and 2003; 10 for Outstanding Voice-Over Performance in 1992 (six), 1993, 1998, 2001 and 2003; and two for Outstanding Music and Lyrics in 1997 and 1998.

Magic & illusion
Art & media

Oldest magic society ⌃⌃

Houdini (Hungary/USA, above) was one of the most famous illusionists in history. Nicknamed the King of Handcuffs, he was especially well known as an escape artist. Apart from inventing and performing illusions, he owned a share in the famous Martinka's magic shop in New York City, USA, and he was president of the Society of American Magicians from 1917 until his death in 1926. This is the oldest magic society in the world and was founded in Martinka's on 10 May 1902 with only 24 members.

Highest annual ⌃⌃
earnings by a magician

David Copperfield (USA, above) had the highest annual earnings of any magician in 2002 with $55 million (£32.7 million) according to the 2003 *Forbes* Celebrity 100 list. The star of TV shows for both ABC and CBS, Copperfield has performed illusions such as making a jet plane disappear and walking through the Great Wall of China.

★ Highest viewing figures for a TV magic show

Magician Doug Henning (Canada) attracted more than 50 million viewers for the first of his eight *World of Magic* one-hour television specials. The show, directed by Walter C Miller (USA), was first transmitted live on NBC in the USA on 26 December 1975, guest starring Gene Kelly (USA). Henning performed spellbinding illusions including a re-creation of Harry Houdini's famous water torture cell, as well as close-up magic.

★ Longest running TV magic show

Dick 'Mr Magic' Williams (USA) presented 1,200 programmes of WMC-TV's *Magicland*, a weekly half-hour magic show that was on air for 23 years between January 1966 and January 1989.

★ Largest illusion ever staged

The largest illusion ever staged was presented by David Copperfield (USA), who created the illusion of vanishing the Statue of Liberty in New York, USA, on his fifth television special, *The Magic of David Copperfield*, aired on CBS in 1983. The illusion was invented by Jim Steinmeyer and constructed by John Gaughan (both USA).

★ Most copied stage illusion

Invented by Robert Harbin (South Africa) in 1965, the Zig Zag Girl is the most popularly performed stage illusion in the world. A girl, standing in an upright cabinet, is apparently cut into three pieces and has the middle of her body pulled to one side. It was copied so quickly that Harbin published a highly priced book in 1970 (limited to 500 copies) that allowed each purchaser to build one version of the prop. It is estimated that at least 15,000 Zig Zag illusions have been built to date, meaning that 14,500 are unauthorized copies.

★ Most escapes from handcuffs

Nick Janson (UK) has escaped from handcuffs locked on him by more than 1,760 different police officers around the world since 1954.

★ Lowest Death Dive escape

In 1997, Australian Robert Gallup was leg-manacled, handcuffed, chained, put into a secured mail bag and then locked in a cage with a 0.74-m² (8-ft²) floor area before being thrown out of a C-123 transport plane at 5,485 m (18,000 ft) above the Mojave Desert, California, USA. With less than a minute before impact and travelling at 240 km/h (150 mph), he escaped from the sack and cage to reach his parachute secured on the outside of the cage and deployed it with enough altitude to land safely.

★ Fastest transformation illusion

Internationally renowned illusionists The Pendragons (both USA) present Houdini's metamorphosis illusion at a speed that would have fooled its inventor. Jonathan Pendragon is locked in a trunk on top of which his wife Charlotte stands. She conceals herself behind a curtain which drops after just 0.25 seconds to reveal her transformation into her husband. She, of course, is now locked in the trunk.

★ Largest magic society

Founded in 1968 in New York, USA, The International Magicians' Society boasts 37,000 members worldwide, including, among others, David Copperfield (USA).

Most expensive magic show ever staged »

Siegfried and Roy at the Mirage, Las Vegas, Nevada, USA, starring the German illusionists Siegfried Fischbacher (near right) and Roy Horn (far right) cost over $28 million (then £16 million) to stage when it opened on 1 February 1990. The show, which featured dozens of wild animals, including an elephant and a giant fire-breathing mechanical dragon, and a cast of 60, closed after its 5,750th performance on 3 October 2003 after Roy was seriously injured by a white tiger called Montacore.

★ **Earliest presentation of 'sawing' a woman in half**
The first illusionist to seemingly saw a woman in half was its inventor Percy Selbit (UK, b. Percy Tibbles) on 17 January 1921 at the Finsbury Park Empire, London, UK.

★ **Most living creatures produced during a magic performance**
Penn & Teller (USA) produced more than 80,000 bees during their television special *Don't Try This At Home* filmed in 1990. In their British TV version of the routine, the bees were replaced with a safer alternative – bluebottle flies.

★ **Longest running theatre of magic**
John Nevil Maskelyne and George Cooke (both UK) founded, produced and starred in the Maskelyne & Cooke magic theatre at the Egyptian Hall, Piccadilly, London, UK, from 26 May 1873 to 10 December 1904. Maskelyne and business partner David Devant (UK) moved the business to St George's

Hall, Langham Place, London, UK, on 2 January 1905 where the daily shows were regularly continued by three generations of the Maskelyne family until 14 October 1933 – a span of more than 60 years.

★ **Longest magic show**
Dr A Alexander (India) performed his magic show for 24 hours on 27–28 February 2004 at Renew 2000 Community Centre, St Antony's Church Complex, Palakkarai, Tiruchirappalli, India, making it the longest by an individual before a paying audience.

★ **Most magical effects in a stage play**
Directed and adapted by Ken Hill (UK), *The Invisible Man*, which opened in the West End at the Vaudeville Theatre, London, UK, on 20 February 1993, featured a total of 53 different magic effects and illusions.

★ **Youngest magician**
The Yamagami Brothers (both Japan, Yoshinosuke b. 11 August 1994 and

Akinoshin b. 1 December 1995) are the youngest professional illusion artists. Their debut appearance was on 17 April 2001 when they were aged 6 years 229 days and 5 years 128 days respectively.

★ **Most non-magicians taught to present a trick in a single location**
Magician Luis de Matos (Portugal) taught 52,000 people a simple method to apparently vanish 52,001 silk handkerchiefs simultaneously at the Estádio do Dragão football stadium, Porto, Portugal. The effect (not the lesson) was shown live on RTP television on 16 November 2003.

★ **Oldest magic shop**
The world's oldest family-run magic business is Davenports, founded in 1898 by Lewis Davenport (UK) who opened his shop on London's Ryles Road in 1903 and another on Mile End Road in 1908. The business was inherited by his son George in 1926 and is now

run by his granddaughter Betty, who took over in 1961. The shop moved to its current location in The Strand in 1984.

★ **Largest magic convention**
The Blackpool Magicians' Club convention is held annually at the Opera House and Winter Gardens, Blackpool, Lancashire, UK, on the last weekend in February. First held in 1952, it attracts over 3,000 people from around the world.

★ **Oldest weekly magic magazine**
Abracadabra, first edited by Goodliffe (UK), was first published on 2 February 1946 in Birmingham, UK. Currently edited by Donald Bevan (UK), issue 3,029 was published on 19 February 2004.

★ **Highest selling magic magazine**
First published in September 1991, *MAGIC: The Magazine for Magicians* is published monthly by Stagewrite Publishing, Inc., Las Vegas, USA, with an international circulation of 9,691.

Greatest ⌃⌃ comic-reading nation

In Japan, 40% of all printed material sold are manga comics (above). Thirteen weekly magazines by the largest publishers, together with 10 biweeklies and about 20 monthlies, represent the core of this industry. Throughout the 1990s, yearly sales of manga reached an average of 600 billion yen (£3.83 million or $5.5 billion), with roughly 60% spent on magazines and 40% on paperbacks. At any given time at least 10 of these magazines reach sales of 1 million or more copies per issue. People of all ages read manga yet currently much of the market is targeted at adults.

Largest first-edition ⌃⌃ print run

The release of JK Rowling's (UK) *Harry Potter and the Order of the Phoenix* (above) on 21 June 2003 marked the largest first-edition print run in history, with a staggering 8.5 million copies.

★ All-time best selling book
Excluding non-copyright works such as the Bible and the Koran, the world's all-time best selling book is *Guinness World Records* (formerly *The Guinness Book of Records*). Since it was first published in October 1955, global sales in some 37 languages have exceeded 100 million (by October 2003).

★ Fastest selling fiction book
Released on 8 July 2000, the 3.8 million initial print run of *Harry Potter and the Goblet of Fire*, JK Rowling's (UK) fourth Harry Potter book, is the fastest selling book in history. The book broke all sales records with an estimated 3 million copies sold after just 48 hours. (There are currently 27.6 million copies of the first three Harry Potter books in print.)

★ Longest running comic
Since its first edition was published on 4 December 1937, *The Dandy* has been published continuously by DC Thomson & Co of Dundee, UK. The weekly comic's best known character is Desperate Dan, an unshaven cowboy from a town called Cactusville, whose favourite food is cow pie.

★ Best selling cookbook
Betty Crocker's Quick and Easy Cookbook is the best selling cookbook of all time with 50 million copies sold since 1950. Betty Crocker of General Mills is one of the most successful corporate trademarks of all time – the name appears on more than 130 General Mills products, sales of which amount to over $500 million (£276.9 million) a year.

★ Longest novel
Published in 2003, *Knickers* by Simon Roberts (UK) contains a total of 14,156,074 characters (each letter counts as one character and spaces are also counted as one character each).

★ Longest poem ever published
The lengthiest poem ever published is the Kirghiz folk epic *Manas*, which appeared in printed form in 1958 but which has never been translated into English. According to the *Dictionary of Oriental Literatures*, this three-part epic runs to about 500,000 lines. Translated excerpts appear in *The Elek Book of Oriental Verse*.

★ Most widely read catalogue
The IKEA catalogue of Swedish flat-packed furniture is the world's most widely read catalogue, with 130 million copies printed every year. It is translated into 28 languages and distributed across 36 countries.

★ Longest kept diary
Ernest Loftus (Zimbabwe) kept a daily diary for over 91 years. He began writing on 4 May 1896 at the age of 12 and continued until his death on 7 July 1987, aged 103 years 178 days.

★ Largest published crossword
In July 1982, Robert Turcot (Canada) compiled a crossword comprising 82,951 squares. It contained 12,489 clues across and 13,125 down, and covered 3.55 m^2 (38.21 ft^2). The first ever crossword was created by journalist Arthur Wynne (UK) and published on 21 December 1913 in the Sunday newspaper *New York World* (USA). It had the shape of a diamond and contained no internal black squares.

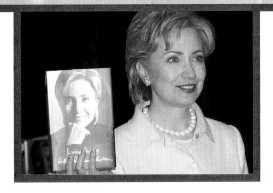

Largest published book ⌄

The world's largest published book, entitled *Bhutan*, weighs 60.3 kg (133 lb), contains 114 full-colour pages and measures 1.52 m high and 2.13 m wide (5 x 7 ft) when opened. It was devised by teams from MIT (Massachusetts Institute of Technology), Acme Bookbinding and the Friendly Planet, and unveiled on 15 December 2003 in New York, USA.

Fastest selling ⌃ non-fiction book

Living History, former first lady Hillary Rodham Clinton's (USA) memoir of her life with

US President Bill Clinton (USA) and his relationship with the intern Monica Lewinsky (USA), is the fastest selling non-fiction book in history, shifting 200,000 copies on its first day of sales in the USA in June 2003.

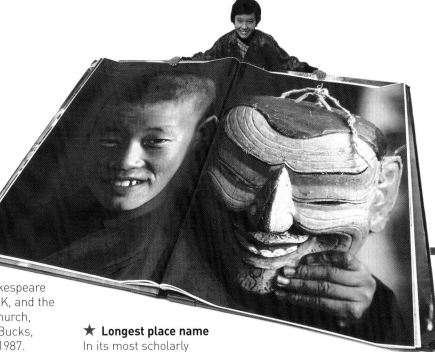

★ Heaviest ever newspaper
The most massive single issue of a newspaper was the Sunday *New York Times* of 14 September 1987, which weighed more than 5.4 kg (12 lb) and contained 1,612 pages.

★ Earliest newspaper to achieve a circulation of a million
The earliest newspaper to achieve a circulation of 1 million copies was *Le Petit Journal*, published in Paris, France. It reached this figure in 1886.

★ Biggest sign language mass participation
A total of 1,920 children signed simultaneously to perform a song on 'World Children's Day at McDonald's 2003'. This event took place in Olympian City, Hong Kong, China, on 5 October 2003.

★ Longest reading-aloud marathon by an individual
Adrian Hilton (UK) recited the complete works of Shakespeare in a 'Bardathon' lasting 110 hr 46 min on the site of the Globe Theatre at the Shakespeare Festival, London, UK, and the Gold Hill Baptist Church, Chalfont St Peter, Bucks, UK, on 16–21 July 1987.

★ Greatest living linguist
The greatest living linguist is Gregg M Cox (USA), who can read and write in 64 languages (speaking 14 fluently) and 11 different dialects.

★ Most common language
The most common first language is Chinese, spoken by more than 1.1 billion people. The 'common speech' (Pûtônghuà) is the standard form of Chinese, with a pronunciation based on that of Beijing.

The most widespread as well as the second most spoken language is English, with a conservative estimate of 800 million speakers. Of these, some 310 million are native speakers, mainly in the USA (about 270 million) and the UK (60 million). The third most spoken language is Spanish.

★ Longest place name
In its most scholarly transliteration, Krungthep Mahanakhon, the 167-letter official name for Bangkok, the capital of Thailand, has 175 letters. The official short version (without capital letters, which are not used in Thai) consists of 111 letters (6 words): *krungthephphramahanakhon bowonratanakosin mahintharayuthaya mahadilokphiphobnovpharad radchataniburirom udomsantisug.*

★ Most complex languages
The Amele language of Papua New Guinea has the most verb forms, with over 69,000 finite forms and 860 infinitive forms of the verb. Haida, the North American Indian language, has the most prefixes (70), and Tabasaran, a language of southeast Dagestan, uses the most noun cases (48). The Eskimo language used by the Inuit has 63 forms of the present tense, and simple nouns have as many as 252 inflections.

★ Language with most consonants
The language with the largest number of distinct consonantal sounds was that of the Ubykhs in the Caucasus, with 81. Ubykh speakers migrated from the Caucasus to Turkey in the 19th century, and the last fully competent speaker, Tevfik Esenc, died in Istanbul in October 1992.

★ Largest postcard
In August 1994, two huge postcards measuring 28.8 m^2 (310 ft^2) were sent by the Canadian National Defence Headquarters to the Canadian headquarters of peacekeeping units, serving in Bosnia and Herzegovina and in Rwanda.

Highest paid « TV actress per episode

As of April 2004, the highest paid TV actresses per episode were Jennifer Aniston (left), Lisa Kudrow and Courteney Cox Arquette (all USA), who played the female leads in *Friends* (NBC, USA) since 1994 and earned approximately $1 million (£703,334) each per episode in the show's final series. Helen Hunt (USA) also reportedly earned $1 million (£610,000) per episode of *Mad About You* (NBC, USA) in the 1990s.

Highest paid ⌃ TV actor per episode

The world's highest paid TV actor per episode is Ray Romano (USA, above), who earned $1.8 million (£1.2 million) per episode of *Everybody Loves Raymond* (CBS, USA) for the eighth series in 2004/05.

★ **Longest running TV variety show**
Sábado Gigante (Univision Television Network, USA) has been broadcast every Saturday evening since 8 August 1962. The Spanish-language show was created and has been continually hosted by Mario Kreutzberger (Chile), or 'Don Francisco' as he is more popularly known. Each three-hour episode is filmed in front of a live audience.

★ **Largest TV contract**
In May 2003, Oprah Winfrey (USA) signed a contract worth $279 million (£175 million) with the American TV station ABC to host *The Oprah Winfrey Show* for an extra two years until 2008. The show is among the highest rated daytime shows, with an average US weekly audience of 26 million.

★ **Longest working career as a TV chef**
Eva Vicenta Uranga Roig Vda. de Zarate (Mexico), or 'Mrs Zarate' as she is better known, hosted her first cookery show, *Cocina*

Al Minuto (Televisora Tapatia, Mexico), on 1 December 1960. She currently presents the same show under the name of *Hasta La Cocina* for Televisa Guadalajara Co. in Guadalajara, Jalisco, Mexico. Mrs Zarate has spent 6,610 hours cooking for TV shows. She was born on 13 July 1920, making her one of the oldest TV presenters in the world.

★ **Longest running TV quiz show**
It's Academic (NBC4 USA) has been on air weekly since 7 October 1961. The show, which features high-school teams competing against each other, was created by Sophie Altman (USA) and entered its 43rd season in autumn 2003.

★ **Longest TV quiz programme**
The longest TV quiz programme began at 8:15 pm on 29 August 2003, finishing 52 hr 45 min later at 1 am on 1 September 2003. The show was broadcast on 9Live (Germany) and co-hosted by Thomas Schürmann, Anna

Heesch, Alida-Nadine Kurras, Robin Bade and Jörg Draeger (all Germany) from the studio in Ismaning, Germany. Callers phoned in to answer a quiz question and hopefully win a cash prize, which increased with each wrong answer. On this occasion, 2,346 callers phoned in to try to win the €1 million (£680,000 or $1.2 million) answering approximately 1,500 questions.

★ **Longest running TV show**
Meet the Press (NBC, USA) was first transmitted on 6 November 1947 and has been aired subsequently each week since 12 September 1948.

★ **Longest time in the same role in a TV series**
Helen Wagner (USA) has played the character of Nancy Hughes McClosky in *As The World Turns* (CBS, USA) since it premiered

on 2 April 1956. The 12,000th episode was broadcast on 6 May 2003.

★ **Longest working career of a TV director on the same programme**
The weekly sports show *Estadio Uno*, produced by SIFAR SA, Uruguay, and currently broadcast on Channel 5 of Sistema Nacional de Televisión, has been directed continuously by Julio Sánchez Padilla (Uruguay) since it was first aired on 5 July 1970.

★ **Most expensive TV programme**
The world's most expensive TV programme, in terms of cost per episode, is *ER* (NBC, USA). At its peak, in January 1998, the makers, Warner Bros (USA), agreed to a three-year deal with NBC for 22 one-hour episodes to be made at a cost of $13.1 million (£8.2 million) each.

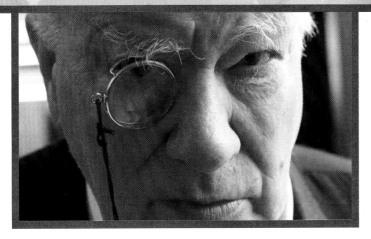

Most durable TV presenter ⌃

Patrick Moore (UK, above) holds records for both the world's most durable TV presenter and the longest running TV show with the same presenter, for his monthly programme *The Sky at Night* (BBC, UK), which he has hosted without a break since 24 April 1957. Episode number 614 was aired on 2 February 2004.

Highest paid TV drama ⌄ actor per episode

Noah Wyle (USA, below) earned approximately $400,000 (£258,000) per episode of *ER* (NBC, USA) for the 2003/04 series. Wyle plays the character of the head doctor, Dr John Carter.

★ **Most prolific TV scriptwriter** Since 1942, the output of Ted (later Lord) Willis is estimated to have been 20 million words. From 1949 until his death in 1992 he wrote 41 TV series, including the first seven years and 2.25 million words of *Dixon of Dock Green*, which ran on BBC Television, UK, from 1955 to 1976. He also wrote 37 stage plays and 39 feature films.

★ **Most successful TV soap** *Dallas* (CBS, USA) began in 1978 as a mini-series. By 1980 it had been watched by around 83 million people in the USA, giving it a share of 76% of the television audience – a record at the time. It had also been seen in more than 90 countries, often in locally dubbed versions. After 11 years and 353 episodes, the last episode was broadcast in the USA on 3 May 1991.

★ **Longest TV talk show marathon** The world record for the longest TV talk show marathon is 30 hours and is held by both Zoltán Kováry (Hungary) and

Vador Lladó (Spain). Kováry continually interviewed guests and presented from 4 pm on 13 February 2003 until 10 pm on 14 February 2003 at the Fix.tv studios, Budapest, Hungary; Lladó of Flaix TV did the same from 3 to 4 May 2002 in Barcelona, Spain.

★ **Longest running sports TV programme** *Scotsport* (Scottish TV, UK) first aired on 18 September 1957 at 10:30 pm and is still running. The weekly show is presented by Jim Delahunt (UK).

★ **Highest fee per minute for an actor in a TV advert** Nicole Kidman (Australia) reportedly earned $3.71 million (£2 million) for acting in a four-minute commercial for Chanel No. 5 in December 2003. This figure represents $928,800 (£500,000) per minute.

★ **Most Emmy Awards for the same show ever** *Sesame Street* (PBS, USA) has won 91 Emmy Awards. The programme premiered on TV

in 1969, and features puppet characters the Muppets, designed by Jim Henson (USA).

★ **Most prolific TV, film and theatre stuntman** Since 1968, Roy Alon (UK) has been credited for working on 893 TV, film and theatre productions as either a stunt co-ordinator, performer or 2nd Unit Director as of 20 February 2004. This total includes 11 theatre productions, 36 commercials, 144 feature films (including all the Superman movies and most of the Bond series) and 701 TV shows.

★ **Longest running children's magazine programme** *Blue Peter* (BBC, UK) was first transmitted from London's Lime Grove Studios on 16 October

1958, and celebrated 45 years on air in October 2003. So far it has had 29 presenters.

★ **Longest running pop show** The first edition of *Top of the Pops* (BBC, UK) was presented by DJ Jimmy Savile (UK) on 1 January 1964. The show celebrated its 2,000th edition on 13 September 2002 and its 40th year on air in January 2004.

★ **Most TV variety shows hosted by same presenter** The most live variety TV shows hosted by the same presenter is 5,000 as of 5 April 2002. Fuji Television Network Inc.'s *Waratte Iitomo!* has been hosted by Kazuyoshi Morita (Japan), aka Tamori, since its first episode on 4 October 1982.

Largest TV audience ⌃ for a space event

The first moonwalk by the *Apollo 11* astronauts was watched on TV by an estimated 600 million people, a fifth of the world's population at the time. The astronauts, Neil Armstrong, Edwin 'Buzz' Aldrin and Michael Collins (all USA, above), were the stars of a parade through New York City, USA, to celebrate their achievement on 14 August 1969.

Most valuable ⌃ TV costume

The Superman suit from the 1955 series *The Adventures of Superman* (above) sold for a record $129,800 (£81,307) at the Profiles in History auction, Los Angeles, California, USA, on 31 July 2003. The suit was worn by George Reeves (USA) in the title role.

★ **Most watched TV network**
The state-owned station China Central Television (CCTV) is transmitted to 90% of all viewers in China. It is estimated that more than 1.1 billion people have access to television in China.

★ **Earliest television sponsor**
On 19 June 1946, Gillette sponsored the broadcast of a boxing match between Joe Louis and Billy Conn (both USA) in New York City, USA.

★ **Earliest colour
TV transmission**
On 3 July 1928, John Logie Baird (UK) showed television images of red and blue scarves, a UK policeman's helmet, a man poking his tongue out, the glowing end of a cigarette and a bunch of roses during a demonstration at his studios in Covent Garden, London, UK.

★ **Earliest underwater TV**
The first public demonstration of underwater TV occurred on 26 August 1952 at the 19th National Radio and Television Exhibition, London, UK. Marconi Siebe Gorman showed model divers working on a sunken ship on monitor sets. The cameras used to film the divers weighed 900 kg (1,984 lb), cost £3,500 ($6,400) and could transmit from depths of 455 m (1,492 ft).

★ **Deepest live-TV broadcast
by a presenter**
Alastair Fothergill (UK) carried out an underwater broadcast at a depth of 2.4 km (1.5 miles) on *Abyss Live* (BBC, UK). The broadcast was televised on 29 September 2002 from inside a MIR submersible, along the Mid-Atlantic Ridge off the east coast of the USA.

★ **Earliest public TV advert**
On 27 June 1941, the first open public TV advertisement ever was broadcast on NBC's WNBT station in New York, USA, for a Bulova watch.

★ **Most awards won
by a TV advert**
The Levi 'Drugstore' 501 jeans television advertisement won 33 awards in 1995. These included a Lion D'Or for director Michel Gondry (France) and a Grand Clio Award for the advert.

★ **Longest running
TV advert**
The Discount Tire Company's 'Thank you' advert, produced by Swartwout Productions (USA), first aired in 1975. The same commercial has been aired continuously every year in parts of the USA.

★ **Longest running
TV chat show**
The Tonight Show (NBC, USA) first aired on 27 September 1954 hosted by Steve Allen (USA). *The Tonight Show With Jay Leno* has been hosted by Jay Leno (USA) since 1992, when he took over from Johnny Carson (USA). Carson began hosting the show in 1962 and moved it to its present location in Hollywood, California, USA.

★ **Longest running TV drama**
Procter & Gamble Productions' *Guiding Light* (CBS, USA) was first aired on CBS on 30 June 1952, and is still shown each week day. It was originally broadcast as a radio serial on WLW Radio in 1937, then made the transition to TV in 1952.

★ **Longest running TV forum**
Question Time (BBC, UK) was first broadcast on 25 September 1979 and still runs weekly in the UK. The programme allows a TV studio audience and viewers at home to question a panel of top decision-makers about current policies and topics.

Largest music TV network ⌃⌃

MTV began broadcasting on 1 August 1981 and is currently transmitted to approximately 340 million households in 140 countries. This means it can be seen by one in three of the world's total TV audience. Britney Spears, Madonna and Christina Aguilera (above, left to right, all USA) are shown here performing at the 20th Annual MTV Video Music Awards in August 2003.

★ GWR TALKS TO
Matt Groening

The Simpsons (FOX, USA), which is now watched in more than 70 countries, had its 326th episode on 22 February 2004. It is the longest running prime-time animated series and had won 20 Emmy Awards as of September 2003, a record for an animated TV series. GWR talks to the creator of this much-loved TV phenomenon, cartoonist Matt Groening (USA).

Congratulations! What's it like to be an official Guinness World Record holder?
It really is an unexpected thrill. I don't care about awards, but to be in the *Guinness World Records* book is really great. It's something I'd never expected, you know, and I'm glad it's a record to be proud of. There are certain records you don't want to have... I'm glad I've not been sitting in baked beans!

The show also has a record for its many guest stars. Why are celebs so keen to appear?
Firstly, it's the easiest gig in showbusiness! You can show up in curlers and barefoot, speak into the microphone and be on your merry way. You can literally phone it in – we've done phone hook-ups with some big stars. But it's more fun when we convince the stars to come in. When Mick Jagger was at the FOX studios, people on the show were very excited. That's why

we do it – to entertain ourselves! We've had Michael Jackson as a 300-lb white guy who thought he was Michael Jackson; we've had Elizabeth Taylor doing the voice of Maggie; Paul McCartney, George Harrison and Ringo Starr.

But of all the people, I think *The Simpsons*' writing team was most excited to have Adam West, the original TV Batman!

What advice do you have for kids who want to work in TV?
My advice to kids who want to work in TV is don't spend all your time watching TV! One of the things about working in TV is that it's like a voracious beast... you need to keep filling it with content. So cram your brain full of culture, history, science and politics, and you'll do very well in TV.

Do you have a favourite episode?
Ah, I like a lot of the very early episodes, particularly ones with Lisa. When Lisa first meets Bleeding Gums Murphy, her saxophone mentor, I was

amazed that the show could actually be moving, given how garish the characters were drawn.

You'll need to last 30 years to beat the record for the longest running comedy show on TV. Do you think you can do it?
Aaah, I hope so! I don't see any end in sight. It doesn't get easier to come up with new stories, but we continue to surprise ourselves. And that's basically our goal – to keep things surprising. It gets harder as the decades roll by. Everybody who likes the show compares the latest episode to their favourite, and it's hard to measure up to the past sometimes. But we're trying!

MATT GROENING

Music & entertainment

Contents

Most weeks at No.1 and No. 2 on US singles chart

For eight weeks, between 20 December 2003 and 7 February 2004, Hip-Hop act OutKast (USA, below) had singles at No.1 and No. 2 on the US singles chart with 'Hey Ya!' and 'The Way You Move' respectively.

Biggest jump to No.1 on US singles chart

Kelly Clarkson (USA, above), winner of *American Idol*, broke a record set in 1964 by The Beatles (UK) when her first single, 'A Moment Like This', jumped from No. 53 to No.1 in October 2002. Its first-week sales of 236,000 were bigger than those for the rest of the Hot 100 combined.

★ GWR TALKS TO
Sir Paul McCartney

Sir Paul McCartney (UK, above) currently holds 22 Guinness World Records – more than any other person. He holds 16 records as a member of The Beatles (UK), the biggest selling group of all time. He also holds world records in his own right, including the earliest live debut performance of a classical work on the Internet (the 75-minute *Standing Stone* broadcast on 19 November 1997), and the record for the largest paying audience for a rock stadium concert, which he achieved on 21 April 1990 when more than 184,000 fans attended his concert at the Maracanã Stadium, Rio de Janeiro, Brazil.

Were you a fan of *Guinness World Records* as a child?
Yes, as kids my friends and I were fans, we had many favourites – tallest, smallest etc, and we used to dip into it for amazing facts. I never thought I'd get a world record myself!

How did you celebrate your first No. 1?
That was 'From Me to You', which hit the top of the UK chart back in 1963. It was a long time coming, so we partied a lot.

Did The Beatles expect to set so many records?
We certainly didn't realize we were going to get into the record book, though we wanted to, like everyone else. It's an honour for a kid who sat in the pub and hoped to be the tiddlywinks champion of the world to get to our level of success.

Why do you think that sales of The Beatles' albums continue to rise?
A lot of the sales are to young people, which is funny because we all assumed it would be a lot of older people like ourselves on a nostalgia trip. Without being too immodest, I think that the writing was very good and it still holds up.

Are there any other world records that you'd like to have a go at?
I'm working on tallest! My main ambition is just to enjoy life.

What advice would you give to anyone wanting to go into the music industry?
Work hard, be true to yourself and love what you do.

★ **Biggest selling single in the world since UK charts began**
The biggest selling single sales since UK charts began on 14 November 1952 is Elton John's (UK) 'Candle In The Wind 1997'/'Something About The Way You Look Tonight', with worldwide sales of 33 million. By 20 October 1997 it had also reached No.1 in 22 countries. All Elton John's artist royalties and PolyGram's profits were donated to the Diana, Princess of Wales Memorial Fund.

★ **Biggest selling single by a group**
'Rock Around The Clock' sold an unaudited 25 million copies. Written by James E Myers (USA), aka Jimmy DeKnight, and Max C Freedman (USA), it was recorded on 12 April 1954 by Bill Haley and His Comets (USA).

★ **Most UK singles to debut at No.1**
Westlife (Ireland) had 12 singles debut at No.1 in the UK chart between 1 May 1999 and 22 November 2003.

Best UK solo album ⟰ chart start

Robbie Williams (UK, above) had five successive No.1s on the UK album chart. The albums, released between September 1997 and November 2002, are: *Life Thru A Lens* (1997), *I've Been Expecting You* (1998), *Sing When You're Winning* (2000), *Swing When You're Winning* (2001) and *Escapology* (2002). From 1 January 2000 to 31 December 2003, he sold 5,608,000 albums in the UK – more than any other UK album act. He has also won a record 14 British Record Industry Trust (BRIT) awards.

★ Most consecutive No.1 singles

From 28 July 1997 to 21 January 2004, 19 consecutive singles by The KinKi Kids (Japan) debuted at No.1 on the Japanese chart.

★ Biggest jump to No.1 on UK singles chart

Irish boy band Westlife's single 'Unbreakable' made an unprecedented leap from No.195 to No.1 on the UK Top 200 in November 2002.

★ Biggest first UK chart week for a single

Will Young's (UK) debut single 'Anything Is Possible'/ 'Evergreen' sold 1,108,269 copies in its first 'chart week' – ie its total sales from 25 February to 2 March 2002 – including 385,000 on its first day of release. It went on to sell an unprecedented 2 million copies in the UK in 15 weeks.

★ Biggest selling UK single by a female group

'Wannabe' by The Spice Girls (UK), released in July 1996, spent seven weeks at No.1 in the UK,

selling 1.2 million copies. The single hit No.1 in a further 31 countries.

★ Most hit singles on UK chart

As of April 2004, Elvis Presley (USA) had scored 135 hit singles on the UK chart.

★ Longest time spent on UK singles chart

The longest time that a single has spent on the UK chart is 124 weeks for 'My Way' by Frank Sinatra (USA), which entered and re-entered the chart ten times between April 1969 and April 1994.

★ Biggest selling album ever

Thriller by Michael Jackson (USA) has registered global sales of over 47 million copies to date since 1982.

★ Biggest selling album on UK chart

Over 4.5 million copies of The Beatles' (UK) *Sgt Pepper's Lonely Hearts Club Band* are reported to have been sold in the UK since its release in June 1967.

★ Most albums on US chart simultaneously

Three bands – The Beatles (UK), The Monkees (USA) and U2 (Ireland) – have all had seven albums on the US Top 200 simultaneously.

★ Best selling debut album in the USA

Boston by Boston (USA), released in 1976, has sold over 16 million copies.

★ Most No.1 albums on US chart by a group

The Beatles had 19 US No.1 albums – more than double the number by Elvis Presley (USA) and The Rolling Stones (UK), both of whom have had nine No.1 albums. In all, The Beatles' albums have spent 133 weeks at the top spot.

★ Biggest all-time sales by a group

The all-time sales for The Beatles have been estimated by EMI at more than 1 billion discs and tapes.

★ Biggest selling teenage artist

Before she turned 20 years old on 2 December 2001, Britney Spears (USA) had global sales of 37 million records.

★ Most vocal edits on a single recording

Brian Transeau (USA) incorporated a total of 6,178 vocal edits in the production of his track 'Simply Being Loved (Somnambulist)', which was released in August 2003. The single spent 11 weeks on the US charts.

Biggest selling ⌃ country album by a group

Since its release in 1998, *Wide Open Spaces* by the Dixie Chicks (USA, above) has sold 10 million copies.

★ Largest paying rock band concert attendance

The Molson Canadian Rocks for Toronto concert, which was held on 30 July 2003 at Downsview Park in Toronto, Ontario, Canada, attracted a paying audience of 489,176. The SARS benefit gig raised $7,590,507 (£3,398,930) from ticket sales.

★ Largest free rock concert attendance

Rod Stewart's (UK) free concert at Copacabana Beach, Rio de Janeiro, Brazil, on New Year's Eve 1994, reportedly attracted an audience of 3.5 million.

★ Largest simultaneous charity rock concert

Live Aid was organized by Bob Geldof (Ireland) and comprised two concerts, simultaneously held in London, UK, and Philadelphia, Pennsylvania, USA, on 13 July 1985. More than 60 of rock music's biggest acts played for free to an estimated 1.5 billion TV viewers watching throughout the world, raising money for African famine relief. Geldof, then lead singer of the Boomtown Rats, was inspired to organize Live Aid after watching a BBC documentary on starvation in Ethiopia.

★ Largest rock star benefit concert

A concert held at Wembley Stadium, London, UK, on 20 April 1992 in memory of rock star Freddie Mercury (UK), who died of AIDS, raised $35 million (£19.96 million) for AIDS charities. It was attended by about 75,000 people and is estimated to have been seen by almost 1 billion people in over 70 countries.

★ Most concerts performed in 50 days

During a tour of the USA, the rock band Jackyl (USA) played 101 concerts in 50 days, from 12 September to 31 October 1998. Jackyl appeared in a total of 59 cities in 26 states.

★ Biggest rock earnings from one venue

The biggest gross from concerts played at a single venue is $38,684,050 (£24,100,163) by Bruce Springsteen (USA) from a series of 10 shows that he performed at Giants Stadium, New Jersey, USA, between 15 July and 21 August 2003. The concerts were seen by a total of 566,560 people.

★ Highest grossing country music tour

Garth Brooks' (USA) three-year 'Sevens' tour, which commenced in March 1997, grossed a total of $105 million (£65.62 million). He performed 350 shows in 100 cities with an average attendance of 55,000 people per show.

★ Most successful male country artist

Garth Brooks (USA) is the most successful country recording artist of all time, with album sales of more than 100 million since 1989. He has also sold more albums than any other solo artist in the USA.

★ Most successful female country artist

Reba McEntire (USA) is the biggest selling female country vocalist in the USA, with eight multi-platinum albums, 16 platinum albums and 23 gold albums by February 2004, from a career spanning more than 25 years. She has sold 48 million albums in total.

★ Most successful country duo

Six albums by Brooks & Dunn (Kix Brooks and Ronnie Dunn, both USA) have sold more than 1 million copies and 17 of their singles have got to No.1 on the country chart, including 'Boot Scootin' Boogie' (1992), 'Little Miss Honky Tonk' (1995) and 'Husbands and Wives' (1998).

Shortest UK Top 10 single »

The shortest single to chart on the UK Top 10 is Liam Lynch's (USA, right) 'United States of Whatever',

which was 1 min 26 sec long and entered the chart on 7 December 2002, peaking at No.10.

Youngest ⌃ platinum album act

Billy Gilman (b. 24 May 1988, USA, above) was 12 years 68 days old

when his debut album *One Voice* was awarded a platinum certificate for achieving 1 million sales in the USA. The album was released on 20 June 2000 and was certified platinum 12 weeks later in August 2000.

★ Longest stay at No.1 by US rock single
Canadian band Nickelback's single 'Too Bad' held the top spot on the US Mainstream Rock chart for a record-breaking 20 weeks between January and May 2002.

★ Most simultaneous album entries in a week on US charts
Seven different albums by US rock group Pearl Jam entered the US Top 200 chart on 17 March 2001. These were part of a series of 23 albums recorded live at different venues around the USA. This feat broke the group's own record of five entries from a series of 25 simultaneously released live albums from concerts held during their successful European tour in 2000.

★ Biggest selling album in the USA by a female solo artist
Since its release on 4 November 1997, Canadian country singer Shania Twain's album *Come On Over* has

sold a total of 19 million copies in the USA and 30 million copies worldwide.

★ Most weeks on US charts for an album by a female artist
Patsy Cline's (USA) *12 Greatest Hits* was still on the US Country catalogue album chart in February 2001, 722 weeks after first entering it. The album spent 251 weeks (almost five years) at No.1 in total.

★ Most weeks on US Adult Contemporary chart
Australian duo Savage Garden's single 'I Knew I Loved You' had spent a record 124 weeks on the US Adult Contemporary chart when it exited in February 2002, beating the record of 123 weeks set by another of their recordings, 'Truly Madly Deeply'.

★ Most platinum RIAA albums by a country music artist
Since 1981, George Strait (USA) has earned 26 Recording Industry Association of America

(RIAA) platinum album awards (for sales of over 1 million copies in the USA) – with 12 of these albums selling more than 2 million copies. His total sales are over 62 million.

★ Slowest climbing act on US charts
Rock group Creed's (USA) track 'Higher' was on the US Hot 100 for a record 36 weeks before it finally climbed into the Top 10 in July 2000.

★ Longest stay on the UK album chart
Fleetwood Mac's (UK/USA) *Rumours* album, released on 26 February 1977, spent 477 weeks on the UK album chart. It included four singles chart entries, though none of them reached the Top 20.

★ Youngest female to top UK album charts
Canadian singer/songwriter Avril Lavigne topped the UK album chart on 11 January 2003 aged 18 years 106 days. The album, *Let Go*, made No.1 in its 18th week on the chart.

★ Longest gap between US chart album hits
There was a gap of 28 years between Santana's No.1 US album *Santana III* of November 1971 and their next No.1 *Supernatural* of October 1999. The latter gave the group phenomenal worldwide success, selling 21 million copies.

★ Shortest music video
In 1994, US metal band Brutal Truth produced a video 2.18 seconds in length to accompany their track 'Collateral Damage'. The video features a sequence of flash frames depicting popular conservative American cultural icons of the late 20th century.

★ Loudest drummer
A peak reading of 109.1 decibels was recorded during a show by The Jerome Experience (France) at the Celtic Warriors 10th Birthday Bash at Woodgreen Animal Shelter, Cambridgeshire, UK, on 12 April 2003. The Jerome Experience is a one-man show featuring drummer Jérôme Dehèdin (France).

Most simultaneous R&B hits

Rapper 50 Cent (aka Curtis Jackson, USA, right) had nine simultaneous entries on the *Billboard* Top R&B/Hip-Hop Singles & Tracks chart on 10 May 2003.

»

Longest span on US R&B chart ⌃

Ray Charles (USA, above) has appeared on the US R&B singles chart for seven decades. He first charted as leader of The Maxine Trio with 'Confession Blues' in April 1949. His latest entry was in July 2002 with 'Mother', a span of 53 years.

★ **Best selling rap/Hip-Hop album in the USA**
The best selling rap/Hip-Hop album ever in the USA is *CrazySexyCool* by TLC (USA), which has achieved sales of 11 million, surpassing MC Hammer's (USA) *Please Hammer Don't Hurt 'Em* (which has sold 10 million units).

★ **Rap artist with the most US No.1 albums**
When *The Black Album* topped the US album charts in November 2003, Jay-Z (aka Shawn Carter, USA) became the only rap act to have scored six No.1 albums.

★ **Fastest selling female debut album**
Ashanti's (aka Ashanti S Douglas, USA) eponymous debut album sold 503,000 copies in its first week on release in the USA in April 2002. In the same week, she became the first female performer to simultaneously hold the top two places on the Hot 100 singles chart with 'Foolish' and 'What's Luv?' (with Fat Joe).

★ **Biggest UK first-week Hip-Hop album sales**
Eminem's (aka Marshall Mathers III, USA) album *The Eminem Show* sold 315,000 copies in its first week on sale in the UK in June 2002. This gave him his second UK No.1 album, a feat that no other rap artist has achieved.

★ **Most successful remix album**
In February 2002, Jennifer Lopez's (USA) album *J To Tha Lo!: The Remixes* became the first remix album to top the US charts, with sales of over 1 million, including 156,000 in its first week.

★ **Best chart start**
Rap artist DMX (aka Earl Simmons, USA) is the only artist whose first five albums have entered the US chart at No.1. The records are *It's Dark And Hell Is Hot* (1998), *Flesh Of My Flesh Blood Of My Blood* (1999), *... And Then There Was X* (2000), *The Great Depression* (2001) and *Grand Champ* (2003).

★ **Most consecutive weeks at No.1 on US singles chart**
'One Sweet Day' by Mariah Carey and Boyz II Men (both USA) topped the US chart for 16 consecutive weeks in 1995.

★ **Oldest MOBO winner**
The oldest Music of Black Origin (MOBO) award winner is BB King (USA), who was 73 years old in 1998 when he picked up the Award for Lifetime Achievement.

★ **Longest stay on US Rap singles chart**
'Hot Boyz' by Missy 'Misdemeanor' Elliott (aka Melissa Elliott), featuring Nas, Eve and Q-Tip (all USA), spent a record 18 weeks at the top of the US Rap chart in 1999–2000.

★ **Longest US singles chart span**
Louis Armstrong (USA) first appeared on a *Billboard* chart on 6 April 1946. His most recent entry to the listings came in 1988, 17 years after his death, with 'What A Wonderful World' from the soundtrack to the film *Good Morning, Vietnam* (USA, 1987). Armstrong also had over 50 hits before the 'official' chart started in 1940, his first being 'Muskrat Ramble' in 1926, thus taking his span of hits to more than 61 years.

★ **Most consecutive weeks at No.1 by the same producer**
Hip-Hop producer Irv Gotti (USA) produced the No.1 single on the US Hot 100 pop chart for a record 19 successive weeks between 23 February and 22 June 2002. CEO of Murder Inc. Records, Gotti has worked with artists such as Ja Rule, Jay-Z, Ashanti, DMX and Fat Joe.

★ **Youngest solo rap artist at No.1 on US R&B and Rap charts**
In July 2000, Lil' Bow Wow (aka Shad Lamar Moss, USA) went to No.1 on the US R&B and Rap charts with 'Bounce With Me' (featuring Xscape), aged only 13 years 4 months.

Most weeks at No.1 ⌃⌃ on US singles chart by a girl band

The single 'Independent Woman', released by Destiny's Child

(USA, above) on 20 November 2000, subsequently spent a record 11 weeks at the top of the US singles chart.

★ **Youngest solo artist at No.1 on US album chart**
Stevie Wonder (aka Steveland Morris, b. 21 May 1950, USA) was 13 years 3 months old when his album *Little Stevie Wonder – The 12 Year Old Genius* topped the US charts in 1963.

★ **Youngest R&B chart entrant**
Hailie Jade Mathers (b. 25 December 1995, USA) became the youngest performer, aged 6 years 210 days, to be credited with an R&B hit when 'My Dad's Gone Crazy' charted in August 2002. She performed on the track with her father, Eminem (USA).

★ **Biggest selling rap artist**
Rap legend 2Pac (aka Tupac Shakur, USA) has certified US album sales of 36 million, and has now had more hits after his death (at the age of 25 in September 1996) than he did while he was alive. The posthumous hits include three US No.1 albums, *The Don Killuminati* (1997), *Until The End*

Of Time (2001) and *Better Dayz* (2002), and an additional 16 US R&B chart singles.

★ **Fastest rap MC**
Rebel XD (aka Seandale Price, USA) beat his own record and rapped 683 syllables in 54.501 seconds on the set of *Guinness World Records: Primetime* in Los Angeles, California, USA, on 24 June 1998.

★ **Fastest selling rap artist**
Eminem's (USA) album *The Marshall Mathers LP* sold 1.76 million copies in its first week in the USA in May 2000.

★ **Highest annual earnings by a rap act**
Eminem (USA) and rapper and producer Dr Dre (aka Andre Young, USA) earned $35 million (then £21.8 million) in 2002, according to the 2003 *Forbes* Celebrity 100 list.

★ **Largest rap group**
With 124 members, Hip-Hop outfit Minority Militia (USA) is the world's largest rap group.

Each member either raps, sings, plays an instrument or produces on their 2001 album *The People's Army*, released on Low Town Records.

★ **Longest working career by a recording artist**
Jazz singer Adelaide Hall (USA) is the most durable recording artist, having released material over eight consecutive decades. Her first record, 'Creole Love Call', was recorded with Duke Ellington on 26 October 1927, and her last was made on 16 June 1991 at the Cole Porter Centennial Gala in London, UK.

★ **Most Grammy awards won by a female artist**
Aretha Franklin (USA) has won 15 Grammys. She received her first in 1967 for Best Female R&B Vocal Performance with the song 'Respect'.

★ **Most Grammy awards won by a solo performer**
Stevie Wonder (USA) has won 19 Grammy awards. Since 1973 he has won Best Male R&B Vocal Performance six times.

★ **Hit act with the most grandchildren**
When soul singer Solomon Burke (USA) entered the US album chart in August 2002 with the Grammy-nominated *Don't Give Up On Me*, he had 65 grandchildren and 10 great-grandchildren.

★ **Earliest jazz record made**
The first jazz record comprised 'Indiana' and 'The Darktown Strutters' Ball' and was released on 31 May 1917. It was recorded for the Columbia label in New York City, USA, in January 1917 by the Original Dixieland Jazz Band, led by Dominic 'Nick' James La Rocca (USA).

Largest animal orchestra

The animal orchestra with the most members is the 12-piece Thai Elephant Orchestra (above), ⌃

which gives concerts at the Thai Elephant Conservation Centre, Lampang, Thailand. The orchestra was founded by Richard Lair and David Soldier (both USA) in 2000, with the aim of conserving the Asiatic elephant species.

★ **Most prolific composer**
Georg Philipp Telemann (Germany) wrote 12 complete sets of services – one cantata every Sunday – for a year, 78 services for special occasions, 40 operas, 600 to 700 orchestral suites, 44 passions, plus concertos, and other chamber music.

★ **Longest working operatic career**
Danshi Toyotake (Japan) sang Musume Gidayu (traditional Japanese narrative) for 91 years from the age of seven. Her professional career spanned 81 years.

★ **Longest opera**
Die Meistersinger von Nürnberg by Richard Wagner (Germany) is the longest of commonly performed operas. A normal uncut version, as performed by the Sadler's Wells company (UK) between 24 August and 19 September 1968, entailed 5 hr 15 min of music.

★ **Largest orchestra**
A total of 6,452 musicians from the Vancouver Symphony Orchestra and music students from all over British Columbia, Canada, played 'Ten Minutes of Nine' – an arrangement by Frederick Schipizky of the 'Ode To Joy' from Beethoven's Ninth Symphony – for 9 min 44 sec at BC Place Stadium, Vancouver, Canada, on 5 May 2000. It was conducted by Bramwell Tovey (UK).

★ **Largest cello ensemble**
A total of 1,013 cellists played in the 'Concert of 1,000 Cellists' held in Kobe, Japan, on 29 November 1998, conducted by Kazuaki Momiyama (Japan). Nine pieces of music were performed, the longest of which was Bach's Suite in D Major at 8 min 26 sec.

★ **Largest simultaneous percussion performance**
A percussive rhythm was played for over six minutes by 10,102 people at an event held at the Hong Kong Coliseum, Hong Kong, China, on 2 July 2002.

★ **Largest full drum-kit ensemble**
The largest complete drum-kit ensemble consisted of 264 participants who gathered to play at Tacoma Narrows Airport, Gig Harbour, Washington, USA, on 29 March 2003 under the direction of Gerard Schwarz (USA), conductor of the Seattle Symphony Orchestra.

★ **Largest drum ensemble**
The largest drum ensemble consisted of 3,140 participants who gathered to play at the opening ceremony of the Hong Kong Drum Festival at Victoria Park, Hong Kong, China, on 13 July 2003.

★ **Largest didgeridoo ensemble**
On 19 April 2003, 210 musicians assembled to play didgeridoos for 20 minutes at the Helitherme Bad Waltersdorf, Austria.

★ **Largest harmonica ensemble**
Organized by CentrumKultury Zamek, 851 harmonica players gathered at the 10th Poznan Blues Festival, Poznan, Poland, to perform 'When the Saints Go Marching In' on 13 September 2003.

★ **Most durable living organist**
Stanley Hayes (UK) has been the organist at St David's Church, Thelbridge, Devon, UK, since 1926, when he was 13. He continues in the post, providing a regular voluntary service for Sunday worship, weddings, funerals and baptisms.

Best selling world music album

The 1998 Grammy award-winning album *Buena Vista Social Club* (1997) has sold over 4 million copies – 1.5 million of which were sold in the USA. The album brought together some of Cuba's best musicians, including Omara Portuondo and Teresita Garcia Caturla (both above), Ibrahim Ferrer and Compay Segundo, as well as inspiring Wim Wender's cinema documentary *Buena Vista Social Club* (Germany, 1999).

Youngest » person at No.1 in the classical charts

In November 1998, Charlotte Church (UK, right) entered the UK classical album charts with her debut album *Voice of an Angel* at the age of 12 years 9 months. The album was certified double platinum in the UK within four weeks of its release.

★ Longest working career of a conductor

Torstein Grythe (Norway) has conducted the Silver Boys Choir of Oslo, Norway, for 63 years from 1940 and still continues to do so at the age of 85.

★ Longest concert by a group

From 21 to 23 September 2002, the group John Jerome Sangamam (India) played for 40 hours at St Montford Indoor Stadium, Mylapore, Chennai, India. The 20-strong band performed over 500 different numbers, all in Tamil.

★ Longest international career of a sitarist

Indian classical sitarist Ravi Shankar's first sitar performance was in Allahabad, India, in 1939, and his first international sitar concert in New York, USA, in 1956. However, Shankar's first international stage appearances in Europe and the USA took place earlier, as a dancer and musical accompanist in his brother

Uday Shankar's troupe in 1932, when he was aged 12. He continues to tour today, with dates in North America in 2004.

★ Best selling Raï artist

Algerian Raï singer Khaled has sold over three million albums worldwide, including *Khaled*, which featured his first international hit 'Didi'. Other albums include *N'ssi N'ssi*, *Sahra* and *Kenza*. The live album *1, 2, 3 Soleils* sold one million copies worldwide. Khaled is also the best selling artist singing in Arabic.

★ Biggest selling bhangra solo artist

Malkit Singh (India) has sold an average of 260,000 copies of each of his albums, totalling sales of over 4.9 million records in his 20-year career. He also holds the record for the most recordings by a bhangra artist.

★ Longest running bhangra band

Bhujhangy, a bhangra band based in Birmingham (UK), have been performing and

recording bhangra albums since 1967. Balbir Singh (UK), who sings with his brother, Dalbir Singh (UK), is the only member of the band's original line-up.

★ Best selling reggae album

Legend (1984), by the late Bob Marley (Jamaica), is the biggest selling reggae album of all time. In the UK, where it topped the chart, it has had certified sales of 1.8 million, and although it did not reach the Top 40 in the USA, it sold more than 10 million copies there.

★ Biggest selling album by a Latin artist

Mexican-born Carlos Santana's *Supernatural* album, released in June 1999, has sold 14 million copies in the USA, and 21 million worldwide.

★ Biggest selling female Latin artist

Cuban-born singer Gloria Estefan has had total album sales estimated at over 35 million.

★ Most albums on Latin chart simultaneously

Shortly after her death on 16 July 2003, the legendary 'Queen of Salsa' Celia Cruz (Cuba) had eight albums in the Top 10 of *Billboard*'s Tropical Latin album chart.

★ Biggest selling male Latin artist

Spanish vocalist Julio Iglesias is the most successful Latin music artist in the world, with reported global sales of more than 200 million albums.

★ Top selling album act in Japan

Utada Hikaru (Japan) is the only Japanese act to sell over two million copies each of three consecutive albums. Her 1999 debut album *First Love* was the biggest ever seller in Japan, shifting over 10 million copies; her second, *Distance*, sold over 5.5 million; and her third, *Deep River* (2002), sold 1.6 million on its first day and 2.3 million in the first five days.

«

Heaviest building re-location on wheels

Built in 1910, the 2,638-tonne (5,816,000-lb) Shubert Theater (left) in Minneapolis, Minnesota, USA, was moved in one piece from Block E to a new site three blocks away on Hennepin Avenue over 12 days by Artspace Projects between 9 and 21 February 1999.

⭐ Furthest building re-location

The linked five-storey Gem Theater (built 1927) and Century Club building (built 1903) in Detroit, Michigan, USA, which weighed 2,495 tonnes (5,500,000 lb), was moved a distance of 563 m (1,850 ft) on 72 dollies, each with eight rubber tyres, in 25 days from 16 October 1997.

⭐ Largest purpose-built theatre

The most capacious purpose-built theatre is the Perth Entertainment Centre, Western Australia. It has 8,500 seats and a main stage area that measures 21.3 x 13.7 m (70 x 45 ft). It was opened on 26 December 1974.

⭐ Largest theatre stage

The world's largest stage is at the Hilton Theater at the Reno Hilton, Reno, Nevada, USA. It measures 53.3 x 73.4 m (175 x 241 ft). The stage has three main lifts, each capable of raising 65.3 tonnes (143,961 lb) and two turntables each with a circumference of 19.1 m (62 ft 6 in).

⭐ Most expensive stage prop

For the musical stage version of *Chitty Chitty Bang Bang*, which opened at the London Palladium, London, UK, on 16 April 2002, the magical flying car of the title cost an estimated £750,000 ($1.07 million) to make. The complete set, including the flying car, was designed by the award-winning set designer Anthony Ward (UK).

⭐ Most theatrical members of a family to appear on stage

A total of 24 direct members of the Hurst family, headed by Mike and Marjorie (both UK), performed at the Kenton Theatre, Henley-on-Thames, Oxfordshire, UK, in a production of *Puss In Boots* on 19 and 20 December 2003. The performers, whose ages ranged from 1 to 63, included the Hursts' six children Timothy, Alexis, Muffin, Bryony, Jonas and Adam, and their spouses Lynsey, Nathan, Ben and Ruth plus their grandchildren Ben, Ellie, Aisling, Cassian, Liberty, Flavia, Emerald, Tabitha, Antigone, Polyanna, Madeleine and Amelie (all UK).

⭐ Longest working career of a theatre director on the same production

Enrique Pineda (Mexico) directed the monologue *La Virgen Loca* (*The Crazy Virgin*), performed by Hosmé Israel (Mexico), since its premiere on 24 August 1974 at the Teatro Rafael Solania, University of Veracruz, Mexico, until it closed on 30 November 2003, a total of 29 years 98 days.

⭐ Longest working career of a theatre producer on the same production

Mildred Ilse (USA), producer of *The Drunkard* (once the world's longest running play), was with the production for its entire run of 26 years 103 days from 6 July 1933 to 17 October 1959, a total of 9,477 performances, in Los Angeles, California, USA.

⭐ Longest working career in the same role

Terence Ranasinghe and his wife Malini (both Sri Lanka) have played the major roles in ER Sarachchandra's (Sri Lanka) *Sinhabahu* in over 5,000 theatre performances from 1961 until 1991 – a total of 30 years.

⭐ Most ardent theatre-goer

Howard Hughes, Prof Emeritus of Texas Wesleyan College, Fort Worth, Texas, USA, attended a record 6,136 theatre shows in the period 1956–87.

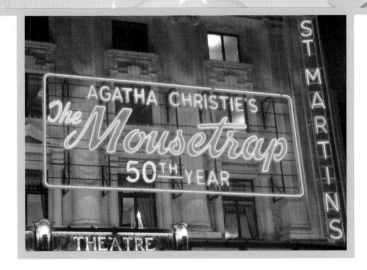

Longest theatrical run ⌃

The longest continuous run of any show in the world is *The Mousetrap* by Dame Agatha Christie (UK).

By 29 February 2004, it had had 21,263 performances at St Martin's Theatre, London, UK (above). The play celebrated its 50th anniversary in 2002.

Largest »
stage lift
system

The stage of the Bellagio Theatre, Las Vegas, Nevada, USA, measures 339 m² (3,650 ft²) and is divided into four sections, supported by four hydraulic lifting systems. Each system raises one of the four sections synchronously (or not) through a pool containing 5.6 million litres (1.24 million gal) of water. The lift system was specially manufactured for Cirque du Soleil's (Canada) 'O', performed in, above and under water (two members, right).

⭑ First professional stage actress

Margaret Hughes (UK, 1643–1719) appeared as Desdemona in Thomas Killigrew's version of *Othello, The Moor of Venice* on 3 December 1660, at a converted tennis court called the Vere Street Theatre, London, UK.

⭑ Highest box office gross for a theatre production

Since first opening at Her Majesty's Theatre, London, UK, on 9 October 1986, Andrew Lloyd Webber's musical *The Phantom of the Opera* has played in 18 countries and taken over £2 billion ($3.2 billion) at the box office.

⭑ Most scripted roles in different locations in one night

On 24 February 2004, as part of Visit London's 'One Amazing Week', Jerry Hall (USA) took on recognized scripted roles to appear at six different London West End theatre productions during the course of a single night. Replacing

a cast member each time, from her first appearance on stage at 7:30 pm to her last entrance at 10:09 pm, she was Monsieur André in *The Phantom of the Opera* at Her Majesty's Theatre; one of four prostitutes in *Les Misérables* at the Palace Theatre; Mr Myers in *Fame* at the Aldwych Theatre; Brenda in *Blood Brothers* at the Phoenix Theatre; one of the six 'Swings' in *Anything Goes* at the Theatre Royal; and finally one of the 24 members of the ensemble in *Chitty Chitty Bang Bang* at the London Palladium.

⭑ Most costume changes demanded by a lead theatrical role

Michael Jibson (UK) achieved 29 complete costume changes during each performance as Joe Casey in the West End musical *Our House*, directed by Matthew Warchus (UK) at the Cambridge Theatre, London, UK, from 28 October 2002 to 16 August 2003. The quick-change costumes and illusion effects were designed by Paul Kieve (UK), allowing the fastest

change to take just four seconds on stage. Assisted in the wings by principal dresser Murray Lane (UK), Warchus made additional partial changes during the 2-hr 10-min show.

⭑ Longest play

The Warp, a ten-part play cycle by Neil Oram performed at the Institute of Contemporary Art, London, UK, on 18–20 January 1979 and directed by Ken Campbell, lasted 18 hr 5 min. Russell Denton (UK) was on stage for all but five minutes.

⭑ Longest running musical

The off-Broadway musical *The Fantasticks* by Tom Jones and Harvey Schmidt (both USA) opened at the Sullivan Street Playhouse, New York, USA, on 3 May 1960 and closed on 13 January 2002, after 17,162 performances.

⭑ Longest one-man show to run in London's West End

An Evening with Tommy Steele opened at the Prince of Wales Theatre, London, UK, on

11 October 1979 and closed on 29 November 1980 – a total of 414 days.

⭑ Largest amateur puppet show

Working 463 puppets, a total of 402 puppeteers from Cockington Primary School (UK) performed the puppet show *Hurucan and the Feathered Snake* at the Riviera International Centre, Torquay, Devon, UK, on 16 July 2003.

⭑ Longest theatrical run for a revue

The greatest number of performances of any theatrical presentation is 47,250 (to April 1986) for *The Golden Horseshoe Revue*, a variety show staged at Disneyland Park, Anaheim, California, USA, from 16 July 1955 to 12 October 1986. It was seen by 16 million people.

⭑ Longest running annual theatre revue

The longest running annual revues were *The Ziegfeld Follies* (USA, 1907–57), which went through 25 editions.

Sport

Contents

Longest touchdown in a Super Bowl

The longest touchdown in Super Bowl history is 85 yards, scored by Muhsin Muhammad (USA, near left), playing for the Carolina Panthers in Super Bowl XXXVIII, on 1 February 2004.

Most yards gained rushing in an NFL game

Jamal Lewis (USA, below) rushed for 295 yards playing for the Baltimore Ravens against the Cleveland Browns on 14 September 2003, scoring two touchdowns.

★ **Most passes completed in a Super Bowl game**
Quarterback Tom Brady (USA) of the New England Patriots threw 32 completed passes in Super Bowl XXXVIII on 1 February 2004 in Houston, Texas, USA.

★ **Most passes received in a Super Bowl career**
Jerry Rice (USA) received 33 passes during his four Super Bowl appearances in 1989–90, 1995 and 2003, playing for the San Francisco 49ers and the Oakland Raiders.

★ **Most field goals by an individual in a Super Bowl game**
The most field goals scored by an individual in a Super Bowl game is four, kicked by Don Chandler (Green Bay Packers) in 1968 and Ray Wersching (San Francisco 49ers) in 1982.

★ **Most team interceptions in a Super Bowl**
In Super Bowl XXXVII, played in San Diego, California, USA, on 26 January 2003, the Tampa Bay Buccaneers made a record five interceptions, returning them for 172 yards and three touchdowns.

★ **Highest aggregate score in the Super Bowl**
The greatest aggregate score of 75 points was achieved in 1995 when the San Francisco 49ers beat the San Diego Chargers 49–26.

★ **Coach with most wins**
The most games won as head coach is 347 by Don Shula (USA) of the Baltimore Colts (1963–69) and Miami Dolphins (1970–95).

★ **Longest NFL field goal**
The longest successful field goal in an National Football League (NFL) game is 63 yards by Tom Dempsey (USA) playing for the New Orleans Saints against the Detroit Lions on 8 November 1970; and by Jason Elam (USA) playing for the Denver Broncos against the Jacksonville Jaguars on 25 October 1998. Dempsey was born with no right hand, and no toes on his right foot (which was his kicking foot). He wore a modified shoe.

★ **Most NFL titles**
The Green Bay Packers have won a record 12 NFL titles, in 1929–31, 1936, 1939, 1944, 1961–62, 1965–67, 1996.

★ **Most points scored in a season**
The most points scored in a season is 176, by Paul Hornung (USA) for the Green Bay Packers in 1960.

★ **Most NFL games played**
George Blanda (USA) played in a record 340 games in a record 26 seasons in the NFL (Chicago Bears 1949–58, Baltimore Colts 1950, Houston Oilers 1960–66 and Oakland Raiders 1967–75).

★ **Highest score in an NFL regular season game**
The highest team score is 72 by the Washington Redskins against the New York Giants (41) at Washington on 27 November 1966. The aggregate score of 113 is also a record.

★ **Most combined yards gained in an NFL season**
Lionel James (USA) gained 2,535 combined net yards in the 1985 NFL season playing for the San Diego Chargers.

★ **Most combined yards gained in an NFL career**
The most combined net yards gained in an NFL career is 21,803 by Walter Payton (USA), playing for the Chicago Bears from 1975 to 1987.

★ **Most touchdowns in an NFL game**
Ernie Nevers (USA) scored six touchdowns playing for the Chicago Cardinals against the Chicago Bears on 28 November 1929, equalled by William Jones (USA) playing for the Cleveland Browns against the Chicago Bears on 25 November 1951, and Gale Sayers (USA) playing for the Chicago Bears against the San Francisco 49ers on 12 December 1965.

Most passes « received in an NFL season

Marvin Harrison (USA, left) received a record 143 passes in the 2002 NFL season playing for the Indianapolis Colts.

★ **Highest combined kick return yardage in an NFL season**
Michael Lewis (USA) of the New Orleans Saints set an NFL combined punt/kickoff return record with 2,432 yards in the 2002 season.

★ **Most passes received in an NFL career**
The most pass receptions in an NFL career is 1,519 by Jerry Rice (USA), playing for the San Francisco 49ers and the Oakland Raiders during 1985–2003.

★ **Most passes received in an NFL game**
Tom Fears (USA) caught 18 passes in an NFL game against the Green Bay Packers on 3 December 1950, playing for the Los Angeles Rams.

★ **Most passes completed in an NFL game**
Drew Bledsoe (USA), playing for the New England Patriots, completed 45 passes in an NFL game against the Minnesota Vikings on 13 November 1994.

★ **Most passes completed in an NFL regular season**
The most passes completed in an NFL regular season is 418 by quarterback Rich Gannon (USA) for the Oakland Raiders in the 2002 season.

★ **Most passes completed in an NFL career**
Dan Marino (USA) completed a total of 4,967 passes between 1983 and his retirement in 2000, playing for the Miami Dolphins. He holds many other records, including most yards gained passing in both a career (61,631) and a season (5,084 in 1984).

★ **Most field goals by an individual in an NFL game**
Jim Bakken (USA) scored seven field goals in an NFL game against the Pittsburgh Steelers in 24 September 1967, playing for the St Louis Cardinals.

★ **Most field goals by an individual in an NFL season**
Olindo Mare (USA) scored 39 field goals in the 1999 NFL season, playing for the Miami Dolphins.

★ **Most field goals by an individual in an NFL career**
Gary Anderson (USA) scored 465 field goals over his NFL career playing for the Pittsburgh Steelers (1982–94), Philadelphia Eagles 1995–96), San Francisco 49ers (1997) and Minnesota Vikings (1999–2001).

★ **Most yards gained passing in an NFL career**
Dan Marino (USA) threw 61,361 yards passing during his NFL career from 1983 to 1999, playing for the Miami Dolphins. In 1998, Marino received the Man of the Year award from the NFL in recognition of his support of various children's charities.

★ **Most yards gained rushing in an NFL career**
Emmitt Smith (USA) of the Dallas Cowboys gained 17,418 yards rushing over his NFL career spanning from 1990 to 2003.

★ **Most sacks made in an NFL career**
Bruce Smith (USA) has made 199 sacks in the course of his NFL career, playing for the Buffalo Bills (1985–2000) and the Washington Redskins (2000–03).

★ **Most NFL career interceptions**
Paul Krause (USA), a free safety from the University of Iowa, is the leading pass interceptor of all time with 81 steals during a 16-season career, playing for Washington Redskins (1964–67) and Minnesota Vikings (1968–79).

★ **Most interceptions in an NFL season**
The most interceptions made in an NFL season is 14 by Dick 'Night Train' Lane (USA) playing for the Los Angeles Rams in 1952, the first fully professional season. He returned them for 298 yards and two touchdowns.

★ **Most games officiated**
Raymond Longden (USA) has officiated at well over 2,000 US football games, more than any other referee. He has officiated in more than 50 games a season since 1947.

Baseball
Sport

Highest paid player «

The richest contract, based on the average annual salary for the duration of the contract, is $25.2 million (£15.9 million) by Alex Rodriguez (USA, left) of the Texas Rangers ($252 million or £159.6 million over 10 years), signed in December 2000. Rodriguez moved to the New York Yankees before the start of the 2004 season, in a complicated deal that sees the Rangers cover the player's wages, paying $67 million (£36 million) of the $179 million (£95 million) left on his contract, and with the Yankees paying him $112 million (£59 million) over the next seven years.

★ Most games played
Pete Rose (USA) played in a record 3,562 games with a record 14,053 at bats for the Cincinnati Reds (1963–78 and 1984–86), Philadelphia Phillies (1979–83) and Montreal Expos (1984).

★ Most consecutive games
Calvin Edwin Ripken Jr (USA) played a record 2,632 consecutive games for the Baltimore Orioles between 30 May 1982 and 19 September 1998.

★ Most sacrifice bunts in a career
The most sacrifice bunts made in professional baseball is 514 by Masahiro Kawai (Japan) during a career spanning 20 years from 1984 to 2003, playing for the Yomiuri Giants in Japan.

★ Longest Major League game
The Chicago White Sox and the Milwaukee Brewers played a game lasting 8 hr 6 min on 9 May 1984. The White Sox eventually won the game 7–6 in the 25th inning.

★ Most strikeouts in a Major League career
Nolan Ryan (USA) pitched 5,714 strikeouts over his career from 1966 to 1993, playing for the New York Mets, the California Angels, the Houston Astros and the Texas Rangers.

★ Most strikeouts in one Major League game
Roger Clemens (USA) pitched 20 strikeouts in one game (9 innings) playing for the Boston Red Sox against the Seattle Mariners on 29 April 1986 and against the Detroit Tigers on 18 September 1996. The record was equalled by Kerry Wood (USA), playing for the Chicago Cubs against Houston Astros on 6 May 1998.

★ Most runs in a Major League career
The most runs scored in a Major League career is 2,295 by Rickey Henley Henderson (USA) up to 2003. Henderson began the first of his 25 seasons to date on 24 June 1979 with the Oakland Athletics, and then went on to play for nine franchises before finishing the 2003 season with the Los Angeles Dodgers.

★ Most doubles in a Major League career
Tris Speaker (USA) hit a record 792 doubles during his career, playing for the Boston Red Sox, the Cleveland Indians, the Washington Senators and the Philadelphia Athletics from 1907 to 1928.

★ Most triples in a Major League career
The most triples hit in a Major League career is 309 by Sam Crawford (USA), playing for Cincinnati Reds and the Detroit Tigers from 1899 to 1917.

★ Most no-hit games pitched in a Major League career
The most no-hitters pitched in a career is seven by Nolan Ryan (USA) between 1973 and 1991.

★ Most Major League games pitched
By the end of the 2003 season, Jesse Orosco (USA) had pitched a total of 1,251 games for the New York Mets, Los Angeles Dodgers, Cleveland Indians, Milwaukee Brewers, Baltimore Orioles, St Louis Cardinals, Minnesota Twins, New York Yankees and San Diego Padres.

★ Most stolen bases in a Major League career
Rickey Henley Henderson (USA) achieved 1,406 stolen bases during his career, from 1979 to 2003, playing for the Oakland Athletics, New York Yankees, Toronto Blue Jays, San Diego Padres, Anaheim Angels, Seattle Mariners, New York Mets, Boston Red Sox and Los Angeles Dodgers.

★ Highest batting average in a Major League career
The highest career batting average is .367 by Tyrus Raymond 'Ty' Cobb (USA), playing for the Detroit Tigers and Philadelphia Athletics between 1905 and 1928.

Most home runs ⌃ in a season

Barry Bonds (USA, above) of the San Francisco Giants scored 73 home runs in the 2001 season.

Oldest Major ≫ League player

Leroy Robert 'Satchel' Paige (USA, right) began playing for the Cleveland Indians in 1948, aged 41. He pitched for the Kansas City Athletics at 59 years 80 days on 25 September 1965.

★ **Most runs batted in in a Major League career**
The most runs batted in in a career is 2,297 by Henry Hank Aaron (USA) from 1954 to 1976.

★ **Most runs in a Major League season**
William Robert Hamilton (USA) scored a record 196 runs playing for the Philadelphia Phillies in 1894.

★ **Most consecutive Major League games batted safely**
Joseph Paul DiMaggio (USA), playing for the New York Yankees, safely batted in 56 consecutive games between 15 May and 16 July 1941.

★ **Most consecutive hits in Major League**
On 19–21 June 1938, Michael Franklin 'Pinky' Higgins (USA) had 12 consecutive hits playing for the Boston Red Sox. Walter 'Moose' Dropo (USA) equalled this on 14–15 July 1952, playing for the Detroit Tigers.

★ **Highest percentage home runs in a career**
During his career (1914–35), George Herman 'Babe' Ruth (USA) hit 714 homers from 8,399 times at bat, the highest home run percentage of 8.5% in Major League history.

★ **Most home runs in a single game**
The most home runs in a Major League game is four, first achieved by Robert Lincoln 'Bobby' Lowe (USA) for the Boston Beaneaters against the Cincinnati Reds on 30 May 1894. The feat has been achieved many times since then.

★ **Most Cy Young Award wins**
The Cy Young Award, given annually since 1956 to the most outstanding pitcher in the major leagues, has gone to Roger Clemens (USA) a record six times. During this time he played for the Boston Red Sox (1986, 1987, 1991), Toronto Blue Jays (1997–98) and New York Yankees (2001).

★ **Most wins of the Most Valuable World Series Player award**
The only men to have won MVP twice are: Sanford 'Sandy' Koufax (USA), playing for the Los Angeles Dodgers (1963, 1965); Robert 'Bob' Gibson (USA), playing for the St Louis Cardinals (1964, 1967); and Reginald Martinez 'Reggie' Jackson (USA), playing for the Oakland Athletics (1973) and New York Yankees (1977).

★ **Oldest World Series player**
Jack Quinn (USA) of the Philadelphia Athletics was 47 years 91 days old when he played on 4 October 1930.

★ **Most durable announcer**
Ernest Harwell (USA) had a 55-year career that began in 1948 with the Brooklyn

Dodgers, followed by the New York Giants (1951–53), Baltimore Orioles (1954–59) and Detroit Tigers (1960–2002). In the course of his career, Harwell announced more than 8,300 Major League baseball games.

★ **Largest replica bat**
The world's biggest ever replica baseball bat is 36.5 m (120 ft) in length and weighs 30,844 kg (68,000 lb) and was made by bat manufacturer Hillerich Bradsby (USA). The bat is modelled on the 'R43' bat made for Babe Ruth in 1927 by the same manufacturer.

★ **Fastest hit in Finnish baseball**
Sami Ahola (Finland) hit a ball at a speed of 174 km/h (108.1 mph) at the Lahti Indoor Arena, Finland, on 20 February 2002.

Basketball
Sport

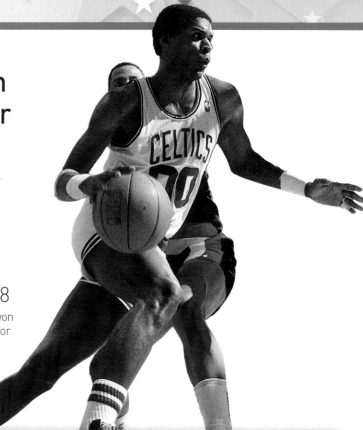

« Most blocks in an NBA career

The greatest number of blocks in a National Basketball Association (NBA) career is 3,830 in 1,238 games by Hakeem Olajuwon (USA, near left), playing for the Houston Rockets (1984–2001) and the Toronto Raptors (2001–02).

Most NBA ⩘ Championship titles

The Boston Celtics have won a total of 16 NBA Championship titles, in 1957, 1959–66, 1968–69, 1974, 1976, 1981, 1984 and 1986. In their last three Championship-winning years, their team included record-breaker Robert Parish (USA, above).

★ **Highest aggregate score in an NBA match**
The highest aggregate score in an NBA match is 370, which occurred when the Detroit Pistons beat the Denver Nuggets 186-184 at Denver, Colorado, USA, on 13 December 1983. The match went into overtime after a 145-145 tie.

★ **Most consecutive NBA wins**
The Los Angeles Lakers won 33 games in succession from 5 November 1971 to 7 January 1972.

★ **Most wins in an NBA season**
In the 1995/96 season, the Chicago Bulls won a total of 72 games.

★ **Most losses in an NBA season**
The highest number of losses incurred in a season was by the Philadelphia 76ers, who were defeated 73 times and won just nine games during an 82-game season.

This run of bad luck included a 20-game losing streak between 1972 and 1973.

★ **Most points in an NBA season**
Wilt Chamberlain (USA) scored 4,029 points while playing for the Philadelphia Warriors in the 1961/62 season.
During this season, Chamberlain also set the record for the highest scoring average in a season, with 50.4 points per game, and scored 1,597 field goals, the most in a season.

★ **Most points scored by an individual in an NBA game**
Wilt Chamberlain (USA) scored 100 points for the Philadelphia 76ers against the New York Knicks on 2 March 1962.

★ **Most three-point field goals in an NBA season**
Dennis Scott (USA) scored 267 three-point field goals for the Orlando Magic in 1996/97.

★ **Most three-point field goals in an NBA career**
Reggie Miller (USA) scored 2,426 three-point field goals for the Indiana Pacers between 1987 and 2004.

★ **Most consecutive NBA games played**
AC Green (USA) played 1,177 consecutive games for the Los Angeles Lakers, Phoenix Suns, Dallas Mavericks and Miami Heat between 19 November 1986 and 20 March 2001.

★ **Most games played in an NBA career**
Robert Parish (USA) played 1,611 regular-season games during his NBA career from 1976 to 1997. He achieved this record over 21 seasons playing for four teams: the Golden State Warriors

(1976–80), the Boston Celtics (1980–94), the Charlotte Hornets (1994–96) and the Chicago Bulls (1996–97).

★ **Most free throws in an NBA career**
The greatest number of free throws made in a career is 9,715 in 1,458 games by Karl Malone (USA) playing for the Utah Jazz (1985–2003) and the Los Angeles Lakers (2003–04).

★ **Most rebounds in an NBA career**
Wilt Chamberlain (USA) had 23,924 rebounds in 1,045 games. During his NBA career he played for the Philadelphia Warriors (1959–62), the San Francisco Warriors (1962–65), the Philadelphia 76ers (1964–68) and the Los Angeles Lakers (1968–73).

Highest point- ⌄ scoring average in an NBA career

The highest point-scoring average for players who have exceeded 10,000 points is 30.1 by Michael Jordan (USA, below), who scored a total of 32,292 points in 1,072 games playing for the Chicago Bulls (1984–98) and the Washington Wizards (2001–03).

★ Most points scored in an NBA career

The greatest number of points scored in an NBA career is 38,387 (at an average of 24.6 points per game) by Kareem Abdul-Jabbar (b. Ferdinand Lewis Alcindor, USA) from 1969 to 1989. This total includes 15,837 field goals that were scored in regular season games and 5,762 points – including 2,356 field goals – that were scored in play-off games.

★ Most NBA play-off appearances in a career

During his playing career, Kareem Abdul-Jabbar (USA) took part in 237 play-off games. He played for the Milwaukee Bucks from 1969 to 1975 and the Los Angeles Lakers from 1975 to 1989.

★ Most fouls in an NBA career

Kareem Abdul-Jabbar committed a total of 4,657 fouls in 1,560 games during a playing career that lasted from 1969 to 1989.

★ Most steals and assists in an NBA career

John Stockton (USA) achieved 3,265 steals in 1,504 games, playing for the Utah Jazz from 1984 to 2003.

Stockton made a total of 15,806 assists in 1,504 games playing for the Utah Jazz from 1984 to 2003, another world record.

★ Tallest player

Suleiman Ali Nashnush (Libya) was reputed to be 2.45 m (8 ft 0.25 in) when he played for his national team in 1962.

★ Longest time to spin a basketball on one finger

Zhao Guang (China) spun a regulation basketball on one finger while maintaining the spin for 3 hr 59 min on 29 January 2003 in Shenyang, China.

★ Longest basketball marathon

A match lasting 26 hr 42 min was played at Warwick Academy, at the Bermuda College Gym, Paget, Bermuda, on 15–16 March 2003. The Blue and White teams played a total of 27 games against each other.

★ Most basketballs dribbled simultaneously by one person

Joseph Odhiambo (USA) dribbled six basketballs simultaneously on 15 August 2000 at his home at Mesa, Arizona, USA. This beat his previous record of dribbling five basketballs at once.

★ Most consecutive shots with head

Eyal Horn (Israel) performed a total of 19 consecutive lay-ups (controlling and shooting the ball using only his head) on the set of *Guinness Rekord TV*, Stockholm, Sweden, on 29 November 2001.

★ Most consecutive free throws

Ted St Martin (USA) scored 5,221 consecutive free throws at Jacksonville, Florida, USA, on 28 April 1996.

★ Most free throws in one minute

David Bergström (Sweden) achieved 48 free throws in one minute at Fyrishov, Uppsala, Sweden, on 2 October 2001. The attempt was filmed by *Guinness Rekord TV*, Sweden.

★ Most three-pointers in one minute

Lea Hakala (Finland) made 19 successful three-point shots in a minute on the set of *Guinness World Records*, Helsinki, Finland, on 22 October 2001.

★ Greatest distance to dribble a basketball in 24 hours

Suresh Joachim (Australia) dribbled a basketball a distance of 156.71 km (97.37 miles) at Vulkanhallen, Oslo, Norway, on 30–31 March 2001.

★ Longest goal thrown in an exhibition match

Iain McKinney (UK) scored a basketball goal from a distance of 27.6 m (90 ft 6 in) playing for the Sheffield Sharks at Ponds Forge, Sheffield, South Yorkshire, UK, on 8 April 1996.

Ice hockey
Sport

Most NHL career wins ⌃⌃ by a goaltender

Having begun his career with the Montreal Canadiens in 1985,

goaltender Patrick Roy (Canada, above) of the Colorado Avalanche had 516 wins up to the end of the 2002 regular season. With 22 shutouts, Roy also holds the record for the most shutouts by a goaltender in NHL playoff history.

★ **Most wins in a National Hockey League (NHL) season**
The Detroit Red Wings achieved 62 wins during the 1995/96 NHL season.

★ **Longest NHL winning streak**
The longest run of winning matches – both home and away – in NHL history is 17 by the Pittsburgh Penguins between 9 March and 10 April 1993.

★ **Fewest defeats in an NHL season**
In the 1976/77 season, the Montreal Canadiens lost just eight games, the fewest ever in a season of 70 or more games, from 80 played (60 wins, 12 ties and a record 132 points).

★ **Most losses in an NHL season**
The San Jose Sharks had 71 losses during the 1992/93 season, including a record 32 games lost at home.

★ **Most points scored in an NHL career**
Wayne Gretzky (Canada) scored 2,857 points for the Edmonton Oilers, Los Angeles Kings, St Louis Blues and New York Rangers between 1979 and 1999. The points total comprise 894 goals and 1,963 assists, achieved in 1,487 games.

★ **Most goals scored in an NHL season**
Wayne Gretzky (Canada) scored 92 goals for the Edmonton Oilers during the 1981/82 season.

★ **Most goals scored by a team in an NHL season**
The Edmonton Oilers scored 446 goals in the 1983/84 season.

★ **Most goals scored by an individual in an NHL game**
Joe Malone (Canada) scored seven goals for the Québec Bulldogs in their game against the Toronto St Patricks in Québec City, Québec, Canada, on 31 January 1920.

★ **Longest NHL suspension for an infraction during a game**
Marty McSorley (USA) of the Boston Bruins incurred a 23-game suspension in February 2000 for hitting Vancouver Canucks' Donald Brashear (Canada) on the head with his stick in a game at Vancouver, British Columbia, Canada, on 21 February 2000.

★ **Most penalty minutes in an NHL career**
In the 17 seasons between 1971 and 1988, Dave 'Tiger' Williams (Canada) had 3,966 penalty minutes – the most in NHL history – playing for the Toronto Maple Leafs, Vancouver Canucks, Detroit Red Wings, Los Angeles Kings and the now-defunct Hartford Whalers.

★ **Most penalties against an individual in an NHL game**
Chris Nilan (USA) had a record 10 penalties called against him when playing for the Boston Bruins against the Hartford Whalers on 31 March 1991.

★ **Most penalties in an NHL game**
The most penalties awarded in any NHL game is 85, when the Edmonton Oilers played the Los Angeles Kings in Los Angeles, California, USA, on 28 February 1990.

★ **Most NHL goaltending appearances**
The most NHL goaltending appearances is 971 by Terry Sawchuk (Canada) for the Detroit Red Wings, Boston Bruins, Toronto Maple Leafs, LA Kings and New York Rangers from 1949 to 1970.

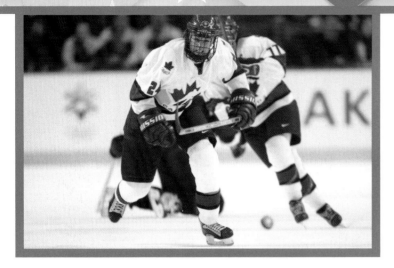

Most women's ice hockey Olympic wins

Women's ice hockey has been contested twice at the Winter Olympics, in 1998 and 2002. The USA beat Canada in the final in 1998, and Canada (above) got revenge by beating the USA in the 2002 final.

Most hat-tricks in an NHL career »

The most hat-tricks scored in an NHL career is 50 by Wayne Gretzky (Canada, right), for the Edmonton Oilers, Los Angeles Kings, St Louis Blues and New York Rangers between 1979 and 1999.

★ **Most goaltending shutouts in an NHL career**
The most goaltending shutouts in an NHL career is 103 by Terry Sawchuk (Canada) for the Detroit Red Wings, Boston Bruins, Toronto Maple Leafs, Los Angeles Kings and New York Rangers from 1949–70.

★ **Most NHL All-Star selections**
Gordie Howe (Canada) was selected 21 times for the NHL All-Star game while playing for the Detroit Red Wings between 1946 and 1979. He played in the first team 12 times and in the second team nine times.

★ **Quickest goal scored in an NHL match**
The quickest goals in an NHL match were scored five seconds after the opening whistle. This record is held by Doug Smail (Canada) for the Winnipeg Jets against the St Louis Blues at Winnipeg, Manitoba, Canada, on 20 December 1981; and by Bryan John Trottier (Canada) for the New York Islanders against the Boston Bruins at Boston, USA, on 22 March 1984; and by Alexander Mogilny (Russia) for the Buffalo Sabers against the Toronto Maple Leafs at Toronto, Ontario, Canada, on 21 December 1991.

★ **Most ties in an NHL season**
The Philadelphia Flyers played 24 tied games over a 76-game season in 1969/70.

★ **Most men's ice hockey Olympic wins**
Ice hockey was first contested at the Winter Olympics in 1920. The most wins is eight by the USSR – in 1956, 1964, 1968, 1972, 1976, 1984, 1988 and in 1992 – as the CIS, when all players were Russian.

★ **Most points scored by an individual in a professional ice hockey game**
A record 10 points in a game has been scored twice by two professional players: Jim Harrison (Canada) with three goals and seven assists for the Alberta (later Edmonton) Oilers in a World Hockey Association (WHA) match at Edmonton, Canada, on 30 January 1973; and Darryl Sittler (Canada) with six goals and four assists for Toronto Maple Leafs against Boston Bruins in an NHL match in Toronto, Ontario, Canada, on 7 February 1976.

★ **Most team Stanley Cup wins**
The Montreal Canadiens have won the Stanley Cup 24 times (1916, 1924, 1930–31, 1944, 1946, 1953, 1956–60, 1965–66, 1968–69, 1971, 1973, 1976–79, 1986 and 1993) from a record 32 finals.

★ **Most individual Stanley Cup wins**
Henri Richard (Canada) had 11 individual Stanley Cup wins for the Montreal Canadiens between 1956 and 1975.

★ **Most points scored in a Stanley Cup series**
Wayne Gretzky (Canada) scored a record 47 points for the Edmonton Oilers in the 1985 Stanley Cup. The points scored comprised 17 goals and 30 assists, which are in themselves records.

★ **Most games played in a professional ice hockey career**
Gordon 'Gordie' Howe (Canada) played 2,421 games in his professional ice hockey career from 1946 to 1979.

★ **Largest ice hockey stick**
An ice hockey stick made by the Millwork Home Centre in Oshawa, Ontario, Canada, measured 13.5 m (44 ft 3.6 in) from the heel of the blade to the top of the shaft on 25 October 2003.

★ **Most durable ice hockey player**
The most durable ice hockey player is James Bernard Hawkins (USA), who began playing in organized hockey leagues in 1932 and played for a total of 71 years.

★ **Ice hockey marathon**
The longest duration for a game of ice hockey is 130 hr 7 min, played at the Moosomin Communiplex, Moosomin, Saskatchewan, Canada, on 13–18 October 2003.

Football 1
Sport

Fastest goal »
in a World Cup
soccer match

The quickest goal in a World Cup finals match, as recognized by the Fédération Internationale de Football Association (FIFA), was timed at 11 seconds. It was scored by Hakan Sukur of Turkey (far right) against the Republic of Korea at Daegu, Korea, on 29 June 2002.

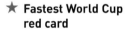

★ **Fastest World Cup red card**
Ion Vladoiu (Romania) was sent off after only three minutes in a World Cup finals match against Switzerland on 22 June 1994 at the Pontiac Silverdome, Detroit, Michigan, USA.

★ **Most World Cup finals goals**
Gerd Müller scored 14 goals in World Cup finals tournaments for West Germany. This total comprises 10 goals in 1970 in Mexico and four in West Germany in 1974, when the host nation went on to lift the trophy.

★ **Most goals in a single World Cup finals**
The most goals scored by an individual player in a World Cup finals tournament is 13 by Just Fontaine (France) in 1958 in Sweden.

★ **Most women's World Cup wins**
A women's World Cup competition was initiated in 1991 and is held quadrennially.

The tournament has been held on four occasions so far. The USA won two of these (1991 and 1999), while the winners in 1995 were Norway with Germany winning in 2003.

★ **Most World Cup clean sheets**
Goalkeeper Peter Shilton (UK) played in 10 World Cup finals matches for England without conceding a single goal over three tournaments and a total of 17 games between 1982 and 1990.

★ **Most countries in FIFA World Cup qualifiers**
A total of 198 federations registered to play in the FIFA qualifiers for the 2002 World Cup, which were held jointly in South Korea and Japan. The soccer federations of Afghanistan,

Burundi, New Guinea, Niger and North Korea were the exceptions.

★ **Most World Cup wins**
FIFA instituted the first World Cup on 13 July 1930 in Montevideo, Uruguay. The tournament is held every four years and has been won five times by Brazil, in 1958, 1962, 1970, 1994 and 2002.

★ **Highest score in an international match**
Australia defeated American Samoa 31–0 in a World Cup qualifying match at Coffs Harbour, New South Wales, Australia, on 11 April 2001.

★ **Youngest scorer in a World Cup finals**
Edson Arantes do Nascimento, better known as Pelé, was aged 17 years 239 days

when he scored for Brazil against Wales, at Gothenburg, Sweden, on 19 June 1958.

★ **Youngest player in a World Cup finals**
The youngest person ever to play in a finals match is Norman Whiteside (UK), who played for Northern Ireland against Yugoslavia aged 17 years 41 days in Zaragoza, Spain, on 17 June 1982.

★ **Oldest player in World Cup finals**
Albert Roger Milla (b. 20 May 1952) played for Cameroon against Russia at Stanford, Palo Alto, California, USA, on 28 June 1994 at the age of 42 years 39 days.
During the course of this match Milla also scored, making him the oldest person ever to score in the World Cup finals.

Most Africa Cup of ⌃ Nations wins

The record for the most wins of the Africa Cup of Nations is four, jointly held by Ghana, who won in 1963, 1965, 1978 and 1982; Egypt, who won in 1957, 1959, 1986 and 1998; and Cameroon (above), who won in 1984, 1988, 2000 and 2002.

Fastest ≫ international hat-trick

Japanese international Masashi 'Gon' Nakayama (right) scored a hat-trick in 3 min 15 sec against Brunei during an Asian Cup qualifying match on 16 February 2000. Nakayama netted on 1 minute, 2 minutes and 3 min 15 sec, bettering the 62-year-old record set by George William Hall (UK), who scored three in 3 min 30 sec for England against Ireland at Old Trafford, Manchester, UK, on 16 November 1938.

★ **Most goals scored by a goalkeeper in one game**
Paraguayan goalkeeper José Luis Chilavert scored a hat-trick of penalties for Vélez Sarsfield in their 6–1 defeat of Ferro Carril Oeste on 28 November 1999 in the Argentine professional league.

Chilavert specializes in penalties and free-kicks. He is the only keeper to have scored in a World Cup qualifying game (against Argentina in Buenos Aires, 1997) and the only one to have taken a direct free-kick in a World Cup (France, 1998).

He also holds the record for the most goals scored by a goalkeeper, with a total of 56 official league and international goals between July 1992 and October 2001. Chilavert currently plays for his country and for the French club Strasbourg.

★ **Most goals scored in an international by an individual**
During the record-breaking 31–0 defeat by Australia of American Samoa,

Archie Thompson (Australia) scored an international record 13 goals.

★ **Oldest regular player**
Enrique Alcocer (Mexico, b. 28 August 1924) is currently the world's oldest regular football player. He plays for the Reforma Athletic Club in Mexico City, Mexico. Alcocer began playing regularly in 1936 for the Grosso Junior and High School in Mexico City, and subsequently played professionally for the Marte Football Club in 1944 in Mexico's first division before joining his current club in 1952.

★ **Largest tournament by players**
The Chappies Little League Cup competition was held in South Africa between March and September 2003, and was contested by 6,023 teams comprising a total of 138,529 players. The tournament is the South African national schools' under-12 competition.

★ **Most durable referee**
Jozsef Magyar (Hungary) regularly refereed competitive football for 50 years. He gained his refereeing qualification in 1953 and officiated his last match on 9 March 2003 in Sitke, Hungary, aged 80.

★ **Most women's international caps**
The greatest number of international appearances by a woman for a national side is 270 by Kristine Lilly (USA), who represented the USA between 1987 and 2004.

★ **Most men's international caps**
The most international appearances for a national team is 171 by Claudio Suarez for Mexico between 1992 and 2003.

★ **Most South American Championships**
Argentina won the South American Championship (known as the Copa América since 1975) a record 15 times between 1910 and 1993.

★ **Most expensive goalkeeper**
In July 2001, Gianluigi Buffon (Italy) transferred between Italian Serie A clubs Parma and Juventus for a record fee of £32.6 million ($46.8 million).

★ **Highest score in a women's international**
The record scoreline of 21–0 has been achieved on four separate occasions: by Japan against Guam at Guangzhou, China, on 5 December 1997; Canada against Puerto Rico at Centennial Park, Toronto, Canada, on 28 August 1998; by Australia against American Samoa and by New Zealand against Samoa – both of these matches took place at Mt Smart Stadium, Auckland, New Zealand, on 9 October 1998.

Most English League Cup wins «

Liverpool (team members Michael Owen, far left, and Steven Gerrard, left; both UK) has won the English League Cup seven times, in 1981–84, 1995, 2001 and 2003.

★ **Largest attendance**
The greatest recorded crowd at any football match was 199,854 for the Brazil against Uruguay World Cup match in the Maracanã Municipal Stadium, Rio de Janeiro, Brazil, on 16 July 1950.

★ **Largest soccer complex**
The National Sports Center at Blaines, Minnesota, USA, has 57 pitches, 55 of which are playable at any one time.

★ **Furthest distance travelled between competitors in the same league**
The furthest distance travelled between two clubs in the top division of a professional national league is 4,794 km (2,979 miles) between the home grounds of the US Major League Soccer teams LA Galaxy and New England Revolution.

★ **Most goals in a Champions League season**
The most goals scored in a UEFA Champions League season is 12 by Ruud van Nistelrooy (Netherlands) for Manchester United in the 2002/03 season.

★ **Fastest Champions League goal**
The fastest goal in a Champions League match was scored by Gilberto Silva (Brazil) in 20.07 seconds playing for Arsenal against PSV Eindhoven in Eindhoven, The Netherlands, on 25 September 2002. Arsenal went on to win the game 4–0.

★ **Most Champions League goals**
The most goals in UEFA Champions League matches is 44 by Raúl González Blanco (Spain) playing for Real Madrid from 1992 until present.

★ **Highest score in a national cup final**
In 1935, Lausanne-Sports beat Nordstern Basel 10–0 in the Swiss Cup final. Two years later, they suffered defeat by the same scoreline at the hands of Grasshopper Club (Zurich) in the 1937 Swiss Cup final.

★ **Most consecutive Champions League match victories**
The longest winning streak in the UEFA Champions League is 11 games by FC Barcelona in the 2002/03 season.

★ **Most Cup Winners' Cups**
The Cup Winners' Cup, contested until 1999 by the winners of the national cups in Europe, was won a record four times by FC Barcelona (1979, 1982, 1989 and 1997).

★ **Most assists in a Major League Soccer season**
Carlos Valderrama (Colombia) made 26 assists in a Major League Soccer season, playing for the Tampa Bay Mutiny in 2000.

★ **Longest clean sheet in goalkeeping**
Abel Resino (Spain) of Atlético de Madrid succeeded in preventing goals being scored past him in top-class competition for 1,275 min (just over 14 matches) during the 1990/91 La Liga season.

The record in international matches is 1,142 min (nearly 13 matches) by Dino Zoff (Italy) from September 1972 to June 1974.

★ **Most domestic league titles**
The most domestic league titles won by a football club is 50, by Rangers FC (UK) in the Scottish Division 1 and Premier Division championships, between 1891 and 2003.

★ **Fastest time to score a hat-trick**
Tommy Ross (UK) scored three goals in 90 seconds for Ross County against Nairn County at Dingwall, Ross-shire, UK, on 28 November 1964.

★ **Most Futsal World Cup titles**
Since it was first held in 1989, the most wins at the Futsal (indoor soccer) World Cup is three by Brazil (1989, 1992 and 1996). The fourth tournament, held in 2000 in Guatemala, was won by Spain, who beat Brazil 4–3 in the final.

Most expensive soccer player »

The highest transfer fee for a player is 13 billion Spanish pesetas (£47 million or $66 million) for Zinédine Zidane (France, right) for his transfer from Juventus to Real Madrid on 9 July 2001.

Most career goals ⌃

Edson Arantes do Nascimento (Brazil, above), better known as Pelé, scored a total of 1,279 goals from 7 September 1956 to 1 October 1977 in 1,363 games. Pelé's best year was 1959, in which he scored 126 goals. The milésimo (1,000th) came from a penalty for his club Santos at the Maracanã Stadium, Rio de Janeiro, Brazil, on 19 November 1969 in his 909th first-class match. He later added two more goals in special appearances.

★ **Unbeaten premiership season**
In the premiership season of 2003/04, Arsenal FC were unbeaten in 38 games, winning 26, drawing 12 and losing none. In the process they scored 73 goals and conceded 26, failing to score on only four occasions.

★ **Most premiership goals**
Alan Shearer (UK) has scored 243 goals in the English Premiership. Shearer began his career with Southampton, before moving to Blackburn Rovers and finally to Newcastle United in July 1996 for a record fee of £15.6 million ($22.4 million).

★ **Longest penalty shootout**
In the Derby Community League (UK) under-10s Cup match between Mickleover Lightning Blue Sox and Chellaston Boys 'B' on 17 January 1998, a total of 66 penalties were taken to decide the tie, which had finished 1–1. The Blue Sox eventually won the marathon shoot-out 2–1, with 35 penalties being saved, the rest going wide of the target.

★ **Most consecutive passes**
The most consecutive soccer passes is 557 and was set by members of the McDonald's Youth Football Scheme, Tsing Yi, Hong Kong, China, on 4 May 2002.

★ **Most goals scored direct from corners**
The most goals scored in a match by an individual direct from corners is three by Steve Cromey (UK) for Ashgreen United against Dunlop FC on 24 February 2002 at Bedworth, Warwickshire, UK, and by

Daniel White (UK) for Street and Glastonbury under-11s against Westfield Boys on 7 April 2002.

★ **Most touches of a football in 30 seconds**
The most touches of a football in 30 seconds, while keeping the ball in the air, is 141 by Ferdie Adoboe (USA) in New York, USA, on 27 August 2003.
The women's record is 137 touches by Tasha-Nicole Terani (USA) in New York, USA, on 27 August 2003.

★ **Fastest ball control marathon distance**
Jan Skorkovsky (Czechoslovakia) kept a football up while running a distance of 42.195 km (26.219 miles) in the Prague City Marathon in 7 hr 18 min 55 sec on 8 July 1990.

★ **Longest ball control with feet, legs and head**
Martinho Eduardo Orige (Brazil) juggled a regulation-size football for 19 hr 30 min non-stop with feet, legs and head without the ball ever

touching the ground at Padre Ezio Julli Gym in Araranguá, Brazil, on 2–3 August 2003.

★ **Longest ball control while lying down**
Tomas Lundman (Sweden) managed to keep a regulation-size football up in the air using his feet while lying on his back for 7 min 36 sec at Angebo Svågagården Hudiksvall, Sweden, on 20 September 2003.

★ **Most football management rejection letters**
The most rejection letters received for football management jobs is 29 by Richard Dixon (UK). Dixon applies only for jobs that are available and has received official letters from clubs such as Tottenham Hotspur, Manchester United, Atlético de Madrid and the English and Cypriot national sides. The hobby began in 2000 when Physical Education teacher Dixon contracted glandular fever and applied for the Millwall job.

Rugby
Sport

Most Super League titles

The most Super League titles won by a team is four by St Helens (above) in 1996, 1999, 2000 and 2002. The Super League is the UK's premier Rugby League competition, instituted in 1996.

★ **Most points by an individual player in a Rugby Union international**
In the World Cup qualifying match between Hong Kong and Singapore at Kuala Lumpur, Malaysia, on 27 October 1994, Hong Kong's Ashley Billington scored 50 points (10 tries).

★ **Most penalties by an individual player in a Rugby Union international**
The record is shared by two players: Keiji Hirose kicked nine successful penalties for Japan against Tonga (44–17) in Tokyo, Japan, on 9 May 1999; and Andrew Mehrtens also kicked nine for New Zealand against Australia (34–15) at Auckland, New Zealand, on 24 July 1999.

★ **Most points in a Rugby Union international career**
Neil Jenkins (UK) scored 1,049 points in 87 matches (1,008 points in 83 matches for Wales, 41 points in four matches for the British Lions) between 1991 and March 2001.

★ **Fastest Rugby Union World Cup try**
Elton Flatley (Australia) scored a try just 18 seconds after kick-off when playing for Australia against Romania on 18 October 2003 at the Suncorp Stadium, Brisbane, Queensland, Australia.

★ **Largest rugby tour**
Between 11 and 14 April 2003, 264 players and coaches from Ealing Rugby Club (UK) played matches on tour in Ireland.

★ **Most women's Rugby Union World Cup titles**
The women's World Cup has been contested four times (1991, 1994, 1998 and 2002). New Zealand has won the title twice, in 1998 and 2002, while USA and England have one win apiece.

★ **Most wins in the Hong Kong Sevens**
First held in 1976, this is the world's most prestigious international tournament for seven-a-side Rugby Union. Fiji has won a record nine times, in 1977–78, 1980, 1984, 1990–92 and 1998–99. For 1997 the contest was replaced by the World Cup Sevens, which Fiji also won.

★ **Highest attendance at a Rugby Union match**
The largest paying attendance for a Rugby Union international is 109,874 for New Zealand's 39–35 victory over Australia at Stadium Australia, Sydney, Australia, on 15 July 2000.

★ **Highest attendance at a Rugby League match**
A total of 104,583 spectators saw a Rugby League double header at Stadium Australia, Sydney, Australia, on 7 March 1999. The Newcastle Knights beat the Manly Sea Eagles 41–18, and the Parramatta Eels beat the St George Illawarra Dragons 20–10.

★ **Most Rugby League World Cup wins**
The Rugby League World Cup competition was first held in 1954. Australia have most wins, with eight, in 1957, 1968, 1970, 1977, 1988, 1992, 1995 and 2000, as well as a win in the International Championship of 1975.

★ **Most Rugby League Challenge Cup wins**
The Rugby League Challenge Cup (inaugurated in the 1896/97 season) has been won a record 17 times by Wigan (in 1924, 1929, 1948, 1951, 1958–59, 1965, 1985, 1988–95 and 2002).

★ **Most National Rugby League (NRL) titles**
The Brisbane Broncos have won two NRL titles, in 1998 and 2000. The NRL is Australia's premier Rugby League competition. Instituted in 1998, it replaced the Australian Rugby League (1995–97), which in turn replaced the New South Wales Rugby League (1908–94).

Biggest Rugby Union World Cup match win ⟱

The largest winning margin recorded in Rugby Union World Cup matches is 142 points, when host nation Australia beat Namibia 142–0 in Adelaide, Australia, on 25 October 2003. Matt Giteau (Australia) is pictured below scoring one of his tries.

Most Rugby Union ⟰ World Cup wins

The William Webb Ellis Trophy (above) is awarded to the winners of the Rugby Union World Cup (instituted in 1987). The most wins is two by Australia, in 1991 and 1999.

★ **Most tries scored in an amateur Rugby League season**
Richard Lopag (UK) scored 169 tries for the Deighton Juniors Under-13 side, West Yorkshire, UK, in the 2001/02 season.

★ **Most hat-tricks in a Rugby League season**
Richard Lopag (UK) of Deighton Juniors Under-13s, Huddersfield, West Yorkshire, UK, scored 43 hat-tricks during the 2001/02 season.

★ **Fastest Rugby League hat-trick**
Chris Thorman (UK) scored a hat-trick of tries within 6 min 54 sec of the start of a match, for Huddersfield Giants against Doncaster Dragons in the semi-final of the Buddies National League Cup at Doncaster, South Yorkshire, UK, on 19 May 2002.

★ **Most rugby tackles in one hour**
Cranleigh RFC Under-11s made 1,644 rugby tackles in one hour on 21 April 2002 at Cranleigh Rugby Club, Surrey, UK.

★ GWR TALKS TO
Jason Leonard OBE

Jason Leonard (UK, below right pictured with his International Rugby Players Association Asprey Special Merit Award, presented in 2002) played in 114 international Rugby Union matches for England between 1990 and 2004. The England prop became the most capped player of all time when he came on for Phil Vickery (UK) in the fourth minute of England's World Cup semi-final victory over France at the Telstra Stadium, Sydney, Australia, on 16 November 2003. England won the match 24–7 with Leonard having been on the pitch for one minute.

Who inspires you?
Muhammad Ali, the Greatest.

Did you always want to be a rugby player?
At school, I wanted to be a footballer – I was a pretty good defender – but then I discovered rugby, and that was that!

If you hadn't pursued a career in rugby what do you think you would have done?
When I left school, I worked in the building trade, so I'd probably have carried on with that.

Did you think your international career would go on this long?
When I started playing for England, back in 1990, 30 caps was considered a great career, so I'm amazed I managed to carry on playing for 14 years! I've recently decided to bow out of competitive rugby, but I've enjoyed every minute and achieved more than I could have ever dreamed of when I started, so I've no regrets.

What is your greatest achievement in rugby?
Winning the World Cup with England in Australia in 2003.

What advice would you give to young sportsmen and women?
Enjoy it, and always give 100%.

Which is your favourite Guinness World Record?
Mine!

Cricket
Sport

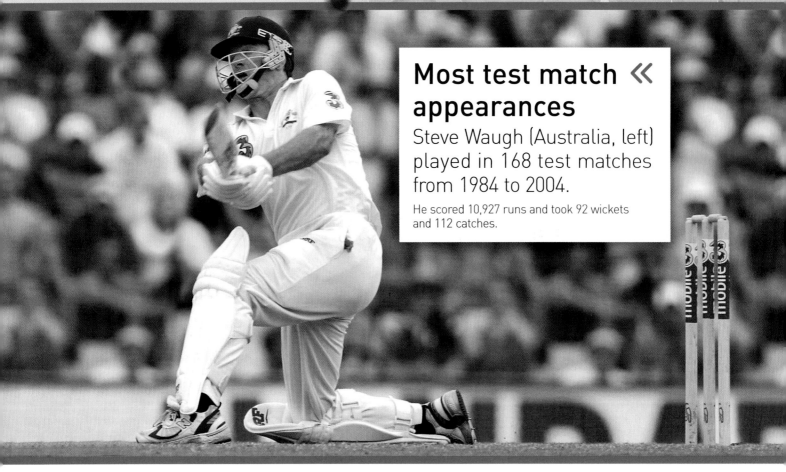

Most test match « appearances

Steve Waugh (Australia, left) played in 168 test matches from 1984 to 2004.

He scored 10,927 runs and took 92 wickets and 112 catches.

★ **Highest test team score**
Sri Lanka scored 952 for 6 against India at Colombo, Sri Lanka, on 4–6 August 1997.

★ **Most runs in test cricket**
Allan Border (Australia) scored a total of 11,174 runs in 156 tests (an average of 50.56) from 1978 to 1994.

★ **Highest test batting average**
Don Bradman (Australia) retired with a batting average of 99.94 after playing for Australia in a total of 52 tests. He scored 6,996 runs in 80 innings between 1928 and 1948.

★ **Highest partnership in a test match**
The highest partnership is 576 for the second wicket by Sanath Jayasuriya at 340 and Roshan Mahanama (both Sri Lanka) at 225 for Sri Lanka against India at Colombo, Sri Lanka, on 4–6 August 1997.

★ **Most test match wickets**
Muttiah Muralitharan (Sri Lanka) is the leading Test match wicket-taker with 521 (average 22.76 runs per wicket) in 89 matches, between August 1992 and May 2004.

★ **Most catches by a wicket keeper in test cricket**
Ian Healy (Australia) made a total of 366 catches (in 119 tests) playing for Australia between 1988 and 1999.

★ **Most catches by a fielder in test cricket**
Mark Waugh (Australia) made 181 catches in 128 tests for Australia between 1990 and 2003.

★ **Most 'ducks' in test cricket**
The player who has the dubious honour of registering the most 'ducks' (a score of nothing) in test cricket is Courtney Walsh (Jamaica) with 43 in 185 innings for the West Indies between November 1984 and April 2001.

★ **Most sixes in a test match innings**
Wasim Akram (Pakistan) hit 12 sixes in his 257 not out for Pakistan against Zimbabwe at Sheikhupura, Pakistan, on 18–20 October 1996.

★ **Most extras conceded in a test match**
The West Indies conceded 71 extras in Pakistan's first innings at Georgetown, Guyana, on 3–4 April 1988. The total comprised 21 byes, eight leg byes, four wides and 38 no-balls.

★ **Most test centuries**
Sunil Gavaskar (India) scored a total of 34 centuries (in 214 innings) playing for India between 1971 and 1987.

★ **Longest test match**
The longest-lasting recorded cricket match was the 'timeless' test between England and South Africa at Durban, South Africa, from 3 to 14 March 1939. Neither side was able to secure victory and the match was abandoned after 10 days (the eighth day was rained off)

because the ship taking the England team home was due to leave. The total playing time was 43 hr 16 min and a record test match aggregate of 1,981 runs was scored.

★ **Most consecutive test wins**
Australia recorded a run of 16 successive test victories when they beat India by 10 wickets at Mumbai (Bombay), India, in March 2001.

★ **Youngest test player**
The youngest test player ever is Hasan Raza (Pakistan, b. 11 March 1982), who made his debut aged 14 years 227 days against Zimbabwe at Faisalabad, Pakistan, on 24 October 1996.

★ **Most catches by a fielder in a World Cup match**
The greatest number of catches in a cricket World Cup match is four by Mohammad Kaif (India) against Sri Lanka in Johannesburg, South Africa, on 10 March 2003.

Highest « test innings

Brian Lara (Trinidad, left) scored 400 not out for West Indies v. England

at Antigua Recreation Ground, St John's, Antigua, on 10–12 April 2004. The innings included four sixes and 43 fours, in a team total of 751-5. Lara became the only player to have set this record twice, having previously scored 375 against the same opposition on the same ground in April 1994.

Fastest bowling ⌃

The highest electronically measured speed for a ball bowled by any bowler is 161.3 km/h (100.23 mph)

by Shoaib Akhtar (Pakistan, above) against England on 22 February 2003 in a World Cup match at Newlands, Cape Town, South Africa.

★ **Most catches by a fielder in a World Cup career**
Ricky Ponting (Australia) made 18 catches in 28 matches between 1996 and 2003.

★ **Most catches by a fielder in a cricket World Cup tournament**
Ricky Ponting (Australia) took 11 catches in the World Cup tournament in South Africa in 2003.

★ **Highest team score in World Cup cricket**
The highest team score in a World Cup match is 398 for 5 by Sri Lanka against Kenya at Kandy, Sri Lanka, on 6 March 1996.
The lowest team score is 36 by Canada against Sri Lanka at Boland Park, Paarl, South Africa, on 19 February 2003.

★ **Most centuries in first-class cricket**
Jack Hobbs (UK) scored 197 centuries out of a total of 1,315 innings while playing for Surrey and England between 1905 and 1934.

★ **Highest individual innings score**
Brian Charles Lara (Trinidad) scored 501 not out in 7 hr 54 min playing for Warwickshire against Durham at Edgbaston, UK, between 3 and 6 June 1994.
During his innings he also broke two other cricketing records: the most runs in a day (390 on 6 June) and the most runs from strokes worth four or more (308, comprising 62 fours and 10 sixes).

★ **Highest individual score in one-day internationals**
Saeed Anwar (Pakistan) scored 194 while playing for Pakistan against India at Madras (Chennai), India, on 21 May 1997.

★ **Most runs off a ball**
Garry Chapman (Australia), partnered by Chris Veal (Australia), scored 17 (all run, with no overthrows) off a single delivery while playing for Banyule against Macleod at Windsor Reserve, Victoria, Australia, on 13 October 1990. Chapman had pulled the ball to mid-wicket, where it disappeared into 25-cm-high (10-in) grass.

★ **Most runs off one over**
The first batsman ever to score 36 runs off a six-ball over was Garfield St Aubrun Sobers (Barbados) off Malcolm Andrew Nash (UK) for Nottinghamshire against Glamorgan at Swansea on 31 August 1968.
Ravishankar Jayadritha Shastri (India) achieved the same feat for Bombay against Baroda at Mumbai (Bombay), India, on 10 January 1985 off the bowling of Tilak Raj Sharma (India).

★ **Longest cricket marathon**
Cricket Club des Ormes (France) played a cricket marathon of 26 hr 13 min at Dol de Bretagne, France, on 21–22 June 2003. Two teams of 12 played six matches in all, with the Young Guns team winning five matches to the Veterans' one.

★ **Oldest umpire**
After playing professionally for Staffordshire, UK, as a younger man, Joe Filliston (UK) applied to become an umpire at the age of 82. The Marylebone Cricket Club (MCC) invited him to umpire for the Lord's Taverners on many occasions and he was still umpiring at the age of 100.

★ **Youngest cricketer to hit six sixes in an over**
The youngest cricketer to hit six consecutive sixes in the same over is Anthony McMahon (UK), who achieved the feat at the age of 13 years 261 days, on 24 May 2003, while playing for Chester-le-Street against Eppleton at Eppleton Cricket Club, Durham, UK.

Highest beach volleyball ⌄ career earnings (AVP tour)

Karch Kiraly (USA, below) has won a record $2,929,158 (£1,872,708) in official Association of Volleyball Professionals (AVP) Tour earnings through to the end of the 2002 season.

Most men's handball ⌃ World Championships won

Two countries have won the men's world title four times. Sweden

(1999 team members, above) won in 1954, 1958, 1990 and 1999, and Romania in 1961, 1964, 1970 and 1974.

★ **Most men's volleyball World Championships**
The USSR has won six titles (in 1949, 1952, 1960, 1962, 1978 and 1982).

★ **Most women's volleyball World Championships**
World Championships were instituted in 1952 for women, and the USSR has won a record five titles (in 1952, 1956, 1960, 1970 and 1990).

★ **Most beach volleyball titles (AVP tour)**
Karch Kiraly (USA) has won a record 143 AVP tour titles through the end of the 2003 season.

★ **Most Olympic medals for men's volleyball**
The record for men is three, held jointly by Yuriy Mikhailovich Poyarkov (USSR), who won gold medals in 1964

and 1968 and a bronze in 1972; Katsutoshi Nekoda (Japan), who won gold in 1972, silver in 1968 and bronze in 1964; and Steve Timmons (USA), who won gold in 1984 and 1988, and bronze in 1992.

★ **Longest volleyball marathon**
The longest game of volleyball played was one of 24 hr 10 min at the Vocational School Centre, Torgau, Germany, on 30 September–1 October 2002.

★ **Handball target shooting**
Jonas Källman (Sweden) hit eight handball targets in 30 seconds on the set of *Guinness Rekord TV*, Stockholm, Sweden, on 27 November 2001.

★ **Most women's World Championships handball titles won**
Three women's titles (all indoor unless stated) have been won by Romania in 1956, 1960 (both outdoor) and 1962; the GDR in 1971, 1975 and 1978; and the USSR in 1982, 1986 and 1990.

★ **Highest score in an international handball match**
In August 1981, the USSR beat Afghanistan 86–2 in the 'Friendly Army Tournament' at Miskolc, Hungary.

★ **Longest handball marathon**
The longest game of handball was 70 hours, set by 12 players from the HV Mighty/Stevo team in Geesteren, Tubbergen, The Netherlands, on 30 August–2 September 2001.

★ **Most women's lacrosse World Championships**
The first World Cup was held in 1982, replacing the World Championships, which had been held three times since 1969. The USA have won a record six times (in 1974, 1982, 1989, 1993, 1997 and 2001).

★ **Most men's lacrosse World Championships**
The USA has won eight of the nine World Championships (in 1967, 1974, 1982, 1986, 1990, 1994, 1998 and 2002).

Canada won the other world title in 1978, beating the USA 17–16 after extra time – in what was the first drawn international match.

★ **Highest score in men's lacrosse**
The highest score in a World Cup match is Scotland's 34–3 win over Germany at Manchester, UK, on 25 July 1994. In the World Cup premier division, the record score is the USA's 33–2 win over Japan at Manchester on 21 July 1994.

★ **Highest score in women's lacrosse**
The highest score by an international team was by Great Britain and Ireland with their 40–0 defeat of Long Island during their 1967 tour of the USA.

★ **Longest lacrosse throw**
The longest recorded lacrosse throw is 148.91 m (488 ft 6 in), by Barnet Quinn (Canada) on 10 September 1892.

Most Champions' trophies in » women's hockey

The women's Champions' trophy, first held in 1987, has been won a record six times by Australia,

They won in 1991, 1993, 1995, 1997, 1999 and 2003. Pictured are Wendy Alcorn (far right), playing for Australia against China (Zhaoxa Chen, near right).

★ **Most korfball World Championships**
The Netherlands has won the World Championships (instituted 1978) a record six times, in 1978, 1984, 1987, 1995, 1999 and 2003.

★ **Highest score in a korfball World Championship final**
The highest team score in the final of the World Championships is 23 by The Netherlands against Belgium (11) in 1999.

★ **Longest korfball marathon**
Members of the korfball club de Vinken at Vinkeveen, The Netherlands, played a game of korfball lasting 26 hr 2 min on 23–24 May 2001.

★ **Biggest winning margin in a korfball World Championship final**
In the final of the Centennial Championship, held in Rotterdam, The Netherlands, on 9 November 2003, there was a winning margin of 13 points, between The Netherlands (22) and Belgium (9).

★ **Most World Games titles won for korfball**
Korfball was first held as part of the World Games in 1985 and the most titles won is five (every occasion the event has been held) by The Netherlands, in 1985, 1989, 1993, 1997 and 2001. In winning these five titles The Netherlands has never lost a match.

★ **Highest score in international women's hockey**
The England women's hockey team beat France 23–0 at Merton, Greater London, UK, on 3 February 1923.

★ **Highest score in international men's hockey**
The highest international score was when India defeated the USA 24–1 in Los Angeles, California, USA, in the 1932 Olympic Games.

★ **Most women's hockey World Cups won**
The Fédération Internationale de Hockey (FIH) World Cup for women was first held in 1974.

The most wins is five by The Netherlands (in 1974, 1978, 1983, 1986 and 1990).

★ **Most men's hockey World Cup titles**
The FIH World Cup for men was first held in 1971. The most wins is four by Pakistan (in 1971, 1978, 1982 and 1994).

★ **Most Champions' trophies in men's hockey**
This competition was first held in 1978 and has been contested annually since 1980 by the top six men's teams in the world. The most wins is eight by Germany (1986–88 as West Germany, 1991–92, 1995, 1997 and 2001).

★ **Most goals scored in a hockey career**
David Ashman (UK) has scored a record 2,326 goals having played for Hampshire, Southampton, Southampton Kestrals and Hamble Old Boys (for whom he has scored 2,165 goals, a record for one club), in 1958–99.

★ **Most goals scored in an international hockey career**
The greatest number of goals scored in international hockey is 267 by Paul Litjens (Netherlands) in 177 games.

★ **Highest attendance for a hockey match**
The match between England and the USA at Wembley, London, UK, on 11 March 1978 was attended by 65,165 people.

★ **Most hockey Olympics umpired**
Graham Dennis Nash (UK) umpired in five successive Olympics (1976–92) and retired after the Barcelona Games, having officiated in a record 144 international matches.

★ **Largest hockey stick**
A hockey stick made by the Jubilee Committee of AMHC Upward, Arnhem, The Netherlands, measured 12.07 m (39 ft 7 in) long and weighed 580 kg (1,278 lb) on 11 September 1999.

Most goals « in an AFL career

Tony Lockett (Australia, left) scored 1,357 goals during his Australian Football League (AFL) career playing for St Kilda and the Sydney Swans from 1983 to 1999.

Most yards passing in ⌃ a Canadian football career

Damon Allen (Canada, above) threw for a record 61,802 yards during his CFL career for Edmonton Eskimos, Ottawa Roughriders, Hamilton Tiger-Cats, Memphis Mad Dogs, British Columbia Lions and Toronto Argonauts from 1985 to 2003.

★ **Most AFL Premiership titles**
Two clubs have won the AFL Premiership 16 times: Carlton, between 1906 and 1995, and Essendon, between 1897 and 2000.

★ **Highest AFL team score**
The AFL record for one team is 239 (37–17) by Geelong against Brisbane on 3 May 1992.

★ **Highest aggregate score in an AFL match**
The highest aggregate record score is 345 points when St Kilda beat Melbourne 204–141 on 6 May 1978.

★ **Most goals kicked in an AFL Grand Final**
Two players have kicked nine goals in an AFL Grand Final: Gordon Coventry (Australia) for Collingwood against Richmond in the 1928 AFL Grand Final and Gary Ablett (Australia) for Geelong against Hawthorn in the 1989 AFL Grand Final.

★ **Most goals scored on a debut**
The greatest number of goals scored on an Australian Rules football debut is 12, by John Coleman (Australia) playing for Essendon against Hawthorn in Round One of the 1949 season.

★ **Most goals by an individual in an AFL season**
The AFL season's record is 150 and has been reached by two players: Bob Pratt (South Melbourne) in 1934 and Peter Hudson (Hawthorn) in 1971.

★ **Most games played in an AFL career**
Michael Tuck (Australia) played 426 AFL games in his career from 1972 to 1991.

★ **Longest winning streak**
Geelong won 23 consecutive games in the AFL Premiership between 1952 and 1953.

★ **Longest losing streak**
University lost 51 consecutive games in the AFL premiership between 1912 and 1914.

★ **Largest disciplinary fines for a single AFL match**
The highest disciplinary fines imposed as a result of a single AFL match is AUS$67,500 (£28,163 or $49,773). The fines were incurred during a match between Western Bulldogs and St Kilda on 4 May 2003. Nine players from each team were fined and one player was banned for three matches.

★ **Most consecutive CFL games played**
Bob Cameron (Canada) played 353 consecutive Canadian Football League (CFL) games for the Winnipeg Blue Bombers between 1980 and 2000.

★ **Most CFL games played in a career**
Lui Passaglia (Canada) played in 408 CFL games for the British Columbia Lions (aka the BC Lions) from 1976 to 2000. He also scored a CFL career record 3,991 points for the BC Lions from 1976 to 2000.

★ **Most points in a CFL game**
Bob McNamara (Canada) scored 36 points for the Winnipeg Blue Bombers against the BC Lions on 13 October 1956.

★ **Most points in a CFL season**
Lance Chomyc (Canada) scored a season record 236 points for the Toronto Argonauts in 1991.

★ **Longest field goal in a CFL game**
The longest field goal in a regular game was 62 yards. It was kicked by Paul McCallum (Canada) for the Saskatchewan Roughriders against the Edmonton Eskimos on 27 October 2001.

★ **Most Grey Cup wins**
The Toronto Argonauts have won the Grey Cup a record 14 times between 1914 and 1997.

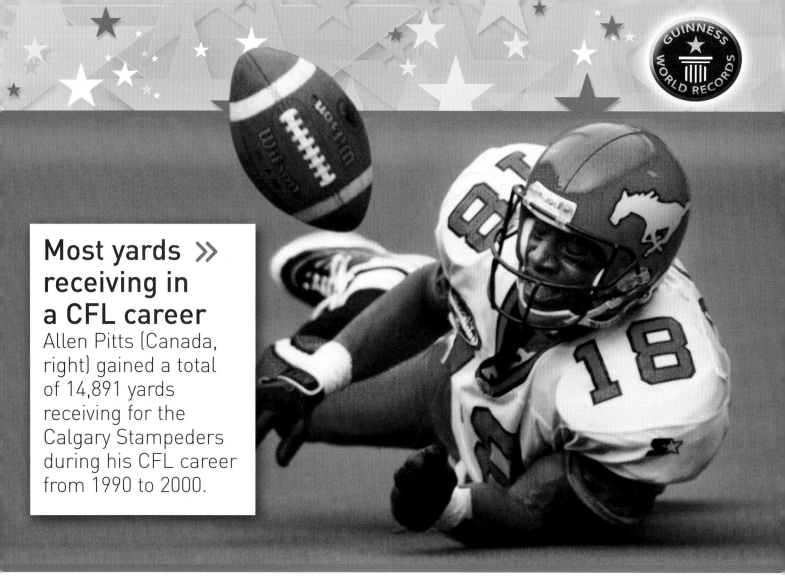

Most yards >> receiving in a CFL career

Allen Pitts (Canada, right) gained a total of 14,891 yards receiving for the Calgary Stampeders during his CFL career from 1990 to 2000.

★ **Most receptions in a CFL season**
Derrell Mitchell (Canada) made a record 160 pass receptions for the Toronto Argonauts in 1998.

★ **Most pass receptions in a CFL career**
The greatest number of passes caught over the course of a CFL career is 972, by Darren Flutie (Canada) playing for the BC Lions, Edmonton Eskimos, and Hamilton Tiger-Cats between 1991 and 2002.

★ **Longest rush in a CFL game**
Two players have gained 109 yards running from the line of scrimmage: George Dixon (Canada) for the Montreal Alouettes against the Ottawa Roughriders on 2 September 1963; and Willie Fleming (USA) for the BC Lions against the Edmonton Eskimos on 17 October 1964.

★ **Longest punt in a CFL game**
Zenon Andrusyshun (Canada) kicked a punt a distance of 108 yards for the Toronto Argonauts against the Edmonton Eskimos on 23 October 1977.

★ **Most punt return touchdowns in a CFL career**
Henry Williams (Canada) returned a total of 26 punts for touchdowns during his CFL career for the Edmonton Eskimos from 1986 to 1999.

★ **Most touchdowns scored in a CFL season**
Milt Stegall (Canada) scored a record 23 touchdowns for the Winnipeg Blue Bombers in 2002.

★ **Most touchdowns scored in a CFL career**
George Reed (Canada) scored a total of 137 touchdowns for the Saskatchewan Roughriders during his CFL career from 1963 to 1975.

★ **Most yards rushing in a CFL career**
George Reed (Canada) rushed for a career-record 16,116 yards for the Saskatchewan Roughriders between 1963 and 1975.

★ **Most kicks blocked in a CFL career**
The greatest number of kicks blocked over the course of a CFL career is 10 by Gerald Vaughn (Canada) while playing for three teams – the Calgary Stampeders, the Winnipeg Blue Bombers and the Hamilton Tiger-Cats – between 1993 and 2002.

★ **Longest pass completion in Canadian football**
The longest pass completion in the CFL covered a distance of 109 yards and has been achieved by three different sets of players: Sam Etcheverry to Hal Patterson (both Canada) for the Montreal Alouettes against the Hamilton Tiger-Cats on 22 September 1956; Jerry Keeling to Terry Evanshen (both Canada) for the Calgary Stampeders against the Winnipeg Blue Bombers on 27 September 1966; and Damon Allen to Albert Jackson (both Canada) for the BC Lions against the Montreal Alouettes on 21 August 2002.

★ **Most Shinty Challenge Cup team wins**
From 1907 to 1986, Newtonmore won the Camanachd Association Challenge Cup (instituted in 1896 and also known as the Scottish Cup) 28 times. Shinty is a game similar to Ireland's hurling and is played almost exclusively in Scotland.

★ **Most Shinty Challenge Cup winners' medals won by an individual**
David Ritchie and Hugh Chisholm (both UK) of Newtonmore have won 12 Challenge Cup winners' medals each.

★ **Highest score in a Shinty cup final**
Kingussie beat Newtonmore 12–1 at Fort William, Highland, UK, in 1997.

★ **Highest individual score in a Shinty cup final**
John Macmillan Mactaggart (UK) scored 10 hails, or goals, for Mid-Argyll in a Camanachd Cup match in 1938.

Fastest »
tennis serve

The fastest tennis service by a man (measured with modern equipment) is 241.4 km/h (150 mph) by Andy Roddick (USA, right) during a Davis Cup match against Stefan Koubek (Austria) at the Mohegan Sun Arena, Uncasville, Connecticut, USA, on 6 February 2004.

★ Fastest serve by a woman
Venus Williams (USA) served at 205 km/h (127.4 mph) during the European Indoor Championships at Zurich, Switzerland, on 16 October 1998.

★ Youngest female world No.1
Martina Hingis (Switzerland, b. 30 September 1980 in the former Czechoslovakia) was 16 years 182 days when she became world No.1 on 31 March 1997. She is also the youngest female Wimbledon champion: she was 15 years 282 days when she won the ladies doubles in 1996 with partner Helena Sukova (Czechoslovakia).

★ Youngest male world No.1
Marat Mikhailovich Safin (Russia, b. 27 January 1980) was 20 years 234 days when he achieved the world No.1 ranking by winning the President's Cup tournament in Tashkent, Uzbekistan, on 17 September 2000.

★ Youngest Davis Cup player
The youngest player to compete in the Davis Cup is Kenny Banzer (Liechtenstein) at the age of 14 years 5 days on 16 February 2000 against Algeria.

★ Most consecutive Davis Cup wins
The USA won a record seven consecutive Davis Cup tournaments in 1920–26. Their reign was brought to an end by France in 1927, who went on to keep the title for six years, the second longest winning streak, before losing to Great Britain in 1933.

★ Most Davis Cup wins
The most wins in the Davis Cup, the men's international team championship, has been 31 by the USA between 1900 and 1995.

★ Oldest Davis Cup player
The oldest player to compete in the Davis Cup is Yaka-Garonfin Koptigan (Togo, b. 23 December 1941) aged 59 years 147 days on 27 May 2001.

★ Most Wimbledon men's singles titles
Pete Sampras (USA) won seven Wimbledon men's singles tennis titles in 1993–95 and 1997–2000.

★ Most Wimbledon singles titles won by a woman
The most Wimbledon singles tennis titles won by a woman is nine by Martina Navratilova (USA) in 1978–79, 1982–87 and 1990.

★ Best wildcard performance at Wimbledon
The best ever performance by a wildcard entrant at the Wimbledon Championships was that of Goran Ivanisevic (Croatia) in 2001. Invited to play in the competition by the All England Club, Ivanisevic, ranked 125th in the world, won the men's singles title by beating Pat Rafter (Australia) 6–3, 3–6, 6–3, 2–6, 9–7 in the final. The Croatian's popular win came in his fourth final appearance, and he also served a record 213 aces throughout the tournament, including 27 in the final.

★ Longest Wimbledon career
The longest Wimbledon tennis career is 55 years and is held by Jean Borotra (France), who competed in the men's singles competition 35 times between 1922 and 1964. He then went on to compete in the men's veteran doubles and the mixed doubles events from 1965 to 1977, retiring when he was 78.

★ Oldest US Open champion
Margaret du Pont (USA, b. 4 March 1918) won the mixed doubles at the age of 42 years 166 days in 1960.

★ Youngest US Open champion
Vincent Richards (USA, b. 20 March 1903) was 15 years 139 days when he won the men's doubles with Bill Tilden (USA) in 1918.

Most French Open ⌃ singles tennis titles won by a man

Björn Borg (Sweden, above) won six French Open singles titles in 1974–75 and 1978–81.

Oldest Wimbledon champion

The oldest main draw Wimbledon tennis champion ≫ is Martina Navratilova (USA, right). She was 46 years 261 days when she won the mixed doubles with Leander Paes (India) on 6 July 2003.

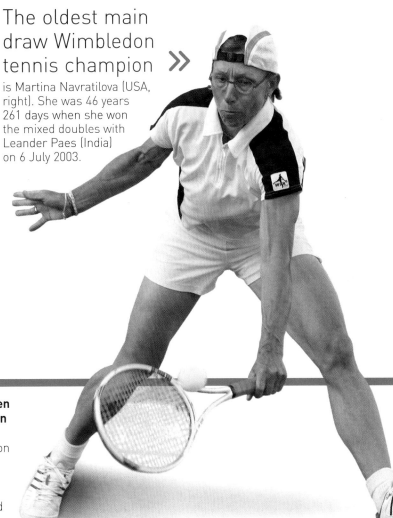

★ **Youngest female to win the US Open singles championship**
Tracey Austin (USA, b. 12 December 1962) was 16 years 271 days when she won the women's singles in 1979.

★ **Youngest male to win the US Open singles championship**
Pete Sampras (USA, b. 12 August 1971) was 19 years 28 days when he won the US Open on 9 September 1990.

★ **Most US Open singles titles won by a woman**
Molla Mallory (née Bjurstedt, Norway) won eight US Open singles tennis titles in 1915–18, 1920–22 and 1926.

★ **Most US Open singles titles won by a man**
The most US Open singles tennis titles won by a man is seven and is shared by Bill Tilden (USA) in 1920–25 and 1929, Richard Sears (USA) in 1881–87, and William Larned (USA) in 1901, 1902 and 1907–11.

★ **Most French Open singles titles won by a woman**
Chris Evert (USA) won seven French Open singles tennis titles in 1974, 1975, 1979, 1980, 1983, 1985 and 1986.

★ **Most Australian Open singles titles won by a man**
Roy Emerson (Australia) won a record six Australian Open singles tennis titles in 1961 and 1963–67.

★ **Most men's wheelchair tennis World Team Cups**
The World Team Cup for wheelchair tennis has been contested annually since 1985. The USA has won the men's competition a record nine times (1985–91, 1995 and 1997).

★ **Most Grand Slam tournament singles titles won**
Margaret Court (Australia) won 24 Grand Slam tournament singles between 1960 and 1973.

★ **Oldest tennis player**
The oldest tennis player is José Guadalupe Leal Lemus (Mexico, b. 13 December 1902), who began playing tennis in 1925 and has been playing regularly ever since, a total of 79 years. Now aged 101, he currently plays every Wednesday at the Club Campestre Morelia, Morelia, Mexico, with a group of doctors 20–25 years his junior.

★ **Longest singles marathon**
The longest competitive singles match lasted 25 hr 25 min and was played between Christian Albrecht Barschel and Hauke Daene (both Germany) on 12–13 September 2003 at Mölln Tennis Club, Mölln, Germany.

★ **Longest doubles marathon**
The longest competitive doubles tennis match lasted 48 hr 6 min and was played between Jaroslaw Kadzielewski and Rafal Siupka, and Mateusz Zatorski and Kamil Milian (all Poland) on 30 August to 1 September 2002 at Giliwice Sports Hall, Poland.

★ **Longest doubles marathon by one pair**
The longest competitive doubles tennis match, by one pair playing against all comers, lasted 26 hours and was played by Mike Geraghty and Francis Power (both Ireland) on 20–21 June 2003 at Galway Lawn Tennis Club, Galway, Ireland.

⩔ Most Uber Cup wins

China holds the record for the most wins at the women's team badminton World Championships for the Uber Cup, instituted in 1956. They won eight times: in 1984, 1986, 1988, 1990, 1992, 1998, 2000 and 2002. Zhou Mi (China, left) played in the 2002 competition.

Most men's ⩓ table tennis World Championship wins

Viktor Barna (Hungary, above) won a record five men's singles table tennis World Championships (1930, 1932–35).

★ **Most badminton World Championships titles**
A record five titles have been won by Park Joo-bong (South Korea), for the men's doubles in 1985 and 1991 and mixed doubles in 1985, 1989 and 1991.

★ **Most mixed team badminton World Championship wins**
The most wins at the mixed world team badminton championships for the Sudirman Cup (instituted in 1989) is four by China, in 1995, 1997, 1999, 2001.

★ **Most badminton World Cup women's singles wins**
Susi Susanti (Indonesia) won five World Cup women's singles tournaments in 1989, 1993–94 and 1996–97.

★ **Most badminton Thomas Cup wins**
The most wins at the men's world team badminton championships for the Thomas Cup (instituted in 1948) is 13 by Indonesia (1958, 1961, 1964, 1970, 1973, 1976, 1979, 1984, 1994, 1996, 1998, 2000 and 2002).

★ **Most badminton World Championship singles titles**
Four Chinese players have each won two individual world titles. Yang Yang won the men's singles in 1987 and 1989, and the women's singles have been won by Li Lingwei in 1983 and 1989; by Han Aiping in 1985 and 1987; and by Ye Zhaoying in 1995 and 1997.

★ **Longest badminton match in competition**
In the final of the men's singles at the 1997 World Championships at Glasgow, UK, on 1 June, Peter Rasmussen (Denmark) beat Sun Jun (China) 16–17, 18–13, 15–10 in a match that lasted 2 hr 4 min.

★ **Shortest badminton match**
Ra Kyung-min (South Korea) beat Julia Mann (England) 11–2, 11–1 in 6 minutes during the Uber Cup in Hong Kong on 19 May 1996.

★ **Oldest badminton player**
Henry Paynter (Canada, b. 24 February 1907) is an active member of the Kelowna Badminton Club, British Columbia, Canada, and was still playing regularly in March 2004, aged 97.

★ **Highest speed of a shuttlecock off a badminton racket**
In tests at Warwickshire Racquets and Health Club, UK, on 5 November 1996, Simon Archer (UK) hit a shuttlecock at a measured speed of 260 km/h (162 mph).

★ **Longest table tennis singles marathon**
The longest marathon singles match was 132 hr 31 min by Danny Price and Randy Nunes (both USA) at Cherry Hill, New Jersey, USA, on 20–26 August 1978.

★ **Longest table tennis doubles marathon**
On 9–13 April 1979, Lance, Phil, and Mark Warren and Bill Weir (all USA) played doubles table tennis for 101 hr 1 min 11 sec at Sacramento, California, USA,

★ **Most women's table tennis World Championships**
Angelica Rozeanu (Romania) won a record six consecutive women's singles table tennis World Championship titles from 1950 to 1955.

★ **Longest table tennis rally**
John Duffy and Kevin Schick (both New Zealand) achieved a table tennis rally lasting 5 hr 2 min 18.5 sec at Whangarei, New Zealand, on 5 November 1977.

★ **Most combined team wins at the racquetball World Championships**
The World Championships were instituted in 1981, have been held biennially since 1984 and are based on the US version of the game. The USA has won a record ten combined team titles, in 1981, 1984, 1986 (tie with Canada), 1988, 1990, 1992, 1994, 1996, 1998 and 2002.

Most men's World team squash titles ⌃

Australia have won eight men's world team titles, in 1967, 1969, 1971, 1973, 1989, 1991, 2001 and 2003. David Palmer (Australia, above) was one of the players in the 2001 World Championship team.

★ **Most women's racquetball World Championship wins**
The most women's racquetball World Championships won by an individual is three by Michelle Gould (USA) in 1992, 1994 and 1996.

★ **Most women's team wins at the racquetball World Championships**
The USA has won nine women's team titles, in 1986, 1988, 1990, 1992, 1994, 1996, 1998, 2000 and 2002.

★ **Most wheelchair racquetball World Championships**
Chip Parmelly (USA) won a record three wheelchair racquetball World Championships, in 1990, 1992 and 1994.

★ **Most men's Real Tennis World Championships**
The first recorded Real Tennis world champion was Clerg (France) in c. 1740. Jacques Edmond Barre (France) held the title for a record 33 years from 1829 to 1962. Pierre Etchebaster (France) holds the record for the greatest number of successful defences of the title with eight during his career (1928–52).

★ **Most women's Real Tennis World Championships**
Instituted in 1985, the women's World Championships has been won six times by Penny Lumley (née Fellows, UK) in 1989, 1991, 1995, 1997, 1999 and 2003.

★ **Oldest Real Tennis court**
The oldest of the surviving active Real Tennis courts in Great Britain is that at Falkland Palace, Fife, built by King James V of Scotland in 1539.

★ **Most squash World Open Championship titles**
Jansher Khan (Pakistan) won a record eight World Open titles, in 1987, 1989, 1990 and 1992–96.

★ **Most squash club championships**
The most club championships won by an individual at the same club is 21 (including a record 17 consecutively) by Carole Cameron (UK) at the Thurso and District Squash Club, Thurso, Caithness, UK, in 1982–85 and 1987–2003.

★ **Most squash World Championships**
Jahangir Khan (Pakistan) won six World Open titles, in 1981–85 and 1988. He has also won the International Squash Rackets Federation world individual title three times, in 1979, 1983 and 1985.

★ **Most women's squash World Championship wins**
The women's title has been won seven times by Australia, in 1981, 1983, 1992, 1994, 1996, 1998 and 2002.

★ **Most women's world team titles for squash**
Sarah Fitzgerald (Australia) has won five women's World Open titles, in 1996–98 and 2001–02.

★ **Longest squash match**
The longest recorded competitive match was one of 2 hr 45 min when Jahangir Khan (Pakistan) beat Gamal Awad (Egypt) 9–10, 9–5, 9–7, 9–2, the first game lasting a record 1 hr 11 min, in the final of the Patrick International Festival at Chichester, West Sussex, UK, on 30 March 1983.

★ **Highest speed of a squash ball**
In tests at Wimbledon Squash and Badminton Club in January 1988, Roy Buckland hit a squash ball by an overhead service at a measured speed of 232.7 km/h (144.6 mph) over the distance to the front wall. This is equivalent to an initial speed at the racket of 242.6 km/h (150.8 mph).

Most men's gold >> medals in the athletics World Championships

The World Championships were inaugurated in 1983, when they were held in Helsinki, Finland. The greatest number of World Championship men's gold medals won by an individual is nine, by Michael Johnson (USA, right), who won the 200 m in 1991 and 1995, the 400 m in 1993, 1995, 1997 and 1999, and the 4 x 400-m relay in 1993, 1995 and 1999.

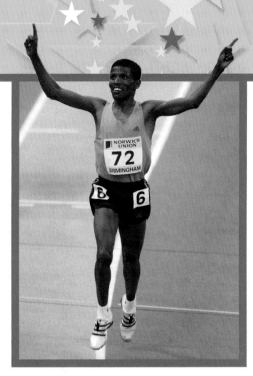

Fastest 10,000 m ⌃

Haile Gebrselassie (Ethiopia, above) ran 26:22.75 for the men's 10,000-m event at Hengelo, The Netherlands, on 1 June 1998. He also holds the record for the fastest 5,000 m (12:39.36).

Men's indoor world records

Event	Record	Name & nationality	Venue	Date
TRACK				
50 m	5.56	Donovan Bailey (Canada)	Reno, USA	9 February 1996
		Maurice Greene (USA)	Los Angeles, USA	3 February 1999
60 m	6.39	Maurice Greene (USA)	Madrid, Spain	3 February 1998
		Maurice Greene (USA)	Atlanta, USA	3 March 2001
200 m	19.92	Frank Fredericks (Namibia)	Liévin, France	18 February 1996
400 m	44.63	Michael Johnson (USA)	Atlanta, USA	4 March 1995
800 m	1:42.67	Wilson Kipketer (Denmark)	Paris, France	9 March 1997
1,000 m	2:14.36	Wilson Kipketer (Denmark)	Birmingham, UK	20 February 2000
1,500 m	3:31.18	Hicham El Guerrouj (Morocco)	Stuttgart, Germany	2 February 1997
1 mile	3:48.45	Hicham El Guerrouj (Morocco)	Ghent, Belgium	12 February 1997
3,000 m	7:24.90	Daniel Komen (Kenya)	Budapest, Hungary	6 February 1998
5,000 m	12:49.60*	Kenenisa Bekele (Ethiopia)	Birmingham, UK	20 February 2004
50-m hurdles	6.25	Mark McCoy (Canada)	Kobe, Japan	5 March 1986
60-m hurdles	7.30	Colin Jackson (GB)	Sindelfingen, Germany	6 March 1994
4 x 200-m relay	1:22.11	Great Britain (Linford Christie, Darren Braithwaite, Ade Mafe, John Regis)	Glasgow, UK	3 March 1991
4 x 400-m relay	3:02.83	USA (Andre Morris, Dameon Johnson, Deon Minor, Milton Campbell)	Maebashi, Japan	7 March 1999
5,000-m walk	18:07.08	Mikhail Shchennikov (Russia)	Moscow, Russia	14 February 1995
FIELD				
High jump	2.43 m (7 ft 11.6 in)	Javier Sotomayor (Cuba)	Budapest, Hungary	4 March 1989
Pole vault	6.15 m (20 ft 2 in)	Sergei Bubka (Ukraine)	Donetsk, Ukraine	21 February 1993
Long jump	8.79 m (28 ft 9.96 in)	Carl Lewis (USA)	New York City, USA	27 January 1984
Triple jump	17.83 m (58 ft 5 in)	Aliecer Urrutia (Cuba)	Sindelfingen, Germany	1 March 1997
Shot-put	22.66 m (74 ft 4 in)	Randy Barnes (USA)	Los Angeles, USA	20 January 1989
Heptathlon	6,476 points	Dan O'Brien (USA) Events: 60 m 6.67 sec; long jump 7.84 m (25 ft 6.2 in); shot-put 16.02 m (52 ft 6.6 in); high jump 2.13 m (6 ft 11.76 in); 60-m hurdles 7.85 sec; pole vault 5.20 m (17 ft 0.7 in); 1,000 m 2:57.96	Toronto, Canada	13–14 March 1993

*From 1 January 1987, the International Athletics Association Federation (IAAF) recognized world indoor records. Prior to that, the best performances had been noted as world bests. After this date, performances needed to better the world best performances to be officially accepted by the IAAF as records.

★ **Most women's gold medals in the athletics World Championships**
Gail Devers (USA) won five World Championship gold medals: for the 100 m in 1993, the 100-m hurdles in 1993, 1995 and 1999, and for the 4 x 100-m in 1997.

★ **Most men's successive World Championship athletics wins in a single event**
Sergei Bubka (Ukraine) won six athletics World Championships in the pole vault event between 1983 and 1997.

★ **Most women's athletics World Championship medals**
Merlene Ottey (Jamaica) won 14 athletics World Championship medals between 1983 and 1997: gold for 200 m in 1993 and 1995 and 4 x 100-m in 1991; silver for 100 m in 1993 and 1995, 200 m in 1983 and 4 x 100-m in 1991; and bronze for 100 m in 1987 and 1991, 200 m in 1987, 1991 and 1997, and the 4 x 100-m in 1983 and 1993.

Most men's athletics ⌃ Olympic medals

Paavo Nurmi (Finland, above right) won 12 Olympic medals (nine gold and three silver) in the Games of 1920, 1924 and 1928.

★ Most men's athletics World Championship medals

Carl Lewis (USA) won a total of 10 World Championship medals. He won eight gold medals – for the 100 m, long jump and 4 x 100-m relay in 1983; the 100 m, long jump and 4 x 100-m relay in 1987; and the 100 m and 4 x 100-m relay in 1991 – as well as silver for the long jump in 1991 and bronze for the 200 m in 1993.

★ Most men's athletics Olympic gold medals

Raymond Clarence Ewry (USA) won 10 Olympic gold medals, in the standing high, long and triple jumps in 1900, 1904, 1906 and 1908.

★ Most women's athletics Olympic gold medals

The most gold medals won by a woman is four, shared by: Francina 'Fanny' Elsje Blankers-Koen (Netherlands) for the 100 m, 200 m, 80-m hurdles and the 4 x 100-m relay, in 1948; Elizabeth 'Betty'

Cuthbert (Australia) for the 100 m, 200 m and 4 x 100-m relay in 1956 and the 400 m in 1964; Bärbel Wöckel (GDR) in the 200 m and 4 x 100-m relay in 1976 and 1980; and Evelyn Ashford (USA) in the 100 m in 1984 and the 4 x 100-m relay in 1984, 1988 and 1992.

★ Most athletics Olympic gold medals in one Games

Paavo Nurmi (Finland) won five gold medals in 1924: in the men's 1,500 m, 5,000 m, 10,000-m cross-country and

the 3,000-m team and cross-country team events.

The most medals won in individual events is four by Alvin Christian Kraenzlein (USA), who won the men's 60 m, 110-m hurdles, 200-m hurdles and long jump in 1900.

★ Most women's athletics Olympic medals

Three women athletes share this record: Shirley Barbara de la Hunty (Australia) won seven medals – three gold, one silver and three bronze – in the 1948, 1952 and 1956 Games.

A re-read of the photo-finish indicates that she finished third, not fourth, in the 1948 200-m event, thus unofficially increasing her medal haul to eight. Irena Szewinska (Poland) won a total of seven medals – three gold, two silver and two bronze – in 1964, 1968, 1972 and 1976, and is the only woman athlete to win a medal in four successive Games. Merlene Ottey (Jamaica) has also won seven medals – two silver and five bronze – in 1980, 1984, 1992 and 1996.

Men's outdoor world records

Event	Record	Name & nationality	Venue	Date
TRACK				
100 m	9.78	Tim Montgomery (USA)	Paris, France	14 September 2002
200 m	19.32	Michael Johnson (USA)	Atlanta, USA	1 August 1996
400 m	43.18	Michael Johnson (USA)	Seville, Spain,	26 August 1999
800 m	1:41.11	Wilson Kipketer (Denmark)	Cologne, Germany	24 August 1997
1,000 m	2:11.96	Noah Ngeny (Kenya)	Rieti, Italy	5 September 1999
1,500 m	3:26.00	Hicham El Guerrouj (Morocco)	Rome, Italy	14 July 1998
1 mile	3:43.13	Hicham El Guerrouj (Morocco)	Rome, Italy	7 July 1999
2,000 m	4:44.79	Hicham El Guerrouj (Morocco)	Berlin, Germany	7 September 1999
3,000 m	7:20.67	Daniel Komen (Kenya)	Rieti, Italy	1 September 1996
5,000 m	12:39.36	Haile Gebrselassie (Ethiopia)	Helsinki, Finland	13 June 1998
10,000 m	26:22.75	Haile Gebrselassie (Ethiopia)	Hengelo, The Netherlands	1 June 1998
20,000 m	56:55.60	Arturo Barrios (Mexico, now USA)	La Flèche, France	30 March 1991
25,000 m	1:13:55.80	Toshihiko Seko (Japan)	Christchurch, New Zealand	22 March 1981
30,000 m	1:29:18.80	Toshihiko Seko (Japan)	Christchurch, New Zealand	22 March 1981
1 hour	21,101 m	Arturo Barrios (Mexico, now USA)	La Flèche, France	30 March 1991
110-m hurdles	12.91	Colin Jackson (GB)	Stuttgart, Germany	20 August 1993
400-m hurdles	46.78	Kevin Young (USA)	Barcelona, Spain	6 August 1992
3,000-m steeplechase	7:55.28	Brahim Boulami (Morocco)	Brussels, Belgium	24 August 2001
4 x 100-m relay	37.40	USA (Michael Marsh, Leroy Burrell, Dennis Mitchell, Carl Lewis)	Barcelona, Spain	8 August 1992
		USA (John Drummond, Andre Cason, Dennis Mitchell, Leroy Burrell)	Stuttgart, Germany	21 August 1993
4 x 200-m relay	1:18.68	USA (Michael Marsh, Leroy Burrell, Floyd Heard, Carl Lewis)	Santa Monica Track Club, Walnut, USA	17 April 1994
4 x 400-m relay	2:54.20	USA (Jerome Young, Antonio Pettigrew, Tyree Washington, Michael Johnson)	New York City, USA	23 July 1998
4 x 800-m relay	7:03.89	Great Britain (Peter Elliott, Garry Cook, Steve Cram, Sebastian Coe)	London, UK	30 August 1982
4 x 1,500-m relay	14:38.80	West Germany (Thomas Wessinghage, Harald Hudak, Michael Lederer, Karl Fleschen)	Cologne, Germany	17 August 1977
FIELD				
High jump	2.45 m (8 ft 0.25 in)	Javier Sotomayor (Cuba)	Salamanca, Spain	27 July 1993
Pole vault	6.14 m (20 ft 1.68 in)	Sergei Bubka (Ukraine)	Sestriere, Italy	31 July 1994
Long jump	8.95 m (29 ft 4.32 in)	Mike Powell (USA)	Tokyo, Japan	30 August 1991
Triple jump	18.29 m (60 ft)	Jonathan Edwards (GB)	Gothenburg, Sweden	7 August 1995
Shot-put	23.12 m (75 ft 10.2 in)	Randy Barnes (USA)	Los Angeles, USA	20 May 1990
Discus	74.08 m (243 ft)	Jürgen Schult (GDR)	Neubrandenburg, Germany	6 June 1986
Hammer	86.74 m (284 ft 7 in)	Yuriy Sedykh (USSR)	Stuttgart, Germany	30 August 1986
Javelin	98.48 m (323 ft 1 in)	Jan Zelezny (Czech Republic)	Jena, Germany	25 May 1996
Decathlon	9,026 points	Roman Sebrle (Czech Republic)	Götzis, Austria	26–27 May 2001
Day 1:		Events: 100 m 10.64 sec; long jump 8.11 m (26 ft 7.25 in); shot-put 15.33 m (50 ft 3.7 in); high jump 2.12 m (6 ft 11.4 in)		
Day 2:		110-m hurdles 13.92 sec; discus 47.92 m (157 ft 2.5 in); pole vault 4.80 m (15 ft 9 in); javelin 70.16 m (230 ft 2 in); 1,500 m 4:21.98		

Fastest man
Sport

The men's 100 m is a classic record that holds a unique place in sport, with the record holder arguably able to claim the title of world's fastest man. The history of this event encompasses many of the greatest names in athletics.

10.2 seconds

In the first edition of *Guinness World Records* (formerly *The Guinness Book of Records*), in 1955 the record for the men's 100 m was 10.2 seconds and was jointly held by six athletes: Jesse Owens (USA, who ran this time in 1936), Harold Davis (USA, 1941), Lloyd LaBeach (USA, 1948), Norwood 'Barney' Ewell (USA, 1948), McDonald Bailey (Trinidad, 1951) and Heinz Fütterer (West Germany, 1954).

Unlike today, many records set before January 1977 were hand-timed using stopwatches that were accurate to the nearest tenth of a second. This meant that an athlete needed to break the record by a clear tenth of a second to set a new record, increasing the odds of joint record holders. Today, automatic electronic timers accurately register up to one hundredth of a second, meaning that it is possible to ratify records with smaller margins than ever before.

In 1956 two further names were added to the 10.2-second record: Americans Bobby Morrow and Ira Murchison both ran times of 10.2 seconds that year. The 10.2-second barrier was finally breached in August 1956 by Willie Williams (USA), and his time of 10.1 seconds was equalled by four other athletes before the 10-second time was eventually set by Armin Hary (West Germany) in 1960.

Under 10 seconds

Electronic timing was introduced at the Mexico Olympics in 1968. The first athlete to have his electronically timed run recognized by the International Athletics Association Federation (IAAF) as a record was Jim Hines (USA), who ran 9.95 seconds for Olympic gold. The IAAF recognized Hines' 9.95 time, but continued to recognize the other 11 athletes who shared or equalled the existing record of 9.9 seconds, until Carl Lewis (USA) ran the 100 m in an amazing time of 9.86 seconds in 1991.

A record-breaking decade

The 1980s saw extraordinary 100-m runs. Calvin Smith (USA) ran 9.93 seconds in 1983 and Carl Lewis equalled this time in 1987 before running a new time of 9.92 at the Seoul Olympics in 1988. Lewis actually finished in the silver medal position behind Ben Johnson (Canada) at the Olympic final, but Johnson failed the subsequent drugs test, and his 9.79 time was disqualified, allowing Lewis to take gold. During the race, Lewis looked over at Johnson three times, which cost him a precious hundredth of a second.

Rivalry

The next six years marked a great rivalry between Carl Lewis and Leroy Burrell (USA), and further hundredths of a second were shaved off the record. Burrell set a new time for the 100 m on 14 June 1991 in New York with 9.90 seconds, but Lewis snatched it back later that year with a new record of 9.86. This race at the World Championships in Tokyo was rated as one of the greatest 100 m of all time, with six athletes beating 10 seconds, and the top two (Lewis and Burrell) beating the listed world record. Burrell broke the record again in 1994 running a time of 9.85, but lost it to Donovan Bailey (Canada) in July 1996 with a time of 9.84. Bailey won this race with an incredible final burst of speed; he was only in fifth place at 50 m, but had moved up to first place by the 90-m mark.

Maurice Greene (USA) dominated the 100 m for the following three years, culminating with his 9.79-second run in June 1999.

Fastest man on Earth

Maurice Green's record was finally broken by Tim Montgomery (USA) on 14 September 2002 in Paris at the IAAF Grand Prix final. Montgomery flew out of the starting blocks, winning in 9.78 seconds (0.42 seconds faster than the record set by Jesse Owens in 1936) and running at an average speed of 36.8 km/h (22.9 mph).

1936
Jesse Owens 10.2 seconds

1960
Armin Hary 10 seconds

1968
Jim Hines 9.95 seconds

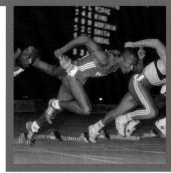

1983
Calvin Smith 9.93 seconds

Men's 100-m record breakers

Time	Athlete	Date	Venue
10.2	Jesse Owens (USA)	20 June 1936	Chicago
10.1	Willie Williams (USA)	3 August 1956	Berlin
10.0	Armin Hary (West Germany)	21 June 1960	Zurich
9.9	Jim Hines (USA)	20 June 1968	Sacramento
9.95	Jim Hines (USA)	14 October 1968	Mexico City
9.93	Calvin Smith (USA)	3 July 1983	Colorado
9.92	Carl Lewis (USA)	24 September 1988	Seoul
9.90	Leroy Burrell (USA)	14 June 1991	New York
9.86	Carl Lewis (USA)	25 August 1991	Tokyo
9.85	Leroy Burrell (USA)	6 July 1994	Lausanne
9.84	Donovan Bailey (Canada)	27 July 1996	Atlanta
9.79	Maurice Greene (USA)	16 June 1999	Athens
9.78	Tim Montgomery (USA)	14 September 2002	Paris

★ GWR TALKS TO
Tim Montgomery

When did you realize that you wanted to pursue a career in athletics?
As a very young child, I knew that I was athletic and pretty fast, but I didn't look at it as the profession for me until later on in my life. I remember when I had to cut the grass and I would run around our huge yard and overexert myself until I would just pass out! I guess I was about 14 when people began to recognize that I had great potential to be a top-class athlete.

Who encouraged you?
My mother was always a great source of motivation and support. She encouraged me to dream big and reach for anything I desired. I also received encouragement from coaches, teachers and many other people.

What's your typical training day?
Very strenuous. We practise six days a week for several hours a day. Every day varies. One day we may be doing intervals and blocks/starts and the next day we have running drills followed by weight training.

Do you have to follow a special diet?
Not really. I train really hard so I don't have to diet. But you have to be sensible and eat healthily or else it could jeopardize your training. I will say, however, that I'm a big fan of pizza!

What do you consider to be your greatest achievement?
The world record is very important to me. I can't describe what it feels like to know that you have beat everyone in the world and that you can be considered the best on the entire planet! Another favourite moment was when I set the world junior record in 1994.

Is it true that you once competed in borrowed shoes and still won?
Yes! My luggage got lost and I had to borrow Marion Jones's shoes. That definitely has to be the most hilarious and odd thing that has ever happened to me.

What does being a record holder mean to you?
To know that you hold one of the most coveted titles in the sport makes you feel like you can touch the sky. It has been a confirmation that if you work hard and be persistent and keep the faith you can overcome even the greatest obstacles.

Who was your idol when you were growing up?
Muhammad Ali. I loved everything about him: his gracefulness in the ring, his attitude, his athletic ability... everything!

What are your future goals?
I'd love to break my own record! On a personal level, I'd like to start up and run the Tim Montgomery Foundation to help young people reach their goals and overcome adversity and other challenges in life.

What advice would you give to youngsters who want to pursue a career in athletics?
If you believe in yourself, what other people think won't matter. If you want to play a sport or break a record, there is nothing stopping you except you.

What gives you your drive?
God, my family and myself. With those three things, I can and will reach all my goals.

2002
Tim Montgomery 9.78 seconds

1991
Carl Lewis 9.86 seconds

1996
Donovan Bailey 9.84 seconds

1999
Maurice Greene 9.79 seconds

Women's outdoor world records

Event	Record	Name & nationality	Venue	Date
TRACK				
100 m	10.49	Florence Griffith-Joyner (USA)	Indianapolis, USA	16 July 1998
200 m	21.34	Florence Griffith-Joyner (USA)	Seoul, South Korea	29 September 1988
400 m	47.60	Marita Koch (GDR)	Canberra, Australia	6 October 1985
800 m	1:53.28	Jarmila Kratochvílová (Czechoslovakia)	Munich, Germany	26 July 1983
1,000 m	2:28.98	Svetlana Masterkova (Russia)	Brussels, Belgium	23 August 1996
1,500 m	3:50.46	Qu Yunxia (China)	Beijing, China	11 September 1993
1 mile	4:12.56	Svetlana Masterkova (Russia)	Zurich, Switzerland	14 August 1996
2,000 m	5:25.36	Sonia O'Sullivan (Ireland)	Edinburgh, UK	8 July 1994
3,000 m	8:06.11	Wang Junxia (China)	Beijing, China	13 September 1993
5,000 m	14:28.09	Jiang Bo (China)	Beijing, China	23 October 1997
10,000 m	29:31.78	Wang Junxia (China)	Beijing, China	8 September 1993
20,000 m	1:05:26.60	Tegla Loroupe (Kenya)	Borgholzhausen, Germany	3 September 2000
25,000 m	1:27:05.90	Tegla Loroupe (Kenya)	Megerkirchen, Germany	21 September 2002
30,000 m	1:45:50.00	Tegla Loroupe (Kenya)	Warstein, Germany	6 June 2003
1 hour	18,340 m	Tegla Loroupe (Kenya)	Borgholzhausen, Germany	7 August 1998
100-m hurdles	12.21	Yordanka Donkova (Bulgaria)	Stara Zagora, Bulgaria	20 August 1988
400-m hurdles	52.34	Yuliya Pechonkina (Russia)	Tula, Russia	8 August 2003
3,000-m steeplechase	9:08.33	Gulnara Samitova (Russia)	Tula, Russia	10 August 2003
4 x 100-m relay	41.37	GDR (Silke Gladisch, Sabine Rieger, Ingrid Auerswald, Marlies Göhr)	Canberra, Australia	6 October 1985
4 x 200-m relay	1:27.46	USA 'Blue' (LaTasha Jenkins, Latasha Colander Richardson, Nanceen Perry, Marion Jones)	Philadelphia, USA	29 April 2000
4 x 400-m relay	3:15.17	USSR (Tatyana Ledovskaya, Olga Nazarova, Maria Pinigina, Olga Bryzgina)	Seoul, South Korea	1 October 1988
4 x 800-m relay	7:50.17	USSR (Nadezhda Olizarenko, Lyubov Gurina, Lyudmila Borisova, Irina Podyalovskaya)	Moscow, Russia	5 August 1984
FIELD				
High jump	2.09 m (6 ft 10.25 in)	Stefka Kostadinova (Bulgaria)	Rome, Italy	30 August 1987
Pole vault	4.82 m (15 ft 9.75 in)	Yelena Isinbayeva (Russia)	Gateshead, UK	13 July 2003
Long jump	7.52 m (24 ft 8.25 in)	Galina Chistyakova (USSR)	St Petersburg, Russia	1 June 1988
Triple jump	15.50 m (50 ft 10.25 in)	Inessa Kravets (Ukraine)	Gothenburg, Sweden	10 August 1995
Shot-put	22.63 m (74 ft 3 in)	Natalya Lisovskaya (USSR)	Moscow, Russia	7 June 1987
Discus	76.80 m (252 ft)	Gabriele Reinsch (GDR)	Neubrandenburg, Germany	9 July 1988
Javelin	71.54 m (234 ft 8 in)	Osleidys Menéndez (Cuba)	Réthymno, Greece	1 July 2001
Heptathlon	7,291 points	Jacqueline Joyner-Kersee (USA) Events: 100-m hurdles 12.69 sec; high jump 1.86 m (6 ft 1.25 in); shot-put 15.80 m (51 ft 10 in); 200 m 22.56 sec; long jump 7.27 m (23 ft 10.25 in); javelin 45.66 m (149 ft 10 in); 800 m 2:8.51 sec	Seoul, South Korea	23–24 September 1988

Most successive wins by a woman in the athletics World Championships

Astrid Kumbernuss (Germany, right) won three successive shot-put events between 1995 and 1999.

★ **Fastest 100 x 1-mile relay**
The record for 100 miles (160 km) by 100 runners is 7 hr 35 min 55.4 sec by the Canadian Milers Athletic Club at York University, Toronto, Ontario, Canada, on 20 December 1998.
The equivalent women's record was set by the Canadian Women's Milers Club who completed a 100 x 1-mile relay in a time of 9 hr 23 min 39 sec on 27 December 1999.

★ **Most athletics world records set on one day**
Jesse Owens (USA) set six world records in 45 minutes at Ann Arbor, Michigan, USA, on 25 May 1935 with a 9.4-sec 100 yd at 3:15 pm, a 8.13-m-long (26-ft 8.25-in) jump at 3:25 pm, a 20.3-sec 220 yd (and 200 m) at 3:45 pm, and a 22.6-sec 220-yd low hurdles at 4 pm (which also included a record for the 200-m hurdles).

★ **Longest winning sequence in a track event**
Ed Moses (USA) dominated the men's 400-m hurdling event for almost 10 years. His record of 122 consecutive wins began on 2 September 1977 and ended when he was beaten by Danny Harris (USA) in Madrid, Spain, on 4 June 1987.

★ **Longest winning sequence in a field event**
Iolanda Balas (Romania) won 150 consecutive competitions at high jump from 1956 to 1967.

★ **Greatest standing long jump**
The farthest long jump from a standing position is 3.71 m (12 ft 2 in) by Arne Tvervaag (Norway) in 1968.

The women's best is 2.92 m (9 ft 7 in) by Annelin Mannes (Norway) at Flisa, Norway, on 7 March 1981.

★ **Greatest standing high jump**
The greatest high jump from a standing position is 1.90 m (6 ft 2.75 in) by Rune Almen (Sweden) at Karlstad, Sweden, on 3 May 1980.
The women's best is 1.52 m (4 ft 11.75 in) achieved by Grete Bjordalsbakka (Norway) in 1984.

★ **Fastest 1,000-mile relay by a team of 10**
Willie Mtolo, Graham Meyer, Jan van Rooyen, Dimitri Grishine, Daniel Radebe, Pio Mpolokeng, Oliver Kandiero, Frans Moyo, Simon Mele and Philip Molefi (all South Africa) ran a 1,000-mile (1,600-km) relay from Cape Town to Johannesburg, South Africa, in 99 hr 3 min 27 sec from 14 to 18 August 2002.

★ **Fastest men's 100 x 1,000-m relay**
A team from the Centro Universitario Sportivo, Bari, Italy, completed a 100 x 1,000-m relay in 5 hr 13 min 21.9 sec on 14 March 1999.

★ **Most participants in a relay race**
A total of 7,175 runners (287 teams of 25) participated in the Batavierenrace from Nijmegen to Enschede, The Netherlands, on 24 April 1999.

Fastest women's indoor 800 m ⌃

Jolanda Ceplak (Slovenia, above) set a new record for the women's indoor 800-m event on 3 March 2002 in Vienna, Austria, with a time of 1 min 55.82 sec.

Women's indoor world records

Event	Record	Name & nationality	Venue	Date
TRACK				
50 m	5.96	Irina Privalova (Russia)	Madrid, Spain	9 February 1995
60 m	6.92	Irina Privalova (Russia)	Madrid, Spain	11 February 1993 9 February 1995
200 m	21.87	Merlene Ottey (Jamaica)	Liévin, France	13 February 1993
400 m	49.59	Jarmila Kratochvílová (Czechoslovakia)	Milan, Italy	7 March 1982
800 m	1:55.82	Jolanda Ceplak (Slovenia)	Vienna, Austria	3 March 2002
1,000 m	2:30.94	Maria Mutola (Mozambique)	Stockholm, Sweden	25 February 1999
1,500 m	3:59.98	Regina Jacobs (USA)	Boston, USA	2 February 2003
1 mile	4:17.14	Doina Melinte (Romania)	East Rutherford, USA	9 February 1990
3,000 m	8:29.15	Berhane Adere (Ethiopia)	Stuttgart, Garmany	3 February 2002
5,000 m	14:39.29	Berhane Adere (Ethiopia)	Stuttgart, Germany	31 January 2004
50-m hurdles	6.58	Cornelia Oschkenat (GDR)	Berlin, Germany	20 February 1988
60-m hurdles	7.69	Lyudmila Engquist (Russia)	Chelyabinsk, Russia	4 February 1993
4 x 200-m relay	1:32.55	SC Eintracht Hamm (Helga Arendt, Silke-Beate Knoll, Mechthild Kluth, Gisela Kinzel, all West Germany) LG Olympia Dortmund Karlsruhe (Esther Möller, Gabi Rockmeier, Birgit Rockmeier, Andrea Philipp, all Germany)	Dortmund, Germany Germany	19 February 1988 21 February 1999
4 x 400-m relay	3:24.25	Russia (Tatyana Chebykina, Svetlana Goncharenko, Olga Kotlyarova, Natalya Nazarova)	Maebashi, Japan	7 March 1999
3,000-m walk	11:40.33	Claudia Iovan (Romania)	Bucharest, Romania	30 January 1999
FIELD				
High jump	2.07 m (6 ft 9.5 in)	Heike Henkel (Germany)	Karlsruhe, Germany	9 February 1992
Pole vault	4.85 m (15 ft 11 in)	Svetlana Feofanova (Russia)	Athens, Greece	22 February 2004
Long jump	7.37 m (24 ft 2.25 in)	Heike Drechsler (GDR)	Vienna, Austria	13 February 1988
Triple jump	15.16 m (49 ft 9 in)	Ashia Hansen (GB)	Valencia, Spain	28 February 1998
Shot-put	22.50 m (73 ft 10 in)	Helena Fibingerová (Czechoslovakia)	Jablonec, Czechoslovakia	19 February 1977
Pentathlon	4,991 points	Irina Belova (Russia) Events: 60-m hurdles 8.22 sec; high jump 1.93 m (6 ft 4 in); shot-put 13.25 m (43 ft 5.75 in); long jump 6.67 m (21 ft 10.75 in); 800 m 2:10.26	Berlin, Germany	14–15 February 1992

★ **Most athletics Indoor World Championship medals**

Merlene Ottey (Jamaica) won six Indoor World Championship medals in individual events: three gold (60 m in 1995 and 200 m in 1989 and 1991), two silver (60 m in 1991 and 200 m in 1987) and one bronze (60 m in 1989).

The men's record is five medals and is held jointly by Ivan Pedroso (Cuba), for the long jump (gold in 1993, 1995, 1997, 1999 and 2001) and Javier Sotomayor (Cuba) for the high jump (gold in 1989, 1993, 1995 and 1999 and bronze in 1991).

★ **Greatest average mileage run daily**

During the year from 1 August 1996 to 31 July 1997, Tirtha Kumar Phani (India) ran every day, running 22,565.76 km (14,021.7 miles) in total. This equates to an average of 61.824 km (38.41 miles) per day.

Highest altitude marathon

The biennial Everest Marathon, ≪
which was first run on 27 November
1987, begins at Gorak Shep at an altitude of 5,212 m (17,100 ft),
and ends at Namche Bazar at 3,444 m (11,300 ft). The men's
record is 3 hr 56 min 10 sec by Hari Roka (Nepal), set in 1999,
and the women's record is 5 hr 16 min 3 sec, set by Anne
Stentiford (UK) in 1997.

Men's ultra-long distance world records

Event	Record	Name, nationality & venue	Date
100 km	6:10:20	Don Ritchie (GB), London, UK	28 October 1978
100 miles	11:30:51	Don Ritchie (GB), London, UK	15 October 1977
1,000 km	5 days 16:17:00	Yiannis Kouros (Greece), Colac, Australia	26 November–1 December 1984
1,000 miles	11 days 13:54:58	Piotr Silikin (Lithuania), Nanango, Australia	11–23 March 1998
24 hours	303.506 km (188.589 miles)	Yiannis Kouros (Australia), Adelaide, Australia	4–5 October 1997
6 days	1,022.068 km (635.083 miles)	Yiannis Kouros (Greece), New York, USA	2–8 July 1984

Women's ultra-long distance world records

Event	Record	Name, nationality & venue	Date
100 km	7:23:28	Valentina Liakhova (Russia), Nantes, France	28 September 1996
100 miles	14:29:44	Ann Trason (USA), Santa Rosa, USA	18–19 March 1989
1,000 km	8 days 00:27:06	Eleanor Robinson (GB), Nanango, Australia	11–18 March 1998
1,000 miles	13 days 01:54:02	Eleanor Robinson (GB), Nanango, Australia	11–24 March 1998
24 hours	240.169 km (149.234 miles)	Eleanor Adams (GB), Melbourne, Australia	19–20 August 1989

★ **Most individual medals won at half marathon World Championships**
The most individual medals won at the IAAF Half Marathon World Championships is eight by Lidia Simon-Slavuteanu (Romania). Between 1996 and 2000 she won three team gold, one team silver, one individual silver and three individual bronze. The men's record is five medals by Hendrick Ramaala (South Africa) – two team gold, one team silver and two individual silver between 1997 and 1999.

★ **Most team wins in the half marathon World Championships**
The most team wins at the IAAF Half Marathon World Championships is seven for men by Kenya (1992–95, 1997, 2000, 2002), and six for women by Romania (1993–97, 2000).

★ **Largest half marathon**
The world's largest half marathon is The BUPA Great North Run between Newcastle-upon-Tyne and South Shields, Tyne and Wear, UK. For the 2000 event held on 22 October, there were 36,822 finishers out of 50,173 entries.

★ **Fastest half marathon speed march**
William MacLennan (UK) completed a half marathon wearing full military combat gear and carrying an 18-kg (40-lb) backpack, in 1 hr 43 min 42 sec at the Redcar Half Marathon, North Yorkshire, UK, on 25 March 2001.

★ **Most marathons run in a calendar year**
The most marathons completed in one year is 100 by Angela Gargano (Italy). Starting with the Dubai Marathon on 11 January 2002, she went on to run 99 more, the last of which was the Maratona di San Silvestro, Italy, on 31 December 2002.

★ **Fastest aggregate time to run a marathon on each continent**
Between 13 February and 23 May 1999, Tim Rogers (UK) ran a marathon on each of the seven continents in an aggregate time of 34 hr 23 min 8 sec. The attempt took 99 days to complete, which is also a record for the shortest duration.

The women's world record is 37 hr 20 sec by Kimi Puntillo (USA), who ran them all between 3 November 1996 and 4 October 1998. The attempt took 700 days to complete – a record in itself.

Fastest 25-km ⌃⌃ and 30-km road races

Naoko Takahashi (Japan, above) ran the 25-km women's road race in Berlin, Germany, in 1 hr 22 min 31 sec on 30 September 2001. At the same event, she also set the record for the 30-km race, finishing in a time of 1 hr 39 min 2 sec.

Most individual cross-country wins »

The greatest number of men's individual cross-country victories in the World Championships is five by Paul Tergat (right) in 1995–99 and John Ngugi (both Kenya) in 1986–89 and 1992.

Men's road race

Event	Record	Name, nationality & venue	Date
10 km	27:02	Haile Gebrselassie (Ethiopia), Doha, Qatar	11 December 2002
15 km	41:29	Felix Limo (Kenya), Nijmegen, The Netherlands	11 November 2001
20 km	56:18	Paul Tergat (Kenya), Milan, Italy	4 April 1998
Half marathon	59:17	Paul Tergat (Kenya), Milan, Italy	4 April 1998
25 km	1:13:14	Rodgers Rop (Kenya), Berlin, Germany	6 May 2001
30 km	1:28:36	Takayuki Matsumiya (Japan), Kumamoto, Japan	16 February 2003
Marathon (26 miles 385 yards)	*2:04:55	Paul Tergat (Kenya), Berlin, Germany	28 September 2003
100 km	6:13:33	Takahiro Sunanda (Japan), Yubetsu, Japan	21 June 1998

* The marathon record printed in the first edition of *Guinness World Records* in 1955 was 2:17:39.4

Women's road race

Event	Record	Name, nationality & venue	Date
10 km	30:21	Paula Radcliffe (GB), San Juan, Puerto Rico	23 February 2003
15 km	46:57	Elana Meyer (RSA), Cape Town, South Africa	2 November 1991
20 km	1:03:26	Paula Radcliffe (GB), Bristol, UK	6 October 2001
Half marathon	1:06:44	Elana Meyer (RSA), Tokyo, Japan	15 January 1999
25 km	1:22:31	Naoko Takahashi (Japan), Berlin, Germany	30 September 2001
30 km	1:39:02	Naoko Takahashi (Japan), Berlin, Germany	30 September 2001
Marathon	2:15:25	Paula Radcliffe (UK), London, UK	13 April 2003
100 km	6:33:11	Tomoe Abe (Japan), Yufutsu, Japan	25 June 2000

★ **Fastest time to complete three marathons in three days**
The fastest combined time for three marathons in three days is 8 hr 22 min 31 sec by Raymond Hubbard (UK). The races were held between 16 and 18 April 1988: Belfast 2 hr 45 min 55 sec; London 2 hr 48 min 45 sec; and Boston 2 hr 47 min 51 sec.

★ **Fastest speed march marathon by an individual**
Chris Chandler (UK) set an individual record in the RAF Swinderby Marathon at Swinderby, Lincolnshire, UK, on 25 September 1992, when he completed the marathon carrying a pack weighing 18 kg (40 lb). His time was 3 hr 56 min 10 sec.

★ **Fastest marathon speed march without rifles**
The fastest time for a team of eight to 10 to complete a marathon while carrying 18-kg (40-lb) backpacks is 4 hr 19 min 7 sec by eight members of 29 Commando Regiment

Royal Artillery at the Luton Marathon, Bedfordshire, UK, on 29 November 1998.

★ **Fastest marathon speed march team with rifles**
A team of nine representing II Squadron RAF Regiment from RAF Hullavington, Wiltshire, UK, completed the London Marathon in 4 hr 33 min 58 sec on 21 April 1991. Each carried a pack weighing at least 18 kg (40 lb), including a rifle.

Fastest «
men's 20-km road walk

Jefferson Pérez, (Ecuador, left) set a new record of 1 hr 17 min 21 sec for the men's 20-km road walk in Paris St-Denis, France, on 23 August 2003.

Men's walking world records

Event	Record	Name & nationality	Venue	Date
TRACK				
20 km	1:17:25.6	Bernardo Segura (Mexico)	Fana, Norway	7 May 1994
30 km	2:01:44.1	Maurizio Damilano (Italy)	Cuneo, Italy	4 October 1992
50 km	3:40:57.9	Thierry Toutain (France)	Héricourt, France	29 September 1997
2 hrs	29,572 m	Maurizio Damilano (Italy)	Cuneo, Italy	4 October 1992
ROAD				
20 km	1:17:21.0	Jefferson Pérez (Ecuador)	Paris St-Denis, France	23 August 2003
50 km	3:36:03.0	Robert Korzeniowski (Poland)	Paris St-Denis, France	27 August 2003

Women's walking world records

Event	Record	Name & nationality	Venue	Date
TRACK				
10 km	41:56.23	Nadezhda Ryashkina (USSR)	Seattle, USA	24 July 1990
20 km	1:26:52.30	Olimpiada Ivanova (Russia)	Brisbane, Australia	6 September 2001
ROAD				
20 km	1:26:22.0	Yang Wang (China)	Guangzhou, China	19 November 2001
	equal	Yelena Nikolayeva (Russia)	Cheboksary, Russia	18 May 2003

★ Longest running race ever

The longest running race ever staged was the 1929 trans-continental race from New York City, to Los Angeles, California, USA, a distance of 5,850 km (3,635 miles). Johnny Salo (Finland) won in 79 days, running from 31 March to 17 June. His elapsed time of 525 hr 57 min 20 sec at an average speed of 11.12 km/h (6.91 mph) left him only 2 min 47 sec ahead of Englishman Pietro 'Peter' Gavuzzi.

★ Oldest marathon

The Boston Marathon was first held on 19 April 1897, when it was run over 39 km (24 miles 1,232 yd). John A Kelley (USA) finished the Boston Marathon 61 times between 1928 and 1992, winning in 1935 and 1945.

★ Most marathons completed

Horst Preisler (Germany) ran 949 races of 26 miles 385 yd or longer between 1974 and 25 March 2000.

★ Most consecutive weekends of marathon running

Richard Worley (USA) ran either a marathon or an ultramarathon (a race longer than marathon distance) for 159 consecutive weekends. The first was the Walt Disney World Marathon in Orlando, Florida, USA, on 5 January 1997, and the last was the Houston Methodist Marathon in Houston, Texas, USA, on 16 January 2000. In the course of the records, Richard ran a marathon in all 50 US states in one year, for three consecutive years.

★ Fastest pram-pushing half marathon

Martin de Scally (South Africa) completed the Vaal Half Marathon in Vereeniging, South Africa, in a time of 1 hr 21 min 1 sec on 2 March 2003 while pushing a pram.

The women's equivalent record is 1 hr 30 min 51 sec by Nancy Schubring (USA) at the Mike May Races Half Marathon, Vassar, Michigan, USA, on 15 September 2001.

★ Fastest pram-pushing marathon

The fastest time to run a marathon while pushing a pram is 3 hr 54 min 36 sec, by Han Frenken (Netherlands) at the Leidsche Rijn Marathon, Utrecht, The Netherlands, on 21 April 2003.

★ Fastest skipping marathon

The fastest time to complete a marathon while skipping rather than running is 5 hr 55 min 13 sec by Ashrita Furman (USA) at the Comox Valley Roads Marathon, Vancouver Island, British Columbia, Canada, on 31 August 2003.

★ Fastest half marathon in a two-person pantomime costume

On 6 October 2002, Paul Donaghy and Steve Langley (both UK) completed the Great North Run, Newcastle, Tyne and Wear, UK, in a time of 2 hr 9 min 13 sec wearing a pantomime camel costume.

Oldest female marathon finisher

Jenny Wood-Allen (UK, below, b. 1911) ran the London Marathon on 14 April 2002 aged 90 years 145 days, in 11 hr 34 min.

Treadmill world records

Event	Record	Name & nationality	Venue	Date
TEAM				
1,000,000 m (Team of 12)	82 hr 46 sec	HMP Downview UK	Sutton, UK	14–17 August 2000
12 hours (women)	161.3 km (100.2 miles)	Australia	Prahran, Australia	5 September 2003
12 hours (men)	178.6 km (110.9 miles)	Australia	Prahran, Australia	5 September 2003
INDIVIDUAL				
24 hours (female)	151.48 km (94.12 miles)	Georgina McConnell (Australia)	Wests Illawerra, Unanderra, Australia	25 November 2003
24 hours (male)	222.41 km (138.2 miles)	Tony Mangan (Ireland)	Dublin, Ireland	25 October 2003
48 hours	372.08 km (231.2 miles)	Tony Mangan (Ireland)	Dublin, Ireland	26 October 2003
1 week	455.83 km (283.2 miles)	David Taylor (Australia)	Wests Illawerra, Unanderra, Australia	30 November 2003
100 km	9 hr 5 min 37 sec	Richard Donovan (Ireland)	Galway, Ireland	31 July 2003
100 miles	16 hr 23 min 16 sec	Andrew Rivett (UK)	Alverthorpe, UK	6 April 2003

Walking backwards world records

Event	Record	Name & nationality	Venue	Date
100 m	13.60	Ferdie Ato Adoboe (Ghana)	Northampton, USA	25 July 1991
200 m	32.78	Timothy Bud Badyna (USA)	Santa Clarita, USA	17 January 2001
1 km	3:36.07	Thomas Dold (Germany)	Messkirch, Germany	13 July 2003
1 mile	6:00:2.35	D Joseph James (India)	Coimbatore, India	10 August 2002
10 km	45:00:31.0	Vangal A Mathiyazhagan (India)	Coimbatore, India	30 May 1999
Marathon	3:53:17.0	Timothy Bud Badyna (USA)	Toledo, USA	24 April 1994
24 hours	153.52 km (95.40 miles)	Anthony Thornton (USA)	Minneapolis, USA	31 December 1988 –1 January 1989

★ **Fastest 10-km road race in a two-person pantomime costume**
Wearing a pantomime camel costume, Simon Wiles and Les Morton (both UK) set a time of 44 min 2 sec for the Percy Pud 10-km race in Loxley, Sheffield, South Yorkshire, UK, on 2 December 2001.

★ **Fastest three-legged marathon**
Identical twins Nick and Alastair Benbow (both UK) set a three-legged running record in the London Marathon with a time of 3 hr 40 min 16 sec on 26 April 1998. They were tied together at the wrist and shared a pair of three-legged running

trousers. They also hold the equivalent half-marathon record: they ran the London Half Marathon in 1 hr 37 min 53 sec on 2 March 2003.

★ **Most siblings to complete a marathon**
The eight Hughes brothers – Richard, Harry, Declan, Owen, Seamus, Patrick, Cathal and Vincent (all Ireland) – competed in and completed the Dublin Marathon on 29 October 1984.

★ **Oldest male marathon finisher**
On 10 October 1976, 98-year-old Dimitrion Yordanidis (Greece) ran a marathon in 7 hr 33 min in Athens, Greece.

★ **Fastest 24-hour running relay by a team of 10**
The greatest distance covered in 24 hours by a team of 10 is 487.343 km (302.281 miles) by Puma Tyneside RC at Monkton Stadium, Jarrow, Tyne and Wear, UK, between 10 and 11 September 1994.

★ **Fastest 100-mile relay by a team of 10**
Ten cadets from the 2331 (St Ives) Squadron Air Training Corps completed 100 miles in relay in 10 hr 21 min 35 sec at the St Ivo Outdoor Centre, St Ives, Cambridgeshire, UK, on 21 September 2003. The team members were

Sgt M Trace, Cwo C Trace, Sgt D Dew, Cpl L McGregor, Cwo J Martin, Sgt B Blewett, Cdt T Philpot, Cpl J Young, Cwo A Owen and Cpl R Jepp.

★ **Fastest backwards run from Los Angeles to New York**
Arvind Pandya (India) ran backwards across the USA from Los Angeles, California, to New York City in 107 days between 18 August and 3 December 1984. Arvind runs backwards in marathons and races all over the world to raise funds for various public causes. He has raised money for good causes in Africa, India and Europe.

Combat
Sport

Most heavyweight boxing world title recaptures ⌃

Three boxers have regained the heavyweight championship of the world twice. Muhammad Ali (USA, above right) first won the title on 25 February 1964, defeating Sonny Liston (USA). Having been stripped of the title by the world boxing authorities on 28 April 1967, he beat George Foreman (USA) on 30 October 1974. He then won the WBA title from Leon Spinks (USA) on 15 September 1978 after losing to him on 15 February 1978.

Evander Holyfield (USA) won the title in October 1990 by defeating James Douglas (USA). He regained the WBA and IBF versions when he beat Riddick Bowe (USA) in November 1993 and regained the WBA version again, on 9 November 1996, when he defeated Mike Tyson.

Lennox Lewis (UK) was awarded the WBC title in January 1993 after the then champion Riddick Bowe (USA) refused to fight him. He then won the WBC title on 7 February 1995, beating Oliver McCall (USA), and regained the WBC, IBF and IBO titles when he defeated Hasim Rahman (USA) on 17 November 2001.

★ Most undefeated boxing matches

Edward Henry Greb (USA) was unbeaten in a sequence of 178 bouts in 1916–23 (including 117 'no decisions', of which five were unofficial losses). Of boxers with complete records, Packey McFarland (USA) had 97 fights (five draws) in 1905–15 without a defeat. Pedro Carrasco (Spain) won 83 consecutive fights from 22 April 1964 to 3 September 1970, drew once and had a further nine wins before his loss to Armando Ramos (USA) in a World Boxing Council (WBC) lightweight contest on 18 February 1972.

★ Longest reign as world heavyweight boxing champion

Joe Louis (USA) was champion for 11 years 252 days, from 22 June 1937 – when he knocked out James Joseph Braddock (USA) in the eighth round at Chicago, Illinois, USA – until announcing his retirement on 1 March 1949. During his reign, Louis made a record 25 defences of his title.

★ Shortest reign as world boxing champion

Tony Canzoneri (USA) was world light-welterweight champion for 33 days, from 21 May to 23 June 1933, the shortest period for a boxer to have won and lost a world title in the ring.

★ Most heavyweight titles won by a former middleweight

This remarkable feat has been achieved only twice in 106 years. The first time was by Robert James 'Bob' Fitzsimmons (UK) when he knocked out James J Corbett (USA) at Carson City, Nevada, USA, on 17 March 1897. Roy Jones Jr (USA) matched this when he beat John Ruiz (USA) for the World Boxing Association (WBA) title by unanimous decision on 2 March 2003 at Las Vegas, Nevada, USA.

★ Heaviest heavyweight boxing world champion

Primo Carnera (Italy), the 'Ambling Alp' who won the title from Jack Sharkey (USA) in New York City, USA, on 29 June 1933, scaled 118 kg (260 lb) for this fight but his peak weight was 122 kg (269 lb).

★ Longest boxing fight

The world title fight (under Queensberry rules) between the lightweights Joe Gans (USA) and Oscar Matthew 'Battling' Nelson (Denmark), the 'Durable Dane', at Goldfield, Nevada, USA, on 3 September 1906 was terminated in the 42nd round when Gans was declared the winner on a foul.

★ Youngest national heavyweight champion

Bill Sutherley (UK) won the Scottish Amateur Boxing Association (ABA) heavyweight title on 23 February 1961, at the age of only 18 years and 11 days.

★ Youngest boxing world champion

Wilfred Benitez (Puerto Rico) was 17 years 176 days when he won the WBA light-welterweight title in San Juan, Puerto Rico, on 6 March 1976.

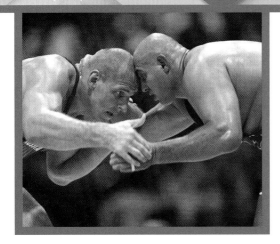

Most World Championship wrestling titles

Aleksandr Karelin (Russia, above left) won a record 12 world titles in the Greco-Roman under-130-kg class between 1988 and 1999.

Largest » Sumo yokozuna wrestler

Hawaiian-born Chad Rowan, alias Akebono (right), became the first foreign rikishi to be promoted to the top rank of yokozuna in January 1993. At 2.04 m (6 ft 8 in) and 227 kg (501 lb) he is the tallest and the heaviest yokozuna in sumo history.

★ Youngest world heavyweight boxing champion

Mike Tyson (USA) was 20 years 144 days when he beat Trevor Berbick (USA) to win the WBC belt at Las Vegas, Nevada, USA, on 22 November 1986. He added the WBA version when he beat James 'Bonecrusher' Smith on 7 March 1987 at the age of 20 years 249 days. He became undisputed champion on 2 August 1987 when he beat Tony Tucker (USA) for the International Boxing Federation (IBF) title.

★ Most knock-outs in a boxing career

The greatest number of finishes classed as 'knock-outs' in a career is 145 (129 in professional bouts) by Archie Moore (USA, b. Archibald Lee Wright).

★ Undefeated heavyweight boxing world champion

Rocky Marciano (USA, b. Rocco Francis Marchegiano) is the only world champion at any weight to have won every fight of his entire completed professional career, from 17 March 1947 to 21 September 1955 (he announced his retirement on 27 April 1956); 43 of his 49 fights were by knock-outs or stoppages.

★ Longest boxing career

Bob Fitzsimmons (UK) had a career lasting more than 31 years (1883–1914). On 20 December 1905, aged 42 years 208 days, he had his last world title bout. Jack Johnson (USA) also had a career of over 31 years, 1897–1928.

★ Most jiu-juitsu team World Championships

The World Council of Jiu-Jitsu Organizations has staged World Championships biennially since 1984. Canada has won the team competition on five occasions (1984, 1986, 1988, 1992 and 1994).

★ Most team kata titles at a karate World Championship

A kata team event was introduced at the 1986 karate World Championships. Of the nine championships held biennially since, in both the men's and women's disciplines, Japan have failed to win on only four occasions out of 16 competitions in both classes.

★ Most countries represented at a karate World Championship

At the 16th staging of the biennial karate World Championships, held in 2002 in Madrid, Spain, 84 countries were represented.

★ Most competitors at a karate World Championship

In 1988, a total of 1,157 competitors took part in the karate World Championships at the ninth staging of the biennial tournament in Cairo, Egypt.

★ Fastest 100-man kumite ('sparring') karate

On 22 March 1995, Francisco Alves Filho (Brazil) defeated 100 consecutive opponents in full-contact knockdown fighting in 3 hr 8 min. He won 26 fights by Ippon (full points), 50 by decision, and drew 24. He did not lose a single fight.

★ Most judo throws in one hour

The most judo throws completed in one hour by a pair is 3,786 by Dale Moore and Nigel Townsend (both UK) at Esporta Health Club, Chiswick Park, Greater London, UK, on 23 February 2002.

★ Most judo throws in 10 hours

Csaba Mezei and Zoltán Farkas (both Hungary) of the Szany judo sport team completed 57,603 judo throws in a 10-hour period at the Szany Sports Hall, Szany, Hungary, on 1 May 2003.

★ Most bout successes in annual sumo tournaments

Yokozuna Mitsugu Akimoto, aka Chiyonofuji (Japan), set a record for domination of one of the six annual tournaments by winning the Kyushu Basho for eight successive years (1981–88). He also holds the record for the most career wins (1,045) and Makunouchi (top division) wins (807).

Women's +75-kg total

Ding Meiyuan (China, below) achieved a record total lift of 300 kg in Sydney, Australia, on 22 September 2000. She also set the +75-kg snatch record with a lift of 137.5 kg in Vancouver, Canada, on 21 November 2003.

Most Olympic « weightlifting gold medals

Three competitors have won a record total of three Olympic weightlifting gold medals: Naim Suleymanoglü (Turkey) at the Olympic Games in 1988, 1992 and 1996; Pyrros Dimas (Greece, left) in 1992, 1996 and 2000; and Akakios Kakiasvili (Greece) in 1992, 1996 and 2000.

In 1992 Kakiasvili was known as Kakhi Kakhiachbili and he represented the EUN/CIS, also known as the Unified Team of the former Soviet Republics.

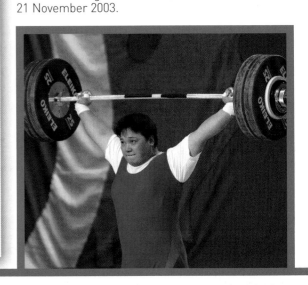

★ Most Olympic weightlifting medals
Norbert Schemansky (USA) won four Olympic weightlifting medals between 1948 and 1964.

★ Youngest weightlifting record breaker
Naim Suleymanoglü (Turkey, b. 23 January 1967) was 16 years 62 days old when he set the world records for clean and jerk, at 160 kg, and combined total, at 285 kg, at Allentown, New Jersey, USA, on 26 March 1983.

★ Most accumulative weight bench-pressed in one hour
Eamonn Keane (Ireland) lifted a total weight of 138,480 kg (305,300 lb) in one hour at World Gym, Marina del Ray, California, USA, on 22 July 2003.

★ Greatest multiple of bodyweight lifted by a man
Lamar Gant (USA) was the first man to deadlift nearly five times his own bodyweight. He lifted 299.5 kg (661 lb), when he weighed 59.5 kg (131 lb), in 1985.

Men's weightlifting world records

Bodyweight	Event	Weight, name & nationality		Venue	Date
56 kg	Clean & jerk	168 kg	Halil Mutlu (Turkey)	Trencín, Slovakia	24 April 2001
	Snatch	138.5 kg	Halil Mutlu (Turkey)	Antalya, Turkey	4 November 2001
	Total	305.0 kg	Halil Mutlu (Turkey)	Sydney, Australia	16 September 2000
62 kg	Clean & jerk	182.5 kg	Maosheng Le (China)	Busan, Korea	2 October 2002
	Snatch	153 kg	Zhiyong Shi (China)	Izmir, Turkey	28 June 2002
	Total	325 kg	World Standard		
69 kg	Clean & jerk	197.5 kg	Guozheng Zhang (China)	Qinhuangdao, China	11 September 2003
	Snatch	165 kg	Georgi Markov (Bulgaria)	Sydney, Australia	20 September 2000
	Total	357.5 kg	Galabin Boevski (Bulgaria)	Athens, Greece	24 November 1999
77 kg	Clean & jerk	210 kg	Oleg Perepetchenov (Russia)	Trencín, Slovakia	27 April 2001
	Snatch	173 kg	Sergey Filimonov (Kazakhstan)	Busan, Korea	4 October 2002
	Total	377.5 kg	Plamen Zhelyazkov (Bulgaria)	Doha, Qatar	27 March 2002
85 kg	Clean & jerk	218 kg	Zhang Yong (China)	Tel Aviv, Israel	25 April 1998
	Snatch	182.5 kg	Andrei Ribakov (Bulgaria)	Havirov, Czech Republic	2 June 2002
	Total	395 kg	World Standard		
94 kg	Clean & jerk	232.5 kg	Szymon Kolecki (Poland)	Sofia, Bulgaria	29 April 2000
	Snatch	188 kg	Akakios Kakiashvilis (Greece)	Athens, Greece	27 November 1999
	Total	417.5 kg	World Standard		
105 kg	Clean & jerk	242.5 kg	World Standard		
	Snatch	198.5 kg	Marcin Dolega (Poland)	Havirov, Czech Republic	4 June 2002
	Total	440 kg	World Standard		
+105 kg	Clean & jerk	263 kg	Hossein Rezazadeh (Iran)	Warsaw, Poland	26 November 2002
	Snatch	213.0 kg	Hossein Rezazadeh (Iran)	Qinhuangdao, China	14 September 2003
	Total	472.5 kg	Hossein Rezazadeh (Iran)	Sydney, Australia	26 September 2000

From 1 January 1998, the International Weightlifting Federation (IWF) introduced modified bodyweight categories, thereby making the then world records redundant. This is the new listing with the world standards for the new bodyweight categories. Results achieved at IWF-approved competitions exceeding the world standards by 0.5 kg for snatch or clean and jerk, or by 2.5 kg for the total, will be recognized as world records.

★ Greatest multiple of bodyweight lifted by a woman using one arm
Cammie Lynn Lusko (USA) became the first woman to lift more than her bodyweight with one arm. She lifted a total weight of 59.5 kg (131 lb) when she had a bodyweight of 58.3 kg (128 lb 7 oz), at Milwaukee, Wisconsin, USA, on 21 May 1983.

★ Most push-ups in one minute
Jack Zatorski (USA) performed 133 push-ups in one minute at Fort Lauderdale, Florida, USA, on 1 March 2003.

Men's 56-kg »
clean and jerk

Halil Mutlu (Turkey, right) lifted a record 168 kg

at Trencin, Slovakia, on 24 April 2001.
He also set the record for men's snatch,
with a lift of 138.5 kg in Antalya, Turkey,
on 4 November 2001, and for the
total, with a lift of 305 kg in Sydney,
New South Wales, Australia, on
16 September 2000.

★ **Most push-ups in
one minute using
the back of the hands**
Steve Bugdale (UK) completed
89 push-ups in one minute at
Plymstock Health and Fitness
Club, Plymouth, Devon, UK,
on 12 May 2003.

★ **Most push-ups in
one hour using the back
of the hand of one arm**
Bruce Swatton (UK) completed
441 one-arm push-ups in one
hour at Plymstock Health and
Fitness Club, Plymouth, Devon,
UK, on 12 May 2003.

★ **Most sit-ups in one minute
using an abdominal frame**
BM Gopikrishnan (India) carried
out 138 sit-ups in one minute
using an abdominal frame at
Somers Town Community
Sports Centre, London, UK,
on 9 December 2003.
Gopikrishnan also holds
the record for most sit-ups in
one hour using an abdominal
frame. He completed 8,367
sit-ups at Gundeldinger Hall,
Basel, Switzerland, on
20 December 2003.

Women's weightlifting world records

Bodyweight	Event	Weight, name & nationality		Venue	Date
48 kg	Clean & jerk	116.5 kg	Zhuo Li (China)	Qinhuangdao, China	10 September 2003
	Snatch	93.5 kg	Zhuo Li (China)	Qinhuangdao, China	10 September 2003
	Total	207.5 kg	Mingjuan Wang (China)	Warsaw, Poland	19 November 2002
53 kg	Clean & jerk	127.5 kg	Xueju Li (China)	Busan, South Korea	20 November 2002
	Snatch	102.5 kg	Ri Song Hui (North Korea)	Warsaw, Poland	1 October 2002
	Total	225 kg	Yang Xia (China)	Sydney, Australia	18 September 2000
58 kg	Clean & jerk	133 kg	Caiyan Sun (China)	Izmir, Turkey	28 June 2002
	Snatch	110 kg	Li Wang (China)	Bali, Indonesia	10 August 2003
	Total	240 kg	Li Wang (China)	Bali, Indonesia	10 August 2003
63 kg	Clean & jerk	138 kg	Natalia Skakun (Ukraine)	Vancouver, Canada	18 November 2003
	Snatch	113.5 kg	Anna Batsiushka (Belarus)	Vancouver, Canada	18 November 2003
	Total	247.5 kg	Xia Liu (China)	Qinhuangdao, China	12 September 2003
69 kg	Clean & jerk	150 kg	Chunhong Liu (China)	Vancouver, Canada	19 November 2003
	Snatch	120 kg	Chunhong Liu (China)	Vancouver, Canada	19 November 2003
	Total	270 kg	Chunhong Liu (China)	Vancouver, Canada	19 November 2003
75 kg	Clean & jerk	152.5 kg	Ruiping Sun (China)	Busan, South Korea	7 October 2002
	Snatch	118.5 kg	Ruiping Sun (China)	Busan, South Korea	7 October 2002
	Total	270 kg	Ruiping Sun (China)	Busan, South Korea	7 October 2000
+75 kg	Clean & jerk	168.5 kg	Dan Sun (China)	Hyderabad, India	31 October 2003
	Snatch	137.5 kg	Ding Meiyuan (China)	Vancouver, Canada	21 November 2003
	Total	300 kg	Ding Meiyuan (China)	Sydney, Australia	22 September 2000

★ **Greatest height attained
on a climbing machine
in one hour**
Paddy Doyle (UK) climbed to
a height of 958.29 m (3,144 ft)
on a 'VersaClimber' machine
in one hour, while carrying
a 18.1-kg (40-lb) pack,
on TV show *This Morning*,
Carlton TV Studios, London,
UK, on 17 October 2002.

★ **Fastest time to climb
the height of Everest
on a machine**
Kelvin Turner (UK) climbed
the equivalent of the height
of Mount Everest (8,850 m
or 29,035 ft) in a time of
2 hr 57 min 56.5 sec on
19 February 2003 at the
LivingWell Health Club,
Redland, Bristol, UK.

★ **Most skips by an
individual in 24 hours**
Jim Payne (Ireland) skipped
141,221 jumps of a rope in
24 hours at City Square
Shopping Centre, Waterford,
Ireland, on 26–27 March 2004.
The attempt was carried out
to raise funds for Our Lady's
Hospital for Sick Children
in Crumlin, Ireland.

Winter sports 1
Sport

Most men's Alpine skiing Olympic medals ⌄

The most Olympic Games medals won by a man is seven by Kjetil André Aamodt (Norway, below) who, in addition to his record three gold medals, has won two silver (for the downhill and combined events in 1994) and two bronze (for the giant slalom in 1992 and the super-giant slalom in 1994).

Most women's ⌃ Alpine skiing Olympic gold medals

Four women have won three Olympic gold medals: Vreni Schneider (Switzerland, above) (giant slalom in 1988, slalom in 1988 and 1994); Katja Seizinger (Germany) (downhill in 1994 and 1998, combined in 1998); Deborah Compagnoni (Italy) (super-giant slalom in 1992, giant slalom in 1994 and 1998); and Janica Kostelic (Croatia) (combined, giant slalom and slalom in 2002).

★ **Highest speed in an Olympic downhill race**
On 13 February 1998 Jean-Luc Crétier (France) attained an average speed of 107.53 km/h (66.81 mph) in the Olympic downhill race at Nagano, Japan.

★ **Fastest World Cup downhill speed**
Armin Assinger (Austria) reached a speed of 112.4 km/h (69.8 mph) at Sierra Nevada, Spain, on 15 March 1993.

★ **Most World Cup downhill wins**
Franz Klammer (Austria) won 25 downhill races from 1974 to 1984.

★ **Longest downhill ski run**
The Weissfluhjoch-Küblis Parsenn course, near Davos, Switzerland, measures 12.23 km (7.6 miles).

★ **Most men's Alpine skiing Olympic gold medals**
The most Alpine skiing Olympic gold medals won by a male is three. The record is shared by Anton 'Toni' Sailer (Austria) for downhill, slalom and giant slalom in 1956; Jean-Claude Killy (France) for downhill, slalom and giant slalom in 1968; Alberto Tomba (Italy) for slalom and giant slalom in 1988 and giant slalom in 1992; and Kjetil André Aamodt (Norway), for super giant slalom in 1992 and 2002 and the combined event in 2002.

★ **Most women's Alpine skiing Olympic medals**
Two women have won five skiing medals in the Olympic Games. In addition to her record three gold medals, Vreni Schneider (Switzerland) won silver in the combined event and bronze in the giant slalom in 1994. Katja Seizinger (Germany) won bronze in the 1992 and 1998 super-giant slalom in addition to her three gold successes.

★ **Most men's Alpine skiing World Championship titles**
The Alpine skiing World Championships debuted at Murren, Switzerland, in 1931. Anton 'Toni' Sailer (Austria) has won a record seven titles: all four titles in 1956 (giant slalom, slalom, downhill and non-Olympic Alpine combination) and the downhill, giant slalom and combined in 1958.

★ **Most women's Alpine skiing World Championship titles**
Christl Cranz (Germany) has won the most Alpine skiing World Championship titles, with seven individual – four slalom (in 1934 and from 1937 to 1939) and three downhill (in 1935, 1937 and 1939) – and five combined (from 1934 to 1935 and 1937 to 1939). She also won the gold medal for the combined in the 1936 Olympic Games.

★ **Highest speed by a skier**
Philippe Goitschel (France) reached a speed of 250.7 km/h (155.77 mph) at Les Arcs, France, on 23 April 2002.

★ **Highest speed by a female skier**
Karine Dubouchet (France) reached a speed of 242.26 km/h (150.53 mph) at Les Arcs, France, in May 1999.

★ **Most World Cup race wins**
The most individual event wins is 86 (46 giant slalom, 40 slalom, from a total of 287 races) by Ingemar Stenmark (Sweden) from 1974 to 1989, including a men's record 13 in one season in 1978/79, of which 10 were part of a record 14 successive giant slalom wins from 18 March 1978 (Ingemar's 22nd birthday) to 21 January 1980.

★ **Most women's World Cup race wins**
Annemarie Moser (née Proll, Austria) won 62 individual event wins from 1970 to 1979, including a record 11 consecutive downhill wins from December 1972 to January 1974. She has also claimed the World Cup Overall Champion title (downhill and slalom events combined) a record six times since the tour began in 1967.

★ **Most men's freestyle World Cup titles**
Eric Laboureix (France) won five men's freestyle World Cup titles, from 1986 to 1988 and 1990 to 1991.

Most 'vertical feet' skied by a man ≪ in 24 hours

On 29 April 1998, Chris Kent, Edi Podivinsky (left), Luke Sauder (all Canada) and Dominique Perret (Switzerland) skied 107,777 m (353,600 ft) in 14 hr 30 min on a slope at Blue River, British Columbia, Canada. They completed the run 73 times and were lifted back to the summit each time by helicopter. Podivinsky is shown here in action at the World Cup in Wengen, Switzerland, in 2000.

★ **Most women's freestyle World Cup titles**
Connie Kissling (Switzerland) won 10 World Cup freestyle titles from 1983 to 1992.

★ **Most freestyle skiing World Championship titles**
The first World Championships were held at Tignes, France, in 1986, when titles were awarded in ballet, moguls, aerials and combined events. Edgar Grospiron (France) has won a record three World Championship titles: moguls in 1989 and 1991 and aerials in 1995. He also won an Olympic title in 1992.
The greatest number of world titles won by a woman is also three by Candice Gilg (France), who won the moguls in 1993, 1995 and 1997.

★ **Most somersaults and twists in a freestyle aerial jump**
The greatest number of twists and somersaults achieved in a freestyle jump was set by Matt Chojnacki (USA), who completed a quadruple-

twisting quadruple back flip at Winter Park Resort, Colorado, USA, on 4 April 2001.

★ **Most Nations Cup wins**
The Nations Cup is awarded according to the combined results of individual performances by men and women in the World Cup. The Cup has been won 22 times by Austria, in 1969, 1973–80, 1982 and 1990–2001.

★ **Farthest vertical distance skied in 12 hours**
The greatest vertical distance skied in a 12-hour period by an individual, skiing both the downhill and the uphill sections, is 10,080 m (33,070 ft) by Manfred Tod (Austria) at Mariazeller Burgeralpe, Austria, on 24 February 2003.

★ **Most 'vertical feet' skied by a woman in 24 hours**
Jennifer Hughes (USA) skied 93,124 vertical metres (305,525 ft) at Atlin, British Columbia, Canada, on 20 April 1998. She was accompanied by snowboarder Tammy McMinn

(USA) during her record attempt and the two women were lifted from the bottom of the run to the top by helicopter.

★ **Longest competitive ski jump by a man**
Andreas Goldberger (Austria) made a ski jump of 225 m (738 ft) at Planica, Slovenia, on 18 March 2000.

★ **Longest ski jump by a woman**
Eva Ganster (Austria) achieved a distance of 112 m (367 ft) in the ski jump at Bischofshofen, Austria, on 7 January 1994.

★ **Most ski flips in 10 minutes**
Tommy Waltner (USA) completed 23 front inverted aerial jumps within 10 minutes on 25 April 2000. The event took place on Aspen Mountain, Colorado, USA, in order to raise money for Waltner's 'Loops for Lupus' campaign.

★ **Largest flare run**
The largest flare run ever consisted of 1,321 skiers and snowboarders who followed a

course of 7 km (4.3 miles) between Piz Martegnas and Savognin, Switzerland, on 1 January 2000 while carrying flares.

★ **Longest ski lift**
The Grindelwald–Männlichen gondola ski lift in Switzerland is 6,239 m (3.88 miles) long.

★ **Most men's medals in Olympic biathlon**
Ricco Gross (Germany) won seven Olympic biathlon medals: three golds (4 x 7.5 km in 1992, 1994 and 1998), three silvers (10 km in 1992 and 1994 and 4 x 7.5 km in 2002) and a bronze (for the pursuit in 2002).

★ **Most women's medals in Olympic biathlon**
Uschi Disl (Germany) won a total of eight Olympic biathlon medals: two golds (4 x 7.5 km in 1998 and 2002), four silvers (3 x 7.5 km in 1992, 4 x 7.5 km in 1994 and 7.5 km in 1998 and 2002) and two bronzes (15 km in 1994 and 1998).

Most men's snowboarding World Cup titles

Mathieu Bozzetto (France, right) has won six titles: the overall in 1999–2000 and the slalom/parallel slalom in 1999–2002.

Highest average ⌃ speed in major 50-km Nordic skiing

The record time for a 50-km race in a major championship is 1 hr 54 min 46 sec by Aleksey Prokurorov (Russia, above) at Thunder Bay, Canada, on 19 March 1994, at an average speed of 26.14 km/h (16.24 mph).

★ **Highest snowboarding speed**
Darren Powell (Australia) reached a speed of 201.907 km/h (125.459 mph) at Les Arcs, France, on 2 May 1999.

★ **Fastest snowboard on a bobsleigh run**
Reto Lamm (Switzerland) surfed down a bobsleigh run on his snowboard at 80 km/h (49.7 mph) at Königssee, Germany, in November 1998 for *Guinness – Die Show der Rekorde*.

★ **Most snowboarding World Cup titles**
The greatest number of titles won is 16 by Karine Ruby (France). She won overall titles in 1996–98 and 2001–02; the slalom/parallel slalom in 1996–98 and 2002; the giant slalom in 1995–98 and 2001; and the snowboard cross in 1997 and 2001.
　The first snowboarding World Cup series began in 1995, with World Championships inaugurated the following year.

★ **Most snowboarding championship titles**
The greatest number of snowboarding titles won (including Olympic titles) is three, by Karine Ruby. She won the giant slalom in 1996, the Olympic title in 1998 (the first year that snowboarding became an Olympic sport) and the snowboard cross in 1997.

★ **Most X-Games snowboarding medals**
Shaun Palmer (USA) has won a record three gold medals at the Winter ESPN X-Games for the Boarder X discipline (1997–99) since the inaugural X Games in 1997. Across all the disciplines he has won a total of six gold medals at the X-Games.
　The most X-Games snowboarding medals won by a woman is six, by Barrett Christy (USA).

★ **Oldest sled dog racing trail**
The oldest established sled dog trail is the 1,688-km (1,049-mile) Iditarod Trail, which runs from

Anchorage to Nome, Alaska, USA. The trail has existed since 1910 and has been the course of an annual race since 1967.

★ **Longest trail in dog sled racing**
The longest race is run on the 2,000-km (1,243-mile) Berengia Trail from Esso to Markovo, Russia, which started as a 250-km (155-mile) route in April 1990. Now established as an annual event, the fastest time to complete the trail was achieved in 1991 by Pavel Lazarev (USSR) in 10 days 18 hr 17 min 56 sec. His time was equivalent to an average speed of 8 km/h (5 mph).

★ **Most ski orienteering World Championship team wins**
Sweden has won the men's relay title six times, in 1977, 1980, 1982, 1984, 1990 and 1996.
　Finland have won the women's relay eight times, in 1975, 1977, 1980, 1988, 1990, 1998, 2000 and 2004.

Vidar Benjaminsen (Norway) has won a record 15 medals, including four gold, two individual and two relay.

★ **Most individual ski orienteering World Championships**
Ragnhild Bratberg (Norway) has won four individual titles: the classic in 1986 and 1990 and the sprint in 1988 and 1990.
　The men's record is also four by Nicolo Corradini (Italy), who won the classic in 1994 and 1996 and the sprint in 1994 and 2000.

★ **Most Nordic skiing Olympic gold medals**
Bjørn Dæhlie (Norway) won eight Olympic gold medals for Nordic skiing (on the flat), for the 15 km, 50 km and 4 x 10 km in 1992; the 10 km and 15 km in 1994; and the 10 km, 50 km and 4 x 10 km in 1998.
　The most Olympic gold medals won by a woman is six by Lyubov Yegorova (Russia), for the 10 km, 15 km and 4 x 5 km in 1992, and the 5 km, 10 km and 4 x 5 km in 1994.

Most « snowboarding Olympic medals

Since the introduction of snowboarding to the Winter Olympics in 1998, the most medals won is two by Ross Powers (USA, left), who won gold for the halfpipe in 2002 and bronze for the same event in 1998; and Karine Ruby (France), who won gold for parallel giant slalom in 1998 and silver for the same event in 2002.

★ **Most World Nordic Championship title wins**

The first World Nordic Championships were those of the 1924 Winter Olympics in Chamonix, France. The most titles won by a woman is 17 by Yelena Välbe (Russia). Her total comprises 10 individual and seven relay wins from 1989 to 1998. With an additional seven medals, her total of 24 is also a record.

The most titles (including those for the Olympics) won by a man is 17 by Bjørn Dæhlie (Norway) – 12 individual and five relay between 1991 and 1998. Dæhlie won a record 29 medals from 1991 to 1999.

★ **Most Olympic Nordic skiing medals**

The greatest number of medals won by a man in Nordic skiing is 12 by Bjørn Dæhlie (Norway), who in addition to his record eight gold medals, also won four silver from 1992 to 1998.

The record for women is 10 by Raisa Smetanina (USSR/CIS) who won four gold (the 5 km in 1980, the 10 km in 1976 and the 4 x 5 km in 1976 and 1992), five silver (the 10 km in 1984 and 1988, the 5 km in 1976, the 20 km in 1984 and the 4 x 5 km in 1980) and one bronze (the 20 km in 1988).

★ **Greatest Nordic skiing distance in 24 hours**

Seppo-Juhani Savolainen (Finland) covered 415.5 km (258.2 miles) at Saariselk, Finland, on 8–9 April 1988.

Kamila Horakova (Czech Republic) achieved a women's record distance of 333 km (206.91 miles) in the event between 12 and 13 April 2000 at the Canmore Nordic Centre, Alberta, Canada.

★ **Most Nordic ski-jumping World Championships**

Birger Ruud (Norway) won five ski-jumping titles in 1931–32 and 1935–37.

Ruud is the only person to have won Olympic events in each of the dissimilar Alpine and Nordic disciplines. In 1936 he won the ski-jumping and the Alpine downhill (which was not then a separate event, but only a segment of the combined event).

★ **Most Nordic combined skiing Olympic gold medals**

The most gold medals won at the Olympic Games is three by Ulrich Wehling (GDR), for the individual in 1972, 1976 and 1980; and Sampaa Lajunen (Finland), for the individual, sprint and relay in 2002. Lajunen also won silver at individual and relay in 1998, for a record total of five medals.

Snowshoe race

Event	Time	Name & nationality	Venue	Date
Men				
100 m	13.23	Keith Sendziak (USA)	Gabriels, New York, USA	27 February 1999
200 m	28.73	Birger Ohlsson (Sweden)	Gabriels, New York, USA	27 February 1999
400 m	1:03.24	Birger Ohlsson (Sweden)	Gabriels, New York, USA	27 February 1999
1,500-m run	5:20.47	Matthew Dougherty (USA)	Saranac Lake, New York, USA	23 February 2002
1,500-m walk	8:37.00	Michel Lavoie (Canada)	St Luc, Québec, Canada	17 February 1996
Women				
100 m	14.98	Mary Shanly (USA)	St Luc, Québec, Canada	17 February 1996
200 m	34.31	Mary Shanly (USA)	St Luc, Québec, Canada	17 February 1996
400 m	1:24.43	Ann Herbowy (USA)	Gabriels, New York, USA	27 February 1999
1,500-m run	6:51.67	Rebecca Harman (USA)	Saranac Lake, New York, USA	23 February 2002
1,500-m walk	10:46.00	Lynn Dextradeur (Canada)	Hull, Québec, Canada	Unknown 1989

Most Olympic Games ⋙ curling wins

Curling became an Olympic sport in 1998. It has only been part of the Olympics twice altogether and to date four countries have won one title each. In 1998, Switzerland won the men's title and Canada won the women's. In the 2002 Games, Norway's men's team (Lars Vaagberg, below) and Great Britain's women's team were the winners.

Fastest lugeing speed ⋀

Tony Benshoof (USA, above) reached a speed of 139.39 km/h (86.6 mph) on the track built for the 2002 Olympics at Park City, Utah, USA, on 16 October 2001. The speed was reached during training for the 2001 Luge World Cup Series.

★ Fastest game of curling
Eight curlers from the Burlington Golf and Country Club curled an eight-end game in 47 min 24 sec, with time penalties of 5 min 30 sec, at Burlington, Ontario, Canada, on 4 April 1986. The time is taken from when the first rock crosses the near hogline until the last rock comes to a stop.

★ Longest curling stone throw
Eddie Kulbacki (Canada) threw a curling stone a distance of 175.66 m (576 ft 4 in) at Park Lake, Neepawa, Manitoba, Canada, on 29 January 1989. The attempt took place on a specially prepared sheet of curling ice on frozen Park Lake a record 365.76 m (1,200 ft) long.

★ Most World Championship and Olympic Games luge wins by a man
The most single-seater World Championship and Olympic titles (instituted in 1953) won is six by Georg Hackl (GDR/ Germany) in 1989, 1990, 1992, 1994, 1997 and 1998. Jan Behrendt and Stefan Krausse (both GDR/Germany) have won a record six two-seater titles, in 1989, 1991–93, 1995 and 1998.

★ Most Olympic gold luge medals by a woman
Steffi Walter (née Martin, GDR) won two gold medals for lugeing, with victories at the women's single-seater luge event in 1984 and 1988.

★ Most luge World Championship titles by a woman
Margit Schumann (GDR) won four luge World Championships, in 1973–75 and 1977.

★ Youngest Olympic bobsleigh champion
William Guy Fiske (USA) was 16 years 260 days old when he won the gold medal with the five-man bobsleigh team during the 1928 Winter Olympics held at St Moritz, Switzerland.

★ Oldest Olympic bobsleigh champion
Jay O'Brien (USA) was 47 years 357 days old when he won the gold medal with the four-man bobsleigh team during the 1932 Winter Olympics held at Lake Placid, New York, USA.

★ Most individual Olympic bobsleigh medals
Bogdan Musiol (GDR) won a record seven individual Olympic bobsleigh medals (one gold, five silver, one bronze) between 1980 and 1992.

★ Most Olympic gold bobsleigh medals won by an individual
Meinhard Nehmer and Bernhard Germeshausen (both GDR) have each won three gold bobsleigh medals, in the 1976 two-man and the 1976 and 1980 four-man events.

★ Most individual World Championship bobsleigh titles
The greatest number of bobsleigh World Championship titles won by an individual is 11 by Eugenio Monti (Italy) between 1957 and 1968. He accomplished this feat by winning eight two-man titles and three four-man titles.

★ Most bobsleigh World Championships by a women's team
A women's bobsleigh World Championships was introduced in 2000 and the sport made its debut at the 2002 Winter Olympic Games. Since 2000 Germany has won the title a record three times, in 2000, 2003 and 2004.

★ Most medals won at the women's bobsleigh World Championships
Since the introduction of the bobsleigh to the World Championships in 2000, the greatest number of medals won by an individual is four by Susi-Lisa Erdmann (Germany). She won gold in 2004 (with Kristina Bader) and in 2003 (with Annegret Dietrich), and bronze in 2001 (with Tanja Hees) and in 2002 (with Nicole Herschmann).

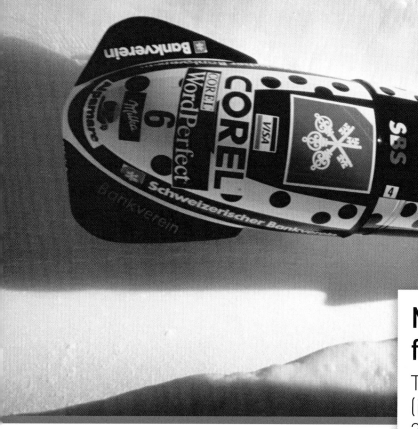

Most wins in the ⌃ four-man bobsleigh

The world four-man bobsleigh title (instituted in 1924) has been won 20 times by Switzerland (above), in 1924, 1936, 1939, 1947, 1954–57, 1971–73, 1975, 1982–83, 1986–90 and 1993. This total includes a record five Olympic victories, in 1924, 1936, 1956, 1972 and 1988.

★ Most wins in the two-man bobsleigh World Championships and Olympic Games

Switzerland have won the two-man bobsleigh title 17 times, in 1935, 1947–50, 1953, 1955, 1977–80, 1982–83, 1987, 1990, 1992 and 1994. They have also had a record four Olympic wins, in 1948, 1980, 1992 and 1994.

★ Fastest Cresta Run completion time

The Cresta Run, which dates from 1884, is 1,212 m (3,977 ft) long and has a drop of 157 m (514 ft). On 13 February 1999, James Sunley (UK) made the run in 50.09 seconds at an average speed of 87.11 km/h (54.13 mph).

★ Most Cresta Run wins

The greatest number of wins in the Cresta Run Curzon Cup competition (instituted in 1910) is eight by 1948 Olympic champion Nino Bibbia (Italy) in 1950, 1957–58, 1960, 1962–64 and 1969; and by Franco Gansser (Switzerland) in 1981, 1983–86, 1988–89 and 1991.

★ Fastest Cresta Run time from Junction

On 17 January 1999, Johannes Badrutt (Switzerland) made a time of 41.02 seconds and covered a distance of 890 m (2,921 ft) on the Cresta Run starting at Junction, the second point of the run from which competitors can officially start.

★ Most Olympic gold figure skating medals by a man

Gillis Grafstrom (Sweden) won three gold medals in 1920, 1924 and 1928, and a silver in 1932.

★ Most Olympic gold figure skating medals by a woman

Sonja Henie (Norway) won three gold medals at the Winter Olympics of 1928, 1932 and 1936.

★ Most Olympic gold figure skating medals as a pair

Irina Rodnina (USSR) won three pairs figure skating Olympic gold medals, with two different partners. In 1972 she won the gold with Alexei Ulanov, and in 1976 and 1980 she won the gold with Alexandr Zaitsev (both USSR).

★ Most figure skating Grand Slams by a man

The most figure skating Grand Slams – which comprise the European, World and Olympic titles – won by a man is two by Karl Schäfer (Austria) in 1932 and 1936.

★ Most figure skating Grand Slams by a woman

Two women have won two figure skating Grand Slams: Sonja Henie (Norway) in 1932 and 1936, and Katarina Witt (West Germany) in 1984 and 1988.

★ Most figure skating pairs World Championship titles

Irina Rodnina won 10 World Championship pairs titles (instituted in 1908) – four with Aleksey Nikolayevich Ulanov in 1969–72 and six with her husband Aleksandr Gennadyevich Zaitsev (all USSR) in 1973–78.

The most ice dance titles (instituted in 1952) won is six by Lyudmila Alekseyevna Pakhomova and her husband Aleksandr Georgiyevich Gorshkov (both USSR) in 1970–74 and 1976. The pair also won the first ever Olympic ice dance title in 1976.

★ Most continuous upright spins by an ice skater

The most continuous upright spins on ice skates on one foot is 115 by Lucinda Ruh (Switzerland) at Chelsea Piers Sky Rink, New York City, USA, on 3 April 2003.

★ Longest jump-flip by a figure skater

Robin John Cousins (UK) achieved 5.81 m (19 ft 1 in) in an axel jump and 5.48 m (18 ft) with a backflip at Richmond Ice Rink, Surrey, UK, on 16 November 1983.

Fastest 500 m speed skating »

Hiroyasu Shimizu (Japan, right) achieved a record time of 34.32 seconds in the men's 500 m speed skating competition at Salt Lake City, Utah, USA, on 10 March 2001.

★ **Greatest ice skating distance in 24 hours**
Martinus Kuiper (Netherlands) skated a total distance of 546.65 km (339.67 miles) at Alkmaar, The Netherlands, on 12–13 December 1988.

★ **Most speed skating sprint World Championship wins**
Igor Zhelezovskiy (USSR/Belarus) has won a record total of six men's sprint titles. His victories came in 1985–86, 1989 and 1991–93.

★ **Most men's speed skating Olympic gold medals**
The greatest number of Olympic gold medals won by a man is five. The record is shared by two speed skaters: Clas Thunberg (Finland) in 1924 and 1928 (including one tied); and Eric Arthur Heiden (USA) who, uniquely, won all his gold medals at one Games at Lake Placid, New York, USA, in 1980. In the process, he broke a world speed record.

★ **Most women's speed skating Olympic gold medals**
The most Olympic speed skating gold medals won by a woman is six by Lidiya Pavlovna Skoblikova (USSR), who won two golds in 1960 and four in 1964.

★ **Most men's World Championship speed skating titles**
The most World Championship speed skating titles won by a man is five. The record is shared between two speed skaters. Oscar Mathisen (Norway) won titles in 1908–9 and 1912–14, while Clas Thunberg (Finland) won in 1923, 1925, 1928–29 and 1931.

★ **Most women's speed skating World Championship titles**
The most titles won by a woman is eight by Gunda Niemann-Stirnemann (Germany) in 1991–93 and 1995–99.

★ **Most speed skating Single Distance World Championship titles**
The Single Distance World Championships were instituted in 1996. Since that time, Gunda Niemann-Stirnemann (Germany) has won 11 titles: the 1,500 m in 1997, the 3,000 m in 1996–99 and 2001, and the 5,000 m in 1997–2001.
   The greatest number of titles won by a man is seven by Gianni Romme (Netherlands). He won the 5,000 m in 1998–2000 and the 10,000 m in 1996–98 and 2000.

Men's speed skating world records

Event	Time	Name & nationality	Venue	Date
500 m	34.32	Hiroyasu Shimizu (Japan)	Salt Lake City, USA	10 March 2001
1,000 m	1:07.18	Gerard van Velde (Netherlands)	Salt Lake City, USA	16 February 2002
1,500 m	1:43.95	Derek Parra (USA)	Salt Lake City, USA	19 February 2002
3,000 m	3:42.75	Gianni Romme (Netherlands)	Calgary, Canada	11 August 2000
5,000 m	6:14.66	Jochem Uytdehaage (Netherlands)	Salt Lake City, USA	9 February 2002
10,000 m	12:58.92	Jochem Uytdehaage (Netherlands)	Salt Lake City, USA	22 February 2002
Short track				
500 m	41.184*	Jean-Francois Monette (Canada)	Calgary, Canada	18 October 2003
1,000 m	1:24.674*	Jiajun Li (China)	Bormio, Italy	2 February 2004
1,500 m	2:10.639*	Hyun-Soo Ahn (Korea)	Marquette, USA	24 October 2003
3,000 m	4:32.646*	Hyun-Soo Ahn (Korea)	Beijing, China	7 December 2003
5,000-m relay	6:43.730	Canada (Eric Bédard, Marc Gagnon, Jean-Francois Monette, Mathieu Turcotte)	Calgary, Canada	14 October 2001
* Subject to ratification by the International Skating Union (ISU) Council				

Fastest women's 1,500 m speed skating ⌄

Anni Friesinger (Germany, below foreground) achieved a time of 1 min 54.02 sec at Salt Lake City, Utah, USA, on 20 February 2002.

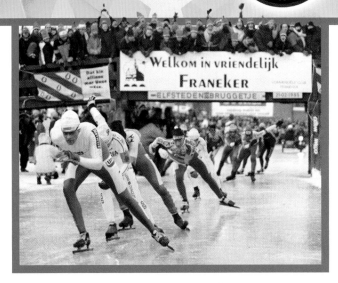

Longest ice skating race

The *Elfstedentocht* ('Tour of the 11 Towns', above), ⌃ which started in the 17th century, covers 200 km (124.27 miles). It was held in The Netherlands in 1909–63, 1985–86 and 1997. As the weather does not permit an annual race in The Netherlands, *Elfstedentocht*s also take place at alternative venues. The record men's time is 5 hr 40 min 37 sec by Dries van Wijhe (Netherlands); the women's record is 5 hr 48 min 8 sec by Alida Pasveer (Netherlands), both at Lake Weissensee, Austria, on 11 February 1989.

★ **Lowest men's speed skating World Championship score**
The lowest, and therefore best, score achieved for the men's World Championship speed skating title is 152.651 points by Rintje Ritsma (Netherlands) in Hamar, Norway, on 6–7 February 1999.

★ **Lowest women's speed skating World Championship score**
The lowest score for a woman is 161.479 points, achieved by Gunda Niemann-Stirnemann (Germany) at Hamar, Norway, on 6–7 February 1999.

★ **Most men's short-track speed skating Olympic medals**
Marc Gagnon (Canada) has won a total of five Olympic medals for short-track speed skating. His record tally comprises three gold medals (for the 500 m in 2002 and the relay in 1998 and 2002) and two bronze medals (for the 1,000 m in 1994 and the 1,500 m in 2002).

★ **Most women's short-track speed skating Olympic medals**
Two women have won five medals. Chun Lee-kyung (South Korea) won four gold medals (the 1,000 m in 1994 and 1998, and the relay in 1994 and 1998) and one bronze (the 500 m in 1998). Yang Yang (China) won four silver medals (the 500 m in 1998, the 1,000 m in 1998 and the relay in 1998 and 2002) and one bronze (the 1,000 m in 2002).

★ **Most wins in men's short-track speed skating World Championships**
The most successful skater in these championships, which were instituted in 1978, has been Marc Gagnon (Canada). He was men's overall champion in 1993–94, 1996 and 1998.

★ **Most wins in women's short-track speed skating World Championships**
In the women's competition the most successful skaters have been Sylvie Daigle (Canada), with victories in 1983 and 1988–90, and Yang Yang (China), who was champion in 1998–2001.

Women's speed skating world records

Event	Time	Name & nationality	Venue	Date
500 m	37.22	Catriona LeMay Doan (Canada)	Calgary, Canada	9 December 2001
1,000 m	1:13.83	Christine Witty (USA)	Salt Lake City, USA	17 February 2002
1,500 m	1:54.02	Anni Friesinger (Germany)	Salt Lake City, USA	20 February 2002
3,000 m	3:57.70	Claudia Pechstein (Germany)	Salt Lake City, USA	10 February 2002
5,000 m	6:46.91	Claudia Pechstein (Germany)	Salt Lake City, USA	23 February 2002
Short track				
500 m	43.671	Evgenia Radanova (Bulgaria)	Calgary, Canada	19 October 2001
1,000 m	1:30.483	Chun-Sa Byun (Korea)	Budapest, Hungary	3 February 2002
1,500 m	2:18.861*	Eun-Ju Jung (Korea)	Beijing, China	11 January 2004
3,000 m	5:01.976	Choi Eun-kyung (South Korea)	Calgary, Canada	22 October 2000
3,000-m relay	4:12.793	South Korea (Park Hye-won, Joo Min-jin, Choi Min-kyung, Choi Eun-kyung)	Salt Lake City, USA	20 February 2002

* Subject to ratification by the ISU Council

Youngest golfer to play ⌃⌃ in the Ryder Cup

Sergio Garcia (Spain, above) competed for Europe in the Ryder Cup in 1999 aged 19 years 8 months and 15 days.

Highest career earnings on the US LPGA Tour ⌃⌃

Annika Sorenstam (Sweden, above) earned $13,199,874 (£7,183,688)

on the US Ladies Professional Golf Association (LPGA) Tour from 1993 to the end of 2003. She also holds the record for the highest season's earnings on the US LPGA Tour, earning $2,863,904 (£1,817,467).

★ **Most British Open titles**
Harry Vardon (UK) won six British Open Titles, in 1896, 1898, 1899, 1903, 1911 and 1914.

★ **Most US Open titles**
Four golfers have won the US Open four times: Willie Anderson (UK) in 1901 and 1903–05; Bobby Jones Jr (USA) in 1923, 1926, 1929 and 1930; Ben Hogan (USA) in 1948, 1950, 1951 and 1953; and Jack Nicklaus (USA) in 1962, 1967, 1972 and 1980.

★ **Most Solheim Cup wins**
The Solheim Cup, the women's equivalent of the Ryder Cup, was first held in 1990 and is contested biennially between the top professional players of Europe and the USA. The

USA has won five times: 1990, 1994, 1996, 1998 and 2002. Europe won three times, in 1992, 2000 and 2003.

★ **Most successful Ryder Cup captain**
The most successful Ryder Cup captain is Walter Hagen (USA) with four wins. Hagen captained the US team to victory in 1927, 1931, 1935 and 1937. He was one of the most colourful sports personalities of his time, and is credited with doing more than any other golfer to influence the perception of his profession.

★ **Lowest score over 18 holes by a woman**
The lowest recorded score on an 18-hole course over 5,600 yd (5,120 m) for a woman is 59

by Annika Sorenstam (Sweden) in the 2001 Standard Register PING tournament at Moon Valley Country Club, Phoenix, Arizona, USA, on 16 March 2001.

★ **Biggest margin of victory in a golf tournament**
The biggest margin of victory in a major golf tournament was achieved by Tiger Woods (USA), who won the 2000 US Open by 15 shots. He finished with a round of 67 to add to rounds of 65, 69 and 71 for a 12-under-par total of 272.

★ **Lowest individual score at the World Cup**
The lowest individual total score for the four rounds of the World Cup is 263 by Tiger Woods (USA) at Kuala Lumpur, Malaysia, from 18 to 21 November 1999.

★ **Most US PGA Driving Distance titles**
Driving distance is the average number of yards per measured drive and is measured on two holes per round. Care is taken to select two holes

that face in opposite directions to counteract the effects of wind, and drives are measured to the point at which they come to rest regardless of whether they are on the fairway or not. John Daly (USA) won 11 US PGA Driving Distance titles from 1991 to 1993 and from 1995 to 2002. His longest average drive was 306.8 yd (280.44 m) in 2002.

★ **Most consecutive holes-in-one**
There are at least 20 cases of holes-in-one (or 'aces') being achieved in two consecutive holes, of which the greatest was Norman L Manley's (USA) unique 'double albatross' on the par-4 330-yd (301-m) seventh hole and par-4 290-yd (265-m) eighth hole on the Del Valle Country Club course, Saugus, California, USA, on 2 September 1964.
An albatross occurs when a player completes a hole three under par, and is therefore a hole-in-one only when hit on a par-4 hole.

Highest career earnings on the US PGA circuit »

Tiger Woods (USA, right) won $41,508,265 (£22,614,807) between August 1996 and March 2004 on the US Professional Golfers' Association (PGA) circuit. He also holds the record for the highest season's earnings on the US PGA Tour, earning $9,188,321 (£6,155,504).

★ **Most holes-in-one by husband and wife at same hole**
John and Jenny Dixon (both UK) scored consecutive holes-in-one during a four-ball competition on the third hole at Knaresborough Golf Club, Knaresborough, North Yorkshire, UK, on 22 August 1996. This was equalled by Elmer and Marilyn James (both USA) on the 16th at Halifax Plantation Golf Club, Ormond, Florida, USA, on 19 April 1998.

★ **Most holes played in 24 hours**
Ian Colston (Australia) played 22 rounds and five holes (401 holes) at Bendigo Golf Club, Victoria, Australia, (par 73 – 6,061 yd or 5,542 m) on 27–28 November 1971.

★ **Most holes played in 24 hours using a cart**
On 6–7 August 1990, David Cavalier (USA) played 846 holes at Arrowhead Country Club, North Canton, Ohio, USA, on a nine-hole course 3,013 yd (2,755 m) in length.

★ **Most holes played in a year**
Leo Fritz (USA) played a record 10,550 holes in 1998.

★ **Most walking golfers on a single course in 24 hours**
The greatest number of walking golfers to complete a full round on the same course on the same day is 491 on the Torrance Course at St Andrews Bay Golf Resort and Spa, St Andrews, Fife, UK, on 8 June 2003.

★ **Largest bunker**
The world's biggest bunker (or 'trap') is Hell's Half Acre on the 585-yd (535-m) seventh hole of the Pine Valley course, Clementon, New Jersey, USA, built in 1912 and generally regarded as the world's most testing course. The hazard starts 265 m (280 yd) from the tee and extends another 137 m (150 yd) to the next section of fairway.

★ **Longest tournament putt**
The longest recorded holed putt in a major tournament is 33.5 m (110 ft) by Jack Nicklaus (USA) in the 1964 Tournament of Champions, and Nick Price (Zimbabwe) in the 1992 US PGA.
Bob Cook (USA) sank a putt measured at 42.74 m (140 ft 2.75 in) on the 18th hole at St Andrews in the International Fourball Pro Am Tournament on 1 October 1976.

★ **Longest non-tournament putt**
On 6 November 2001, Fergus Muir (UK) sank a putt measuring 114.3 m (375 ft) on the Eden Course at St Andrews Links, Fife, UK.

★ **Longest golf carry with one hand**
Petri Takkunen (Finland) drove a golf ball 236.22 yd (216 m) using only one hand at Ruukkigolf, Pohja, Finland, on 16 June 2003.

★ **Greatest distance between two rounds of golf played on the same day**
The greatest distance between two rounds of golf played on the same day is 12,063 km (7,496 miles) by Larry Olmsted (USA), who played two full 18-hole rounds at New South Wales Golf Club, Sydney, Australia, and then Pelican Hill Golf Club, Newport Beach, California, USA, on 18 February 2004.

★ **Fastest round of golf by an individual**
With great variations in the lengths of golf courses, speed records are of little comparative value, even for rounds under par. The fastest round played when the golf ball comes to rest before each new stroke is 27 min 9 sec by James Carvill (UK) at Warrenpoint Golf Course, County Down, UK, who completed 18 holes over 6,154 yd (5,628 m) on 18 June 1987.

★ **Fastest round of golf by a team**
The WBAP News/Talk 820 (USA) team of golfers completed 18 holes in 8 min 47 sec at Bridlewood Golf Club, Flower Mound, Texas, USA, on 12 August 2003. A total of 95 golfers took part on an 18-hole course measuring 6,021 yd (5,505 m) in length.

Most water polo ⌃ World Championships

Water polo was first held at the World Swimming Championships in 1973. The most wins is two by Italy (1978 and 1994; above, back), the USSR (1975 and 1982), Yugoslavia (1986 and 1991) and Spain (1998 and 2001).

Largest « 'paddle-in' wave surfed

A wave measuring 50 ft (15.2 m) in height from trough to crest was ridden by Taylor Knox (USA, left) at a break known as Killers at Todos Santos Island off Ensenada, Mexico, on 22 February 1998. Knox caught the wave by using an arm-powered paddle-in rather than being towed.

★ Most water polo Olympic medals
Five players share the record of three gold medals: George Wilkinson in 1900, 1908 and 1912; Paulo 'Paul' Radmilovic and Charles Sidney Smith in 1908, 1912 and 1920 (all GB); and Desz Gyarmati and György Kárpáti (both Hungary) in 1952, 1956 and 1964.

Paul Radmilovic also won a gold for the 4 x 200-m freestyle relay swimming in 1908.

★ Most water polo goals in an international game
The greatest number of goals scored by an individual in a water polo international is 13 by Debbie Handley for Australia (16) against Canada (10) at the World Championship in Guayaquil, Ecuador, in 1982.

★ Longest water polo marathon
A match lasting 24 hours was played by Rapido 82 Haarlem at the De Planeet pool, Haarlem, The Netherlands, from 30 April to 1 May 1999.

★ Longest water-skiing marathon
Ralph Hildebrand and Dave Phillips (both Canada) water-skied simultaneously for 56 hr 35 min 3 sec around Indian Arm, Rocky Point, British Columbia, Canada. They completed their feat on 12 June 1994 after covering a distance of 2,152.3 km (1,337.46 miles) at an average speed of 48 km/h (30 mph). While skiing at night they used infrared binoculars and spotlights.

★ Most barefoot water-skiing World Championships
The record is held jointly by Kim Lampard (Australia), for wins in 1980, 1982, 1985 and 1986, and Jennifer Calleri (USA), who won in 1990, 1992, 1994 and 1996.

The most titles won by a man is three by Brett Wing (Australia), in 1978, 1980 and 1982, and Ron Scarpa (USA), in 1992, 1996 and 1998.

The team title has been won six times by the USA, in 1988, 1990, 1992, 1994, 1996 and 1998.

★ Largest wave surfed (unlimited)
The largest wave successfully surfed had a face 70 ft (21.3 m) in height. It was ridden by Pete Cabrinha (USA) at a break known as Jaws (Peahi) on the North Shore of Maui, Hawaii, USA on 10 January 2004. He was towed into the wave using a wave runner.

★ Most amateur surfing World Championships
Surfing's World Amateur Championships were inaugurated in May 1964 at Sydney, Australia. The greatest number of titles won is three by Michael Novakov (Australia), who won the kneeboard event in 1982, 1984 and 1986.

★ Longest surfboard ride on a river bore
The longest recorded rides on a river bore have been set on the Severn bore, UK. The Official British Surfing Association distance record for riding a surfboard is 9.1 km (5.7 miles) by David Lawson (UK) from Windmill Hill to Maisemore Weir (both Gloucestershire, UK) on 29 August 1996.

★ Longest continuous journey by a kite surfer
Fabrice Collard, Kent Marincovik and Neil Hutchinson (all USA) travelled a distance of 88 nautical miles (163 km or 101.3 miles) between Key West, Florida, USA, and Varadero, Cuba, on boards pulled by kites on 21 December 2001.

Their journey, during which they were not permitted to touch any other vessel, lasted 8 hr 38 min at an average speed of 12 knots (22 km/h or 14 mph).

★ Most windsurfing World Championships
From 1979 to 1983, Stephan van den Berg (Netherlands) won five windsurfing world titles.

★ Longest windsurfing marathon
Sergiy Naidych (Ukraine) windsurfed for 71 hr 30 min at Radyschev Lake, Simerferopol, Crimea, Ukraine, from 6 to 9 June 2003.

Most men's professional surfing World Championships »

The most Association of Surfing Professionals (ASP) Tour World Championship titles won by a man is six by Kelly Slater (USA, right), in 1992 and 1994–98.

The equivalent women's title has been won six times by Layne Beachley (Australia) from 1998 to 2003.

★ **Longest windsurfing journey**
Steve Fisher (USA) crossed the Pacific from California to Hawaii on *Da Slipper II*, a highly modified 5.4-m-long (17-ft 8-in) windsurfer. The 2,269-nautical mile (4,203-km or 2,612-mile) journey took a total of 47 days and Steve arrived on a beach on Maui, Hawaii, on 3 September 1997.

★ **Fastest time to windsurf across the Atlantic**
Sergio Ferrero (Italy) windsurfed across the Atlantic from the Canary Islands to Barbados, a distance of approximately 2,600 nautical miles (5,000 km or 3,100 miles) in 24 days from 6 to 30 June 1982.

★ **Most consecutive days spent surfing**
Dale Webster (USA) has surfed every day since 2 September 1975, passing his 10,407th consecutive day of surfing on 29 February 2004. He set himself the condition that a 'surf' should consist of catching at least three waves to shore.

Water-skiing – Men's world records

Event	Score	Name/Nationality	Venue	Date
Slalom	1 buoy/9.75-m line	Jeff Rogers (USA)	Charleston, South Carolina, USA	31 August 1997
		Andy Mapple (GB)	Miami, Florida, USA	4 October 1998
		Jamie Beauchesne (USA)	Charleston, South Carolina, USA	6 July 2003
Tricks	12,320 points	Nicolas Le Forestier (France)	Chaugey, France	13 July 2003
Ski fly	91.1 m (298 ft 10 in)	Jaret Llewellyn (Canada)	Orlando, Florida, USA	4 May 2000
Jump	71.9 m (235.ft 9.6 in)	Jimmy Siemers (USA)	Lago Santa Fe, Texas, USA	10 August 2003
Overall	2,818.8 points	Jaret Llewellyn (Canada)	Seffner, Florida, USA	29 September 2002

Water-skiing – Women's world records

Event	Score	Name/Nationality	Venue	Date
Slalom	1 buoy/10.25-m line	Kristi Overton Johnson (USA)	West Palm Beach, Florida, USA	14 September 1996
Tricks	8,630 points	Tawn Larsen Hahn (USA)	Wilmington, Illinois, USA	11 July 1999
Ski fly	69.4 m (227 ft 7 in)	Elena Milakova (Russia)	Pine Mountain, Georgia, USA	26 May 2002
Jump	56.6 m (186 ft)	Elena Milakova (Russia)	Rio Linda, California, USA	27 July 2002
Overall	2,854.01 points	Elena Milakova (Russia)	Hazelwood Ski World, Lincolnshire, UK	29 July 2001

Barefoot water-skiing – Men's world records

Event	Score	Name/Nationality	Venue	Date
Jump	27.4 m (89 ft 9.6 in)	David Small (GB)	Mulwala Water Ski Park, New South Wales, Australia	8 February 2004
Slalom	20.5 crossings of the wake in 15 sec	Brian Fuchs (USA)	Liverpool, New South Wales, Australia	April 1994
Tricks	9,550 points	David Small (GB)	Mulwala Water Ski Park, New South Wales, Australia	5 February 2004

Barefoot water-skiing – Women's world records

Event	Score	Name/Nationality	Venue	Date
Jump	20.6 m (67 ft 6.9 in)	Nadine de Villiers (RSA)	Roodeplaat Dam, South Africa	4 March 2000
Slalom	17.0 crossings of the wake in 15 sec	Nadine de Villiers (RSA)	Wolwekrans, South Africa	5 January 2001
Tricks	4,400 points	Nadine de Villiers (RSA)	Wolwekrans, South Africa	5 January 2001

Eskimo rolls

Event	Record	Name & nationality	Venue	Date
Fastest 1,000 (no paddle)	31 min 55 sec	Colin Hill (UK)	Durham, UK	12 March 1987
Fastest 1,000 (paddle)	34 min 43 sec	Ray Hudspith (UK)	Newcastle Upon Tyne, UK	20 March 1987
Fastest 100 (no paddle)	2 min 39 sec	Colin Hill (UK)	London, UK	22 February 1987
Fastest 100 (paddle)	3 min 7 sec	Ray Hudspith (UK)	Tyne and Wear, UK	3 March 1991
Fastest 100 (female, paddle)	3 min 42 sec	Helen Barnes (UK)	London, UK	2 August 2000
Most consecutive	1,796	Randy Fine (USA)	Florida, USA	8 June 1991
Tandem (paddle) (one minute)	23	Emmanuel Baclet & Yann Hascoet (France)	Benodet, France	29 July 2003

Rowing world records

Event	Time	Name & nationality	Regatta	Date
Men				
Single sculls	6:36.33	Marcel Hacker (Germany)	Seville, Spain	2002
Double sculls	6:04.37	Luka Spik, Iztok Cop (Slovenia)	St Catharines, Canada	1999
Quadruple sculls	5:37.68	Italy	Indianapolis, USA	1994
Coxless pairs	6:14.27	Matthew Pinsent, James Cracknell (GB)	Seville, Spain	2002
Coxless fours	5:41.35	Germany	Seville, Spain	2002
*Coxed pairs	6:42.16	Igor Boraska, Tihomir Frankovic, Milan Razov (Croatia)	Indianapolis, USA	1994
*Coxed fours	5:58.96	Germany	Vienna, Austria	1991
Coxed eights	5:22.80	The Netherlands	St Catharines, Canada	1999
Women				
Single sculls	7:07.71	Roumiana Neykova (Bulgaria)	Seville, Spain	2002
Double sculls	6:38.78	Georgina Evers-Swindell, Caroline Evers-Swindell (New Zealand)	Seville, Spain	2002
Quadruple sculls	6:10.80	Germany	Duisburg, Germany	1996
Coxless pairs	6:53.80	Georgeta Andrunache, Viorica Susanu (Romania)	Seville, Spain	2002
*Coxless fours	6:25.47	Canada	Vienna, Austria	1991
Coxed eights	5:57.02	Romania	Lucerne, Switzerland	1999
Men's lightweight				
*Single sculls	6:47.97	Karsten Nielsen (Denmark)	St Catharines, Canada	1999
Double sculls	6:10.80	Elia Luini, Leonardo Pettinari (Italy)	Seville, Spain	2002
*Quadruple sculls	5:45.18	Italy	Montreal, Canada	1992
*Coxless pairs	6:29.97	Christian Yantani Garces, Miguel Cerda Silva (Chile)	Seville, Spain	2002
Coxless fours	5:45.60	Denmark	Lucerne, Switzerland	1999
*Coxed eights	5:30.24	Germany	Montreal, Canada	1992
Women's lightweight				
*Single sculls	7:15.88	Marit van Eupen (Netherlands)	Lucerne, Switzerland	1999
Double sculls	6:50.63	Berit Christoffersen, Lene Andersson (Denmark)	Copenhagen, Denmark	1995
*Quadruple sculls	6:29.55	Australia	Seville, Spain	2002
*Coxless pairs	7:18.32	Eliza Blair, Justine Joyce (Australia)	Aiguebelette, France	1997

* denotes non-Olympic boat classes

Fastest single sculls ⌃

Roumiana Neykova (Bulgaria, above) set a record of 7 min 7.71 sec for the single sculls in Seville, Spain, in 2002.

★ **Most men's World & Olympic canoeing titles**
The men's record is 13 by Gert Fredriksson (Sweden), 1948–60, Rüdiger Helm (GDR), 1976–83, and Ivan Patzaichin (Romania), 1968–84.

★ **Most canoeing gold medals won at a single Olympic Games**
The most gold medals at one Games is three by Vladimir Parfenovich (USSR) in 1980 and Ian Ferguson (New Zealand) in 1984.

★ **Most consecutive kayak cartwheels**
Koya Morita (Japan) set a record of 264 consecutive cartwheels in a kayak at Tama River, Ome-shi, Japan, on 17 August 2003. One kayak cartwheel is a full 360° rotation – vertically rather than horizontally.

★ **Greatest distance by canoe in 24 hours**
Ian Adamson (USA) paddled 327.1 km (203.3 miles) in a canoe on the Colorado River from Gore Canyon, Colorado, to Potash, Utah, USA, between 7 and 8 June 1997.

The record for the same time canoeing on the ocean is held by Randy Fine (USA), who paddled 194.1 km (120.6 miles) along the Florida coast on 26–27 June 1986.

★ **Fastest 75-ft descent by canoe**
Shaun Baker (UK) descended a vertical height of 22.86 m (75 ft) in 19.9 seconds in a canoe on a river in Snowdonia, UK, on 26 August 2000.

★ **Most women's Olympic & World canoeing titles**
Birgit Fischer (GDR/Germany) won seven Olympic gold medals between 1980 and 2000. She also won three silver medals for a record total of 10 medals. In addition, she won 29 world titles between 1979 and 1998, for a record 34 titles overall.

Apnea – freediving world records

	Depth	Name & nationality	Venue	Date
Constant weight				
Men	95 m (311 ft)	Herbert Nitsch (Austria)	Dellach, Millstatter See, Austria	4 September 2003
Women	70 m (229 ft)	Tanya Streeter (UK)	Guadeloupe, France	11 May 2001
Constant weight without fins				
Men	61 m (200 ft)	Stig Åvall Severinsen (Denmark)	Puerto de la Cruz, Venezuela	28 September 2003
Women	43 m (141 ft)	Mandy-Rae Cruickshank (Canada)	Vancouver, Canada	1 September 2003
Variable weight				
Men	120 m (393 ft)	Patrick Musimu (Belgium)	Playa del Carmen, Mexico	12 November 2002
Women	122 m (400 ft)	Tanya Streeter (UK)	Turks and Caicos	21 July 2003
No limits				
Men	162 m (531 ft)	Loic Leferme (France)	Nice, France	20 October 2002
Women	160 m (525 ft)	Tanya Streeter (USA)	Turks and Caicos	17 August 2002.
Free immersion				
Men	101 m (331 ft)	Carlos Coste (Venezuela)	Puerto de la Cruz, Venezuela	4 October 2003
Women	71 m (232 ft)	Annabel Briseno (USA)	Kona, Hawaii, USA	15 November 2003
Dynamic apnea with fins				
Men	200 m (656 ft)	Peter Pedersen (Denmark)	Randers, Denmark	18 July 2003
Women	150 m (492 ft) (25 m pool)	Nathalie Desreac (France)	Réunion Island, France	14 November 1998
	150 m (492 ft) (50 m pool)	Natalia Molchanova (Russia)	Limassol, Cyprus	26 May 2003
Dynamic apnea without fins				
Men	166 m (544 ft)	Stig Åvall Severinsen (Denmark)	Aarhus, Denmark	19 July 2003
Women	100 m (328 ft)	Renate De Bruyn (Netherlands)	Eindhoven, The Netherlands	10 October 2003
Static apnea				
Men	8 min 24 sec	Stephane Mifsud (France)	Rouen, France	8 November 2003
Women	6 min 21 sec	Annabel Briseno (USA)	Kona, Hawaii, USA	13 November 2003

 # GWR TALKS TO
Tanya Streeter

Freediver Tanya Streeter (UK, right) currently holds three freediving world records: the no-limits freedive (160 m or 525 ft), freediving with a constant weight (70 m or 229 ft) and the variable weight freediving record of 122 m (400 ft), which she set on the Atlantic islands of Turks and Caicos on 21 July 2003. Freediving involves staying under water for as long as possible on just one breath. Some freediving records require diving to incredible depths.

How and when did you first become interested in freediving?
I grew up on a Caribbean island and I was a good snorkeller. Technically, snorkelling is freediving; any time you take a breath and go under water you are freediving. I started freediving when I was 25. I was inspired by people around me who knew more about the sport than I did.

What's your training regime?
A huge part of this sport is about fitness and being in peak physical condition. Much of my training is endurance based: I do a lot of spinning (static cycling), and lots of aerobic training to get my cardiovascular system working efficiently. Then there's the conditioning work, getting my body used to not breathing, and operating without breathing during the course of the dive; this work is often pool-based. Finally, freediving is largely dependent on mental strength, so I need to train myself mentally, which is probably the hardest part.

Is it fair to say that freediving is an extreme sport?
No, absolutely not. People think that because we can hold our breaths for so long, or dive so deep, we must in some way be super-human, or are attempting to do very extreme things, when really what we're attempting to do is on the extreme edge of human potential. Most people will have tried to swim as far as they can under water on one breath: when you compare their 40 seconds with our six minutes, what freedivers do seems impossible.

Freediving is also a very controlled environment isn't it?
It is. We have to consider every element of the dive. People breathe instinctively; once you take away that option, it makes you think about absolutely everything you're going to need to do to be able to breathe again. It's highly, highly controlled.

What do you consider your greatest achievement so far?
I don't think that my achievement in my sport has actually been at the forefront for me, it's the fact that I have the opportunity to inspire people. I get lots of e-mails from people who have read about me and were inspired, and I get much more emotional satisfaction from that than I ever have done from a world record. I train very hard and I face every human fear that everyone else faces when embracing challenges. But it's the personal experience and the journey to those goals that stay with you. Never giving up on a goal has taught me the most.

What advice would you give someone wanting to freedive?
Safety. You must never do any breath-hold activity alone, even if it's just holding your breath in a pool. You must get some instruction, because it's more complicated than it seems. Many freedivers like myself are happy to give advice, but this sport should only be done with at least one companion, never alone.

Swimming
Sport

Women's swimming (short course)

Event	Time	Name & nationality	Venue	Date
50-m freestyle	23.59	Therese Alshammar (Sweden)	Athens, Greece	18 March 2000
100-m freestyle	52.17	Therese Alshammar (Sweden)	Athens, Greece	17 March 2000
200-m freestyle	1:54.04	Lindsay Benko (USA)	Moscow, Russia	7 April 2002
400-m freestyle	3:59.53	Lindsay Benko (USA)	Berlin, Germany	26 January 2003
800-m freestyle	8:13.35	Sachiko Yamada (Japan)	Nishinomya-shi, Japan	24 January 2004
1,500-m freestyle	15:43.31	Petra Schneider (GDR)	Gainesville, USA	10 January 1982
4 x 50-m freestyle	1:37.52	The Netherlands (Hinkelien Schreuder, Annabel Kosten, Chantal Groot, Marleen Veldhuis)	Dublin, Ireland	12 December 2003
4 x 100-m freestyle	3:34.55	China (Le Jingyi, Na Chao, Shan Ying, Nian Yin)	Gothenburg, Sweden	19 April 1997
4 x 200-m freestyle	7:46.30	China (Xu Yanvei, Zhu Yingven, Tang Jingzhi, Yang Yu)	Moscow, Russia	3 April 2002
50-m butterfly	25.36	Anna-Karin Kammerling (Sweden)	Stockholm, Sweden	25 January 2001
100-m butterfly	0:56.34	Natalie Coughlin (USA)	New York, USA	22 November 2002
200-m butterfly	2:04.04	Yu Yang (China)	Berlin, Germany	18 January 2004
50-m backstroke	26.83	Hui Li (China)	Shanghai, China	2 December 2001
100-m backstroke	0:56.71	Natalie Coughlin (USA)	New York, USA	23 November 2002
200-m backstroke	2:03.62	Natalie Coughlin (USA)	New York, USA	27 November 2001
50-m breaststroke	29.96	Emma Igelström (Sweden)	Moscow, Russia	4 April 2002
100-m breaststroke	1:05.09	Leisel Jones (Australia)	Melbourne, Australia	28 November 2003
200-m breaststroke	2:17.75	Leisel Jones (Australia)	Melbourne, Australia	29 November 2003
100-m medley	58.80	Natalie Coughlin (USA)	New York, USA	23 November 2003
200-m medley	2:07.79	Allison Wagner (USA)	Palma de Mallorca, Spain	5 December 1993
400-m medley	4:27.83	Yana Klochkova (Ukraine)	Paris, France	19 January 2002
4 x 50-m medley	1:48.31	Sweden (Therese Alshammar, Emma Igelström, Anna-Karin Kammerling, Johanna Sjöberg)	Valencia, Spain	16 December 2000
4 x 100-m medley	3:55.78	Sweden (Therese Alshammar, Emma Igelström, Anna-Karin Kammerling, Johanna Sjöberg)	Moscow, Russia	5 April 2002

Men's 200-m ⌃ short course backstroke

Aaron Peirsol (USA, above) completed the men's 200-m short course backstroke in a record time of 1 min 51.17 sec in Moscow, Russia, on 7 April 2002. He also holds the record for the long course race over the same distance, with a time of 1 min 55.15 sec, recorded in Minneapolis, USA, on 20 March 2002.

★ **Most Olympic diving medals**
The most medals won by a diver is five. Klaus Dibiasi (Italy) won three gold and two silver (1964–76), and Greg Louganis (USA) won four golds and one silver (1976, 1984 and 1988). Dibiasi is the only diver to win the same event (highboard) at three successive Games (1968–76). Two divers have won highboard and springboard doubles at two Games: Patricia Joan McCormick (née Keller, USA) in 1952 and 1956, and Louganis in 1984 and 1988.

Men's swimming (short course)

Event	Time	Name & nationality	Venue	Date
50-m freestyle	21.13	Mark Foster (GB)	Paris, France	28 January 2001
100-m freestyle	46.74	Aleksandr Popov (Russia)	Gelsenkirchen, Germany	19 March 1994
200-m freestyle	1:41.10	Ian Thorpe (Australia)	Berlin, Germany	6 February 2000
400-m freestyle	3:34.58	Grant Hackett (Australia)	Sydney, Australia	18 July 2002
800-m freestyle	7:25.28	Grant Hackett (Australia)	Perth, Australia	3 August 2001
1,500-m freestyle	14:10.10	Grant Hackett (Australia)	Perth, Australia	7 August 2001
4 x 50-m freestyle	1:25.55	The Netherlands (Mark Veens, Johan Kenkhuis, Gijs Damen, Pieter van de Hoogenband)	Dublin, Ireland	14 December 2003
4 x 100-m freestyle	3:09.57	Sweden (Johan Nystr-öm, Lars Frolander, Mattias Ohlin, Stefan Nystrand)	Athens, Greece	16 March 2000
4 x 200-m freestyle	6:56.41	Australia (William Kirby, Ian Thorpe, Michael Klim, Grant Hackett)	Perth, Australia	7 August 2001
50-m butterfly	22.74	Geoff Huegill (Australia)	Berlin, Germany	
100-m butterfly	50.02	Cavic Milorad (Serbia and Montenegro)	Dublin, Ireland	12 December 2003
200-m butterfly	1:50.73	Frank Esposito (France)	Antibes, France	8 December 2002
50-m backstroke	23.31	Matthew Welsh (Australia)	Melbourne, Australia	2 September 2002
100-m backstroke	50.58	Thomas Rupprath (Germany)	Melbourne, Australia	8 December 2002
200-m backstroke	1:51.17	Aaron Peirsol (USA)	Moscow, Russia	7 April 2002
50-m breaststroke	26.20	Oleg Lissogor (Ukraine)	Berlin, Germany	26 January 2002
100-m breaststroke	57.47	Ed Moses (USA)	Stockholm, Sweden	23 January 2002
200-m breaststroke	2:02.92	Ed Moses (USA)	Berlin, Germany	17 January 2004
100-m medley	52.63	Peter Mankoc (Slovenia)	Antwerp, Belgium	15 December 2001
200-m medley	1:54.65	Jani Sievinen (Finland)	Kuopio, Finland	21 April 1994
400-m medley	4:02.72	Brian Johns (Canada)	Victoria, Canada	21 February 2003
4 x 50-m medley	1:34.46	Germany (Thomas Rupprath, Mark Warnecke, Fabian Friedrich, Carstein Dehmlow)	Dublin, Ireland	11 December 2003
4 x 100-m medley	3:28.12	Australia (Matthew Welsh, Jim Pipes, Geoff Huegill, Ashley Callus)	Melbourne, Australia	4 September 2002

Women's swimming (long course)

Event	Time	Name & nationality	Venue	Date
50-m freestyle	24.13	Inge de Bruijn (Netherlands)	Sydney, Australia	22 September 2000
100-m freestyle	53.77	Inge de Bruijn (Netherlands)	Sydney, Australia	20 September 2000
200-m freestyle	1:56.64	Franziska van Almsick (Germany)	Berlin, Germany	3 August 2002
400-m freestyle	4:03.85	Janet Evans (USA)	Seoul, South Korea	22 September 1988
800-m freestyle	8:16.22	Janet Evans (USA)	Tokyo, Japan	20 August 1989
1,500-m freestyle	15:52.10	Janet Evans (USA)	Orlando, USA	26 March 1988
4 x 100-m freestyle relay	3:36.60	Germany (Franziska van Almsick, Petra Dallmann, Sandra Volker, Kathrin Meibner)	Berlin, Germany	29 July 2002
4 x 200-m freestyle relay	7:55.47	GDR (Manuela Stellmach, Astrid Strauss, Anke Möhring, Heike Friedrich)	Strasbourg, France	18 August 1987
50-m butterfly	25.57	Anna-Karin Kammerling (Sweden)	Berlin, Germany	31 July 2000
100-m butterfly	56.61	Inge de Bruijn (Netherlands)	Sydney, Australia	17 September 2000
200-m butterfly	2:05.78	Otylia Jedrejczak (Poland)	Berlin, Germany	2 August 2002
50-m backstroke	28.25	Sandra Voelker (Germany)	Berlin, Germany	17 June 2000
100-m backstroke	59.58	Natalie Coughlin (USA)	Fort Lauderdale, USA	13 August 2002
200-m backstroke	2:06.62	Krisztina Egerszegi (Hungary)	Athens, Greece	25 August 1991
50-m breaststroke	30.57	Zoe Baker (UK)	Manchester, UK	30 July 2002
100-m breaststroke	1:06.52	Penny Heyns (South Africa)	Sydney, Australia	23 August 1999
200-m breaststroke	2:22.99	Hui Qi (China)	Hangzhou, China	13 April 2001
200-m medley	2:09.72	Wu Yanyan (China)	Shanghai, China	17 October 1997
400-m medley	4:33.59	Yana Klochkova (Ukraine)	Sydney, Australia	16 September 2000
4 x 100-m medley relay	3:58.30	USA (Megan Quann, Jenny Thompson, BJ Bedford, Dara Torres)	Sydney, Australia	23 September 2000

Men's swimming (long course)

Event	Time	Name & nationality	Venue	Date
50-m freestyle	21.64	Alexander Popov (Russia)	Moscow, Russia	16 June 2000
100-m freestyle	47.84	Pieter van den Hoogenband (Netherlands)	Sydney, Australia	19 September 2000
200-m freestyle	1:44.06	Ian Thorpe (Australia)	Fukuoka, Japan	25 July 2001
400-m freestyle	3:40.17	Ian Thorpe (Australia)	Fukuoka, Japan	22 July 2001
800-m freestyle	7:39.16	Ian Thorpe (Australia)	Fukuoka, Japan	24 July 2001
1,500-m freestyle	14:34.56	Grant Hackett (Australia)	Fukuoka, Japan	29 July 2001
4 x 100-m freestyle relay	3:13.67	Australia (Michael Klim, Chris Fydler, Ashley Callus, Ian Thorpe)	Sydney, Australia	16 September 2000
4 x 200-m freestyle relay	7:04.66	Australia (Grant Hackett, Michael Klim, William Kirby, Ian Thorpe)	Fukuoka, Japan	27 July 2001
50-m butterfly	23.44	Geoff Huegill (Australia)	Fukuoka, Japan	27 July 2001
100-m butterfly	51.81	Michael Klim (Australia)	Canberra, Australia	12 December 1999
200-m butterfly	1:54.58	Michael Phelps (USA)	Fukuoka, Japan	24 July 2001
50-m backstroke	24.99	Lenny Krayzelburg (USA)	Sydney, Australia	28 August 1999
100-m backstroke	53.60	Lenny Krayzelburg (USA)	Sydney, Australia	24 August 1999
200-m backstroke	1:55.15	Aaron Peirsol (USA)	Minneapolis, USA	20 March 2002
50-m breaststroke	27.18	Oleg Lisogor (Ukraine)	Berlin, Germany	2 August 2002
100-m breaststroke	59.94	Roman Sloudnov (Russia)	Fukuoka, Japan	23 July 2001
200-m breaststroke	2:10.16	Mike Barrowman (USA)	Barcelona, Spain	29 July 1992
200-m medley	1:55.94	Michael Phelps (USA)	Maryland, USA	9 August 2003
400-m medley	4:09.09	Michael Phelps (USA)	Barcelona, Spain	27 July 2003
4 x 100-m medley relay	3:33.48	USA (Aaron Peirsol, Brendon Hanson, Michael Phelps, Jason Lezak)	Yokohama, Japan	29 August 2002

★ Most diving World Championships

Greg Louganis (USA) won five world titles – highboard in 1978, and highboard and springboard in 1982 and 1986 – and four Olympic gold medals in 1984 and 1988. Philip George Boggs (USA) also won three golds in one event, for springboard in 1973, 1975 and 1978.

★ Most men's Olympic swimming medals

Mark Spitz (USA) won nine gold medals: the 100-m and 200-m freestyle (1972), the 100-m and 200-m butterfly (1972), 4 x 100-m freestyle (1968 and 1972), the 4 x 200-m freestyle (1968 and 1972) and the 4 x 100-m medley (1972). All but one of these (the 4 x 200-m freestyle of 1968) were also new world records. He also won a silver (100-m butterfly) and a bronze (100-m freestyle) in 1968, giving him a record 11 medals in all.

★ Most individual Olympic swimming gold medals

Krisztina Egerszegi (Hungary) won five gold medals: 100-m backstroke (1992), 200-m

Most women's Olympic medals ⌃

Three women have won eight medals. Dawn Fraser (Australia, above right) won four golds and four silvers (1956–64); Kornelia Ender (GDR) won four golds and four silvers (1972–76); and Shirley Babashoff (USA) won two golds and six silvers (1972–76).

backstroke (1988, 1992 and 1996) and 400-m medley (1992).

Five men have four Olympic golds: Charles Meldrum Daniels (USA) for 100-m freestyle (1906 and 1908), 220-yd freestyle (1904) and 440-yd freestyle (1904); Roland Matthes (GDR) for 100-m and 200-m backstroke (1968 and 1972); Mark Spitz (USA) for 100-m and 200-m freestyle, and 100-m and 200-m butterfly (1972); Tamás Daryni (Hungary) for 200-m and 400-m medley (1988 and 1992); and Aleksandr Popov (Russia) for 50-m and 100-m freestyle (1992 and 1996).

★ Farthest distance swum

Martin Strel (Slovenia) swam the Mississippi River, USA, from its source in northern Minnesota to the Gulf of Mexico, between 4 July and 9 September 2002. He swam a total of 3,797 km (2,360 miles) in 68 days.

Most show >> jumping World Cup wins

The show jumping World Cup (instituted 1979) has been won three times by Hugo Simon (Austria) in 1979, 1996 and 1997; and Rodrigo Pessoa (Brazil, right) in 1998–2000. Pessoa's wins were all on the same horse, Gandini Baloubet du Rouet (right).

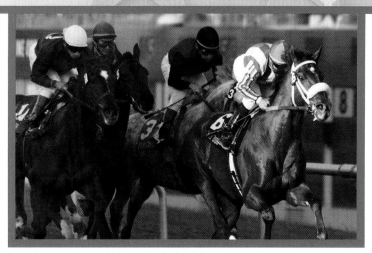

Most horse racing ⌃ career wins by a jockey

Laffit Pincay Jr (USA, above far right) rode a total of 9,531 winners from 16 May 1964 to 1 March 2003.

Pincay announced his retirement aged 56 at the end of April 2003, nearly two months after breaking his neck in a fall at Santa Anita, California, USA.

★ **Most men's show jumping World Championships**
The most show jumping World Championships won by a man is two, by Hans Günter Winkler (Germany) in 1954 and 1955 and Raimondo d'Inzeo (Italy) in 1956 and 1960.

★ **Most women's show jumping World Championships**
Janou Tissot (France) won two World Championship titles on Rocket in 1970 and 1974.

★ **Most show jumping World Championship team titles**
The most show jumping team World Championship titles is two and the record is shared by France in 1982 and 1990, Germany in 1994 and 1998, and the USA in 1986 and 2002.

★ **Most Badminton wins**
The Badminton Three-Day Event (instituted 1949) has been won six times by Lucinda Green (UK) in 1973 (on Be Fair), 1976 (Wide Awake), 1977 (George), 1979 (Killaire), 1983 (Regal Realm) and 1984 (Beagle Bay).

★ **Jockey with most St Leger wins**
Between 1821 and 1846, jockey Bill Scott (UK) won the St Leger (instituted 1776), the world's oldest classic race, nine times.

★ **Fastest time to run the St Leger**
In 1926, Coronach ran the St Leger in a time of 3 min 1.6 sec. This was equalled by Windsor Lad in 1934.

★ **Fastest time to run the Epsom Derby**
In 1995, Lammtarra ran the Epsom Derby in 2 min 32.3 sec.

★ **Fastest time to run the Kentucky Derby**
Secretariat, ridden by Ron Turcotte (Canada), ran a record time of 1 min 59.4 sec on 5 May 1973 at Churchill Downs, Kentucky, USA.

★ **Greatest total prize money for a day's racing**
The Dubai World Cup race meeting at Nad Al Sheba, Dubai, United Arab Emirates, held annually in March, has total

prize money of $15.25 million (£10.62 million). Since 2002, the seven-race meeting has included the world's richest race, the Dubai World Cup.

★ **Highest amount won in a single race**
The highest amount won in one horse race is $3.6 million (£2.03 million) for the Dubai World Cup by: Dubai Millennium, 2000; Captain Steve, 2001; Street Cry, 2002; Moon Ballard 2003; and Pleasantly Perfect, 2004.

★ **Oldest horse to win a race**
Al Jabal, a pure-bred Arabian horse, ridden by Brian Boulton and owned by Andrea Boulton (both UK), was 19 years old when he won the Three Horseshoes Handicap Stakes on 9 June 2002 at Barbury Castle, Wiltshire, UK.

★ **Most polo World Championships**
Argentina have won three polo World Championships: in 1987 in Argentina, 1992 in Chile and 1998 in the USA.

★ **Most goals in polo World Championships**
Argentina have scored 35 goals during final matches of the polo World Championships.

★ **Highest rodeo earnings**
Ty Murray (USA) holds three records for rodeo earnings: he has record career earnings of $2,931,227 (£1,870,624) won between 1989 and 2002; he won the most prize money in a single season with $377,358 (£240,692) earned in 1998; and he won the most money at a single rodeo with a win of $124,821 (£79,716) at the National Finals Rodeo in Las Vegas, Nevada, USA, in 1993.

★ **Highest bull riding score**
Wade Leslie (USA) scored 100 points out of a possible 100 on Wolfman Skoal at Central Point, Oregon, USA, in 1991.

★ **Highest bareback riding score**
Wes Stevenson (USA) scored 94 out of a possible 100 on Kesler Rodeo's Cover Girl in Dallas, Texas, USA, in 2002.

Highest saddle bronc score ∧∧

The highest scored saddle bronc ride is 95 out of a possible 100 by Glen O'Neill (Australia, above) on Franklin's Airwolf at Innisfail, Alberta, Canada, in 1996; and also by Doug Vold (USA) on Transport at Meadow Lake, Saskatchewan, Canada, in 1979.

★ GWR TALKS TO
Tony McCoy

Jockey Tony McCoy (UK, above) holds the record for the most steeplechase wins in a career, with 2,078 winners ridden between 1992 and May 2004. He has also won more steeplechase races in a season than any other jockey, with 289 in 2001/2002.

What first got you interested in horses and how old were you when you started riding?
My dad had horses and I thought that I'd like to ride them – I was fortunate enough to have my own ponies. I also liked watching it on

TV. I first sat on a horse when I was about seven or eight but I started racing at the age of 16 – the age you have to be to compete legally.

What do you do to keep fit for your sport?
With riding every day I don't really have to do anything to keep fit. If you do a certain activity a lot, that keeps you fit for that activity. If I was having time off I'd use my gym.

What's your favourite memory from your career so far?
That would be a few years ago when I broke Sir Gordon Richards' 55-year record for the most wins in a season – he was champion flat jockey 26 times.

Is your record for steeplechase wins in a career as special?
Yes, it's a different type of record. Every record you hold is special, but with this one, so many great

jockeys before me set it, like John Francome, Peter Scudamore, Richard Dunwoody; and being able to say that I've brought home more winners than them means a lot as they were the people I looked up to when I was younger.

So are they also your idols?
They are definitely, very much so, and I'm very lucky now as they're my friends as well, even though when I was young and growing up I looked up to them a lot.

What's your favourite racecourse?
For me personally, Cheltenham because it's just got a brilliant atmosphere. Liverpool's not too bad either.

What's the most races you've ridden in one day?
The most in one day is 11. The most wins in one day is five.

What keeps you going? What's your motivation?
I love doing it and the day I don't enjoy doing it I won't do it. Anyone that's lucky enough to earn their living from their sport would tell you how lucky they are.

If you had to name one major goal that you haven't achieved so far, what would it be?
I have to win the Grand National. It's not really happening at the moment. It's one of the biggest courses and one of the biggest sporting events in the world.

You're an inspiration to those wishing to get involved in the sport. Is that important to you?
If you can help young children or get them involved in any sport it's great, and if they have as much luck as I have had, then they're going to be very lucky people.

Greatest « paragliding altitude gain

Robbie Whittal (UK, left) achieved a record height gain of 4,526 m (14,849 ft) at Brandvlei, South Africa, on 6 January 1993. As a comparison, Boeing 747s normally cruise at 10,000 m (32,808 ft).

The greatest height gained with a paraglider by a female is 4,325 m (14,189 ft) by Kat Thurston (UK) over Kuruman, South Africa, on 1 January 1996.

Most parachutists to ⌃ jump from a balloon

Thirty members of Paraclub Flevo (above), Lelystad, The Netherlands, jumped from a balloon over Markelo, The Netherlands, on 10 May 2003.

★ **Longest free-fall parachute jump**
Eugene Andreev (USSR) holds the official Fédération Aéronautique Internationale (FAI) record for the longest free-fall parachute jump after falling for 24,500 m (80,380 ft) from an altitude of 25,458 m (83,523 ft) near the city of Saratov, Russia, on 1 November 1962.

★ **Largest FAI-approved free-fall parachute formation**
A free-fall formation consisting of 357 skydivers from more than 40 countries was formed over Takhli, Thailand, on 6 February 2004. The event was organized by World Team '04 and formed part of the Thailand Royal Sky Celebration, which was supported by the Royal Thai Air Force and took place in honour of the Thai royal family.

★ **Most parachute descents**
On 13 July 2003, Don Kellner (USA) made his 34,000th free-fall skydive in accordance with the US Parachute Association basic safety requirements. He made his first jump on 14 June 1961.

Cheryl Stearns (USA) holds the corresponding women's record, with a total of 15,560 descents as of August 2003.

★ **Most people to tandem parachute in 24 hours**
The greatest number of tandem parachute jumps performed from the same airfield in a 24-hour period is 41, achieved at The Big Jump 2001 event at Hinton Airfield, Banbury, Oxfordshire, UK, on 16 September 2001.

★ **Largest canopy formation**
The largest canopy formation consisted of 70 parachutes and was formed by an American-led international team over Lake Wales, Florida, USA, on 29 November 2003. The formation involved 15 'layers' of parachutes stacked on top of one another, with each parachutist in contact with the canopy of the person below them.

★ **Highest static-line parachute jump with a round canopy**
Graham Spicer and Martin Cruickshank (both UK) completed a static-line parachute jump using round canopies from an altitude of 9,235 m (30,300 ft) over Yolo County, California, USA, on 19 September 2002. Both men are members of the Association of British Military Parachutists.

★ **Longest flight by powered parachute (absolute)**
The official FAI record for the longest distance flown in a single hop by powered parachute is 644 km (400 miles), by Juan Ramon Morillas Salmeron (Spain), from Almonte, Huelva, Spain, to Minuesa, Teruel, Spain, on 21 June 1998.

★ **Fastest speed in a paraglider over a 25-km triangular course**
The fastest speed achieved over a 25-km (15.53-mile) triangular course for an official FAI world record is 28.26 km/h (17.55 mph) by Patrick Berod (France) at Albertville, France, on 27 June 1995.

The fastest speed achieved by a woman is 22.75 km/h (14.13 mph) by Fiona Macaskill (UK) at Plaine Joux, France, on 24 April 2003.

★ **Greatest distance in a paraglider**
On 21 June 2002, William Gadd (Canada) travelled a distance of 423.4 km (263.08 miles) by paraglider, from Zapata, Texas, to south of Ozona, Texas, USA.

The greatest distance flown by a woman in a paraglider is 285 km (177.1 miles) by Kat Thurston (UK) from Kuruman, South Africa, on 25 December 1995.

★ **Greatest distance in a tandem paraglider**
Richard Westgate and Jim Coutts (both UK) flew a tandem paraglider for a total distance of 220.4 km (136.95 miles) without landing from Quixada, Brazil, to Bom Principio, Brazil, on 30 November 2000.

Greatest absolute altitude ⋏ in a glider

Robert Harris (USA) achieved a height of 14,938 m (49,009 ft) in a glider over California City, USA, on 17 February 1986.

The women's single-seater glider world record for absolute altitude was set by Sabrina Jackintell (USA), who achieved a height of 12,637 m (41,460 ft) over Black Forest Gliderport, Colorado Springs, USA, on 14 February 1979.

★ Greatest height gain in a tandem paraglider

The height gain record for a tandem paraglider is 4,380 m (14,370 ft), achieved by Richard and Guy Westgate (both UK) at Kuruman, South Africa, on 1 January 1996.

★ Most men's hang-gliding World Championships

World championships for hang-gliding were first held in 1976. The most individual wins is three by Tomas Suchanek (Czech Republic) in 1991, 1993 and 1995, and Manfred Ruhmer (Austria) in 1999, 2001 and 2003.

The women's hang-gliding World Championships were first held in 1987. The most individual wins is three by Kari Castle (USA) in 1996, 2000 and 2002.

★ Greatest distance flown in a hang-glider

The greatest distance flown when setting an official FAI hang-gliding record is 700.6 km (435.33 miles) by Manfred Ruhmer (Austria) from Zapata, Texas, to Lamesa, Texas, USA, on 17 July 2001.

★ Greatest straight distance in a hang-glider by a woman

The FAI straight-line distance record by a woman in a hang-glider is 403.5 km (250.7 miles), achieved by Kari Castle (USA) at Zapata, Texas, USA, on 28 July 2001.

★ Greatest return distance in a hang-glider

Rohan Holtkamp (Australia) achieved a record out-and-return distance of 330.6 km (205.4 miles) at Eucla, Australia, on 12 February 1998.

The farthest out-and-return distance travelled by a woman with a hang-glider is 143.85 km (89.38 miles), achieved by Tascha McLellan (New Zealand) at Forbes, Australia, on 3 January 1999.

★ Greatest distance in triangular hang-gliding

Tomas Suchanek (Czech Republic) achieved a record triangular-course distance of 357.12 km (221.9 miles) at Riverside, New South Wales, Australia, on 16 December 2000.

The equivalent women's record is 167.2 km (103.9 miles), achieved by Nichola Hamilton (UK) on 2 January 1997 at Croydon Hay, New South Wales, Australia.

★ Greatest height gain in a hang-glider

Larry Tudor (USA) achieved a height of 4,343 m (14,250 ft) over Owens Valley, California, USA, on 4 August 1985.

Judy Leden (UK) achieved the equivalent women's record with a height of 3,970 m (13,025 ft) on 1 December 1992 at Kuruman, South Africa.

★ Most consecutive loops in a hang-glider

Chad Elchin performed 95 consecutive loops at the Highland Aerosports flight park at Ridgely, Maryland, USA, on 16 July 2001. Elchin was towed to 4,846 m (15,900 ft) and looped his Aeros Stealth Combat non-stop down to

213 m (700 ft), at speeds ranging from 28 km/h to 128 km/h (17–80 mph).

★ Fastest speed in a glider

The highest average speed reached in a glider when setting an official FAI world record is 247.49 km/h (153.78 mph) by James and Thomas Payne (both USA) when setting the out-and-return course of 500 km (310 miles) speed record at California City, USA, on 3 March 1999.

★ Greatest altitude gain in a glider

The greatest height gain in a glider is 12,894 m (42,303 ft) by Paul F Bikle (USA) over Lancaster, California, USA, on 25 February 1961.

The equivalent record for women is a height of 10,212 m (33,504 ft), achieved by Yvonne Loader (New Zealand) at Omarama, New Zealand, on 12 January 1988.

Highest women's team FITA outdoor recurve score ⌄

In 1992 the South Korea women's team (Kim Soo-nyung [below], Cho Youn-jeong and Lee Eun-kyung) scored 4,094 points from a possible 4,320 in the single FITA round, women's team category in Barcelona, Spain. The international governing body of archery, the Fédération Internationale de Tir à l'Arc (FITA), was founded in 1931. FITA regulates archery around the world through more than 125 member associations.

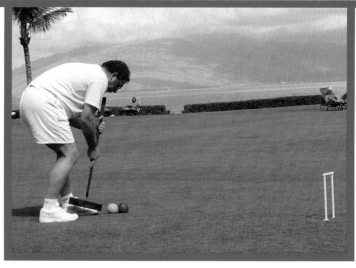

Most MacRobertson ⌃ Shield wins

The MacRobertson Shield (instituted 1925) has been won a record 12 times by the Great Britain croquet team (GB team member David Foulser, above): 1925, 1937, 1956, 1963, 1969, 1974, 1982, 1990, 1993, 1996, 2000 and 2003.

Archery indoor records

Event	Pts	Name & nationality	Venue	Date
18 m				
Men	597	Michele Frangilli (Italy)	Nîmes, France	January 2001
Women	591	Lina Herasymenko (Ukraine)	Istanbul, Turkey	March 1997
25 m				
Men	598	Michele Frangilli (Italy)	Gallarate, Italy	November 2001
Women	592	Petra Ericsson (Sweden)	Oulu, Finland	March 1991

Archery men (single FITA rounds)

Event	Pts	Name & nationality	Venue	Date
FITA	1,379	Oh Kyo-moon (South Korea)	Wonju, South Korea	Nov 2000
90 m	337	Jang Yong-ho (South Korea)	New York, USA	July 2003
70 m	347	Choi Young-kwang (South Korea)	Hongseong, South Korea	Aug 2002
50 m	351	Kim Kyung-ho (South Korea)	Wonju, South Korea	Sept 1997
30 m	360/17	Kye Dong-hyun (South Korea)	Cheongju, South Korea	Sept 2002
Team	4,074	South Korea (Jang Yong-ho, Choi Young-kwang, Im Bong-hyun)	New York, USA	July 2003

Archery women (single FITA rounds)

Event	Pts	Name & nationality	Venue	Date
FITA	1,388	Park Seong-hyun (South Korea)	Yechoen, South Korea	March 2003
70 m	348	Lee Hee-jeong (South Korea)	Cheongju, South Korea	Oct 2001
60 m	350	Kim Jo-soon (South Korea)	Wonju, South Korea	Sept 1998
50 m	350	Park Seong-hyun (South Korea)	Yechoen, South Korea	March 2003
30 m	360/14	Lee Hyun-jeong (South Korea)	Cheongju, South Korea	Oct 2001
Team	4,094	South Korea (Kim Soo-nyung, Lee Eun-kyung, Cho Yuon-jeong)	Barcelona, Spain	Aug 1992

★ Highest archery score in 24 hours

The highest point score in 24 hours shooting FITA 18 rounds is 26,064 by Michael Howson and Stephen Howard (both UK) at Oakbank Sports College, Keighley, West Yorkshire, UK, on 11–12 November 2000.

★ Longest rifle shooting marathon

Five members of the St Sebastianus Schützenbruderchaft Ettringen 1901 eV shooting club shot for 26 hours at Ettringen, Germany, on 20–21 September 2003. The five members were: Karl Westhoften, Rainer Lanz, Dieter Franken, Christian Lanz and Manfred Savelsberg (all Germany), who shot from three positions – prone, standing and kneeling – and followed all International Shooting Sport Federation (ISSF) regulations.

★ Highest skeet shooting score by a woman

Svetlana Demina (Russia) set a world record on 1 June 1999 with her score of 99 (75 + 24) in the women's skeet-shooting event held in Kumamoto City, Japan.

★ Highest men's trap shooting score

Marcello Tittarelli (Italy) shot an incredible 150 out of 150 (125 + 25) in the men's trap shooting 125 targets on 11 June 1996 at the World Cup in Suhl, Germany. In the trap events, named after the device that launches clay targets into the air, a bank of three traps is set at varying heights and angles within a trench in front of each shooter. The shooter does not know which of the three traps will release next. As each target is released, the shooter is allowed two shots.

★ Highest men's rifle shooting score (50 m, three positions)

With an overall score of 1,287.9, Rajmond Debevec (Slovenia) set a world record for the men's rifle 50 m (3 x 40 shots) in Munich, Germany, on 29 August 1992.

Youngest professional ⌃ snooker World Champion

Stephen Hendry (above, UK, b. 13 January 1969) became the youngest professional snooker World Champion at 21 years 106 days on 29 April 1990.

★ **Most croquet World Championship wins by an individual**

The first croquet World Championships were held at the Hurlingham Club, London, UK, in 1989 and have been held annually since. The most wins is four by Robert Fulford (UK) in 1990, 1992, 1994 and 1997.

★ **Most national croquet titles won by an individual**

Bob Jackson (New Zealand) won the New Zealand croquet Open Championship Singles title 14 times – 1975, 1978, 1982–84, 1989, 1991–92, 1995, 1997–99 and 2002–03.

★ **Longest indoor bowls marathon**

Six members of Arnos Bowling Club, Southgate, UK, played indoor bowls for a record 36 hours on 20–21 April 2002.

★ **Highest tenpin bowling pinfall in one lane over 24 hours**

The highest pinfall achieved in tenpin bowling on one lane in 24 hours is 36,781 by 12 bowlers at Go Bowling, Dunstable, Bedfordshire, UK, between 21 and 22 August 2003.

★ **Longest tenpin bowling marathon**

The longest tenpin bowling marathon is 52 hr 15 min by Fred Miller (UK) at the AMF Bowling Centre in Wigan, Lancashire, UK, between 28 February and 2 March 2003.

★ **Most darts World Championship titles**

The most darts World Championship titles won is 11 by Phil Taylor (GB). He won the World Darts Organization (WDO) championship in 1990 and 1992, and the Professional Darts Corporation (PDC) championship in 1995–2002 and 2004.

★ **Fastest snooker 147 break**

The fastest 147 snooker break in a professional tournament is 5 min 20 sec by Ronnie O'Sullivan (UK) during the 1997 World Championships held at Sheffield, South Yorkshire, UK, on 21 April 1997. The only way to get a 147 clearance is to pot the black ball after every red, then clear the coloured balls in order: yellow, green, brown, blue, pink and black.

★ **Highest break in snooker**

Wally West (UK) recorded a break of 151 in a snooker match at the Hounslow Lucania, London, UK, in October 1976. The break involved a free ball, which created an 'extra' red, when all 15 reds were still on the table. In these very exceptional circumstances, the maximum break is 155.

★ **Longest billiards marathon**

Pierre De Coster (Belgium) played billiards against all comers for 181 hr 8 min at SK Kampenhout clubhouse, Kampenhout, Belgium, from 3 to 10 June 2003. De Coster played a total of 820 games, winning 518.

★ **Longest pool marathon by a team**

A four-man team played pool for 120 hours at the Heritage Inn, Brooks, Alberta, Canada, from 15 to 20 January 2003. The team members were Jack Nemeth, Doug Webster, Harlan Ivarson and Doug Prenevost (all Canada).

★ **Longest pool marathon by an individual**

Raf Goossens (Belgium) played pool against all comers for 75 hr 19 min 17 sec at Café St-Jozef, Kampenhout, Belgium, from 19 to 22 February 2003.

Motor sports 1
Sport

Largest NASCAR ⌃ Speedway

Talladega Superspeedway (above) in Alabama, USA, is the largest National Association for Stock Car Auto Racing (NASCAR) Speedway. The tri-oval-shaped track is 4.28 km (2.66 miles) long, has a banking angle of 33° and can house more than 143,000 seated guests and thousands more in the 87-hectare (215-acre) infield.

The track opened as Alabama International Motor Speedway in 1969 and was built at a cost of more than $4 million [then £1.66 million].

★ Most wins in a NASCAR season

Richard Petty (USA) won 27 races in 1967. During the same season, Petty also set the mark for the most consecutive wins, with 10.

Petty holds a number of other NASCAR records. He won a record 200 race victories during his NASCAR career, which lasted from 1958 to 1992, and achieved an unrivalled 126 pole positions during this time, winning 61 races from the front of the grid.

Petty also started 1,184 races during his career, more than any other NASCAR driver.

★ Most NASCAR titles

Since the NASCAR Championship was first held in 1949, two drivers have won it a total of seven times: Richard Petty (USA) in 1964, 1967, 1971–72, 1974–75 and 1979; and Dale Earnhardt (USA) in 1980, 1986–87, 1990–91 and 1993–94.

★ Most consecutive NASCAR Championships

Eight drivers have won back-to-back NASCAR Championships, but only one, Cale Yarborough (USA), has won three Championships consecutively, between 1976 and 1978.

★ Most Formula One Grand Prix wins by a driver

Michael Schumacher (Germany) won a total of 70 Formula One Grand Prix races between 1991 and 2003.

Schumacher holds the record for the most points scored in a Formula One career, with 1,038 points from 1991 to 2003.

He also holds the record for the greatest number of points scored by a driver in a Formula One season, after scoring 144 points in 2002.

During the same season, Schumacher also won an unrivalled 11 Formula One Grand Prix.

★ Most consecutive wins of the same Grand Prix

Ayrton Senna (Brazil) took first place in the Monaco Grand Prix a total of five times in a row between 1989 and 1993.

Senna's exceptional career was tragically cut short when he was killed on 1 May 1994 while competing in the San Marino Grand Prix.

★ Most consecutive Formula One pole positions

Alain Prost (France) had seven consecutive Formula One pole positions in the 1993 season driving for the Williams-Renault team. Prost was also world champion that year.

★ Most Formula One pole positions in season

The greatest number of Formula One pole positions in a season by one driver is 14 by Nigel Mansell (UK). Driving for the Williams-Renault team in 1992, Mansell won the World Championship before switching over to Indy cars the following year, winning the 1993 Indy car series at his first attempt.

★ Most Formula One pole positions in a career

The greatest number of Formula One pole positions is 65 by Ayrton Senna (Brazil) from 161 races (including 41 wins), from 1985 to 1994, for the Toleman, Lotus, McLaren and Williams teams.

Most World Drivers' Championship wins ⌄

Inaugurated in 1950, the World Drivers' Championship has been won a record six times by Michael Schumacher (Germany, below) in 1994–95 and 2000–03.

Most wins by an ⌃ individual at the Le Mans 24-hour race

Jacky Ickx (Belgium, above left) won the Le Mans 24-hour race six times, in 1969, 1975–77 and 1981–82.

★ **Most Formula One fastest laps in a season**
The greatest number of fastest laps recorded by one driver in a Formula One season is nine by Mika Hakkinen (Finland) in 2000 while driving for the McLaren-Mercedes team.

Hakkinen finished the World Drivers' Championship second that year with 89 points. Michael Schumacher (Germany) won the Championship with a total of 108 points.

★ **Oldest Grand Prix driver**
The oldest ever Grand Prix driver was Louis Alexandre Chiron (Monaco, 1899–1979), who finished sixth in the Monaco Grand Prix on 22 May 1955 at the age of 55 years 292 days.

★ **Youngest Grand Prix driver**
The youngest driver ever to qualify for a Grand Prix was Michael Christopher Thackwell (New Zealand, b. 30 March 1961). He took part in the Canadian Grand Prix on 28 September 1980 at the age of 19 years 182 days.

★ **Oldest Formula One world champion**
Juan Manuel Fangio (Argentina, b. 24 June 1911) won his last World Championship on 4 August 1957 at the age of 46 years 41 days.

★ **Youngest Formula One world champion**
The youngest ever Formula One world champion was Emerson Fittipaldi (Brazil, b. 12 December 1946), who won his first World Championship on 10 September 1972 aged 25 years 273 days.

★ **Youngest driver to claim a Formula One World Championship point**
When he finished in sixth place in the Brazilian Grand Prix on 26 March 2000, Jenson Button (UK, b. 19 January 1980) was only 20 years 67 days old.

Button originally finished in seventh position, out of the points, but after McLaren driver David Coulthard (UK) was disqualified from his second-place finish, Button was promoted to a points-scoring position.

★ **Most Formula One Grand Prix retirements**
The greatest number of race retirements in Formula One is 135 by Andrea de Cesaris (Italy), during a career that spanned 14 years from 1980 to 1994.

De Cesaris also has the dubious honour of holding the record for most Grand Prix races (208) without a victory.

★ **Most Grand Prix wins by a constructor**
As of the end of the 2003 season, Ferrari (Italy) had won 166 Formula One Grand Prix races.

★ **Most Formula One Constructors' World Championship titles**
Ferrari have won 13 Formula One Constructors' World Championship titles, in 1961, 1964, 1975–77, 1979, 1982–83 and 1999–2003.

★ **Most points by a constructor in a Formula One season**
In the 2002 Formula One season, the Ferrari team amassed 221 World Championship points. The team's drivers that year were Michael Schumacher (Germany) and Reubens Barichello (Brazil).

The Ferrari team won 15 races out of 17 and wrapped up both the drivers' and the constructors' titles in record time.

★ **Most wins by a constructor in a Formula One season**
The greatest number of wins by a constructor in a Formula One season is 15. This feat has been achieved by two teams: McLaren in 1988 and Ferrari in 2002.

★ **Most team wins at the Le Mans 24-hour race**
Porsche have won the Le Mans 24-hour race on 16 occasions, in 1970–71, 1976–77, 1979, 1981–87, 1993 and 1996–98.

Most superbike World Championship « pole positions

Troy Corser (Australia, left) achieved 28 pole positions in the superbike World Championships from 1995 to 2001.

Most motorcycle World Championship 250-cc titles ⌃

Two riders have won the 250-cc World Championship four times: Max Biaggi (Italy, leading above) from 1994 to 1997 and Phil Read (UK) in 1964, 1965, 1968 and 1971.

★ **Longest motorcycle race circuit**
The 'Mountain' circuit on the Isle of Man, over which the principal TT (Tourist Trophy) races have been run since 1911 (with minor amendments in 1920), has 264 curves and corners and measures 60.72 km (37.73 miles).

★ **Most superbikes World Championship race wins by a manufacturer**
Ducati (Italy) won 219 superbikes World Championship races from 1988 to 2004.

★ **Most superbikes World Championship titles won by a manufacturer**
Ducati have won 12 superbikes World Championships manufacturers' titles, in 1991–96 and 1998–2003.

★ **Most superbikes World Championship pole positions by a manufacturer**
In the superbikes World Championships between 1988 and 2004, Ducati (Italy) achieved a record 118 pole positions.

★ **Most superbikes World Championship titles**
Carl Fogarty (UK) won four superbikes World Championship titles, in 1994, 1995, 1998 and 1999.

★ **Most superbikes World Championship race wins**
Carl Fogarty (UK) won a record 59 races in superbikes World Championships between 1992 and 1999.

★ **Most sidecar World Championship titles**
The most sidecar World Championship titles won by the same pair is five, by Klaus Enders and Ralph Engelhardt (both Germany) riding a BMW machine in 1967, 1969 and 1972–74.

★ **Most 500-cc motocross World Championship titles**
Two riders have both won five 500-cc motocross World Championships: Roger de Coster (Belgium) in 1971–73 and 1975–76, and Joel Smets (Belgium) in 1995, 1997–98, 2000 and 2003.

★ **Most 250-cc motocross World Championship titles**
Joël Robert (Belgium) won six 250-cc motocross World Championships, in 1964 and 1968–72. Between 25 April 1964 and 18 June 1972 he won a record 50 250-cc Grand Prix.

★ **Most 125-cc motocross World Championship titles**
The 125-cc class of the motocross World Championship has been won three times by three riders: Gaston Rahier (Belgium) in 1975–77, Harry Everts (Belgium) in 1979–81 and Alessio Chiodi (Italy) in 1997–99.

★ **Most motorcycle World Championship 500-cc titles**
The most motorcycling World Championship 500-cc titles won is eight by Giacomo Agostini (Italy) from 1966 to 1972 and in 1975.

★ **Most motorcycle World Championship 350-cc titles**
Giacomo Agostini (Italy) won seven motorcycling World Championship 350-cc titles from 1968 to 1974.

★ **Most motorcycle World Championship 125-cc titles**
Angel Roldán Nieto (Spain) won seven motorcycling World Championship 125-cc titles, in 1971, 1972, 1979 and 1981–84.

★ **Most motorcycle World Championship 80-cc titles**
Jorge Martinez (Spain) won three motorcycling World Championship 80-cc titles from 1986 to 1988. This class ran for only six years between 1984 and 1989.

★ **Most motorcycle World Championship 50-cc titles**
Angel Roldán Nieto (Spain) won six motorcycling World Championship 50-cc titles in 1969, 1970, 1972 and 1975–77.

★ **Lowest elapsed time for a National Hot Rod Association (NHRA) drag racing Pro Stock motorbike**
Angelle Savoie (USA) covered 440 yd in 7.049 seconds on her Suzuki Pro Stock motorbike at Matthews, Louisiana, USA, in May 2002.

Most rally World Championship race wins ⌃⌃

Two drivers have each won 25 World Championship races: Colin McRae (UK) in 1993–2002 and Carlos Sainz (Spain, driving above) in 1990–2003.

★ **Fastest speed for an NHRA Pro Stock motorbike**
Matt Hines (USA) achieved 312.37 km/h (194.10 mph) on a Suzuki at Englishtown, New Jersey, USA, in May 2001 – the highest terminal velocity for a petrol-driven piston-engined motorcycle (Pro Stock) .

★ **Lowest elapsed time for an NHRA Pro Stock car**
Greg Anderson (USA) covered 440 yd in 6.670 seconds driving a Pontiac Grand Am at Concord, North Carolina, USA, on 18 May 2003.

★ **Fastest speed in an NHRA Pro Stock car**
Set by Greg Anderson (USA) at Concord, North Carolina, USA, on 18 May 2003, the highest terminal velocity for a Pro Stock car is 333.42 km/h (207.18 mph).

★ **Lowest elapsed time for an NHRA Top Fuel drag racer**
Anthony Schumacher (USA) covered 440 yd in 4.441 seconds in a McKinney dragster at Long Grove, Illinois, USA, on 4 October 2003. Top Fuel cars run on 90% nitro-methane and 10% methanol, also known as racing alcohol. As a result, the engine is about 2.4 times as powerful as a similar displacement engine running gasoline and produces at least 8,000 horsepower.

★ **Fastest speed for an NHRA Top Fuel drag racer**
The highest terminal velocity at the end of a 440-yd run is 536.31 km/h (333.25 mph) by Douglas Kalitta (USA) at Ypsilanti, Michigan, USA, on 9 November 2003 in a McKinney dragster.

★ **Lowest elapsed time in an NHRA funny car**
John Force (USA) covered 440 yd in 4.721 seconds in a Ford Mustang at Yorba Linda, California, USA, on 1 June 2003. Funny cars are rear-wheel-driven dragsters with a massive front-mounted engine and huge, distinctive rear wheels.

★ **Fastest speed in an NHRA funny car**
Gary Scelzi (USA) reached 529.76 km/h (329.18 mph) from a standing start over 440 yd in a Dodge Stratus at Fresno, California, USA, on 28 September 2003.

★ **Most rally World Championship race wins in a season**
Didier Auriol (France) won a record six rally World Championship races in 1992.

★ **Youngest rally World Championship driver**
The youngest driver to compete in a Fédération Internationale de l'Automobile (FIA) World Championship rally is Jari-Matti Latvala (Finland), who was 18 years 61 days when he drove in the 50th Acropolis Rally, Athens, Greece, on 6–8 June 2003.

★ **Most rally World Championship race wins by a manufacturer**
Lancia (Italy) won 73 rally World Championship races from 1972 to 2004.

★ **Most rally World Championship wins by a manufacturer**
Lancia (Italy) won 11 rally World Championship titles between 1972 and 1992.

★ **Most Dakar Rally wins**
Ari Vatanen (Finland) has won the Dakar Rally a record four times, first in 1987 and then on three more occasions from 1989 to 1991.

★ **Most Dakar Rally bike category wins**
Stéphane Peterhansel (France) had a record six wins in the bike category of the Dakar Rally in 1991–93, 1995 and 1997–98.

Most Tour de France wins

Lance Armstrong (USA, right) »
has won the Tour de France a record
five times in 1999–2003. He shares
this record with Jacques Anquetil (France) in 1957,
1961–64; Eddy Merckx (Belgium) in 1969–72 and 1974;
Bernard Hinault (France) in 1978–79, 1981–82 and 1985;
and Miguel Indurain (Spain) in 1991–95.

★ **Fastest women's 200 m, unpaced, flying start**
The fastest unpaced 200 m cycled from a flying start is 10.831 seconds by Olga Slyusareva (Russia) in Moscow, Russia, on 25 April 1993.

★ **Fastest men's 200 m, unpaced, flying start**
Curtis Harnett (Canada) cycled a distance of 200 m in 9.865 seconds from an unpaced flying start in Bogotá, Colombia, on 28 September 1995.

★ **Fastest women's 500 m, unpaced, flying start**
The fastest unpaced 500 m cycled from a flying start is 29.655 seconds, by Erika Salumäe (USSR, now Estonia), in Moscow, USSR, on 6 August 1987.

★ **Fastest men's 500 m, unpaced, flying start**
Arnaud Duble (France) finished the men's 500 m unpaced in 25.850 seconds from a flying start in La Paz, Bolivia, on 10 October 2001.

★ **Fastest women's 500 m, unpaced, standing start**
The fastest unpaced 500 m cycled from a standing start is 34.000 seconds, by Yong Hua Jiang (China), in Kunming, China, on 10 August 2002.

★ **Fastest men's 1 km, unpaced, standing start**
The world record time for the 1-km cycle is 58.875 seconds by Arnaud Tournant (France) at La Paz, Bolivia, on 10 October 2001.

★ **Fastest women's 3 km, unpaced, standing start**
The world record for the 3-km Women's Individual Cycling Pursuit race is 3 min 30.816 sec, set by Leontien Zijlaard-van Moorsel (Netherlands) at the 2000 Olympic Games held in Sydney, Australia, on 17 September 2000.

★ **Fastest men's team 4 km, unpaced, standing start**
The Australian team consisting of Peter Dawson, Graham Brown, Mark Renshaw and Luke Roberts cycled 4 km in 3 min 59.583 sec. The time was set at the Commonwealth Games in Manchester, UK, on 1 August 2002.

★ **Fastest men's 4-km, unpaced, standing start**
Chris Boardman (UK) cycled a distance of 4 km in 4 min 11.114 sec at Manchester, UK, on 29 August 1996.

★ **Greatest distance cycled in 24 hours**
The 24-hour record behind pace is 1,958.196 km (1,216.8 miles) by Michael Secrest (USA) at Phoenix International Raceway, Arizona, USA, on 26–27 April 1990. Solo and unpaced, Secrest achieved a distance of 857.36 km (532.74 miles) over the same time at the Olympic Velodrome, California State University, Carson, USA, on 23–24 October 1997.

★ **Farthest cycling in an hour, unpaced, standing start**
The official Union Cycliste Internationale (UCI) one-hour record of 49.441 km (30.72 miles) was set in Manchester, UK, on 27 October 2000 by Chris Boardman (UK).

★ **Greatest distance cycled in one hour by a woman, unpaced, standing start**
The official UCI one-hour record by a woman is 45.094 km (28.02 miles) by Jeanie Longo (France) in Mexico City, Mexico, on 7 December 2000.

★ **Longest one-day cycle race**
The longest one-day 'massed start' road race is the Bordeaux–Paris event in France, which is 551–620 km (342–385 miles) long, depending on the route.

★ **Fastest cycling end-to-end**
Andy Wilkinson (UK) cycled between Land's End, Cornwall, and John O'Groats, Highland, UK, in 1 day 21 hr 2 min 18 sec from 29 September to 1 October 1990.
The holder of the women's record is Pauline Strong (UK). She finished the distance in 2 days 6 hr 49 min 45 sec from 28 to 30 July 1990.

Biggest winning ⌃ margin in a Tour de France

The greatest time gap between the winner and the runner-up

at the finish of a Tour de France is 28 min 27 sec, between Fausto Coppi (Italy, above left) and Stan Ockers (Belgium) in 1952.

★ **Fastest trans-Europe two-person relay cycle**
Kevin Moreland and Guy Lawton (both UK), supported by the Twisting Compass Team, cycled in relay from Tarifa, Spain, to North Cape, Norway, in a time of 9 days 20 hr 43 min from 6 to 16 July 2002.

★ **Youngest Tour de France winner**
Henri Cornet (France) was aged 19 years 350 days when he won the Tour de France in 1904. Cornet actually finished the race in fifth position, but was awarded the victory after the first four riders were all disqualified.

★ **Oldest Tour de France winner**
Firmin Lambot (Belgium) was 36 years 4 months when he won the Tour de France in 1922.

★ **Closest Tour de France race**
The closest Tour de France race ever was in 1989 when, after 3,267 km (2,030 miles) over 23 days (1–23 July), Greg LeMond (USA) completed

the Tour in 87 hr 38 min 35 sec, beating Laurent Fignon (France) to the finish in Paris by 8 seconds.

★ **Most Tour de France stage wins**
Eddie Merckx (Belgium) has 34 Tour de France stage wins. Merckx also shares the record for the most overall Tour victories with five won in 1969–72 and in 1974.

★ **Fastest average speed in the Tour de France**
During the 1999 Tour, Lance Armstrong (USA) cycled at an average speed of 40.276 km/h (25.026 mph).

★ **Most Tour of Spain wins**
The most wins in the Tour of Spain cycling race is three by Tony Rominger (Switzerland) from 1992 to 1994.

★ **Most Tour of Italy wins**
The most Tour of Italy wins is five and is shared by Alfredo Binda (Italy) in 1925, 1927–29 and 1933; Fausto Coppi (Italy) in 1940, 1947, 1949 and

Most downhill ⌃ mountain-biking World Championships won by a woman

Anne-Caroline Chausson (France, above) has won 10

downhill World Championships – three in the junior championship from 1993 to 1995 and seven in the senior class from 1996 to 2002.

1952–53; and Eddy Merckx (Belgium) in 1968, 1970 and 1972–74.

★ **Fastest trans-Australia cycling**
Tomio Uranyu (Japan) cycled from Perth, Western Australia, to Sydney, New South Wales, in 9 days 23 hr 25 min from 28 March to 7 April 1992.
   The women's record is held by Helen Shelley (Australia), who cycled the distance in 13 days 2 hr 55 min from 24 April to 7 May 1999.

★ **Fastest cyclist on snow**
The fastest ever speed attained cycling downhill on snow or ice is 212.139 km/h (132 mph),

by downhill mountain bike racer Christian Taillefer (France) on a Peugeot cycle at the speed ski slope in Vars, France, in March 1998.

★ **Most downhill mountain-biking World Championships wins**
Nicolas Vouilloz (France) had a record 10 World Championship wins – three in the junior championships from 1992 to 1994 and seven in the senior class in 1995–99 and 2001–02.

★ **Most downhill mountain-biking World Cup event wins**
Nicolas Vouilloz (France) won 16 World Cups from 1992 to 2001.

Wheel skills
Sport

Highest air on a skateboard ⌄

Professional skateboarder Danny Way (USA, below) performed a 5.56-m (18-ft 3-in) method air off the top of a 6-m (20-ft) quarterpipe at Point X Camp near Aguanga, California, USA, on 17 April 2002. The height was measured from the top of the ramp.

★ Longest skateboard journey

The longest recorded journeys by skateboard were completed by Jack Smith (USA) in July 1976 and again in July 1984, when he covered just under 4,830 km (3,000 miles) between Lebanon, Oregon, and Williamsburg, Virginia, USA.

★ Highest skateboarding ollie

On 6 February 2000, Danny Wainwright (UK) popped the highest ollie at 113 cm (44.5 in) off flat ground to win the Reese Forbes Ollie Challenge at the ASR Show, Long Beach, California, USA.

★ Highest skateboard drop into a quarterpipe

Adil Dyani (Norway) dropped into a 5.5-m-high (18-ft) quarterpipe ramp from a height of 9.15 m (30 ft) on a skateboard at Oslo, Norway, on 4 October 2003. The drop was effectively made from 3.65 m (12 ft) above the lip of the ramp.

★ Highest skateboarding jump

Trevor Baxter (UK) cleared a bar set at 1.65 m (5 ft 5 in) by jumping off a moving skateboard and landing on it after it had passed under the bar, at Grenoble, France, on 14 September 1982.

★ Fastest speed on a skateboard

Gary Hardwick (USA) reached 100.66 km/h (62.55 mph) in a standing position at Fountain Hills, Arizona, USA, on 26 September 1998.

★ Fastest speed on a street luge

The highest speed set for riding a skateboard in a prone position is 126.12 km/h (78.37 mph) by Roger Hickey (USA) on a course near Los Angeles, California, USA, on 15 March 1990.

★ Longest 50-50 rail grind on a skateboard

The longest skateboard rail grind is 10.31 m (33 ft 10 in) by Chad Fernandez (USA) on the *Today* show in New York City, USA, on 25 August 2003.

★ Most continuous skateboard revolutions

Richard Carrasco (USA) completed a total of 142 continuous 360° revolutions on a skateboard on 11 August 2000 in Santa Ana, California, USA.

★ Longest ramp jump on a skateboard

Danny Way (USA) performed a 19.8-m (65-ft) skateboard jump between two ramps at Point X Camp near Aguanga, California, USA, on 16 April 2002.

★ Highest BMX vertical air

Mat Hoffman (USA) achieved a 8.07-m (26-ft 6-in) air from a 7.3-m-tall (24-ft) quarterpipe ramp on 20 March 2001, in Oklahoma City, USA. Hoffman was towed by a motorcycle in the run-up to the jump to reach the required speed.

★ Highest bunny hop

Bruno Arnold (France) achieved the highest ever bunny hop on a mountain bike, clearing a

Longest ⌃ BMX backflip

On 9 February 2002, Allan Cooke

(USA, above) performed a 16.45-m (54-ft) backflip on his BMX between two specially constructed ramps at Point X Camp near Aguanga, California, USA.

1.17-m-high (3-ft 10.2-in) horizontal bar without using a ramp on the set of *L'Été de tous les Records*, Le Touquet, France, on 24 July 2003.

★ Highest vertical drop on a bicycle

Walter Belli (Italy) and David Cachón Labrador (Spain) both rode their BMX bicycles off a 4-m-high (13-ft 1-in) platform and continued to cycle upon landing without their feet touching the ground on the set of *El Show de los Récords*, Madrid, Spain, on 5 December 2001. In accordance with the record rules, they were not allowed a run-up before dropping off the platform.

Highest Moto X ⌃ Step Up jump

The greatest height achieved in the XGames Moto Cross Step Up event is 10.67 m (35 ft) by Tommy Clowers (USA, above) on 18 August 2000. The feat is a motorcycle high-jump, in which riders must try to clear a bar placed at the top of a steep take-off ramp. This record is the equivalent of jumping on to the roof of a two-storey building. In the photo above, Clowers is performing a trick called a mulisha air.

★ **Highest ramp jump on a BMX bike**

Timo Pritzel (Germany) and Jesús Fuentes (Spain) cleared a bar 5.12 m (16 ft 9.5 in) above floor level using BMX bicycles on the set of *El Show de los Récords*, Madrid, Spain, on 21 September 2001.

★ **Longest power-assisted ramp jump by bicycle**

Professional stunt rider Colin Winkelmann (USA) jumped his BMX bicycle 35.63 m (116 ft 11 in) after being towed to a speed of approximately 100 km/h (60 mph) behind a motorcycle at Agoura Hills, California, USA, on 20 December 2000 for the *Guinness World Records: Primetime* TV show.

★ **Longest standing jump on a mountain bike**

Marc Caisso (France) achieved a standing bike jump distance of 2.9 m (9 ft 6 in) on his mountain bike at the studios of *L'Émission des Records*, Paris, France, on 26 October 2000.

★ **Longest endo with feet off the pedals**

Martti Kuoppa (Finland) was able to maintain a wheelie on the front wheel of his BMX for 23.25 seconds, while covering a distance of 100 m (328 ft) and without his feet touching the bike's pedals, on 26 June 2001 at Helsinki, Finland.

★ **Most BMX gyrator spins in one minute**

The record for the greatest number of gyrator spins in one minute is 29 by Sam Foakes (UK) for BBC1's *Blue Peter* at London, UK, on 11 March 2002.

★ **Farthest distance on a unicycle in one hour**

Dieter Dölling (Germany) covered 10.650 km (6.617 miles) in one hour around an indoor track on 11 July 1998.

★ **Fastest 100 m on a unicycle**

Peter Rosendahl (USA) covered 100 m (328 ft) in 12.11 seconds, at a speed of 29.72 km/h

(18.47 mph), from a standing start at Las Vegas, Nevada, USA, on 25 March 1994.

★ **Most skipping revolutions in one minute on a unicycle**

Amy Shields (USA) performed 209 skips (or rope revolutions) on a unicycle in one minute at St Paul, Minnesota, USA, on 23 February 2002.

★ **Highest inline skate ramp jump**

José Félix Hormaetxe Henry (Spain) cleared a bar set at 4.5 m (14 ft 9 in) on inline skates at the studios of *El Show de los Récords*, Madrid, Spain, on 14 December 2001.

★ **Farthest distance on inline skates in one hour**

Massimilliano Sorrentino (Italy) covered 37.425 km

(23.254 miles) on inline skates in one hour at Rieti, Italy, on 27 July 2003.

★ **Longest and fastest journey on inline skates**

Russell 'Rusty' Moncrief (USA) crossed the USA on inline skates in 69 days 8 hr 45 min from 5 January to 15 March 2002. He started out from Crescent Beach, near Jacksonville, Florida, and completed his journey at Soltana Beach, near San Diego, California, after covering 4,175 km (2,595 miles).

★ **Greatest distance on inline skates in 24 hours**

Kimberly Ames (USA) covered 455.55 km (283.07 miles) in 24 hours on inline skates at Portland, Oregon, USA, on 2 October 1994.

Unusual sports

Most consecutive bog snorkelling World Championships ⌄

Steve Griffiths (UK, below) is the only person to have won the bog snorkelling World Championship three times, consecutively, from 1985 to 1987. This annual event takes place in the dense Waen Rhydd Peat bog on the southern outskirts of Llanwrtyd Wells, Powys, UK.

Most toe wrestling ⌃ World Championships

Alan Nash (UK) has won five toe wrestling World Championships, in 1994, 1996–97, 2000 and 2002. The women's category has been won four times by Karen Davies (UK) from 1999 to 2002. The Championships are held annually on the first Saturday in June at Ye Olde Royal Oak, Wetton, Staffordshire, UK. Contestants must push an opponent's foot to the other side of a specially constructed ring called a 'toerack' using only their toes.

★ Most entrants at a bog snorkelling World Championships

Entrants in the bog snorkelling World Championships have to complete two lengths of a 54.8-m (60-yd) trench cut through a peat bog as quickly as possible, wearing snorkels and flippers. On 25 August 2003, 96 people entered the competition at Waen Rhydd peat bog, Llanwrtyd Wells, Powys, UK. Fifteen-year-old Philip John (UK) won in a record time of 1 min 35 sec.

★ Farthest distance to throw a rolling pin

Lori La Deane Adams (USA) threw a rolling pin weighing 970 g (2 lb) a distance of 53.47 m (175 ft 5 in) at Iowa State Fair, Iowa, USA, on 21 August 1979.

★ Farthest haggis hurl

Alan Pettigrew (UK) threw a haggis (of minimum weight 680 g or 1 lb 8 oz) a distance of 55.11 m (180 ft 10 in) at Inchmurrin, Argyll, UK, on 24 May 1984.

★ Fastest 40-m walk on water

The fastest time to walk 40 m (131 ft) on water using self-propelled buoyancy shoes was 1 min 10.8 sec. It was achieved by the team Gemini Dawn on 11 April 2003 at the Royal Commonwealth Pool, Edinburgh, UK. The event was part of the 2003 Edinburgh Science Festival.

★ Most sheep shorn manually in eight hours

The record for the most sheep shorn manually with scissors and handblade in eight hours is 50. János Marton (Hungary) achieved the feat, without any breaks, on 26 April 2003 at Hódmezővásárhely Animal Husbandry Show, Hódmezővásárhely, Hungary.

★ Farthest dyno climbing by a man

In dyno climbing, participants launch themselves from one set of handholds to a higher set with no intermediate holds. Matt Heason (UK) achieved a distance of 2.6 m (8.53 ft) in the Bendcrete Dyno Competition held at the Edge Climbing Centre, Sheffield, South Yorkshire, UK, on 20 April 2002.

★ Farthest dyno climbing by a woman

The farthest distance achieved by a woman is 1.9 m (6.233 ft) by Katherine Schirrmacher (UK) at the Bendcrete Dyno Competition held at the Edge Climbing Centre, Sheffield, South Yorkshire, UK, on 20 April 2002.

★ Longest football pitch

The annual Shrovetide Football Match has been played for more than 300 years. It is a game short on rules and long on physical contact between the two teams from Ashbourne, Derbyshire, UK: the Up'ards (those born north of the River Henmore) and the Down'ards (those born south of the river). The goals are the waterwheels at Clifton (target for the Down'ards) and Stursdton (target for the Up'ards) 4.8 km (3 miles) apart. The most goals in modern times was three in a day, but one a day is average.

★ Greatest competitive distance flown in a career by a pigeon

Brazilian Beauty, a blue-check hen owned by Robert Koch (South Africa), flew 41,050 km (25,507 miles) during a competitive career that lasted from 1990 to 1997.

★ Longest shaft achieved by a man in kiiking

The aim of kiiking, a sport native to Scandinavian and Baltic countries, is to complete a 360° revolution on a swing. Success is measured by the length of the shafts of the swing – the longer the shafts the better. The longest shaft used to successfully complete a rotation is 7.01 m (23 ft) by Andrus Aasamäe (Estonia) at Rakveres, Estonia, on 16 July 2000.

★ Longest shaft achieved by a woman in kiiking

The longest shaft used to successfully complete a rotation in kiiking by a woman is 5.86 m (19 ft 2.7 in) by Kätlin Kink (Estonia) at Pärnus, Estonia, on 2 September 2001.

World Championships with the heaviest participants

The World Elephant Polo Association (WEPA) was founded in 1982 and has hosted a championship tournament (above) every year since. Elephant polo is played by riders on elephants, four to a team. The invitational tournament is held every December on a grass airfield in Megauly, on the edge of the Royal Chitwan National Park in Nepal.

★ Most pea-shooting World Championships

Mike Fordham (UK) won a total of seven pea shooting World Championships, in 1977–78, 1981, 1983–85 and 1992.

★ Most coal-bag carrying titles by a man

Terry Lyons (UK) holds the record for the most titles at the annual Coal Carrying Championship race at Gawthorpe, West Yorkshire, UK, held on Easter Monday every year. Lyons carried a 50-kg (110-lb) bag of coal over the 1,012.5-m (3,322 ft) course and won the race every year between 1977 and 1985 inclusively, with the sole exception of 1980, when the race was won by Colin Claypole (UK).

★ Fastest individual coal-bag carrying by a man

On 1 April 1991, David Jones (UK) carried a 50-kg (110-lb) bag over the course of the annual Coal Carrying Championship race at Gawthorpe, West Yorkshire, UK, in 4 min 6 sec.

★ Fastest individual coal-bag carrying by a woman

Ruth Clegg (UK) holds the women's record for the annual Coal Carrying Championship race at Gawthorpe, West Yorkshire, UK, carrying a 20-kg (44-lb) bag over the course in 5 min 4 sec on 6 April 2002.

★ Most horseshoe pitching World Championship wins by a man

Ted Allen (USA) won a total of 10 horseshoe pitching World Championships between 1933 and 1959. Since their inception, the Championships have been played at irregular intervals, but have been held every year since 1946.

★ Most horseshoe pitching World Championships wins by a woman

Vicki Chappelle Winston (USA) won an unrivalled 10 horseshoe pitching World Championships in the women's category. She won the first of her titles in 1956, and the last in 1981. Her other championship wins were in 1958–59, 1961, 1963, 1966–67, 1969 and 1975.

★ Most ringers in a horseshoe pitching World Championship game

The term 'ringer' describes a horseshoe that comes to rest encircling the stake.The most ringers scored by an individual in a horseshoe pitching World Championship games is 175 by Glen Henton (USA) in 1965.

★ Longest horseshoe pitching winning streak

The longest winning streak in the horseshoe pitching World Championships is 69 games by Fernando Isais (USA) between 1950 and 1952.

★ Largest Wellington boot race

The most participants to take part in and finish a race while wearing Wellington boots is 981. The race was held at Waimea College, Nelson, New Zealand, on 3 September 2003.

★ Most extreme ironing World Championships

On 20–21 September 2002, the inaugural extreme ironing World Championships, organized by the German Extreme Ironing Section (GEIS), was held in Munich, Germany. It was won by Inga Kosak (Germany) with a score of 522. Participants are scored on style and textile, and against the clock, over five disciplines: Forest, Water, Rocky, Urban and Freestyle.

Index

This index concentrates on the subjects of the records (eg kissing, chocolates, tortoises) rather than the type of record (eg highest, longest, widest). Personal names of record holders are not included. Page numbers in bold type indicate the main entry on a topic. Page numbers in italic type indicate an interview with or feature on the person named.

steeplechase (track athletics) 229, 232
steeplechasing (horseracing) 259
stick insects 68
sticks
  hockey (field hockey) 221
  ice hockey 211
  ice-lolly 107
stinging nettles 75
stirrup bone (stapes) 18
stock cars, NASCAR speedway (motor sport) 264
stock exchanges 90
stolen bases, baseball 206
stomach, objects in 20
stones (biological), gallstones & bladder stones 18
stones (geological) see rocks & stones
stop-motion animations, movies 180
stoppies & endos (front-wheel wheelies)
  BMX 271
  motorcycles 135
stored-program computers 161
storms, geomagnetic 50
stout drinking 112
strain 121 (microbe) 67
Stratosphere Giant (tree) 74, 75
streamliners 130
street luge 270
Streeter, Tanya *255*
strength
  humans **34–5**, **240–1**, 268
  spiders 69
stride length, ostriches 63
strikeouts, baseball 206
string balls 105
stripping shovels 143
strong nuclear force 148
studios, movies 179
stuntmen 178, 179, 187
stylites (pole-sitters) 97
subatomic particles 146, 148, 149
submarine mountain ranges 56
submarine telephone cables 154
submersibles 40, 137
'Sue' (*Tyrannosaurus rex*) 59
Suez Canal 123
suitcases, bending iron bars into suitcases 35
suits (clothing) 171
sumo wrestling 239
Sun & solar phenomena 48, 50, 51, 146
  see also solar energy
sunfish 66
sunflowers 76, 77
sunspot data 146
Super Bowl (American football) 204
Super League (rugby league) 216
superbikes 266
supermarket trolley pushes 32
supermodels 171
supernovas 46
supersonic speeds
  aircraft 138, 139, 141, 164, 165
  cars 132, 133
surface-effect ships (SES) 164
surfing (water sport) 252, 253
surgery 20, 21, 40, 160
survival **40–1**
suspension bridges 122
suspensions (sports) see disciplinary actions (sports)
sustainability (environment) 84
sweets & confectionery 94, 112, 113, 114, 115
swifts & swiftlets 62, 63
swimming **256–7**
  birds 62
swings, kiiking swings 272
Swiss Cup (football) 214
switchboards 155
synagogues 96

table tennis **226**
tackles, rugby football 217
tags & labels collections 107
taikonauts (Chinese astronauts) 157
tails, dinosaurs 58
taipans 71
Taipei 101 (building) 120, 121
takes & retakes, movies 178, 179
talk & chat shows, television 187, 188
talkies (movies) 174, 180, 181
tandem parachuting & paragliding 260, 261
tankers, oil tankers & crude carriers 137
tanks & tank battles 86, 162
target handball 220
target sports see specific sports (eg archery)
tarsiers 60
tattoos 171
taxation 80, 81
tea & tea bags 94, 114
tea cup catching while unicycling 26
teaching & education 93, 183
team sports & activities **32–3**
  see also specific sports (eg baseball)
tearing telephone directories 35
teddy bears 108
teeth
  balancing motorcycle on 35
  brushing (mass-participation event) 31
  coconut husking with 112
  elephant's dental caps 105
  hippos' canines 60
  regrowth 21
  vehicle pulling with 34
  weightlifting with 35
telecommunications see communications
telegraph 155
telephone directory tearing 35
telephones & telephone calls 90, 94, 103, 154, 155
telescopes 147, 159
  observations 46, 47, 48, 49
television **186–9**
  actors 186, 187
  advertising, commercials & sponsorship 187, 188
  animation & cartoon series 181, 187, 189
  audiences 182, 187, 188
  communications towers & masts 121, 123
  costumes 188
  Emmy Awards 181, 187
  magic shows 182, 183
  marathon events 37, 187
  music programmes & networks 154, 187, 189
  programme presenters 25, 61, 186, 187, 188
  screen size 160
  set ownership 95
  telephone votes 154
  televised trials (legal cases) 88
  wildlife programmes 61
temperatures
  absolute zero & temperatures close to it 46, 146, 149
  astronomical objects 46, 47, 48, 49, 158
  birds 63
  human endurance 38, 40
  lava 52
  melting & boiling points 148
  microbes 67
  oceans 56
  weather & climate 51
temples 96, 150
10,000 m (track athletics) 228, 229, 232

tennis 25, **224–5**
  Real Tennis 227
  table tennis **226**
  tennis ball holding 26, 72
tenpin bowling 110, 263
tenrecs 60
terns 63
Test cricket 218, 219
Texas skips 37
text messages 155
TGV trains 128
thank-yous by Oscar winners 177
The Simpsons (television programme) 181, 189
theatre **200–1**
  magic shows 183
  make-up 98
  plays 183, 185, 201
theme parks & rides 95, **126–7**
Thermohaline Conveyor 56
thigh bone (femur) 18, 19
31-legged races 32
Thomas Cup (badminton) 226
three-day events (horse riding) 258
three-legged marathon running 237
360-degree spins, cars 131
throws
  basketball free throws 208, 209
  cow pats 26
  discus (athletics) 229, 232
  haggis 272
  hammer (athletics) 229
  horseshoe pitching 273
  javelin (athletics) 229, 232
  judo 239
  lacrosse 220
  rolling pins 272
  shot-put (athletics) 228, 229, 232, 233
Thrust SSC (supersonic car) 132, 133
Tibetan bridges 122
tiddlywinks 110
tides 57
tightrope balancing & skipping 26, 38
time
  day length 49, 53
  dilation 149
  measurement 102, 105, 119, 230
titles & championships see specific sports (eg basketball)
toads 65
tobacco 94
tobogganing & bobsleigh 246, 247
toes
  cats 73
  toe wrestling 272
tomatoes 76, 77, 99
tombs & cemeteries 97
tongues
  dogs 72
  humans 14
tools, flint knapping 151
Top Fuel drag racing 267
Top Thrill Dragster (roller coaster) 127
topiary gardens 125
tops, spinning tops 108
tornadoes 50, 51
Torosaurus 58
tortoises 70
touchdowns
  American football 204
  Canadian football 223
touchscreens, computers 160
Tour de France (cycle race) 268, 269
Tour of Italy (cycle race) 269
Tour of Spain (cycle race) 269
tourism 24, 95
tournaments see specific sports (eg tennis)
tours & concerts 152, 153, 192, 194, 199
towels 104
towers
  air-traffic control 119
  buildings (skyscrapers) 39, 118, 119, **120–1**

communications towers & masts 121, 123
LEGO, playing cards & related constructions 26, 108, 110, 111
toxins see poison, venom & toxins
toys **108–9**
  retail consultants 24
  yo-yos 102, 106, 109
track & field events (athletics) **228–37**
tracks
  Hot Wheels 108
  model railways 128
  NASCAR Speedway 264
traffic jams 95
trails, sled dog racing 244
trains
  road & overland supply trains 142
  transport system see railways & trains
trampolining 26
trans-America running 236, 237
trans-Australia cycling 269
transatlantic crossings
  by air 138, 141
  by sea 137, 253
transfer fees, football (soccer) 215
transformation illusions 182
transplant surgery 20, 21
transport see specific types (eg cars)
transporters, crawler-transporters 142
trap-shooting 262
trapdoor spiders 69
travel
  tourism 24, 95
  see also journeys; specific forms of travel (eg air travel)
treadmill running 237
trees 74, 75
  deforestation & reforestation 84
  fruit trees 76
  hedges & mazes 125
  tree planting 33
treks 42, 43
trials (legal cases) 88
trials motorcycles 134
triangular course hang-gliding & paragliding 260, 261
tries, rugby football 216, 217
triple jump (athletics) 228, 229, 232, 233
triples hit, baseball 206
trolley pushes, supermarket 32
trophies see cups; prizes & awards; world cups
trucks 131, 142, 143
  truck pulls (strength events) 34
truffles (fungi) 103
tuba playing 36
tuna 66
tunnels 123
  bridge-tunnels 122
turf (grass) 102
turkeys 85
turtles 70
tusks 58, 105
TV see television
twins 15, 22, 237
twists (food), sesame twists 114
twists (jumps), freestyle skiing 243
two-man bobsleigh 247
typing 29
  text messages 155
Tyrannosaurus rex 58, 59
tyres 143

Uber Cup (badminton) 226
UEFA Champions League (football) 214
ultra-long distance events (athletics) 232, 234, 236

Acknowledgments

Special thanks go to the following people for their work during the production of this year's edition:

Jim Booth, Nicky Boxall, James Bradley, Caroline Butler, Scott Christie, Ann Collins, Chris Darley, Sam Fay, Marco Frigatti, Lisa Gibbs, Sophie Gimber, Simon Gold, James Herbert, Mary Hill, Laura Hughes, Caius Julyan, Peter Laker, Joyce Lee, Scott Lindsay, Anthony Liu, Andi Mercer, Shazia Mirza, Rob Molloy, Alistair Richards, David Roberts, Nicola Savage, Malcolm Smith, Ryan Tunstall, Kate White, Sophie Whiting.

The team also wishes to thank the following individuals and organizations:

Academy of Motion Picture Arts and Sciences, Ernest Adams, AIDA (Association Internationale pour le Développement del'Apnée), Dr Leslie Aiello, Airports Council International, Amnesty International, Dr Martyn Amos, Jorgen Vaaben Andersen, Anritsu, Antietam Recreation Centre, Vic Armstrong, Gee Armytage, Sir David Attenborough, Australia Zoo, Ron Baalke, Capt Mike Baker, Bank of England, Ken Bannister, Mike Bannister, Dr Peter Barham, Peter Baroody, Brenda Barton (World Food Program), BBC, Guenter Bechly, Bryan Berg, Gabe Bevilacqua, Jackie Bibby, Aase Bjerner, Richard Boatfield, Ian Bottomley (Royal Armouries, Leeds), Dr Richard Bourgerie, BP, Britannica Book of the Year, British Academy of Film & Television Arts, British Airways, British Antarctic Survey, British Board of Film Classification, British Flydog Association, British Geological Survey, British Llamaand Alpaca Association, British Museum, British National Space Centre, Prof John Brown, BT, Dr Robert Angus Buchanan, Prof Michael Burrows, CAIDA, Caltech, Cambridge University, Cancer Research UK, Dr Robert Carney, Casella CEL inc., John Cassidy, Keisha Castle-Hughes, CERN, Dr Franklin Chang-Diaz, Dr Hubert Chanson, Prof Phil Charles, Janina Chilcot, Chinese Embassy (London), Christie's, CIA World Factbook, Admiral Roy Clare, Isabelle Clark, Richard Clark, Stephen Clarke, Bridget Clifford (Royal Armouries Library, Tower of London), CMR/TNS Media Intelligence, Competitive Media Reporting/TNS Media Intelligence, ConocoPhillips, Dr Mike Coughlan, Dr Paul Craddock, Sarah Crane (Bernard Matthews plc), Dr Phillip Cribb, Crufts, Prof Mike Cruise, Cushman, Wakefield Healey & Baker, Dr Pam Dalton, Danmarks Kaninavlerforening (DK), Prof Kris Davidson, Dr Ashley Davies, Jim DeBosh, Deutschland GmbH for RTL, Dr David Dilcher, Discovery News,

Martin Dodge, Gary Duval, Edinburgh Science Festival, EETimes, Dr Farouk El-Baz, Dr Cynan Ellis-Evans, Mark Elmore, Elysium, Dr John Emsley, Encyclopaedia Britannica, Louis Epstein, ESA, eTForecasts, Exeter University, FAI (Fédération Aeronautique Internationale), Dr Xiaohui Fan, David Feldman, FIA (Fédération Internationale de l'Automobile), Sir Ranulph Fiennes, FIM (Fédération Internationale de Motocyclisme), FINA (Fédération Internationale de Natation Amateur), Max Finberg, Sarah Finney, Firefly Encyclopedia of Birds, FIRS (Fédération Internationale de Roller Skating), FIS (Fédération Internationale de Ski), FISA (Fédération Internationale des Sociétés d'Aviron), FITA (Fédération Internationale de Tir a l'Arc), Forbes, Brian Ford, Ford Press Office, Foreign &Commonwealth Office, Freemont Street Experience, Jono Friedman, Keith Friedman, Arran Frood, Ashrita Furman, Tim Furniss, Drew Gardner, Bill Gates, Martin Gedny, Geological Society of London, Dr Richard Ghail, Lois Gibson, Andy Gillard (Scootering magazine), Globastat, Carlos Gómez, Antonio González, Kim Goodman, Stephanie Gordon, Steve Gould, Visual Impact, Chris Gravett, Woburn Abbey, GRF, Matt Groening, Cornelius Growweblaar, Prof John Guest, Guinness World Records: Die Grössten Weltrekorde – Endemol, Guinness World Records: Fifty Years, Fifty Records – Granada for ITV, Dr Jim Gunson, Stuart Haggard, Nicholas Hall (Royal Armouries, Fort Nelson), Mary Hanson, Andy Harris, Ziggy Harrison-Tikisci, Colin Hart, Harvard-Smithsonian Center for Astrophysics, Roger Hawkins, Peter Haynes, Ron Hildebrant, Peter Hillary, Sir Edmund Hillary, Dr Paul Hillyard, Neil Holloway, Adam Honeywill, Hoovers, Dr David Horne, Graham Hudson, Paul Hughes, IAAF (International Association of Athletics Federation), IHPVA (International Human Powered Vehicle Association), IMDB, Imperial College London, Institute of Nanotechnology, Intel, International Energy Agency, International Tea Committee Ltd ISAF (International Sailing Federation), IWF (International Weightlifting Federation), IWSF (International Water Ski Federation), Jetstream Servers, Prof Steve Jones, Cathie Jung, Sandra & Myles Kannemeyer, Emily Kao, Robin Karpan (Alton Museum of History of Art), Dr Nichol Keith, Keo Films, Michael Kettman, Paul Kieve, Prof Joseph Kirschvink, Naomi Kitchener, Ron Klemenic, Jay Koch, Sir John Kreb, Arthur M Kyengo, L'Été De Tous Les Records – R et G Productions for France 3, Lancaster University, Steve Landis, Dr Rolf Landua, Dr Roger Launius, Bernard Lavery, Peter Lavinger, Andy Lee, Alain Leger, Jason Leonard, Dr Melinda Lewis, Martin Lindsey,

Martin Lockheed,Los Alamos National Laboratories, Dr Robert Loss, Louisiana State University, Dané Ludik, Dr Karl Lyons, The Magnificent Seven, Simone Mangaroo, Prof Giles Marion, Brian Marsden, Dr Jim Marshall, Jenny Marshall, Jessie Masson, Dave McAleer, Sir Paul McCartney, Tony McCoy, Grant McLachlan, Dr Alan McNaught, Medlowlands Stadium, The Met Office, Mi2g, Microsoft Corporation, Lucy Millington, Alice Mills, Chris Mills, Rosie Mills, Dr Edgar Mitchell, Hia Mofmann, Monell Chemical Senses Center, Tim Montgomery, Dr Sir Patrick Moore, Prof Jon Morse, Mosaique crew, Pam & Gary Mount, Munich Re, Sal Murillo, Munt Martin, NASA, National Academy of Sciences, National Federation of Master Window & General Cleaners, National Geographic, National Hamster Council, National Maritime Museum, National Physical Laboratory, National Science Foundation, Natural History Museum, Randy Nelson, NetNames, FFG Neustrashimy, Dr Ted Nield, A C Nielsen, NOAA, Richard Noble, Henry Northcroft, Barry Norman (WKVL Amusement Research Library), Andrew Nottage, Oracle, Oxford University, PADI (Professional Association of Diving Instructors), PAF, Morag & Stephen Paskins, John Payne, Jack Pearce, Giles Porter (Visual Impact), PPARC, Carla Prashad (Ascent Media Group), Productschap voor Gedistilleerde Dranken, Publishers Weekly, Salvador Pujol Miralles, Qinetiq, Lee Redmond, John Reed (WSSRC – sailing governing body), Prof Sir Martin Rees, William, Benjamin & Jeremy Rees, Victoria Reeves, Regional Planetary Image Facility (University College London), Iain Reid, Ian Ridpath, Graeme Rimer (Royal Armouries), Dan Roddick, Dr Mervyn Rose, Ros Rossington, Andrew Rotz, Mary Rotz, Royal Astronomical Society, Royal Botanical Gardens, Kew, Royal Horticultural Society, The Royal Institution, Royal Philips Electronics, Royal Society of Chemistry, Russia Monitor, Rutherford Appleton Laboratory, Ryan Sampson, Jeff Saward (Caerdroia – The Journal of Mazes and Labyrinths), Science Museum (London), Search Engine Watch, Istvan Sebestyen, Dr Paul Selden, Prof Dick Selley, SETI Institute, Bill Sharp, Dr Craig Sharp, Brunel University, Dr Seth Shostak, Dr Martin Siegert, Siemens, Frank Simon, The Smithsonian Institution, Peter Smithurst (Royal Armouries, Fort Nelson), Sotheby's, Lara Speicher, Graham Spicer, SpinaHering Marcelo (World Food Program), Statistics Iceland, Tanya Streeter, Peter Strongwater, Strongwater Studios, Danny Sullivan, Greg Swift, The Tate Modern, Debbie Tawse, Charlie Taylor, Heather Tinsley, Turhune Orchards,

UIM (Union Internationale Motonautique), UK Planetary Forum, Prof Martin Uman, UN Factbook, United Nations Centre for International Crime Prevention, University of Bath, University of Birmingham, University of Boston, University of Colorado, University of Dundee, University of Florida, University of Greenwich, University of Hertfordshire, University of Oklahoma, University of Southampton, US Drug Enforcement Agency, Melga van der Herwe, Juhani Virola, Geoff Wald, Dr David Wark, Prof Kevin Warwick, Dr David Webb, Mark Wells (Controller, Entertainment, Granada), Kelly Wessel (WFDF –World Flying Disc Federation), Wildlife Campus (South Africa), Prof Andrew Willmott, Punch Wilson, Richard Winter, Prof Richard Wiseman, Greg Wood, The World Bank Group, World Footbag Association, World Health Organization, World Meteorological Organization, World Sailing Speed Record Council, World Tourism Organization, World Wildlife Fund, Malaysia, Prof Joshua Wurman, www.EverestNews.com, www.globastat.com, www.landspeed.com, www.nationmaster.com, www.nua.com, Dr David Wynn-Williams, Robert Young.

Additionally to the many (too many to list individually) websites, periodicals and newspapers around the world for their help.

Picture credits

4   (see pp 80, 73, 131, 144, 190, 180, 103, 239)
6   Getty Images (2), Rex Features (2), Betty Halvagi, Drew Gardner/Guinness World Records
8   Getty Images, Corbis
9   Getty Images, Rex Features
10 Topham Pictures, C/o RTL/Gregorowius, Primetime, Drew Gardner/Guinness World Records
12 (see pp 27, 22, 28, 37, 38)
14 Rex Features, Corbis
15 Corbis, Drew Gardner/Guinness World Records.
16 Corbis (3)
17 Corbis (2), Associated Press, Guinness World Records
18 Science Photo Library (2)
19 Science Photo Library
20 Drew Gardner/Guinness World Records
21 Rex Features (2)
22 Rex Features, Corbis
23 Rex Features
24 Drew Gardner/ Guinness World Records, NewsPix
25 Rex Features, c/o Susan Jones
26 Drew Gardner/Guinness World Records
27 Drew Gardner/Guinness World Records (3)
28 c/o Banana George
29 c/o Lee Stewart, Getty Images
30 c/o NYAA Youth Achievement Award Council
31 c/o Renshi Manoj Gupta Liu Dawei, Xiahua News Agency
32 © Richard Creed
33 c/o Ian Kershaw, c/o Royal Marine Reserves
34 c/o David Huxley, c/o Chad Netherland
35 Drew Gardner/Guinness World Records
36 c/o Sanjeev Babu
37 c/o Cunning Stunts, Drew Gardner/Guinness World Records
38 Rex Features
39 Rex Features (2)
40 Associated Press, P A Photos
41 Reuters
42 c/o Chris & Erin Ratay, Rex Features, Getty Images
43 Drew Gardner/Guinness World Records
44 see (pp 73, 75, 51, 71)
46 © Lynette Cook
47 Science Photo Library (2)
48 NASA/JPL (2)
49 NASA/JPL/Malin Space Science Systems NASA/JPL
50 Science Photo Library, Reven Wurman, Science Photo Library
51 Science Photo Library
52 Alamy, Corbis
53 National Geographic Image Collection

54 © Simon Freshfield, Associated Press (3), Corbis
55 Getty Images, Associated Press, Corbis
56 Science Photo Library
57 NASA / Visible Earth, Corbis
58 Associated Press
59 Corbis
60 NHPA
61 Alamy (2), Rex Features
62 Corbis (2)
63 RSPB Images
64 Nature Picture Library, Alamy
65 Alamy
66 Corbis, Alamy
67 Corbis, Ardea
68 Corbis
69 c/o Yoichiro Kawamura, NHPA, Corbis
70 Rex Features, Alamy
71 Corbis
72 c/o Charles Dodman, c/o Linda Skeels-Hopson
73 © Lori Cope/*Country World Newspaper*, c/o Janice Wolf
74 Corbis (2), Rex Features
75 Nature Picture Library
76 c/o Aharon Shemoel
77 Rex Features (2)
78 (see pp 80, 85, 83, 91, 87)
80 Corbis (2)
81 Getty Images
82 P A Photos, Getty Images
83 Rex Features
84 Still Pictures, Rex Features
85 Associated Press
86 Associated Press
87 Getty Images, Rex Features
88 Rex Features, National Geographic, Image Collection
89 Alamy, Tiffany Gibson
90 Getty Images (2)
91 Getty Images (2)
92 Corbis (2)
93 Corbis
94 Getty Images, Alamy
95 Corbis
96 Corbis (2)
97 Getty Images
98 Drew Gardner/Guinness World Records
99 Rex Features (2)
100 (see pp 103,102,107,110)
102 c/o Duncan Toys Company, Rex Features
103 Corbis
104 c/o Game Show Network, c/o John J Bain
105 c/o Calgary Zoo, c/o Giancarlo Francenella
106 Drew Gardner/Guinness World Records, c/o Lucky Meisenheimer
107 Drew Gardner/Guinness World Records
108 Christie's Images, Rex Features
109 Christie's Images
110 Drew Gardner/Guinness World Records, c/o Del Lawson

111 c/o Newmarket Recreation
112 c/o The Odeon Leicester Square, c/o Hyatt Regency Hotel Vancouver
113 © North News and Pictures, Newcastle Upon Tyne, Rex Features
114 c/o Windsor Certified Farmers Market
115 c/o Nestle Italy, c/o Mohegan Sun Hotel
116 (see pp 131,120,126,141,143)
118 Corbis, Getty Images
119 Alamy
120 © Cliff Tan Anlong, Catholic High School, Singapore (all illus), Corbis (2), Alamy
121 © Torsten Jacobi, Alamy
122 Corbis
123 Corbis, Getty Images
124 Garden Picture Library c/o Stewarts GardenLands
125 Corbis
126 Corbis
127 Rex Features, c/o Cedar Point Amusement Park
128 c/o Northlandz
129 Getty Images, National Railway Museum/Science & Society Picture Library
130 Dempsey's World Record Associates, Corbis
131 c/o Dodge
132 Rex Features, from the Collections of The Henry Ford, Corbis (2) Getty Images/Hulton Archive
133 Rex Features (2), Corbis (2)
134 © John Cassidy, c/o Brad Graham
135 c/o Tom Wiberg, c/o Triumph
136 c/o Stone Manganese, Marine Ltd., Getty Images/Hulton Archive
137 Corbis
138 Getty Images/ Hulton Archive
139 Corbis (2)
140 Getty Images (2)
141 Corbis (2)
142 NASA/KSC
143 Corbis, Drew Gardner/Guinness World Records
144 Getty Images
145 (see pp 148, 150, 159), c/o U.S. Navy
146 Science Photo Library
147 c/o Argonne National Laboratory, CCLRC Rutherford, Appleton Laboratory
148 Corbis, Science Photo Library
149 Science Photo Library
150 Alamy
151 Corbis, Rex Features
152 Alamy, © Jason Grow
153 Getty Images
154 Getty Images
155 Corbis (2)
156 Novosti, Getty Images/ Hulton Archive, Corbis, Associated Press

157 NASA (3), NASA/KSC, Getty Images
158 NASA/KSC
159 NASA/JSC, NASA
160 Corbis
161 Getty Images, c/o Toshiba
162 © The Board of Trustees of the Armouries (2)
163 Getty Images
164 c/o U.S. Navy
165 c/o U.S. Navy (2)
166 (see pp 180,170,178,182,186)
168 Rex Features
169 Getty Images, Rex Features
170 Corbis, c/o Laura Mitchell
171 c/o Santa Marinella, Drew Gardner/Guinness World Records
172 *The Matrix Reloaded* © 2003 WV Films LLC
173 Rex Features, *The Lord of the Rings: The Return of the King* © MMIII NLP All rights reserved Photo by Pierre Vinet Photo appears courtesy of New Line Productions, Inc.
174 Corbis (2)
175 *X2* © 2003 Twentieth Century Fox All Rights Reserved
176 Getty Images
177 Getty Images
178 © Roy Alon Stunts, Corbis
179 P A Photos
180 Rex Features
181 © Disney Enterprises, Inc./ Pixar Animation Studios Ronald Grant Archive
182 Getty Images, Associated Press
183 Rex Features
184 Associated Press, Corbis
185 Rex Features, National Geographic Image Collection
186 Getty Images (2)
187 Rex Features, Getty Images
188 Getty Images, Corbis
189 Getty Images (see p 189 for *The Simpsons*)
190 London Features International
191 Getty Images, (see pp 195, 199, 201)
192 Rex Features, Getty Images (2)
193 Getty Images
194 Rex Features
195 Getty Images (2)
196 Rex Features, Getty Images
197 Rex Features
198 Rex Features
199 Rex Features, London Features International
200 c/o Artspace Projects, Inc.
201 Rex Features (2)
202 see (pp 251,204,215,242,267)
204 Getty Images (2)
205 Getty Images
206 Getty Images
207 Getty Images (2)
208 Getty Images (2)

209 Getty Images
210 Getty Images
211 Getty Images (2)
212 Getty Images
213 Getty Images (2)
214 Getty Images
215 Getty Images (2)
216 Getty Images
217 Getty Images (3)
218 Getty Images
219 Getty Images (2)
220 Getty Images, Associated Press
221 Getty Images
222 NewsPix, Associated Press
223 Reuters
224 Getty Images
225 Getty Images (2)
226 Getty Images, Getty Images/Hulton Archive, Hulton Archive
227 NewsPix
228 Getty Images (2)
229 Getty Images
230 Getty Images (2), Associated Press, Getty Images
231 Getty Images, Corbis, Getty Images (2)
232 Getty Images
233 Getty Images
234 Getty Images
235 Associated Press, Getty Images
236 Getty Images
237 P A Photos
238 Getty Images
239 Getty Images, Rex Features
240 Corbis, Getty Images
241 Getty Images
242 Getty Images, Corbis
243 Getty Images
244 Getty Images (2)
245 Getty Images
246 Getty Images (2)
247 Getty Images
248 Corbis
249 Reuters (2)
250 Getty Images (2)
251 Getty Images
252 Getty Images (2)
253 Getty Images
254 Getty Images
255 Associated Press
256 Getty Images
257 Getty Images
258 Reuters, Corbis
259 Reuters, Getty Images
260 Airsport Photo Library, c/o Paraclub Flevo
261 Airsport Photo Library
262 Empics, Leo Nikora
263 Getty Images
264 Getty Images
265 Getty Images (2)
266 Getty Images (2)
267 Getty Images
268 Corbis
269 Corbis, Getty Images
270 Getty Images, Corbis
271 Buzz Pictures
272 Rex Features (2)
273 Getty Images

Be a record breaker!

If you think you've got what it takes to be a Guinness World Record holder, then we want to hear from you!

1. Decide which record you want to break

If you think you have what it takes to join our exclusive record-breaking club, then read on. There are thousands of records to choose from. You could gather a large group of people to break a mass participation record, or perhaps you have an unusual collection. You might even suggest something new. If this is the case, what we are looking for is a challenge that is inspiring, interesting, requires skill and is likely to attract subsequent challenges from people all around the world.

2. Make an application

You need to contact us BEFORE you make your attempt – do not send us any evidence or documentation before we have assessed your proposal. Every Guinness World Record is governed by a unique set of rules that MUST be followed. You need to apply for these rules before you can make an attempt. If you have a new record idea, you need to find out if we have accepted your proposal before you attempt the record. If we like your idea, we will draw up rules specifically for your attempt in order to set a standard for all subsequent challenges. The easiest and fastest way to make an application is via our website. Click on the link that says 'Make a Record Attempt', this will take you to an online

application form. You'll be asked to choose a password which we will send you with a membership number to allow you access to our new tracking system. Through this you can monitor the progress of your claim and ask any questions about your record attempt. If you don't have Internet access, you can contact us by post. Ensure that you have provided adequate contact details. Please be aware that proposals received this way take much longer to process than those received via the website.

Our website:
www.guinnessworldrecords.com

Write to us:
Guinness World Records
338 Euston Road
London NW1 3BD
UK

Call us: +44 (0) 870 241 6632
Fax us: +44 (0) 20 7891 4501

3. Wait until you hear from us

Once your application has been processed, your proposal will be passed on to one of our specialist researchers. If the application is successful, we will email you with the corresponding rules and regulations that must be strictly adhered to for the attempt to be considered. We'll also send you some

general guidelines that explain the evidence you need to provide to have your record attempt verified. If we reject your proposal we will explain why and, if appropriate, suggest an alternative idea.

4. Organizing the record attempt

We can provide you with advice and guidance regarding record-related queries. As long as there is no violation of the guidelines, your record attempt can be organized in any way you choose. Guinness World Record adjudicators are able to attend events but we will charge a fee for this. Please remember that all record attempts are undertaken at the sole risk of the competitor and Guinness World Records cannot be held responsible for any liability arising out of any record attempt.

5. Have your attempt verified

Once you've completed your attempt, you must send us a package containing all the verification documents we have requested (ie photographs, videos, witness statements and, where required, other more specialized items that will depend on your specific record attempt). All evidence must be sent to our mailing address, clearly marked with your membership number and claim identification number, (which will have been provided in prior correspondence). If your claim passes all inspections, including a final scrutiny from the Keeper of the Records, you will be declared a Guinness World Record holder! Please bear in mind that with over 60,000 claims coming in every year, it can take some time to process every claim – so please be patient!

6. Recognition of your attempt

All Guinness World Record holders receive a complimentary certificate to commemorate their achievement. We cannot guarantee that any specific record will appear in our book, as the record selection changes annually. But as long as you hold on to your current world record, there is always the chance that your record could appear in a future edition.

Good luck!